EXPLAINING ECONOMIC GROWTH
Essays in Honour of Angus Maddison

CONTRIBUTIONS
TO
ECONOMIC ANALYSIS

214

Honorary Editor:
J. TINBERGEN

Editors:
D. W. JORGENSON
J. -J. LAFFONT

NORTH-HOLLAND
AMSTERDAM • LONDON • NEW YORK • TOKYO

EXPLAINING
ECONOMIC GROWTH
Essays in Honour of Angus Maddison

Edited by

Adam SZIRMAI
Bart VAN ARK
Dirk PILAT
Faculty of Economics
University of Groningen
The Netherlands

1993

NORTH-HOLLAND
AMSTERDAM • LONDON • NEW YORK • TOKYO

ELSEVIER SCIENCE PUBLISHERS B.V.
Sara Burgerhartstraat 25
P.O. Box 211, 1000 AE Amsterdam, The Netherlands

338.9
E962

(Tel: 508-750-8400
Fax:)

ISBN: 0 444 89495 0

INTRODUCTION TO THE SERIES

This series consists of a number of hitherto unpublished studies, which are introduced by the editors in the belief that they represent fresh contributions to economic science.

The term "economic analysis" as used in the title of the series has been adopted because it covers both the activities of the theoretical economist and the research worker.

Although the analytical methods used by the various contributors are not the same, they are nevertheless conditioned by the common origin of their studies, namely theoretical problems encountered in practical research. Since for this reason, business cycle research and national accounting, research work on behalf of economic policy, and problems of planning are the main sources of the subjects dealt with, they necessarily determine the manner of approach adopted by the authors. Their methods tend to be "practical" in the sense of not being too far remote from application to actual economic conditions. In additon they are quantitative.

It is the hope of the editors that the publication of these studies will help to stimulate the exchange of scientific information and to reinforce international cooperation in the field of economics.

The Editors

Preface

This volume presents the proceedings of the conference "Explaining Economic Growth" held from 8 to 10 April 1992 at the University of Groningen. The conference was organised in celebration of the 65th birthday of Angus Maddison, Professor at the Faculty of Economics of the University of Groningen since 1978. This book is dedicated to him by friends, colleagues and pupils, in friendship and in recognition of his past and present achievements in the field of research on economic growth and its explanations.

We gratefully acknowledge financial support for the conference from the Royal Dutch Academy of Sciences, the University of Groningen, the Faculty of Economics of the University of Groningen and the Stichting Groninger Universiteits Fonds. We thank Monique Tjiong for her assistance in the preparation of the camera-ready copy.

In the final stage of the processing of the manuscript, the sad news reached us of the death of Edward Denison, one of the contributors to this volume. We remember Denison as a pioneer in growth accounting and as a source of inspiration to scholars working in this field.

> Adam Szirmai
> Bart van Ark
> Dirk Pilat

Participants Conference
"Explaining Economic Growth"

Bart van Ark
University of Groningen
The Netherlands

Wilfred Beckerman
Balliol College
United Kingdom

Derek Blades
OECD, Paris
France

Peter Boomgaard
KITLV, Leiden
The Netherlands

Nicholas Crafts
University of Warwick
United Kingdom

Edward Denison
The Brookings Institution
United States

J.W. Drukker
University of Groningen
The Netherlands

Éva Ehrlich
Institute for World Economics
Budapest, Hungary

Rainer Fremdling
University of Groningen
The Netherlands

Jan Willem Gunning
Free University, Amsterdam
The Netherlands

Alan Heston
University of Pennsylvania
United States

André Hofman
ECLAC, Santiago
Chile

John Kendrick
George Washington University
United States

Steven Keuning
Central Bureau of Statistics
The Netherlands

Jan Kregel
University of Bologna
Italy

Angus Maddison
University of Groningen
The Netherlands

Kees van der Meer
NRLO, The Hague
The Netherlands

Stanislav Menshikov
Erasmus University
The Netherlands

Chris de Neubourg
University of Limburg
The Netherlands

Douglass North
Washington University
St. Louis, United States

Mary O'Mahony
NIESR, London
United Kingdom

Sir Alan Peacock
David Hume Institute
Edinburgh, United Kingdom

Jan Pen
University of Groningen
The Netherlands

Dirk Pilat
University of Groningen
The Netherlands

Leandro Prados de la Escosura
Universidad Carlos III
Madrid, Spain

Gé Prince
University of Groningen
The Netherlands

Luc Soete
MERIT Institute, Maastricht
The Netherlands

Elmer Sterken
University of Groningen
The Netherlands

Adam Szirmai
University of Groningen
The Netherlands

Kimio Uno
Keio University
Japan

Victor Urquidi
Colegio de Mexico
Mexico

Hans-Jürgen Wagener
University of Groningen
The Netherlands

Edward Wolff
New York University
United States

Jan Luiten van Zanden
Free University, Amsterdam
The Netherlands

Contents

Preface vii

List of Conference Participants viii

Introduction
Adam Szirmai 1

I. PROXIMATE AND ULTIMATE SOURCES OF GROWTH

1. The Growth Accounting Tradition and Proximate
   Sources of Growth
   Edward F. Denison 37
2. The Ultimate Sources of Economic Growth
   Douglass C. North 65
3. Is Economic Growth Still Desirable?
   Wilfred Beckerman 77
4. Technology and Growth: The Complex Dynamics
   of Catching Up, Falling Behind and Taking over
   Luc Soete and Bart Verspagen 101
5. How Much Does Capital Explain?
   John W. Kendrick 129
6. The Role of Education in Productivity Convergence:
   Does Higher Education Matter?
   Edward N. Wolff and Maury Gittleman 147

II. COUNTRY EXPERIENCES OF ECONOMIC GROWTH

7. Explaining Japan's Postwar Economic Growth -
   The Contribution of Growth Accounting
   Dirk Pilat 171
8. Economic Growth in Indonesia, 500-1990
   Peter Boomgaard 195
9. Comparative Productivity in Manufacturing:
   A Case Study for Indonesia
   Adam Szirmai 217
10. Economic Development in Latin America in
    the 20th Century - A Comparative Perspective
    André Hofman 241

11. The Dutch Economy in the Very Long Run -
    Growth in Production, Energy Consumption and Capital
    in Holland (1500-1805) and the Netherlands
    Jan Luiten van Zanden 267
12. Long-Run Economic Growth in Spain since 1800:
    An International Perspective
    Leandro Prados de la Escosura 285
13. Economic Growth in Eastern Central Europe
    after World War II
    Éva Ehrlich 301
14. Was the Thatcher Experiment Worth It?
    British Economic Growth in a European Context
    Nicholas F.R. Crafts 327

III. MEASURING LEVELS OF ECONOMIC PERFORMANCE

15. What can be Learned from Successive ICP
    Benchmark Estimates?
    Alan Heston and Robert Summers 353
16. The ICOP Approach - Its Implications and Applicability
    Bart van Ark 375
17. Comparing Capital Stocks
    Derek W. Blades 399

IV. POLICY PERSPECTIVES

18. Liberalism and Economic Growth
    Sir Alan Peacock 413
19. Keynesian Stabilisation Policy and Post War
    Economic Performance
    Jan A. Kregel 429
20. The Developmentalist View
    Victor L. Urquidi 447
21. The "Socialist Experiment" and Transformation
    towards the Market
    Stanislav Menshikov 467

Author Index 485

Subject Index 491

Explaining Economic Growth
A. Szirmai, B. van Ark and D. Pilat
© 1993 Elsevier Science Publishers B.V. All rights reserved.

Introduction

Adam Szirmai*
University of Groningen

1. Economic Divergence since the Fifteenth Century

In the fifteenth century differences in average per capita income between countries and regions were far smaller than at present. In most regions, whether in Europe, Asia, the Middle East or South America, the great majority of the population lived off the land and was never very far removed from subsistence levels.[1] Standards of living and technology in advanced Asian societies such as China, India or Indonesia were at least as high as in late medieval Europe (see the article by Boomgaard in this book, see also Elvin, 1973; Maddison, 1971). If a mid-fifteenth century observer would have had to predict the locus of economic breakthroughs in the world economy, the obvious candidate would have been China, rather than Europe (cf. Ronan and Needham, 1978). Nevertheless the breakthrough did take place in Europe, while China experienced centuries of relative stagnation.

From the sixteenth century onwards Western Europe experienced a dual process of internal economic growth and external economic and political expansion, resulting in the present world economic order, characterised by great disparities in income levels and a high degree of economic, political and social interdependence. This process was unique in two senses. For the first time in history part of mankind permanently broke through the vicious circles of poverty which had kept people close to subsistence levels from time immemorial.[2] In Western Europe and areas of Western settlement centuries of sustained increase in per capita incomes followed. In the second place earlier processes of political and economic expansion were followed by periods of contraction and decentralisation. The European penetration of the world led to a permanent interdependence of the world economic order. This

---

* I have benefited greatly from detailed comments on a first draft of this introduction by my co-editors Bart van Ark and Dirk Pilat and by Nanno Mulder.

[1] One of the exceptions was Holland where the share of non-agricultural labour was already rather high in the early sixteenth century (see the contribution by Jan Luiten van Zanden to this volume).

[2] For a dissenting view stressing economic growth in medieval Britain since the domesday book, see Snooks (1992).

interdependence will persist long after Western countries and countries of Western settlement may have lost their economic lead.

How can one explain the economic breakthrough in feudal Europe and the long and accelerating process of increase in per capita incomes? Why were other areas unable to meet the Western challenge, lagging in their growth of capita income, thus becoming what is now euphemistically called "developing economies". These classic questions form the long-run context for the modern study of economic growth.

In April 1992 a three day conference in honour of Angus Maddison was held at the University of Groningen. The theme of this conference was "Explaining Economic Growth". The conference papers are now being published in this book. In the following introduction, I will review the central issues discussed in the papers and at the conference.[3]

2. The Relationship between the Conference Topics and the Work of Angus Maddison

Angus Maddison has devoted the major part of a long and distinguished career to the study of economic growth. Working in the tradition of Kuznets, Abramovitz, Denison and Kendrick he has published an endless stream of influential books and articles on economic growth in all its ramifications. The conference "Explaining Economic Growth" was organised around themes and approaches which are prominent in his work. With no pretence at making a complete assessment of Maddison's scientific *oeuvre*, I will start by mentioning some important characteristics of his work and show how they are reflected in this book.

a. A first topic prominent in his work is growth accounting and explanation of growth, stagnation, convergence and divergence. Some of his publications focus explicitly on growth accounting (e.g. Maddison, 1972, 1987). In most of his other publications the argument is phrased in terms of a growth accounting framework (e.g. Maddison, 1970; 1991). In addition, Maddison has written widely about the more ultimate sources of growth, such as national and international institutions, characteristics of international economic and political orders, economic policies and technological diffusion from leading to follower countries (cf. Maddison, 1971, 1988). These topics form Part I of the book. The opening articles by Denison and North are devoted to a general discussion of proximate and ultimate sources of growth. The articles by Soete and Verspagen, Kendrick and Wolff deal with the

---

[3]   Thanks are due to Nanno Mulder who prepared a summary of the conference discussions. I have made no attempt to reproduce the discussions in full, but I have tried to include the most important issues under debate in the introduction.

contributions of technology, capital and education, respectively. Two recent growth accounting exercises are included in the present volume, one by Dirk Pilat on Japanese growth from 1953 to 1989 and one by André Hofman on Latin American growth from 1950-1989.

b. In order to explain growth, one should be able to measure it with some degree of accuracy. Maddison has always stressed the vital importance of quantitative empirical work in a Kuznetsian vein. In contrast to many in the economics profession, who tend to take statistics as manna descending from statistical bureaus, he has put great effort into the creation of a reliable statistical data base which will be invaluable for future researchers in the field of economic growth. Most articles in this book reflect a similar involvement in fundamental quantitative work. In particular the papers by Boomgaard, Crafts, Ehrlich, Hofman, Pilat, Prados de la Escosura, Szirmai and van Zanden in Part II are devoted to studies of growth experience, presenting recent empirical information on growth performance in various regions of the world economy and various historical periods.

c. A third characteristic of Maddison's work is its exceptional diversity and scope. Starting with his well-known *Economic Growth in the West* (1964), Maddison has published books on Japan and the USSR (1969), India and Pakistan (1971), Latin America, the Caribbean and the OECD (1986), Brazil and Mexico (Maddison and Associates, 1992), Indonesia (Maddison and Prince, 1989), economic policy in developing countries (1970), economic development in advanced countries (1982, 1991) and economic development in the world economy (1989). The editors have tried to reflect the richness of this comparative approach in this book, which includes articles on Western European, Eastern European, Latin American and Asian countries.

d. A fourth hallmark of Maddison's work is his interest in long-run trends in economic performance, covering at least decades, and preferably even centuries. His recent *Dynamic Forces of Capitalist Development* (1991) spans the period 1820-1989, with the introductory chapters going back to 1400. His *World Economy in the Twentieth Century* (1989) presents trends of economic development in the world economy from 1900 to 1989. Several of the contributions to this volume were invited with this long-run focus in mind. In his studies of long-run economic development, Maddison has always tried to straddle the disciplines of economics and economic history. In his view, economists can gain better understanding of contemporary economic problems by placing them in historical perspective. Economic historians can benefit from the application of modern analytical economic concepts and theories to historical data. The contributors to this volume accordingly include distinguished representatives of both disciplines.

e. In order to compare levels of economic performance at given moments in time, quantitative international comparisons of real output and productivity are necessary. Maddison has done a considerable amount of research on international comparisons from an industry of origin perspective (Maddison, 1952, 1967, 1983; Maddison and van Ark, 1988, 1989) and has stimulated younger colleagues to pursue this line of research. A whole session of the conference was devoted to the methodological problems involved in international comparisons. The papers of this session - by Heston and Summers, van Ark, and Blades - are reproduced in Part III.

f. A question of considerable interest is to what extent economies are converging on or diverging from each other in the long run. In his magnum opus *Dynamic Forces in Capitalist Development: A Long-Run Comparative View* (1991), Maddison emphasises the importance of catch up effects in post-war economic growth in the advanced capitalist countries. The topics of catching up, falling behind, convergence and divergence are explicitly discussed by Soete and Verspagen, and Wolff. They are also referred to in most of the other papers in this volume. In order to understand such patterns in economic performance, a comparative approach is an important tool. Maddison has always defended the fruitfulness of a comparative approach for an understanding of economic trends and problems in different countries. His comparisons not only involve different countries, but also different historical periods (cf. his *Two Crises: Latin America and Asia*, 1929-38 and 1973-83, 1985).

g. Finally, Maddison has devoted considerable attention to the role of policy in economic performance (e.g. Maddison, 1964, 1970, 1991, chapter 6.). His primary interest is in the broad outlines of economic strategies and their impact on economic development in the long run, rather than on the day to day debates on specific policy measures. Particularly, by studying policy in a comparative setting as one of the many factors directly or indirectly influencing economic performance, one is better able to assess the relative success or failure of policy approaches. In Part IV of this book, the role of economic policy is discussed from different perspectives in papers by Peacock, Kregel, Urquidi and Menshikov.

3. The Desirability of Growth

Most scholars of growth take both the desirability and the feasibility of economic growth for granted. They think that the historical record has shown Malthusians to have been wrong about limits to growth in the past (cf. Maddison, 1982, 1991). They expect Malthusian pessimists to be wrong about future prospects. On a global level food production has outstripped population growth for the past two centuries. Technological change has more than counterbalanced diminishing returns. Repeated predictions of the exhaustion of natural resources, whether referring to coal, oil or minerals have so far not materialised (cf. the paper by Beckerman in this book). When resources became scarce, price increases made the exploitation of new or alternative resources economically feasible.

Nevertheless, the desirability and feasibility of economic growth are once again being questioned. The first line of criticism suggests that economic growth as such does not necessarily contribute to welfare. This approach states that indicators of life expectancy, literacy, infant mortality, income inequality etc. are more important than GDP per capita in assessing economic welfare.[4] The second line of attack emphasises environmental limits to growth which increasingly have to do with the carrying capacity of the earth as whole. These critics point to negative effects of continued growth such as global warming, holes in the ozone layer, acid rain, disappearance of tropical rain forests, diminishing diversity of species and irreversible pollution of oceans, soils, atmosphere and drinking water.

Wilfred Beckerman's paper in this volume offers a spirited defense of economic growth. He claims that much of the anti-growth literature bases itself based on unproven statements with regard to environmental limits and disregards the economic costs of draconian anti-growth measures. Beckerman's main point is that, as measured by a multitude of environmental indicators - clean air, clean water, urban degradation - , the richer a country, the less environmental pollution there is. There is a conflict of interests between people in poor countries, who have an interest in improving their standards of living and people in rich countries who are worried about global environmental consequences of growth. As regards social indicators, Beckerman argues that they are highly correlated with GDP per capita (see also Beckerman, 1974).

Beckerman's critics at the conference, among whom his discussant Jan Pen, argued that he focused too exclusively on the distributive aspects of environmental pollution. They were more concerned with the possibly irreversible environmental effects of continued population growth and growth of GDP per capita at a global level.

4. Proximate Sources of Growth

In growth accounting, the proximate sources of growth are divided into the growth of inputs such as physical capital, labour and land and the productivity of those inputs. Labour input can be adjusted to include changes in working hours and in the quality, composition and educational level of the labour force. Capital can be augmented to include changes in the composition of

---

[4] See for instance the *Human Development Report* of the UN published since 1990, see also the paper by Nicholas Crafts in this book.

assets and embodied technological change. The factors of production are weighted to arrive at measures of total factor input. In a neo-classical framework, factor shares in national income are usually taken as weights. The part of growth attributed to changes in total factor productivity is the residual unexplained by changes in (augmented) factor inputs. Subsequently, some scholars try to add factors explaining part of growth and thus reducing the size of the unexplained residual. Such factors include the reallocation of resources from sectors with low productivity to sectors with high productivity, economies of scale, changes in capacity utilisation, costs of regulation, effects of reductions in international trade barriers and effects of weather on farm production (see e.g. Abramovitz, 1989; Denison, 1967; Kendrick, 1981; Maddison, 1987 and papers by Kendrick, Pilat and Hofman in this book). The remaining residual is a "measure of our ignorance" (Abramovitz, 1956, p. 11). Among others it can include measurement errors and the effects of disembodied technological change. One of the factors influencing the rate of technological change is the distance to the most advanced country in terms of technology and productivity. The theory of the catch-up effects suggests that follower countries can experience rapid technological change and increases in productivity by copying technology from the leader country (e.g. Maddison, 1987).

In his contribution to this volume Edward Denison traces the history of and the reaction of the profession to growth accounting. He also highlights some of the controversies surrounding it. Depending on the definition chosen and the period and country under consideration, growth of the physical capital stock can account for a very substantial part of GDP growth. For instance, Kendrick's estimate for the contribution of capital to GDP growth in the period 1960-1990 period in OECD countries is 40 per cent (p. 139).[5] Given the importance of capital, it is not surprising that many of the controversies in growth accounting discussed by Denison have to do with the measurement of the contribution of capital to growth.

Over the years an important issue with regard to capital is the question to what extent capital stock measures should be adjusted to incorporate quality improvement due to technological change. Denison takes the position that this should not be done. Capital should be seen in relation to the financial resources set aside in an economy for saving and investment. If one incorporates technological change in the measurement of the stock of capital, the contribution of capital will seem larger and the contribution of embodied technological change as a separate source of growth will not be visible. Other scholars, including John Kendrick in his contribution to this book, prefer to adjust measures of capital stocks for quality change.

---

[5]   All non-dated references are references to articles included in this volume.

A second issue of importance in assessing the contribution of capital is the choice of an appropriate measure of aggregate output. According to Denison, the contribution of capital will be inflated at market prices, because indirect business taxes and transfer payments are included in the earnings of capital. He also prefers to use net rather than gross stocks, which will tend to show larger shares for capital. Kendrick, on the other hand, defends the use of gross concepts, because the decline in output producing capacity of aging capital goods is exaggerated by the net measure.[6] It is not surprising that Kendrick arrives at substantially higher estimates for the contribution of capital (see Kendrick, p. 136 ff.) than Denison. The most extreme difference is found for the period 1929-48 for the USA. For this period Denison finds a contribution of capital to growth of less than 4 per cent versus the 17 per cent found by Kendrick.

A third issue relates to the definition of capital. If one includes consumer durables owned by households and institutions in the capital stock as is done by Christensen and Jorgenson (1970), the role of capital will become more important and changes in total factor productivity will be proportionally smaller. An issue discussed by both Denison and Kendrick is the role of capacity utilisation. If increases in capacity utilisation are included in the measurement of capital, the role of capital becomes more important.[7]

Not all differences in concepts and estimates are of a fundamental nature.[8] As long as the procedures involved are kept transparent, one can reconstruct one concept from another and reconcile different estimates. For instance, whether one relegates embodied technological change to the residual, or adjusts capital input, one is still studying the same phenomenon.

In several publications John Kendrick (e.g. Kendrick, 1976) has argued for a wider concept of capital, which includes so-called human or intangible capital. This wider concept of capital refers to both non-human or tangible capital goods and human or intangible capital goods. The latter consist of technological knowledge accumulated by investments in research and development, human intangible stocks accumulated by workers as a result of investments in education, training, health, safety and mobility, plus tangible

---

[6] Christensen, Cummings and Jorgenson (1980) also prefer the gross concept. As labour is not depreciated, a net concept of capital implies asymmetric treatment of labour and capital inputs.

[7] Some issues raised in the discussion were the choice for GDP or GNP as the income aggregates to be explained. Kimio Uno suggested that one should consider nominal production aggregates as well as real ones. Nominal aggregates are those economic actors are faced with.

[8] The conceptual differences between Kendrick and Denison discussed here, should not obscure the fact that they are working very much in the same tradition.

capital goods in the educational system (Kendrick pp. 141/2). This wider concept of capital can explain about five-sixths of US economic growth in the period 1948-1969.

In a thoughtful comment on Kendrick's paper Mary O'Mahony made the connection between the broader concept of capital championed by Kendrick and the work of new growth theorists such as Lucas, Romer and Barro, who all focus heavily on investment in knowledge, research and development, technology and human capital (Romer, 1986; Lucas, 1988; Barro, 1991). Several articles in this book touch, though often briefly, on the debate between the so-called "new" growth theory and the older mainstream theory of growth associated with the names of Solow and Denison. To clarify this debate, I think it is useful to make a distinction between theoretical modelling of growth and more empirically oriented work on growth.

The orthodox neo-classical model of growth assumes diminishing marginal returns to each of the factors of production and constant returns to scale for all factors of production. In the long run this implies that as the capital to labour ratio increases, diminishing marginal returns will result in zero growth of per capita income. Thus all levels of per capita income would tend to converge as leading economies run into diminishing returns. Diminishing returns can be offset by technological change, which is treated in the theory as an exogenously determined factor (Solow, 1957). However, as new growth theorists emphasise, new technologies are available everywhere in the world and technologies can diffuse from advanced to less advanced countries. Therefore, the neo-classical growth theory pre-supposes convergence of per capita incomes in the world economy (Romer, 1986; Solow, 1991).

Theoretically the discussion between new and older growth theory focuses on the treatment of technological change in the production function (cf. Ehrlich, 1990). In neo-classical growth models technological change is relegated to the residual. The new growth theory claims to be able to endogenise technological change. Investment by profit maximising firms and individuals takes place not only in tangible capital goods, but also in stocks of knowledge and human capital. The production of goods and services through the application of knowledge in production is subject to increasing returns to scale, due to the positive external effects of knowledge in production. The greater the level of the initial investment in knowledge and human capital, the greater the returns to further investments. The production of knowledge itself is subject to decreasing returns, otherwise there would be no limits to the achievable growth rate at all. Thus, the new theory offers an explanation of divergence in economic performance. Countries with a head start in accumulation of human capital and knowledge will tend to forge ahead. In another form, an old notion from development economics surfaces again, namely the idea of vicious circles and backwash effects on the one hand and virtuous circles and cumulative causation on the other hand (Myrdal, 1957; Nurkse, 1953). But while the early formulations, such as Nurkse concentrated on the shortage of savings in poor countries, new growth theory focuses on increasing returns. Advanced countries have increasing returns, which are lacking in more backward countries.

From an empirical point of view, however, new growth theory seems less new, than from the perspective of growth modelling. Many of the ideas presented as new, have long been present in various strands of empirical research. Though the coefficients used to weight factor inputs in growth accounting often derive from a neo-classical framework, growth accounting is theoretically eclectic and not limited to neo-classical assumptions about diminishing returns. For instance, some growth accountants make adjustments for economies of scale and for Keynesian factors such as use of capacity. Growth accountants have long been aware of the importance of investments in human capital and technological change. Following Denison, it has become standard practice to incorporate human capital in the measures of labour input, thus allowing one to measure the contribution of human capital to output growth. Economists of education such as Becker and Schultz already emphasised the importance of investment in human capital in the sixties. With regard to technological change, Kuznets gave a clear analysis of the role of feedback effects of the application of inventions on the facilitation of additional knowledge and invention, in an article on two hundred years of US growth originally published in 1977 (Kuznets 1979, p. 13). In growth accounting, one of the ways in which one can try to capture part of technological change is by adjusting estimates of capital input for embodied technological change. Empirical research on growth, to some extent irrespective of the theoretical debate, has tried to unscramble the contributions of different sources of growth, such as embodied and disembodied technical change, innovation and diffusion and investments in human capital. So far, new growth theory has had but little to contribute to the empirical side of the debate.

Even at the theoretical level, Solow, one of the founding fathers of neo-classical growth theory, has recently pointed out that orthodox theories of growth are not necessarily inconsistent with divergence. The availability of modern technology does not mean that technological diffusion takes places automatically to less developed economies. In absence of institutional changes these economies may be unable to assimilate new technologies (Solow, 1991). It is precisely such points which are taken up in the papers by Soete and Verspagen on technological diffusion and Douglass North on institutions in this book.

In her comment on Kendrick's paper, Mary O'Mahony also raised the issue of the use of econometric techniques in growth accounting. The coefficients used to weight the inputs of capital and labour in orthodox growth accounting derive from the standard Cobb Douglas production function with diminishing returns to each of the factors of production and constant returns to all the factors of production. Assuming that factors of production are remunerated according to their marginal products, the weights of capital and labour equal the shares of the factors of production in value added. However, if the assumption of decreasing returns to scale is relaxed, other weights may be required. To estimate these weights, one needs econometric techniques.

A similar point was made by Kimio Uno in his comment on Denison's paper. In addition he argued for a more disaggregated approach where the sources of growth were studied in different sectors.[9] Finally, Uno pointed to the possibility of dynamic interactions between the sources of growth which cannot be captured in standard growth accounting (see also Abramovitz, 1989). He argued that econometric techniques can uncover the interactions between separate inputs and can incorporate the role of demand in growth models.

In the discussion, critics of econometric techniques in growth accounting generally pointed to the lack of robustness of coefficients, a certain lack in transparency in econometric approaches, and the direction of intellectual energy and creativity away from the arduous empirical work on the construction of data themselves. Many of the contributors to growth accounting in this volume represent the tradition that it is of the greatest importance to present the data and estimates in such a transparent fashion, that one can experiment with alternative sets of weights in order to gain a better understanding of the sensitivity of the results to different assumptions.

5. Catch-up, Convergence and Divergence

In his empirical work on advanced economies Maddison (e.g. 1987, 1991) has stressed the importance of catch-up effects. In the post-war period catch-up effects enabled Japan and Western European economies to grow more rapidly than the US, because they could apply technology developed in the leader country without having to bear the costs of research and development. The catch-up hypothesis in its simple form suggests a relationship between the distance in per capita income or per capita productivity to the leader country (representing the productivity frontier in the world economy) and the growth rate of per capita income. The lower the initial level the faster a country will grow.

[9] For instance some Japanese sectors such as electrical machinery and equipment have large residuals, while others such as the services have a negative residual. Economies of scale are prominent in iron and steel and less so in other sectors.

Catch up and falling behind and convergence and divergence[10] are the central themes of the paper by Soete and Verspagen on technology and the paper by Wolff on education. These papers try to explain why some countries grow faster than others and which factors contribute to our understanding of processes of convergence and divergence.

The paper by Soete and Verspagen argues for an empirical approach. It starts with a critical discussion of the unrealistic nature and the restrictive assumptions of both older and newer growth models. It introduces a "probit model" of technological diffusion, which is highly relevant for the analysis of convergence and divergence. This model states that new technologies will be adopted by economies if their income per capita exceeds some critical level. Beyond this level, processes of catch up and convergence will predominate. Below this level, processes of falling behind and divergence will operate. In addition to this threshold level of income per capita, the authors point to the importance of the historical institutional framework within which new technology is either assimilated or rejected. They stress the importance of the concepts of technological distance and the capability to assimilate knowledge. In addition, they give some emphasis to the penalties of technological leadership, a phenomenon often stressed in the catch-up literature (for an early formulation, see Veblen, 1915). In advanced countries, new technologies have to compete with investments in existing technologies, which act as a brake on technological change.

The paper presents a variety of measures of dispersion (Theil coefficient, average deviation from leading countries) and a variety of indicators of economic performance (GDP, GDP/capita, R and D intensity, number of patents, investment rates). On the basis of a cluster analysis for the post-war period countries are divided into five clusters: leading elite countries, two catching up clusters and two falling behind clusters. The remainder of the article focuses on a subset of countries belonging to the catching-up clusters. For OECD countries and Asian NICs catch-up effects are very pronounced, but for OECD countries the possibilities for further catching-up seem to be exhausted in the eighties.

While the Soete and Verspagen paper focuses primarily on catch up, the paper by Wolff deals more with convergence. Following a recent paper by Mankiw, Romer and Weil (1992), Wolff distinguishes between "unconditional convergence" and "conditional convergence". Unconditional convergence is the notion implicit in orthodox neo-classical growth theory that sooner or later

---

[10] Catch-up and falling behind refer to changes in the distance from the leader country in terms of per capita income or productivity. Convergence and divergence refer to measures of dispersion in income per capita or productivity within or between groups of countries. This distinction is not always clearly made.

all countries in the world will attain the same per capita income. The theory of conditional convergence suggests that, within groups of countries with similar levels of investment and educational attainment, countries with lower initial per capita income will experience more rapid growth rates of per capita income. Thus convergence within groups may go hand in hand with increased divergence between groups.

Like Soete and Verspagen, Wolff starts by regressing growth rates on the income gap in the initial situation between a country and the leading country. The sub-sample of countries with the highest relative income per capita shows the strongest convergence effects and the most significant coefficients. As more countries are included in the analysis, the unconditional convergence effects become weaker and the coefficients are less often significant. Wolff goes on to assess the effects of primary, secondary and tertiary education variables on growth rates. He concludes that countries with similar educational levels tend to converge amongst themselves, "though not catching up with countries whose educational levels are higher" (p. 154). Thus for poor countries, lack of education is one of the influences which tend to swamp the advantages of backwardness. One of the aims of the paper is to assess the relative importance of primary, secondary and tertiary education. At low income levels, both primary and secondary education have a significant independent influence on growth. In upper middle income levels only secondary education is important. Among the industrial market economies, university enrolment was the only significant education variable, but surprisingly enough its importance seems to be diminishing over time. Another intriguing finding of the paper is that enrolment variables perform better in the analysis than variables measuring educational attainments, even though the latter variables are theoretically more closely related to the concept of human capital. Finally, in terms of goodness of fit the conditional convergence model performs better for the period prior to 1980. This suggests a diminution of catch-up effects over time.

The article by Wolff is characteristic of a "maximalist" approach to growth analysis, where researchers try to include as many countries as possible in the statistical analysis, using publicly available data bases. Like Soete and Verspagen and many other researchers, Wolff makes use of the Summers and Heston data set (Summers and Heston, 1988). In practice there may be something of a trade-off between the size of the country sample and the reliability of the estimates.[11] The more countries one includes, the harder

---

[11] For instance gross enrolment rates are very unreliable indicators of the level of schooling in most less developed countries. In the case of the Soete and Verspagen paper some participants in the discussion were surprised to see the USSR and Hungary classified in the "leading elite" cluster between 1973 and 1988.

it is to gain intimate knowledge of the statistical materials for each country.

The article by Nicholas Crafts focuses on the relative performance of the United Kingdom within a sample of 19 OECD countries in the post war period. Crafts also uses a "conditional convergence" framework and shows that growth rates within the sample are related to the initial distance to the United States, holding growth of labour input and investment ratios constant (cf. Dowrick and Nguyen, 1989). He pays particular attention to the value of the residuals for each country in the regression equation. If the residuals are positive, countries are doing better than would be expected on basis of a simple catch-up hypothesis. This is the case for the UK in the period 1973-1987. Crafts has not included human capital variables in his regression equations, but concludes that improved productivity performance in the UK in the Thatcher period cannot be attributed to increases in investment in physical capital, nor to increases in human capital. The main explanation for productivity improvement is a shakeout of unproductive labour. There are no signs of increases in human capital formation or investment in research and development in the UK. Neither are there any indications that the productivity shock, which lowered the capital output ratio, had a permanent effect on the growth rate of capital, with long and cumulative effects on the growth rate due to Romer type external effects.

6. Ultimate Sources of Growth

Knowledge of the proximate sources of growth is a bridge towards a systematic study of the more ultimate factors underlying the accumulation of stocks of human and physical capital, knowledge and technology (cf. Maddison, 1988). Both growth accounting and growth theory contribute to our understanding of growth by analysing the direct relationships between growth and the inputs into the production process. In addition, these approaches pay attention to variables which influence the productivity of factors of production, such as e.g. economies of scale, technological change or resource allocation. However, the conditions underlying the accumulation of factors of production, the efficiency of their use and of technological change, are taken for granted.

The article by Douglass North deals with precisely such questions. His starting point is the astonishing divergence in economic performance between different regions in the world economy. Like new growth theorists he engages in a polemic against a version of orthodox neo-classical theory, which assumes that free movement of factors of production will result in convergence in the long run. Like new growth theorists, North sees a crucial role for technological change: "The ultimate source of growth..is, in fact, the knowledge and skills a society invests in" (p. 70). However, for North it is not enough to state that individuals and firms invest in knowledge and that technological change is endogenous to the production function. One has to ask when and under what conditions economic actors will be motivated to invest in knowledge (and tangible capital). North focuses on the kind of institutions which will promote efficient behaviour, both in the short run (allocative efficiency) and in the long run (adaptive efficiency). Institutions are defined as the humanly devised constraints that structure human interaction. They are made up of formal rules, informal constraints and enforcement characteristics (p. 66). Institutions provide a framework of incentives and opportunities for the emergence of different types of organisations. Technological change and increasing interdependence have led to increasing transaction costs, both in exchange relations and within productive organisations. In the Western world the rise of relatively flexible institutions has mitigated the tension between technological change and organisations.

In addition to providing a framework for the development of organisations, institutions provide perceptions of reality. Following Herbert Simon, North distinguishes between instrumental rationality, which is based on the postulate of an objective description of the world, and procedural rationality, which is based on subjective perceptions of reality. Once incentives and perceptions are locked into an adaptively inefficient pattern, incremental change will take a society along a less efficient path of development. Thus institutions are characterised by "path dependence". Path dependence and incremental change can help explain the persistent differences in economic performance in time and space.

The role of ultimate sources of growth surfaced in several of the conference papers and in the discussions during the conference. Among the factors mentioned were: demographic change, religious influences on attitudes towards work and saving - a new version of traditional Weberian themes is offered by Hofstede in his analysis of the contribution of the Confucian ethic to growth in East Asian countries (Hofstede, 1984, 1991) - , the role of state formation processes as a prerequisite for the functioning of efficient markets, the function of pressure groups in the Olsonian tradition, attitudes towards income, risk and leisure, the changing quality of management, the role of urbanisation and of course the role of government policy. However, Denison was right in concluding (p. 45) that the quantitative information needed to link more ultimate sources of growth systematically to more proximate sources is still lacking.

Apart from the diffusion of technology, attention primarily focused on the internal sources of growth. Some authors, however, also discussed the role of international economic and political orders. Boomgaard raised the question to what extent colonialism was responsible for economic stagnation in Indonesia, while Hofman paid attention to the effects of developments in the international economic order on Latin American development.

7. Experience of Economic Growth

The articles on growth experiences included in Part II of this book have a number of characteristics in common. In the first place, they summarise the most recent empirical evidence on economic performance in the regions discussed, evidence often generated by the authors themselves. In the second place, they apply modern national accounting concepts to the study of long-run historical processes of growth. In the third place, they all deal with the sources of growth and stagnation, catch up and falling behind discussed in sections 4, 5 and 6 above. The sample of countries includes Japan, an example of explosive growth and catch up, the Netherlands and the UK, both early leaders in the process of Western growth and Indonesia which experienced growth till 1500 and relative stagnation since then. The paper by Crafts raises the question whether government policy in the UK in the Thatcher years succeeded in reversing the pattern of relative decline of the post-war years. The economic development of Spain since 1880 is analysed as a process of failed catch up in a country at the Southern periphery of Europe. The papers on Latin America and Eastern Europe show some interesting parallels, tracing a pattern of rapid growth based on growth of factor inputs till the end of the seventies, followed by decline and stagnation thereafter.

The article by Peter Boomgaard traces processes of economic growth in the very long run in Indonesia. Using fragmentary historical sources on trade, urbanisation, political organisation, inscriptions and exports, Boomgaard concludes that there was a period of almost uninterrupted economic growth from 500-1500, though with shifts in the centre of gravity of economic and political activity. Unfortunately he is unable to indicate to what extent growth of output and population is accompanied by growth of per capita income.

At an early stage Java in particular was characterised by a relatively high level of cultural, political and economic sophistication. There was settled agriculture and wet rice cultivation. There was international trade in luxury agricultural products, which even reached the Roman empire. There were states with complex structures and increasing monetisation from 1300 onwards.

From the standpoint of convergence and divergence an important conclusion is that the level of economic development in Java between 1000 and 1500 was not much different from that of the commercial areas of Europe, India and China.[12]

---

[12] A similar point has been made by among others Elvin (1973) and Wallerstein (1974) for medieval China and Maddison for Moghul India (1971). In terms of technology, the general opinion was that late medieval China was more advanced than most areas of the world.

In explaining the differential performance of Europe and Indonesia since 1500, Boomgaard points to urbanisation as one of the important "ultimate" sources of growth. The most important difference compared to medieval Europe was the relatively low degree of urbanisation in Indonesia and the absence of a hierarchy of markets. In Europe towns combined a variety of functions, such as market place, concentration of trades and artisans, religious functions, political functions and military functions. In Indonesia all these functions were separated. Local ports tended to develop into separate city states. Cities lacked permanence. At various stages, the lack of urbanisation promoted decentralisation and delayed industrialisation.

A second factor of importance is colonialism, though Boomgaard is very cautious in assessing its long-run effects, pointing to the emotional and ideological biases involved in the discussion. His conclusion is that on balance the period from 1500-1800 was not one of expansion. On the one hand, the Dutch East India company formed a dynamic sector of the economy, on the other it pushed Javanese entrepreneurs out of more rewarding activities, sapping the dynamism of the indigenous economy. The East India company from 1600 onwards and the later colonial regime in the nineteenth and twentieth century also contributed to slower growth through capital drain from Indonesia to the Netherlands (cf. Maddison, 1989b). Though Boomgaard characterises the period from 1800 onwards as one of moderate to high growth, Indonesia entered the modern era of interdependence as one of the countries with the lowest per capita income in the world.

In my own paper I discuss the rapid growth of industrial production in Indonesia since 1966. Starting from a very low base, growth rates of over 10% per annum were achieved for more than two decades. The pattern of industrialisation was resource and labour intensive and until recently highly inward looking. Applying industry of origin methods, I have estimated that productivity per person employed in Indonesian manufacturing was 9.7 per cent of that in the USA in 1987.

In an article on Dutch economic growth van Zanden summarises the latest quantitative evidence of Dutch growth performance from 1500 till the beginning of the twentieth century. He identifies two main periods of growth. There was a period of very rapid growth of between 1580 and 1670, with per capita income increasing between 30 and 60 per cent. The second period was after 1850, when a normal rate economic growth resumed after a long intervening period of relative stagnation. Starting from the high level attained in the second half of the seventeenth century, per capita income remained constant or even exhibited some decline till the end of the eighteenth century. According to van Zanden the availability of unlimited supplies of labour from peripheral provinces and from outside the Netherlands depressed wages. The availability of cheap labour was one of the factors which inhibited growth of per capita output prior to 1850. Per capita growth resumed in the first half of the nineteenth century, but only slowly, as population grew rapidly as well.

In the seventeenth century the Netherlands had become the world productivity leader (see also Maddison, 1991, p. 30/31). Given the relatively short period of rapid growth between 1580 and 1670 van Zanden concludes there must have been substantial economic growth prior to 1500 and that the level of per capita income in 1500 must already have been rather high. By this time a majority of 60 to 70 per cent of the working population of Holland was already working outside the agricultural sector. Like Boomgaard van Zanden stresses the importance of urbanisation. In 1580 no less than 45 per cent of the total population of Holland was living in cities. This rose to 59 per cent by 1670. The period of very rapid growth between 1580 and 1670, was thus associated with rapid urbanisation and also with growth of population.

Presenting data on energy consumption and prices, van Zanden rejects the hypothesis that the availability of cheap energy in the form of peat contributed to rapid growth in the seventeenth century. On the contrary, the relative price of peat rose and the energy intensity of production declined. Only in the nineteenth century did the availability of cheap fuel lead to drastic increases in the energy intensity of production during the process of industrialisation.

Van Zanden also presents data on holdings of financial capital, showing in particular how accumulation of financial capital continued even during the long period of stagnation of per capita income growth between 1650 and 1790.

After playing a crucial role in the early phase of the European expansion overseas, the economic importance of Spain declined. Spain was unable to convert the immense wealth streaming in from its overseas colonies into productive activities. Economic and political leadership shifted to North Western Europe in the sixteenth and early seventeenth century. Over the past two centuries, however, Spain has evolved from a declining imperial power to an emerging but relatively backward nation at the Western European periphery (Prados de la Escosura, p. 285). Prados de la Escosura picks up the quantitative story Spanish economic growth in 1800 and presents new long term estimates of growth of GDP per capita. His estimates are made from the production side and show a more rosy picture for the period 1860-1980, than previous estimates made from the expenditure side. One of the reasons for the differences is that Prados has been able to pay more attention to service production.

On average GDP per capita increased by 0.8 per cent per annum, with rapid growth from 1860 to 1890 and from 1913 to 1929. Compared to previous estimates, Prados' estimates also show less decline in GDP per capita between 1929 and 1950. Nevertheless, he interprets Spanish growth and development as an example of non-convergence. Taking levels of real output per capita in 1985 from Summers and Heston (1991), Prados, compares trends in GDP in Spain with those in the USA, Germany, France, and Italy. In spite of a low initial level of per capita income, Spain did not show any signs of catch up before 1960. Spain was characterised by relatively low levels of accumulation of human and physical capital, delayed release of labour from agriculture and a closed and inward looking economy. In particular the decade of the fifties was a decade of failed catching up, as a comparison with Italy's performance brings out.[13] Prados identifies the period between Franco's death in 1975 and the admission of Spain to the EEC as a second period of failed catch up.

The other extreme in terms of catch up is Japan, the prime example of a late developer which has achieved such fast rates of growth that it is now approaching the world productivity leader the USA in several branches of economic activity. In the period 1953-1973 GDP per capita increased at almost 7.5 per cent per year. Per capita growth slowed down after 1973, but still continued at a respectable rate of over 3 per cent per year. In certain branches of manufacturing such as machinery and transport equipment Japan has by now even become the productivity leader (Pilat and van Ark, 1991).

Pilat applies Denison's growth accounting framework to identify the proximate sources of growth of GDP for the period 1953-1989. Their importance varies from subperiod to subperiod. For the first period 1953-1960, business labour input was the most important factor. Next in order of importance were increases in the capital stock and improved resource allocation due to structural change. In the second period, from 1960 to 1973, the dominant factor was the rapid growth of the non-residential capital stock, accounting for 43 per cent of GDP growth.

Over the whole period 1953-1989, growth of factor inputs accounted for 68 per cent of GDP growth in Japan. Labour inputs accounted for 24 per cent and capital inputs for 44 per cent. The most important source of growth was fixed non-residential capital. Increases in total factor productivity accounted for 32 per cent of GDP growth. Within this category the residual factor advances in knowledge and n.e.c. contributed most to growth. When growth slowed down after 1973, the role of factor inputs became more important, especially in the years immediately after 1973.

Moving to more ultimate causes of Japan's rapid growth, Pilat emphasises the advantages of relative backwardness, combined with a capability to assimilate modern technology developed in the pre-war period. Relative backwardness opened opportunities for structural change and rapid advances

---

[13] In the discussion Nicholas Crafts disputed this assessment of Spain's performance, pointing among others to figures on Spain presented in the paper by André Hofman.

in knowledge. New technology also entered the production process through capital accumulation. In the early post-war years the gap between actual and potential output caused by war-time destruction also contributed to growth.[14] Pilat goes on to discuss the role of buoyant demand, exceptionally high savings and low rates of interest in Japanese capital accumulation. The Confucian ethic and government policy have also undoubtedly contributed to growth, but these factors are so entwined with others that their effects are hard to assess in a quantitative sense.

One of the important questions in economic history concerns the divergence of North and South American economic performance since the middle of the nineteenth century. In the mid-nineteenth century there were considerable similarities between these regions. Both regions were thinly populated, resource rich and experienced massive immigration. The regions were not incomparable in per capita income and primary exports played an important role in economic development. Among the explanations of this divergence are the differences in the institutional structures inherited from the period of colonial penetration and different complexes of attitudes and mentalities associated with Protestant and Catholic countries of colonisation (Hartz, 1964). Other factors mentioned are negative external influences and neo-colonial drain (Cardoso and Faletto, 1979). Argentina was the most famous example of a country expected to attain Western standards of living by 1950, which failed to do so.

The article by André Hofman takes 1900 as its starting point. He analyses economic performance of six Latin American countries - Argentina, Brazil, Chile, Colombia, Mexico and Venezuela - in the twentieth century, comparing them with Asian NICs, Iberian Europe and advanced industrial economies.

According to Hofman per capita income in Latin America stood at 29 per cent of the US level in 1900, indicating that considerable divergence must have taken place in the second half of the nineteenth century. For the greater part of the twentieth century Hofman's paper highlights the relatively successful development of Latin American economies. Up to 1929 Latin America experienced rates of growth per capita at least as high as the advanced industrial countries (1.9 per cent per annum from 1900-1913, 1.6 per cent between 1913-1929). Growth was primarily export led. Initially Latin American countries were hard hit by the depression of 1929, but most countries recovered rapidly due to successful import substitution. In the thirties Latin American countries performed much better than Asian countries (cf. Maddison, 1985). Till 1950 per capita growth rates were higher than in several European countries.

---

[14] This point was emphasised by Kees van der Meer, the discussant of Pilat's paper.

In the post-war period all countries in the world economy were characterised by rapid growth of per capita income. But till 1973 growth in Latin America was slower than in European countries and Asian NICs, though somewhat higher than in the USA. Looking at individual countries, relative positions of Argentina and Chile declined quite substantially, while the relative positions of the other countries improved. In terms of catch up Latin America's average position relative to the USA remained by and large unchanged between 1900 and 1980, which points to a long period of growth. In terms of per capita income the large Latin American countries were among the richest of the so-called developing economies in the post-war period.

What Hofman's paper brings out effectively is the disastrous impact of the lost decade of the 1980s. During this period GDP declined by 0.6 per cent per year. At the end of the decade GDP per capita stood at 24 per cent of the USA against 29 per cent at the beginning of the century. Latin America's relative position also deteriorated dramatically in comparison with Asian and Western European countries. Hofman's article also shows clearly how long-run economic performance in Latin America was affected by phases of development in the world economy (cf. Maddison, 1989).

One of the interesting findings of the Hofman study for the post-war period is the slow growth of total factor productivity, compared to Asian NICs and advanced capitalist countries, in particular after 1973. Changes in national income were driven primarily by changes in factor inputs. After 1980 total factor productivity growth was even negative, pointing to a decline in the efficiency of the use of inputs. In other words, disembodied technological progress must have played a less important role in Latin America than elsewhere. This implies that the potential for rapid absorption of new technology from leading countries has up till now not been fully exploited.

To some extent the slow growth of total factor productivity may be due to the fact that Hofman incorporated part of technological progress in his measure of capital input, making upward adjustments for vintage effects. Also much of technological change in Latin America is embodied in imported capital goods. Other possible explanations lie in low initial levels of education, technology and capacity to innovate, misallocation of resources, inefficient management and an institutional structure resistant to change.[15]

In her contribution to this book Eva Ehrlich focuses on economic performance in Eastern Central Europe. She begins by stressing that the unity of this region was artificially created by the cold war division of Europe, which put this area within the sphere of influence of the Soviet Union and imposed the Stalinist model of economic development. Within the region a

---

[15] These points were mentioned by the discussant of the Hofman paper, Victor Urquidi.

distinction can be made between relatively developed countries in the pre-war period such as Czechoslovakia, Hungary and Poland and the Balkan countries Jugoslavia, Bulgaria and Romania. The first three countries embarked earlier on the path of industrialisation, and in particular the Czech part of Czechoslovakia had approached Western European levels of economic development. In the Balkan countries agriculture was more important and the overall initial level of economic development in the post-war period was lower. Ehrlich presents her own estimates of economic growth in the post war period based on the physical indicator method (see e.g Ehrlich, 1969, 1991). These estimates are generally lower than officially published estimates based on net material product concepts.

The overall picture is one of rapid growth and industrialisation till the middle sixties, continued growth at a slower pace till 1975 and stagnation followed by collapse in the period 1975-1990. Till 1980 these countries show a moderate amount of catch up, which proved to be transient in the eighties, when the distance to the advanced countries increased dramatically (cf. Hofman's analysis of Latin American growth experience). This pattern of initial catch up followed by stagnation under the Stalinist model of economic development - characterised by elimination of markets, central planning, priority for massive investment in heavy (defence) industry and collectivisation of agriculture - can be explained by what Ehrlich calls a model of exhaustive growth. At an early stage rapid growth can be achieved by massive mobilisation of resources for investment in capital stock and extensive use of energy. Because of neglect of infrastructure and stagnation of technical change, modernisation of products and modernisation of production technology, the growth model exhausts itself and ends up in stagnation. Rephrasing Ehrlich's analysis in terms of proximate and ultimate causes, one could say that the Stalinist model creates institutions which subsequently discourage efficient allocation of resources and technological progress. Given the lack of technological progress, the system runs into diminishing returns. There are intriguing parallels between Ehrlich's model of exhaustive growth and Hofman's analysis of slow growth of total factor productivity in post-war Latin America.

In his already mentioned article on the United Kingdom in the Thatcher years, Crafts tackles the question whether relative economic decline can be arrested. The United Kingdom was the world productivity leader till approximately 1890, when it was overtaken by the USA. In the twentieth century, the United Kingdom experienced slow productivity growth (see also Maddison, 1991). Though it participated in the acceleration of per capita growth rates in the post-war "golden age" till 1973, its growth rates were among the lowest of the advanced industrial countries. Crafts argues that a shakeout of unproductive labour in manufacturing in the 1979-1989 period

definitely contributed to increased productivity per capita and improvement in
per capita growth rates both in absolute terms and in comparison with other
countries. The price of this shakeout was a substantial increase in
unemployment. In terms of loss of output, Crafts thinks this was more than
compensated by increased productivity. An overall assessment of the period in
terms of welfare effects, however, depends on the weights one attaches to
unemployment and increases in inequality and other social indicators, relative
to productivity increases. Looking at a variety of social indicators - such as
life expectancy at birth, fatal accidents, satisfaction with the environment,
incidence of poverty and inequality - in a comparative context, Crafts comes
to a less negative assessment of the welfare consequences of Thatcherian
policies, than most critics of the Thatcher regime. However, he seriously
doubts whether the productivity shock will have a long run effect on capital
accumulation, technological change and the growth rate.

8. International Comparisons of Levels of Economic Performance

Level comparisons are an essential ingredient of international comparisons of
economic performance. They provide benchmarks for an assessment of the
relative standing of economies at given moments of time. It is well known
that exchange rates have some serious disadvantages as conversion factors in
international level comparisons. Exchange rates fluctuate widely due to capital
movements. They are subject to policy interference and they are primarily
influenced by the movements in tradables, rather than non-tradables. Research
efforts have therefore long been directed at developing alternative conversion
factors.

   The best known approach to international comparisons is the International
Comparisons Project (ICP) of the United Nations, which has been adopted by
a variety of international organisations such as Eurostat and OECD (see e.g.
Kravis, Summers and Heston, 1982). The ICP approach is an expenditure
approach, in which prices are collected in a great number of countries for a
specified basket of final goods and services. On the basis of these prices
purchasing power parities (PPPs) are calculated for aggregate national income
and for different components of final demand. These purchasing power
parities have been used to construct data sets for the post-war period in
"international dollars" (see Summers and Heston, 1988, 1991). These data
sets are now being used by numerous scholars making international
comparisons, including several of the authors in the present volume (Wolff,
Soete and Verspagen, Prados and indirectly Crafts and Hofman).

   The ICP tradition is represented in this book by an article by Heston and
Summers. Heston and Summers tackle one of the pressing issues in
international comparisons, namely the discrepancies between relative growth

rates of GDP per capita calculated from national time series and implicit relative growth rates calculated from successive benchmark comparisons. By and large Heston and Summers are of the opinion that implicit relative growth rates based on subsequent benchmarks should be preferred. However, for the 24 OECD countries discussed in the present article, they qualify this conclusion, particularly for the short run. Over short periods of five years "substantial variations may show up in benchmarks that are not necessarily informative about growth" (p. 356).

The mirror image of inconsistencies between growth rates of real GDP calculated directly and via benchmarks, are inconsistencies between benchmark purchasing power parities and PPPs updated or backdated from earlier or later benchmarks using national price indices.

Heston and Summers go one step further. Instead of comparing retropolated PPPs with earlier benchmark PPPs, they divide PPPs by the exchange rate to get comparative price levels (CPLs). As PPPs and exchange rates tend to move together, they argue that CPLs will be more stable than PPPs.[16] Heston and Summers compare comparative price levels backdated with national price indices from the latest 1990 benchmark, with comparative price levels based on earlier benchmarks. Again they find considerable discrepancies. They argue that exchange rate shocks offer a partial explanation of such discrepancies. Exchange rate shocks affect the relative prices of tradables and non-tradables in a country, without influencing real trends in production in the short term. Benchmark comparisons of real income are influenced by appreciation or depreciation of the currency. National time series reflect only the trends in real production.

A second important issue raised in the Heston and Summers paper is, whether price levels and price structures converge in the catching-up process. Angus Maddison has frequently defended the use of Paasche price indices for international comparisons, using US prices to make international comparisons. He argued that price structures would tend to converge on that of the world leader as time went by. In earlier ICP benchmark studies the degree of price similarity also tended to increase as income levels of countries approached each other (see Kravis, Heston and Summers, 1982). However, the data presented by Heston and Summers in the present article show no empirical evidence for such convergence. Comparative price levels do not converge as countries come closer to each other in income levels and price structures do not become more similar. On the whole, price structures in the world economy have tended to diverge rather than converge between 1970 and 1985.

---

[16] This step was criticised by the discussant of the paper, Wilfred Beckerman, who argued that the switch to comparative price levels did not contribute to the clarity of the argument.

The main alternative to the expenditure approach to international comparisons is the industry of origin approach, whereby level comparisons are made sector by sector, industry by industry. In his paper Bart van Ark distinguishes two methods within the industry of origin approach, one based on comparisons of physical quantities, the second based on quantity weighted price ratios. At present, the latter method is the most common one. Since Rostas' pioneering work (Rostas, 1948), it was thought that the industry of origin approach was too labour intensive to be widely applicable. However, in recent years a research team assembled by Maddison at the University of Groningen has demonstrated the feasibility of the industry of origin approach in a research project entitled International Comparisons of Output and Productivity (ICOP). Van Ark gives an overview of the research done in the ICOP project. He discusses its methodology, main results and some of its important problems.

The ICOP approach enables one to make productivity comparisons on a sectoral basis. It uses unit values from industrial censuses to derive price ratios for matched items. These price ratios are aggregated into unit value ratios at higher levels of aggregation such as industries, branches and sectors of the economy. Thus, the ICOP approach is particularly suitable for the study of convergence or divergence of productivity levels at the sectoral level. Such sectoral comparisons are more difficult in an expenditure approach, where the PPPs are based on price data for final goods and services. In addition, the ICOP approach can serve as a valuable cross check for comparisons from the expenditure side.

So far, the ICOP studies have been binary comparisons, usually with the USA as the reference country. Price comparisons are weighted either at weights of the reference country or the other country, bringing out the effects of differences in economic structure. The Fisher average of price ratios at the weights of the two countries is used as a summary measure.[17] Recently Pilat and Prasada Rao (1991) have shown, however, that the multilateral techniques developed in the ICP project can also be applied to ICOP data.

Van Ark discusses three important problems encountered in the ICOP project, namely the quality problem, the problem of double deflation and the consistency of benchmarks and time series. To what extent are the items listed in production censuses, the primary source for industry of origin comparisons, comparable in quality? To what extent can quality adjustments be made,

---

[17] Derek Blades suggested comparing countries with very different structures via a chain of intermediary countries, so that the basket of products is not so different per comparison (e.g. Mexico-Spain, Spain-France, France-USA). Van Ark disagreed arguing that this procedure would obscure the effects of differences in economic structure.

if necessary? The quality problem is also discussed in my own paper which applies the ICOP methodology in a comparison of Indonesian and US manufacturing. One would expect large quality differences between economies at different levels of development. But the Indonesian data provide insufficient detail to assess the extent of quality differences. The second problem refers to double deflation. With the exception of studies on agriculture and distribution, output PPPs have been used to convert value added in most ICOP studies. It would be preferable to have separate PPPs for inputs, but so far, data problems have stood in the way of achieving double deflation. The third problem is that of the inconsistencies between benchmarks and time series also discussed by Heston and Summers. Van Ark discusses various statistical sources of discrepancy. He disagrees with the conclusion that the ideal solution would be to make annual benchmarks to assess dynamic economic performance. He argues for a compromise between regular updating of benchmark comparisons and the use of national time series for extrapolation between benchmarks. The paper concludes with a novel exercise in level accounting. Van Ark tries to account for differences in productivity levels, using capital intensity, firm size and economic structure as explanatory variables. In the case of a Japan/USA comparison 85 per cent of the productivity gap can be explained by these variables. In a Germany/USA and a UK/USA comparison most of the differences remain unexplained.

Apart from the problem of the appropriate conversion factor, international comparisons are hampered by differences in concepts and methods of measurement. These differences are particularly important in the case of the measurement of capital. Capital stock estimates are usually made through the Perpetual Inventory Method, which cumulates annual investments over time. But the assumptions made in different countries concerning service lives and depreciation patterns differ greatly. In several publications (e.g Maddison, 1992), Maddison has favoured standardising the capital stock estimates by applying common assumptions to the underlying investment data from different countries.

The paper by Derek Blades questions this approach. Blades' position, in particular with regard to service lives, is that the national estimates are empirically based and that there are indeed considerable national differences in service lives of capital goods. Some countries keep machinery and structures in use far longer than other countries. Standardised estimates of the capital stock may well be more biased, than estimates using nationally based service lives.

Blades' position was in turn criticised by Mary O'Mahony who argued that for the United Kingdom the empirical basis of the official capital stock estimates is extremely shaky and that researchers are unable to check the plausibility and reliability of the data. A second counterargument offered in favour of standardisation was that, especially for developing economies and for earlier historical periods empirical information on service lives and depreciation patterns is simply lacking. For instance, in the case of Hofman's capital stock estimates for Latin American countries, there is no alternative to the application of standardised assumptions. No official estimates are available and there is no reason to assume that service lives in developing economies such as the Latin American ones are longer than in advanced economies. They may just as well be shorter.[18]

A synthesis between the conflicting points of view would be to use standardised estimates, when data are lacking or estimates are deemed untrustworthy. When detailed examination of the empirical data supports the view that service lives or depreciation patterns differ in different countries, one could deviate from the standardised assumptions.

9. The Role of Policy

Four authors examine the role of policy in economic performance from different policy perspectives. The paper by Sir Alan Peacock presents a liberal perspective on growth. Kregel focuses on the potential contributions of a Keynesian approach to economic policy. The paper by Urquidi presents an evaluation of the developmentalist strategies followed by Latin American countries since the thirties. The paper by Menshikov analyses the breakdown of the Soviet communist model of development and the dire problems involved in the present transition to a market economy.

The four perspectives form a continuum running from a minimalist role of the state in the case of the liberal perspective to pervasive central planning in the communist strategy. In keeping with the present day intellectual climate Peacock's paper is the least unapologetic of the four. He asserts that liberal ideas are totally integrated in mainstream economic analysis. This holds both for the analysis of the importance of market institutions for an efficient allocation of resources and for the assumptions of modern growth accounting and growth theory. In Peacock's view these are all foreshadowed in the work of Adam Smith. Even the external effects of investment in technology - much emphasised in the contemporary discussion - are analysed in the *Wealth of Nations*.

Peacock begins with the statement that from a liberal perspective economic growth is not a goal in itself. It is the outcome of a multitude of individual

---

[18] Several participants, including Menshikov and Urquidi gave anecdotal examples of new machinery cannibalised for spare parts or rusting unused, in both Eastern Europe and Latin America. Average service lives might just as well be shorter, rather than longer in such countries.

decisions with regard to work and savings patterns. In the political sphere collectivist action to encourage growth is only acceptable if it is in response to voter demands in the political markets for policy. If there is a demand for growth oriented policies, then the liberal perspective on the functioning of the economy holds that limited state intervention will be more conducive to growth, than a more activist approach. According to Peacock the full liberal programme can already be found in the writings of Adam Smith. Smith is in favour of limited government action in removing barriers to competition and creating a stable environment for economic activity. In particular, the government has a role in creating and enforcing institutional arrangements which favour security of property and enforcement of contracts. Also "good" government can contribute to the infrastructure of communications and transport. But the public sector should be kept in check to prevent a reduction of savings through excessive taxation. In particular, Peacock is critical of developmentalist approaches in developing countries which assign a major role to the state. Following Deepak Lal (1983), liberals believe that "getting prices right" is more important than promoting growth by planning, regulation and government expenditure and investments.

Peacock does not indicate to what extent post-war economic policy in European countries should be characterised as "liberal". Therefore it is hard to assess the claim that limited government is more conducive to growth than activist government. Peacock quotes empirical research by Scully (1989), which asserts that growth performance is negatively associated with the size of public expenditures. But, as some of his critics noted during the conference, Peacock seems to take this idea as more or less self-evident.

Kregel returns to the writings of Keynes to establish the outlines of Keynesian economy policy. He defends Keynes against the charge of supporting "simple deficit spending". He argues that the basic characteristic of Keynesian policy is countercyclical public investment spending. In order to achieve this, the government budget should be divided into a current expenditure budget and a capital budget. Under normal conditions, the current budget should run a surplus, to be transferred to the capital budget. In periods of recession an offensive policy should be followed in which deficits on the capital budget compensate for exogenous cyclical changes in investment spending. One of the central points in Kregel's paper is that real Keynesian countercyclical investment policies have never really been put into practice. Thus one cannot assess the impact of "real" Keynesian policy. The division of the government budget into a current and a capital account has never been made. While the share of government expenditure in gross domestic product in OECD countries has increased in the post-war period, public investment as a percentage of GDP has declined. It is the share of social security transfer payments which has gone up. Kregel advocates a reversal in the trend towards increasing transfer payments, combined with increased capital investment by the government. In addition Keynesian policy calls for lower interest rates. Kregel argues that the time is ripe for a real Keynesian economic policy.

Victor Urquidi traces the origins of the "developmentalist approach" back to last quarter of the nineteenth century, when developmentalist regimes such as that of Porfirio Diaz in Mexico promoted economic development through public works, subsidies for infrastructural investment, concessions for the development of natural resources and measures favouring industrialisation. The rationale for this approach, then as in later years, was that Latin American economies such as Argentina, Brazil and Mexico, were very vulnerable to external economic and financial fluctuations. From the great depression of the 1930s onwards, nationalistic economic policies were formulated in which state enterprise, planning, regulation and intervention in markets and import substitution were important elements. These trends were strengthened during world war II. After the war, the ECLAC secretariat and Raoul Prebisch provided the explicit theoretical underpinnings, pointing to adverse terms of trade for primary products.

The developmentalist approach is clearly associated with the structuralist view that in developing economies economic change is inhibited by obstacles, bottlenecks and constraints. To break through the institutional constraints of underdevelopment requires government planning and large scale efforts to industrialise. Efforts need to be coordinated (planning) and a gradualist approach should be rejected in favour of a big push.

In his evaluation of developmentalist practice Urquidi is somewhat ambivalent. On the one hand, he makes it clear that developmentalist policy was far from unsuccessful in its earlier phases. After the war rapid growth and industrialisation got under way in many Latin American countries. On the other hand, Urquidi agrees with the modern consensus that in the long run inward looking policies and import substitution resulted in overprotection, highly improductive economic structures and wasteful government expenditures. As the article by Hofman in this book illustrates, the economic performance of inward looking Latin American economies in the past twenty years compares badly with that of more outward looking Asian economies. In addition, the record of developmentalism in terms of equity is very bad. In spite of an egalitarian rhetoric, inequalities remained very large under developmentalist policies and the poorest segments of the population benefited little from economic growth.

Urquidi goes on to discuss recent "neo-structuralist" formulations, which call for a reduced role of government, a greater role of markets and a stronger outward orientation and finds them "not quite convincing" (p. 461). He suggests that there is no clear break with the past and that old ideas have been adapted to the realities of the new situation. Nevertheless, Urquidi fiercely defends developmentalism and neo-structuralists against frontal attacks on the role of government by neo-liberals. Following authors such as Seers,

Sen, Singer and the ECLAC (UN-ECLAC, 1990), he points to the active role of governments in several of the Asian NICs. Urquidi believes that the worst features of developmentalism should be corrected. But he sees a continuing task for governments in the overall coordination of the economy, in combating structural rigidities and in striving for equity.

There are certain parallels between Urquidi's discussion of developmentalism and Menshikov's analysis of the Socialist experience. On the one hand, Menshikov makes it clear that the socialist model has completely broken down. On the other hand he is firmly opposed to the shock treatment proposed by some people as the best way to achieve a rapid transition to a market economy.

Menshikov's analysis of the breakdown of the Stalinist model is complementary to Ehrlich's analysis in Part II of this book. The elimination of private property and the market resulted in an hierarchical and monopolistic managerial bureaucracy. Central planning, intended in theory to achieve balanced growth in the economy, soon lost touch with the reality of productive activity. In order to survive and fulfil plan targets, firms were obliged to engage in overexploitation of resources, activities in the shadow economy and bureaucratic bargaining and manipulation. The system degenerated into planned anarchy. The basic point Menshikov makes is that the Stalinist model itself inevitably produces a shadow economy.

For Menshikov, the fact that Stalinist socialism is dead, does not mean that all variants of socialism are doomed. He argues that socialism can and even must adapt to the market. Like Kregel who stated that true Keynesian policies had not yet been tried, Menshikov claims that market socialism has never yet been given a chance. A system of market socialism, in which a private sector co-exists with and competes with a dominant public sector operating under liberalised planning, has never been put into practice.

Menshikov's analysis of the failure of economic reform in the former Soviet Union is one of the most interesting parts of his paper. In the first place, the Stalinist command economy gave rise to a shadow economy which was speculative rather than productive. The extreme liberalisation of prices under Yeltsin gave operators in the shadow economy further opportunities to exploit shortages, while supply was unresponsive to price increases. Menshikov criticises the timing of reform measures. Price liberalisation should have followed economic stabilisation and privatisation, rather than preceding it. He rejects shock therapy and total liberalisation of prices.

Priority should be given to the creation of a market infrastructure, economic stabilisation and the creation of a de-monopolised private sector. State firms should be privatised in a non-monopolistic fashion. The shadow economy should be legalised. Measures should be taken to improve the price elasticity of supply. Any plans for a transition to a market economy should take the existing structure of the economy as their point of departure. Because efforts at reform have so far disregarded this existing structure of the economy, perverted socialism risks being transformed into a perverted and improductive form of monopolistic competition. If a market infrastructure is not in place, and in particular if there is no network of wholesale distribution, liberalisation will mean nothing but the transformation of state firms into new monopolies and oligopolies which can exploit scarcity. The shadow economy is so tied up with the corrupted public sector that liberalisation in the present circumstances only creates new opportunities for manipulation of scarcity.

Not everyone will necessarily agree with Menshikov's harsh assessment of the shadow economy and his rejection of price liberalisation and shock therapies. But his paper certainly provides an illustration of how a long-run economic strategy such as the Stalinist model in the Soviet Union resulted in institutional arrangements which have an independent influence on the further course of events, even after the political system underlying them has crumbled away. Thus economic policy, conceived of as a strategy for development sustained over a long period, takes its place among the ultimate sources of growth and stagnation, which play a prominent role in this book.

I would like to conclude this introduction with three final observations. In the first place, the papers included in the volume testify to the extremely lively state of affairs in research on economic growth. In the second place, it is worth noting how much of a common framework and language was to be found in the conference papers, notwithstanding the diversity in topics, periods, regions and approaches. Finally, this collection of papers serves to bring out the prominent role of Angus Maddison in present day debates and contemporary research on economic growth and its explanations. This volume is dedicated to him, not only in recognition of his past contributions, but also to celebrate his continued involvement in the study of economic growth.

References

Abramovitz, M. (1956), "Resource and Output Trends in the United States since 1870", *American Economic Review*, Vol. 46, May, pp. 5-23.

Abramovitz, M. (1989), "Thinking about Growth", in: M. Abramovitz, *Thinking about Growth*, Cambridge University Press, Cambridge, pp. 3-79.

Barro, R.J. (1991), "Economic Growth in a Cross Section of Countries", The *Quarterly Journal of Economics*, Vol. 106, pp. 407-443.

Beckerman, W. (1974), *In Defence of Economic Growth*, Cape, London.

Cardoso, F.H. and E. Faletto (1979), *Dependency and Development in Latin America*, University of California Press.

Christensen, L.R. and D.W. Jorgenson (1970), "U.S Real Product and Real Factor Input, 1929-1967", *The Review of Income and Wealth*, March, pp. 19-50.

---, D. Cummings, D.W. Jorgenson (1980), "Economic Growth, 1974-73: An International Comparison", in: J.W. Kendrick and B.N.Vaccara, *New Developments in Productivity Measurement and Analysis*, University of Chicago Press, Chicago/London, pp. 595-698.

Denison, E.F. (1967), *Why Growth Rates Differ: Postwar Experience in Nine Western Countries*, Brookings Institution, Washington.

Dowrick, S. and D.T. Nguyen (1989), "OECD Comparative Economic Growth 1950-85: Catch-Up and Convergence", *American Economic Review*, Vol. 79, pp. 1010-1030.

Ehrlich, E. (1969), Dynamic International Comparison of National Incomes Expressed in Terms of Physical Indicators, *Osteuropa Wirtschaft*, Nr. 1, Köln.

--- (1991), *Országok versenye, 1937-1986* (Competition Among Countries, 1937-1986), Közgazdasági és Jogi Könkiadó, Budapest.

Ehrlich, I. (1990), "The Problem of Development: Introduction", *Journal of Political Economy*, Vol. 98. No 5, Supplement, pp. S1-10.

Elvin, M. (1973), *The Pattern of the Chinese Past*, Stanford University Press, Stanford.

Hartz, L. (ed.) (1964), *The Founding of New Societies: Studies in the History of the United States, Latin America, South Africa, Canada and Australia*, Harcourt, Brace and World, New York.

Hofstede, G. (1984), *Culture's Consequences. International Differences in Work Related Values*, Sage Publications, Beverly Hills.

--- (1991), *Cultures and Organisations*, McGraw Hill, London, 1991.

Kendrick, J.W. (1976), *The Formation and Stocks of Total Capital*, The National Bureau of Economic Research, New York.

--- (1981), "International Comparisons of Recent Productivity Trends", in: W. Fellner (ed.), *Essays in Contemporary Economic Problems*, American Enterprise Institute, Washington, D.C., pp. 125-170.

Kravis, I., A. Heston and R. Summers (1982), *World Product and Income*, Johns Hopkins, Baltimore.

Kuznets, S. (1979), "Two Centuries of Economic Growth. Reflections on U.S. Experience", in: S. Kuznets, *Growth, Population and Income Distribution. Selected Essays*, W.W. Norton and Co., New York/London, pp. 1-24.

Lal, D. (1983), *The Poverty of "Development Economics"*, Hobart Paperback, No. 16, Institute of Economic Affairs, London.

Lucas, R.E. (1988), "On the Mechanics of Economic Development", *Journal of Monetary Economics*, Vol. 22, pp. 3-42.

Maddison, A. (1952), "Productivity in Canada, the United Kingdom and the United States", *Oxford Economic Papers*, October, pp. 235-42.

--- (1964), *Economic Growth in the West*, Allen and Unwin, London.

--- (1967), "Comparative Levels of Productivity in the Developed Countries", *Banca Nazionale del Lavoro Quarterly Review*, December, pp. 3-23.

--- (1969), *Economic Growth in Japan and the U.S.S.R.*, Allen and Unwin, London.

--- (1970), *Economic Progress and Policy in Developing Countries*, Allen and Unwin, London.

--- (1971), *Class Structure and Economic Growth: India and Pakistan since the Moghuls*, Allen and Unwin, London.

--- (1972), "Explaining Economic Growth", *Banca Nazionale del Lavoro Quarterly Review*, September, pp. 211-262.

--- (1982), *Phases of Capitalist Development*, Oxford University Press, Oxford.

--- (1983), "Comparison of Levels of GDP per Capita in Developed and Developing Countries, 1700-1980", *Journal of Economic History*, March, pp. 27-41.

--- (1985), *Two Crises: Latin America and Asia, 1929-38 and 1973-83*, OECD, Development Centre, Paris.

--- (ed.) (1986), *Latin America, The Caribbean and the OECD*, OECD, Development Centre, Paris.

--- (1987), "Growth and Slowdown in Advanced Capitalist Economies: Techniques of Quantitative Assessment", *Journal of Economic Literature*, Vol. XXV, pp. 647-698.

--- (1988), "Ultimate and Proximate Growth Causality: A Critique of Mancur Olson on the Rise and Decline of Nations", *Scandinavian Economic History Review*, No. 2, pp. 25-29.

--- (1989), *The World Economy in the Twentieth Century*, OECD, Paris.

--- (1989b), "Dutch Income in and from Indonesia 1700-1938", *Modern Asian Studies*, pp. 645-70.

--- (1990), "Measuring European Growth: The Core and the Periphery", in: E. Aerts and N. Valerio (eds.), *Growth and Stagnation in the Mediterranean World*, Leuven University Press, pp. 82-118.

--- (1991), *Dynamic Forces in Capitalist Development. A Long-Run Comparative View*, Oxford University Press, Oxford.

--- (1992), "Standardised Estimates of Fixed Investment and Capital Stock at Constant Prices: A Long-Run Survey for 6 Countries", Paper presented at Twenty Second General Conference of IARIW, Flims, September.

--- and B. van Ark (1988), *Comparisons of Real Output in Manufacturing*, Policy, Planning and Research Working Papers, WPS5, World Bank, Washington, D.C.

Maddison, A. and B. van Ark (1989), "International Comparison of Purchasing Power, Real Output and Labour Productivity: A Case Study of Brazilian, Mexican and US Manufacturing, 1975", *Review of Income and Wealth*, March, pp. 31-35.

--- and Associates (1992), *The Political Economy of Poverty, Equity and Growth. Brazil and Mexico*, Oxford University Press, New York.

--- and G. Prince (eds.) (1989), *Economic Growth in Indonesia, 1820-1940*, Foris Publications, Dordrecht, Holland.

Mankiw, F, D. Romer and D. Weil (1992), "A Contribution to the Empirics of Economic Growth", *Quarterly Journal of Economics*, Vol. 107, pp. 407-438

Myrdal, G., (1957), *Economic Theory and Underdeveloped Regions*, Duckworth & Co., London.

Nurkse, R. (1953), *Problems of Capital Formation in Underdeveloped Countries*, Oxford University Press, New York.

Pilat, D. and B. van Ark (1991), "Productivity Leadership in Manufacturing, Germany, Japan and the United States, 1973-1989", *Research Memorandum*, No. 456, Institute of Economic Research, Groningen.

--- and D.S Prasada Rao (1991), "A Multilateral Approach to International Comparisons of Real Output, Productivity and Purchasing Power Parities in Manufacturing" *Research Memorandum*, No. 440, Institute of Economic Research, Groningen.

Romer, P.M. (1986), "Increasing Returns and Long-Run Growth", *Journal of Political Economy*, Vol. 94, No. 5, pp. 1002-1037.

Ronan, C.A. and J. Needham (1978), *The Shorter Science and Civilisation in China, Vol. 1. An Abridgment of Joseph Needham's Original Text*, Cambridge University Press, Cambridge.

Rostas, L. (1948), *Comparative Productivity in British and American Industry*, National Institute of Economic and Social Research, Cambridge University Press, London.

Scully, G. (1989), "The Size of the State, Economic Growth and the Efficient Utilization of National Resources", *Public Choice*, Vol. 63, No. 2, November, pp. 149-64.

Snooks, G.D. (1992), "Great Waves of Economic Change: Very Long-Run Growth in Britain, 1086-1990", Paper presented to the 22nd IARIW conference, Flims, Switserland, September.

Solow, R.M., (1957), "Technical Change and the Aggregate Production Function", *Review of Economics and Statistics*, Vol. 39, pp. 312-20.

--- (1991), "New Directions in Growth Theory", in: B. Gahlen, H. Hesse, H.J. Ramser und G. Bombach (Hrsg.), *Wachstumstheorie und Wachstumspolitik. Ein neuer Anlauf*, Mohr/Siebeck, Tübingen, pp. 3-17.

Summers, R. and A. Heston (1988), "A New Set of International Comparisons of Real Product and Price Level Estimates for 130 Countries, 1950-1985", *Review of Income and Wealth*, Series 34, No. 1, March, pp. 1-25.

--- and --- (1991), "The Penn World Table (Mark 5): An Expanded Set of International Comparisons, 1950-1988", *Quarterly Journal of Economics*, Vol. CVI, No. 2, May.

United Nations (1991), *Human Development Report 1991*, Oxford University Press, New York.

United Nations, Economic Commission for Latin America and the Caribbean (1990), *Changing Production Patterns and Social Equity*, Santiago de Chile.

Veblen, T. (1915, 1962), *Imperial Germany and the Industrial Revolution*, reprinted by A.M. Kelley (ed.), Macmillan, New York.

Wallerstein, I. (1974), *The Modern World-System. Capitalist Agriculture and the Origins of the European World-Economy in the Sixteenth Century*, Academic Press, New York.

Part I

Proximate and Ultimate
Sources of Growth

Explaining Economic Growth
A. Szirmai, B. van Ark and D. Pilat
© 1993 Elsevier Science Publishers B.V. All rights reserved.

The Growth Accounting Tradition and Proximate Sources of Growth

*Edward F. Denison**
Brookings Institution

This narrative begins late in 1959 with a meeting in Washington of the Research Advisory Board of the Committee for Economic Development (CED), an organization of business executives. The Advisory Board, consisting of academic economists, recommended that the research staff of CED explore ways to raise the American growth rate, which was widely regarded as unsatisfactory. I had joined this small staff in 1956 and drew the assignment. The result was publication in January 1962 of my *The Sources of Economic Growth in the United States and the Alternatives Before Us*. Two papers emerging from this project became available before then: a paper for the President's Commission on National Goals, written jointly with Herbert Stein, then Director of CED's Research Division (Stein and Denison, 1960); and a paper delivered at the 1961 annual meetings of the American Economic Association, entitled "How to Raise the High Employment Growth Rate by One Percentage Point" (Denison, 1962a).[1]

---

[*] To confine this history of "growth accounting" to a manageable scope the term is used narrowly; much analysis that is necessary for or closely related to growth accounting is omitted. Developments in national income and wealth measurement are excluded as, consequently, is indispensable work of official statisticians and many others. Also excluded are estimates confined to a division of output growth between total input and output per unit of input. Together, these limitations eliminate major contributions of John Kendrick, Simon Kuznets, and Angus Maddison, among many others. Production functions fitted by correlation analysis, models of growth, and analyses of productivity by industry and final product are also omitted. Some minor methodological issues introduced by Dale Jorgenson and various associates are not discussed; as Jorgenson (1990) makes clear, we often disagree on procedures. The development of growth accounting or developments in growth analysis around 1960, when growth accounting was starting, are briefly discussed in two previous articles of mine (1984a and 1987) and two by Angus Maddison (1972 and 1987). Zoltan Roman (1982) and Maurice Scott (1989) include growth accounting in broader descriptions of the development of productivity and growth analysis.

[1] Besides presenting estimates of the effect on the growth rate and the costs of various possible courses of action, the former paper discussed the desirability of high growth as a national goal.

Prior to joining CED's staff, I had spent the 1941-56 period at the Department of Commerce, where I devoted much of my time in the earlier years to estimating components of national income and product, analyzing the trends they revealed, and - with several others - developing the format of the national income and product accounts adopted by the United States that became part of the basis for the United Nations accounts.[2] This experience was invaluable. It resulted in intimate familiarity with the meaning, definition, and derivation of the official series available to measure the output of nations. If one is to analyze the behavior of these series, one must know how they are compiled.

The Sources of Economic Growth investigated three main topics: the sources of United States growth from 1909 to 1958 and during subperiods; the probable future growth rate from 1960 to 1980, which was calculated by adding the contributions expected from the various growth sources; and, most important, the amount by which the future growth rate, whatever it would be otherwise, could be altered by possible actions to affect each source of growth.

Later studies saw many improvements in my methodology but the main ingredients were already present. Let me mention a few, beginning with output measurement.

Actual output was sharply distinguished from potential output, although growth accounting techniques were not used to calculate potential output until a decade later.[3] I measured actual output by constant-price national income, also called net national product at factor cost.

Three characteristics make national income preferable to other candidates. First, unlike gross national product, national income is measured after deduction of capital consumption. Although no production series can, by itself, measure welfare, it is more desirable to maximize net product, the amount available for consumption and additions to the capital stock, than to

---

[2] Among my colleagues were Milton Gilbert (Chief of the National Income Division), Daniel Creamer, George Jaszi, William H. Shaw, Charles F. Schwartz, and Dwight B. Yntema. Richard Stone from the United Kingdom (who with J.R. Meade had prepared the original national accounts published with the 1941 British budget) and George Luxton from Canada participated in the formulation of the national accounts. See Duncan and Shelton (1978) for a description of this period and Denison (1947) for a description of definitional decisions reached at the meetings with Stone and Luxton.

[3] Estimates of potential output and potential man hours by J.W. Knowles of the staff of the Congressional Joint Committee on the Economic Report were discussed, but sources of growth of potential output were not prepared. Business cycle peaks were selected to bound periods for which the sources of growth of actual output were presented.

maximize gross product, a duplicated measure. Moreover, actions that raise gross product but lower net product are possible. For example, diverting gross investment from long-lived to short-lived assets by tax breaks for depreciation may raise the gross rate of return and gross investment while reducing the net rate of return and net investment. Second, unlike domestic product, national income cannot be raised by diverting investment abroad to investment at home even though the rate of return is lower at home so that the shift reduces income available to the nation's residents for consumption or investment.[4] Third, unlike valuation at market prices, valuation at factor cost prevents a shift in the composition of output between lightly taxed and heavily taxed (or subsidized) products from changing measured output.[5]

The methodology in *The Sources of Economic Growth* was firmly grounded upon principles of cost minimization and marginal productivity analysis and in particular on the principle of proportionality, which states that under fairly realistic conditions the earnings of employed inputs are proportional to their marginal products. Earnings were used as weights to combine total labor, capital, and land into a measure of total factor input, and also to combine different types of labor, capital and land into aggregate measures for these separate inputs. The best procedure available was sought to obtain a quantity series for each input (which was multiplied by the input's weight to obtain its contribution to output) and to appraise the effect on output of changes in each determinant of output per unit of input.

Apart from the weighting scheme, the series for the different sources of growth were estimated independently of one another. Hence, if anyone preferred a method of deriving the contribution of any output determinant that differed from mine, he could replace my estimate for that determinant without changing any others except the growth accounting residual.[6] That residual is an estimate of the combined contributions made to growth by advances in knowledge of how to produce at low cost and of miscellaneous output determinants for which separate estimates have not been made. The residual

---

[4]   In November 1991 the U.S. Department of Commerce, as a result of adopting the United Nations System of National Accounts, shifted from gross national product to gross domestic product as the production measure it stresses. I consider this unfortunate.

[5]   In practice this seems to have little effect on growth rates or a properly conducted analysis. Use of market prices to measure output has, however, misled several analysts into overweighting capital in computing total factor input. They obtained the earnings of capital and land, used as their weight, by subtracting labor earnings from output valued at market prices without eliminating indirect business taxes and certain smaller items.

[6]   Maddison (1972) followed this practice for several determinants in amending my estimates from *Why Growth Rates Differ* (Denison, 1967b).

also picks up the net error in the other estimates.

My methodology at that time incorporated three important assumptions. One was needed to estimate the effect of changes in the distribution of employed persons by amount of education. Among workers of the same age and sex, I assumed that three-fifths of the difference in the average earnings of persons with different amounts of education resulted from the difference in education and two-fifths from differences in other attributes of individuals that were associated with education. Later I was able to eliminate the need for this assumption by adjusting directly for differences in scholastic aptitude, socioeconomic status, color, region, farm or nonfarm employment, and full-year employment in addition to age and sex (Denison, 1974, pp. 43-47 and 218-59).

A second assumption concerns the effect of changes in the work year. Over a wide range of hours there is an efficiency offset to reductions in full-time working hours, so that when hours are reduced the quality-adjusted amount of work performed in an hour increases, and total labor input is reduced less than total hours. The size of this efficiency offset to shorter hours declines as hours are progressively shortened. I assumed a particular curve conforming to this pattern. Subsequent studies retained such an assumption but refined the estimates in a number of ways.

The third assumption was that the economy operated under conditions of increasing returns to the size of the national market such that a change in any other output determinant that would have raised private national income by 1 per cent under constant returns to scale actually raised it by 1.1 percent. With some slight modification this assumption has been retained in my later studies.[7] Gains from economies of scale were shown as a separate source in tables showing the sources of growth but estimates of the gain that could be achieved by a favorable change in any growth determinant were stated after allowance for their augmentation by economies of scale.

In all my books I have tried to describe fully the derivation of my estimates - approaching as closely as is feasible to the ideal, the reader's ability to reproduce every number. This practice is essential if quantitative economics is to progress, not only because it permits evaluation of procedures but also to allow one investigator to build upon the work of another. Full description, with reasons for choices, requires space if a subject is extensive, and this is why articles are so often less satisfactory than books. Full description has become part of the growth accounting tradition as practiced by all major participants.

---

[7] In one study (Denison, 1974) I estimated the size of the gains from economies of scale by correlation analysis but later (Denison, 1979b) returned to the original assumption.

The *Sources of Economic Growth in the United States* provided a menu of choices available to increase the growth rate, indicating what change would be required in each determinant to raise the growth rate over the next 20 years by one-tenth of a percentage point, or by the maximum amount possible if this were less than one-tenth of a point. Perhaps the most important conclusion of this first study was that large changes in the determinants of growth would be required to raise the long term growth rate by even tenths of a percentage point. This became less surprizing once one recognized that the changes in output determinants that underlay the existing growth rate were very large.

The second page of the book pointed out that it is concerned exclusively with economic growth in the United States during the twentieth century. Conclusions reached for the United States in this century, I wrote, cannot be transferred to other places and times. However, I suggested that application of similar analytical techniques to the study of growth in other countries would be fruitful, and that comparisons of the results for different countries would be enlightening. Anticipating the distinction drawn in this volume, and by Maddison (1991, pp. 10-11), between direct determinants of growth and background influences, which usually change over longer periods though sometimes abruptly, I wrote:

"Existing political institutions, the general framework of law and of business and financial organization, prevailing attitudes of individuals toward income, work, and provision for the future, religious beliefs, and standards of conduct governing dealings among individuals provide an environment within which production takes place that I regard as given in its fundamentals, though constantly adapting to changing circumstances..."

I have been fortunate throughout my career in having reading committees and advisory committees that included highly competent economists who were receptive to new approaches. Thus Solomon Fabricant, Paul Samuelson, and Herbert Stein were on the reading committee for the book, and Milton Friedman, Neil H. Jacoby, Isador Lubin, Paul Samuelson, and Charles L. Schultze on the advisory panel for the Stein-Denison paper for the President's Commission on National Goals.

Reviewers of the book criticized particular points or estimates but nearly all endorsed the general approach. Review articles by Simon Kuznets (1962) in *Challenge* magazine and by Moses Abramovitz (1962) in the *American Economic Review* along with reviews in other professional journals, including reviews by Wilfred Beckerman (1962) and Douglas North (1963) among participants in the present conference, drew the attention of economists to the book. A *Washington Post* editorial (February 18, 1962) about the book's findings, coverage elsewhere in the daily and business press, and a chapter in J.J. Servan-Schreiber's best selling *Le defi americain* (1967) reached a broader audience. President Kennedy, an enthusiastic promoter of growth, read the *Post* editorial. In response to his inquiry, Robert Solow, then on the staff of the President's Council of Economic Advisers, wrote him a memorandum agreeing with much of my analysis of the effect of measures to stimulate growth. *Newsweek* magazine of March 25, 1963, probably with some exaggeration, referred to me as the man whose "monumental survey last year has convinced President Kennedy that a 5 per cent rate in the U.S. is probably out of reach. His finding so impressed the Administration that it lowered its growth target, starting talking of 4 per cent as a good number to shoot for." Emphasis on education as a source of growth may have strengthened support for educational spending and opportunities.[8]

The book was followed by a good deal of research by others that applied its approach to other countries. Some writings, mainly unpublished dissertations, attempted a complete study while others provided estimates for individual growth sources - often for education, which I had found to be of major importance in the United States. I sometimes encountered planners in Europe using back-of-the-envelope calculations, based on my techniques, to approximate the likely effect on growth of adopting some measure under consideration.

The Sources of Economic Growth inevitably raised the question, if it is so hard to raise the American growth rate, how did some countries obtain growth rates several percentage points higher than the United States? Joseph Pechman and Robert Calkins of The Brookings Institution, where I had written my doctoral dissertation for Brown University back in 1939-40, attracted me to the Brookings staff late in 1962, with my first project to be a study of growth in Western Europe. The project's end result was a 1967 book, entitled *Why Growth Rates Differ: Postwar Experience in Nine Western Countries.* It was obvious in advance that the study would have to consider international differences in **levels** of output per worker if differences in **growth rates** were to be interpreted properly. I therefore selected the nine countries covered by the OECD study, conducted by Milton Gilbert and Associates, entitled *Comparative National Products and Price Levels.*[9] This splendid study furnished bilateral comparisons between the United States and each of eight European countries of the quantities and prices of GNP and

---

[8]   A doctoral dissertation at the University of Maryland (Lewis, 1989) examines the book's analysis of and influence on education.

[9]   The "associates" were Wilfred Beckerman, John Edelman, Stephen Marris, Gerhard Stuvel, and Manfred Teichert. Irving Kravis had collaborated with Gilbert in an earlier pathbreaking study of five of the countries. Similar studies for later years, used in "level" comparisons in later growth accounting studies, have been conducted at the University of Pennsylvania by Kravis, Alan Heston, Robert Summers, Zoltan Kenessey, and others.

about 250 GNP components. It provided alternative comparisons based on weights for each of the paired countries and on both factor cost and market price valuations. I converted the estimates for GNP at factor cost to a national income basis and adjusted them to refer to 1960. The study covered the United States, Belgium, Denmark, France, Germany, the Netherlands, Norway, the United Kingdom, and Italy.

During my tenure at the Commerce Department I had been active in the International Association for Research in Income and Wealth. At its biennial sessions I met economists responsible for national income and wealth estimates of other countries. Without the assistance of these friends in supplying and explaining details of national statistics I could not have carried out this study. Odd Aukrust, Kjeld Bjerke, P.J. Bjerve, Jacques Mayer, and Rolf Krengel are among the many to whom I am particularly indebted. It was my good fortune that Jean-Pierre Poullier joined me in the study soon after it began. His knowledge of European institutions, languages and sources was extremely helpful.

The Economic Council of Canada wanted me to add Canada to my list of countries. When this proved impractical Donald J. Daly of the Council staff initiated a comparison project for Canada, which was carried out by Dorothy Walters. Daly and Walters kept in touch with me throughout our investigations and followed procedures similar to mine, so that our results are comparable. Their investigation resulted in two books by Walters (1968 and 1970).[10]

Not long after starting the study I learned that the Social Science Research Council was sponsoring an investigation of long-term growth in the United States, several European countries and Japan. Scholars in each country were to investigate growth in their own countries over as long a period as possible - usually back to the mid-nineteenth century - and a volume by Simon Kuznets and Moses Abramovitz drawing together the findings from the countries was planned. I was fortunate enough to be invited to a meeting of this group at Salsjobaden, Sweden at which plans for the SSRC project were reviewed and progress reported. I described some of my own early results. The ground rules for authors of the individual country studies were that they were free to pursue any line of inquiry they chose but all were to include certain types of estimates and analysis so as to allow comparison and integration. These included sources-of-growth estimates such as I had prepared for the United States and was developing for Europe.[11]

---

[10] E.C. West prepared the comparison of output levels in the United States and Canada.

[11] The role of demand was, I believe, another.

None of the SSRC country studies were finished until after my *Why Growth Rates Differ* was published in 1967, and in the event only three were completed.[12] However, these were all admirable studies: by Carré, Dubois, and Malinvaud for France (1975; French edition, 1972); by Ohkawa and Rosovsky for Japan (1973); and by Matthews, Feinstein, and Odling-Smee for Britain (1982). My own studies have tried to answer the question, what determinants were responsible for higher growth rates in one period than another, but the long time span covered by the SSRC studies permitted them to focus on the fascinating question, which was part of their common assignment, "What determinants explain why growth rates were much higher after World War II than in the preceding century?"

The SSRC studies lead me to a topic I would otherwise defer. Growth accounting establishes a comprehensive nonduplicating classification of direct determinants of output, measures changes in each determinant, and calculates the effect of each change upon output. Examples of direct determinants are the amounts and characteristics of labor, capital, and land used in production, the state of knowledge as to how to produce at low cost, the amount of misallocation of resources, and the size of markets. The more satisfactory growth accounting studies go further and use the growth accounting classification and results as a framework for a broader discussion. They attempt to go as far as information, time, and energy permit to explain the changes that occur in the many determinants of growth, or the differences that appear between areas. I have tried to do this in my main publications and the three SSRC volumes were particularly successful in doing so.

Looking for more ultimate causes is, however, a seemingly endless quest. For example, the education of **employed** persons increased in the 1960s because the education received by young persons entering employment had been increasing for more than half a century and, consequently, greatly exceeded the education of workers who retired. Depending on the country, the increase in education may have come because compulsory schooling requirements were introduced, raised, or better enforced, because voluntary attendance increased, or both. Which of these it was greatly affected the extent to which distributions of employed persons by amount of education were concentrated within a narrow range in the 1960s. Changes in compulsory and voluntary education may have reflected changes in public attitudes, the ability of parents to afford extra schooling, or efforts of religious bodies and philanthropic organizations to establish schools. But what was behind each of **these** changes? A seemingly endless succession of links lies behind changes in every source of growth.

---

[12] Articles presenting partial results for other countries were published. The planned summary volume was not written.

Some investigators choose to start from the other end, with what they regard as the most fundamental determinants of changes in a nation's output, perhaps religious beliefs, governmental structure, and attitudes toward income and leisure, toward the opposite sex and children, toward science, or toward change in general. If one started in this way one could, in principle, reverse the procedure of the growth accountant. One could trace the effect of each attitudinal or institutional change to its effect upon each direct determinant of output, use the growth accountant's techniques to measure the positive or negative effects of the induced change in each direct determinant, and group the changes so as to obtain the contribution to growth of each of the more ultimate determinants of output. In fact, much of the knowledge needed to make the quantitative links from ultimate to proximate sources of growth is lacking and this prevents comprehensive estimates of the sources of growth classified according to ultimate sources. But it does not prevent qualitative evaluations and generalizations such as are reached by North and other economic historians, or Mancur Olson's views on the increasing rigidity of economies until they are violently shaken up.

Between publication of the *Sources of Growth* and that of *Why Growth Rates Differ* I participated in three conferences dealing with the economics of education. One, in Chicago, whose proceedings were published in the *Journal of Political Economy* (1962), included papers by Theodore W. Schultz, Gary Becker, Jacob Mincer, and Burton Weisbrod, all of whom had pioneered research in this field.[13] Another contributor was Selma Mushkin, who soon thereafter induced me to write a paper (Denison, 1964a) for OECD's Study Group in the Economics of Education, which held a meeting in Paris that was long remembered by its participants for its spirited discussion.[14] The meeting resulted in an OECD publication called *The Residual Factor and Economic Growth*. My paper, after summarizing my estimates of the sources of growth in the United States, compared the contribution of education to postwar growth in the United States, United Kingdom, and Italy. Edmund Malinvaud and Erik Lundberg were among those selected in advance to discuss this paper; John Vaizey, Nicholas Kaldor, and Thomas Balogh were its severest

---

[13] My own contribution to this conference was a summary of the education chapter of my *Sources of Economic Growth*.

[14] As an inducement to write this paper Mushkin promised to arrange the preparation of time series for the amount of education held by employed persons, which were needed for *Why Growth Rates Differ*. This was done very satisfactorily by A.M. Arnesen for Norway, Rose Knight for the United Kingdom, E. Raymaekers for Belgium, and Michel Debeauvais and Associates for France.

critics.[15] The debate centered, among other things, on the acceptability of using earnings to measure differences in relative marginal products. The same paper was made available at a third conference on the economics of education held by the International Economic Association in France in 1963, with a number of the same participants but also many others.[16]

Why Growth Rates Differ was previewed at the 1966 American Economic Association meetings (Denison, 1967a), with Charles P. Kindleberger as discussant, and published in 1967. The book examined mainly the period from 1950 to 1962. It analyzed the sources of growth and of international differences in growth rates of national income and national income per person employed in the nine countries covered; the sources of differences between levels of national income per person employed in the United States and each of the European countries in 1960; and the relationship between levels and growth rates.

The findings were numerous and complex so the following capsule summary is unavoidably inadequate. First, in an international study it is necessary to pay great attention to price weights. Second, gains from eliminating the overallocation of labor to farming and nonfarm self-employment were systematically important in explaining international differences in growth rates, and were closely related to the fraction of the labor force in these activities when the period began. Third, all major growth sources except education contributed more to growth of national income per person employed in Europe than in the United States. Fourth, the separately estimated determinants accounted for nearly all of the difference between growth rates in the United States and the European countries. This suggested that incorporation of knowledge into production was not a major cause of the higher European growth rates in 1950-62. France and Italy were exceptions, but even there the residual differed only modestly from other countries. Fifth, European countries obtained higher growth rates than the United States in this period not because, on balance, they did more to obtain growth but because they operated under conditions that were different with respect to factor proportions, to amount of resource misallocation, to the existing level of technology, management, and general efficiency in the use of resources, and

---

[15] Comments of Malinvaud and Lundberg are published. Also published is a summary of conference discussions written by Tibor Scitovsky and Robert Neild. A paper by Jan Tinbergen and H.C. Bos presenting a planning model for educational requirements for economic growth was, like my paper, severely attacked (especially by Thomas Balogh) and strongly defended.

[16] See Robinson and Vaizey (1966). The paper as published there omitted an important addition dealing with earnings differentials that appears in the OECD volume. The paper was also reprinted by UNESCO and others.

to economies of scale. Sixth, with output valued in United States prices (which minimizes the European output shortfall) in 1960 national income per person employed was below the United States level by over 40 percent on average in Northwest Europe and 60 percent in Italy. The amounts of these gaps that separately estimated determinants explained, individually and collectively, varied among countries but in all cases much of the gap remained in the residual.

Output per person employed in Northwest Europe in 1960 was only at the United States level of 1925. Separately estimated determinants were more favorable in 1960 Europe than in the 1925 United States but residual productivity was much lower. The difference in the residual, it will be recalled, is after elimination of the effects not only of differences in inputs, measured as comprehensively as possible, but also of differences in resource misallocation and economies of scale. Some combination of output determinants not isolated (although I speculated about them) was evidently so adverse in Northwest Europe in 1960 as to offset the advantage of being able to draw upon an extra 35 years' accumulation of managerial and technological knowledge. Knowledge itself that was available to the United States became available to Europe quickly. Alec Cairncross (1966, 1992) is right to stress the difficulty of successfully adopting foreign practices without also coopting their personnel, but even so most of the 1960 residual seemingly must be ascribed to other determinants, probably involving less efficiency within firms. No similar study for the three most recent decades is available, but it is probable that this 1960 efficiency gap by now has largely disappeared along with most of the gap in national income per person employed.

Shortly after *Why Growth Rates Differ* was published, I wrote a chapter (Denison, 1968), largely based on the same research but focused on the United Kingdom, for a Brookings survey of the outlook for that country.

Like all my books, *Why Growth Rates Differ* repeatedly cautioned readers about possible errors in data utilized and in my estimates, and tried to distinguish findings that seemed well founded from those that were less so. Other growth accounting studies have done the same. I think and hope that injection of a healthy dose of skepticism, without discouraging bold assumptions when they are unavoidable, has become part of the growth accounting tradition. So has realization that to ignore a growth determinant, and thus to assume implicitly that something has not changed, is no less an assumption than is an explicit judgement.

Why Growth Rates Differ was widely and enthusiastically reviewed in the countries it covered, and in many others as well, in both professional journals and periodicals of general circulation. This stimulated further interest in growth accounting, particularly in academic circles but also in policy making. Findings were cited in testimony before United States Congressional Committees and in reports of the U.S. Council of Economic Advisers.

Poullier and I met in Brussels with the Belgian Cabinet Committee on Economic Growth. I also met in Paris with the staff of the French Planning Commission. Results were cited in an Australian parliamentary inquiry.

The growth source for which my estimates have been disputed most over the years is capital.[17] A number of issues have arisen, and my estimates are said to be both too low and too high. Some of the disagreement is over classification, some over the choice of an output measure, and some over substance.

My estimates of the contribution of fixed nonresidential business capital to the growth rate, excluding a separate allowance for associated economies of scale, are approximately the products of the growth rates of the stock of such capital, valued in constant prices, and the percentages of national income that such capital earns.[18] In constructing series for the capital stock, different capital goods are equated by their costs at a common date. The contributions of inventories are measured similarly. The contributions of dwellings and international assets are based directly on the output ascribed to the assets in the aggregate output series used.

Some seven arguments that my estimates of the contribution of physical capital are too small, none of which I have accepted, can be identified.

The first issue, raised by several persons including Angus Maddison (1972) in a delayed review of *Why Growth Rates Differ*, concerns embodiment. It was argued that when advances in knowledge permit later vintages of capital goods to have higher marginal products than capital with the same production cost in earlier vintages, the quantity of capital should be counted as increasing proportionally, thus transferring part of the contribution of advances in knowledge to capital.[19] This procedure divorces cause from effect. I want to identify the contribution of capital, or investment, with saving and I want the contribution of advances in knowledge to be

[17] I discussed the contribution of capital to growth in industrial countries separately in (Denison, 1976a and 1980).

[18] More exactly, this calculation is first made for nonresidential business. The growth rate used for fixed private nonresidential capital is the weighted average of the growth rates of the gross and net stock, weighted 3 and 1, respectively, in an effort to approximate the course of capital services. The resulting estimate of the contribution of such capital to the growth rate of nonresidential business national income is multiplied by the ratio of nonresidential business national income to total national income to obtain the contribution to the growth rate of total national income. (Denison, 1985, pp. 50-52, 84-88, 103-4). Earlier estimates were only slightly different.

[19] This is sometimes described as measuring capital by method 3 rather than by method 1, from Denison (1957) or by J instead of K, from a 1960 article by Solow. (See Denison, 1974, p. 55).

comprehensive, with "embodied" knowledge included.[20] Fulton could build a steamboat having a higher marginal product than boats that had equal production costs but were propelled by sails, oars, or poles because he and others invented the steamboat, not because his boat required more postponing of consumption. Preferences as to classification aside, moreover, the contribution of embodied new knowledge, like a capital stock series that equates different vintages by their marginal products, defies measurement. It is impractical either to adjust capital goods price indexes to include "unmeasured" quality change or to separate embodied from disembodied knowledge. Estimates which purport to include embodied knowledge in capital's contribution actually derive from sheer assumption as to the importance of embodiment or from totally inadequate correlation analysis. Furthermore, this procedure would have no implication for policy even if it could be implemented.

The second issue, also related to embodiment, concerns the average age of capital goods. It is argued that when the average age of capital goods is reduced by one year, with composition held constant, output is raised by an amount equivalent to the contribution of one year's advance in embodied knowledge in addition to the capital contribution based on the rate of return. Under very special circumstances, such as prevailed in some countries immediately after World War II, this position can be correct and significant, and I allowed for it in *Why Growth Rates Differ*. But under ordinary circumstances, as I showed in the same book and earlier in "The Unimportance of the Embodied Question" (Denison 1964b), changes in average age are too small to affect growth rates appreciably even if the underlying argument were correct.[21] In addition, the argument itself is flawed. Different types of capital goods experience very different amounts of quality improvement and hence of obsolescence. Opportunities for the greatest gains from investment include the replacement of capital goods that have suffered substantial obsolescence. Gross investment sufficient to hold the average age of capital constant would provide ample gross investment to absorb the better opportunities. Consequently, the gain in the average quality of the capital stock that is supposed to derive from an increment to investment that reduces the average age of capital is not realized. Instead, the difference in average age is largely offset by a reduction in the average amount of quality improvement incorporated in new capital. (See Denison, 1964b and 1967b, pp. 144-50 and Harberger, 1964, pp. 69-70).

The third to sixth issues can be described in the historical context of the

---

[20] See Denison (1972a).

[21] Also see Hulten (1992).

discussion of an article by Dale Jorgenson and Zvi Griliches, who had concluded that there had been almost no postwar increase in American productivity; factor inputs accounted for almost all output gains. They did not secure this result by embodying the fruits of new knowledge into capital, as many readers supposed, but by other statistical procedures. Four main issues involving capital emerged in an interchange between these writers and me in the *Survey of Current Business* from 1969 to 1972 (Jorgenson and Griliches, 1972; Denison, 1972b), in the course of which they changed their estimates.[22]

The first and quantitatively most important explanation of their vanished productivity growth concerned capital utilization. Murray Foss (1963) had shown that the average hours that power-driven equipment in manufacturing and mining establishments are used had increased substantially. Jorgenson and Griliches simply assumed that the average hours of all capital, even dwellings, had increased at the same rate as hours of this segment of power-driven equipment. When challenged, Jorgenson and Griliches eliminated the adjustment for inventories, dwellings and land. They retained it for all nonresidential structures and equipment in all industries but greatly reduced their estimate of the hours increase. In all, 84 percent of the adjustment was removed. In addition to the facts, I questioned their classification of all gains from increased use of capital as a contribution of capital, mainly because the changes were not related to saving. I regard a 1984 book by Foss on capital utilization and growth as definitive on this topic. Using data from Foss, who had made a similar calculation for nonfarm nonresidential business national income, I later calculated that increased capital utilization contributed only 0.03 percentage point to the growth of national income in nonresidential business in 1929-48, 0.04 in 1948-73, and 0.02 in 1973-76. These are generous estimates, based on the assumption that increased use did not shorten service lives.

The second reason that Jorgenson and Griliches obtained such a large contribution from capital is that they calculated the earnings of capital, which determine its weight in total input, by subtracting the earnings of labor from GNP at market prices. The effect was to count indirect business taxes, business transfer payments, and the statistical discrepancy in the national accounts as earnings of capital and hence to overweight capital in total input. This is not an unusual error - Solow, for example, made the same error in calculating his initial production functions (Denison, 1962b, p. 104) - but it was especially damaging here because Jorgenson and Griliches's utilization adjustment made their capital input grow very fast. In revising their estimates,

---

[22] An earlier interchange (Griliches and Jorgenson, 1966; Denison, 1966) had already described most of these issues.

Jorgenson and Griliches eliminated most sales and excise taxes from capital income but retained property taxes, whose classification I had suggested was debatable, and a number of other items (Denison, 1972b, p. 100).

Third, Jorgenson and Griliches, like many others, measured output gross of capital consumption, that is, by GNP. Because all of the increase in capital consumption is counted as a contribution of capital, use of GNP instead of net product yields a much larger contribution to the growth rate from capital and lower contributions from all other determinants, even if capital consumption grows at the same rate as GNP. With a shift toward short-lived assets, capital consumption has actually grown faster than national product. I have already stated why GNP is an inappropriate output measure.

In the course of the interchange, Jorgenson and Griliches replaced their estimates with new ones by Laurits Christensen and Jorgenson (1970). Elimination of most of the utilization adjustment and removal of most indirect business taxes and transfer payments from the capital weight would have restored the residual and removed most of the difference between their estimates and mine. But Christensen and Jorgenson offset part of the change by moving consumer durables owned by households and institutions into the business sector and imputing a return on those assets. The fourth issue concerns this expansion of the scope of the estimates to include the services of consumer durables. Depreciation on consumer durables is huge even with straight line depreciation because these assets are short-lived, and Christensen and Jorgenson maximized its size by use of an accelerated depreciation pattern. All of the increase in the constant-dollar value of this imputed depreciation, in addition to the smaller increase in net income that was imputed to ownership of consumer durables, is counted as a contribution of capital.[23] It is measurement of output gross of depreciation that makes the effect of this extension of scope so big.

Other points affecting capital's contribution that I shall skip over entered into this exchange with Jorgenson and Griliches. These included the treatment of capital gains in calculating income shares, the choice of weighting schemes for output and input, and the depreciation formula.

Jorgenson and changing associates have continued to calculate series which show an exceptionally large contribution from capital because they use GNP to measure output and include in the business sector the use of consumer durables. Martin N. Baily and Charles L. Schultze (1990, pp. 385-95) have shown that there is a negligible difference between the results obtained for 1948-79 by Jorgenson, Gollop, and Fraumeni (1987) and by me (1985) when they refer to the same scope and concept of output. Griliches, meanwhile, has

---

[23] This is in addition to capital's contribution to the production of consumer durables.

directed the program in productivity at the National Bureau of Economic Research since 1978 and has continued his research on education and on research and development. A recent book (Griliches 1988) summarizes his findings, cites his (and other) publications, and reprints a number of his older papers.

The final (and seventh) main argument for adjusting the contribution of capital upward was introduced by Maurice Scott (1989). Scott believes that after investments are undertaken investors see opportunities for further investments of which they were unaware before, and which yield as much as their previous investments did. He argues that advances in knowledge are proportional to, and caused by, investment so it is impossible to separate the contribution made by the two to growth, and their combined contribution is really a contribution of investment. I provided strong reasons to reject these views in a review article of Scott's book (Denison 1991) and need not repeat them here. Like Paul Romer and Robert Lucas, Scott is an original contributor to the "new growth theory" if one follows Robert Solow (1992, p. 10) in identifying that theory with the assumption that some output determinant or other is not subject to diminishing returns.

While I have rejected arguments that my procedures understate the contribution of capital to growth, I have accepted (Denison, 1974 and 1989) an argument, presented most effectively by Thomas K. Rymes in several books and articles, that my past estimates overstate the contribution of capital. Suppose that new knowledge permits more capital goods, unchanged in design, to be produced with no increase in the factor inputs used in their production. The usual procedures (including mine) will show the capital stock increasing as the extra capital goods enter the stock and will credit capital (and total input) with the resulting gains in national product. This occurs even though the increases in output of capital goods result from advances in knowledge, not from saving in the fundamental sense of forgoing consumption. Alexandra Cas and Rymes (1991, p. 5), estimated that this caused the 1961-80 growth rate of GNP per unit of factor input in the Canadian private economy to be understated by 0.47 percentage point, or 28 percent, and the contribution of capital to be overstated by the same 0.47 point.[24] On a net product or national income basis, the misstatement would be much smaller because depreciation increases less than it does when the usual measure is used.

---

[24] This book makes a major contribution to the measurement of productivity by industry and end product, subjects omitted from this paper, as well as to the measurement of capital.

Much of the 1971 conference of the International Association for Research in Income and Wealth was devoted to factor input and productivity, with emphasis on growth accounting and questions it raised. Two issues of the *Review of Income and Wealth* (1972a and 1972b) contain many of the papers delivered. Daniel Creamer and Rymes discussed capital input, Donald Daly weighting of inputs to calculate total factor input, and I "Classification of the Sources of Growth."[25] Besides papers by Kendrick on intangible capital and Rolf Krengel and Joachim Frohn on industry productivity estimates, Ned Nadiri summarized and discussed growth accounting estimates, not all complete, for 26 countries. Significant growth accounting studies upon which he drew that I do not mention elsewhere include those by Sam Bowles and Evangelos A. Voloudakis for Greece, and by Hector Correa, who was the first to introduce an allowance for health and nutrition into labor input, for nine Latin American countries.[26] Zoltan Roman provided original estimates for Hungary, which follow a classification only partly reconcilable with that for other countries, and Hisao Kanamori a fine study of the sources of growth in Japan.[27]

My own opportunity to study Japanese growth came later, when Brookings undertook the comprehensive study that culminated in a book titled *Asia's New Giant* (Patrick and Rosovsky, editors, 1976). William Chung, who had written his doctoral dissertation on Japanese growth (Chung, 1970), joined me. Our part of the project resulted in a chapter in the general book and a separate volume, *How Japan's Economy Grew So Fast* (Denison and Chung, 1976).

Although Japan's high growth rate was partly due to rapid employment growth, the growth rate of real national income per person employed was also extremely high: 7.2 percent in Japan in 1953-71 as against 2.3 percent in the United States in 1948-73, after elimination of the effects of certain irregular factors and differences in estimation procedures. Chung and I found that education, miscellaneous labor input components, and land together

---

[25] I consider this an important paper because much of the disagreement about growth sources stems from differences, often unrecognized, in classification. The invited discussant, Wilfred Beckerman, appeared less sure of the topic's significance at the time but included a Spanish translation in a volume he edited (Beckerman, 1976).

[26] The applicability of Correa's procedures for health and nutrition to advanced countries is discussed in Denison 1967, pp. 114-15 and 404-05. Subsequent application of growth accounting techniques to Argentina and other Latin American countries by Rodolfo E. Biasco also deserves mention.

[27] Kanamori's results were broadly consistent with those reached later by Denison and Chung (1976), but he did not disaggregate the contribution of output per unit of input. Earlier studies were published in Japanese by Kazushi Ohkawa and by T. Watanabe and S. Ekaizu; Kanamori compares their findings with his.

contributed 0.2 percentage point more to growth of output per worker in the United States; all other determinants contributed 5.2 percentage points more in Japan. This difference divides as follows: average hours, 0.4 points; age-sex composition, 0.3; capital per worker, 1.3; improved labor allocation, 0.7; economies of scale, 1.6; advances in knowledge and miscellaneous determinants included in the residual, 0.9 (Denison 1984a, table 6).

A comparison with ten European and North American countries showed no single factor was responsible for Japan's having the highest growth rate of national income per person employed. Instead, Japan received a larger contribution than any of the ten other countries from all of five major categories of growth sources - the increase in labor input, the increase in capital input, reallocation of labor from farming and nonfarm self employment, the incorporation of new knowledge into production, and economies of scale - with the sole exception that Italy gained slightly more from labor reallocation.

In 1970 the **level** of national income per person employed in Japan was only 55 percent of the United States level by the comparison most favorable to Japan, use of United States price weights. Chung and I combined estimates of the sources of the differences in the level of output per person employed with the sources of differences in growth rates to project the Japanese growth rate into the future. To do so we assumed that, as the United States advantage in level over Japan with respect to each determinant disappeared, the Japanese advantage in growth rates with respect to that determinant would also disappear.

The first really thorough study of the sources of growth in a large low-income country was prepared for India as a doctoral dissertation by Bakul H. Dholakia and published in 1974. It was admirably complete and carefully done. Dholakia covered the twenty years from 1948-49 to 1968-69. He compared his results for India with mine for the United States and Northwest Europe. He followed the basic methodology I had used and his results appear to be largely comparable to mine. Labor, capital, and output per unit of input contributed about equally to Indian growth over Dholakia's whole period. Dholakia's book was unknown to me for years after its appearance, and still seems not to be widely known.[28]

My estimates of the sources of growth in the United States were updated through 1969 in a Brookings book titled *Accounting for United States Eco-*

---

[28] Dholakia omits an estimate for India of what I called "economies of scale associated with income elasticities" and consequently obtains a contribution from the residual that may be slightly larger than otherwise would have been the case. Nevertheless, the residual was smaller than in the United States or Northwest Europe.

nomic Growth, 1929-1969 (Denison 1974). It provided complete annual data. Methodology and sectoring were substantially improved. An innovation was the extension of the sources-of-growth analysis to provide series for potential national income and GNP which, I believe, are superior to series based on alternative methodologies. The series were calculated by estimating each year the difference between the actual value of each output determinant and the value it would have taken if the pressure of demand upon available resources had been at a standardized high employment level.[29] Estimates of the gap between actual and potential output and its components are useful for short-run cyclical analysis, and the presentation of annual series for potential output and its determinants, and of the sources of growth of potential output, improve analysis of long term growth. In this and later books I have considered estimates of the sources of growth that refer to potential output more illuminating than those that refer to actual output and given them at least equal emphasis.

Growth accounting became familiar to economists in the communist countries rather quickly. A Russian translation of *Why Growth Rates Differ*, with a long introduction by Valentin M. Kudrov which included considerable information about the Soviet Union, was published in 1971 and widely distributed. I was told later that a serious effort had been made to produce estimates of the sources of growth in the Soviet Union comparable to mine for the West but that it was unsuccessful, perhaps because the official national income series was unsuitable for use as an output measure. Partial estimates appeared for East European countries, in addition to Roman's estimates for Hungary. In 1987 a small group of Chinese economists and engineers led by Shi Qingqi began a study of the sources of growth in postwar China, on which I advised. A brief preliminary report, including tentative estimates, was completed and a meeting to discuss it was held in January 1990, but to my great regret the group was disbanded before necessary modifications were made. I understand that a different group using the Jorgenson-Christensen methodology was at work at the same time.

A study by Kim Kwang-suk and Park Joon-kyung for the Korea Development Institute, to which I served as an adviser, resulted in 1979 and 1985 books on sources of growth in South Korea. The latter covers 1962-83 and is an excellent study of a period of fast growth, made the more useful because comparable to my studies for the United States, Western Europe and Japan, Walters' for Canada, and, to a large extent, Dholakia's for India. It is interesting to compare the sources of Korean growth with those of Japan about a decade earlier. In its first period of very rapid growth, 1963 to 1972,

---

[29] See Denison (1974, 1979b, and 1985).

Korea followed closely the pattern of growth sources evidenced in Japan in its first such period, 1953 to 1961. Strikingly, however, comparison of the following decade, that is, of 1972-82 in Korea with 1961-71 in Japan, showed several major differences. Among other changes, the residual estimate for advances in knowledge and miscellaneous determinants held up and even increased in Japan in 1961-71 but plunged in Korea after 1973, as it did almost everywhere including Japan.[30] Whatever happened after 1973, it was sufficient to override any similarities of growth patterns at the same stage of development but different dates among advanced and rapidly developing countries. Only increases in contributions from other growth sources, especially labor input, enabled Korea, unlike most countries, to maintain its high growth rate of total national income after 1973.

Indeed, after 1973 the whole world changed. Almost everywhere growth rates of actual and potential national income, both total and per person employed, fell sharply. Two of my books (Denison, 1979b and 1985) and several articles (e.g. Denison, 1979a, 1983, and especially 1984b) examined the slowdown period in the United States. Detailed estimates in the first book ended with 1976, in the second with 1982.[31] Three additional sources of output-per-unit-of-input growth, or rather retardation, were separated from the residual. These represented costs of environmental controls, employee safety and health legislation, and crime (Denison, 1978 and 1979b). Separately estimated determinants explained only about half of the retardation in the growth of output per person employed up to 1982 (Denison, 1985, p. 37), with a large number of determinants each explaining a small amount. The other half of the retardation appears in the residual. I labeled the latter half a "mystery" and the label was widely adopted.

Although growth accounting left the cause of much of the slowdown unassigned, it was nevertheless invaluable in analyzing even this portion. Dozens of alleged explanations were being advanced and most were accompanied by a proposal by some interest group for a cure at the expense of some other group or the public purse. Assembling information and

---

[30] Estimates for Japan by Kanamori and Associates (1983) showed a large drop in their residual from 1960-70 to 1970-80.

[31] Like my earlier books these and the preceding one (Denison, 1974) benefitted greatly from comments on drafts, including those by Abramovitz, Fabricant, Kendrick, and Schultze, who had also reviewed earlier manuscripts, as well as Jack Alterman, Jerome Mark, George Jaszi, Peter Clark, Robert Aaron Gordon, Arthur Okun, and George Perry. Reviewers were again generous.
Findings from the 1985 book were previewed and discussed at a June 1984 conference at Rolleboise, France, that was organized by the World Bank and OECD. Proceedings were summarized in a report edited by Jacques de Bandt (1985).

analyzing it by growth accounting techniques, often aided by other kinds of economic analysis, showed definitively that most of the explanations asserted either could not have contributed to the slowdown at all or else could have explained only a small amount of it (Denison, 1979b, especially chapter 9; 1984b; and 1985, chapter 3). Among the latter, the energy price rises were the most important but they could not have accounted for more than 0.1 or 0.2 percentage point of the growth rate reduction in the United States.[32] Neither the amount of organized research and development expenditures nor its rate of return was a factor. Only a few candidates for culprit or culprits could not be eliminated; I discussed them in the 1985 volume. Among them is the quality of management. A discussion of management in that book concludes as follows (Denison, 1985, pp. 46-47).

"The position that American management took the wrong turn is only informed opinion, and obviously it is contested. I do not know whether this belief is correct, but I do find it sufficiently plausible, the importance of management great enough, and the timing of the change consistent enough, to include it among the more probable main causes of the slowdown in the growth of residual productivity. As with most other explanations, however, the suddenness of the change in the growth rate is a difficulty. Nor is it obvious how management deterioration relates to the international character of the productivity slowdown, although multinational corporations might have contributed to dissemination of the criticized practices among Western free-market economies. "

During this period Kendrick was associated with the American Enterprise Institute, where he analyzed the slowdown in American productivity by use of growth accounting (Kendrick, 1979) and arranged for others, including me, to do so (Denison, 1984b).[33] Particular mention should be made of articles by Kendrick (1981) and Maddison (1984) that examine the productivity slowdown in a number of countries.[34] In his most recent book, Maddison (1991) relies on both growth accounting techniques and historical interpretation as he provides a panoramic view of long-term growth, postwar acceleration, and subsequent retardation. This was preceded by his 1987 *Journal of Economic Literature* article which both surveyed growth accounting and provided numerous estimates for 1913-50, 1950-73 and 1973-84.

---

[32] Jorgenson (e.g. 1984) has persistently ascribed dominant importance to energy prices.

[33] Denison (1985) commented on some of Kendrick's estimates.

[34] Maddison's paper appeared in a conference volume edited by Kendrick (1984) that contained several other articles on the slowdown. Papers for a second AEI conference arranged by Kendrick, held in 1986, were mainly concerned with productivity by industry. They were not published.

In my view, the mystery surrounding much of the productivity slowdown remains. In a review article of *Accounting for Slower Economic Growth* Richard Stone (1980) recommended that I should make my best guess as to the causes of the retardation and adjust my tables accordingly. I have been unwilling to do so because I lack confidence in any surmise I might make.[35] Rather, it has been my practice to let my tables stand as initially compiled, without introduction of adjustments to make estimates appear more consistent or palatable, and instead to introduce speculations about any odd behavior of the residual in the text.

I have two regrets about the development of growth accounting. The clear lesson from growth accounting - and not only from growth accounting - is that there are several main and many smaller sources of growth, and many ways to affect the growth rate, each way by a rather small amount. My first regret is that growth accounting has not lastingly diverted a great many economists from a single-minded devotion to raising saving and investment as **the** road to higher growth, to be achieved (if at all) not only at the expense of consumption but also of efficient resource allocation, equity, and equality.[36] Adam Smith and Alfred Marshall knew better than this. If one were **forced** to choose a single growth source as most important in the long run, the choice would have to be advances in knowledge. Regrettably, it is not clear how they can be accelerated very much.

My second regret is that growth accounting has nowhere been institutionalized in such a way that comprehensive annual time series including recent years are continuously available. Expanded, as in my more recent books, to embrace potential as well as actual output and the sources of difference between them, current annual series could provide a basis for improving short-run as well as long-run analysis and policy formulation.[37] A menu of choices to alter the growth rate of potential output is rarely subject to rapid change, but this too would benefit from regular updating.

Let me now offer a final apology for skipping the contributions of many scholars, whether this results from my need to restrict the subject or from my

---

[35] Stone's recommendation is less appealing than his earlier proposal to eliminate discrepancies in the national accounts by adjusting all components of income and product in proportion to the products of the estimate for each component and its estimated percentage error margin.

[36] Among many recent exceptions are Becker (1992), Cairncross (1975, 1992), and Lucas (1988).

[37] Questions about productivity that growth accounting can (and, each in at least one study, does) help answer, were posed in a previous paper (Denison, 1984a, p. 7). They are worded in terms of American growth but are equally applicable to other countries. Similar questions can be asked about total output.

ignorance of parts of the world-wide literature. I also ask your indulgence for emphasizing activities in which I participated and my own points of view. If the reader finds this paper is better viewed as a personal history than as a history of the sources of growth, I hope that he will find that it nevertheless reports a major part of developments in growth accounting. Other papers in this volume, I trust, will comprize the next noteworthy event in growth accounting's history.

References

Abramovitz, M. (1962), "Economic Growth in the United States", *American Economic Review*, Vol. 52, No. 4, pp. 762-782.

Baily, M. and C. Schultze (1990), "The Productivity of Capital in a Period of Slower Growth", *Brookings Papers on Economic Activity*, Microeconomics, pp. 369-406.

Becker, G. (1992), "The Adam Smith Address: Education, Labor Force Quality, and the Economy", *Business Economics*, Vol. 27, No.1, pp. 7-12.

Beckerman, W. (1962), "The Sources of Economic Growth in the United States and the Alternatives Before Us", *The Economic Journal*, Vol. 72, No. 288, pp. 935-938.

--- (ed.) (1976), Separata del Volumen 1/1976 de la *Revista Espanola de Economia*.

Cairncross, A. (1966), *Economics and Economic Policy*, Basil Blackwell Ltd., Oxford.

--- (1975), *Inflation, Growth and International Finance*, State University of New York Press, Albany.

--- (1992), "From Theory to Policy Making: Economics as a Profession", *Banca Nazionale del Lavoro Quarterly Review*, No. 180, pp. 3-20.

Carré, J.J., P. Dubois, and E. Malinvaud (English edition 1975), *French Economic Growth*, Stanford University Press, Stanford.

Cas, A. and T. Rymes (1991), *On Concepts and Measures of Multifactor Productivity in Canada, 1961-1980*, Cambridge University Press, Cambridge.

Christensen, L. and D. Jorgenson (1970), "U.S. Real Product and Real Factor Input, 1929-1967", *The Review of Income and Wealth*, Vol. 16, No. 2, pp. 19-50.

Chung, W. (1970), *A Study of Economic Growth in Postwar Japan for the Period 1952-1967: An Application of Total Productivity Analysis*, New School for Social Research, New York (mimeo).

De Bandt, J. (1985), *Long-Run Growth Prospects for Industrial Countries Conference: Proceedings*, The World Bank and OECD, Washington (mimeo).

Denison, E. (1947), "Report on Tripartite Discussions of National Income Measurement", in: *Studies in Income and Wealth*, Vol. 10, University Press for the National Bureau of Economic Research, Cambridge, pp.3-22.

--- (1957), "Theoretical Aspects of Quality Change, Capital Consumption and Net Capital Formation", in: *Studies in Income and Wealth*, Vol. 19, Princeton University Press for National Bureau of Economic Research, Princeton, pp. 215-261, 281-284.

--- (1962a), "How to Raise the High Employment Growth Rate by One Percentage Point", *American Economic Review*, Vol. 52, No. 2, pp. 67-75.

--- (1962b), *The Sources of Economic Growth in the United States and the Alternatives Before Us*, CED Supplementary Paper No. 13, Committee for Economic Development, New York.

--- (1964a), "Measuring the Contribution of Education (and the Residual) to Economic Growth," in: OECD Study Group in the Economics of Education, *The Residual Factor and Economic Growth*, OECD, Paris, pp. 13-55, 77-100.

--- (1964b), "The Unimportance of the Embodied Question", *American Economic Review*, Vol. 54, No. 2, Part 1, pp. 90-94.

--- (1966), "Discussion" (of paper by Griliches and Jorgenson), Vol. 56, No. 2, *American Economic Review*, pp. 76-78.

--- (1967a), "Sources of Postwar Growth in Nine Western Countries", *American Economic Review*, Vol. 67, No. 2, pp. 325-332.

--- (1967b), *Why Growth Rates Differ: Postwar Experience in Nine Western Countries*, Brookings Institution, Washington. Also 1971, Translation into Russian with Introduction by V. Kudrov, Progress Publishing House, Moscow.

--- (1968), "Economic Growth", in: R. Caves and Associates, *Britain's Economic Prospects*, The Brookings Institution, Washington, pp. 231-278.

--- (1972a), "Classification of Sources of Growth", *Review of Income and Wealth*, Vol. 18, No. 1, pp. 1-25.

--- (1972b), "Some Major Issues in Productivity Analysis: An Examination of Estimates by Jorgenson and Griliches" (reprinted from May 1969 *Survey of Current Business, Part II*) and "Final Comments", *Survey of Current Business*, Vol. 52, No. 5, Part 2, pp. 37-63 and 95-110.

--- (1974), *Accounting for United States Economic Growth, 1929-1969*, The Brookings Institution, Washington.

--- (1976), "The Contribution of Capital to the Postwar Growth of Industrial Countries", in: *U.S. Economic Growth from 1976 to 1986: Prospects, Problems, and Patterns*, Vol. 3, *Capital*, Studies Prepared for the Use of the Joint Economic Committee, Congress of the United States, November 15, pp. 45-83.

Denison, E. (1978), "Effects of Selected Changes in the Institutional and Human Environment Upon Output per Unit of Input", *Survey of Current Business*, Vol. 58, No. 1, pp. 21-44.

--- (1979a), "Where Has Productivity Gone?" in W.Fellner, Project Director, *Contemporary Economic Problems 1979*, American Enterprise Institute, Washington, pp. 71-77. Reprinted from *Basis Point*, Vol. 3, No. 1 (1978).

--- (1979b), *Accounting for Slower Economic Growth: the United States in the 1970s*, The Brookings Institution, Washington.

--- (1980), "The Contribution of Capital to Economic Growth", *American Economic Review*, Vol. 70, No. 2, pp. 220-224.

--- (1983), "The Interruption of Productivity Growth in the United States", *The Economic Journal*, Vol. 93, No. 372, pp. 56-77.

--- (1984a), "Productivity Analysis through Growth Accounting", in: A. Brief (ed.), *Productivity Research in the Behavioral and Social Sciences*, Praeger Publishers, New York, pp. 7-55.

--- (1984b), "Accounting for Slower Economic Growth: An Update", in: J. Kendrick (ed.), *International Comparisons of Productivity and Causes of the Slowdown*, American Enterprise Institute and Ballinger Publishing Co., Cambridge.

--- (1985), *Trends in American Economic Growth, 1929-1982*, The Brookings Institution, Washington.

--- (1987), "Growth Accounting", in: *The New Palgrave: A Dictionary of Economics*, The Stockton Press, Vol. II, pp. 571-574, New York.

--- (1989), *Estimates of Productivity Change by Industry: An Evaluation and an Alternative*, The Brookings Institution, Washington.

--- (1991), "Scott's A New View of Economic Growth: A Review Article", *Oxford Economic Papers*, Vol. 43, No. 2, pp. 224-236.

--- and W. Chung (1976), *How Japan's Economy Grew So Fast*, The Brookings Institution, Washington.

Dholakia, B. (1974), *The Sources of Economic Growth in India*, Good Companions, Baroda (India).

Duncan, J. and W. Shelton (1978), *Revolution in United States Government Statistics 1926-1976*, Government Printing Office, Washington.

Foss, M. (1963), "The Utilization of Capital Equipment: Postwar Compared with Prewar", *Survey of Current Business*, Vol. 43, No. 6, pp. 8-16.

--- (1984), *Changing Utilization of Fixed Capital: An Element in Long Term Growth*, American Enterprise Institute, Washington.

Gilbert, M. and Associates (1958), "Comparative National Products and Price Levels: A Study of Western Europe and the United States", OEEC, Paris.

Griliches, Z. (1988), *Technology, Education, and Productivity*, Basil Blackwell Ltd., New York.

62   *Edward F. Denison*

Griliches, Z. and D. Jorgenson (1966), "Sources of Measured Productivity Change: Capital Input", *American Economic Review*, Vol. 56, No. 2, pp. 50-61.

Harberger, A. (1964), "Taxation, Resource Allocation, and Welfare", in: *The Role of Direct and Indirect Taxes in the Federal Revenue System*, Princeton University Press for the National Bureau of Economic Research and Brookings Institution, Princeton.

Hulten, C. (1992), "Growth Accounting When Technical Change Is Embodied in Capital", *American Economic Review*, Vol. 82, No. 4, pp. 964-980.

Jorgenson, D. (1984), "The Role of Energy in Productivity Growth", in: J. Kendrick (ed.), *International Comparisons of Productivity and Causes of the Slowdown*, American Enterprise Institute, Washington, pp. 279-334.

--- (1990), "Productivity and Economic Growth", in: E. Berndt and J. Triplett (eds.), *Fifty Years of Economic Measurement*, Studies in Income and Wealth, Vol. 54, University of Chicago Press for the National Bureau of Economic Research, Chicago, pp. 19-118.

---, F. Gollop and B. Fraumeni (1987), *Productivity and U.S. Economic Growth*, Harvard University Press, Cambridge.

--- and Z. Griliches (1972), "The Explanation of Productivity Change" (reprinted with corrections from *The Review of Economic Studies*, July 1967), "Issues in Growth Accounting: A Reply to Edward F. Denison", and "Final Reply", *Survey of Current Business*, Vol. 52, No. 5, Part 2, pp. 3-36, 65-94 and 111.

Journal of Political Economy (1962), Supplement to October issue, Vol. 70, No. 5, Part 2.

Kanamori, H. and Associates (1983), *Japanese Economy in 1990 on a Global Context*, The Japan Economic Research Center, Tokyo.

Kendrick, J. (1979), "Productivity Trends and the Recent Slowdown: Historical Perspective, Causal Factors, and Policy Options", in: W. Fellner, Project Director, *Contemporary Economic Problems 1979*, American Enterprise Institute, Washington, pp. 17-69.

--- (1981), "International Comparisons of Recent Productivity Trends", in: W. Fellner, Project Director, *Contemporary Economic Problems, 1981-1982 Edition*, American Enterprise Institute, Washington, pp. 125-170.

--- (ed.) (1984), *International Comparisons of Productivity and Causes of the Slowdown*, American Enterprise Institute and Ballinger Publishing Company, Cambridge.

Kuznets, S. (1962), "The Sources of Economic Growth", *Challenge*, April, pp. 44-45.

Lewis, M. (1989), *Denison Revisited: Education and Economic Growth Once Again*. Unpublished Ph.D. dissertation, University of Maryland, College Park, MD.

Lucas, R. (1988), "On the Mechanics of Economic Development", *Journal of Monetary Economics*, Vol. 22, No.1, pp. 3-42.

Maddison, A. (1972), "Explaining Economic Growth", *Banca Nazionale del Lavoro Quarterly Review*, No. 102, pp. 211-262.

--- (1984), "Comparative Analysis of the Productivity Situation in the Advanced Capitalist Countries", in: J. Kendrick (ed.), *International Comparisons of Productivity and Causes of the Slowdown*, American Enterprise Institute and Ballinger Publishing Company, Cambridge, pp. 59-92.

--- (1987), "Growth and Slowdown in Advanced Capitalist Economies: Techniques of Quantitative Assessment", *Journal of Economic Literature*, Vol. 25, No.2, pp. 649-698.

--- (1991), *Dynamic Forces in Capitalist Development,* Oxford University Press, Oxford.

Matthews, R., C. Feinstein and J. Odling-Smee (1982), *British Economic Growth 1856 - 1973*, Stanford University Press, Stanford.

North, D. (1963), "The Sources of Economic Growth in the United States and the Alternatives Before Us", *The Journal of Economic History*, Vol. 23, No. 3, p. 352.

Ohkawa, K. and H. Rosovsky (1973), *Japanese Economic Growth*, Stanford University Press, Stanford.

Patrick, H. and H. Rosovsky (eds.) (1976), *Asia's New Giant: How the Japanese Economy Works*, The Brookings Institution, Washington.

Review of Income and Wealth (1972a), papers by E. Denison, D. Daly, D. Creamer, T. Rymes, and J. Kendrick, Vol. 18, No. 1.

Review of Income and Wealth (1972b), papers by M. Nadiri, H. Kanamori, R. Krengel, J. Frohn, Z. Roman, and A. Gaathon, Vol. 18, No. 2.

Robinson, E. and J. Vaizey (eds.) (1966), *The Economics of Education*, International Economic Association, MacMillan, London.

Roman, Z. (1982), *Productivity and Economic Growth*, Akademiai Kiado, Budapest.

Scott, M. (1989), *A New View of Economic Growth*, Clarendon Press, Oxford.

Servan-Schreiber, J. (1967), *Le Defi Americain*, Denoel, Paris.

Solow, R. (1960), "Investment and Technical Progress", in: K. Arrow, S. Karlin, and P. Suppes (eds.), *Mathematical Methods in the Social Sciences, 1959*, Stanford Univesity Press, Stanford, pp. 89-104.

--- (1992), *Policies for Economic Growth*, SAIS, The Johns Hopkins University, Washington.

Stein, H. and E. Denison (1960), "High Employment and Growth in the American Economy", in: *Goals for Americans: Programs for Action in the Sixties*, Report of the President's Commission on National Goals, Prentice

Hall for the American Assembly, Washington, pp. 163-90.

Stone, R. (1980), "Whittling Away at the Residual: Some Thoughts on Denison's Growth Accounting - A Review Article", *Journal of Economic Literature*, Vol. 18, No. 4, pp. 1539-1543.

Walters, D. (1968), *Canadian Income Levels and Growth: An International Perspective*, Economic Council of Canada, Queen's Printer, Ottawa.

--- (1970), *Canadian Growth Revisited, 1950-67*, Economic Council of Canada, Queen's Printer, Ottawa.

Explaining Economic Growth
A. Szirmai, B. van Ark and D. Pilat
© 1993 Elsevier Science Publishers B.V. All rights reserved.

The Ultimate Sources of Economic Growth

Douglass C. North*
Washington University, St. Louis

I

The word "ultimate" in the title given to me for this volume honoring Angus Maddison has the sobering ring of a Wagnerian opus. Ultimate sources may take us to the origins of the universe, the physical characteristics of the planet, the evolution of the human species, and the underlying traits of the human character. I have nothing so grandiose in mind. The sources I have in mind are more mundane and proximate - though probably not as proximate as those of Ed Denison since they are customarily the exogenous variables in standard economic models. They are the demographic, technological, and institutional sources of economic growth. It will surely not surprise you if I concentrate on the last of these three.

What I shall attempt to explain is the economic diversity of the human condition across space and time that Angus Maddison's research has illuminated. This diversity is puzzling because the economic theory that we employ implies that with the trade of goods, services, and productive factors it should not persist. Clearly something is missing in that theory. At a minimum institutions and the costs of transacting are missing; but also missing is the fallibility of the human mind. The neo-classical world is not only frictionless but also one populated by omniscient beings. My focus therefore is on both the way institutions evolve and the way humans process the information they receive. And finally it is about time. Let me elaborate on each of those factors before I turn to apply them to some recent history as a prelude to erecting an - albeit loose and incomplete - scaffold of the ultimate sources of economic growth.

Institutions

Institutions provide the incentive structure of a society. They are the humanly devised constraints that structure human interaction. Together with the technology employed they determine the costs of producing and transacting and therefore total costs. Neoclassical theory confined costs to production costs on

---

* This essay expands on a number of themes originally developed in my *Institutions, Institutional Change and Economic Performance* (1990).

the implicit assumption that it was costless to define and enforce the property rights over goods and services or the performance of agents. Transaction costs are all those costs involved in measuring the multiple dimensions of what is being traded (in product and factor markets) and the cost of enforcing those trades. It is institutions that define the property rights that determine the measurement costs and that specify the mechanisms that determine the effectiveness of the enforcement of property rights.

Institutions are made up of formal rules (constitutions, laws, regulations) and informal constraints (conventions, norms of behavior, and self imposed codes of conduct) and of their enforcement characteristics. They exist to reduce uncertainty in human exchange. The uncertainty arises because of the complexity of the problems of human interaction and the mental constructs humans develop to decipher that complexity.

Information Processing

The uncertainty that underlies institution formation is associated with the behavior of others with whom one is interacting. The more complex the human interaction the more demanding are the institutional requirements necessary to structure the resultant exchange. In simple exchange involving repetitive human interaction, customs and traditions establish the coordinates of the exchange process. They become embedded in the culture of a society and are intergenerationally transferred. Beyond cultural standards of behavior there is the local "learning" that resolves exchange problems unique to particular local conditions. Together these two sources of information processing - customs and local learning - are called folk psychology in the cognitive science literature. They are non scientific and refer to our everyday mundane understanding of ourselves and others. They can, and do, result in widely divergent perceptions of the world and "the way it works." They suffice for exchange in "simple" societies. But as exchange becomes more complex and impersonal the informational demands increase and so do the complexity of the problems to be solved. The informational requirements of impersonal exchange entail the ability to measure and enforce contractual agreements across space and time. The complexity of the problems arises from the interaction of large numbers of people formed into political, social, and economic units.

Time

Time should take care of all these problems. It should do so because evolutionary theory suggests that maladapted policies and institutions will give way to more successful ones. Armen Alchian's classic essay on "Uncertainty, Evolution and Economic Theory" (1950) was broadly interpreted as implying that competition would weed out inefficient institutions in competition with more efficient ones. But this efficient interpretation of institutional evolution as embodied in my earlier study (North and Thomas, 1973) was unable to account for the widespread existence and persistence of economies that failed to grow. We do learn from outcomes inconsistent with expectations and, indeed, with the enormous decline in information costs of the modern world this learning process may be accelerating - as the remarkable events in central and eastern Europe of the past half dozen years attest. But the former centrally planned economies have learned what does not work but there is no guarantee that they have or will learn how to realize a set of institutions that does work because the informational requirements and the complexity of the problems to be solved have also been growing. To see why, we must turn to some recent history.

II

We live in the midst of the second economic revolution - a revolution which began in the late nineteenth century and is still continuing. That revolution is the wedding of science and technology, which is the underlying determinant of modern productivity. It is a revolution because it is a fundamental change in the stock (and flow) of knowledge, which entails an equally fundamental change in the organization of human beings and the structure of societies.

The development of the disciplines of physics, chemistry, biology, genetics is the source of the growth in the stock of scientific knowledge. The systematic application of these disciplines to the basic economic problem of scarcity has not only purged the Malthusian specter of diminishing returns from our purview but has created the vision of a potential world of plenty. To achieve that potential however, entails a restructuring of economic, social, and political institutions and organizations in order to realize the increasing returns attributes of the technology in which this scientific knowledge is embodied.[1]

The technology requires occupational and territorial specialization on an unprecedented scale and in consequence the number of exchanges grows exponentially. In order to realize the gains from the productive potential associated with a technology of increasing returns one has to invest enormous resources in transacting. In the United States, for example, the labor force grew from 29 million to 80 million between 1900 and 1970; during that period production workers grew from 10 million to 29 million, while white collar workers (the great majority of whom are engaged in transacting) increased from 5 million to 38 million. The transaction sector (that part of transaction costs that goes through the market and therefore can be measured) in the United States in

---

[1] See Chapter 13 "The Second Economic Revolution" in my *Structure and Change in Economic History* (1981) for an elaboration of this argument.

1970 made up 45 percent of GNP.[2] The increasing size of the transaction sector reflected not only the growth of whole sectors of the economy devoted to transacting such as banking and finance but also the growth within firms of increasing resources devoted to transacting as embodied in the employment of lawyers, accountants, managers, clerks, and so forth.

Let me briefly elaborate some of the measurement and enforcement problems that account for the size of the transaction sector. Necessary to be able to realize the gains of a world of specialization are control over quality in the lengthening production chain and a solution to the problems of increasingly costly principal/agent relationships. Much technology indeed is designed to reduce transaction costs by substituting capital for labor or by reducing the degrees of freedom of the worker in the production process and by automatically measuring the quality of intermediate goods. An underlying problem is that of measuring inputs and outputs so that one can ascertain the contribution of individual factors and the output at successive stages of production. For inputs there is no agreed upon measure of the contribution of an individual input. Equally there is room for conflict over the consequent payment to factors of production. For output, not only is there residual unpriced output, that is waste and pollutants, but also there are complicated costs of specifying the desired properties of the goods and services produced at each stage in the production process.

Firms using this new technology have large fixed capital investments with a long life and (frequently) low alternative scrap value. As a result the exchange process embodied in contracts has to be extended over long periods of time, which entails uncertainty about prices and costs and the possibility of opportunistic behavior on the part of one of the parties to the exchange. A number of organizational problems emerge from the use of this new technology.

First, increased resources are necessary to measure the quality of output or the performance of agents. Sorting, grading, labeling, trade marks, warranties, licensing, time and motion studies and a variety of other techniques to measure the performance of agents are all, albeit costly and imperfect, devices to measure the characteristics of goods and services and the performance of agents. Despite the existence of such devices the dissipation of income is evident all around us in the difficulties of measuring the quality of automobile repairs, of evaluating the safety characteristics of products and the quality of medical services, or of measuring educational output. The problems of evaluating performance are even more acute in hierarchies because of the difficulties of achieving low cost measurement of the multiple dimensions of the agent's performance.

Second, while team production permits economies of scale to be realized, it does so at the cost of worker alienation and shirking. The "discipline" of the factory is no more than a response to the control problem of shirking in team

---

[2]   John Wallis and Douglass North (1986).

production. From the perspective of the employer the discipline consists of rules, regulations, incentives, and punishments essential to effective performance. Innovations such as time and motion studies are methods of measuring individual performance. From the viewpoint of the worker they are inhuman devices to foster speedups and exploitation. Since there is no agreed upon measure of output that constitutes contract performance, both are right.

Third, the potential gains from opportunistic behavior increase and lead to strategic behavior both within the firm (labor-employer relations, for example) and in contractual behavior between firms. Everywhere in factor and product markets the gains from withholding services or altering the terms of agreement at strategic points offer large potential gains.

Fourth, the development of large scale hierarchies produces the familiar problems of bureaucracy. The multiplication of rules and regulations inside large organizations to control shirking and principal/agent problems results in rigidities, income dissipation, and the loss of flexibility essential to adaptive efficiency.

Finally there are external effects: the unpriced costs reflected in the modern environmental crisis. The interdependence of a world of specialization and division of labor increases exponentially the imposition of costs on third parties.

The restructuring necessary to take advantage of this technology entails a complete alteration of economic organization as Chandler (1977) has eloquently described. But the economic restructuring itself entails a fundamental restructuring of the entire society in order to create efficient economic markets This technology and accompanying scale economies entails specialization, minute division of labor, impersonal exchange and urban societies. Uprooted are all the old informal constraints built around the family, personal relationships, and repetitive individual exchanges. Indeed the basic traditional functions of the family - education, employment (the family enterprise), and insurance - are either eliminated or severely circumscribed. New formal rules and organizations and an increased role of government replace them.

The contention of Marxists was that problems that resulted from this restructuring were a consequence of capitalism and that the inherent contradictions between the new technology and the consequent organization of capitalism would lead to its demise. The Marxists were wrong that the problems were a consequence of capitalism; they are ubiquitous to any society that attempts to adopt the technology of the second economic revolution. However, as the foregoing paragraphs have attempted to make clear, Marxists were right in viewing the tension arising between the new technology and organization as a fundamental dilemma.[3] These tensions have only partially been resolved in the

---

[3] It is surely one of the great ironies of history that Karl Marx who first pointed out the necessity of restructuring economic and political organization in order to be able to

market economies of the Western world. The growth of government, the disintegration of the family, the incentive incompatibility problems in many modern political and economic hierarchical organizations are all symptoms of the consequent problems besetting Western economies.

However, the relative flexibility of the institutions of the Western world - both economic and political - has mitigated these problems. Adaptive efficiency, while far from perfect in the Western world, accounts for the degree of success that such institutions have experienced. The basic institutional framework has encouraged the development of political and economic organizations that have replaced (however imperfectly) the traditional functions of the family; mitigated the insecurity associated with a world of specialization; evolved flexible economic organization that has induced low cost transacting; resolved some of the incentive incompatibilities of hierarchies and encouraged creative entrepreneurial talent; and tackled (again very imperfectly) the external effects that are not only environmental but also social in an urban world.

III

How does one create an institutional framework (i.e. devise and put in place a set of property rights) that can realize the potential of the new technology? It is not just "getting the prices right" at a moment of time (allocative efficiency) that is our objective, but getting them right over time (adaptive efficiency). To accomplish that objective requires much more than transferring assets from public to private hands (important as that task is). It also entails the development of a legal system that will embody the correct incentives (for adaptive efficiency); the creation of effective and impartial enforcement by that legal system; the development of organizations made up of entrepreneurs who will invest in the kind of skills and knowledge essential to sustained productivity increase. It also entails the establishment of a polity that will broadly support and enforce the new property rights; will undertake those investments essential to sustained productivity increase that are privately unprofitable because of public goods or free riding attributes; and will mitigate the insecurities and uncertainties associated with a competitive, interdependent world.

Now all of that is a tall order and if one looks to the way in which the institutional framework evolved in the "successful" economies as a guide to policy one will be hard put to derive many lessons. The ultimate source of growth in this essay is, in fact, the knowledge and skills a society invests in. The rise of the Western world was a consequence of the skills and knowledge deemed worthwhile acquiring by the political and economic organizations of the medieval

---

realize the potential of a new technology should have been responsible for the creation of societies that foundered on this precise issue.

and early modern Western world. They were responsible not only for the directly productive activities of economic organizations but for the development of the military technology which led to the hegemony of the West. But this ultimate source of growth is of limited help in immediate policy determination. The reason is that the framework evolved over a long period of time and much of it was accidental in the sense that it was guided by the short run interests of political and economic entrepreneurs that had long run unanticipated consequences.

There are two fundamentally intractable problems in creating adaptively efficient institutions about which we know very little - aligning the informal constraints with the formal rules and creating and maintaining a polity that will support adaptively efficient institutions. Let me take each in turn.

It is not just the formal rules that make for low transaction costs. The costs of measurement and enforcement of the complex contracts essential to a successful economy would be prohibitive in a world populated by individuals with the behavioral assumptions we employ in economics. If individuals maximized at every margin so that they would cheat, lie, steal, or kill their competitor whenever it paid, it is hard to imagine that the costs of transacting would not foreclose modern economies. Equally if individuals have been brought up with norms that eschewed competition, individual initiative, the incentive structure of market economies, they will be hard put to adjust when the formal rules change. Informal constraints, unlike formal rules, cannot be changed overnight. They evolve slowly. Broadly speaking people must believe in an institutional framework - must consider it "fair" - in order that the informal constraints will be aligned with and reinforce the formal rules (and therefore provide for low cost transacting). The greater the degree of incompatibility between the formal rules and the informal constraints the greater will be the instability of the polity. That brings me to the second problem.

Much of the new political economy has assumed, implicitly or explicitly, that political markets operate like economic markets and that the same efficiency characteristics obtain. They do not and there is no way that I know of to get them to "behave" like efficient economic markets. Let me put the argument in a transactions cost framework. When it is costless to transact, the efficient competitive solution of neo-classical economics obtains. It does so because the competitive structure of efficient markets leads the parties to arrive costlessly at the solution that maximizes aggregate income. To the extent that these conditions are approximated in the real world it is because competition is strong enough via arbitrage and efficient information feedback to approximate the Coase zero transaction conditions and the parties can realize the gains from trade inherent in the neo-classical argument. It is difficult and rare to get economic markets with such characteristics. What would it take to get political markets to approximate the zero transaction cost model of efficient economic exchange? The conditions are easily stated.

The only legislation or regulation enacted would be that which increased aggregate income and in which the gainers compensated the losers at a transaction cost that is low enough to make it worthwhile. The informational and institutional requirements are:

1. The affected parties would have the information and correct model to know not only what bills affected them but also the amount of gains or losses they would incur.
2. The results would be communicated to their agent (the legislator) who would faithfully vote accordingly.
3. His or her vote would be weighted by the net gains or losses of the constituents and only legislation would be enacted in which the net gains exceeded the net losses by an amount that was more than the transaction cost of compensating the losers.

The institutional structure most favorable to approximating such conditions is a modern democratic polity with universal suffrage. Vote trading, log rolling, and the incentive of an incumbent's opponents to bring his or her deficiencies before constituents and hence reduce agency problems all contribute to better outcomes.

But look at the disincentives built into the system. Rational voter ignorance is not just a buzzword of the public choice literature. But not even the most dedicated voter could acquire the information to be vaguely informed about the myriad bills that affect his or her welfare; there is no way that the constituent (or even the legislator) could ever possess accurate models to weigh the consequences. Agency theory provides abundant, if controversial, evidence of the degree to which legislators act independently of constituent interests. Whereas legislators may trade votes on the basis of the perceived number of votes he or she stands to gain or lose, that is frequently a long way from reflecting the net gains or losses of the constituency. And how often is there an incentive to compensate losers? There is a vast difference between better and efficient outcomes.[4]

IV

We need to model the way choices are made in both the polity and the economy, to adjust our thinking to recognize the intractability of the problems we confront and the limited means available to solve them if we are to come to grips with the organizational problems arising from the second economic revolution. What is the difference between the new institutional economics approach and the traditional economist's account - after all both accounts use neo-classical price

---

[4] See the author's "A Transaction Cost Theory of Politics", *The Journal of Theoretical Politics*, Fall 1990, for an elaboration of this argument.

theory? The difference is that the former abandons a crucial assumption of neo-classical theory and incorporates a crucial feature about the characteristics of institutions. Abandoned is instrumental rationality; incorporated are the characteristics of institutions that produce path dependence.

By instrumental rationality we mean that the actors have correct theories by which to interpret the world around them or if they have initially incorrect theories the information feedback that they receive will lead the actor to revise their theories to correct theories. Herbert Simon (1986, pp. 25-40) has accurately summarized the implications of such an assumption as follows:

"If we accept values as given and constant, if we postulate an objective description of the world as it really is, and if we assume that the decisionmaker's computational powers are unlimited, then two important consequences follow. First we do not need to distinguish between the real world and the decisionmaker's perception of it: He or she perceives the world as it really is. Second, we can predict the choices that will be made by a rational decisionmaker entirely from our knowledge of the real world and without a knowledge of the decisionmaker's perceptions or modes of calculation (we do, of course, have to know his or her utility function).

If, on the other hand, we accept the proposition that both the knowledge and computational ability of the decisionmaker are severely limited, then we must distinguish between the real world and the actor's perception of it. That is to say, we must construct a theory (and test it empirically) of the processes of decision. Our theory must include not only the reasoning processes but also the processes that generate the actor's subjective representation of the decision problem, his or her frame.

The rational person in neo-classical economics always reaches the decision that is objectively, or substantively, best in terms of the given utility function. The rational person of cognitive psychology goes about making his or her decisions in a way that is procedurally reasonable in the light of the available knowledge and means of computation."

The implications of procedural rationality as opposed to instrumental rationality are far reaching for our understanding of economics and economic history. Institutions are unnecessary in a world of instrumental rationality; ideas and ideologies don't matter; and efficient markets - both economic and political-characterize economies. Procedural rationality on the other hand maintains that the actors have incomplete information and limited mental capacity by which to process that information and in consequence develop regularized patterns of exchange to structure exchange. There is no implication that the consequent institutions are efficient (in the sense of providing low cost transacting). In such a world ideas and ideologies play a major role in choices and transaction costs result in imperfect markets.

What does it mean to say that institutional matrices are characterized by path dependence? The explanation is derived from the symbiotic relationship between institutions and organizations. The institutional framework determines the opportunity set. That is, the political and economic organizations have come into existence because of the opportunities created by the institutions (and the other traditional economic constraints). That opportunity set in turn will shape the kinds of knowledge and skills that organizations will invest in (either directly or indirectly through the polity) in order to survive. The result is a set of reinforcing mechanisms such as network externalities, economies of scope, and complementarities that bias incremental costs and benefits in favor of those organizations that are broadly consistent with the institutional framework; correspondingly, they make choices that would run counter to the institutional framework unprofitable.

The idea of path dependence was first elaborated by W. Brian Arthur (1988) and Paul David (1985) to explain the way increasing returns of new technologies locked the players into a particular (and not necessarily optimal) path. The concept has even more applicability to institutional evolution. Economies once on a particular path find it very hard to fundamentally alter the direction because of the built in characteristics of institutions described above. The striking comparison between the institutional evolution of Spain and England and the downstream consequences for Latin and North American subsequent history are a striking illustration of the role of path dependence.[5]

If economies were not characterized by institutions and if instrumental rationality characterized human decision making then the problem of modern economic growth would be reduced to a matter of preferences. Political entrepreneurs not only would know the political and economic policies that would direct them on to an adaptively efficient path, but also could overnight transform the institutional framework to create the proper incentive structure. Because institutions do result in "lock-in" and the actors proceed on the basis of limited information and subjective models as guides to choices, the paths of economies diverge widely and persistent poor performance can continue.

Both of these characteristics of institutions are crucial to the divergent patterns of economic performance over space and time. 1) Procedural rationality means that the subjective models of the actors that are responsible for the way they process information, shape the way individuals perceive problems and hence shape the choices they make. In this context the ideas, ideologies, dogmas, myths that people believe in matter. 2) Path dependence implies that the organizations that evolved as a response to the institutional framework will make the incremental decisions that are shaping downstream development. Since their

---

[5]   For an elaboration of this brief historical reference see North (1990), Chapter 12.

perceived interests are broadly consistent with the existing institutional structure
the resultant policies will tend to perpetuate the current direction of the economy
whether growth or stagnation.

V

Let me conclude by stating five propositions that do, I believe, define the sources
of institutional change that ultimately determine economic growth:
1. The continuous interaction between institutions and organizations in the
   economic setting of scarcity and hence competition is the key to institutional
   change.
2. Competition forces organizations to continually invest in skills and knowledge
   to survive. The kinds of skills and knowledge individuals and their
   organizations acquire will shape evolving perceptions about opportunities and
   hence choices that will incrementally alter institutions.
3. The institutional framework provides the incentives that dictate the kinds of
   skills and knowledge perceived to have the maximum pay-off.
4. Perceptions are derived from the mental constructs of the players.
5. The economies of scope, complementarities, and network externalities of an
   institutional matrix make institutional change overwhelmingly incremental and
   path dependent.

References

Alchian, A. (1950), "Uncertainty, Evolution and Economic Theory", *Journal of Political Economy,* Vol. 58, No. 1, pp. 21-221.

Arthur, W.B. (1988), "Self-Reinforcing Mechanisms in Economics", in: P.W. Anderson, K. Arrow, and D. Pines (eds.), *The Economy as an Evolving Complex System,* Addison-Wesley, Reading, pp. 9-29.

Chandler, A.D. (1977), *The Visible Hand,* Harvard University Press, Cambridge.

David, P. (1985) "Clio and the Economics of QWERTY", *American Economic Review,* Vol. 75, No. 1, pp. 332-337.

North, D.C. (1981), *Structure and Change in Economic History,* Norton, New York.

--- (1990), "A Transactions Cost Theory of Politics", *Journal of Theoretical Politics,* Vol. 2, No. 4, pp. 355-367.

--- and R. Thomas (1973), *The Rise of The Western World: A New Economic History,* Cambridge University Press, Cambridge.

Simon, H. (1986), "Rationality in Psychology and Economics", in: R. Hogarth and M. Reder (eds.) *Rational Choice,* University of Chicago Press, Chicago, pp. 25-40.

Wallis, J. and D.C. North (1986), "Measuring the Transaction Sector in the American Economy, 1870-1970", in: S.E. Engerman and R.E. Gallman (eds.), *Long Term Factors in American Economic Growth*, University of Chicago Press, Chicago, pp. 95-148.

Explaining Economic Growth
A. Szirmai, B. van Ark and D. Pilat
© 1993 Elsevier Science Publishers B.V. All rights reserved.

Is Economic Growth Still Desirable?

Wilfred Beckerman
Balliol College, University of Oxford

1. The Early Anti-Growth Movement

I have two reasons for being delighted to contribute to this volume to honour the work done by my very old friend and sometime colleague, Angus Maddison. First, we are all very much in his debt for the perseverence and skill with which he has studied the determinants of economic growth over the long run historical past, combining statistical ingenuity with the vision of the historian. But to judge by much of the current scepticism as to the beneficial effects on human welfare of economic growth, one might conclude that the chief value of Maddison's work would have been not so much to provide guidance as to how to promote growth but how to stop it. This, I believe, would be a terrible mistake, which brings me to my second reason for welcoming the invitation to write this article.

This is that I very much welcome an opportunity to return to a topic on which I published a book nearly twenty years ago. This book, *In Defence of Economic Growth*[1], was largely devoted to refuting the widespread arguments to the effect that continued economic growth was undesirable for one reason or another. The harmful effects of economic growth were alleged to include relatively tangible effects, such as damage to the physical environment, or the exhaustion of raw material supplies, as well as more intangible harmful effects on the quality of life.

But, on the whole, the environmental concerns that had been in the forefront of the debate in the advanced countries in the late 1960s and early 1970s, had been relatively local environmental issues - such as pollution of rivers, or of beaches as a result of discharges from the rivers or neighbouring urban conglomerations, or unpleasant local atmospheric conditions in towns and cities. True, international pollution, such as that caused by acid rain and some ocean pollution from oil-tankers, was also on the agenda. But these appeared to be less alarming than the recent concern with the ozone layer or global warming resulting from the "greenhouse effect". Threats of species extinction or of a loss of bio-diversity also now appear prominently in the growth-versus-the environment debate.

---

[1] *In Defence of Economic Growth*, Cape, London, 1974, US edition under title *Two Cheers for the Affluent Society*, St Martin's Press, New York, 1975.

But behind these differences in the technical arguments deployed in the debate one fundamental feature of the debate has remained unchanged. This is that different sides in the debate correspond closely to differences in relative incomes. In the late 1960s and early 1970s the anti-growth movement was largely a middle class movement in the more affluent countries. Many of their concerns were brilliantly formulated by Mishan (1967), who enumerated various alleged shortcomings of economic growth. Pollution of the environment was only one of them. Others included congestion of travel facilities and holiday resorts, and other forms of externality, as well as less tangible effects, such as the subordination of nobler social values to the pursuit of commercial objectives and the consequent deterioration in society's moral standards.

It is true that for some groups in society economic growth brought some deterioration in certain components of their standards of living. Economic growth means change and when the world changes some people tend to lose out. In particular, the middle classes found it more difficult to get domestic servants, the roads were beginning to get cluttered up with the cheap and badly maintained cars of the poor, and their favourite holiday resorts - Greek islands, Italian hill towns, or wherever - were becoming transformed by the millions of less affluent tourists on cheap package holidays. To the middle classes in the advanced countries, therefore, it might well appear that, on balance, economic growth was bad for their welfare.

One of the consequences of the widespread concern with the impact of economic growth on the environment was the U.N. World Conference on the Environment in Stockholm, in 1972. But at this conference the developing countries made it perfectly clear that development was given greater priority in their objectives and policies than concern for the environment. Slowing down economic growth in the interests of protecting the environment might appear to be worthy cause to the more affluent groups in the rich countries but was certainly not on the agenda of the developing countries.

In fact, even in the advanced countries it was never clear that it was on the agenda for the majority of the population, and not largely a middle class movement. The vast majority of the working classes in the developed countries appreciated only too well the benefits of the improvements in the living standards that technological advance could bring. For them the washing machines and automobiles which some environmental groups affected to despise represented a release from drudgery and an opening up of mobility. And the virtual elimination of malnutrition and many fatal diseases associated with poverty in the advanced countries undoubtedly made a major contribution to the welfare of the majority of the working population in these countries. Insofar as the members of this section of the population were concerned with the environment at all, it was their inadequate housing or the dirty, noisy and dangerous conditions in which many of them worked that they worried about.

But the noise levels or safety precautions in factories have never appeared in the lists of environmental concerns that are prominent in the environmentalist literature, and improvements in these aspects of the environment have been largely obtained by pressure from trade unions. And by the end of the 1960s, almost all the most prominent components of the environment in the more advanced countries were improving.[2]

The improvements that were taking place in the environment in Britain and - with some time lag - in many other industrialised countries were, of course, partly to the credit of the environmental movements. But they also reflected changing social and economic conditions that both raised environmental concern in the hierarchy of priorities of the population in advanced countries and increased the means available to deal with the environment.[3] Without economic growth, the environments in most of the Western world would have remained as bad as they had been in the 19th century and as bad as the environments that were - and are - still found in most of the poor cities of the world.

2. Economic Growth and Resources

Paradoxically, at the same time as the undesirability of continued economic growth was being proclaimed it was also often maintained - usually by the same people - that continued economic growth was also impossible on account of an impending shortage of raw materials or food supplies, or of environmental catastrophe. It was never clear why such groups of people were so alarmed at the prospect that economic growth was both undesirable and impossible, for it would have presumably been much more alarming if it had been either undesirable but inevitable, or desirable but impossible. A situation in which something was both undesirable but impossible would seem, on the face of it, to be highly satisfactory.

Nevertheless, much attention was given to the warnings about the inevitable constraints on growth that were formulated precisely in *The Limits to Growth*, a study commissioned by the "Club of Rome" (Meadows et. al., 1972). This study purported to show, amongst other things, that continued economic growth in the short run would eventually lead to exhaustion of non-renewable resources, so that we would condemn future generations to very low standards of living when resource scarcity became serious. This has led to the current fashion for the concept of "sustainable" development. To the economist the major flaws in the methodology of these predictions were glaringly obvious. Known estimates of resources at any point of time would relate only to those

---

[2] For details see my *In Defence of Economic Growth* (1974), pp. 65-68 and 122-133.

[3] See for example Ashby and Anderson (1981) and Brimblecombe (1987).

resources which had been worth while discovering. As long as the equilibrium price did not make it worth while searching for additional supplies nobody would be carrying out such a search. If, on the other hand, it appeared that demand was outrunning supplies, the price would tend to rise. This would set in motion numerous feedback effects familiar to economists.

These would include increased exploration, and increased extraction of resources that had hitherto not been worthwhile extracting. There would also be economies in the use of the materials and a switch to close substitutes. One way or another the market would tend to reduce demand and increase supply. And, indeed, the history of resource supplies and demands over the last century or more confirmed this sequence of events. Furthermore, many prophecies of impending exhaustion of supplies had been made during the last century or more, based on a simple comparision of rates of consumption with current estimates of "known" reserves, and all of them had been falsified by events.

And during the roughly two decades that have passed since *The Limits to Growth* and similar doomsday pronouncements were published, it has become abundantly clear that their predictions, too, have been falsified. For example, in *The Limits to Growth* 1970 world supplies of lead were put at 91 million metric tons. Between 1970 and 1989 the world consumed 98.5 million metric tons. Yet by 1989 total known reserves of lead instead of being negative were actually 125 million tons. Exactly the same applies to natural gas and zinc, in that cumulative world consumption during the period 1970-89 has equalled or exceeded the 1970 "known reserves", yet the known reserves at the end of the period were greater than at the outset.[4]

Similarly, the balance between world supply and demand for food has not developed along the lines of the doomsday predictions. World food output over the last twenty years - as, indeed, over the preceding twenty years as well - has continued to rise faster than world population. Food output per head, therefore, has continued to grow.[5] It is true that this does not apply to every area of the globe and that this has not prevented human factors - such as civil wars, blatant discrimination, and so on - from leading to massive food shortages in particular regions. But the fact that human stupidity and evil is capable of leading to disasters is nothing new and has nothing to do with the "Limits to Growth" thesis.

---

[4] 1970 reserve estimates in Meadows et. al. (1972), pp. 56-59; consumption data from *Metal Bulletin's Prices and Data* (Surrey, U.K., 1990), p. 255 and *passim*; 1989 known reserves from *The World Almanac* (1990), p. 130 (derived from U.S. Bureau of Mines data).

[5] UNCTAD, *Handbook of International Trade and Development Statistics*, 1989, p. 456, Table 6.5.

During the last few years, however, most environmental movements have either abandoned or played down their opposition to economic growth in general. Whilst still attacking the alleged excessive importance attached to the growth objective by most governments, the emphasis has switched to the concept of "sustainable growth". In a later section of this article I criticise this concept on the grounds that it is not easily morally defensible or very operational. But whether or not the criticisms of the concept that I put forward are valid, there appear to be serious weaknesses in two of the main ingredients of the "sustainable growth" line of argument, in addition to those mentioned already. One of these is the threat of species extinction and the other is the threat to the global climate.

3. Preservation of Species

Most varieties of the concept of "sustainable" growth include some reference to the need to pass on to future generations an environmental stock that is equivalent, in some sense, to that which we have inherited. Leaving aside the philosophical problems that arise in connection with the notion of inter-generational justice, there are some obvious questions that have to be faced in evaluating how operational the concept of "sustainable growth" can be as far as its application to species conservation is concerned.[6] The case for preserving intact the existing number of species has usually been based on two distinct arguments. The first of these is simple compassion and concern for all living beings. The second is the value to the human race of preserving species, in the interests of preserving a gene bank that may turn out some day to be useful on account of medicinal properties.

As regards the first argument, most of us would agree that inflicting suffering or death on any living creature is a terrible thing. But it surely makes no difference to any particular individual creature faced, say, with the danger of imminent death at the hands of some hunter or of somebody destroying his usual habitat, whether he is almost the last surviving member of some species or whether, in fact, there are countless millions of fellow members of the same species roaming the Earth.

So if we are concerned about species loss it must be on account of our welfare - not that of the species - i.e. the second argument mentioned above namely that we want to preserve species diversity on account of their possible contribution to some unknown and unidentified medical advance. But this is, of course, a straightforward investment problem. If there is no opportunity cost involved in preserving species then, of course, by all means let us preserve them (though, personally, I could do without cockroaches). But to

---

[6] For a recent survey of the philosophical issues see Pasek (1992).

the economist the question is how much growth has to be sacrificed in the interests of species preservation. To sacrifice some economic growth on the grounds that "...one never knows, some day some particular species - like some particular plant - may turn out to have medicinal properties" involves comparing the relative probability of the returns involved in making some sacrifice of resources in the interests of species preservation with that of investment in some other activity - such as continuing with, or increasing, present research expenditures including medical research. If one could identify which particular species ought to be preserved it would be an easier task. But to sacrifice economic growth in order to preserve all the species, most of which are likely to contribute nothing, is hardly a rational procedure, particularly when what is to be sacrificed includes resources that could be devoted to medical research if that were some over-riding objective. How many scientists would agree that the probability of success in their own line of research is less than that in spending the equivalent amount of resources on species preservation, so that their own research budgets should be scrapped?

4. The Greenhouse Effect

The most widely dramatised complaint about the harmful environmental consequences of economic growth is the alleged threat that economic growth poses to the global climate. In particular, it is argued that unless drastic action is taken to curb the use of energy and/or switch to forms of energy that produce much less carbon dioxide, if any, economic growth will greatly increase concentrations of carbon dioxide in the atmosphere, with a resulting threat to the global climate, including, notably, "global warming" caused by the "greenhouse effect". This particular danger, together with the thinning of the ozone layer, has captured the headlines and the imagination of a wide section of the community. For it is argued that what is at stake here is the whole future of the human race. Whilst, in developing countries, local pollution may be a very serious matter, it is implied that it cannot compare in gravity with global environmental deterioration that threatens continued survival of the human race.

It is true that the human race is polluting the atmosphere on an unparalleled scale in general and, in particular, is even succeeding in increasing the carbon concentration of the atmosphere at a rate that could conceivably have harmful effects on human welfare if continued indefinitely (or at least until all reasonably accessible resources of fossil fuels have been burnt up). Hence it is right that research into these effects - both scientific and economic - and into the measures that might be needed to combat them, if necessary, should be high up on any agenda for environmental policy. But this does not mean that there is a valid case now for panic action and for the hasty implementation of draconian measures to slow down economic growth, either directly or indirectly through massive cuts in energy consumption. The reasons for this are numerous and I have set them out in detail elsewhere, so I shall retrict myself here to two or three brief remarks.[7]

First, as regards the scientific evidence for the danger of severe climate change resulting from the accumulation of greenhouse gases, it should be noted, first of all, that most reputable scientists seem to agree that there are still major gaps in their understanding of the global warming phenomenon in general and, in particular, the relationship between carbon dioxide and global warming, with corresponding very large differences in the predictions made by alternative climate models.[8]

In particular, very little is known yet about the role of cloud cover in preserving the heat balance in the atmosphere and the way in which this would be affected. The same applies to the role of the surface-sea interface and the mixing of the deep oceans, which happen to be the biggest single depository of carbon. Much further research is needed into this. Furthermore, whereas there is general agreement to the effect that global warming will lead to increased precipitation (though wide disagreement as to the amount) the economic effects, which are mainly on agriculture, depend crucially on the geographical distribution of this increased rainfall. It makes all the difference if the extra rain comes down in Ireland or in the Sudan (though "Murphy's law" would suggest that it will be the former).

Meanwhile, most economic estimates of the effects of global warming have been based on what was in 1990 the consensus scientific view (as embodied in the 1990 report of the International Panel on Climate Change) to the effect that, in the absence of special measures to reduce the emissions of greenhouse gases - notably of CO_2 - the CO_2 concentration in the atmosphere would double by the end of the next century, and possibly earlier, and the average global temperature could rise by between $1.5°$ and $4.5°$ - i.e. a mean value of about $3°$ (Celsius). And most economic estimates of the effects of "business as usual" scenarios take this as a benchmark degree of climate change. These estimates suggest that the damage done to economic output would be a negligible proportion of world output - i.e. less than 1 per cent of world output. By contrast, estimates of the loss of output that would result from the draconian measures widely advocated in order to bring about drastic cuts in CO_2 emissions suggest that these would be of an order of magnitude higher.[9]

---

[7] See my chapter "Global Warming: A Sceptical Economic Assessment" in Helm (1991).

[8] For example, whilst all the main models predict that there will be increased precipitation as a result of global warming the estimated increases in precipitation range from +3 percent to +15 percent!

[9] See my references to these estimates in Beckerman (1992).

None of this means that there is no need for any action at all to curb global warming. For example, William Nordhaus has estimated that the optimal policy for the reduction in greenhouse gases would include cutting out the production of CFCs, eliminating uneconomic excessive deforestation and a reduction of about 10 per cent in emissions of CO_2 by the adoption of policies - such as carbon taxes - that create economic disincentives to the use of fossil fuels (Nordhaus, 1990). Carbon taxes would, of course, provide a further stimulus to more research into renewable forms of energy, such as harnessing wind, tide and solar energy and the development of photovoltaics. Technical progress over the last decade or two in these areas suggest possibilities for genuinely economically viable economies in the use of conventional carbon intensive fuels. For example, the latest *World Development Report* of the World Bank states that "in high insolation areas the costs of electricity from solar energy seem likely to become competitive with those of nuclear power within the next ten years or so (even neglecting their advantages in reducing environmental costs) and probably with those of fossil fuels over the long term".[10]

In short, there is simply no reason to believe that the global warming threat constitutes a case for deliberately slowing down economic growth or even taking drastic action to achieve sharp reductions in CO_2 emissions. Even if past trends in energy use continued unabated the resulting economic damage will not be catastrophic or even anywhere near as large as the costs of draconian action to prevent it. Furthermore, past trends in energy use need not persist even if economic growth is maintained. The carbon emissions/ economic output ratio is likely to decline considerably and economically viable research into renewable energy sources can greatly cut the world's dependence on fossil fuels. In fact, it is precisely economic growth, with the technical progress in all areas that invariably accompanies it, that is the best guarantee that an economical shift to non-fossil fuels takes place.

5. Income Levels and Environmental Quality

(a) The General Relationship

The *prima facie* reasons for expecting economic growth to be good for the environment, on the whole, as well as bad for it in specific instances and particular time periods, hardly need elaboration. As people get richer their priorities change and the environment moves up in the hierarchy of human needs. When their basic needs for food, water, clothing and shelter are

---

[10] World Bank (1992). See also Anderson (1991) and Overseas Development Institute (1992).

satisfied they can begin to attach importance to other ingredients in total welfare, including, eventually, the environment. And this shift in expenditure priorities is easier insofar as richer countries will be more able to afford them.

Furthermore, the pattern of output in advanced countries has been changing in a direction that tends to impose less of a burden on the environment than was the case at earlier stages of their development. At higher levels of income industry accounts for a smaller share of GDP, and services, which are relatively non-polluting, account for an increasing share. Even within industry there has tended to be a shift away from the highly polluting heavy industries, including metallurgy and heavy engineering, towards high-tech, high value-added industries, employing large amounts of very skilled human capital and with smaller inputs of energy or raw materials.[11]

Nevertheless, the relationship between higher incomes and the state of the environment is not always a simple monotonic one. The dynamics of economic growth are often more complex. In some cases, higher incomes immediately lead to better environments, as when societies can begin to afford to devote more resources to the provision of clean water and sanitation and the like. In other cases, the initial effect can be harmful, as when it is associated with the installation of heavily polluting industries or rapid influx of population into cities in countries which are too poor to meet the resulting fast rise in claims on the urban infrastructure. In the longer run these problems also appear to be overcome in richer countries, but they are sometimes replaced by other forms of pollution, such as the emission of carbon and nitrogen oxides or the acute problems of disposing of increasing municipal waste.[12]

The complexity of the relationship is partly a technical matter, partly a matter of the preference patterns of individuals, but is also partly a matter of the political and social circumstances determining the relationship between, on the one hand, the speed with which the environment deteriorates in the early stages of economic growth and the extent to which the authorities in any country react to the deterioration. Nevertheless, as far as the main thesis of this paper is concerned, the conclusion is unaffected, namely that, in the

---

[11] Gordon Hughes argues, in "Are the Costs of Cleaning up Eastern Europe Exaggerated?", (draft of paper for the World Bank and the Commission of the European Communities, November 1990, page ii), that insofar as Eastern European economies develop along the lines of the currently advanced Western economies their pollution intensities, and possibly levels, will decline precisely on account of this shift in economic structure that seems to characterise economic growth in almost all countries of the world.

[12] For an excellent exposition, accompanied by some striking graphical illustrations, see World Bank (1992), "Overview", Figure 2.

longer run, economic growth leads to an improvement in the environment but
that countries may pass through phases, in the course of their growth, in
which the environment gets worse, and that the extent and duration of this
negative relationship depends to a large extent on policies. In short, there is
nothing inevitable about environmental damage as a consequence of economic
growth.

(b) The State of the Environment in Developing Countries

Although data deficiencies rule out precise calculations, it is quite clear that
the general situation as regards water supplies, sanitation and urban air
pollution is far worse in developing countries than in more advanced
countries. For example, water supply and sanitation is still a major problem,
with at least 1 billion people in developing countries not having access to safe
drinking water, and at least 2 billion having no access to satisfactory
sanitation.[13]

The serious welfare effects on developing countries of inadequate water
and/or sanitation supplies are indisputable - in spite of much uncertainty
concerning the precise relationship between water supplies and health. For
example, it appears that about one to one and a half billion people are affected
by water-related diseases in one form or another - notably schistosomiasis,
hookworm, diarrhea, ascariasis, guinea worm and trachoma.[14] And infant
mortality alone on account of diarrhea, which has a strong relationship to
clean water supplies and sanitation facilities, is reckoned to be about 5 million per annum.[15]

Similar conclusions can be drawn concerning air quality in developing
countries. The combination of industrialisation - often without the benefit of
the latest pollution reduction technologies - and rapid urbanisation,
accompanied often by dramatic increases in urban motorised transport has led
to acute air pollution problems in many cities. One of the best known cases is

---

[13] These are the estimates contained in *Global Consultation on Safe Water and Sanitation for the 1990s*, which were published in 1990 and were lower than earlier World Bank estimates published in 1988, both for 1980 and for projections to 1990. The higher estimates correspond more closely to another estimate according to which over 1.5 billion people in the world still do not have access to safe drinking water, in Briscoe and De Ferranti (1988).

[14] Briscoe and De Ferranti (1988), p. 1; a breakdown by these diseases is given in Esrey et. al. (1990), p. vii, but no total is shown. Presumably there is considerable overlap in that people suffering from one of the diseases are also likely to be suffering from one or more of the others.

[15] This estimate refers to mortality among children below five years of age. See Esrey et. al. (1990) and Snyder and Merson (1982).

Sao Paulo, of course, where, by the early 1970s, air pollution had become so severe that there were noticeable increases in mortality. Even worse air pollution was experienced in Cubatao, on account of a combination of the mix of industries located there and unfavourable meteorological conditions.[16]

An aspect of air pollution that is less widely known is the severity of indoor air pollution in rural areas in many developing countries associated with the extremely pollution-intensive character of traditional cooking and heating techniques (notably reliance on biomass fuels). This is believed to be partly responsible for the fact that over 5 million children die every year from acute respiratory illness which is most prevalent in rural areas of developing countries.[17] This is about as many as the number of children who die every year from diarrhea on account partly of inadequate water and sanitation services.

(c) Water Supplies and Income Levels

Figure 1 below shows the percentage of the population with access to safe drinking water in countries with different income levels, in 1975 and 1985.[18] As one would expect, higher incomes tend to be associated with a higher proportion of the population having access to safe drinking water.[19] There has also been some progress in almost all countries over the period 1975 to 1985, in spite of the rapid growth of the population of most developing countries during this period. It can be seen that there is both a generally much higher percentage of the population with access to safe drinking water in the top two quintiles, and that in all quintiles, the rise in incomes between 1975 and 1985 was accompanied by a rise in this percentage.

---

[16] World Bank Operations Evaluation Department, *Environmental Aspects of Selected Bank-Supported Projects in Brazil: The World Bank and Pollution Control in Sao Paulo*, September 4 1990, pp. 11-12 (confidential).

[17] See foreword by John D. Spengler in Smith (1987), p. vii.

[18] For various reasons figures for individual countries are not strictly comparable so that a more reasonable picture of the income/water supply relationship is provided by grouping countries into broad income bands.

[19] Similar correlations between income and water supplies is shown in the UN Economic and Social Commission for Asia and the Pacific, *State of the Environment in Asia and the Pacific*, vol. 2.

FIGURE 1
Drinking Water and Income, 1975 and 1985
Quintile Grouping in 1987 US$

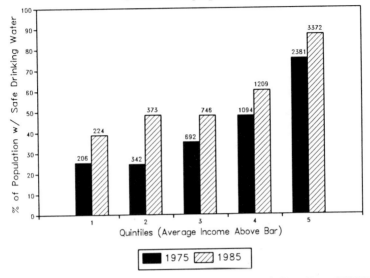

Source: World Bank, Bank Social and Economic Data Base (BESD).

Although satisfactory sewerage and sanitation arrangements are more difficult to define and hence to represent in a simple number, figure 2 below also confirms what one would expect, namely that an increase in incomes is the best way of increasing access to the sanitation facilities that most people in advanced countries would take for granted as normal attributes of a minimum standard of living.[20]

In the longer run, when incomes approach the levels enjoyed currently by advanced countries, one must assume that similar degrees of access to sanitation will be achieved. But it is clear that very rapid urbanisation poses special problems, even if average incomes are rising, so that in the short-to-medium run the conflict between economic growth and the environment can be more pronounced. And, as discussed in more detail below, rapid urbanisation - which seems inevitable whatever is happening to incomes per head - means that the medium run conflict might last for quite a long time in some cases.

---

[20] And it should not be forgotten that the data shown in figure 2 refer to the **average** situation in the countries in question. Within these countries there are then major differences between income groups with respect to their access to decent sanitation.

FIGURE 2
Rural-Urban Sanitation and Income 1985, Country Income
Quintiles in 1987 US$

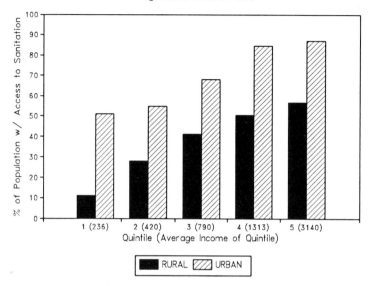

Source: World Bank, Bank Social and Economic Data Base (BESD).

(d) Air Quality and Income Levels

(i) SO_2. If cities are grouped into broad bands corresponding to the income levels of the countries in which they are located a fairly clear pattern emerges, as can be seen in figure 3. In the earlier years covered by the observations in question (around late 1970s) the ambient concentrations of SO_2 in the atmosphere were greater the higher the income band. But by the end of the period covered (usually mid or late 1980s) the position had been reversed. As can be seen in the right hand side of the diagram, this corresponded to a decline in SO_2 concentrations of about 8.9 per cent per annum in the high income countries and a rise of about 3.7 per cent in the low income countries. Taking all the 33 cities covered in the data on SO_2 ambient air quality published by the Global Environment Monitoring System (GEMS) of the United Nations "...27 have downward (at least 3 per cent per year) or stationary trends and 6 have upward trends (at least 3 per cent per year) with most improvements noted in cities of developed countries" (UNEP/WHO, 1988, p. 15).

FIGURE 3
Urban SO2 Concentrations, Cities Grouped by Income Level

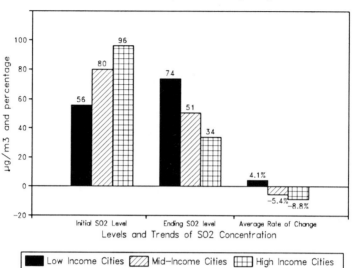

Source: GEMS, *Air Quality in Selected Urban Areas*, WHO, Geneva, various issues 1973-82; UNEP (1991), *Environmental Data Report*, third edition, London. For income figures: World Bank, Economic and Social Database (BESD); United Nations, State of the Environment in Asia and the Pacific, Bangkok, draft.

(ii) SPM or smoke. Similarly, for concentrations of suspended particulate matter or smoke, of the 37 cities covered in the GEMS data, 19 had downward trends, 12 were more or less stationary and only 6 had upward trends. Indeed, measured by the number of days on which the WHO guidelines for SPM or smoke were exceeded during the course of the year, the preponderance of cities in developing countries is overwhelming.[21] For those cities for which adequate data are available the following diagram shows that cities in low income countries had ambient concentrations of SPM or smoke that were much higher than those in the richer countries. And, again, it is in the richer countries that SPM concentrations have fallen.

---

[21] The six worst cities, taking the average of 1980-84, in the GEMS ranking, were Teheran, Shenyang, Calcutta, Beijing, Xian and New Delhi, with Bombay, Kuala Lampur and Bangkok not far behind. In these cities SPM and smoke levels exceeded 230 $\mu g/m^3$ (this being the WHO guideline for the 98th percentile - i.e. exposure level that should not be exceeded more than 2 percent of the time, or 7 days a year) for anything between 200 days and 300 days per year (UNEP/WHO, 1988, Figure 4.9, p. 33).

FIGURE 4
Urban SPM Concentrations, Cities Grouped by
Income Level

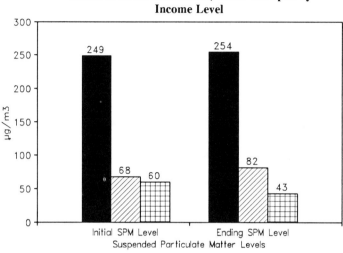

Source: GEMS, *Air Quality in Selected Urban Areas*, WHO, Geneva, various issues 1973-82; UNEP (1991), *Environmental Data Report*, third edition, London. For income figures: World Bank, Economic and Social Database (BESD).

(iii) NO_x and CO. The picture is slightly more confused when one turns to two other pollutants, namely carbon monoxide (CO) and nitrous oxides (NO_xs), since emissions of these, particularly the CO, are heavily influenced by the automobile - both the numbers and the speeds at which they are able to circulate.[22] Furthermore, the limitations on inter-city comparability of measures of these pollutants are particularly severe. Nevertheless, some overall difference can be observed between poor and rich country cities. For example, trends in ambient NO_2 concentrations in most developed countries' cities are now stable or declining, in spite of sustained increases in automobile numbers. By contrast, although data are scarce it appears that trends are generally rising in cities in developing countries.[23] The picture is roughly the

---

[22] Up to a point the emission of pollutants from automobiles falls off rapidly as their speed increases, so that a major cause of urban air pollution from automobiles is traffic congestion. See Faiz et. al. (1990), tables 19 (p. 42), 20 (p. 43) and 21 (p. 46).

[23] Faiz et. al. (1990), p. 43. Even here, however, there are notable exceptions, namely Singapore.

same for CO ambient concentrations. Data are only available for cities in eleven countries and CO concentrations are declining in all of them. With one exception - Santiago - the cities are all in high income countries. By contrast, fragmentary data on a few individual cities in developing countries confirm the rise in concentrations of these pollutants.

(iv) lead. Another important pollutant from mobile sources has been lead. Relatively accurate indicators are available of the amounts of lead in gasoline in individual countries and it can be seen that in recent years almost all industrialised countries have taken effective measures of one kind or another to reduce lead emissions from automobiles, often with striking results. For example, the total quantity of lead used in gasoline in the USA was cut from 170,000 tons in 1975 to 40,000 tons in 1984, and Japan has made even greater progress. By contrast "few developing countries have yet made significant reductions in petrol lead content..." (UNEP/WHO, 1988, p. 60). There have been no or negligible falls in lead levels in petrol in Africa and South- and Central America and the Caribbean, whereas there has been a big fall in Europe and North America, and quite a big fall in Asia, even without taking account of the consumption of unleaded petrol in these countries (UNEP/WHO, 1988, p. 60).

In general, therefore, although one cannot say precisely how overall "air quality" should be defined, or at exactly what income level individual aspects of air quality begin to improve with further growth, it is fairly clear that it does so sooner or later. How much sooner or later - i.e. at what point in time or level of income - urban air conditions reach a point when effective policies are introduced will depend on a host of variables, including technical, social and political variables.

In short, there is overwhelming evidence for the positive relationship between income levels and the components of the environment that are most important for the large majority of the world's population. It is true that the dynamics of the economic growth/environmental pollution relationship are complex, and depend partly on the responsiveness of governments to environmental concerns. But there is still little doubt that, in the longer run, the best way to get a clean environment is to be rich. As far as global pollutants are concerned, the global warming threat has been greatly exaggerated; we are not facing imminent catastrophe if we do not immediately adopt draconian measures to reduce CO_2 emissions; there is plenty of time to think and to do research into alternative less polluting forms of energy. Slowing down economic growth would, if anything, only slow down the technical progress that is needed to reduce the world's dependence on fossil fuels.

6. Economic Growth and Welfare

Of course, economic growth could harm human welfare in ways unrelated to the effects of growth on the environment. As mentioned at the outset of this article, it is also sometimes asserted that growth has other harmful consequences on the "quality of life". But not many components of the "quality of life" are easily measurable, although various attempts have been made to supplement national income data by socio-economic indicators, such as literacy rates, infant mortality rates, life expectancy, and so on. Attempts have also been made to combine these and other socio-economic indicators into "composite indices" of the quality of life.

As I argued in my 1974 book, the historical evidence up to that point was that economic growth had been accompanied by improvements in the main measurable ingredients of the "quality of life", notably those relating to health (Beckerman, 1974, chapter 3). During the last twenty years there have been many more systematic studies of the correlation between incomes per head and either individual ingredients of the quality of life or of composite indices. These studies all confirm that whilst the correlation is not perfect it is always positive and statistically significant. This is the case, for example, in the recent Dasgupta and Weale analysis, which shows positive correlations between per capita national income and individual indicators, such as life expectancy at birth, the adult literacy rate, and even with indices of political and civil liberties (though the direction of causation here is open to question).[24]

A new and very recent composite index - the "Human Development Index" - produced by the UNDP also confirms a strong positive correlation between incomes per head and an index that gives equal weight to incomes, life expectancy and literacy. As the *Human Development Report 1991* says "Human development requires economic growth - for without it, no sustained improvement in human well-being is possible", although it goes on to add that "but while growth is necessary for human development, it is not enough. High growth rates do not automatically translate into higher levels of human development" (p. 1). At another point it states that "the best way to promote human development is to increase the national income and to ensure a close link between economic growth and human well-being" (p. 3).

Indeed, the strength of the correlation between per capita national income and the aggregate Human Development Index has been the source of the criticism of the index by McGillivray (1991), who argues that the strength of this correlation demonstrates that the index is superfluous. However, given that the correlation between this index and incomes per head is not unity, this

---

[24] Dasgupta and Weale (1992), especially Table 3, p. 124.

conclusion seems unwarranted and the authors of the index are justified in claiming that their results do show that up to a point significant improvements in human development can sometimes be achieved without commensurate increases in incomes per head.

If anything, the real weakness of these composite indices is a much more general conceptual issue, namely the lack of any sound theoretical basis for weighting together the different components of any such composite index of human welfare. The conceptual difficulties are of two kinds. First, there is the arbitrariness of the weighting system used, by comparison with the clear theoretical foundations for the weights used in aggregating different components of national income and expenditure. I have set out my views on this elsewhere and need not repeat them here (see Beckerman, 1968).

Secondly, there are major problems of conceptual commensurability. The problem of incommensurability between different components of an individual's welfare is a well-known problem in philosophy - notably in connection with the feasibility of a utilitarian calculus - and it has spilled over into economics (and sometimes vice versa). Various objections to commensurability have been raised. For example, it can be argued, as does Charles Taylor, that the conventional prudential components of an individual's (or a society's) welfare or utility function - i.e. those that directly affect the individual's welfare "...such as the pursuit of wealth, or comfort, or the approval of those who surround us" - are not comparable with other objectives, such as concern for human liberty, respect for personal integrity, or charity and altruism. The latter are higher level objectives because they correspond to moral imperitives of a quasi-Kantian nature (Taylor, 1982, p. 135).

To others incommensurability may be more a question of how far we have smooth, continuous welfare functions. As Raz puts it, this approach to incommensurability would simply amount to defining it such that "A and B are incommensurate if it is neither true that one is better than the other nor true that they are of equal value".[25] And there are other apparent justifications for questioning the degree of commensurability among components of human welfare as diverse as, for example, longevity, human freedom, and income per head, that make it difficult to defend any attempt to include in a composite index certain features of the quality of life that some commentators would like to include.[26]

Thus, one way or another, there are difficulties in establishing any

---

[25] See Raz (1985/86), p. 117. For a later and fuller discussion of this approach see Raz (1986), Chapter 13.

[26] See a particularly valuable survey of different concepts of incommensurability in Griffin (1986), chapter V.

acceptable composite index of human welfare that goes beyond the economist's concept of national income. But, at the same time, it appears that such indices as are available are highly correlated with national income per head, as are also measurable individual components of human welfare. It follows from this that economic growth may not be everything in life but there is no evidence for the view that, in the longer run, it detracts from human welfare, and there is overwhelming evidence to the effect that it is accompanied by increases in human welfare defined more widely.

7. "Sustainable growth"

Once upon a time the concept of sustainable growth had a fairly precise meaning - at least in economics. In a pioneering study by Nordhaus and Tobin (1972), an attempt was made to adjust conventional measures of economic growth for variables such as changes in leisure, or some of the alleged disamenities of economic growth. This study focussed attention on "sustainable growth", which was interpreted as allowing for depreciation of the capital stock as conventionally defined in economics. The concept has, however, been taken over to mean leaving future generations the same environment as that which we have inherited.

Of course, there is a prior ethical question of what future generations will have done to deserve their inheritance of a vast man-made stock of physical and human capital - including notably scientific and technical knowledge? After all, I have inherited a vast stock of man-made environmental assets of one kind or another, but, try as I may, I cannot remember having done anything special to deserve it. Hence, I would not feel that I had been badly done by if I had inherited less. In fact, there are some things in this world of which I would have gladly inherited less. But the extent of our moral obligations to future generations, if any, raises difficult philosophical problems that lie outside the scope of this paper.[27]

Leaving aside, therefore, these philosophical issues, there are relatively obvious difficulties in the interpretation of "sustainability". For example, one "hard" version of the "sustainability" concept is that we should bequeath to future generations the same amount of every single component of the environment that one can identify. This definition of the capital stock is at least reasonably clear and precise, if totally impossible to measure in practice. But surely, few people would suscribe to the value judgement that we have a moral obligation to pass on to posterity every single one of the over 2 million species of beetles that are believed to exist even if it meant prolonging the suffering imposed on millions of children in the developing world today on

---

[27] See Pasek (1992) for full discussion.

account of a failure to spend more on improving the water supply and sanitation, health care and nutrition.

Of course, as Pearce et. al. (1989) point out in *Blueprint for a Green Economy* (Annex 1), there is a whole range of definitions of "sustainability", most of which seem to be in terms of a "sustainability" constraint that would be much more morally acceptable, in that they do allow for some trade-offs. For example, the sustainability constraint is often interpreted as a requirement to leave to future generations a stock of assets that gives it some predetermined level of potential for welfare, such as that existing today. Beetles might give way to improvements in other aspects of the environment, such as clean water supplies and sanitation. But whilst this concept of sustainability is far more acceptable, ethically, (leaving aside the philosophical problems of putting it into the framework of some acceptable theory of inter-generational justice) the moral acceptability is bought at a very high price. This is that - as Dasgupta and Mäler (1990) point out - this concept of sustainability is totally devoid of informational content. For in the absence of any knowledge of future preference patterns and technological possibilities it is impossible to know what substitutions would permit the same level of welfare to be obtained from different combinations of assets - more trees and less insects? more machines and less fish?

Thus the aggregative concept of "sustainable growth" that is so widely encountered these days in any environmental discussion seems to be either (i) morally indefensible, or (ii) devoid of operational value. For we simply have no basis for judging what the trade-offs would be in the future between, say, work and leisure, certain forms of economic activity and others, economic welfare as against non-economic welfare of the kind one may obtain from the environment, and so on. Since the goal cannot be defined, therefore, there is no answer to questions such as "how do we achieve sustainable develop-ment?". Scientists, even social scientists, should not expect to be taken seriously if they go around asking unanswerable and meaningless questions.

8. Conclusions

There seems little doubt that there is some conflict of interest between richer and poorer groups in society, between rich countries and poor countries, and between future generations and those alive today as regards the relative priority that should be given to economic growth and other components of human welfare. But there is evidence that, in general, incomes per head are positively and significantly correlated with other ingredients of human welfare, such as infant mortality, literacy rates, life expectancy and so on. On income-welfare grounds, therefore, there seems no reason to reject the traditional objective of pursuing the goal of economic growth. Indeed, so clear has been the historical relationship in what are now the advanced countries between economic growth and the specific components of human welfare such as those mentioned above that one is driven to the conclusion that much of the opposition to the growth objective reflects the particular concerns of the more affluent groups in society whose welfare may well be threatened by economic growth in one way or another.

More recently, however, there has been much concern with the undoubtedly major impact that growing economic activity is having on the Earth's environment. This concern is perfectly justified up to a point, in that in the absence of pressure to deal with the negative externalities of an environmental character that are produced by economic activity, this particular market failure would proceed unchecked and welfare could be reduced. However, it is necessary to put the environmental issue into proper perspective.

In particular, to give priority to highly speculative global environmental issues in general and to global warming in particular, in the interests of future generations who are likely to be far richer than we are today, and to take drastic action in pursuit of this goal, however costly it may be in terms of current living standards and the immediate improvement in these living standards, would represent an unjustified sacrifice of the clearly apparent interests of billions of very poor people today. These comprise mainly people in developing countries, where local environmental conditions are flagrantly incomparably worse than those that the majority of people in the advanced countries have ever experienced. Furthermore, evidence has been presented to show that there is also a positive correlation between per capita income levels and the quality of those components of the environment - notably access to clean water, sanitation and urban air quality - that matter most to the populations of developing countries.

This does not mean that global environmental effects of economic growth should be totally ignored. Every assistance must be given to developing countries to adopt technologies that do not waste energy and that are less intensive in carbon dioxide emissions - provided they are also economically viable - in order that they can raise their levels of energy consumption per head in pursuit of higher levels of prosperity. Furthermore, reasonable and economically justifiable research into renewable forms of energy must also be supported, particularly as more of such forms of energy use appear to offer prospects of significant economically viable contributions to energy supplies.

At the same time all countries, including the advanced countries, should take appropriate action to reduce the excessive externality effects of all forms of polluting activities. That there is a market failure here which drives a wedge between economic welfare and some wider concept of welfare is undeniable. But all this is a far cry from the evangelical spirit in which the world is being asked to face up to the need for unlimited sacrifices and to mend its wicked ways if the future of the human race is to be secured. And it is a far cry from the doubts that are often expressed as to the value of economic growth in adding to human welfare.

Human beings will no doubt often misuse the opportunities that continued economic growth will provide. But the chief case for economic growth is that it increases the range of choices and opportunities open to human beings. That they will often choose badly is not a reason for depriving them of that choice.

References

Anderson, D. (1991), *Energy and the Environment: An Economic Perspective on Recent Technical Developments and Policies*, Special Briefing Paper 1, Wealth of Nations Foundation, Edinburgh.

Ashby, E. and M. Anderson (1981), *The Politics of Clean Air*, Clarendon Press, Oxford.

Beckerman, W. (1968), *An Introduction to National Income Analysis*, 3rd Edition, Weidenfeld and Nicholson, London.

--- (1974), *In Defence of Economic Growth*, Cape, London.

--- (1975), *Two Cheers for the Affluent Society*, St Martin's Press, New York.

--- (1991), "Global Warning: A Sceptical Economic Assessment", in: D. Helm, *Economic Policy towards the Environment*, Blackwell, Oxford.

--- (1992) "Economic Growth and the Environment: Whose Growth? Whose Environment?", *World Development*, Vol. 20, No. 2, April.

Brimblecombe, P. (1987), *The Big Smoke*, Routledge, London.

Briscoe J. and D. De Ferranti (1988), *Water for Rural Communities*, World Bank.

Dasgupta, P. and K-G. Mäler (1990), "The Environment and Emerging Development Issues", in: *The World Bank Economic Review, Proceedings of the World Bank Annual Conference on Development Economics*.

--- and M. Weale (1992), "On Measuring the Quality of Life", *World Development*, Vol. 20, No. 1, January.

Esrey, S.S., J.B. Potash, L. Roberts and C. Shiff (1990), *WASH Technical Report, No. 66*, Report prepared for the Office of Health, Bureau for Science and Technology, U.S. Agency for International Development, Washington D.C., July.

Faiz, A, K. Sinha, M. Walsh and A. Varma (1990), *Automotive Air Pollution*, Policy, Research and External Affairs, World Bank Working Papers, Transport, WPS 492, August.

Griffin, J. (1986), *Well-Being*, Clarendon Press, Oxford.

Hughes, G. (1990), *Are the Costs of Cleaning Up Eastern Europe Exaggerated?*, draft of paper for the World Bank and the Commission of the European Communities, November.

International Panel on Climate Change (1990), Impacts Assessment of Climate Change, World Meteorological Organization/United Nations Environment Programme, Geneva.

McGillivray, M. (1991), "The Human Development Index: Yet Another Redundant Composite Development Indicator", *World Development*, Vol. 19, No. 10, October.

Meadows, D.H. et. al. (1972), *The Limits to Growth*, Universe, New York.

Metal Bulletin's Prices and Data (1990), Surrey, UK.

Mishan, E.J. (1967), *The Costs of Economic Growth*, Staples Press, London.

Nordhaus, W.D. (1990), "To Slow or Not to Slow: The Economics of the Greenhouse Effect", draft, February 1990.

--- and J. Tobin (1972), *Is Economic Growth Obsolete?*, NBER.

Overseas Development Institute (1992), *The Energy Industry and Global Warming: New Roles for International Aid*, London.

Pasek, J. (1992), "Our Obligations to Future Generations: Some Philosophical Issues", *World Development, Special Issue on the Environment*, Vol. 20, No. 4, April.

Pearce, D., A. Markandya and E. Barbier (1989), *Blueprint for a Green Economy*, London.

Raz, J. (1985/86), "Value Incommensurability: Some Preliminaries", *Proceedings of the Aristotelian Society*, New Series, Vol LXXXVI.

--- (1986), *The Morality of Freedom*, The Clarendon Press, Oxford.

Smith, K.R. (1987), *Biofuels, Air Pollution, and Health*, Plenum Press, New York and London.

Snyder, J.D. and M.H. Merson (1982), "The Magnitude of the Global Problem of Acute Diarrhoeal Disease: A Review of Active Surveillance Data", *Bulletin of the World Health Organisation*, Vol. 60, pp. 605-613.

Taylor, C. (1982), "The Diversity of Goods", in: A. Sen and B. Williams, (eds.) *Utilitarianism and Beyond*, Cambridge University Press.

UNCTAD (1989), *Handbook of International Trade and Development Statistics*.

UNEP (1991), *Environmental Data Reports*, third edition, London.

UNEP/WHO (1988), Global Environment Monitoring System (GEMS), *Assessment of Urban Air Quality*.

UNEP/WHO, Global Enviroment Monitoring System (GEMS), *Air Quality in Selected Urban Areas*, various issues, Geneva.

United Nations (1989), *State of the Environment in Asia and the Pacific*, Vol. 2, draft, Bangkok.

--- (1991), *Human Development Report 1991*, New York and Oxford.

World Bank (1990), *Global Consultation on Safe Water and Sanitation for the 1990s*, (background paper to Sept. 1990 New Delhi conference Global Consultation on Safe Water and Sanitation for the 1990s, sponsored by UNDP).

World Bank (1990), Operations Evaluation Department, *Environmental Aspects of Selected Bank-Supported Projects in Brazil: The World Bank and Pollution Control in Sao Paulo*, September 4.

--- (1992), *World Development Report 1992. Development and the Environment*, Washington D.C.

Explaining Economic Growth
A. Szirmai, B. van Ark and D. Pilat

Technology and Growth: The Complex Dynamics of Catching Up, Falling Behind and Taking Over

*Luc Soete and Bart Verspagen**
Maastricht Economic Research Institute on Innovation and Technology (MERIT)

1. Introduction

Over the post-war period research on economic growth has come to be dominated by theoretical approaches which are strongly model-oriented, and whose empirical content is generally limited to broad tests of the consistency of the real world with established or, in more recent times, new growth models. In such approaches empirical tests which do not fit the theoretical model, can only be expressed in terms of paradoxes or the more down to earth question of the economic theorist who wonders "what's wrong with reality". In many ways this is a logical and natural trend. Opposed to the costs, efforts and time involved in carrying out new, original empirical research, theoretical modelling often appears to be the easy road to academic progress and fame in economics.

It is from this perspective that Angus Maddison's research, with that of a very select group of other empirical researchers, some of whom have contributed to this volume, stands out by its overriding immediate empirical concern and historical content. From this perspective, the title of this volume *Explaining Economic Growth* describes well the underlying motivation and spirit of much of Maddison's research, even though it gives insufficient credit to what has already been explained about economic growth, mainly thanks to Maddison's numerous investigations into the broad long-term macro-economic empirical regularities in growth and development.

Of course, the choice of the subject of economic growth has itself much been influenced by growth theory, and in particular the old growth models of the 1950s and their "residual" evidence. However, particularly in the field of growth and development and the accompanying patterns of structural change, much old and even some of the new theoretical work, has been dominated by an overriding concern to reduce the complexities of the real world to easily quantifiable relationships, which can be fitted into some straightforward

---

* We thank Marjolein Caniëls for research assistance.

modelling framework. In doing so, many of the pioneering investigations on the complex dynamics linking growth, structural change and technical change associated with the names of Schumpeter, Kuznets and Gerschenkron, to name but a few, have often become totally neglected.

In this article, we address in particular the issue of technical change and economic development. We will do so not from a long term historical perspective - to do so would require Maddison's detailed historical knowledge on data and empirical evidence which we lack - but from a relatively short term empirical perspective (the last 25 years) in a spirit which nevertheless could still be called Maddisonian.

Technical change itself has often been the major factor behind structural change and the emergence of new phases of development in different countries. In a first section we centre therefore on a number of issues related to technical change. These highlight features which have often been neglected in traditional neo-classical growth analyses and, as illustrated by some of the empirical evidence gathered by Maddison, they warrant a different approach focusing more on the disequilibrium yet endogenous nature of technical change. In a second section we briefly review some of the recent new growth and development contributions, allowing, contrary to the standard neo-classical growth model, for a more endogenous treatment of technical change. Our review brings to the forefront the fact that these models, while stressing some of the dynamic "increasing return" features of knowledge and technical change, remain nevertheless dominated by notions of equilibria and uniformity between countries, which do not fit some of the disruptive characteristics of technical change and its diffusion. In the third section we then present some of our own empirical evidence. The latter is two-fold. First we bring together evidence on the variety of converging and diverging growth patterns both over time and between large geographical areas; second we present evidence on variety in innovative and imitative behaviour of various (groups of) countries. Our empirical analysis is purely descriptive. Its aim is to illustrate the wide variety of growth performance, rather than to try explain it.

2. Technical Change: From Innovation to Diffusion and Imitation

2.1. Technical Change: Some Crucial Features

When discussing the contribution of technical change to growth and development, it is essential to recognise that the economic impact of technical innovations and their diffusion can be dramatically different. In this context, it is useful to make a couple of distinctions.

First, at the level of **innovation**, it is essential to recognise that there is a widespread difference in the impact of such technological advances. Thus, there are many innovations which have very widespread societal effects and might even change the whole quality of life, but whose measurable economic effects are small or at best indirect in terms of macro-economic growth and efficiency. Examples abound. The innovation of an oral contraception device had a major impact on sexual behaviour in the 1960s and 1970s in most countries, giving rise to some fundamental debates about medical and social ethics. Its economic impact was at best indirect through greater participation of women in the labour market.

On the other hand, there are many innovations with significant, but widely divergent economic impact. Thus there are innovations which find applications in only one sector: a so-called "localised" impact (e.g., the float glass process introduced by Pilkington's in the 1960s), and those which effect many or all sectors of the economy: a so-called "pervasive" impact (e.g., the microprocessor or the electronic computer). In any discussion of the impact of technical change on growth, including productivity growth, it is essential to be aware of this wide variation in the economic impact of technological advances.

Second, with respect to technology **diffusion**, there is of course a striking degree of methodological similarity between the typical epidemic diffusion model, and the models of industrial growth and economic development, developed in the thirties by among others Kuznets (1930) and Schumpeter (1934). In many ways this is not surprising. The concepts of "imitation" and "bandwagon effects" so crucial to the diffusion literature, are also central to many of the more structural accounts of economic growth, where the S-shaped diffusion pattern is similar to the emergence and long term rise and fall of industries. An attempt at linking the two theories was made in Freeman, Clark and Soete (1982).

The critique of the standard diffusion model led to the application of "Probit analysis" in developing alternative models of inter-firm diffusion. The central assumption underlying the probit model is that an individual consumer (or firm) will adopt an innovation at a time his income (size) exceeds some critical level. This critical or tolerance income level (or size) represents the actual tastes of the consumer (the receptiveness of the firm) which, in turn, can be related to any number of personal or economic characteristics. Over time, though, with the increase in income level and assuming an unchanged income distribution, the critical income level will fall with an across-the-board change in tastes in favour of the new product, due both to imitation, more and better information, band-wagon effects, etc.

The relevance of the probit model for industrial growth theory is self-evident. A "critical" income per capita level is a concept which can be introduced in a straightforward manner in development theories of the stages of economic growth. Replacing the concept of individuals by countries, differences in growth performance between countries can be explained and expected. Considering both the extreme variation in a country's ability to take risks and assess new innovations (the variation in consumer tastes in the probit model), and the extreme levels of income inequality at the world level, it should come as no surprise that growth at the world wide level (diffusion) has been a widely diverging pattern, and that many countries, even with the fall over time in the "critical" income level for industrialisation, might have fallen behind rather than caught up.

From an economic perspective the static, demand-focused nature of the standard diffusion model is questionable. Once the importance of supply factors is recognised, it becomes more apparent how past investment in old, established technologies can slow down the diffusion of new innovations, past investment not only in physical capital but also in human capital, even "intellectual" capital. The importance of past investment in, and existing commitment to, a technology which is being displaced, in slowing down the diffusion of a new technology, points also towards the phenomenon of inter-technology competition. New technology will compete on disadvantageous terms against existing technology. As Rosenberg (1976) and others have observed, the diffusion of steam power in the last century was significantly retarded by a series of improvements in the existing water power technology which further prolonged the economic life of the old technology.

2.2. *International Technology Diffusion: Catching Up, Falling Behind and Taking Over*

The voluminous literature on the subject of international technology diffusion and technological "catching up" can be seen as a straightforward application of the epidemic diffusion model discussed in the previous section.[1] Again, we do not intend to review this literature here. The basic conclusion that arises from it is that technologically backward countries are in an advantageous situation, because they can assimilate technology spill-overs into higher growth rates, and converge rapidly to the per capita income level corresponding to the technological frontier.

The automatic way in which international diffusion of knowledge is assumed to take place in most of these contributions has been criticised in studies based on more in depth historical research on the emergence of technological and economic leadership and the process of taking over, or the

---

[1] See among others Posner (1961), Freeman (1963, 1965), Gomulka (1971, 1991), Cornwall (1976), Abramovitz (1979), Baumol (1986) and Dowrick and Nguyen (1989).

use or adoption of particular technologies.[2] To a large extent, the arguments found in this latter part of the literature link up with the critique of the basic (epidemic) diffusion model discussed above. However, some convergence between these two strands of literature seems to be taking place (Abramovitz, 1986; Perez and Soete, 1988). As highlighted by Maddison (1989), this convergence puts the emphasis clearly back on the historical institutional framework within which the process of imitation/technological catching up takes place, including the role of historical accidents, developmental constraints, be they primarily economic (such as the lack of natural resources) or more political in nature, the role of immigration (Scoville, 1951) and other "germ carriers", and the crucial role of governments (see Yakushiji, 1986).

A model taking these considerations into account, was developed and tested in Verspagen (1991). The model stresses the importance of the concepts of technological distance and the capability to assimilate knowledge spill-overs in the development process. Its nonlinear specification leads to a bifurcation scheme, in which countries lagging too far behind the frontier, and lacking enough assimilation capabilities, will fall behind rather than catch up. Despite the simple nature of the model, the specification is rich enough to encompass both automatic catching up (as a special case), and a probit-like development pattern. Empirical tests of the model showed that among the factors contributing to the assimilation capability education of the labour force is a most prominent one (see also Baumol et al., 1989, on this matter).

Besides being important for the distinction between catching up or falling behind, the implications of such a development view based on historical and institutional factors are also far-reaching at the other end of the growth spectrum. The possibilities for taking over and forging ahead are also highly dependent on factors influencing the successful adaptation and diffusion of new technologies. The vast majority of new technologies will originate primarily from within the technologically most advanced countries. However, there are good reasons to expect that the intra-national diffusion of such a major new technology might well be hampered by the various factors mentioned earlier, the new technology competing (in its diffusion) on disadvantageous terms. Thus, previous investment outlays in the existing technology and the commitment to the latter on the part of management, the skilled labour force and even the "development"-part of R&D activities geared towards improvements upon existing technology, might all hamper the diffusion of a new technology. These brakes to diffusion might even be so strong that the new technology will diffuse more quickly elsewhere, i.e., to a country less committed, both in terms of actual production and investment, to

---

[2] See for example Landes (1969), Hobsbawn (1970), Rosenberg (1970), Ames and Rosenberg (1963), Habakkuk (1962) and von Tunzelmann, (1978).

the older technology. At the same time, as diffusion proceeds, some of the crucial dynamic returns to scale (incremental innovations), resulting for example from user-feedback information will further shift the technological advantage to the country in which the new technology is diffusing more rapidly.

The industrialisation process of Germany, France, the US and a number of smaller European countries in the 19th century, provides ample support for this view, as Maddison (1991) has illustrated. The dramatic decline in the UK's position from an absolute technological leadership, producing more steam engines than the whole of the rest of the world put together in the mid-19th century, is a powerful illustration of this phenomenon. It points amongst others to some of the advantages of late industrialisers, both in terms of catching up with present technological leaders, as well as in terms of acquiring foreign technology at a more competitive price. In recent times, as we shall see in section 3, this has been most obvious in the case of Japan in the 1960s and 1970s, and South Korea in the 1980s. In their rapid industrialisation the world's best-practice productivity levels were achieved over a very short time in steel, cars, electronics, numerically controlled machine tools, and most recently in computers, largely on the basis of initially imported technology. Nevertheless the scarcity of such successful examples of taking over illustrates how non-automatic and exceptional processes of effective technological catching up and leapfrogging are.

Most of these phenomena are hard to catch in the narrow formalism that has become customary in economics. However, the recent so-called new growth theories have tried to capture some of the ideas on increasing returns to scale on which we have elaborated above. Still, the question remains whether the ideas on technical change that have been effectively integrated into this plethora of new theoretical models are rich enough to be able to cope with the more qualitatively inspired ideas on catching up, falling behind and overtaking exposed above. It is this question which we will address in a preliminary way in the next section.

3. Growth Theory: From Old to New Interpretations[3]

Whereas the basic neo-classical growth model (Solow, 1970) treats the rate of technological change as an exogenous parameter, the new neo-classical growth theories follow earlier work in the Schumpeterian tradition by assuming that

[3] This section is largely based on Verspagen (1992). More exact references can be found there.

innovation is an endogenous phenomenon.[4] The crucial argument about innovation in these models follows Arrow's (1962) idea, which was further developed in the industrial economics literature (see Kamien and Schwartz, 1982; Scherer and Ross, 1990), in assuming that part of an innovation consists of externalities flowing to competitors. In this view, only part of the pay-offs of an innovation introduced by an individual firm can be appropriated by this firm.

The start of the new growth models is the assumption that technological advances flow from (private) investment in research and development (R&D) activities. Using intertemporal profit (or utility) maximisation, an optimal investment path for R&D activities is computed by the entrepreneur. However, since part of the knowledge that flows from these investments can also be used by competitors (externalities), the amount of R&D undertaken is sub-optimal from an (aggregate) welfare perspective. The growth rate of production (income, welfare) for society as a whole can be increased by governmental policies taking the form of R&D subsidies.[5] Besides the normative welfare effect, the externalities associated with innovation lead to increasing returns to scale. In simple terms, if one firm doubles its inputs (including R&D), output will more than double, due to knowledge spill-overs.

Broadening the application of the new growth theories to the open economy case leads also to important conclusions with regard to trade and technology policy. In line with strategic trade theory (see Soete, 1991), the basic conclusion is that the arguments in favour of free trade no longer have unlimited validity with respect to time and place. In some specific cases trade policies, in the form of tariffs, or technology policies, in the form of research subsidies, may influence aggregate economic growth or welfare by changing the factor proportions devoted to research and/or manufacturing. The exact outcomes of the policy measures are not, however, very clear-cut from the international perspective. A lot depends on the comparative advantages with regard to technology and manufacturing activities.

The basic mechanism that leads to these conclusions is the general equilibrium framework that is applied in the new growth models. As shown most clearly in Lucas (1988), the single most important difference between the basic Solow model with exogenous technological change and a model based solely on the above principles of endogenous innovation, is exactly the

---

[4]   The most basic contributions are in Romer (1986, 1990), Lucas (1988) and Aghion and Howitt (1990). An application to the issue of international growth is most prominent in Grossman and Helpman (1991).

[5]   In the model in Aghion and Howitt (1990), it is possible that too much is invested in R&D. This is caused by the negative externality corresponding to the so-called business stealing effect.

difference between first-best and second- or third-best growth paths. The basic ideas about the nature of the growth process in the Solow model (i.e., balanced growth) are neatly reproduced in the new growth theory.[6]

This view of the growth process seems to be challenged by the ideas of disruptive structural changes connected with technological change and its (international) diffusion, which were exposed in the previous section, and which are also present in Maddison's (1982, 1991) ideas on phases of economic growth. There seem to be two distinct sources for those different views on the development process.

First, at the level of the basic assumptions underlying the distinct theoretical approaches, it is the equilibrium tendency stemming from (intertemporal) profit or utility maximising agents that makes the difference. Implicitly combined with rational technological expectations, this leads to a theoretical bias against possibilities for lock-in sub-optimal growth paths, path dependency etc., which seem so important when looking at longer term international growth patterns.

Second, it is the characterisation of the nature of technological change itself that is different in the two approaches. The representation of innovation in the new growth models is one of a gradual nature, corresponding to the Solow-model idea of a fixed rate of technological progress. Although this rate is endogenised in the new growth theory, it is still more or less fixed (over time). The development view exposed in the previous section, however, is rooted in the Schumpeterian idea of major fluctuations in the rate of technological change over time (see also Dosi, 1982; Freeman, Clark and Soete, 1982).

Resolving this controversy on the nature of growth (theories) requires above all empirical research. However, both of the theories outlined have their own specific problems related to empirical implication of the ideas. The rather stylised nature of the new growth models leads to clearly unrealistic conclusions, such as the often obtained hypothesis that the size of the resource base (i.e., population) is a factor leading to faster growth. Also, the math-

---

[6] Space considerations force us to generalise more on this subject than may be appropriate. Aghion and Howitt (1990) provide a spectrum of growth possibilities ranging from a "no growth" trap, via a "growth cycle" to "balanced growth". In general, however, the nature of growth paths predicted by the new growth theory can be characterised as balanced growth, as indicated by the following quotation from Romer (1989, p. 4): "Even though [the model] departs from the competitive, price taking assumption that has become standard in equilibrium models, it starts from an explicit specification of preferences, an aggregate technology, and an equilibrium concept. (..) the rationale for this modeling strategy is that it offers the most power for generalising across different types of evidence to reach conclusions about causality".

ematical ingenuity applied in the new growth model comes at the expense of some very limiting assumptions. Capital in the usual sense, for example, as a stock variable is absent in most of the models. Applying these models to empirical data in the usual econometric sense would require much less stylised formulations, or would lead to indirect tests of the theories (as in Romer, 1989).[7] Problems involved in testing the implications of Schumpeterian theory mainly come down to problems with regard to clear formalisation of the arguments (see Gomulka, 1991).

The scope for further integration of some of the ideas of new growth theory with a more detailed analysis of the differentiated role of science and technology in specific sectors is undoubtedly a promising avenue for further research in this area. However, this will not be done in the rest of this article. Instead, we concentrate on presenting some empirical evidence which highlights some of the aspects of the relation between technological change and economic growth in an international setting, thus connecting the various theoretical issues to empirical facts.

4. International Growth and Technological Change: An Empirical Interpretation

4.1. Catching Up or Falling Behind?

As a first way of getting some feeling for the relation between growth rates and technology in the world, this section will summarise the available evidence by trying to detect some regularities in growth performance across countries. The ideas discussed in section 2.2 raise the question whether a (negative) relation between initial income and growth (flowing from a mechanistic view on international diffusion) is valid for a large set of countries, including the Least Developed Countries (LDCs).

Figure 1 plots the change in the per capita income gap vis à vis the USA against the initial income gap in 1960, for 114 countries. The income gap is defined as the natural logarithm of the ratio of per capita income in the USA to per capita income of the other country.[8] Each point corresponds to a particular country, classified into "Oil exporters", "Newly Industrialising Countries", "Developed Market Economies" and "Other" following traditional

---

[7] Space prevents us from reviewing here some of the more recent econometric literature on so-called real business cycles. Many of those econometric growth tests, while staying within a multiple equilibria framework, come up with conclusions very similar to ours. See in particular Durlauf and Johnson (1992).

[8] See Verspagen (1991) for data and for more details on the construction of the growth rates.

World Bank or UN definitions. The lines drawn in the figure are (linear) regression lines for the different sub-samples of countries. Note that a negative change of the income gap implies convergence, or catching up, while a positive change implies falling behind. Hence, negatively sloped regression lines are consistent with convergence.

FIGURE 1
Catching Up and Falling Behind in the World Economy, 1960-1985

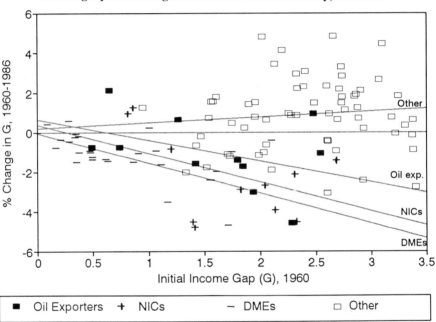

If there is any systematic pattern in the total scatter of points in the graph, it is the variance, which grows bigger the larger the per capita income gap becomes. Thus, the countries close to the world economic and technological frontier (as measured by the performance of the USA) show smaller (absolute) growth rate differentials relative to this frontier than those further away from it.

Obviously, the results in figure 1 indicate that there is a dichotomy between catching up and falling behind at the world level (or at least the part of the world included in our sample). Some of the countries facing the largest initial gaps (the developing countries) have also experienced the largest increases in the gap, which is exactly opposite to what the catching up hypothesis predicts.

However, within one or more groups of countries, the catching-up hypothesis seems to make some sense. Obviously, catching up makes sense for the group of DMEs, and to a lesser extent also for NICs and oil-exporters. Thus, in terms of the results here, there seems to be some indication that catching up is only a relevant phenomenon for the group of DMEs, NICs and oil exporters.

The impression from the graph is confirmed by a more formal analysis. While the lines drawn are regression lines for sub-samples of the total of 114 countries, running a regression for the total sample, and applying a Chow F-test for the hypothesis that this regression fits the data as well as the four separate regressions, yields an F-statistic of 7.59, which rejects the null-hypothesis at the 1 per cent level.

In order to get a first general impression about the possible causes of the dichotomy between catching up and falling behind, the last part of this section presents some additional data and methods. The technique used is cluster analysis. For two periods 1960-1973 and 1973-1988,[9] the average annual growth rate of GDP per capita and population, the average level of R&D intensity, the average share of investment in national income, and the initial level of catching up potential are calculated for each country for which data are available.[10] In order to rule out the influence of scale, each of the variables is scaled on the interval 0-1, with the smallest value in the sample equal to 0 and the largest equal to 1. Then a distance matrix for the countries in 5-dimensional space (each variable represents one dimension) is calculated.[11] This distance matrix is used in a cluster analysis.

Thus, the 1960-1973 world can neatly be divided into three major groups: falling behind, catching up and leading countries. With regard to the question of catching up or falling behind, it seems that investment intensity is a crucial factor. Countries that have (not) been able to catch up are characterised by high (low) rates of investment. R&D intensity seems to be less important for catching up, as both the catching up groups are not characterised by high R&D intensities. Only the technologically leading countries are characterised by high R&D intensities. The role of population growth is unclear.

---

[9] The periodisation is chosen arbitrarily, although the break in 1973 is of course not coincidental.

[10] Data sources and -definitions are as follows: GDP (per capita) and investment shares are taken from Summers and Heston (1991). R&D is defined as total (including higher education and governmental) R&D and is taken from UNESCO and OECD. The catching up potential is defined as the logarithm of the ratio of GDP per capita in the USA to the GDP per capita in the other country in the initial year. See figure 1.

[11] Euclidean distances were used.

FIGURE 2
Economic Performance in Different Clusters, 1960-1973

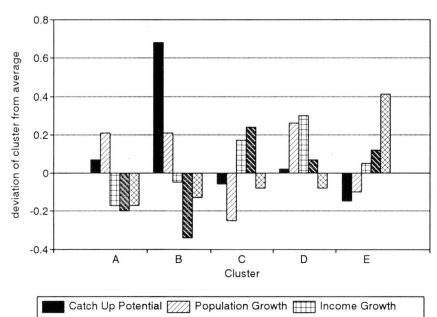

The clusters and their members are the following:[12]

A. "The Falling Behind Countries" (n=24)
    Argentina, Central African Republic, Colombia, Ecuador, Guatemala, India, Iran, Jordan, Madagascar, Mauritius, Mexico, New Zealand Nigeria, Pakistan, Peru, Philippines, Senegal, Sri Lanka, Sudan, Thailand, Trinidad & Tobago, Turkey, Uruguay, Venezuela.
B. "The Worst Falling Behind Countries" (n=2)
    Egypt, Malawi.
C. "The Catching Up Countries" (n=15)
    Austria, Bulgaria, Cyprus, Denmark, Finland, Greece, Iceland, Ireland, Italy, Jamaica, Malta, Norway, Portugal, Spain, Yugoslavia.
D. "The Strongly Catching Up Countries" (n=3)
    Israel, Korea, Singapore.

---

[12] Note that due to the clustering methodology, which does not weight the variables involved in any way, countries may occasionally be grouped under intuitively wrong headings.

E. "The Leading Elite" $(n=14)^{13}$
   Australia, Belgium, Canada, Czechoslovakia, France, Hungary, Japan, Netherlands, Sweden, Switzerland, UK, USA, USSR, West Germany.

The results of the cluster analysis for the period 1960-1973 allow us to identify five clusters. Figure 2 presents the characteristics of these clusters. One (small) group has realised high growth rates with high population growth, while elsewhere (especially outside the catching up group) there is a negative relation between population growth and economic growth. There also seems to be a negative relation between the size of the catching up potential and the capability to catch up, suggesting a "critical" value of the catching up potential along the lines outlined above. With regard to the European countries, it can be noted that additional evidence (see for example the results in the next subsections) indicates that even for those present in the leading group, catching up potential relative to the USA was a phenomenon that strongly favoured growth performance during this period, although on a smaller scale than the countries in the catching up groups.

The same clustering exercise can be repeated for the 1973-1988 period, now with a marginally different set of countries (for reasons of data availability). The results of this exercise is that it is again suitable to divide the sample in five different clusters. However, this time the growth performance of the separate clusters is different from the 1960-1973 period. The characteristics of the clusters are represented in Figure 3. The clusters and their members are as follows:

A. "The Established Falling Behind Countries" $(n=9)$
   Central African Republic, Guatemala, India, Madagascar, Malawi, Nigeria, Rwanda, Senegal, Sudan.

B. "The Missed Opportunities Falling Behind Countries" $(n=6)$
   Argentina, Chili, El Salvador, Guyana, Jamaica, Trinidad & Tobago.

C. "The Newly Catching Up Countries" $(n=19)$
   Brazil, Colombia, Congo, Costa Rica, Ecuador, Egypt, Indonesia, Iran, Jordan, Mauritius, Mexico, Pakistan, Panama, Peru, Philippines, Sri Lanka, Thailand, Turkey, Venezuela.

D. "The Established Catching Up Countries" $(n=23)$
   Australia, Austria, Belgium, Canada, Cyprus, Czechoslovakia, Denmark, Finland, Greece, Iceland, Ireland, Italy, Korea, Malta, New Zealand, Norway, Poland, Portugal, Rumania, Seychelles, Singapore, Spain,

---

[13] While interpreting the presence of the centrally planned economies in this group, one should keep in mind that due to differences in statistical concepts used in communist and market economies, the data may be less comparable in this respect than was implicitly assumed.

Yugoslavia.
E. "The Leading Elite" (n=12)
   France, Hungary, Israel, Japan, Netherlands, St. Lucia, Sweden,
   Switzerland, UK, USA, USSR, West Germany.

FIGURE 3
Economic Performance in Different Clusters, 1973-1988

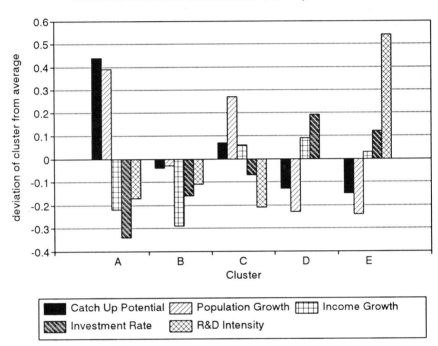

One sees a number of interesting differences with regard to the previous
period. First, there are a number of switches of countries from one group to
another. Most obvious is the switch of several "falling behind"- countries in
the first period to one of the catching up groups in the second. This includes
many NICs (Egypt, Thailand and most South American countries). They have
realised an active industrialisation process, which resulted among other things
in high investment levels and high growth rates. On the other hand, there are
a number of countries (mostly incidental) whose position deteriorated: from
catching up to falling behind (Jamaica, Trinidad and Tobago), from leading to
catching up (Australia, Belgium, Canada, Czechoslovakia).
    Considerations of space force us to leave these switches largely un-
discussed. As the results in Baumol et al. (1989), the contribution by Wolff
and Gittleman to this volume and Verspagen (1991) indicate, education might

be a relevant variable in explaining these switches. It can also be noted that they illustrate the general point about the dynamic structural adjustments caused by the process of technological change and its international diffusion discussed in section 2. Moreover, an important lesson that can be drawn from these switches is that there seems to be scope for influencing growth performance, either by governmental policies, or by changes in cultural or entrepreneurial variables. The dichotomy between successfully switching from falling behind to catching up and remaining in a falling behind situation is illustrative in this respect.

A second difference between the two periods is the distinction between catching up groups. In the first period, there were two catching up groups, which were quite similar with regard to all variables in the analysis, except population growth. In the second period, there is one group (the established catching up countries), which is characterised by high investment, the classic (previous period) characteristic of catching up. The other (newly catching up) countries seem to have much lower investment levels, but rapid population growth. Note also that the scope for catching up has decreased considerably, since the growth rate differences between leaders and catching up countries have diminished.

4.2. Technology and Growth in the Catching Up Part of the World

The last two sections focus on a subset of countries which belong to the catching up groups in the cluster analysis above. In order to describe the trends in convergence or divergence in international growth and technological capabilities, we will use statistics on GDP (denoted by Q), population (N), business enterprise R&D expenditures (R), and patents granted (P).[14] Using these variables, we define R&D intensity as R/Q, and GDP per capita as Q/N.

Two indicators will be used. First, a convergence coefficient C which is defined as follows:

---

[14] Data sources are as follows. R&D statistics as well as GDP used to calculate R&D intensities: OECD; Patents: US Patent and Trademark Office; GDP and population used in secular analysis: Maddison (1991); GDP and population used in postwar-only analysis: Summers and Heston (1991). Country samples are as follows: OECD: jpn, usa, can, bel, dnk, fra, deu, grc, irl, ita, nld, prt, esp, gbr, aus, nzl, aut, fin, nor, swe, tur, yug, che; Asia: jpn, tha, mys, sgp, phl, kor, hkg; South America: mex, col, bra, arg, ury; technological leaders: deu, fra, jpn, gbr, usa, nld, swe, che.

$$C_t = \frac{1}{n}\sum_{i=1}^{n} \frac{Y_t^f - Y_{it}}{Y_t^f} \tag{1}$$

whereby Y stands for R&D intensity and/or GDP per capita. Subscripts t and i $(1..n)$ denote time and countries, respectively. The superscript f denotes the frontier value, which is defined as the maximum of $(Y_{1t}..Y_{nt})$ in each period t.

The convergence coefficient gives the mean value across countries of the percentual deviation from the frontier. If countries with low per capita GDP levels are growing faster (catching up), C will fall. Thus, a decreasing value of C indicates convergence (catching up), while an increasing value points to divergence.

Second, we will define an entropy coefficient E (also known as the Theil coefficient) as follows:[15]

$$E_t = \sum_{i=1}^{n} X_{it} \ln(1/X_{it}) \tag{2}$$

In this equation, X stands for a country's share in total GDP, or patents. The Theil entropy coefficient is an indicator of concentration. Large values of the indicator go with low concentration, low values with high concentration. Thus, at a given point in time, E only gives an indication of the (spatial) distribution of some variable across the country sample. However, it is the time path of E that is of interest for the analysis here. An increasing trend in E over time indicates that the variable under consideration becomes less concentrated over time, which is interpreted as convergence, a decreasing trend in E denotes divergence. For variables which have a clear (short term) relation to the growth rate of population, like GDP (per capita), C is the better indicator because it is able to distinguish between population growth and other factors (technology) as sources for growth.[16] However, for variables which bear a less clear relationship to population growth (like patents), and consequently, for which it does not make much sense to express them in per capita terms, E is a better indicator.

First, we consider Maddison's (1991) long-run data for a subsample of OECD countries, which gives an overview of the trends in convergence/ divergence over the 20th century. In figure 4, time trends for C for per capita

---

[15] Slightly different variants of the Theil entropy coefficient exist. The one used here is often found in the literature on market structure, as for example in Kleinknecht and Verspagen (1989).

[16] Because the definition of entropy uses shares, the entropy of per capita GDP is not a very useful concept.

GDP[17] and E for GDP are given. An impressionistic view of the time series seems to suggest that there are four main periods which differ with regard to convergence/divergence patterns. In the first period (1900-1920), there is no real trend in either of the series. As argued in Maddison (1991), this is the period in which the USA slowly begins to take over technological (i.e. productivity) and economic leadership from Great Britain. The second period corresponds to the 1920s, in which some (very) weak signs of convergence are visible. Then follows the Great Depression of the 1930s and the second world war, which have a dramatic impact on both our indicators C and E. The period 1930-1950 is therefore not very useful from an analytical point of view.

FIGURE 4
Convergence and Divergence in GDP and GDP per Capita,
Sub-Sample of OECD Countries, 1900-1990

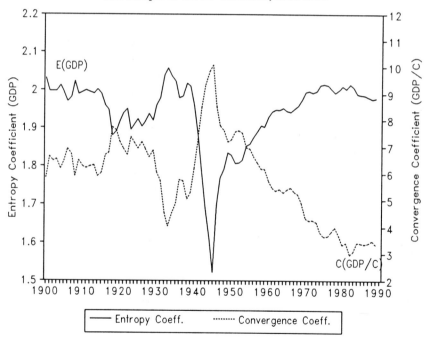

Around 1950, the dispersion in (per capita) GDP seems to have settled back again at levels comparable with the pre-1930 period. From that point

---

[17] Population figures used are the ones in Maddison (1991), corrected for territorial changes.

onwards a very strong trend of convergence sets in. The figure shows that this period has indeed been an exceptional one from an historical point of view, and that a large part of the growth in the lagging countries must be explained by a catching up effect.

The last part of the time series in the graph seems to suggest that from the mid-1970s onwards the catching up effect is becoming less important. The convergence trend weakens, and the scope for catching up seems to be diminishing considerably. The combination of this and the previously mentioned strong convergence trend makes the postwar period in general, and the most recent decade in particular a rather interesting setting to study the dynamics of imitation, innovation and catching up.

4.3. The Post-war Period and Recent Decades: From Convergence to Divergence?

Figure 5 gives the trends in C for per capita GDP in a larger sample of countries, including the OECD and Asian and South American NICs over the postwar period. For the line describing regional growth trends in Asia, Japan is used as the frontier country.[18] Following Soete and Verspagen (1991), the technologically leading countries are defined as those with R&D intensity in 1967 of 1 per cent or more.

The lines show that the strong postwar convergence trend that had been observed in the previous figure also holds, with the exception of South America and Asia, for the different samples of countries considered in figure 5. However, at the end of the period, the trends flatten, and the latest years even show signs of divergence in some cases. Convergence is strongest in the total group of countries and the sample of OECD-countries, indicating the large catching up potential that has arisen from the huge difference in per capita GDP. The specific stabilisation problems in South America cause the fluctuations around the weak trend in that group. Asia seems to be a special case, with divergence until the early 1970s (mainly caused by the strong growth of Japan) and convergence afterwards (caused by the catching up of the NICs). Even within the group of technological leaders, there has been enough scope for convergence until the mid-1970s, indicating the supremacy of the USA in the earlier period.

---

[18] In South America, there is not a clear leading country in terms of GDP per capita, so that the USA has been used as the leader. Note that the samples exclude Southern American and Asian Less Developed Countries (LDCs), including countries such as Peru and India. Thus, the described trends only hold for parts of these continents.

FIGURE 5
Convergence and Divergence in Per Capita GDP, Catching Up Countries,
1950-1990

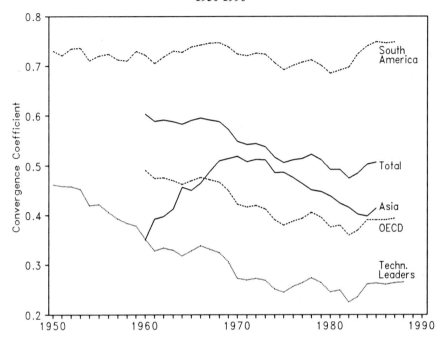

TABLE 1
Structural Breaks in Per Capita GDP Convergence Patterns[a]

Country group	3 breaks assumed	2 breaks assumed	1 break assumed
Total	1969 1976 1982	1969 1982	1982
OECD	1970 1978 1983	1970 1984	1983
Technological leaders	1961 1970 1982	1964 1974	1974
Asia	1965 1970 1983	1970 1983	1970
South America	1961 1969 1981	1965 1981	1980

[a] Within each colunm, the break pattern suggested is the one that maximises the Chow F-statistic for the given number of breaks. In the calculation of the statistic, the minimum period length is restricted to 3 years. All breaks observed are statistically highly significant. Breaks are denoted by the first year of the "new" period.

In order to test for the presence of structural breaks in the convergence patterns in figure 5, linear trends were estimated for different periods in time, and Chow F-statistics were calculated to test for the significance of these breaks. Table 1 gives the optimal break configuration for each of the series.

Obviously, the breaks that occur in the beginning of the 1970s or 1960s are related to different values of the intercept of the curves, leaving the sign of the slope more or less unaffected (Asia is the exception) and making them less interesting for the analysis here. The breaks occurring in the mid-1970s (technological leaders) and beginning of the 1980s (others except Asia), however, correspond to trend-reversals.

The structural breaks in some of the series for the convergence coefficients suggest that the relation between innovation, imitation and catching up has changed over the last three decades. In order to investigate this phenomenon further, we will now turn to innovation indicators. Our basic hypothesis is that both R&D and patent statistics show different aspects of the same process of industrial innovation and its diffusion through the economic system. As such, patents involve novelty (by definition), so that they measure the earlier stages of a process leading from novelty/invention, through development, testing and engineering, to full-scale innovation. R&D is an input into the technological process. As such, it is not only related to innovation (invention), but also to imitation (Cohen and Levinthal, 1989). Thus, R&D is not only related to innovation, but also to its diffusion. The strong positive trend in Korean R&D intensity seems to be illustrative for the latter phenomenon.[19] However, one would ideally like to have another indicator measuring the impact of innovation diffusion more adequately. Since such an indicator is not available, however, we will concentrate on R&D and patents, keeping in mind some of the disadvantages mentioned.

Figure 6 shows the trends in C for R&D intensity. The frontier R&D intensity used is an envelope of Swiss, German and USA values for different years. Since no time series for R&D were available for Asian and South American NICs (except Korea[20]), the figure is restricted to the OECD countries and Korea.

In general, R&D intensity has risen over the 1970s and 1980s (for more details see Soete and Verspagen, 1991), although at different rates in different countries. Total R&D intensity, especially in the USA has been strongly influenced by military research, which is itself highly dependent on government support. The decline of military spending was one of the main factors behind the exceptional (i.e., downward) trend in R&D intensity of the

---

[19] The increase in Korean R&D intensity is impressive. It has risen from 0.5 per cent in 1980 to almost 2 per cent in 1988. Despite this drastic increase, the influence on aggregate convergence/divergence patterns is small, as indicated by the similarity of the lines in the figure for the OECD and OECD plus Korea.

[20] Korea refers to South Korea throughout.

US over the late 1960s and 1970s, which caused Switzerland (and shortly Germany) to be the R&D intensity leaders.

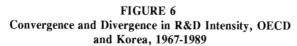

FIGURE 6
Convergence and Divergence in R&D Intensity, OECD
and Korea, 1967-1989

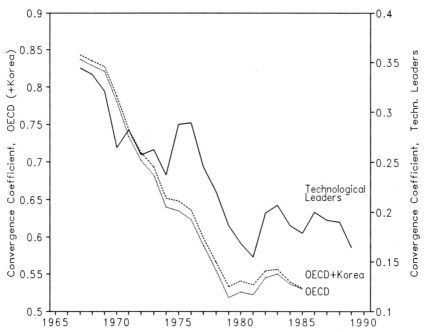

The lines all show that convergence is an adequate description of the movement of R&D intensities until around 1980. After that, the trend flattens, although the most recent data again indicate a weak convergence trend. This pattern seems to fit closely the convergence pattern of growth of the OECD and the technologically leading countries identified in figure 5. Whether it was the R&D convergence that caused the income convergence, or the convergence of per capita income levels that led to the convergence in R&D spending is an issue which we do not attempt to answer here.[21]

Finally, we turn to patents as a second innovation indicator. Patent data are available for all countries used in the sample of Figure 5, so that they give a more complete overview than R&D data. Moreover, patents measure a

---

[21]   There exists a voluminous econometric literature which has attempted to shed some light on this causality. For one such attempt see Patel and Soete (1987, 1988).

different aspect of innovation, as they are clearly related to invention, and are a barrier against imitation. Therefore, they are assumed to measure a different aspect of the relation between innovation, imitation and catching up.[22]

Since national patents cannot be used in an international context due to differences in novelty requirements, we use aggregate USA patents, dated by year of granting. However, the use of patents issued by one national patent office has the drawback that trends in patenting might reflect trends in internationalisation rather than innovative capabilities, and that domestic inventors have a home market advantage.[23]

Trends in E over time are given in Figure 7. Concentrating first on the country groups for which R&D data are available, it seems like the halt of

FIGURE 7
Convergence and Divergence in International Patenting,
Catching Up Countries, 1963-1989

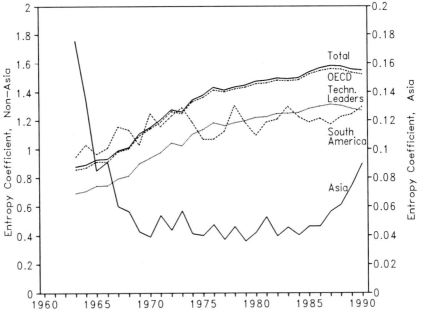

---

[22] In the empirical application of the model in Verspagen (1991), which was discussed briefly above, patents are used as an indicator of the increase of a knowledge gap, as opposed to technological spill-overs (imitation) which reduce the gap.

[23] For a more detailed discussion on the usefulness of patents as indicators of innovation, see Dosi, Pavitt and Soete (1990).

convergence of R&D intensity around 1980 has not left any significant traces in the series for patents. Patenting activity seems to be converging until the late 1980s, when a weak trend towards concentration of patenting seems to set in. The decline of the slope that seems to occur in the OECD and techno-logically leading group of countries in the mid-1970s cannot be attributed to the R&D trends, especially in light of the average lag of around 2 years between patent applications and grants. With regard to the countries that were not present in the previous figure, the trends observed are quite different from each other. In South America convergence seems to obtain until the mid-1970s, and after that the trend is flat. The heavy fluctuations in the line for this continent are caused by the small numbers, which means that small absolute deviations cause large percentual deviations. For Asian countries, the rise of Japan as a technological leader (and indeed later the largest patenting country after the USA), caused a diverging trend in the 1960s. Entropy reached an absolute minimum (close to zero) around 1970, and remained on that level until the late 1980s. After that, increased patenting in the Asian NICs led to convergence.

TABLE 2
Structural Breaks in Technology Indicators Convergence Patterns[a]

Country group	3 breaks assumed			2 breaks assumed		1 break assumed
A. R&D intensity						
OECD	1969	1974	1980	1971	1980	1980
Technological leaders	1975	1982	1987	1975	1982	1979
OECD + Korea	1965	1970	1983	1970	1983	1970
B. Patenting						
Total	1969	1977	1988	1969	1977	1977
OECD	1969	1977	1988	1969	1977	1977
Technological leaders	1969	1977	1988	1977	1988	1977
Asia	1966	1968	1987	1968	1987	1968
South America	1974	1978	1981	1975	1980	1975

[a] Within each column, the break pattern suggested is the one that maximises the Chow F-statistic for the given amount of breaks. In the calculation of the statistic, the minimum period length is restricted to 3 years. All breaks observed are statistically highly significant. Breaks are denoted by the first year of the "new" period.

Table 2 suggests that, contrary to the suggested relation between the breaks in per capita income growth and R&D intensity, patenting seems to be more loosely connected to income convergence. The case of Asian NICs (and Japan) is perhaps the best one to illustrate the dynamics of imitation, innovation and growth. The Asian NICs have been able to switch from a situation of falling behind to one of catching up during the 1970s (see figure 5). The evidence with regard to patenting indicates that the exploitation of the catching up potential in this case was mainly related to imitation, rather than to expansion of original research and inventions. However, as the dramatic upsurge since 1986 in figure 7 in the patent entropy measure (E) for the Asian NICs illustrates, the Asian NICs have started a rapid and increasing effort in technological investments aimed at moving the technological frontier itself, rather than just imitation.

5. Conclusions

In this paper, we hope to have illustrated that, using a number of different conceptual tools on available macro-economic and technological data, the general patterns of economic growth and technological development, which a large number of countries (114) have displayed over the postwar period, point to a wide variety of development and growth paths. This variety holds between the major different categories of countries we considered (technologically leading countries, OECD countries, Asian and South American NICs, LDCs) as well as over time.

With respect to the latter, it is worth emphasising, that while our analysis was not long-term in focus as in the Maddison tradition, and was limited primarily to the postwar period, this shorter time period, nevertheless contained many interesting features from a longer term growth and technology perspective. First of all, the period covering the 1950s, 1960s and beginning of the 1970s appears clearly as a historically unique period of convergence in growth and technological catching-up in the present DMEs and Asian NICs. Second, over the last decade since the mid-1970s this convergence pattern has clearly come to an end in the OECD countries. Both measures calculated point to an end of this major feature of postwar growth: the convergence of income levels and R&D-spending.

By contrast, in the regional area of Asia (Japan and the Asian NICs), the convergence pattern in growth is of a more recent origin (beginning of the 1970s) and seems to continue. From a technological perspective using patent data, a technological innovation catching-up process seems only to have started over the last decade in those countries. This clearly is not the case with respect to the South American NICs, where both convergence in terms of GDP per capita or technological innovation did not really take off.

In our view the variety in paths of growth and development, convergence and divergence, also illustrates the limited usefulness of theoretical analyses in this area which focus on concepts such as balanced or equilibrium growth. Such notions seem so far removed from the complexity of the real world that one may well wonder whether progress in the theoretical equilibrium modelling of growth could ever mean progress in economists' capacity to explain growth.

References

Abramovitz, M.A. (1979), "Rapid Growth Potential and its Realisation: The Experience of Capitalist Economies in the Postwar Period", in: E. Malinvaud (ed.), *Economic Growth and Resources, Vol. 1 The Major Issues*, Proceedings of the Fifth World Congres of the International Economic Association, Macmillan, London, pp. 1-51.

--- (1986), "Catching Up, Forging Ahead and Falling Behind", *Journal of Economic History*, Vol. 46, pp. 385-406.

Aghion, P. and P. Howitt (1990), *A Model of Growth through Creative Destruction*, NBER Working Paper, No. 3223.

Ames, E. and N. Rosenberg (1963), "Changing Technological Leadership and Industrial Growth", *Economic Journal*, Vol. 73, pp. 214-36.

Arrow, K. (1962), "Economic Welfare and Allocation of Resources for Invention", in: R. Nelson (ed.), *The Rate and Direction of Inventive Activity*, NBER, Princeton University Press, Princeton.

Baumol, W.J. (1986), "Productivity Growth, Convergence, and Welfare: What the Long Run Data Show", *American Economic Review*, Vol. 76, pp. 1072-1085.

--- et al. (1989), *Productivity and American Leadership. The Long View*, MIT Press, Cambridge Mass..

Cohen, W.M. and D.A. Levinthal (1989), "Innovation and Learning: The Two Faces of R&D", *Economic Journal*, Vol. 99, pp. 569-596.

Cornwall, J. (1976), *Modern Capitalism: Its Growth and Transformation*, Martin Robertson, London.

Dosi, G. (1982), "Technological Paradigms and Technological Trajectories: a Suggested Interpretation of the Determinants and Directions of Technical Change", *Research Policy*, Vol. 11, pp. 147-162.

---, K. Pavitt and L. Soete (1990), *The Economics of Technical Change and International Trade*, Harvester Wheatsheaf.

Dowrick, S. and D.T. Nguyen (1989), "OECD Comparative Economic Growth 1950-85: Catch-Up and Convergence", *American Economic Review*, Vol. 79, No. 5, pp. 1010-1030.

Durlauf, S.N. and P.A. Johnson (1992), *Local versus Global Convergence across National Economies*, NBER Working Paper, No. 3996.

Freeman, C. (1963), "The Plastics Industry: a Comparative Study of Research and Innovation", *National Institute Economic Review*, No. 26.

--- (1965), "Research and Development in Electronic Capital Goods", *National Institute Economic Review*, Vol. 34.

---, J. Clark, and L. Soete (1982), *Unemployment and Technical Innovation*, Pinter Publishers, London.

Gomulka, S. (1971), *Inventive Activity, Diffusion and the Stages of Economic Growth*, Aarhus, Skrifter fra Aarhus Universtets Okonomiske Institut, No. 24, Institute of Economics.

--- (1991), *The Theory of Technological Change and Economic Growth*, Routledge, London/New York.

Grossman, G. and E. Helpman (1991), *Innovation and Growth. Technological Competition in the Global Economy*, MIT Press, Cambridge Mass..

Habakkuk, H. (1962), *American and British Technology in the Nineteenth Century*, Cambridge University Press, Cambridge.

Hobsbawn, E.J. (1967), "Custom, Wages and Work-Load in Nineteenth Century Industry", *Labouring Men*, Doubleday, New York.

Kamien, M. and Schwartz, N. (1982), *Market Structure and Innovation*, Cambridge University Press, Cambridge.

Kleinknecht, A. and B. Verspagen (1989), "R&D and Market Structure: The Impact of Measurement and Aggregation Problems", *Small Business Economics*, Vol. 1, pp. 297-301.

Kuznets, S. (1930), *Secular Movements in Production and Prices*, Houghton Mifflin, Boston.

Landes, D. (1969), *The Unbound Prometheus*, Cambridge University Press, Cambridge.

Lucas, R. (1988), "On the Mechanics of Economic Development", *Journal of Monetary Economics*, Vol. 22, pp. 3-42.

Maddison, A. (1982), *Phases of Capitalist Development*, Oxford University Press, Oxford/New York.

--- (1989), *The World Economy in the 20th Century*, OECD Development Center, Paris.

--- (1991), *Dynamic Forces in Capitalist Development. A Long-Run Comparative View*, Oxford University Press, Oxford/New York.

Metcalfe, J.S. (1981), "Impulse and Diffusion in the Study of Technological Change", *Futures*, Vol. 12.

Patel, P. and L. Soete (1987), "Technological Trends and Employment in the UK Manufacturing Sectors", in: C. Freeman and L. Soete (eds.), *Technical Change and Full Employment*, Basil Blackwell, Oxford.

--- and L. Soete (1988), "The Contribution of Science and Technology to Economic Growth: A Critical Reappraisal of the Evidence", *STI Review*, December, No. 4, pp. 121-166.

Perez, C. and L. Soete (1988), "Catching up in Technology: Entry Barriers and Windows of Opportunity", in: G. Dosi et al. (eds.), *Technical Change and Economic Theory*, Frances Pinter, London.

Posner, M. (1961), "International Trade and Technical Change", *Oxford Economic Papers*, Vol. 13.

Romer, P. (1986), "Increasing Returns and Long Run Growth", *Journal of Political Economy*, Vol. 94 , October, pp. 1002-1037.

--- (1989), "What Determines the Rate of Growth of Technological Change?", World Bank Working Paper WPS 279, Washington D.C..

--- (1990), "Endogenous Technological Change", *Journal of Political Economy*, Vol. 98, pp. S72-S102.

Rosenberg, N. (1970), "Comments" in: R. Vernon (ed.), *The Technology Factor in International Trade*, NBER/Columbia University Press, New York.

--- (1976), *Perspectives on Technology*, Cambridge University Press.

Scherer, F.M. and D. Ross (1990), *Industrial Market Structure and Economic Performance*, Third Edition, Boston, Houghton Mifflin Company.

Schumpeter, J.A. (1934), *The Theory of Economic Development*, Harvard University Press.

Scoville, W. (1951), "Minority Migration and the Diffusion of Technology", *Journal of Economic History*, Vol. II, pp. 347-360.

Soete, L. (1991), *Technology in a Changing World*, OECD, Paris.

Soete, L. and B. Verspagen (1991), "Recent Comparative Trends in Technology Indicators in the OECD Area", in: OECD, *Technology and Productivity. The Challenge for Economic Policy*, Paris, pp. 249-274.

Solow, R.M. (1970), *Growth Theory: An Exposition*, Oxford University Press, Oxford.

Summers, R. and Heston, A. (1991), "The Penn World Table (Mark 5): An Expanded Set of International Comparisons, 1950-1988", *Quarterly Journal of Economics*, Vol. CVI, No. 2, pp. 327-368.

Verspagen, B. (1991), "A New Empirical Approach to Catching up or Falling behind", *Structural Change and Economic Dynamics*, Vol. 2, No. 2, pp. 359-380.

--- (1992), "Endogenous Innovation in Neo-Classical Growth Models. A Survey", *Journal of Macroeconomics*, Vol. 14, No. 4, forthcoming.

Von Tunzelmann, N. (1978), *Steam Power and British Industrialisation to 1860*, Clarendon Press, Oxford.

Yakushiji, T. (1986), "Technological Emulation and Industrial Development", paper presented at the Conference on Innovation Diffusion, Venice, 17-21 March.

Explaining Economic Growth
A. Szirmai, B. van Ark and D. Pilat
© 1993 Elsevier Science Publishers B.V. All rights reserved.

How Much Does Capital Explain?

John W. Kendrick
The George Washington University

If capital is defined as income and/or output producing capacity, it is obvious that the growth of capital must be an important part of the explanation of economic growth - the more so the more inclusive the definition of capital. Even accepting the conventional definition of capital as material and nonhuman, capital compensation accounts for upwards of one-third of gross factor cost in the United States and most other OECD countries in recent decades.

Using capital share weights, the contribution of material nonhuman capital to economic growth in the United States and in 17 other OECD countries is calculated and discussed in the second section of this paper. Using a comprehensive concept and measure of capital and correspondingly adjusted real gross product estimates, the total capital contribution to economic growth is recomputed for the United States based on earlier work of the author (Kendrick, 1976) and discussed in the concluding section of the paper.

The scope and content of the concepts and measures of output (real product), capital, and the capital weights, all affect the estimates of capital's contribution to economic growth. Accordingly, the following first section of the paper discusses alternative concepts and measures with special reference to those that were selected as a basis for the subsequent analysis.

Concepts and Measures of Output and Capital

Real Gross Product

It is usual to measure the rate of "economic growth" in terms of real gross **domestic** product (GDP). For purposes of production and productivity analysis, it is easier to match outputs and inputs in the domestic economies than when net factor income from abroad is added to GDP to obtain GNP. **Gross** domestic income and product estimates accord symmetrical treatment of labor and capital in that capital consumption allowances are not deducted from the compensation of either factor input - though from a welfare standpoint net income is preferable. **Market price** weights for real outputs are preferable for welfare analysis, but GDP at factor cost is theoretically preferable for production and productivity analysis. From a practical viewpoint, however, it is difficult to adjust prices and price deflators for indirect business taxes less subsidies. Experiments in the United States and Canada for selected years indicate that the movements of real gross product in constant unit factor costs do not differ much from movements of real product at constant market prices anyway.

A major problem in using real GDP for growth analysis is that for the nonbusiness sectors of general governments, households and private nonprofit institutions, gross product is estimated in terms of labor compensation in current values and labor input (hours worked or number of workers) weighted by base-period average compensation for the real input estimates. No account is taken of capital compensation and input. Only in the business sector is product measured predominantly in terms of outputs independent of factor input proxies, and with the associated factor costs including not only labor compensation but also capital compensation as determined in markets. For this reason, productivity measures are frequently confined to the private domestic business economy.

Even in the business sector, factor price deflators (mainly wage rates) are sometimes used, especially in the finance and services industry groups because of difficulties in defining output units and therefore in measuring physical units or pricing them to get deflators for current values. So, in effect, the resulting deflated values are really input measures. In the case of rental real estate, the real values generally are estimated to parallel the movements of the real capital stocks involved, also without allowance for productivity changes.

From the viewpoint of accuracy in estimating real product and productivity, it could be argued that the outputs which are moved by inputs should be omitted from the real product and input measures. Some analysts have removed rental real estate from business product when estimating productivity. One point in favor of the old Ricardian "material product" concept was greater ease and accuracy in measurement. But outputs in the bulk of the service sectors can be measured as well as units of tangible commodities. With the secular increase in the share of services in GDP, more would be lost in omitting them than would be gained from greater accuracy in real product and capital share estimates. Besides, there are problems in measuring outputs of both commodities and services, such as quality changes and outputs of custom-made products, so that accuracy cannot be a *sine qua non* in economic accounts.

For the United States, I use the official estimates by the Bureau of Economic Analysis (BEA) of real GDP originating in the private business economy, as adjusted by the Bureau of Labor Statistics (BLS) for its estimates of multi-factor productivity (1982, 1991). Estimates for the 18 OECD countries shown subsequently are those assembled by the Economics and Statistics Department of the OECD for use in its estimates of total-and-partial-productivity ratios in the business sector (December 1991).

The analyst can try to measure capital's contribution more comprehensively and add imputed capital rentals to income in the nonbusiness sectors to match an expansion of capital estimates to include that owned by households, institutions, and governments as well as by business. Actually, in the final section of this paper I go farther and estimate the contribution of **total** capital, nonhuman and human, used in all sectors to produce both money and imputed income whose scope is consistent with that of the capital estimates discussed in the next section. The expanded estimates of national product and wealth (capital) are fully described in my book *The Formation and Stocks of Total Capital* (1976).

At least half a dozen expanded systems of national income and wealth accounts, including mine, are summarized in Robert Eisner's *Total Incomes Systems of Accounts* (1989). All the systems expand the accounts by adding imputations for many non-market activities beyond the modest number included in the United Nation's *Standard System of National Accounts* (SNA) which are confined largely to those with significant market counterparts. The current revision of the SNA, however, adds flexibility by making provision for "satellite accounts" that can supplement the core accounts.

Some national income accountants such as Nordhaus and Tobin even include imputations for the value (opportunity cost) of leisure time. In my own work extending the accounts, I have drawn the line by confining imputations to economic activities. It could be argued, however, that if so-called consumer durable goods, which deliver direct consumption services in addition to helping with economic activities of households, are included in capital then it would be logical also to include the value of time spent in enjoying the capital services in national income and product.

The imputed rentals on the non-business capital goods are obtained as the sum of depreciation and the implicit interest on the net stocks at current replacement costs. In constant prices, the real rentals are moved by the real capital estimates. This means there is no allowance for changes in the capital/output ratios, which probably imparts some downward bias to the real product numbers, but not as much as the use of labor input without allowance for increases in labor productivity, since the capital/labor ratio has risen in virtually all sectors and industries in progressive economies.

Downward bias in real product estimates shows up in the productivity ratios, of course. Given the increases in labor and capital inputs, the contribution of capital growth as a percentage of real adjusted GDP growth is higher than it would be if downward biases could be eliminated; the contribution of productivity growth is lower.

Real Capital Stocks and Services

As C.J. Bliss put it, "When economists reach agreement on the theory of capital, they will shortly reach agreement on everything else" (1975, p. vii). All this section can do is to lay out the concepts of capital underlying the measures I use to assess the contribution of capital to production and growth. By the narrow definition, capital is viewed as produced commodities, namely structures, equipment and inventory stocks, required for production over future periods. It is the expected future income to which capital goods contribute, discounted to the present, that determines its value. Since this is also the basis for valuing land and other natural resources, land is usually included with the produced agents as part of tangible nonhuman capital. Financial assets are merely claims to wealth, not the real productive capital we are concerned with here.

By a broader definition, capital includes all agents, including humans, with capacity to produce income and/or product in future years. In the final section we look at the contribution of total capital, nonhuman and human, to the expanded measures of income discussed above. We also include nonbusiness material capital. Although the services of household and government capital goods are not priced in markets, they are often the same as those purchased from firms, or provided by durable goods leased from firms by households, institutions, or governments, Inclusion of all the tangible durables and inventory stocks as capital, and their purchases as investment, is in accord with the principle that national income and wealth accounts should be invariant to institutional change including shifts in sectors of purchase or ownership. BEA (1987) now publishes estimates of U.S. fixed reproducible tangible wealth owned by all sectors, by major type. To these, I added land estimates from Kendrick (1976) updated through 1990 by the author.

The difficulty of measuring material capital in real terms is suggested by J.B. Clark's comparison of capital with a waterfall which remains basically the same though the constituent drops of water are continually changing; the stock of capital, when maintained, remains a source of productive power even though it is embodied in a succession of physical instruments. Pigou viewed capital similarly as a material entity comprising heterogenous capital goods "capable of maintaining its quantity while altering its form" (1935, p. 239).

In preparing constant-price-weighted quantity aggregates of various types of capital goods, BEA follows, in effect, the method described by Edward Denison (1957, pp. 215 ff.) as estimating "the amount it would have cost in the base period to produce the **actual** stock of capital goods existing in the given year. For durable capital goods not produced in the base year, one must substitute the amount it would have cost to produce them if they had been known and actually produced."

The Denison approach is consistent with the way BLS adjusts its price indexes for changes in models or "qualities" of the goods. These indexes are used by BEA as deflators for equipment outlays as part of the procedure for estimating real stocks by the perpetual inventory method. The ratio of the cost of a new model to that of the old, as estimated by producers, indicates the percentage of quality improvement; the extent to which price increases more than unit cost counts as a pure price change. If producer cost data are not available and the change in quality is judged to be significant, the entire price change is counted as a quality change. If the prices of both old and new qualities are available for an overlap period, the difference is ascribed to quality. The latter case is analogous to hedonic price adjustments, whereby various characteristics of goods are priced, usually by multiple regression techniques, in order to construct price indexes that take account of changing characteristics of goods over time. BEA uses hedonic methods to prepare price deflators for computers, and for residential structures. Allan Young of BEA (1989, pp. 108-15), considers the use of hedonic adjustments be consistent with the Denison approach described above, but Denison does not.

Note that the BEA capital stock estimates only partially reflect quality improvement. To the extent that the improvements in capital goods are costless, technological advances show up in the productivity residual. Since personal and collective consumption goods and services are generally not adjusted for quality improvements, such technological advances do not show up in the real product and productivity estimates. Shifts in composition of purchases among qualities of a product carrying different price tags do affect the deflated values. Prices of completely new products are carried back to the base period by indexes of the prices of similar products.

Apart from conceptual problems, there are a number of sources of possible inaccuracy in capital estimates obtained by the perpetual inventory method used by BEA and OECD which underlie our analysis. Chief among these are the assumed average economic lives of durables, the mortality patterns used to estimate discards, and the depreciation curves applied to arrive at net stocks. The estimates are particularly sensitive to errors or changes in economic lives. The capital stock estimates must therefore be regarded as approximations to what would be obtained by complete inventories. Even the latter have problems of valuation of aging assets for which there are no organized markets.

Because of the conceptual and statistical problems in estimating weighted quantity aggregates of capital goods, indirect methods have been advocated by some economists, notably Joan Robinson (1956). Robinson would use embodied labor-time; others favor capacity measures, or consumption foregone. As I argued over 30 years ago (Kendrick, 1961), the alternative measures encounter problems and ambiguities as great as those met in estimating real capital *per se*. And since the alternative aggregates are not capital goods, their movements differ from those of the preferred concept given technological progress (1961, p. 110): "The physical capital stock rises more rapidly than the volume of labor or total inputs required to reproduce it at current technology; the physical stock rises less rapidly than its average output capacity or its capacity to contribute to real value-added; and physical stock rises either more or less rapidly than its real value in terms of consumption goods and services depending on relative productivity changes in the two sectors".

For analysis of production and **growth**, real gross capital stocks are the appropriate measure. If adequately maintained, capital goods retain their output-producing capacity over their lifetimes with little diminution. Net capital stocks reflect the depreciation of net income producing capacity of fixed assets as they age. The depreciation of individual capital goods is much greater than any decline in output-producing capacity. Goldsmith and Denison have suggested averaging real gross and net stocks, but in my opinion that still gives too sharp a decline in output capacity due to increased downtime for maintenance and repair, etc. It is better to use real gross stocks as a basis for analyzing the input and contribution of capital to output growth. Any significant change in the average age or age-structure of fixed capital can be taken into account as a supplemental variable.

Some analysts try to adjust fixed capital for changes in rates of utilization of capacity before relating to output. That is not necessary if growth is measured between two periods with comparable utilization rates. Otherwise, the real capital stocks should be adjusted, or rates of utilization used as a separate variable to help explain changes in the productivity of capital or its contribution to changes in output.

It is important to distinguish between capital stocks and services, as stressed by Usher (1980). The latter, or factor inputs, are the appropriate measure for determining the productivity, or contribution of the factors (capital) to production and its growth. The services of the productive factors may be viewed as the time rate of use of the factors times the base period compensation of each per unit of time reflecting the value of the marginal product of the factor in that period.

Thus, labor input is usually measured as worker-hours weighted by base-period average hourly labor compensation. Capital input, if the real stocks are not adjusted for utilization rates, is obtained as the real gross stocks weighted by the base-period gross rate of return. If index numbers are used, the inputs are weighted by the base-period shares of human (labor) and nonhuman capital in gross factor cost (income and product).

The use of gross, rather than net property income (preferred by Denison), substantially increases the weight of capital in total factor input, resulting in higher rates of growth in input and less in total factor productivity since capital has grown faster than labor in all OECD countries since 1950. Further, depreciable capital has grown faster than nondepreciable capital. This is accentuated by the fact that real gross fixed capital stocks have grown faster than net stocks in recent times as depreciation has grown relative to the stocks.

If inputs are estimated and weighted by industry within the business economy, the weighted inputs tend to rise faster than inputs without internal weights. This reflects the fact that inputs tend to move towards the industries in which rates of remuneration are higher (e.g. from agriculture to nonagricultural pursuits). Jorgenson (1987) calls the effects of the relative inter-industry shifts "changes in quality." This does not seem appropriate in the case of nonhuman capital in the sense of technological improvements. It is more appropriate for human input to the extent that industry differences in rates of labor compensation reflect differences in levels of education, training, experience, aptitudes and other qualitative aspects of human capital.

We prefer to use factor share weights rather than coefficients (output elasticities) obtained by multiple regression analysis. Experiments referred to in an earlier work (Kendrick, 1976, p. 117) indicate that when using several independent variables, the coefficients appeared unreasonable and varied depending on specification of the function.

The Contribution of Material Capital Services to Growth

Using estimates of the real services of tangible nonhuman capital of the type described in the previous section, we are now ready to present some estimates of their percentage contributions to economic growth in the United States, and in up to 17 other OECD countries.

A Century of U.S. Economic Growth

The estimates of output, inputs, and productivity ratios contained in table 1 for the period 1948-1990 are published regularly by the Bureau of Labor Statistics (1982 and 1991). They are extended from 1948 back to 1890 by comparable estimates for the same components contained in this author's volumes on U.S. productivity trends for the National Bureau of Economic Research (1961 and 1976).

The contribution of the growth of real gross capital services to the growth of real gross product in the U.S. private domestic business economy over the century 1890-1990 averaged 33.4 per cent. This is calculated from the almost 3 per cent average annual rate of growth of real capital, weighted by its 37.1 per cent share in gross domestic income, divided by the 3.3 average rate of growth in real gross product. (See table 1A). The proportion contributed by the 1.1 per cent rate of increase in labor input (not shown in the table) was about 10 percentage points less. The 1.5 per cent rate of increase in the "total factor productivity" residual accounted for the remaining 44 per cent of the growth rate (as shown in table 1B), exclusive of a small interaction term.

Note that BLS measures labor input in terms of hours worked, without internal weights on an industry, occupational or other basis. This seems inconsistent with the capital input estimates which are weighted by industry. An advantage of labor hour input is that the input does not vary depending on the degree of detail in which weighting is carried out. The 33-industry detail in which I weighted labor hours in the NBER productivity studies resulted in labor input rising by an average of about 0.3 per cent a year more than straight hours. Weighting in much more detail for the period 1948-79, Jorgenson (1987) got considerably higher rates of increase in "labor quality". Denison (1974) also adjusted labor input for quality, consisting primarily of rising educational levels, although capital input was not so adjusted except to the extent that higher quality capital goods were given higher base-period unit cost weights.

John W. Kendrick

TABLE 1
The Role of Capital in Growth of Real Product and Productivity
U.S. Private Domestic Business Economy, 1890-1990 by Subperiod

Part A Capital and Growth of Real Product

Period	Real Gross Product	Inputs		Weight of Capital (ratios)	Weighted Capital	
		Labor	Capital		Rate of growth (%)	Contribution to economic growth (%)
	(average annual rate of growth)					
1890-1915	3.44	1.85	3.48	0.416	1.45	42.1
1915-1929	4.18	1.26	2.25	0.405	0.91	21.8
1929-1948	2.40	0.41	1.05	0.380	0.40	16.6
1948-1973	3.66	0.60	3.91	0.321	1.26	34.4
1973-1981	2.01	1.26	4.03	0.304	1.23	60.9
1981-1990	3.15	1.85	3.00	0.306	0.92	29.1
1890-1990	3.26	1.13	2.95	0.371	1.08	33.1
1948-1990	3.24	0.99	3.74	0.320	1.20	37.0

Part B: Capital and Productivity Growth

Period	Labor Productivity (% rate of growth)	Capital/Labor Substitution		TFP Residual	
		Rate of growth (%)	Contribution to labor productivity growth (%)	% rate of growth	Contribution to economic growth (%)
1890-1915	1.55	0.67	33.2	0.88	25.6
1915-1929	2.88	0.40	13.9	2.48	59.3
1929-1948	1.99	0.67	33.8	1.32	55.0
1948-1973	3.04	1.06	34.7	1.98	54.1
1973-1981	0.75	0.83	111.0	-0.06	
1981-1990	1.28	0.35	27.0	0.93	29.5
1890-1990	2.10	0.66	31.4	1.44	44.2
1948-1990	2.22	0.89	40.1	1.36	43.0

Sources: 1948-1990: U.S. Bureau of Labor Statistics; 1890-1948: John W. Kendrick (1961), *Productivity Trends in the United States*.

In any case, I extrapolated the BLS estimates back by labor hours, and the total factor productivity (TFP) numbers are affected accordingly. That is, the TFP growth rates average about 0.2 percentage points more than those published using internally-weighted labor input estimates.

Looking just at the post-war period 1948-1990, the growth of real capital was higher than in the earlier epoch, averaging 3.7 per cent a year. The output growth rates of about 3.2 per cent were almost exactly the same in both epochs. Despite a lower weight, the capital contribution of 37.0 per cent was more than 4 percentage points higher than the average for the century. The labor contribution was still a bit over one-fifth. The productivity residual fell a little but still contributed about 42 per cent to economic growth.

The rate of increase in so-called "labor productivity" actually increased in the 1948-1990 period compared with the average for the century, as shown in table 1B. The reconciliation item between the rates of change in TFP and labor productivity is the rate of substitution of capital for labor, calculated as the growth rate of the capital/labor ratio weighted by the capital share in gross factor income. The growth of real capital relative to labor input 1948-1990 contributed about 40 per cent to the growth of labor productivity compared with 31 per cent for the century as a whole.

The relative importance of the non-human and human inputs and of the TFP residual varied over the sub-periods. Growth of both factor inputs was strong prior to World War I, but it was only after 1914 that TFP growth accelerated significantly. Indeed, the residual contributed more than half the growth rate from 1914 through 1973. The marked slowing in the capital growth rate between 1929 and 1948 was due to the great depression and World War II. But at around 4 per cent a year from 1948 through 1980, it exceeded the pre-1915 rate. The bulge in the calculated contribution of capital in the 1973-1981 period of slowdown in growth of output, and disappearance of TFP gains reflects the lag in adjustment of capital outlays to the significant deceleration of production. Since 1981, the contribution of capital to growth is almost back to its historic norms, but is has been tempered by the Tax Reform Act of 1986, that repealed most of the special investment incentives that had been enacted in the Economic Recovery Tax Act of 1981.

It is instructive to analyze the difference between my estimates of the capital contribution with those of Denison (1974) for the 1929-69 period. Since Denison's estimates relate to the nonresidential business economy, deducting the services of residential structures from both output and capital reduces the capital share. His real national income estimates show a bit more growth than my real gross product numbers, and his real capital input shows a bit less growth, particularly in the 1929-1948 sub-period when net stocks grew less rapidly than gross. But the chief reason for his much lower estimates of the contribution of capital was his use of capital compensation weights net of depreciation. On balance, his 3.73 per cent capital contribution (his table 8-2) was only about one-fourth of my 17 per cent. His 15.6 per cent for 1948-69 is closer to half the contribution calculated by my approach.

In a narrow sense, relevant to welfare analysis, capital consumption is not desired for its own sake, as Denison argues. But in a broader sense it is part of the process of "creative destruction" in a dynamic economy whereby old and increasingly inferior fixed capital goods, technologically speaking, are gradually replaced by new and improved ones. Moreover, the gross capital compensation weights are symmetrical with the labor compensation weights, the depreciation allowance part of which is largely invested in new and more productive human capital. Even if depreciation were deducted from both labor and nonhuman capital compensation, while the relative weight of capital might drop somewhat, it would still be significantly higher than it is under the asymmetrical treatment.

The Contribution of Capital in Other OECD Countries

Some historical background on the contributions of capital and other sources of growth is provided by Angus Maddison for six countries for the period 1913-1984, by sub-period, in his classic article "Growth and Slowdown in Advanced Capitalist Economies: Techniques of Quantitative Assessment" (1987). Dividing his estimates of the average annual percentage point contributions of the quantities of capital, including residential, by the growth rates of real GDP yield the following results:

	1913-50	1950-73	1973-84
		(percentages)	
France	29.2	21.4	55.0
Germany	20.0	27.5	61.3
Japan	34.8	26.6	57.4
Netherlands	26.7	24.9	64.6
U.K.	26.4	32.8	72.6
U.S.A	19.4	27.4	36.6

Although the United States showed the lowest percentage contribution in the early sub-period, this was due chiefly to is higher rate of growth of output reflecting the marked acceleration of productivity. But with the acceleration of growth in productivity and real product in the other countries 1950-73 (with the temporary exception of the U.K.), capital contribution was generally lower there than in the U.S.. Although all the countries reduced capital accumulation after 1973, it was cut back less than the slowdown in output growth. Thus, there was a relative increase in the capital contribution as measured without allowance for lower rates of utilization of capital stocks.

In 1967, Denison published his important work, *Why Growth Rates Differ*, applying his growth accounting techniques to eight other Western countries for the period 1950-62, and later to Japan (1976, with W.K. Chung). Subsequently, I extended his analysis through 1979 using my own version of growth accounting

(Kendrick, 1981). The average contribution of capital growth to growth of real gross business product in eight other countries 1960-73 was 35.8 per cent, compared with 37.9 in the United States. In the 1973-79 sub-period of slowdown in growth, the capital contribution rose to 54 per cent in the six countries in which output growth rates did not fall below capital growth rates. The U.S. capital contribution percentage rose less than it did abroad - and the United States was one of the few countries to show a marked pickup in growth of real product and productivity after 1981.

Recently an important body of estimates of outputs and inputs, including capital, for the business economies of 18 OECD countries for the years since 1960 has become available. They are unpublished, but underlie the total - and partial - productivity rates of change published in the *OECD Economic Outlook*, most recently in the December 1991 issue.

TABLE 2
The Role of Capital in Growth of Real Product and Productivity
18 OECD Countries, 1960-1990

Part A Capital and Growth of Real Gross Product

Country	Real Gross Product	Inputs		Weight of Capital (ratios)	Weighted Capital	
		Labor	Capital		Rate of growth (%)	Contribution to economic growth (%)
	(average annual rate of growth)					
United States	3.15	1.95	3.49	0.32	1.12	35.5
Japan	6.39	1.15	8.86	0.23	2.04	31.9
Germany	3.12	-0.01	4.26	0.31	1.32	42.3
France	3.85	0.06	3.86	0.31	1.20	31.1
Italy	4.25	0.08	4.11	0.27	1.11	26.1
United Kingdom	2.67	0.04	3.11	0.31	0.96	36.1
Canada	3.92	2.13	4.71	0.35	1.65	42.0
Austria	3.41	-0.35	5.63	0.30	1.69	49.6
Belgium	2.85	-0.40	3.49	0.30	1.05	40.7
Denmark	3.01	-0.16	4.17	0.29	1.21	40.2
Finland	3.65	-0.37	3.93	0.33	1.30	35.6
Greece	4.81	0.06	6.93	0.30	2.08	43.2
Netherlands	2.53	0.02	3.18	0.33	1.05	41.4
Spain	3.92	-0.24	7.00	0.26	1.82	46.5
Sweden	2.41	-0.13	3.63	0.29	1.05	43.8
Switzerland	2.70	0.74	4.59	0.26	1.19	44.3
Australia	3.19	1.58	4.16	0.34	1.42	44.4
New Zealand	2.93	1.38	3.79	0.32	1.21	41.3
Average	3.47	0.42	4.61	0.30	1.38	39.8

140   *John W. Kendrick*

(TABLE 2, continued)

Part B Capital and Productivity Growth

Country	Labor Productivity (% rate of growth)	Capital/Labor Substitution		TFP Residual	
		Rate of growth (%)	Contribution to labor productivity growth (%)	% rate of growth	Contribution to economic growth (%)
United States	1.17	0.48	41.2	0.69	21.8
Japan	5.23	1.80	34.4	3.43	53.7
Germany	3.12	1.32	42.4	1.71	54.8
France	3.78	1.18	27.8	2.58	67.0
Italy	4.17	1.08	25.9	3.05	72.0
United Kingdom	2.63	0.95	36.1	1.68	62.8
Canada	1.76	0.89	50.3	0.88	22.5
Austria	3.80	1.79	47.1	2.02	59.2
Belgium	3.00	1.18	39.3	1.84	71.3
Denmark	3.17	1.26	39.7	1.93	64.1
Finland	4.04	1.43	35.3	2.52	70.7
Greece	4.75	2.06	43.4	2.68	55.7
Netherlands	2.50	1.05	42.0	1.40	55.3
Spain	4.16	1.89	45.4	2.31	58.2
Sweden	2.54	1.09	43.0	1.45	60.2
Switzerland	1.94	0.99	51.1	0.96	35.6
Australia	1.58	0.88	55.7	0.72	22.5
New Zealand	1.55	0.76	49.0	0.52	17.7
Average	3.05	1.23	40.3	1.80	51.9

Source: Based on estimates by OECD (1991). Calculations subject to rounding errors.

Table 2A shows for the 18 countries the rates of change between 1960 and 1990 of the same variables shown in table 1 above for the United States. To summarize briefly with reference to the simple averages for the 18 nations, economic growth averaged about 3½ per cent per annum over the 30-year period. Gains in TFP accounted for a bit over half of the growth. A 4.6 per cent average rate of increase in real capital contributed 39.8 per cent to the growth rate. Thus, labor contributed only about 10 per cent which is not surprising given the average employment growth of less than 0.65 per cent a year. In fact, employment declined in 7 countries as did the total for the 13 European countries.

Output per worker grew at an average annual rate of 3.05 per cent. The substitution of capital for labor averaged 1.23 per cent a year, accounting for about 40 per cent of the growth of labor productivity. The fact that mean labor productivity less mean capital/labor substitution does not exactly equal mean TFP (with allowance for rounding errors) reflects the fact that simple rather than weighted averages were used for the variables (see table 2B)

The table shows the considerable inter-country dispersion in the variables. Economic growth varied from average annual rates of 2.4 per cent in Sweden to 6.4 per cent in Japan. Growth rates of real capital vary from 3.1 per cent in the U.K. to the outlier of 8.9 per cent in Japan. Because of the positive correlation between rates of growth in real product and real capital, there is less variation in the contributions of capital to economic growth. The numbers vary from lows of 26 per cent in Italy and 31 per cent in France to almost 50 per cent in Austria.

The degree of positive correlation between rates of change in labor productivity and in the capital/labor ratio (or in the rate of factor substitution) is particularly significant, as shown in table 2B. As a consequence, there is less dispersion in the contributions of capital/labor substitution to labor productivity growth in the various countries - which range from 26 per cent in Italy to almost 56 per cent in Australia. Dispersion in rates of growth in the TFP residual ranges from less than one per cent a year in Oceania, Canada, and the United States to more than three per cent in Italy and Japan.

Although it is not the focus of this paper, I have documented elsewhere (Kendrick, 1990) that the degree of dispersion in **levels** of labor productivity in OECD countries has declined substantially since 1950. There is a close negative correlation between levels of real product per worker in 1950 and rates of growth in that variable for the several countries. The growth accounting results reported in that article indicate that the narrowing of the productivity gaps between the United States and the other OECD countries was the result mainly of two related factors: increases in capital per worker; and technology catch-up.

Total Capital and Economic Growth

If capital is defined as income-and-output producing capacity for current and future periods, then it follows that the growth of real potential income and product (or actual, if capital is adjusted for rates of utilization of capacity) should be largely, if not entirely, explained by the growth of the services of real total capital stocks. This idea had been expressed in the early 1960s by Theodore W. Schultz, Harry Johnson, the present writer and others (see Kendrick, 1976, Preface and Chapter 1). As Harry Johnson put it at a 1963 OECD conference (1964, p. 121): "The conception of economic growth as a process of accumulating capital in all the manifold forms that the broad Fisherian concept of capital allows is a potent simplification of the analytical problem of growth, and one that facilitates the discussion of growth policy...".

As data permitted, I began in the mid-1960s to prepare estimates of all the significant types of real investment and capital stocks. They consisted of the non-human tangibles, specified earlier, and intangible stocks of technological knowledge accumulated by investments in research and development (R&D); and human intangible stocks accumulated by workers as a result of investments in education, training, health, safety, and mobility, plus tangible human capital created through outlays required to rear children to working age. Beginning at 16, opportunity costs of further schooling were estimated and counted as part of educational investments. Estimates of domestic income/product were broadened for consistency with the expanded capital concept. As noted earlier, the rental value of non-business capital goods was estimated, and estimates were also added of the investments charged by private firms to current expense and the opportunity costs of individuals engaged in investments in self.

To come to the bottom line, the growth rates of real gross product and total capital are shown in the following table (drawn from Kendrick, 1976, table 5-1, p. 113).

	1929-69	1929-48	1948-69
	(average annual percentage rates)		
Real GNP, as adjusted	3.4	2.7	4.0
Real total capital	2.8	2.2	3.5
Tangible	2.4	1.8	3.1
Intangible	3.8	3.2	4.3
Residual	0.6	0.5	0.5

The table shows that total capital, explained about five-sixths of the economic growth rate 1929-69, and somewhat more in the sub-period 1948-69. This compares with less than half explained by the conventional tangible factor inputs. A major reason is the much more rapid growth of intangibles than of tangibles, which explains much of the growth of the usual TFP measures.

Studies of certain types of intangible investment, particularly R&D, indicate considerably higher rates of return than on tangible investments. If adequate data had been available to weight tangible and intangible capital, the weighted aggregate would probably have risen more than the unweighted, further reducing the residual.

It is not surprising that there is a residual, since a number of forces not directly related to investment and capital affect economic growth. Chief among these is economies of scale, which Denison estimates accounts for around one-tenth of the growth rate. Evidence adduced by Murray Foss (1984) suggests that there has been an upward trend in the rate of utilization of fixed capital in the United States due to increases in numbers of shifts worked. The efficiency of labor may have increased with declining average hours of work over the period studied. The effects of informal R&D, and learning-by-doing are not included in capital estimates, nor is computer software which has become important since 1969. Economic efficiency in allocation of resources may have increased due to increasing inter-product and international competition. On the other hand, the residual would be larger if outputs could be adequately adjusted for improvements in quality, and if output prices instead of input prices were used as deflators in more of the industries alluded to above. Note that the residual declined as a per cent of the output growth rate between the two subperiods.

It is not fair to compare the contribution of total capital with the earlier estimates of the contributions of nonhuman capital alone. Therefore, we have rearranged the estimates to show the human and nonhuman components of total capital. We are also able for this paper to weight the two by the labor and nonhuman capital compensation shares of factor income gross of capital consumption but net of maintenance expenses, as derived from table A-5 in Kendrick (1976, p. 163).

	1929-69	1929-48	1948-69
Human capital			
Real stocks, growth rate	3.18	1.65	3.67
Weight	.456	.421	.488
Weighted rate	1.45	1.12	1.79
Contribution to GNP growth (%)	42.6	41.5	44.8
Nonhuman capital			
Real stocks, growth rate	2.53	1.73	3.26
Weighted rate	1.38	1.00	1.67
Contribution to GNP growth (%)	40.6	37.0	41.8
Total capital services	2.83	2.12	3.46
Residual	.57	.58	.54
Share of GNP growth rate (%)	16.8	21.5	13.5

Weighting does not affect the movement of aggregate capital much, but it makes possible the estimation of the contributions of each type of capital to the growth rate of the expanded real GNP estimates. The contribution of nonhuman capital was 40.6 per cent over the period as a whole, and a bit more in the second subperiod. It is about 95 per cent of the proportionate contribution of human capital 1929-69, but somewhat less in the second subperiod.

In conclusion, it appears that the contribution of nonhuman capital to economic growth is not much higher by the total capital approach than it is by the conventional approaches surveyed earlier. The inclusion of real intangible capital mainly affects the movement of real human capital, increasing its contribution to growth and decreasing the residual by removing from the latter a chief cause of advancing productivity - improvements in the quality of human capital and labor input.

References

Bliss, C.J. (1975), *Capital Theory and the Distribution of Income*, North Holland Publishing Company.

Denison, E.F. (1957), "Theoretical Aspects of Quality Change Capital Consumption, and Net Capital Formation", *Problems in Capital Formation, Studies in Income and Wealth*, Vol. 19, Princeton University Press, Princeton.

--- (1974), *Accounting for United States Economic Growth 1929-1969*, The Brookings Institution, Washington.

--- (1967), *Why Growth Rates Differ: Postwar Experience in Nine Western Countries*, The Brookings Institution, Washington.

--- and William K. Chung (1976), *How Japan's Economy Grew so Fast*, The Brookings Institution, Washington.

Eisner, R. (1989), *The Total Incomes System of Accounts*, University of Chicago Press.

Foss, M.F. (1984), *Changing Utilization of Fixed Capital: An Element in Long-Term Growth*, American Enterprise Institute, Washington.

Johnson, H.G. (1964), "Comments", in: OEDC, *The Residual Factor and Economic Growth*, Paris, p. 221.

Jorgenson, D.W., F.M. Gollop and B. Fraumeni (1987), *Productivity and U.S. Economic Growth*, Harvard University Press, Cambridge MA.

Kendrick, J.W. (1961), "Some Theoretical Aspects of Capital Measurement", *The American Economic Review*, Vol. 61, no. 2, May, pp. 102-111.

--- (1976), *The Formation and Stocks of Total Capital*, The National Bureau of Economic Research, New York.

--- (1981), "International Comparisons of Recent Productivity Trends", in: William Fellner (ed.), *Essays in Contemporary Economic Problems: Demand, Productivity, and Population*, American Enterprise Institute, Washington, pp. 125-70.

--- (1990), "International Comparisons of Productivity, Trends, and Levels", *Atlantic Economic Journal*, Vol. 18, no. 3, September, pp. 42-54.

Maddison, A. (1987), "Growth and Slowdown in Advanced Capitalist Economies", *Journal of Economic Literature*, Vol. 25, no. 2, June, pp. 649-698.

OECD (1991), *Economic Outlook*, OECD, Paris, December, Table 48, p. 136.

Pigou, A.C. (1935), "Net Income and Capital Depletion", *Economic Journal*, June, p. 239.

Problems of Capital Formation: Concepts, Measurement, and Controlling Factors, Studies in Income and Wealth, Vol. 19, (1957), Princeton University Press for the National Bureau of Economic Research, Princeton, NJ.

Robinson, J. (1956), *The Accumulation of Capital*, Macmillan, London.

Usher, D. (ed.), (1980) *The Measurement of Capital*, Studies in Income and Wealth, Vol. 45, University of Chicago Press and NBER, Chicago.

U.S. Department of Commerce (June 1987), "Fixed Reproducible Tangible Wealth of the United States, 1925-85", Government Printing Office, Washington.

U.S. Department of Labor (1982), "Trends in Multifactor Productivity, 1948-81", *Bulletin 2178*, Bureau of Labor Statistics, Washington.

--- (1991) "Multifactor Productivity Measures, 1990", *USDL 91-412*, Bureau of Labor Statistics, August, Washington.

Young, A.H. (1989), "BEA's Measurement of Computer Output", *Survey of Current Business*, July, pp. 108-115.

Explaining Economic Growth
A. Szirmai, B. van Ark and D. Pilat
© 1993 Elsevier Science Publishers B.V. All rights reserved.

The Role of Education in Productivity Convergence: Does Higher Education Matter?

Edward N. Wolff and Maury Gittleman
New York University

1. Introduction

Previous explanations of the productivity convergence process almost all involve the so-called "advantages of backwardness", by which it is meant that much of the catch-up can be explained by the diffusion of technical knowledge from the leading economies to the more backward ones (see Gerschenkron, 1952, and Kuznets, 1973, for example). Competitive pressures in the international economy ensure rapid dissemination of superior productive techniques from one country to another. Through the constant transfer of knowledge, countries learn about the latest technology from each other, but virtually by definition the followers have more to learn from the leaders than the leaders have to learn from the laggards. Indeed, those countries that are so far behind the leaders that it is impractical for them to benefit substantially from the leaders' knowledge will generally not be able to participate in the convergence process at all, and many such economies will find themselves falling even further behind.

This mechanism has two implications: First, it means that countries which lag (somewhat) behind the leaders can be expected to increase their productivity performance toward the level of the leading nations. We would expect an **inverse** relation between a country's initial productivity level and its rate of productivity growth. Second, the mechanism tends to undermine itself as the gap in productivity between follower countries and countries in the vanguard is gradually eliminated. That is, the rate of catch-up should slow down as the productivity gap is closed.

It should be stressed at this point that being backward does not itself guarantee that a nation will catch up. Other factors must be present, such as strong investment, an educated and well trained work force, research and development activity, a developed information sector, a suitable product mix, developed trading relations with advanced countries, foreign investment by multi-national corporations, a receptive political structure, low population growth, and the like.

Indeed, recently, researchers such as Mankiw, Romer, and Weil (1992) have distinguished between what they call "unconditional" and "conditional" convergence. The former is characterized by the notion that all nations of the world will eventually attain the same level of average productivity in the long term. The latter view, in contrast, maintains that, **given** other characteristics such as the country's investment rate and educational attainment, countries with lower initial productivity will experience more rapid growth rates of productivity. In other words, countries with **similar** investment rates, educational attainment, and the like, will eventually approach the same level of productivity.

Almost all studies have concluded that unconditional convergence is a very weak force, explaining very little about relative rates of productivity growth among all nations, and we will provide some evidence of this below. However, almost all studies have found that conditional convergence is a very strong force, explaining between 40 and 70 per cent of the variation in country growth rates, depending on the variables and sample of countries employed.

In this paper, we present new evidence on the role of education in the convergence process. Previous work has shown that the quantity of education provided by an economy to its inhabitants is one of the major influences determining whether per capita income in that society is growing rapidly enough to narrow the gap in per capita income with the more prosperous economies (see, for example, Baumol, Blackman, and Wolff, 1989, Chapter 9, or Barro, 1991). Maddison in his work has also drawn attention to the important role played by education in the economic development of nations in the twentieth century (see, for example, Maddison, 1989, Chapter 6). This is important for policy because it suggests that a country can do a great deal to improve its performance in the convergence arena by increasing the resources it devotes to education.

However, what is not so clear from previous work is the comparative role of primary school, secondary school, and higher education in the catch-up process. Many studies (such as Mankiw, Romer, and Weil, 1992, or Helliwell and Chung, 1991) simply use the proportion of the relevant age group enrolled in secondary schools as the "educational variable" in such convergence studies. However, in many such studies there is no justification given for the use of this variable as opposed to primary school or tertiary school enrollment.

We also add a new variable to the analysis of education in the convergence process. Almost all previous studies (including Baumol, Blackman, and Wolff, 1989, Chapter 9) have used educational **enrollment rates**, defined as the percentage of school age children currently enrolled in school, as the measure of educational input. In this study, we include measures of the educational **attainment** of the labor force, defined as the percentage of the active labor force who have attained a certain level of schooling. To our mind, the latter is the more appropriate indicator of schooling input, since it reflects the educational achievements of the current labor force, whereas enrollment rates reflect those of the future labor force. As we shall see below, there are marked differences in results from the use of these two indicators.

Further, we believe that the use of educational attainment by specific educational levels (primary, secondary, and university) is preferable to the use of estimates of aggregate "human capital" of the labor force, as has been done in some studies (for example, Barro and Sala-y-Martin, 1992, Lichtenberg,

1992, and Benhabib and Spiegel, 1992) for two reasons. First, human capital estimates do not enable one to separate out the effects of the different types of skills provided at different levels of education on economic growth. Second, such aggregates almost always rely on a common rate of return to education both by educational level and across countries of the world, whereas many studies have shown that returns to education decline by schooling level and are lower in more developed countries.

The purpose of this paper is to ferret out the respective roles of these three educational levels in the catch-up process on the basis of both enrollment and attainment data. Of particular interest is the apparent lack of importance of higher education in the convergence process. Two dimensions are considered. First, does the relative importance of these three educational variables depend on the level of development of a country - industrialized, middle-income or low-income status? Second, do these effects vary over time, from the 1950s to the 1980s?

The remainder of the paper is divided into three parts. The first of these provides descriptive statistics on educational enrollment and attainment by the level of development of countries. The next provides econometric results on the effects of educational enrollment and attainment on per capita income growth. Implications are drawn in the last part.

2. Educational Enrollment and Attainment by Level of Development

We begin with summary statistics on both enrollment rates and attainment rates for selected years. On the basis of the World Bank definitions, we have divided the countries in our sample into four groups: (1) industrial market economies, (2) upper middle income countries (including centrally planned and two high income oil exporting economies), (3) lower middle income countries, and (4) low income countries.[1] It is first of interest to compare changes over time in enrollment rates by country group (see table 1).[2] Among the industrial market economies, there was almost 100 per cent enrollment at the primary school level and almost no variation among countries in this group. In contrast, the average secondary school enrollment rate increased from 62 per cent in 1965 to 89 per cent in 1983. The dispersion among countries in this group likewise declined, from a coefficient of variation (the ratio of the standard deviation to the mean) of 0.21 in 1965 to 0.15 in 1983. The largest dispersion was found on the higher

---

[1]   It should be noted that World Bank country groupings change over time, depending on their growth rates in per capita income. To standardize the analysis, we have used the World Bank's 1986 definitions.

[2]   It should be noted that we use "gross" enrollment rates throughout the analysis conducted in this paper. See the definition in Footnote b of Table 1.

education level. In 1965, on average, only 15 per cent of college-age adults were enrolled in tertiary school, with the U.S. the highest at 40 per cent and Spain the lowest at 6 per cent. However, by 1983, the average enrollment rate had increased to 30 per cent, with the U.S. still leading at 56 per cent and Ireland the lowest at 22 per cent. Dispersion also fell sharply over this period, from a coefficient of variation of 0.51 in 1965 to 0.27 in 1983.

TABLE 1
Enrollment and Attainment Rates by Educational Level and Country Group, Selected Years, 1960-1983[a]

A. Enrollment Rates[b]

	Primary School		Secondary School		Higher Education	
	1965	1983	1965	1983	1965	1983
Industrial Market Economies						
Mean	1.04	1.01	0.62	0.89	0.15	0.30
Std. Deviation	0.10	0.04	0.13	0.13	0.07	0.08
Coeff. of Var.	0.10	0.04	0.21	0.15	0.51	0.27
Number	19	19	19	19	19	19
Upper Middle Income, High Income Oil Exporters and Centrally Planned Countries						
Mean	0.93	1.03	0.33	0.61	0.06	0.15
Std. Deviation	0.20	0.10	0.16	0.16	0.05	0.07
Coeff. of Var.	0.22	0.10	0.48	0.25	0.76	0.51
Number	23	23	23	23	23	23
Lower Middle Income Countries						
Mean	0.76	0.97	0.15	0.36	0.04	0.10
Std. Deviation	0.28	0.20	0.12	0.17	0.04	0.09
Coeff. of Var.	0.37	0.20	0.79	0.48	0.99	0.90
Number	34	34	34	34	34	34
Low Income Countries						
Mean	0.44	0.64	0.07	0.16	0.01	0.02
Std. Deviation	0.23	0.24	0.08	0.12	0.01	0.02
Coeff. of Var.	0.52	0.37	1.14	0.70	2.01	1.02
Number	32	32	32	32	32	32
All Countries						
Mean	0.75	0.89	0.25	0.45	0.05	0.12
Std. Deviation	0.32	0.24	0.23	0.30	0.06	0.12
Coeff. of Var.	0.42	0.27	0.93	0.66	1.22	0.97
Number	108	108	108	108	108	108

TABLE 1 (Continued)

B. Attainment Rates[c]

	Primary School		Secondary School		Higher Education	
	1960	1979	1960	1979	1960	1979
Industrial Market Economies						
Mean	0.90	0.92	0.22	0.53	0.05	0.13
Std. Deviation	0.08	0.09	0.14	0.19	0.04	0.09
Coeff. of Var.	0.09	0.10	0.62	0.35	0.84	0.65
Number	9	19	15	19	16	19
Upper Middle Income, High Income Oil Exporters and Centrally Planned Countries						
Mean	0.57	0.72	0.11	0.30	0.02	0.07
Std. Deviation	0.28	0.21	0.09	0.15	0.02	0.04
Coeff. of Var.	0.49	0.29	0.80	0.51	0.91	0.56
Number	23	21	21	21	21	21
Lower Middle Income Countries						
Mean	0.39	0.52	0.05	0.13	0.01	0.03
Std. Deviation	0.21	0.23	0.04	0.08	0.01	0.03
Coeff. of Var.	0.54	0.45	0.78	0.60	1.30	0.96
Number	31	34	31	34	31	34
Low Income Countries						
Mean	0.15	0.29	0.03	0.08	0.00	0.01
Std. Deviation	0.16	0.17	0.04	0.08	0.00	0.01
Coeff. of Var.	1.05	0.59	1.75	0.97	0.84	0.92
Number	25	31	25	32	25	32
All Countries						
Mean	0.42	0.56	0.09	0.22	0.02	0.05
Std. Deviation	0.31	0.30	0.10	0.20	0.02	0.06
Coeff. of Var.	0.73	0.52	1.19	0.92	1.48	1.22
Number	88	105	92	106	93	106

[a] The division of the countries into groups follows the World Bank convention. Source: World Bank, *World Development Report 1986*, table 1, pp. 180-1.

[b] The enrollment rate used here is defined as the total enrollment of students of all ages in primary school, secondary school, and higher education, as a proportion of the total population of the pertinent age group. The enrollment rates are gross and may therefore exceed 100 per cent. Source: World Bank, *World Development Report 1986*, table 29, pp. 236-7.

[c] The educational attainment rate is defined as the proportion of the population 25 and over who have attained the indicated level of schooling or greater. Results are based on the combined benchmark and estimated data. See the Appendix for sources and methods.

Among upper middle income countries, the patterns were quite similar. The average primary school enrollment rate increased from 93 per cent to 100 per cent over this period, with dispersion, as measured by the coefficient of variation, falling in half. Secondary school enrollment rates almost doubled, from an average of 33 per cent to 61 per cent, and dispersion fell by half. The average enrollment rate in higher education more than doubled, from 6 per cent to 15 per cent (with Israel in the lead in 1983 at 34 per cent) and dispersion fell by a third.

Similar patterns are evident for the lower middle income group. Primary enrollment rates neared 100 per cent in 1983, secondary enrollment rates more than doubled, as did tertiary school enrollment, reaching a high of 35 per cent in Ecuador in 1983. Dispersion fell for all three educational levels, though the decline was relatively modest for higher education. Low income countries also saw enrollment increase at both the primary school (from 44 per cent to 64 per cent) and secondary school (from 7 per cent to 16 per cent) levels, but the average enrollment rate grew from only 1 per cent to 2 per cent for higher education. The coefficient of variation also fell substantially at all three levels.

Differences between these groups of countries are also striking. In 1983, average primary school enrollment rates were at or near 100 per cent in industrialized, upper income, and middle income countries, and had reached almost two-thirds in low income ones. The coefficient of variation among all countries fell from 0.42 in 1965 to 0.27 in 1983. Thus, differences in primary school enrollment had narrowed among the countries of the world. On the other hand, there were still large differences at the secondary school level in 1983, from a high of 89 per cent for industrialized countries, to 61 per cent for the upper middle income group, 36 per cent for the lower middle income group, and only 16 per cent for low income countries. Though dispersion in secondary enrollment rates among all countries fell between 1965 and 1983, it was still quite high in 1983, at 0.66. The variation was even greater at the tertiary school level in 1983, from a high of 30 per cent for the industrialized group, to 2 per cent for the low income countries, and an overall coefficient of variation of 0.97.

Not surprisingly, intra-group dispersion was lowest at all schooling levels for the industrialized countries, second lowest for middle income countries, third lowest for lower middle income ones, and highest for low income nations. Moreover, for all four country groups, dispersion was lowest at the primary school level, typically twice as great at the secondary school level, and, again about twice as great at the higher education level.

Educational attainment rates (Panel B) are, not surprisingly, lower than the corresponding enrollment rates, since enrollment rates have been increasing over time (that is, attainment rates for the adult population in a given year reflect the enrollment rates when the adults were children). However, changes over time and differences between groups of countries present a similar picture on the basis of attainment rates. Between 1960 and 1979, average attainment rates rose at all three educational levels for all groups of countries.[3] Secondary school attainment rates more than doubled for all four country groups, and higher education attainment rates tripled, except for low income countries. The dispersion in attainment rates fell at all three educational levels for all four groups (except higher education for the low income countries). Moreover, in 1979 intra-group dispersion in educational attainment was lowest for primary school attendance and highest for higher education, as were differences in average attainment rates among the four groups of countries.[4]

On the surface, it would appear that the fact that differences in enrollment and attainment rates were by far greatest at the tertiary school level should have some bearing on the relative growth of these countries over the postwar period. This is the variable of key interest here, and we now turn to the regression results.

3. The Role of Education in the Convergence Process

We make use of the Summers-Heston dataset in the empirical analysis. Summers and Heston (1988) have provided data on per-capita GDP for 63 countries for the period 1950-1985, and for 111 countries for the 1960-85 period. Moreover, the series are updated through 1988 for 108 countries (data available on diskette). Combining the Summers-Heston data with World Bank data on education results in slightly smaller sample sizes for the relevant periods. The GDP figures for different countries are expressed in "1980 international dollars" (1985 international dollars for the 1960-88 data) on the basis of relative purchasing power parity (PPP) exchange rates. The resulting statistics are referred to as real per-capita GDP (RGDP).

Since there is a trade-off between time coverage and country coverage, we will report results on the basis of different country samples for different time periods. However, where we are concerned with changes in coefficient values over time, we will work with constant country samples. Most of our basic results will be reported for the 1960-85 period, since this is the period of maximum country coverage. However, we will also extend some of the regressions back to 1950 and up through 1988 for the smaller country samples.

---

[3] Maddison (1989, pp. 77-78) reports similar results for mean schooling levels for his sample of countries.

[4] Results for attainment rates reported in this paper are based on the combined benchmark and estimated data (see the Appendix for details). Results based on benchmark data alone are quite similar to those reported for the combined sample, unless otherwise indicated.

Our standard estimating equation will be of the form:

$$\ln(RGDP_1/RGDP_0) = b_0 + b_1 RGDP_0 + b_2 EDUCATE + \epsilon \qquad (1)$$

where $\ln(RGDP_1/RGDP_0)$ is the percentage increase in RGDP over from time 0 to time 1, $RGDP_0$ is RGDP at the beginning of the period, and EDUCATE a measure of educational input. The convergence hypothesis predicts that the coefficient b_1 will be negative (that is, countries further behind at the beginning will show more rapid increases in GDP per capita). For the education variable, EDUCATE, we use six alternative measures: enrollment rates for formal **primary** education, for **secondary** education, and for **higher** education, and the three corresponding educational attainment rates. Enrollment rates are recorded as of the beginning of the period (or the earliest date available in the period), while attainment rates are recorded as of the midpoint of the period under consideration (or the closest year available), since this is more representative of the average educational input for the period.

Results are reported for both the 1950-85 and the 1960-85 periods (see table 2). It is first of interest to consider the unconditional convergence equation, with a constant and initial RGDP as the only independent variables (top lines of Panels A and B). For the 1950-85 period, the coefficient of initial RGDP is negative but insignificant, while for the 1960-85 period the coefficient is negative and significant at the 5 per cent level, but the R^2 is only 0.06 (only 6 per cent of the differences explained). Thus, by itself, catch-up is a very weak force among all countries of the world.

One of the prime reasons, besides low investment rates, for the relatively weak catch-up of the less developed countries to the industrialized countries over the postwar period was the failure of the lagging countries to keep up with, absorb and utilize new technological and product information, and to benefit from the international dissemination of technology. Countries only slightly behind the leaders, in contrast, have been eminently successful in doing so. One of the elements that one may well expect to explain an economy's ability to absorb information and new technology is the education of its populace.

With the inclusion of the education variable, the coefficient of initial RGDP is negative and significant at the one or five per cent level in four of the six cases for the 1950-85 period and at the one per cent level in all cases for the 1960-85 sample. Thus, in effect, countries with similar educational levels were shown quite consistently to be converging among themselves, in terms of RGDP, though not catching up with countries whose educational levels were higher.

TABLE 2
**Regressions of Growth in Real GDP per Capita (RGDP) on Initial RGDP
And Educational Enrollment and Attainment Rates, 1950-85 and 1960-85[a]**

Dependent Variable	Constant	Initial RGDP	Educ. Var.	R^2	Adjust R^2	Std Err Of Reg	Samp Size	Education Variable
A. 1950-85 Period								
R85/50	0.822** (9.06)	-0.172 (0.45)		0.003	-0.013	0.438	63	
R85/50	-0.149 (0.71)	-0.669 (1.83)	0.295** (4.98)	0.295	0.271	0.372	63	PRIM-ENRL$_{1965}$
R85/50	0.510** (6.78)	-1.689** (4.72)	1.766** (7.89)	0.511	0.495	0.310	63	SCND-ENRL$_{1965}$
R85/50	0.759** (8.98)	-0.073* (2.07)	3.126** (3.63)	0.183	0.156	0.400	63	UNIV-ENRL$_{1965}$
R85/50	0.223 (1.72)	-1.597** (3.53)	1.303** (5.44)	0.363	0.339	0.361	55	PRIM-ATTN$_{1970}$
R85/50	0.703** (7.54)	-1.185* (2.13)	1.623** (3.44)	0.176	0.147	0.409	60	SCND-ATTN$_{1970}$
R85/50	0.796** (8.49)	-0.254 (0.44)	2.257 (1.23)	0.032	-0.002	0.441	61	UNIV-ATTN$_{1970}$
B. 1960-85 Period								
R85/60	0.524** (10.4)	-0.246* (2.59)		0.058	0.049	0.478	111	
R85/60	-0.205* (2.01)	-0.435** (5.42)	0.988** (7.78)	0.396	0.385	0.385	111	PRIM-ENRL$_{1965}$
R85/60	0.255** (4.37)	-0.461** (5.34)	1.192** (6.72)	0.336	0.323	0.404	111	SCND-ENRL$_{1965}$
R85/60	0.380** (6.69)	-0.325** (3.63)	2.688** (4.45)	0.204	0.189	0.442	111	UNIV-ENRL$_{1965}$
R85/60	0.175* (2.29)	-0.389** (4.46)	0.742** (5.64)	0.303	0.289	0.423	100	PRIM-ATTN$_{1970}$
R85/60	0.350** (5.55)	-0.380** (4.12)	1.340** (4.63)	0.229	0.213	0.441	104	SCND-ATTN$_{1970}$
R85/60	0.437** (7.48)	-0.348** (3.63)	4.034** (3.30)	0.155	0.138	0.460	105	UNIV-ATTN$_{1970}$

Notes to table 2
ᵃ t-ratios are shown in parentheses below the coefficient estimate. Key:
Dependent variable: $\ln(RGDP_{85}/RGDP_{50})$ or $\ln(RGDP_{85}/RGDP_{60})$, as indicated.
$RGDP_t$: RGDP per capita in year t, measured in units of $10,000s (1980 international prices). Source: Summers and Heston (1988), diskettes.
$PRIM\text{-}ENRL_{1965}$: Gross enrollment rate in primary school in 1965. Source: World Bank (1986), table 29.
$SCND\text{-}ENRL_{1965}$: Gross enrollment rate in secondary school in 1965. Source: World Bank (1986), table 29.
$UNIV\text{-}ENRL_{1965}$: Gross enrollment rate in higher education in 1965. Source: World Bank (1986), table 29.
$PRIM\text{-}ATTN_{1970}$: Proportion of the population age 25 and over who have attended primary school or higher in 1970. See the Appendix for sources and methods.
$SCND\text{-}ATTN_{1970}$: Proportion of the population age 25 and over who have attended secondary school or higher in 1970. See the Appendix for sources and methods.
$UNIV\text{-}ATTN_{1970}$: Proportion of the population age 25 and over who have attended an institution of higher education in 1970. See the Appendix for sources and methods.
* significant at the 5 per cent level, 2-tail test.
** significant at the 1 per cent level, 2-tail test.

For the 1960-85 period, the coefficients of the education variables are uniformly positive and significant at the one per cent level. However, primary school education appears to have a somewhat stronger effect than secondary school education (as indicated by the t-ratio and the R^2 statistics), and both are considerably stronger than higher education. Moreover, enrollment rates are uniformly stronger than educational attainment rates. On the surface, this result appears anomalous, since the attainment rates are a direct indicator of the human capital input into production, whereas the enrollment rates are an indicator of future educational input. However, as we shall see below, this result is fairly consistent in our analysis. In the conclusion, we shall offer some reasons for it.

For the 1950-85 period, no clear pattern emerges. On the basis of enrollment rates, the strongest effect comes form secondary schooling, whereas, on the basis of attainment rates, the strongest effect is from primary schooling. Both levels dominate university education and, indeed, on the basis of attainment rates, the variable is statistically insignificant. Moreover, enrollment rates appear to exert a stronger effect on growth than attainment rates at the secondary and higher education levels but not at the primary school level. It is not clear why the results for the 1950-85 period differ so much from those for 1960-85. However, it should be noted that the sample of countries for the 1950-85 period is smaller and likely unrepresentative. Moreover, economic developments during the 1950s still reflected recovery from the devastation of World War II.

A. Investment and Education.

We next consider the role of investment in the convergence process. The explanatory variable that will be used is INVRATE, the average investment rate, defined as the ratio of investment to GDP, both in 1980 international dollars, averaged over the period of analysis (1960-85 in table 3). The estimating equation then becomes:

$$\ln(RGDP_1/RGDP_0) = b_0 + b_1 RGDP_0 + b_2 INVRATE + b_3 EDUCATE + \epsilon \quad (2)$$

As shown in table 3, primary school enrollment appears to be a slightly stronger determinant of growth than secondary school enrollment, once differences in investment rates are controlled for. However, the differences in statistical results between primary school and secondary school enrollment rates are not great. On the other hand, once investment rates are controlled for, the higher education enrollment rate becomes statistically insignificant in explaining growth in per capita income.

TABLE 3
Regressions Of Growth in RGDP on Initial RGDP, the Investment Rate, And Educational Enrollment and Attainment Rates, 1960-85[a]

Constant	Initial RGDP	INVRATE	Educ. Var.	R^2	Adj. R^2	Std Err	Samp Size	Education Variable
-0.37** (3.64)	-0.388** (5.14)	0.028** (4.95)	0.551** (3.71)	0.50	0.49	0.36	102	PRIM-ENRL$_{1965}$
-0.13 (1.39)	-0.373** (4.47)	0.031** (4.86)	0.474* (1.98)	0.46	0.44	0.38	102	SCND-ENRL$_{1965}$
-0.15 (1.63)	-0.330** (4.20)	0.034** (5.78)	0.758 (1.40)	0.45	0.43	0.38	102	UNIV-ENRL$_{1965}$
-0.18 (1.81)	-0.342** (4.25)	0.032** (4.82)	0.288 (1.82)	0.44	0.43	0.39	94	PRIM-ATTN$_{1970}$
-0.17 (1.63)	-0.316** (3.84)	0.037** (5.91)	0.246 (0.72)	0.44	0.42	0.39	96	SCND-ATTN$_{1970}$
-0.18 (1.74)	-0.302** (3.71)	0.039** (6.83)	0.232 (0.20)	0.43	0.42	0.39	97	UNIV-ATTN$_{1970}$

[a] The dependent variable is $\ln(RGDP_{85}/RGDP_{60})$. t-ratios are shown in parentheses below the coefficient estimate. See notes to table 2 for the key. In addition, INVRATE: ratio of investment to GDP (both in 1980 international dollars for the Summers-Heston data) averaged over the appropriate period (1960-85 here). Source: Summers and Heston (1988), diskettes.
* significant at the 5 per cent level, 2-tail test.
** significant at the 1 per cent level, 2-tail test.

The results for educational attainment rates are striking. Primary school attainment is not statistically significant at the 5 per cent level, though it is at the 10 per cent level. Both the secondary school and the university attainment rates are quite insignificant. Thus, it appears that once differences in investment rates among countries are considered, educational attainment has little direct effect on economic growth among countries. However, as we shall show below, both attainment rates and enrollment rates may have an indirect effect.

B. *The Role of Education by Level of Development and Period.*

For the next part of the analysis, we consider the role of educational enrollment and attainment rates over different periods of time and for different groups of countries. There are several reasons to believe that the effects of education might vary across these two dimensions. First, technology in the world economy has changed since the end of World War II. Indeed, some have argued (for example, David, 1991) that a fourth industrial revolution occurred during the 1970s with the widespread introduction and adoption of computers and computer-driven technology.

An implication of this is that new technologies are becoming more and more information-based. Baumol, Blackman, and Wolff (1989) documents this trend for the U.S. (Chapter 7). They found that between 1960 and 1980, knowledge workers (defined as producers of knowledge, including scientists and engineers) were the fastest growing occupational group, at 3.5 per cent per year, followed by data workers (defined as users of knowledge, including secretaries and clerks) at 3.1 per cent per year. In contrast, noninformation (all other) employment grew at 1.1 per cent per year (also, see Reich, 1991). Also, according to this study, the median schooling of information workers in 1980 was 13.1 years (one year of university). If the U.S. experience is not atypical, these results suggest that other industrialized nations have fast been moving toward information economies, with the implication that university education should be rising in importance as a source of growth in the world economy over the postwar period.

Second, skill requirements will generally vary depending on the level of development of a country. For low income countries, literacy and "numeracy" may constitute the crucial skill needs, thus emphasising the importance of primary education. In middle income countries, more specialized and advanced skills are required (the ability to operate and maintain fairly complex machinery, for example), thus suggesting the preeminence of secondary education. In high income countries, scientific and computing skills and, in general, professional skills, play a predominant role, thus implying the primary importance of university education.

Third, the variation in educational levels has itself changed both across countries and over time. Insofar as there has been growing convergence (decreasing dispersion) in educational attainment among the countries of the world and for groups of countries at similar levels of development, the importance of this factor in explaining cross-country differences in growth rates will likewise decrease over time. As documented in Section 2 of the paper, there was convergence at all three educational levels between the early 1960s and the mid-1980s. However, by 1983, the degree of dispersion was low for primary school enrollment but moderate for secondary school enrollment and still substantial for tertiary enrollment. A similar story holds for attainment rates. These results suggest that primary education differences were likely to have been most important during the early part of the postwar period; secondary school differences most important during the middle part of the period; and differences in university education most important in recent years.

The regression results are shown in three stages: first, for all countries of the world for different time periods; second, by level of development for the whole period; and, third, by time period for industrialized and upper middle income countries. Table 4 shows the regression results for the full sample of countries in different time periods. As suggested above, primary school enrollment is the most important educational variable for the 1960-80 period, whereas secondary school enrollment appears slightly stronger than primary enrollment for the 1970-88 period. For the 1979-88 period, the only statistically significant educational variable is secondary enrollment. University education enrollment is not significant in any time period.

The results are similar for attainment rates. The primary school attainment rate is the only significant educational variable for the 1960-80 period; the secondary school attainment rate is the only significant education variable for the 1970-88 period; and there is no significant attainment variable for the 1979-88 period, (though secondary school attainment is close). As before, the enrollment rate variables perform better in these regressions than the corresponding attainment rates. It is also interesting to note that the "convergence model" performs much better (as measured by the goodness of fit) for the 1960-80 period than either the 1970-88 or the 1979-88 period. This finding suggests a diminution of the "catch-up" effect over time.

Table 5 shows regression results for the 1960-88 period for different groups of countries. Among both the industrial market economies and the combined industrial market and upper income economies, it is clear that university enrollment is the predominant educational variable in explaining differences in RGDP growth rates. Primary school and secondary school enrollment rates are both statistically insignificant. However, the attainment rate for higher education is insignificant, as are the other attainment rate variables. Among the lower middle income and the lower income groups of countries, both the primary school and the secondary school enrollment rates are statistically significant. For both of these country groups, university enrollment and all three educational attainment variables are insignificant.

TABLE 4
Regressions of RGDP Growth on Initial RGDP, the Investment Rate,
and Education for All Countries and Various Time Periods, 1960-88[a]

	Enrollment Rates, 1965			Mid-Year Attainment Rates[b]		
	PRIM	SCND	UNIV	PRIM	SCND	UNIV

A. All Countries, 1960-80

Coeff. of Educ. Var.	0.527**	0.390	0.664	0.326*	0.234	0.402
t-ratio of Educ. Var.	(4.18)	(1.87)	(1.10)	(2.38)	(0.81)	(0.39)
R^2	0.47	0.40	0.38	0.39	0.38	0.37
Adjusted R^2	0.45	0.38	0.36	0.37	0.36	0.35
Sample Size	104	104	104	93	95	96

B. All Countries, 1970-88

Coeff. of Educ. Var.	0.338*	0.742*	0.789	0.207	0.704*	1.101
t-ratio of Educ. Var.	(2.43)	(2.52)	(0.92)	(1.08)	(2.29)	(1.28)
R^2	0.25	0.27	0.21	0.20	0.26	0.22
Adjusted R^2	0.22	0.24	0.18	0.17	0.23	0.19
Sample Size	82	82	82	79	80	80

C. All Countries, 1979-88

Coeff. of Educ. Var.	0.164	0.403*	0.525	0.018	0.327	0.520
t-ratio of Educ. Var.	(1.75)	(2.20)	(1.03)	(0.16)	(1.65)	(1.02)
R^2	0.26	0.28	0.25	0.22	0.26	0.25
Adjusted R^2	0.24	0.25	0.22	0.19	0.23	0.22
Sample Size	82	82	82	79	80	80

[a] The dependent variable is $\ln(RGDP_1/RGDP_0)$ for the indicated time period. Separate equations are run for each educational variable. A constant term, initial RGDP, and INVRATE are also included as independent variables in each equation, but the coefficients are not shown.
[b] 1970 attainment rates for Panel A; 1979 attainment rates for panels B and C.
* significant at the 5 per cent level, 2-tail test.
** significant at the 1 per cent level, 2-tail test.

Table 6 shows regression results for university education by time period for the most developed countries. For industrial market economies as a group, university education fails to appear as a significant determinant of growth for any sub-period, though it is significant for the full 1960-88 period (table 5). However, among the combined sample of industrial market and upper middle income economies, university enrollment is statistically significant at the one per cent level over the 1950-88 period and at the five per cent level over the 1950-70 time period but becomes insignificant for the 1970-88 period. This result is contrary to what was expected, since we hypothesized that university education would become more important over time. Moreover, the university attainment rates are uniformly insignificant.

TABLE 5
Regressions of RGDP Growth on Initial RGDP, the Investment Rate, and Education for Various Country Samples, 1960-88[a]

	Enrollment Rates, 1965			Attainment Rates, 1970		
	PRIM	SCND	UNIV	PRIM	SCND	UNIV

A. Industrial Market Economies, 1960-88

	PRIM	SCND	UNIV	PRIM	SCND	UNIV
Coeff. of Educ. Var.	-0.033	0.178	1.534*	1.512	0.049	0.017
t-ratio of Educ. Var.	(0.07)	(0.55)	(2.26)	(1.50)	(0.13)	(0.01)
R^2	0.55	0.56	0.66	0.61	0.53	0.53
Adjusted R^2	0.46	0.47	0.60	0.50	0.43	0.43
Sample Size	19	19	19	14	18	18

B. Industrial Market and Upper Middle Income Economies, 1960-88

	PRIM	SCND	UNIV	PRIM	SCND	UNIV
Coeff. of Educ. Var.	0.649	0.636	2.309*	0.531	0.754	2.160
t-ratio of Educ. Var.	(1.33)	(1.77)	(2.41)	(1.18)	(1.45)	(1.38)
R^2	0.42	0.44	0.49	0.42	0.42	0.42
Adjusted R^2	0.35	0.38	0.43	0.34	0.36	0.35
Sample Size	32	32	32	27	31	31

C. Lower Middle Income Countries, 1960-88

	PRIM	SCND	UNIV	PRIM	SCND	UNIV
Coeff. of Educ. Var.	0.780*	1.593*	0.728	0.573	1.808	3.548
t-ratio of Educ. Var.	(2.87)	(2.20)	(0.35)	(1.72)	(1.36)	(0.88)
R^2	0.35	0.27	0.10	0.21	0.18	0.13
Adjusted R^2	0.26	0.17	-0.02	0.10	0.05	0.00
Sample Size	25	25	25	25	24	24

D. Low Income Countries, 1960-88

	PRIM	SCND	UNIV	PRIM	SCND	UNIV
Coeff. of Educ. Var.	0.834*	2.678*	5.310	-0.263	0.453	-0.209
t-ratio of Educ. Var.	(2.34)	(2.58)	(1.24)	(0.66)	(0.29)	(0.13)
R^2	0.41	0.44	0.27	0.60	0.59	0.58
Adjusted R^2	0.29	0.33	0.12	0.51	0.50	0.49
Sample Size	21	21	21	18	18	18

[a]   The dependent variable is $\ln(RGDP_{88}/RGDP_{60})$. Separate equations are run for each educational variable. A constant term, initial RGDP, and INVRATE are also included as independent variables in each equation, but the coefficients are not shown. Results for the upper middle income group of countries are not shown separately because the sample size is too small.
*   significant at the 5 per cent level, 2-tail test.
**   significant at the 1 per cent level, 2-tail test.

TABLE 6
Regressions of RGDP Growth on Initial RGDP, the Investment Rate, and University Education for Selected Country Samples and Time Periods, 1950-88[a]

	Univ. Enrollment Rates, 1965			Univ. Attainment Rates[b]		
Period:	1950-88	1950-70	1970-88	1950-88	1950-70	1970-88

A. Industrial Market Economies

Coeff. of Educ. Var.	2.149	1.144	0.628	0.888	4.592	0.094
t-ratio of Educ. Var.	(1.98)	(1.29)	(1.26)	(0.45)	(1.76)	(0.23)
R^2	0.70	0.68	0.34	0.61	0.70	0.27
Adjusted R^2	0.64	0.61	0.21	0.53	0.62	0.12
Sample Size	19	19	19	18	16	19

B. Industrial Market and Upper Middle Economies

Coeff. of Educ. Var.	3.496**	2.017*	0.960	1.512	4.465	0.795
t-ratio of Educ. Var.	(3.48)	(2.69)	(1.29)	(0.66)	(1.92)	(1.22)
R^2	0.70	0.61	0.33	0.55	0.59	0.35
Adjusted R^2	0.66	0.57	0.26	0.49	0.54	0.28
Sample Size	27	30	33	26	25	31

[a]   The dependent variable is $\ln(RGDP_1/RGDP_0)$ for the indicated time period. Separate equations are run for each time period. A constant term, initial RGDP, and INVRATE are also included as independent variables in each equation, but the coefficients are not shown.
[b]   The 1970 attainment rates are used for the 1950-88 period; the 1960 attainment rates are used for the 1950-70 period; and the 1979 attainment rates are used for the 1970-88 period.
*   significant at the 5 per cent level, 2-tail test.
**   significant at the 1 per cent level, 2-tail test.

For the final part of the analysis, we look at the relationship between investment rates and educational levels to see if the presence of a well-educated workforce serves to stimulate capital spending. We employ a regression analysis in which the dependent variable is the average investment rate over the period of the analysis and the independent variables are a constant and one of the six educational variables.[5]. The analysis is conducted for three time periods for the full sample of countries. The results, shown in table 7, are striking. As speculated above, investment rates are positively and significantly influenced by the educational level of the population. All three educational levels are significant at the one per cent level and, most importantly, both the enrollment rates and the

---

[5]   An alternative form was also used, including initial RGDP as an independent variable along with the constant term and education. The results are not materially altered by the addition of initial RGDP.

attainment rates are significant at the one per cent level. Secondary education
generally has the strongest effect of the three educational levels, while university
education has the weakest effect, though the differences are not great. Moreover,
the attainment rates appear now with equal force to the enrollment rates.

TABLE 7
Regressions of the Investment Rate on Education for All Countries
And Various Time Periods, 1960-88[a]

	Enrollment Rates, 1965			Mid-Year Attainment Rates[b]		
	PRIM	SCND	UNIV	PRIM	SCND	UNIV
A. All Countries, 1960-80						
Coeff. of Educ. Var.	0.154**	0.248**	0.673**	0.149**	0.302**	0.912**
t-ratio of Educ. Var.	(6.63)	(8.62)	(5.89)	(6.86)	(5.97)	(4.47)
R^2	0.31	0.43	0.26	0.34	0.28	0.18
Adjusted R^2	0.30	0.42	0.25	0.33	0.27	0.17
Sample Size	102	102	102	93	95	96
B. All Countries, 1970-88						
Coeff. of Educ. Var.	0.136**	0.212**	0.491**	0.162**	0.217**	0.484**
t-ratio of Educ. Var.	(5.64)	(7.62)	(4.36)	(7.40)	(7.23)	(4.27)
R^2	0.28	0.42	0.19	0.42	0.40	0.19
Adjusted R^2	0.28	0.41	0.18	0.41	0.39	0.18
Sample Size	82	82	82	79	80	80
C. All Countries, 1979-88						
Coeff. of Educ. Var.	0.130**	0.196**	0.436**	0.147**	0.201**	0.460**
t-ratio of Educ. Var.	(5.40)	(6.81)	(3.82)	(6.66)	(6.65)	(4.13)
R^2	0.27	0.37	0.15	0.37	0.36	0.18
Adjusted R^2	0.26	0.36	0.14	0.36	0.35	0.17
Sample Size	82	82	82	79	80	80

[a] The dependent variable is INVRATE, the average ratio of investment to GDP for the indicated time period. Separate equations are run for each educational variable. A constant term is also included in each equation, but its coefficient is not shown.
[b] 1970 attainment rates for Panel A; 1979 attainment rates for panels B and C.
* significant at the 5 per cent level, 2-tail test.
** significant at the 1 per cent level, 2-tail test.

4. Conclusions and Implications

What can be concluded about the importance of schooling as a determinant of economic growth? It was shown here that among all countries, all three educational enrollment and attainment rate variables are statistically significant at the one per cent level over the 1960-85 period when the investment rate was not included in the analysis. In previous work (Baumol, Blackman, and Wolff, 1989, Chapter 9), secondary education, was stressed as being the most important determinant of growth, over both that of primary and tertiary levels. However, this analysis was conducted without the inclusion of an investment rate variable.

When the investment rate is included in the regression analysis for the full sample of countries, only primary school enrollment remains significant at the one per cent level. Secondary school enrollment becomes significant at the five per cent level, while university enrollment and all the educational attainment variables become insignificant. Subsequent regression analysis revealed that a country's investment is positively and significantly related to both enrollment rates and educational attainment rates. This result suggests that there are complementarities between investment and the availability of a trained labor force, as measured particularly by secondary education. The availability of an educated populace appears to act as a stimulus to investment, thereby exerting an indirect effect on economic growth.

When the sample of countries is segregated into those at similar levels of development, we find that among the industrial market economies and upper middle income countries, the university enrollment rate is the only statistically significant educational variable in explaining the growth of per capita income. Among the lower middle income and low income countries, both primary and secondary school enrollment rates are significant but university enrollment is not. However, none of the attainment variables is significant.

When we considered particular time periods, we found that among all countries primary school enrollment was the most important educational variable in the early part of the postwar period but secondary school enrollment was the most important in the later part. Among the industrial market economies and upper middle income countries alone, university enrollment was apparently more important in the earlier part of the postwar period than the later part. Here, again, none of the educational attainment rates is significant.

The results reported here appear to cast some doubt on the earlier convergence literature which saw education as a major factor promoting economic growth among the countries of the world. There are, in particular, two major puzzles. First, why are educational enrollment rates almost uniformly more powerful as explanatory factors in per capita income growth than educational attainment rates, where the latter are more clearly a better indicator of the educational input into production? The likely reason is that causation runs both ways, with positive feedbacks between GDP growth and educational attainment. Indeed, high or rising enrollment rates, in particular, might, indeed, be an **effect** of growth, rather than a determinant of growth. In other words, countries which have experienced the most rapid growth in GDP are likely the ones which have been able to expand their educational system the most.

Moreover, educational attainment appears to act indirectly as a factor promoting growth through its positive effect on investment. Indeed, the evidence presented above suggests strong complementarities between investment and the availability of a trained labor force. Thus, there appear to be cumulative feedback effects between economic growth, educational attainment, and investment, with each complementing and stimulating the other. This is the subject of a forthcoming book by Baumol and Wolff.

The second puzzle is the seeming lack of importance of university education as a source of growth. This is particularly apparent in per capita income growth regressions involving all countries of the world. Among the advanced economies, university enrollment does exert a significant effect on growth but this effect seems to have diminished over the postwar period rather than increasing. One possible explanation is that the skills acquired in university education are becoming less relevant to productivity growth. For example, several studies have reported results showing that per capita GDP growth is **negatively** related to the number of lawyers per capita of a country. Over time, university education may encourage more rent-seeking activities than directly productive ones.

There is also the possibility that higher education may perform more of a screening function than a training function. As enrollment rates rise, a higher proportion of university graduates may become over-schooled relative to the actual tasks they perform in the workplace. Thus, despite the fact that the advanced countries are moving more and more towards becoming information economies, the training provided in the university may be becoming less applicable to the actual functions of the work place.

For developing countries, it appears that primary emphasis should be given to improvement of both the quantity and quality of primary and secondary education. These two levels are likely to be the main ingredients in promoting their economic growth for the foreseeable future.

166   *Edward N. Wolff and Maury Gittleman*

Appendix
Sources and Methods in the Calculation of Educational Attainment Rates

Our data on educational attainment rates are divided into two groups: our so-called "benchmark data" and our so-called "estimated data".

Benchmark Data.

The basic data on educational attainment were derived from two sources: (1) UNESCO, *Statistics of Educational Attainment and Literacy, 1945-74*, Statistical Reports and Studies, No. 22, table 5, "Educational Attainment by Age and Sex, 1945 Onwards"; and (2) *UNESCO Statistical Yearbook 1990*, table 1.4, "Percentage distribution of population 25 years of age and over, educational attainment and by sex." UNESCO tabulates the data into six categories, according to the percentage of the population whose highest level of schooling attended is: (1) no schooling; (2) first level, incomplete; (3) first level, completed; (4) second level, first cycle; (5) second level, second cycle; and (6) postsecondary. Because the data for some of these categories were often combined (particularly the two first level and the two second level categories), we calculated the following three variables for each country: (1) the proportion of the population aged 25 and over that had attended some primary school or beyond; (2) the proportion that had attended some secondary school or beyond; and (3) the proportion that had attended some postsecondary school.

For the regression analysis, educational attainment rates were required for years 1950, 1960, 1970 and 1979. For countries for which benchmark data were available for some years but missing for others, we imputed missing values as follows: (1) If the missing year fell within three years of a date for which actual benchmark data were available, we used the value for that date. (2) If not, the missing value was calculated on the basis of geometric (growth rate) interpolation between the two nearest dates available.

Estimated Data.

For many countries, there were no benchmark data available on educational attainment rates. These missing values, which we call "estimated values", were imputed on the basis of a regression of available educational attainment rates for year t on educational enrollment ratios (collected from various UNESCO Statistical Yearbooks) for year t and for 15 years prior and on per capita income for year t. We collected data on enrollment data for every five years from 1950 (the earliest date available) through 1975. Enrollment ratios for the third level were not available for 1950 and 1955 though they were available for 1960 through 1975. The regressions provided quite a good fit, with the R^2 usually well in excess of 0.8. The predicted values from the regressions, after constraining them to be between 0 and 100, were then substituted for the missing data.

References

Abramovitz, M. and P.A. David (1973), "Reinterpreting Economic Growth: Parables and Realities", *American Economic Review*, Vol. 53, pp. 428-439.

Barro, R.J. (1991), "Economic Growth in a Cross Section of Countries", *Quarterly Journal of Economics*, Vol. 105, pp. 407-443.

--- and X. Sala-y-Martin (1992), "Convergence", *Journal of Political Economy*, Vol. 100, pp. 223-51.

Baumol, W.J. and E.N. Wolff (forthcoming), *Productivity, Feedbacks, and Long-Term Growth*, MIT Press, Cambridge, MA.

---, S.A.B. Blackman, and E.N. Wolff (1989), *Productivity and American Leadership: The Long View*, MIT Press, Cambridge, MA.

Benhabib, J. and M.M. Spiegel (1992), *Growth Accounting with Physical and Human Capital Accumulation*, Research Report 91-66, C.V. Starr Center for Applied Economics, New York University.

David, P.A. (1991), "Computer and Dynamo: The Modern Productivity Paradox in a Not-Too-Distant Mirror", in: *Technology and Productivity: The Challenge for Economic Policy*, OECD, pp. 315-48.

Gerschenkron, A. (1952), "Economic Backwardness in Historical Perspective", in: B.F. Hoselitz (ed.), *The Progress of Underdeveloped Areas*, University of Chicago Press, Chicago.

Helliwell, J.F. and A. Chung (1991), *Convergence and Growth Linkages between North and South*, mimeo.

Kuznets, S. (1973), *Population, Capital, and Growth: Selected Essays*, W.W. Norton and Company, New York.

Lichtenberg, F. (1992), *Have International Differences in Educational Attainment Levels Narrowed?*, paper presented at the Conference on Historical Perspectives on the International Convergence of Productivity, New York University.

Maddison, A. (1989), *The World Economy in the 20th Century*, OECD, Paris.

Mankiw, F., D. Romer and D. Weil (1992), "A Contribution to the Empirics of Economic Growth", *Quarterly Journal of Economics*, Vol. 107, pp. 407-38.

Reich, R. (1991), *The Work of Nations*, Knopf, New York.

Summers, R. and A. Heston (1988), "A New Set of International Comparisons of Real Product and Prices: Estimates for 130 Countries, 1950-1985", *Review of Income and Wealth*, Series 34, pp. 1-26.

World Bank (1986), *World Development Report 1986*, Oxford University Press, New York.

Part II

Country Experiences of
Economic Growth

Explaining Economic Growth
A. Szirmai, B. van Ark and D. Pilat
© 1993 Elsevier Science Publishers B.V. All rights reserved.

Explaining Japan's Postwar Economic Growth - The Contribution of Growth Accounting

*Dirk Pilat**
University of Groningen

1. Introduction

Except for the United States and the United Kingdom, Japan is probably the country for which the most growth accounting studies have been made. This is not surprising. Japan is the first non-Western country which has caught up in income levels with the industrialised West[1], it is a country which has achieved remarkable high growth rates over a prolonged period of time, and it is a country for which statistical material is relatively abundant. Especially the period between 1950 and 1973 has received a great deal of attention from growth accountants. Studies by Kanamori (1972), Ohkawa and Rosovsky (1973), Denison and Chung (1976) and Nishimizu and Hulten (1978) are but a few of the many studies available. The period after 1973 is covered by fewer studies. Growth in Japan slowed down and returned to levels comparable with Western experience. Most of the studies available for that period (for instance Maddison, 1987; Englander and Mittelstadt, 1988) are of a comparative nature, often with the United States as reference country.

This paper applies growth accounting techniques to identify the main sources of economic growth in Japan in the postwar period. The method used is comparable to that used by Denison and Chung (1976), which is one of the most detailed studies available. The paper first briefly outlines the main features of economic growth in this period. Next, estimates of sources of growth in Japan for the period from 1953 onwards, based on Denison's growth accounting framework, are provided for various sub-periods.

Although growth accounting can help to identify the proximate sources of growth, it is less useful in identifying the ultimate sources of growth (see Maddison, 1987). In the final section some of the links between proximate and ultimate growth causality will be examined for the Japanese case.

---

* I am grateful for comments from Bart van Ark, Angus Maddison, Kees van der Meer, Eddy Szirmai, Kimio Uno and other conference participants. This research is supported by the Dutch Foundation for Scientific Research (NWO).

[1] Disregarding a few oil-producing countries, which are rather special cases.

Table 1 shows some basic trends for the postwar period. The first two sub-periods, 1953-1960 and 1960-1973 are characterised by extremely high growth rates of GDP of 8 to 10 per cent on an annual basis. Labour input, including hours worked, also expanded, causing slightly lower growth rates of labour productivity. In the period 1953-1973 growth accelerated. According to Ohkawa and Rosovsky (1973) this acceleration was part of a longer 'trend acceleration', which started at the beginning of this century.

TABLE 1
Main Indicators of Japanese Growth Experience
(Annual Compound Growth Rates, 1953-1989)

	GDP at Market Prices	GDP per Capita	GDP per Person Engaged	GDP per Hour Worked	Fixed Non-Residential Capital Stock	Fixed Capital Stock per Person Employed
1953-1960	8.25	7.14	6.01	4.80	6.67	4.45
1960-1973	8.83	7.56	7.04	7.44	12.45	10.60
1973-1979	3.35	2.25	2.78	3.23	7.72	7.13
1979-1989	4.18	3.55	3.15	3.20	6.98	5.92
1953-1973	8.63	7.41	6.67	6.51	10.39	8.41
1973-1989	3.87	3.06	3.01	3.21	7.26	6.37
1953-1989	6.49	5.46	5.03	5.03	8.99	7.50

Sources:
GDP 1953-1955 from Ohkawa and Rosovsky (1973), 1955-1989 (new SNA) from EPA, *Report on National Accounts from 1955 to 1989*, Tokyo, 1991; population from Maddison (1991); employment 1953-1954 from Statistics Bureau, Management and Coordination Agency, *Labour Force Survey*, various issues, 1955-1989 from EPA, *op. cit.*; hours worked for non-agricultural industries from Ministry of Labour, *Monthly Labour Survey*, various issues, for agriculture from Statistics Bureau, *op. cit.*; fixed non-residential capital stock 1953-1965 from Ohkawa and Rosovsky (1973), 1965-1989 from EPA, *Gross Capital Stock of Private Enterprises, 1965-1989*, Tokyo, 1991.

The 1973 oil crisis and the following recession caused a slowdown in growth in Japan. Labour input growth stagnated and annual hours worked declined up to 1975. Later in this period, growth picked up again to levels of 5 to 6 per cent annually. The final period, 1979-1989, is characterised by reasonably steady growth of 4 per cent on average. Labour input is still increasing, although hours worked are slowly declining. Over the whole period 1953-1989, GDP at market prices increased almost tenfold, and GDP per person almost sevenfold.

Another characteristic of high growth is the extremely fast growth in fixed capital stock, especially in the second sub-period, 1960-1973. Over the whole period 1953-1989, fixed capital stock increased twenty-two fold. Japan's share of capital formation in total GDP rose extremely fast, from 13.2 per cent in 1953 to 34.7 per cent in 1973, one of the highest percentages in the world. Between 1973 and to 1983 the share of capital formation in GDP declined, to 27.4 per cent in 1983, but since then it has been rising again, to 32.4 per cent in 1989 (EPA, 1991).

Growth has varied quite a lot between sectors. Some subsectors of manufacturing have now reached the edge of world technology and show high productivity levels (Pilat, 1991; Pilat and van Ark, 1991). Other sectors, for instance agriculture and distribution, are lagging in performance and are much further removed from international best practice. The implication of this wide variety in performance is that the following discussion of sources of growth in Japan at the aggregate level masks a broad range of experiences in different sectors of the economy. More detailed growth accounting studies for subsectors (Nishimizu and Hulten, 1978; Uno, 1987) can help to explain the diversity of growth in Japan.

2. Estimating the Sources of Growth, 1953-1989

2.1. Introduction

Japan has an abundance of statistical sources, which provide an opportunity to make detailed estimates of growth, difficult to make in most other countries. The methodology of growth accounting has been spelled out in various studies (Denison and Chung, 1976; Maddison, 1987). Here only a brief introduction is provided.

The growth rate of output is broken down in the contribution of factor inputs (labour, capital and land) and output per unit of input. The contribution of factor inputs is based on the growth rate of each factor input and its corresponding factor share. That part of growth, which can not be explained by the growth of factor inputs, is output per unit of input[2], although it is possible to make further imputations based on other evidence. The methodology used here is mainly based on that used by Denison and Chung (1976). We distinguish two sectors, namely non-residential business and the

---

[2]   Or: "total factor productivity".

whole economy.[3] Output in non-residential business is determined in the
market. It excludes government and non-profit services, and also services
from dwellings. Output in government and non-profit services is produced by
one production factor only, namely labour. Services from dwellings are also
produced by only one production factor, namely residential capital stock. The
estimates for the whole economy include these two sectors.

2.2 Basic Data

Output

Growth accountants use various output concepts in their measurement.[4] I
have chosen to use gross domestic product (GDP) at factor cost as the basic
output concept. This concept is more appropriate for the analysis of the
productive capacity of the economy than net domestic product. Also, the
current Japanese output series are based on GDP. Although these are based on
market prices, information on taxes and subsidies is also supplied. The latest
revisions of the Economic Planning Agency (EPA, 1991b) provide estimates
back to 1955, based on the new system of national accounts (SNA, see UN,
1968). The data for 1953 and 1954 are based on the old SNA and are derived
from Ohkawa and Rosovsky (1973). Output in government and non-profit
services can also be derived from the EPA data, whereas the 1953-1954 data
were derived from Denison and Chung (1976). Output in services from
dwellings was derived from detailed data received from EPA (October 1990)
for the period 1970-1989 and from Denison and Chung for the period 1953-
1969.

Labour Input

The estimates for labour input consist of a number of elements. Employment
for 1955-1989 can be derived from the EPA data. Data for 1953-1954 are
derived from the *Labour Force Survey* (LFS, Statistics Bureau, Management
and Coordination Agency). Hours worked are based on a detailed estimate of
actual hours worked for 1975 (Pilat, 1991), and are linked to series for
monthly hours worked, derived from the *Monthly Labour Survey* (MLS,
Ministry of Labour). These series are made for nine separate sectors and
weighted with employment weights from the LFS. The MLS excludes series

---

[3] This paper mainly describes the estimates for the economy as a whole. The basic
     indices for non-residential business are available from the author.

[4] See the contributions of Denison and Kendrick to this volume for a more elaborate
     discussion.

for agriculture and government, which are derived from the weekly estimates in the LFS. Together these series provide an estimate of total hours worked.

Next, the labour input series are adjusted for changes in the age-sex distribution of the work force. Since earnings in the neoclassical analysis reflect the productivity of each worker, changes in the composition of the workforce, between young and old, and between female and male, affect average productivity. The distribution of employment over age and sex can be derived from the LFS, and detailed weights can be derived from the *Basic Survey of the Wage Structure* (BSWS, Ministry of Labour). This source has been used by other studies for a similar purpose (Denison and Chung, 1976; Imamura, 1990).

An adjustment for changes in the educational level of the workforce is made using the distribution of the labour force over types of education, based on the 1950, 1960, 1970 and 1980 *Population Census* (Statistics Bureau, various issues) and the *1987 Employment Status Survey* (Statistics Bureau). The 1980 and 1987 sources show only four levels of education, but a more detailed breakdown was derived using the procedure outlined in Denison and Chung (1976, Appendix H). The same reasoning applies here. Since persons with higher levels of education receive higher earnings, neoclassical analysis suggests that their productivity is also higher. A change in the composition of the workforce towards higher educational levels will increase the relative productivity of the workforce, and thus have a positive effect on growth. The earnings weights by level of education are derived from Denison and Chung.

Employment in government and non-profit services was derived from EPA data for 1955-1989. 1953 and 1954 are from Denison and Chung's estimates.

Capital Input

The current official capital stock estimates (EPA, 1991a) for Japan are partly based on national wealth surveys and partly on investment series. The latest national wealth survey was made in 1970. Unfortunately, the series do not provide a breakdown by type of asset and are only published as constant price estimates. Furthermore, they cover only fixed private assets and exclude residential capital. The current official estimates only go back as far as 1965. For the period 1953-1965 figures from Ohkawa and Rosovsky (1973) are available. An estimate for inventories was based on annual changes in inventories at constant 1985 prices from EPA (October 1991) and on a benchmark estimate for 1985 of inventories in 1985 prices from the same source. Residential capital stock was derived from Maddison (1991b), who calculated this based on a perpetual inventory method with a 40 year life of assets, rectangular retirement and adjustment for war damage.

No adjustment for vintage effects is made, although the Japanese data show a decline in the average age of fixed capital stock in the period 1955-1970.

TABLE 2
Trends in Output and Input, Japan, 1953-1989, 1953=100

	GDP at Market Prices	Labour Input					Capital Input		Total Factor Input (b)
		Business Employ-Ment	Annual Hours Worked	Age-Sex Compo-sition	Educa-tion	Non-Business Employ-Ment	Non-Residential Capital Stock (a)	Residential Capital Stock	
1953	100.0	100.0	100.0	100.0	100.0	100.0	100.0	100.0	100.0
1954	105.5	100.6	101.5	100.8	100.5	107.6	104.2	103.1	104.0
1955	118.5	104.1	102.6	102.3	101.1	99.5	108.5	106.8	108.3
1956	126.0	106.5	104.7	104.6	101.6	103.9	113.0	111.1	114.5
1957	135.4	110.0	105.6	105.1	102.2	108.5	119.4	115.9	120.4
1958	144.0	111.2	106.5	102.4	102.7	111.9	128.4	121.4	123.7
1959	156.3	112.8	107.3	102.9	103.3	114.5	137.7	127.8	129.1
1960	174.2	115.5	108.4	103.6	103.8	120.4	149.0	135.9	136.6
1961	192.2	117.2	108.5	106.0	104.4	129.7	165.0	146.0	146.0
1962	205.1	119.2	107.5	106.5	104.9	137.5	185.5	157.7	154.9
1963	221.1	120.5	107.1	107.9	105.4	142.2	207.2	171.7	164.3
1964	242.3	122.4	107.5	108.4	106.0	149.5	230.0	189.2	174.4
1965	255.0	124.9	106.5	108.7	106.5	152.9	254.6	211.2	183.8
1966	280.2	128.0	106.7	108.6	107.1	155.9	279.6	236.2	194.0
1967	310.2	131.1	107.2	109.1	107.6	159.3	308.6	264.7	206.2
1968	343.7	133.0	106.7	109.2	108.2	162.8	345.6	299.4	217.9
1969	384.5	134.8	105.7	109.4	108.8	166.7	392.1	340.9	231.0
1970	424.4	137.1	104.8	109.7	109.3	168.2	449.5	388.6	246.0
1971	444.6	137.8	104.3	109.1	110.0	172.5	515.3	440.6	260.3
1972	483.4	138.3	104.1	109.7	110.7	177.7	582.5	499.1	275.0
1973	523.5	141.2	103.2	114.0	111.5	184.9	646.5	567.4	295.9
1974	514.8	140.1	99.8	111.0	112.2	191.6	708.8	636.1	297.0
1975	527.7	139.4	98.1	112.1	112.9	197.1	773.7	700.5	305.3
1976	550.3	140.4	99.5	110.7	113.6	200.7	833.1	768.1	315.7
1977	570.5	142.0	99.8	111.9	114.4	204.2	885.7	838.8	328.3
1978	595.4	143.2	100.2	113.8	115.1	209.8	937.1	911.5	342.1
1979	638.0	144.6	100.5	113.3	115.9	213.0	990.8	986.3	351.6
1980	669.7	145.3	100.3	113.5	116.6	218.4	1052.0	1057.7	361.1
1981	695.4	146.3	100.1	113.5	117.0	223.0	1117.7	1124.6	369.7
1982	716.2	147.4	100.2	114.5	117.3	225.4	1182.9	1190.0	380.6
1983	736.4	149.8	100.3	116.6	117.7	227.5	1247.5	1252.9	395.3
1984	769.8	150.2	101.4	117.5	118.0	228.8	1315.9	1313.3	407.0
1985	809.4	151.3	100.9	118.6	118.3	226.5	1425.2	1374.3	418.6
1986	822.6	152.6	101.0	117.6	118.7	228.1	1543.0	1439.4	428.9
1987	862.5	154.0	101.3	119.9	119.1	229.2	1644.7	1513.4	445.7
1988	917.8	156.6	100.7	119.9	119.4	231.5	1751.8	1598.3	458.0
1989	960.7	160.0	100.0	119.4	119.8	231.1	1864.1	1688.5	470.0

Notes:
(a): Fixed capital stock plus inventories.
(b): Includes land, which is assumed to have remained constant.
Sources: See text.

Land

There is no need to calculate the contribution of land separately, since the Japanese land area has not changed much since 1950.

Total Factor Input

The series of output and factor inputs are presented in table 3. They show an almost tenfold increase in GDP in the period 1953-1989 and a very fast growth of fixed and residential capital stock.

A series of total factor input can be derived as follows. First the growth rate of each factor input is weighted by its factor share in the corresponding year.[5] These weighted growth rates are summed to the growth rate of total factor input and a continuous index can be derived from the annual growth rates. This index is shown in the final column of table 2.

2.3 Factor Shares

GDP at factor cost consists of compensation of employees, fixed capital consumption and operating surplus. The first two components are easily distributed to labour and capital respectively. The third component, operating surplus, poses some difficulties. It must be divided between labour, capital and land income. I have adopted a rather simple approach to the problem. First, land income is assumed to be a fixed 5 per cent of non-residential GDP at factor cost, which is close to the estimate by Denison and Chung. Next, operating surplus is divided between agricultural income and non-agricultural income. For agricultural income it is assumed that 60 per cent of operating surplus consists of labour. This gives a total labour share for agriculture around 60 per cent of GDP at factor cost. This is slightly lower than Denison and Chung's estimate, but higher than that used by Hayami and Yamada (1991). For non-agricultural income it is assumed that labour compensation of self-employed and family workers is the same as that of employees. The labour data are available from previously discussed sources. The remainder of the operating surplus can then be allocated to capital income.

---

[5] For the calculations for the whole economy, five factor shares are available and five main factor input series are calculated, namely those for business labour input, non-business labour input, non-residential capital, residential capital and land. The index for business labour input is based on the multiplication of the four basic indices for employment, hours worked, age-sex composition and education. The index of total non-residential capital is based on the total value in constant yen of fixed capital stock and inventories.

To reduce larger outliers, three-year moving averages of the factor shares were taken as the final shares. For 1953 and 1989, the averages of 1953-1954 and 1988-1989, respectively, were used. The factor shares for benchmark years are presented in table 3.

Total labour income, which includes labour income in government and non-profit institutions declined slightly up to 1969 from 65 to 57 per cent of total GDP at factor cost. From 1969 onwards a fast rise brought its share up to almost 70 per cent. Since 1982 there has been a slight drop again, due to a rising share of residential capital and fixed capital stock in total income. Since land income is an almost constant share of total factor income, the trends in capital income are a mirror image of those of labour income.

TABLE 3

Gross Domestic Product at Factor Cost by Income Share
Whole Economy, 1953-1989, 3-Year Moving Averages

	Labour Income			Capital Income			Land Income
	Business Sector	Govern- ment & Non-profit Insti- tutions	Total	Non- Resi- dential	Resi- dential	Total	
1953	55.95	9.31	65.26	26.78	3.61	30.39	4.35
1960	53.15	7.63	60.78	29.30	5.59	34.89	4.34
1973	54.54	8.58	63.13	26.42	6.20	32.61	4.26
1979	58.19	10.46	68.65	20.29	6.93	27.22	4.13
1989	55.54	10.03	65.57	22.42	7.90	30.32	4.10

Source: See text.

As the output concept used here is gross domestic product, instead of Denison's net domestic product, the income shares show a larger capital share. Since capital stock has grown faster than labour input in the 1953-1989 period, this implies that the contribution of capital to growth can also be expected to be larger than in Denison's framework. The range of capital shares for Japan used in previous studies is wide. A recent survey by Maddison (Maddison, 1987, table 8), shows the lowest estimate of capital income for Japan at 23.7 per cent of total factor income (Denison and Chung, 1976 for 1950-1962) and the highest at 39.2 per cent (Christensen, Cummings and Jorgenson, 1980 for 1952-1973). A large part of these differences is caused by differences in output concepts.

2.4 Output per Unit of Input

By dividing the output series in table 2 by the total factor input series, a series of output per unit of input can be derived. This series still shows fast growth, which implies that a substantial part of output growth remains unexplained. Several methods can be followed to explain a further part. It is possible to impute contributions of other factors to growth, providing that they are not covered by factors already included. Maddison (1987) discusses nine such factors, based on mixed evidence. They are: changing economic structure, catch-up, foreign trade effects, economies of scale, energy effects, effects of natural resource discovery, costs of regulation and crime, labour hoarding and dishoarding and capacity effects. Although not all of these are considered important in the Japanese case, Maddison explains some 40 per cent of Japanese growth in the period 1950-73 with these factors.

Denison and Chung (1976) use a range of additional sources of growth, most of which are similar to Maddison's factors. They are: economies of scale, gains from reallocation of resources, reduction in international trade barriers, effects of weather on farm output and changes in capacity utilisation.

I have chosen to include only some of the factors considered by Maddison and Denison and Chung, since several others made only made neglible contributions to growth.

Improved Resource Allocation

Structural change is regarded as one of the main characteristics of economic growth. It can also make a significant contribution to growth in itself. A movement of production factors from sectors with low to sectors with high productivity levels increases the average productivity level of the economy, and therefore makes a positive contribution to growth.

Denison and Chung distinguish two effects. The first is caused by agricultural workers moving out of agriculture to other sectors of the economy. The second is the reduction of the number of self-employed and family workers outside agriculture. Both agricultural workers and self-employed and family workers outside agriculture are in general regarded as workers with low productivity. Output will increase if they move to jobs with higher productivity, outside agriculture, or from self-employment to employee status.

The first effect is calculated as follows.[6] The share of agricultural income and labour input in total income and labour input are derived from sources

---

[6]   See Denison and Chung (1976), Appendix J, for an extensive discussion.

quoted above. Agricultural labour input is adjusted for hours worked, but no adjustments are made for age-sex effects or education. For each year, two estimates are made. First, an estimate is made of the fall in agricultural income resulting from the actual fall in labour input. The assumption is made that for every per cent that labour input falls, agricultural income falls by half its labour share. Since agricultural labour income is approximately 60 per cent of total agricultural income, this implies that agricultural income falls by approximately 0.3 per cent for each per cent that labour input falls. This assumption is slightly different from that by Denison and Chung, who assumed a 0.25 per cent fall in agricultural income for each per cent fall in labour input. Both percentages are below the actual labour share, implying an underutilisation of labour in the agricultural sector. If labour was fully utilised, each percentage point fall in labour input would result in a 0.6 per cent fall in output.

Second, an estimate is made of the rise in non-agricultural output resulting from the inflow of former agricultural workers. Here no underutilisation is assumed, implying that a one per cent increase of labour input results in an increase of non-agricultural output by the full non-agricultural labour share. The two estimates are added to give a growth rate of the total effect of improved resource allocation from agricultural labour input. From the growth rates a continuous index can be derived.

The second effect of improved resource allocation is based on the declining share of self-employed and family workers in the non-agricultural sector. It is assumed that one employed person in the non-agricultural sector produces the same output as two self-employed persons and family workers. This is again slightly different from Denison and Chung's assumption, who suggested that each employee can produce the same output as four self-employed persons and family workers. I found this assumption not suitable for the whole period, since resource allocation improved substantially especially in the period since 1973 and underutilisation was much less pronounced than in the previous period. For each year, the percentage drop in the share of self-employed and family workers is multiplied by the saving in labour input (50 per cent). This is multiplied by the share of labour in the non-agricultural sector to arrive at an estimate of the increase in output for each year. Finally, a continuous index can be derived from the annual growth rates.

Effect of Weather on Farming

This is a minor factor, which mainly influenced Japanese growth in 1955. Adjustments can be made by calculating a five-year moving average of agricultural output and substituting that for the original series. The difference between the two output indices can be regarded as the effect of weather on agricultural output.

Table 4
Output per Unit of Input
Whole Economy, 1953=100

	Output per Unit of Input	Improved Allocation from Agricultural	from Self-Employed	Effect of Weather	Economies of Scale on Agricultural Output	Advances in Knowledge & n.e.c.
1953	100.0	100.0	100.0	100.0	100.0	100.0
1954	101.5	100.5	99.9	100.3	100.2	100.6
1955	109.3	100.6	100.0	102.8	100.4	105.2
1956	109.7	101.6	100.2	101.2	100.7	105.7
1957	112.2	102.2	100.4	100.7	100.9	107.7
1958	116.5	103.0	100.6	100.8	101.0	110.5
1959	121.4	103.9	100.6	101.3	101.3	113.2
1960	128.0	104.3	100.8	101.2	101.5	118.6
1961	132.4	104.7	101.0	101.4	101.9	121.4
1962	133.7	105.2	101.1	101.2	102.2	121.6
1963	136.2	106.0	101.1	100.8	102.4	123.2
1964	140.8	106.4	101.0	101.0	102.7	126.2
1965	140.9	106.9	101.2	100.9	103.0	125.3
1966	146.9	107.5	101.3	101.2	103.3	129.1
1967	153.1	107.8	101.2	101.2	103.6	133.8
1968	160.8	108.4	101.2	101.1	103.9	139.7
1969	169.8	108.7	101.2	101.3	104.2	146.4
1970	176.0	109.2	101.3	100.8	104.5	151.1
1971	174.3	109.8	101.5	100.5	104.8	148.6
1972	179.4	110.2	101.5	101.1	105.0	151.0
1973	180.6	110.7	101.5	101.3	105.4	150.4
1974	177.0	110.8	101.7	101.1	105.4	147.5
1975	176.6	110.9	101.7	101.1	105.6	146.7
1976	178.2	111.1	101.7	101.0	105.7	147.6
1977	177.6	111.3	101.7	100.9	105.9	146.7
1978	177.9	111.4	101.5	101.0	106.2	146.7
1979	185.5	111.8	101.5	101.1	106.3	152.1
1980	189.6	112.2	101.6	100.9	106.4	154.8
1981	192.3	112.4	101.8	100.9	106.6	156.3
1982	192.4	112.5	101.9	101.0	106.7	155.6
1983	190.5	112.7	102.1	101.0	106.9	153.2
1984	193.4	112.9	102.3	101.1	107.1	154.6
1985	197.8	113.0	102.6	101.1	107.2	157.4
1986	196.2	113.2	102.7	101.0	107.4	155.8
1987	197.9	113.3	102.6	101.1	107.6	156.7
1988	205.0	113.5	102.6	101.0	107.7	161.8
1989	209.1	113.6	102.8	101.1	107.8	164.3

Source: See text.

2.5 Results

Table 5 shows the growth estimates for the whole economy, by sub-period, and table 6 shows the share of each growth component in total growth. The growth rates shown in table 6 cannot be derived directly from table 2 and 4, since a number of compositional effects have to be accounted for. First, total growth is distributed between total factor input

TABLE 5
Growth of GDP and Contribution of Sources of Growth
Whole Economy, 1953-1989, by sub-period

	1953-1960	1960-1973	1973-1979	1979-1989	1953-1973	1973-1989	1953-1989
GDP Growth Rate	8.25	8.83	3.35	4.18	8.63	3.87	6.49
Contribution to Growth:							
Factor Inputs	4.59	6.10	2.90	2.96	5.57	2.94	4.39
Business Labour Input	2.52	1.34	0.36	1.07	1.75	0.80	1.32
- Employment	1.22	0.84	0.25	0.59	0.97	0.46	0.74
- Hours Worked	0.68	-0.20	-0.23	-0.03	0.11	-0.11	0.01
- Age-Sex Composition	0.30	0.40	-0.04	0.31	0.37	0.18	0.28
- Education	0.32	0.29	0.38	0.19	0.30	0.26	0.29
Non-Business Labour Input	0.24	0.27	0.24	0.09	0.26	0.14	0.21
Non-Residential Capital Input	1.62	3.77	1.68	1.40	3.01	1.50	2.33
- Fixed Non-Residential Private Capital	1.45	3.26	1.50	1.33	2.62	1.39	2.07
- Private Inventories	0.17	0.50	0.18	0.07	0.39	0.11	0.26
Residential Capital Input	0.21	0.73	0.62	0.41	0.55	0.49	0.52
Land	0.00	0.00	0.00	0.00	0.00	0.00	0.00
Output per Unit of Input	3.66	2.73	0.45	1.22	3.06	0.93	2.10
Improved Resource Allocation	0.73	0.53	0.16	0.29	0.60	0.24	0.44
from Agricultural Inputs	0.61	0.48	0.16	0.16	0.53	0.16	0.36
from Non-Agricultural Self-Employed	0.11	0.06	-0.00	0.13	0.08	0.08	0.08
Effect of Weather on Farming	0.18	0.01	-0.04	-0.00	0.07	-0.02	0.03
Economies of Scale	0.22	0.30	0.14	0.14	0.27	0.14	0.21
Advances in knowledge & n.e.c.	2.54	1.89	0.18	0.78	2.12	0.56	1.42

Source: See text.

TABLE 6
Explanatory Power of Sources of Growth, in Percentages
Whole Economy, 1953-1989, by sub-period

	1953-1960	1960-1973	1973-1979	1979-1989	1953-1973	1973-1989	1953-1989
GDP Growth Rate	100.0	100.0	100.0	100.0	100.0	100.0	100.0
Factor Inputs	55.6	69.1	86.6	70.9	64.6	76.0	67.6
Business Labour Input	30.5	15.1	10.9	25.5	20.3	20.7	20.4
- Employment	14.8	9.5	7.4	14.2	11.3	12.0	11.5
- Hours Worked	8.2	-2.3	-6.9	-0.7	1.2	-2.7	0.2
- Age-Sex Composition	3.7	4.6	-1.1	7.4	4.3	4.7	4.4
- Education	3.8	3.3	11.4	4.6	3.5	6.8	4.4
Non-Business Labour Input	2.9	3.1	7.0	2.1	3.0	3.7	3.2
Non-Residential Capital Input	19.6	42.6	50.2	33.4	34.9	38.9	36.0
- Fixed Non-Residential Private Capital	17.5	36.9	44.8	31.7	30.4	36.0	31.9
- Private Inventories	2.1	5.7	5.4	1.7	4.5	2.9	4.1
Residential Capital Input	2.5	8.2	18.5	9.8	6.3	12.7	8.0
Land	0.0	0.0	0.0	0.0	0.0	0.0	0.0
Output per Unit of Input	44.4	30.9	13.4	29.1	35.4	24.0	32.4
Improved Resource Allocation	8.8	6.0	4.8	7.0	7.0	6.2	6.8
from Agricultural Inputs	7.4	5.4	4.8	3.8	6.1	4.1	5.6
from Non-Agricultural Self-Employed	1.3	0.6	-0.0	3.1	0.9	2.1	1.2
Effect of Weather on Farming	2.1	0.1	-1.1	-0.1	0.8	-0.4	0.5
Economies of Scale	2.7	3.4	4.2	3.5	3.1	3.7	3.3
Advances in knowledge & n.e.c.	30.8	21.4	5.5	18.8	24.5	14.4	21.8

Source: Derived from table 5.

and output per unit of input, based on the growth rates of both indices. The growth rate of total factor input is then distributed between the five main factor inputs, based on their weighted growth rates. The growth rate of business labour input is divided into its four components based on the growth rate of each component. The growth rate of non-residential capital input is distributed between fixed capital and inventories based on their value shares. Finally, output per unit of input is distributed over its components based on the growth rate of each component.

In all four sub-periods, more than 50 per cent of growth can be explained from increased factor inputs. In the period 1953-1960, business labour input is the most important contributor to growth, with positive contributions from all four components. In this period hours worked increased considerably, giving a strong positive effect on growth. Capital input, especially fixed capital, is also an important contributor in this subperiod. Improved resource allocation contributed 0.7 per cent to the overall growth rate. This is the only period in which a significant contribution of weather to output growth can be identified. Also, the contribution of advances in knowledge and n.e.c. is very high, with a share of more than 30 per cent of total growth.

The second sub-period, 1960-1973, is dominated by the increase in capital input, especially fixed non-residential capital stock. As table 1 shows, fixed capital stock increased with an annual growth rate of almost 12.5 per cent in this period. Residential capital also turned into a significant source of growth. The contribution of hours worked turned negative in this period and has since had a negative contribution to growth. The other labour components where all positive, with important contributions from education and age-sex effects. The effect of improved resource allocation diminished somewhat, reflecting the diminished share of agriculture in the Japanese economy. This dropped from 16 per cent to 5 per cent of total GDP from 1953 to 1973, and from 35.5 to 10.8 per cent of total hours worked in the same period. The effect of advances in knowledge and n.e.c. dropped as well, but remained an extremely important source of growth.

After 1973, growth slowed down. In the period 1973-1979, almost 90 per cent of growth can be explained from increased factor inputs. The growth of total capital input explained almost 70 per cent of total growth. The effect of improved education was considerable and the contribution of improved resource allocation remained significant. The contribution of advances in knowledge and n.e.c. was almost negligible.

In the period 1979-1989, more than 70 per cent of growth can be explained from increased factor inputs. However, the share of advances in knowledge and n.e.c. picked up considerably and explained more than 18 per cent of growth.

For the whole period 1953-1989, the most important single factor in growth is fixed non-residential capital, explaining 36 per cent of growth. The next factor in importance are advances in knowledge and n.e.c., explaining almost 22 per cent of growth. Important other factors are the growth of business employment (11.5 per cent), residential capital stock (8 per cent) and improved resource allocation (6.8 per cent).

Contributions of approximately 4 per cent of total growth each are made by the changing age-sex composition of the labour force, improved education and inventories. Smaller effects are those for employment growth in government and non-profit organisations, and for economies of scale, explaining only 3 per cent of growth each, and the effect of weather on farm output, which explains only 0.5 per cent of growth. The effect of hours worked on growth for the period as a whole is almost zero.

It is difficult to make precise comparisons between these estimates and those of earlier studies. A great variety of output and input concepts is used, many different time-periods have been analysed and various data-sources are utilised. Work by Nishimizu and Hulten (1978) and Jorgenson and Nishimizu (1978) for instance, is difficult to compare with the present study, since these studies use gross output, and therefore include intermediate input as a source of growth.

TABLE 7

Results of Some Previous Studies on Japan's Postwar Economic Growth
Output Growth and Contribution to Output Growth, in percentages

	(1) 1955 -68	(2) 1953 -71	(3) 1950 -73	(4) 1960 -73	(5) 1953 -73	(6) 1973 -84	(7) 1973 -89
Growth Rate of Output	10.10	8.77	9.37	10.90	8.63	3.78	3.87
Contribution to Growth of:							
Total Factor Input	4.03	3.95	4.68	6.40	5.57	3.36	2.94
Labour Input	1.31	1.85	1.61	1.64	1.91	0.81	0.94
Capital Input	2.72	2.10	3.07	4.78	3.56	2.55	1.99
Output per Unit of Input	6.10	4.82	4.69	4.50	3.06	0.42	0.93

Sources:
Col. (1) from Kanamori (1972), table 3; Col. (2) from Denison and Chung (1976), table 4.6; Col. (3) and (6) from Maddison (1987), table 20; Col. (4) from Christensen, et.al. (1980), table 11.11; Col. (5) and (7) from present study, table 5.

Some more or less comparable studies are shown in table 7. Kanamori (1972) works with GNP as his output concept. His study stresses output per unit of input as the main source of growth. He uses rather high labour shares of more than 70 per cent of total income, explaining the low contribution of capital in his study. Denison and Chung's study is probably the most comparable to the present study, but the use of national income as output concept instead of the gross domestic product used here generates a rather different set of estimates. An other difference is caused by the procedures for the estimation of the contributions of economies of scale and improved resource allocation.

Maddison's results are roughly comparable to mine, although my factor input series explain a larger share of growth than his. Christensen et al. also show roughly comparable results, partly because of their very high capital share in total output.

Basically, most studies show capital input and output per unit of input, sometimes broken down in further components, as the main explanatory factors of Japanese economic growth. Some studies identify output per unit of input with technical change (Jorgenson, 1988), but this seems a somewhat rough catch-all concept. Within the present definition of output per unit of input, several studies also stress the importance of structural change (or improved resource allocation). In addition, labour input growth, both quantitative and qualitative is usually identified as an important, but not dominant source of growth.

3. Explaining Growth from the Growth Accounting Results

Growth accounting can identify proximate causes of growth, but gives less information about ultimate growth causality.[7] Ultimate causes of growth are the basic underlying forces of the economy, such as culture, demography, history, institutions, international circumstances, economic policy, etcetera. It is important to identify the links between proximate and ultimate causes, to assess whether growth was caused by a set of unusual and unique circumstances, or was due to manmade influences and policy. Such links do not have to be direct. They may involve a complicated chain of action and reaction. The aim of this section is to discuss some of the links between proximate causes of economic growth, discussed in the previous section, and the underlying ultimate causes. The space provided here is too limited to make a full analysis, but the most important links are briefly discussed.

The first and probably most important explanatory factor for Japan's high rate of economic growth in the postwar period was her relative economic backwardness.[8] This allowed her to benefit from technologies and ideas developed in other, more advanced, countries. The positive effect of this factor in the postwar period was linked to the fact that Japan had already experienced a considerable period of high growth before World War II. In that time, the "social capability" (Abramovitz, 1989) for growth had been

---

[7] See Maddison (1987, 1988) for a discussion of proximate and ultimate growth causality.

[8] See Gerschenkron (1962); Baumol, Blackman and Wolff (1989) and Abramovitz (1989) for extensive discussions of this factor.

formed. Japan's workforce and management had learned to adapt and
assimilate foreign technology, her institutions had adapted to new ideas and
the need for higher educational requirements, and her government had learned
to adopt effective stimulating policies (Johnson, 1982). Before World War II
most of the basic framework for Japan's postwar economic miracle was put in
place. This economic backwardness was further enhanced by the effects of
World War II. The lack of communication between Japan and other
industrialised countries, and the spurt in technical progress made in the United
States during the war, increased the gap between Japan and other
industrialised countries.[9]

Although the proximate causes of growth do not include this factor
directly[10], its effect can be seen in at least two growth components. First,
Japan's backwardness opened large opportunities for improved resource
allocation and structural change. Second, the technology gap between Japan
and the more advanced countries contributed to rapid advances in knowledge.

The next factor in importance has been the fast growth of the capital stock
in Japan. Investment in new capital stock is the means to expand the
productive capacity of the economy, and the way by which new technology
can enter the production process. As such it is one of the driving forces in
economic growth.

Capital formation is the result of demand and supply-side influences. The
demand for capital from Japanese companies in the post-war period has been
large. They operated in a highly favourable environment, especially in the
period of high growth, 1953-1973. The world economy was booming, the
domestic market grew fast and the investment climate was stable. Even
following the slowdown after 1973, the domestic climate remained favourable.
Japanese consumers are highly fashionable and buy new, and expensive
products, much sooner after their introduction than most Western consumers.
Also, the life-time of most consumer durables is rather short in Japan. This
leads to a reasonable rate of return even for risky investments in new
products.

Access to capital has been easy, with low interest rates and easy borrowing
from financial institutions (Minami, 1986). Partly this was the result of the
close ties between enterprises and financial institutions. Partly, it was the
'result of government policy designed to keep interest rates low. Recently, the

---

[9]   During the war a large part of Japan's productive capacity was destroyed. This
      resulted in a great gap between real output and potential output. In the
      reconstruction period after the war this "backlog" relative to potential contributed
      to very high growth rates. However, this reconstruction effect must be
      distinguished from the effect of economic backwardness in general.

[10] Unlike Maddison (1987).

stock market has also provided a means for enterprises to acquire cheap capital (Ito, 1992). In addition, recent work by Ando and Auerbach (1988, 1990) found considerable differences between the cost of capital in Japan and the United States. They related this to the much higher savings rate in Japan, compared with the United States, and imperfections in the flow of capital between the two countries.

A great number of surveys have been made by economists trying to explain the high rate of savings in Japan, although most of these deal with personal savings. A survey by Shinohara (1970) pointed to the following factors. First, due to insufficient insurance and government funding, Japanese have to save more for old-age, sickness and schooling, than in most other industrialised countries. Second, the high price of housing forces Japanese to reserve considerable funds for the possible procurement of their own home. Thirdly, a large part is saved out of bonuses, which constitute a large share of annual salaries. Fourthly, the large numbers of self-employed in Japan save a greater share of their income than employees. Fifthly, the Japanese traditional consumption pattern has only slowly adjusted to their high and fast growing income. Horioka (1990) also surveys a large number of factors, and distinguishes between cultural, demographic and socioeconomic, institutional, economic and government induced factors. He finds that the age structure of the population, the bonus system and the high rate of growth explain a substantial part of the large gap between Japanese saving rates and those of other industrialised countries. Recently Horioka (1991) suggested the life-time savings theory as the most important explanatory factor for Japan's high savings rate. Especially the small share of elderly and the low dependency ratio of Japan in the early postwar period, contributed to the high savings rate. With the current aging of the Japanese population, he expects a decline in the Japanese savings rate.

Household savings in Japan are channeled to postal savings or bank deposits.[11] Postal savings are directly managed by government, whereas the use of private savings can also be influenced by the Japanese government. The saving-investment mechanism is therefore an important method for the Japanese government to influence access to capital and direct investment flows to targeted industries.

The third factor in importance has been the growth in the labour force. A number of factors have been at work here. First, population growth has been more than 1 per cent annually since 1953. On the other hand, with the rise in education, a large number of persons of working age stayed outside employment for a considerable period. Together with the declining share of females, partly caused by the reduced share of agriculture, this caused a lower

---

[11] See Uno (1987) for a discussion of the saving-investment mechanism.

participation rate, dropping from 70 per cent in 1953 to 62.8 per cent in 1989.

Since 1953, the average age of the Japanese workforce has increased, to an average of 41.8 years in 1989. With the declining share of female workers, this explains the rising age-sex contribution to labour input.

In the analysis of proximate causes of growth, increased education only takes a modest position. This is partly due to the fact that a number of educational improvements were already made before and during the war (Lincoln, 1988). In addition, the increase in the average standard of education of the workforce may underestimate the increased training of Japanese workers in their companies. In 1984, 82.5 per cent of all Japanese enterprises provided training to their employees, up from 76.7 per cent in 1976 (Ishikawa, 1991). From 1973 to 1983, the annual average increase of expenses for education and training in firms was almost 12 per cent (Ishikawa, 1991).

Where does this leave government policy, often regarded as the main actor in Japan's high growth period?[12] Especially the role of the Ministry of International Trade and Industry has received a great deal of attention. MITI's role has especially been strong in the shaping and directing of industrial policy, often in close consultation with private enterprise. The purposes of industrial policy have changed over time (Komiya, Okuno and Suzumura, 1988). In the period directly following the war its purpose was reconstruction and the achievement of economic independence. In later years industrial policy stressed heavy industry. In recent years, MITI has become less interventionist and its policy focus has gradually changed to structural adjustment and technology policy (see also Okimoto, 1989). Apart from MITI, the Ministry of Finance and the Bank of Japan have also played an important role, for instance in the targeting of investment funds.

There is therefore no denying that government policy has been extremely important. Its role has been to maintain a stable and favourable investment climate, to stimulate exports and make industries more competitive in the world market, to keep interest rates and inflation low, and to stimulate capital formation and technological improvements. All these factors have greatly influenced Japan's growth in the postwar period, and it is extremely difficult to guess what Japan's growth rate would have been if government policy would have been much less active. It is so much intertwined with all the other components of the postwar 'miracle', that its effect on its own is difficult to assess.

A similar reasoning can be applied to the cultural background of Japan's

---

[12] For instance, Johnson (1982).

success.[13] The Confucian focus on learning and education has helped in the adoptation and diffusion of technology, although the Confucian method of learning with its stress on discipline and repetition is now often regarded as inadequate for a country on the edge of world technology. In addition, the group-oriented Japanese culture has helped to maintain stable labour relations.

The slowdown in growth after 1973 can be traced to a number of the previously discussed sources (see also Lincoln, 1988). The gap between Japan and the world productivity leader, the United States, had declined considerably, leaving less opportunities for adaptation of foreign technology and forcing increased expenditure on domestic research and development. Furthermore, the share of the agricultural sector had diminished considerably, leaving less opportunities for improved resource allocation. The labour surplus situation of the 1950s and 1960s was also degrading into one of occasional shortages. The growth of population was slowing down and Japan's population started aging.

Other important changes after 1973 were the deteriorated international environment, expressed in high inflation, exchange-rate uncertainty, high energy prices and reduced international demand. These affected the high rate of capital formation in Japan negatively, leading to a decline of the rate of capital formation, which lasted up to 1983.

This article has shown that the success of the post-war Japanese economy can be explained in a growth accounting framework. In addition, some links can be found between the proximate causes of growth and more ultimate causality.

References

Abramovitz, M. (1989), *Thinking About Growth*, Cambridge University Press, Cambridge.

Ando, A., and A.J. Auerbach (1988), "The Cost of Capital in the United States and Japan: A Comparison", *Journal of the Japanese and International Economies*, Vol. 2, pp. 134-158.

Ando, A., and A.J. Auerbach (1990), "The Cost of Capital in Japan: Recent Evidence and Further Results", *Journal of the Japanese and International Economies*, Vol. 4, pp. 323-350.

Baumol, W.J., S.A. Batey Blackman and E.N. Wolff (1989), *Productivity and American Leadership: The Long View*, MIT Press, Cambridge.

---

[13] See Dore (1987) for an analysis of the effect of Confucianism on Japanese economic growth.

Christensen, L.R., D. Cummings and D.W. Jorgenson (1980), "Economic Growth, 1947-1973: An International Comparison", in: J.W. Kendrick and B.N. Vaccara (eds.), *New Developments in Productivity Measurement and Analysis*, University of Chicago Press, Chicago, pp. 595-691.

Denison, E.F., and W.K. Chung (1976), *How Japan's Economy Grew so Fast*, The Brookings Institution, Washington D.C.

Dore, R.P. (1987), *Taking Japan Seriously - A Confucian Perspective on Leading Economic Issues*, Athlone Press, London.

Englander, A.S. and A. Mittelstadt (1988), "Total Factor Productivity: Macro-economic and Structural Aspects of the Slowdown", *OECD Economic Studies*, Vol. 10, 8-56, OECD, Paris.

Gerschenkron, A. (1962), *Economic Backwardness in Historical Perspective*, Harvard University Press, Cambridge.

Griliches, Z. and V. Ringstad (1971), *Economies of Scale and the Form of the Production Function*, North Holland, Amsterdam.

Hayami, Y., S. Yamada, et.al. (1991), *The Agricultural Development of Japan - A Century's Perspective*, University of Tokyo Press, Tokyo.

Horioka, C.Y. (1990), "Why is Japan's Household Saving Rate so High? A Literature Survey", *Journal of the Japanese and International Economies*, Vol. 4, No. 1, pp. 49-92.

--- (1991), "The Determinants of Japan's Saving Rate: The Impact of the Age Structure of the Population and Other Factors", *The Economic Studies Quarterly*, Vol. 42, No. 3, pp. 237-253, September.

Hulten, C.R. (ed.) (1990), *Productivity Growth in Japan and the United States*, University of Chicago Press, Chicago.

Imamura, H. (1990), "Compositional Change of Heterogeneous Labor Input and Economic Growth in Japan", in: C.R. Hulten (ed.), *Productivity Growth in Japan and the United States*, University of Chicago Press, Chicago, pp. 349-376.

Ishikawa, T. (1991), "Vocational Training", *Japanese Industrial Relations Series No. 7*, The Japan Institute of Labour, Tokyo.

Ito, T. (1992), *The Japanese Economy*, MIT Press, Cambridge.

Johnson, C. (1982), *MITI and the Japanese Miracle*, Stanford University Press.

Jorgenson, D.W. (1988), "Productivity and Economic Growth in Japan and the United States", *American Economic Review*, Vol. 78, May, pp. 217-222.

--- and N. Nishimizu (1978), "US and Japanese Economic Growth, 1952-1974: An International Comparison", *Economic Journal*, Vol. 88, December, pp. 707-726.

Kanamori, H. (1972), "What Accounts for Japan's High Rate of Economic Growth", *Review of Income and Wealth*, Vol. 18, June, pp. 155-171.

Komiya, R., M. Okuno and K. Suzumura (eds.) (1988), *Industrial Policy of Japan*, Academic Press, Tokyo.

Lincoln, E.J. (1988), *Japan - Facing Economic Maturity*, The Brookings Institution, Washington D.C.

Maddison, A. (1987), "Growth and Slowdown in Advanced Capitalist Economies: Techniques of Quantitative Assessment", *Journal of Economic Literature*, Vol. 25, June, pp. 649-698.

--- (1988), "Ultimate and Proximate Growth Causality: A Critique of Mancur Olson on the Rise and Decline of Nations", *Scandinavian Economic History Review*, Vol. 36, No. 2, pp. 25-29.

--- (1991a), *Dynamic Forces in Capitalist Development*, Oxford University Press, Oxford.

--- (1991b), "Standardised Estimates of Fixed Investment and Capital Stock at Constant Prices: A Long Term Survey for 6 Countries", Groningen, mimeographed.

Minami, R. (1986), *The Economic Development of Japan - A Quantitative Study*, Macmillan Press, London.

Nishimizu, M., and C.R. Hulten (1978), "The Sources of Japanese Economic Growth, 1955-1971", *The Review of Economics and Statistics*, Vol. 60, pp. 351-361.

Ohkawa, K., and H. Rosovsky (1973), *Japanese Economic Growth*, Stanford University Press, Stanford.

Okimoto, D.I. (1989), *Between MITI and the Market: Japanese Industrial Policy for High Technology*, Stanford University Press, Stanford.

Pilat, D. (1991), "Levels of Real Output and Labour Productivity by Industry of Origin, A Comparison of Japan and the United States, 1975 and 1970-1987", *Research Memorandum, No. 408*, Institute of Economic Research, Groningen.

--- and B. van Ark (1991), "Productivity Leadership in Manufacturing, Germany, Japan and the United States, 1973-1989", *Research Memorandum, No. 447*, Institute of Economic Research, Groningen.

Pratten, C. (1988), "A Survey of the Economies of Scale", *Economic Papers*, No. 67, EEC, Brussels.

Shinohara, M. (1970), *Structural Changes in Japan's Economic Development*, Kinokuniya, Tokyo, 1970.

Syrquin, M. (1984), "Resource Reallocation and Productivity Growth", in: M. Syrquin, L. Taylor and L.E. Westphal (eds.), *Economic Structure and Performance - Essays in Honor of Hollis B. Chenery*, Academic Press Inc., Orlando.

Uno, K. (1987), *Japanese Industrial Performance*, North Holland, Amsterdam.

Statistical Sources:

Bureau of Economic Analysis (1986), *The National Income and Product Accounts of the United States, 1929-1982*, Washington D.C.

--- (various issues), *Survey of Current Business*, Washington D.C.

Economic Planning Agency (1990), "Output, Input and Value Added in Constant Prices by Industry, 1970-1988", print-out, Tokyo, October 20th.

Economic Planning Agency (1991a), *Gross Capital Stock of Private Enterprises, 1965-1989*, Tokyo, March.

--- (1991b), *Report on National Accounts from 1955 to 1989*, Tokyo, October.

Ministry of Labour (various issues), *Basic Survey of the Wage Structure*, Tokyo.

--- (various issues), *Monthly Labour Survey*, Tokyo

Statistics Bureau, Management and Coordination Agency (various issues), *Labour Force Survey*, Tokyo.

---, Management and Coordination Agency (various issues), *Population Census of Japan*, Tokyo.

--- (various issues), *Employment Status Survey*, Tokyo.

Explaining Economic Growth
A. Szirmai, B. van Ark and D. Pilat
© 1993 Elsevier Science Publishers B.V. All rights reserved.

Economic Growth in Indonesia, 500-1990

Peter Boomgaard
KITLV, Leiden

1. Introduction

This article is not an attempt to estimate per capita GDP growth over a period of 1500 years. No matter how interesting such an estimate might be thought to be, we simply do not have the data for such an exercise. I could have given such estimates for Java after 1815 and for the so-called Outer Islands (all parts of Indonesia outside Java) after 1930. However, in view of the fact that already so many scholars have recently published their estimates, or data upon which per capita GDP estimates could be based, I have refrained here from doing so.[1]

Instead, I have used the space alotted to me for two related though analytically distinct topics. In the first place I try to identify, for the period under consideration, phases of growth, stagnation, and decline. Secondly, I attempt to trace the factors that may have influenced the overall growth performance and its various phases. These topics will be dealt with in a comparative perspective.

Beforehand, I should point out that our knowledge of economic growth in Indonesia is very unevenly distributed as to time and place. For Java, data on the 5th through 8th centuries are scarce. For the period 800-1350, source material is relatively abundant, though far from easy to interpret. Between 1350 and 1600, information of this kind is more rare. The period 1600-1800 is again relatively well endowed, though not as abundantly as the 19th and 20th centuries.[2] Data on the pre-1900 Outer Islands are few and far between, with the exception of data on localities with a strong Dutch presence, such as Ambon. Statements on economic development of the Outer Islands prior to 1900, therefore, are mostly rather speculative and hypothetical.

Prior to 1800 or even 1900, it is often hardly possible to distinguish between extensive growth (growth of population at constant real per capita income) and intensive growth (growing real income per capita).

---

[1] See e.g. Boomgaard (1989a); Boomgaard and Gooszen (1991); Boomgaard and van Zanden (1990); Booth (1988); Laanen (1989); Maddison (1989).

[2] Statistical data on 20th-century Java are, as a rule, more reliable than those of the 19th century. There is a serious gap, however, between 1940 and 1960.

Before discussing phases of economic development, I will give a short sketch of Indonesia in the 5th century.

2. Indonesia in the 5th century

Our knowledge of anything Indonesian prior to the 5th century AD is so patchy that I have chosen the year 500 as my base-line. This is a rough indication of the period we are dealing with, not an exact reference to a specific occurrence. Neither am I implying that Indonesian economic development, however defined, started from scratch around 500. When we get our first bits of more revealing information dating from the 5th century, we are already confronted with states, kings, a script, the construction of water-works, and foreign commerce, and it must be assumed that the building up of these properties had taken time.

Most of our early information on the Indonesian economy is derived from non-Indonesian sources on maritime trade. Thus we know that a number of Asian products reached the Roman Empire, of which at least one (cloves) must have come from Indonesia because it did not grow anywhere else. White sandal-wood, nutmeg and mace came almost certainly from Indonesia.[3] Other products, such as cinnamon, various gum-resins (benzoin, camphor), and eagle-wood might have been shipped from Indonesia, but could also have arrived from other places (Miller, 1969, pp. 34-64; Warmington, 1974, pp. 199-216).

Prior to the 5th century, there was also some trade between Indonesia on the one hand, and India, mainland Southeast Asia and China on the other, although in the latter case probably via Funan (mainland Southeast Asia). The distribution of imported artifacts (Southern Sumatra, Java, and places around the Banda Sea) suggests that this international trade may have been connected to the spice-trade of the Moluccas, perhaps carried out by Javanese and Sumatran skippers.[4]

In the 5th century we encounter the oldest inscriptions in the archipelago, namely in East Kalimantan (Borneo) and in West Java. They are written in Sanskrit, in Pallava script, bearing testimony of Hindu influence from India, and referring to 'kingdoms' which were equally copied after Indian models.

---

[3]   It is possible that before 500 AD 'real' (white) sandal-wood was also an exclusively Indonesian product (Jones, 1984, p. 28). 'True' nutmeg and mace (*Myristica fragrans*) were also exclusively Indonesian, but it is possible that the Romans obtained, partly or largely, products that were somewhat similar to the real thing, namely the fruit of *M. malabarica*, from India (Miller, 1969, pp. 58-60).

[4]   Bellwood (1985), pp. 280-289; Christie (1991a), p. 25; Wolters (1967), pp. 49-85.

Chinese sources dating from the same period mention 'kingdoms' in West Java and Southeastern Sumatra.[5]

This information, taken together, points in the direction of relatively high levels of cultural, political and economic sophistication, at least locally. The more the pity, therefore, that we know next to nothing about fifth-century Indonesian agriculture. We may assume that some sort of permanent agriculture was practised in the immediate vicinity of the ports-of-trade which formed the nuclei of the 'kingdoms' mentioned. We may also assume that in Java rice cultivation was important, given the fact that it figures prominently in epigraphical sources from the 8th century onward. One gets the impression from the early inscriptions that wet rice cultivation on *sawah* (bunded fields, constructed to hold water) was one of the mainstays of Java's economy, and it is hardly likely that this was a novel phenomenon in the 8th century.[6] Nevertheless, the whole issue is rather problematic since no rice remains from the Indonesian archipelago predating the year 500 have been found as yet (Bellwood, 1985, p. 234). Yet, it seems safe to assume that in fifth-century Java rice was important, though not necessarily wet rice (as opposed to dry rice under permanent or shifting cultivation) and not necessarily on irrigated (as opposed to rain-fed) *sawah*.

3. 500-1500

Between the 5th and 10th century, both Sumatra and Java witnessed periods of economic expansion. In the 7th century the Sumatran state Śrivijaya and the Javanese state Ho-ling seem to have been equally strong as competitors for international commerce, but during the first half of the 8th century Śrivijaya was the stronger mercantile state. However, the late 8th and the 9th centuries witnessed a period of Javanese ascendancy. Śrivijaya did not recover until the tenth century (Christie, 1982, pp. 29-33).

Measured by their remaining monuments, however, Java must have had a much higher level of economic development and population density than Sumatra. The famous Borobudur and the impressive Prambanan complex, dating from the 8th and 9th century respectively, are products of Central Javanese states, contrasting sharply with the handful of statues and inscriptions found in the area where Śrivijaya's capitals must have been located.

In the 10th century, Java's political centre of gravity shifted from Central to East Java, probably owing to a series of disasters in Central Java and due

---

[5] Hall (1985), pp. 39-41; Naerssen (1977), pp. 18-26; Wolters (1967), pp. 159-228.

[6] Boomgaard (1989b), pp. 317-319; Christie in press (a); Jones (1984), p. 61 and p. 83; Setten (1979), pp. 1-9.

to the increased importance of international trade to Javanese rulers, which made the location of the *kraton* (court) in East Java more expedient. During the same period, Sumatran Śrivijaya also resumed its role as an important emporium in the international trade. The natural calamities in Central Java and the shift in location of the *kraton* in combination with trade-wars between Sumatra and Java do not seem to have resulted in economic stagnation in tenth-century Indonesia.[7]

Destruction of the capital in East Java (1016) and economic rivalry between the Southern Indian Chola and Śrivijaya, probably resulting in the destruction of the latter's capital (1025), do not seem to have caused more than a temporary lull in their trading activities (Christie, 1982, pp. 445-447).

By the late 12th century, Śrivijaya (the second) was past its prime and eastern Javanese ports had taken over its leading role, while northern Sumatran harbours started to participate in the international trade through the Straits of Malacca. Most indicators seem to suggest that East Java became increasingly prosperous between 1000 and 1400, due to the growing role of its ports-of-trade in international commerce, and backed up by political unification since the 13th century. This culminated in the fourteenth-century state of Majapahit, an 'empire' with a large number of more or less dependent political entities throughout the archipelago.[8]

We are rather well informed about Java during this period. Sedentary wet rice cultivation (on *sawah*) seems to have been the basis of this society, but we also find frequent references to dry rice and other crops, such as taro, betel and cotton. Mention is also made of other productive lands, such as 'dry' land under permanent or shifting cultivation, garden plots, orchards, pasture land, brush land, forests and marshes. It is not clear what proportion of the population was involved with slash-and-burn and hunting-gathering, because the state was only marginally interested in these people. We may assume, however, that it was a fairly large proportion.

This society was certainly not exclusively 'agricultural'. In the sources we encounter large and varied numbers of full-time and part-time specialists in transport, trade and industry. It was also a society with a well developed, dense network of markets. From at least the 9th century onward, coins of gold, silver and baser metals had circulated in Java. After 1300, Chinese copper coins of low denomination took over the role of the earlier coinage. This low value cash, much better adapted to an economy with frequent exchange and/or market transactions, points to a process of increased monetisation. In such a relatively highly monetised economy, it does not come

---

[7] Christie (1982), pp. 440-443; Christie (1991a), pp. 26-28; Hall (1985), pp. 120-128; Jones (1984), pp. 28-31; Wolters (1967), pp. 248-253.

[8] Christie (1982), pp. 448-450; Christie (1991a), p. 27; Hall, (1985) pp. 120-135.

as a surprise that imported ceramics (from China) and textiles (from India) could be found all over the country, and that indigenous specialists produced large quantities of - probably somewhat cheaper - ceramics and textiles that had been copied from these examples, for the growing demand of the ever increasing wealthy non-elite segements of the population.[9]

And there was of course the state. Or rather, a number of states, each of them fairly complex in structure, with an impressive number of dignitaries and tax-collectors or tax-farmers, and a Hinduist and/or Buddhist clergy. Although probably not merchants themselves, the rulers were quite involved with internal and external trade, through a system of monopolies and tax-exemptions.[10]

However, there are no traces of a hierarchy of markets, and cities were small and late in arriving.[11] I will return to this subject presently.

After 1400, the state and the ports went their separate ways. The state of Majapahit started to desintegrate, and the ports-of-trade developed into city-states that reputedly continued to prosper. One wonders, however, whether frequent conflicts between these cities and their hinterlands, and the arrival of Islam may not have slowed down their growth (Christie, 1991, p. 27; Hall, 1985, pp. 250-260). Such a slow-down is not to be found in the literature. The state of Majapahit came to an end shortly after 1500 .

Summarising the literature on the period 500 to 1500 in Indonesia, one gets the impression that, at least for Java, this was a period of almost uninterrupted growth. Even in periods of political turmoil, such as the early 11th and 15th centuries, there are no references in the literature that suggest more than short-term stagnation or decline. There is nothing to suggest that the 14th century, a period of plague and famine in Europe, India and China, caused any setbacks in Java. The *Pararaton*, a Javanese historical chronicle, lists numerous volcanic eruptions between 1300 and 1500, but the only famine it mentions is dated 1426. Indeed, the plague seems to have taken the overland trade-route from China to Europe, and the fourteenth and fifteenth-centuries trade in the Indian Ocean was thriving.[12]

Of course we have to remain very cautious in our conclusions, because the

---

[9] Christie (1991b); Christie in press (a,b); Jones (1984), pp. 23-42; Pigeaud (1960/1963), Vol. IV, p. 494; Wicks (1986).

[10] On state control over rice see Pigeaud (1960/1963), Vol. IV, p. 386 and p. 503; Wicks (1986), p. 50.

[11] For a different point of view, see Reid (1988), p. 18, who considers the Southeast Asian cities of this period as relatively large.

[12] Brandes/Krom (1920), pp. 129-200; Chaudhuri (1985), p. 63; Gibb (1929), p. 264; Gibb (1971), p. 695, p. 717, p. 720, p. 734; McNeill (1979), pp. 159-170; Reid (1988), pp. 57-58.

data are fragmentary and the literature based upon these data does not seem to be much interested in things like economic stagnation or decline, but for the time being it is difficult to avoid the conclusion that Java went through a millennium of almost uninterrupted growth, combined with diversification and specialisation.

Southeastern Sumatra was in decline from the 13th century onward, and nothing remained to show for its phase of prosperity. At the same time, Northern Sumatra became increasingly more involved in international trade. This development did not lead to the formation of a state comparable to Majapahit or city-states of any permanence comparable to those on Java, with the exception of the incipient city-state and sultanate of Aceh. In the Moluccas we encounter the tiny sultanates of Ternate and Tidore, products of the spice-trade. The remainder of the archipelago is shrouded in darkness.

The question of why Java was doing well, while the other areas in the archipelago were much less successful is too complicated - as far as the answer is known - to be answered here in full. Differences in geomorphology, climate, position along the trade-routes and trade-winds, all played a role. Largely due to these differences, the relations between population, trade and state in Java were not the same as those in Sumatra.

In Sumatra, the state was basically a port-of-trade which functioned as an entrepôt for foreign and indigenous traders. It thrived as long as it could tax the regularly arriving traders. Links between the city-state and its hinterland were weak. Forest products from the hinterland formed only a small part of the total maritime trade-flow going through its harbour, and income from taxes levied on these forest products represented an equally insignificant proportion of total state income. The state was not able or willing to tax the subsistence produce of its hinterland population, which consisted pre-dominantly of shifting cultivators and hunters-gatherers. Any major change in trade-routes, therefore, spelt doom for the state: its sources of income dried up quickly, and the hinterland population stopped sending its produce to the port for lack of buyers. If such a city-state was no longer an entrepôt, it lacked the means to generate its own demand and supply for maritime trade. Apart from all that, this type of state could never commandeer the labour-force necessary for the construction of large buildings, which could have functioned as a major prop for a 'theater state'.

In Java we encounter the felicitous combination of a moderately taxed sedentary peasantry and artisanat, a state rice-trade monopoly linked to foreign and indigenous maritime trade, and a state willing and able to impress its subjects with its splendour. Taxes on rice were probably the most important source of income for Java's rulers, so that a major shift in trade-routes was not as lethal as in the case of the Sumatran states. Tax income of this type of state was not seriously threatened when foreign produce was no longer bulked in its harbours, and its hinterland population was always able to generate its own supply and demand for maritime trade.[13]

But for the absence of major cities, Java between 1000 and 1500 would not have been much different from the commercial areas of Europe, India and China. As I have dealt with this problem more extensively elsewhere, I will summarise my arguments here. In this section I will also summarise some of the arguments put forward by Jan Wisseman Christie, who mentions the same phenomenon, and explains it along broadly similar lines (Boomgaard, 1989b, pp. 323-326; Christie, 1991a).

The most important factor seems to be that a number of functions or institutions, which in many other areas of the world (notably the Middle East, Greece and Rome during Antiquity, and Mediaeval and (Early) Modern Europe) were often found together in one place, thus constituting a large city, were kept separate in pre-1400 Java. The most important cities in Europe were walled in, had therefore a military function, contained often large temples or churches, the palaces and mansions of the ruler and the aristocracy, several markets for local commerce, concentrations of craftsmen, traders and other specialists, and a port-of-trade orientated towards export. All these elements are present in thirteenth and fourteenth-century Java, but never together in one place. The large temple complexes were always, and the smaller ones almost always far away from population centres. The capital of Majapahit was not much more than a court-town, there was no wall around the whole 'town', and it was not a port-of-trade. The capital did have a market, but the large majority of markets were rural ones, and there are no indications for hierarchies of markets, such as have been attested for China and Europe.

The lack of a market hierarchy - and therefore potential cities - may be related to two factors. In the first place, there was a system of circulating markets, on a five day schedule, covering the more important villages, serviced by a group of merchants who were both retail and wholesale traders. In the second place, the fiscal regime for artisans and traders, posed limits upon the number of tax-exempt professionals per village, thus stimulating the spread of these activities all over the country, but discouraging larger concentrations.

Various factors contributed to the moderate size of capitals. The court relied largely on tax farming of a decentralised nature, thereby keeping in check the growth of a central bureaucracy. Local communities were very much responsible for their own taxes, which stimulated local economic growth, but also local autonomy. Furthermore, there were frequent shifts in

---

[13] Explanations along the same lines can be found in Hall (1985), pp. 1-20; Leur (1967), pp. 104-107 and Naerssen (1977), pp. 27-33. On the lack of permanence of states in Sumatra see also Abu-Lughod (1989), pp. 293-294.

locations of the court-towns, partly owing to civil wars, partly to the Javanese belief that certain occurrences rendered a place 'unlucky' and therefore unfit as the residence of a ruler. This behaviour could be observed until far into the 18th century.

In the 15th century we witness the growth of a number of coastal cities, to the detriment of the state. In this respect the 15th century was a period of transition, and I will deal with urbanisation in the next section. Perhaps owing to the late arrival and limited size of cities, industrial development was also restricted, although certainly not absent. In the next section I will return to this topic as well.

Foreign demand and international trade had been one of the motors of economic growth in Indonesia between 500 and 1500. Foreign traders could be found in all important harbours in the archipelago. Along with them they brought specialists in statecraft and Hindu-Buddhist religion, who helped local Indonesian rulers to copy - with adaptations - Indian kingship models. To a certain degree, therefore, economic development in Indonesia could be regarded as the result of export-led growth. Indonesia exported rice, spices and forest produce in exchange for (precious) metals and industrial products.

However, there was also an indigenous growth-component, namely Java's rice-producing sedentary peasantry, backed up by the state with its rice-trade monopoly and the large-scale coastal merchants who traded Javanese rice for the spices of the Moluccas. Indonesian ships and merchants were heavily involved in inter-island and international commerce. Where the state and the ports-of-trade - as in Java - survived the varying fortunes of international trade, they established a link between the indigenous and the external factors of growth.

This state, moreover, was not the state that is associated with 'Oriental Despotism' or the 'Hydraulic Society'. Irrigation was largely undertaken and supervised by local communities, not state-imposed, and administrative and fiscal arrangements left local communities and merchants sufficient leeway.[14] One feature that may have been 'despotical', was the influence of the ruler on the rice-trade, and, perhaps, rice cultivation. I will return to it in the next section.

4. 1500-1800

The most prominent feature of the 'transitional' period from 1400 to 1600 is the growth of cities, particularly those on Java's north-coast. My estimate is that the proportion of people living in towns of over 10,000 inhabitants

---

[14] For a more detailed discussion see Boomgaard (1989b), pp. 317-322 and Christie (1985) and (1986).

increased from ca. 1 per cent around 1400 to 3 or 4 per cent around 1600. It seems plausible to explain this increase in terms of a growing demand for rice and spices, from the newcomer Malacca and from Europe and the Middle East respectively. It is much more difficult to establish whether this urbanisation also had an internal Javanese component. However, with an estimated population of five million and a rather diversified and monetised economy, it is hard to avoid the assumption that some of this urban growth might have been generated internally. The period witnessed the rise of a number of coastal city-states which were both court-towns and ports-of-trade, and, being newly established sultanates, also local centres of religious worship. Javanese cities, therefore, were becoming more like 'real' cities (Boomgaard, 1989b, pp. 326-328).

Nevertheless, it is far from certain that this was a period of uninterrupted growth. After the decline of Majapahit, no single state with a comparable authority emerged, and this period of split sovereignty was dominated by constantly warring city-states. During the 16th century, Javanese fleets attempted several times to oust the recently arrived Portuguese from Malacca, only to be soundly defeated each time, with serious consequences for Javanese shipping and commerce.[15] Particularly the 16th century, therefore, might have been a period of stagnation or of low growth-rates at best.

Outside Java, the city-states and ports-of-trade of Aceh (North Sumatra) and Makasar (South Sulawesi [Celebes]) were doing rather well during the 16th century. Rice cultivation developed in the areas surrounding these cities (Reid, 1988, pp. 24-25). Rice had also been grown in Sumatra and Sulawesi before 1500, but it is less clear whether this had ever been so evidently connected to an expanding urban market.

For the period after 1600 the flow of information on Indonesia is much larger than for the preceding century. Nevertheless, it is almost impossible to decide whether even for Java, so privileged in documentation, the period 1600 to 1800 was one of economic growth, stagnation, or decline. The possibility of an unequivocal judgement is, moreover, complicated by the suspicion of ideological biases in the literature. If a writer regards colonialism per se as detrimental to the local economy, Java, therefore, must have been declining economically between 1600 and 1800. Starting with Java, I will deal with a number of indicators for economic development in order to arrive at some sort of overall estimate for the whole period.

Given the many inter-Javanese wars, the periodical Javanese-Dutch conflicts and a (relatively small) number of epidemics and famines between

---

[15] A detailed description of Java's naval position, the inter-Javanese and Javanese-Portuguese conflicts around 1500 can be found in Cortesão (1967). For the 16th century see Ricklefs (1981), pp. 33-40.

1600 and 1750, population growth cannot have been high. After ca. 1750 the growth-rate of the population increased, with the exception of Eastern Java between 1770 and 1800, owing to military campaigns. Urbanisation continued, although most urban centres of 1600 had more or less disappeared by 1800. The growth of the urban population was largely due to newcomers such as Batavia (Jakarta), Semarang, Yogyakarta and Surakarta. Only the fifth growth-pole, Surabaya, had also been an important trading-centre at the beginning of the period. Urban instability, therefore, had again become a feature of Javanese society, that set it apart from other economically advanced societies. The reasons were the same as before 1400: lack of integration of urban functions. Therefore, when an urban centre lost its most important function, such as being a court-town or a port-of-trade, it could not rely on the presence of two or three other functions for survival (Boomgaard, 1989b, pp. 326-329).

Cities may also have lacked permanence because the (urban) rich do not seem to have invested much in large and imposing stone or brick structures. In Indonesia, as in the whole of Southeast Asia, the rich displayed their wealth and high status by acquiring large numbers of slaves. These slaves were sometimes gainfully empoyed, but more often than not the noblemen-cum-merchants (*orang kaya*) had difficulties in feeding their large retenue. This phenomenon may have had many side-effects. It was an obstacle to capital accumulation in the hands of the most enterprising elements in the society. It also restricted urban growth, because it did not generate the demand for all sorts of construction workers and other artisans, typical for wealthy urban centres in Europe, the Middle East, India and China during the same period.

Of course, this preference for slaves over more permanent status markers is begging the question. This is not the place to tackle this issue, and I will restrict myself to one possible element in the explanation, namely the constant supply of slaves from many regions inside and outside the archipelago.[16]

Turning to agriculture, it must be said that production statistics are not available, but we do have occasional references to the amounts of rice being exported. The amazing conclusion to be be drawn from these - admittedly rather dubious - statistics, is that Java's exportable rice surplus was more or less constant during three centuries, periods of continuous warfare apart, namely some 20,000 metric tons per annum on average.

---

[16] A good and fairly recent introduction to the problems of slavery in Southeast Asia is Reid (1983); on slavery in Java see also Boomgaard (1990). On the importance of slavery in Southeast Asia and Indonesia before 1400, the opinions are divided (Bouchon and Lombard, 1987, pp. 66-67; Casparis, 1986, pp. 10-11; Christie, 1986, p. 77).

It is far from easy to explain this phenomenon. It does not seems to be the result of agricultural diversification. Although there is, for the whole period, evidence for the production and export of non-rice crops, there is no proof for a major shift away from rice.[17] Rather the reverse: there is some evidence that the proportion of land under rice had been increasing between 1500 and 1750, to the detriment of other subsistence crops.[18] At the same time, there had been some measure of population growth. This can only mean that the proportion of rice being exported was decreasing, or that yields per family and/or hectare were dropping, or both (Boomgaard, 1989b, pp. 330-339). I will discuss a number of factors that may have been responsible for this development.

In the first place, there were not many incentives for intensification of land-use. Although Java was probably as densely populated as Western Europe during the same period, a Javanese peasant family needed less agricultural land than its European counterpart, due to differences in yields per hectare of their respective staple crops. Population growth, therefore, did not lead to land-shortage and intensification and diversification of agricultural production, except locally.

Furthermore, there is not much evidence of 'improving landlords'. There was no feudal-cum-manorial system in Java and no land-owning aristocracy that might be interested in investing in agricultural improvement in order to obtain a higher income from its rural properties. If we want to characterise Javanese society in comparable terms, it would be with Max Weber's notion of 'prebendalism'. Under this system rulers assigned tax-income and other rights from certain villages to their aristocracy in exchange for military or civil services of the latter. These rights could be reassigned at the ruler's pleasure, and the aristocracy formed no hereditary links with specific areas. Ownership of the land was vested in the peasantry.[19] I am inclined to regard this prebendal system rather than the absence of economies of scale in rice-cultivation (Bray, 1986) as the explanation for the scarcity of large-scale rice-farming.

---

[17] Long lists of non-rice crops, being exported from almost all Javanese harbours to Batavia, can be found in the various volumes of the *Daghregister*, covering selected years between 1624 to 1682.

[18] In the 18th century, the areas under coffee and sugar expanded. In comparison with rice, however, the proportion of the arable lands, claimed by these crops was small.

[19] There were traces of a feudal/manorial system in areas such as Banten and the Priangan (Western Java); in the same areas we find indications for large-scale rice-farming in the 17th and 18th/19th centuries respectively (Boomgaard, 1989b, p. 339).

Urbanisation may have been another factor if we want to explain stagnating rice-exports. As Java's urban sector was expanding, the cities must have absorbed an increasing share of total rice production.

It is also possible that the indigenous states forced their people to grow rice. Rice growing must have been profitable in many areas before there was ever a question of compulsory cultivation. However, by priming the pump of foreign demand this led to vested interests of the state in rice production and so to an extension of rice cultivation into areas that were more suited to other products. Although I cannot prove that the indigenous rulers routinely forced their peasantry to grow rice, their crucial role in the rice-trade strongly suggests that this was indeed normal policy. It is certain that the VOC (Vereenigde Oostindische Compagnie, or United [Dutch] East-Indian Company) and its successor, the Netherlands-Indies government, made use of these tactics at least from 1790 onward.

If such a policy was indeed applied, it may have led to a number of interrelated developments. As rice moved into less appropriate areas, returns to land and labour dropped. This development in itself could have caused the surplus per capita to decrease, but an additional downward pressure on the surplus might have been caused by arbitrary levies - for which we do have evidence - which could have induced peasants in the more fertile areas to stop producing a marketable surplus. As this must have made it even harder for the ruler or the VOC to acquire the desired amounts of rice, a vicious circle of pressure and tacit resistance seems to have been born. A possible way out could have been the construction of large-scale irrigation projects, but there is no evidence that the indigenous rulers or the VOC were more interested in such infrastructural investments than Java's pre-1500 rulers had been (Boomgaard, 1989b, pp. 340-341).

Finally, it should be mentioned that cultural preferences for rice, which are well-attested for the 19th century, may have had similar effects, namely expansion into areas less suited to rice production, and therefore a lower surplus per capita (Boomgaard, 1989a, pp. 101-107).

Turning to the non-agricultural sectors of the economy, we will have to make do, again, with rather crude data.[20]

Starting with the secondary sector, it is clear that a notable proportion of the population must have been engaged in 'industrial' activities. In the 15th and 16th centuries, the Javanese were an important seafaring nation, with 'colonies' in places such as Malacca and Patani. They probably built most of their own ships, and foreigners came to Java's shores to buy them. The larger ships, however, seem to have been built outside Java. With the arrival of the

---

[20]   Unless otherwise stated, the data on the non-agricultural sectors have been taken from Boomgaard (1990) and (1991).

Dutch around 1600, shipbuilding expanded at first, increasingly under Dutch supervision. For Javanese shipping, the early decades of the 17th century were a rather bleak period, because the ruler of the inland state of Mataram was waging war against and conquering the coastal city-states. In the course of time, the VOC gradually replaced what was left of Javanese maritime trade, until the latter was largely restricted to the coast and the rivers. Shipbuilding under Javanese supervision kept pace with these developments, and in the 18th century only the smallest vessels were still being constructed by the Javanese themselves.

It is possible that the total volume of ships being built was larger around 1800 than it was ca. 1600. Owing to economic difficulties the VOC had to scale down its building programme from the 1770s onward, but private Dutch, Chinese and Javanese shipbuilding continued and might even have increased. The sector as a whole, therefore, may have shown some growth over a period of two centuries. Although management had largely shifted from the Javanese to the Dutch and the Chinese, the shipwrights were still mostly Javanese.

The Javanese also produced large amounts of textile. High quality cloth was imported from India and some Javanese cloth was exported, although it cannot be said that production was geared towards export. Most production came from female home-weavers, who produced largely for family consumption. Yet, production was certainly sensitive to fluctuations in prices and quantities of imported high-quality cottons, and Javanese production was seen to increase when imports dropped or became too expensive. There are indications that production for the market rose around 1750, and it seems likely that these textiles came from workshops and from engrossers, who acquired it under some putting-out arrangement with 'cottage industry' weavers. After 1700, the Javanese also produced large quantities of cotton-yarn for export. This production, however, had nothing to do with favourable market opportunities. It was part of the levies that the VOC had designed in order to obtain a number of trade goods at low cost.

Given these data, it is not unreasonable to assume that total production of yarn and cloth had increased somewhat between 1600 and 1800. It is, however, less obvious that production per capita rose as well.

Around 1800, some textile production was carried out in manufactures, large establishments where sometimes hundreds of people were working together. These manufactures had been established by the Dutch. Something of that nature existed in the Mataram *kraton* around 1650, where hundreds of women produced cloth for the ruler's extensive household. These two examples apart, it is rather dubious whether technology and scale of textile production changed much between 1600 and 1800.

Finally, I should mention the tertiary sector in which thousands of people earned a living. The people involved in shipping were already mentioned. Maritime trade also implies the existence of hundreds of dock-workers. Merchants and traders supplied the goods for the inland markets, the transportation of which was taken care of by thousands of carters and carriers. It is impossible to say whether the proportion of people employed in this sector increased.

What we do know about the tertiary sector is that the majority of people employed in it were 'free labourers'. Slavery was still in existence, but it was on its way out. Corvee labour was still important and would remain so for another century. Nevertheless, the supply of slaves and corvee labourers taken together was not sufficiently large to meet the demand for labour outside agriculture. Although there were always complaints about the available numbers of wage-labourers and their willingness to stay on the job for prolonged periods of time, it is clear that around 1800 large numbers of people were temporarily or permanently available for non-agricultural work. It would be unwise to underestimate the financial and 'cultural' attractions of city-life which 'pulled' these people away from their villages, but we cannot disregard the possibility of push-factors either. Land-shortages were not typical for Java as a whole, but locally easy access to land (and water) may have been problematical.

Taken as a whole, the period 1500 to 1800 does not seem to have been one of expansion. Low population growth, if any, up to 1750, with some increase in the second half of the 18th century. Some urbanisation, but with a lack of stability of urban centres. No intensification in agriculture, and a stagnating exportable surplus of rice. Perhaps some growth in shipbuilding and textile production, but probably not per capita. In so far as the scale of enterprise in these branches had been increasing, this had only occurred in establishments with Dutch or Chinese management. The presence of wage-labour was probably not entirely new, but the numbers involved turned it into a novel structural feature with important consequences for the future. If there was any growth of income per capita at all, it cannot have been much.[21]

What was the role of the VOC in all this? There is not much doubt that they constituted the most dynamic sector of the economy, together with the Chinese, for whom they had created an appropriate 'niche' in this 'plural economy'. The Dutch and the Chinese introduced new technologies, organisational skills and capital, which strengthened the non-agricultural sectors, and led to the introduction or expansion of some cash crops (coffee, sugar). However, they also pushed the Javanese out of the more rewarding economic activities and increased the burden of taxation and corvee levies.

---

[21] In a recently defended dissertation, Nagtegaal (1988) comes to a similar conclusion for the period 1680 to 1743.

In the other regions of the archipelago, we witness the ups and downs in the growth of various states, such as the ports-of-trade and sultanates of Aceh, Jambi and Palembang and the inland state of Minangkabau in Sumatra, the sultanates of Banjarmasin, Pasir and Kutai in Kalimantan, and the city-states of Makasar and Bone in Sulawesi.[22] The development of two older states, Ternate and Tidore in the Moluccas, was effectively curbed by VOC attempts to protect its spice-monopoly.

Many of the more successful city-states combined their role in inter-island and international maritime transport and trade with attempts to strengthen their agricultural basis by stimulating the production of pepper and rice. This was often done in combination with slave-raiding, in order to satisfy their demand for agricultural labour, which would not be met by the population of their hinterlands. Nevertheless, these inland populations should not be regarded as totally insulated groups. Those who lived in the more accessible areas often had trade contacts with the ports, and the rulers of the city-states tried to draw them into their fiscal orbit. Although often at loggerheads, rulers and 'backwoods' people also created mutually beneficient trade-links. The rulers were interested in forest products, gold and diamonds, which they traded for foodstuffs, tobacco, salt, fire-arms and other industrial products, such as textiles and the well-known 'mirrors and beads'. Although most of this exchange took the form of barter, it would be wrong to assume that international maritime trade had left these people untouched.

The role of the VOC in these processes was, again, ambiguous. On the one hand Batavia's position as a staple-market for almost anything that could be shipped, and where small quantities, imported in equally small local craft could be bulked, stimulated the creation and maintenance of a constant flow of commodities from these remote areas. On the other hand, the very presence of the VOC curbed the sultanates in their attempts to expand their political and mercantile sphere of influence. Imports of manufactured items from Europe, India and China, often by VOC ships, may have destroyed some local industries (e.g. Reid, 1988, pp. 107-114).

5. 1800-1990

As the basic facts of this period are much better known than those of the previous centuries, this section can be brief.

If we take the export figures as our starting point, the following sub-

---

[22] There is a dearth of recent studies dealing with the economic history of the Outer Islands prior to the 1870s. Some fascinating insights can be found in Reid (1988), but we are waiting for the sequel to this volume, which will deal more explicitly with economic factors. For the political developments see Ricklefs (1981).

periods can be distinguished (table 1).[23]

To economic historians of the West, this periodisation looks familiar. It seems reasonable to assume that it was heavily influenced by European developments.

Roughly speaking, these periods coincide, at least as regards Java, with phases in the development of real income per capita, with some qualifications. In Java, income per capita probably declined during the period 1800-1835. The growth between 1835 and 1875 was largely due to a higher input of labour, which means that real income per hour worked was probably stable. For the period 1875-1895, stagnation of exports led almost certainly to declining real income per capita, at least in Java, with its high rates of population growth (Boomgaard and van Zanden, 1990, pp. 48-51). Up to the 1950s, data on income per capita for the Outer Islands are much too shaky to alow firm statements.

TABLE 1
Phases of Economic Growth, 1800-1990

1800-1835: stagnation;
1835-1875: growth
1875-1895: stagnation
1895-1925: growth
1925-1965: decline and stagnation
1965-1990: growth

Taken as a whole, this was a period of growth and development. Starting with the agricultural sector of Java, we can distinguish three phases of development in the production of foodcrops. Up to 1930, growth in this sector came largely from the expansion of arable lands (extensification), although some of the growth was due to increased double cropping and slightly rising yields per hectare (up to 1880). Between 1930 and 1960, growth was predominantly generated by an increased cropping ratio (intensification), whereas the high growth-rate of the 1970s and 80s was the product of increasing yields per harvest per hectare. In the Outer Islands the intensification phase seems to have been skipped.[24]

Irrigation, after 1850 increasingly under state management, played an

---

[23] Periodisation based on data from Booth (1988); Clemens and Lindblad (1989), pp. 29-30; Korthals (1991). Up to 1874, (published) export data are only available for Java, but I have assumed that development of the Outer Islands followed roughly the same course as Java.

[24] Both the terminology and the periodisation have been taken from Booth (1988), p. 37; some modifications of her 'model' are based on Boomgaard and van Zanden (1990).

important role in Java's ability to feed its own rapidly growing population. For the first time in Javanese history the label 'Hydraulic society' could be used. Colonial and post-colonial governments combined this with measures to control the cultivation of and the trade in rice. Government control of at least the rice-trade seems to have been a constant in Java's economic development from a very early period onward.

Nevertheless, we also witness in Java a shift away from rice and into roots and tubers, particularly cassava, and maize, owing to the fact that the population was growing faster than irrigated arable lands. Although this shift meant in some ways a drop in the quality of the diet, it also enabled those who had insufficient access to *sawah* to fulfil their calory requirements. This shift, in combination with double cropping and expanding irrigation, goes a long way to explain that throughout the period the Javanese peasantry had - often just - enough to eat. The late 1840s and the middle 1940s apart, Java was not hit by famines that affected a large proportion of the island. On the other hand, food consumption per capita did not improve much either between 1800 and 1960/70. In so far as the agricultural sector was able to produce a surplus, it did not come from the production of foodstuff. From 1870 onward, Java was even importing rice. Rice exports were no longer the engine of Javanese economic expansion. After the 1830s, this function had been taken over by cash crops for the European market, such as sugar, coffee, indigo, tobacco, tea, copra and rubber.

A sure sign of development is, of course, a decreasing share of agriculture in GDP and labour-force. In both cases, the 50 per cent mark was reached in the 1960s.[25] If we take a closer look at the development of the share of agriculture in the Javanese labour-force, we must conclude that this was hardly a gradual process. There was a fairly sharp drop between 1800 and 1875, stagnation between 1875 and 1960, and only in the 1960s was the downward tendency resumed.[26]

This seems to imply that after the growth-spurt in the years 1835-1875, caused by the so-called Cultivation System, the development of the non-agricultural sectors stagnated for almost a century, at least regarding the creation of job opportunities over and above the growth-rate of the population. Although it is certainly true that the period 1875-1960 was not one of vigerous industrial development, registered full-time labour participation in the non-agricultural sectors did not faithfully reflect the magnitude of the labour-force. An increasing number of peasant-cultivators spent an equally

---

[25] The GDP data are for Indonesia, the labour-force data for Java.

[26] The data are taken from Boomgaard (1991), p. 34; Booth (1988), p. 31 and p. 246; White (1991), p. 44.

increasing proportion of their time on non-agricultural side-lines, owing to the falling size of average landholdings.

This phenomenon, nowadays called informal sector, and still typical for most tropical countries, was related to two other developments. In the first place, profits from the export-crops were largely remitted to the mother-country, making for a low rate of local capital formation. Technological development, therefore, the motor of industrial development in the West, was slow or absent, and the industrial sector was not a source of increased productivity and higher returns to labour. In the second place, around 1875 wage-labour had become readily available. During and after the trade depression of the period 1875-1895 it also became gradually cheaper. One could, therefore, argue for a low-level equilibrium trap, caused by low investment rates and cheap labour. One could even - perhaps perversely - argue that the 'Hydraulic society', with its emphasis on the availability of the bare minimum requirements for survival, prevented even lower wages and large-scale rural-to-urban migration, which might have stimulated industrialisation and could have made it more competitive with cheap imports from Europe and Japan.

This gloomy scenario might contain some elements of the situation that seems to obtain at the moment. At a first glance, the Indonesian economy is in good shape. High growth-rates of GDP per capita, even after the oil-boom petered out, although it is a moot point whether the Indonesian economy suffered from the 'Dutch disease'.[27] At the same time, real income per capita seems to be growing and the proportion of people below the poverty-line has dropped considerably (Cheetham and Peters, 1991). An abundant inflow of foreign capital is kept up, particulary from Japan and the NICs.

This, however, points to the darker side of the Indonesian economy, namely its abysmally low wages, and its large informal sector, which acts as a buffer between agriculture and the other sectors. At the same time, government is deregulating rice-production, in accordance with outside suggestions, thereby abandoning a policy-instrument that might date back to the 10th century.

It is difficult to reconcile these two sides of one economy. Yet, it seems to have been the road to sustained development in other Asian countries.

6. Conclusions

Continuous growth between 500 and 1500, stagnation or very low growth-rates between 1500 and 1800, and modest to high growth between 1800 and

---

[27] Compare Booth (1988), pp. 154-155, pp. 209-210, pp. 247-248, with Pangestu (1990).

1990, with Kondratieff-like ups and downs. That is the gradually emerging image of the Indonesian, and particularly the Javanese economy, as it developed over the last 1500 years or so.

In many instances, foreign trade appeared to be one of the engines of growth, but without a local growth-pole such as Java's sedentary, rice-growing peasantry, this growth was rather ephemeral. In the period 1500 to 1800, foreign trade failed to counterbalance the negative effects of internecine warfare and the ousting of the Javanese element from the more lucrative activities. After 1800, its beneficient influence was only intermittently felt.

Government interference with the trade in and/or the production of rice may had negative and positive effects. In combination with the absence of 'improving landlords' and abundance of land, it may have prevented diversification into other crops. In the 19th and 20th centuries it may have kept famines abay, although some would argue that it also prevented large-scale out-migration from the rural areas, thus slowing down urbanisation and industrialisation.

The 'drain' of capital, both in the period 1600-1800 and thereafter, also contributed to low rates of growth. Although the low urbanisation-rates prior to the 1960s were no doubt linked to the capital-drain, the phenomenon as such was much older. If one is looking for indigenous sources of 'underdevelopment', the lack of cities might head the list.

References

Abu-Lughod, J.L. (1989), *Before European Hegemony. The World System A.D. 1250-1350*, Oxford University Press, New York/Oxford.
Bellwood, P. (1985), *Prehistory of the Indo-Malaysian Archipelago*, Academic Press, Sydney (etc.).
Boomgaard, P. (1989a), *Children of the Colonial State; Population Growth and Economic Development in Java 1795-1800*, CASA Monographs, No. 1, Free University Press, Amsterdam.
--- (1989b), "The Javanese Rice Economy 800-1800", in: A. Hayami and Y. Tsubouchi (eds.), *Economic and Demographic Development in Rice Producing Societies. Some Aspects of East Asian Economic History, 1500-1900*, Keio University, Tokyo, pp. 317-344.
--- (1990), "Why Work for Wages? Free labour in Java, 1600-1900", *Economic and Social History in the Netherlands*, Vol. 2, pp. 37-56.
--- (1991), "The Non-Agricultural Side of an Agricultural Economy, Java 1500-1900", in: P. Alexander, P. Boomgaard and B. White (eds.), *In the Shadow of Agriculture; Non-Farm Activities in the Javanese Economy, Past and Present*, Royal Tropical Institute, Amsterdam, pp. 14-40.

Boomgaard, P. and A.J. Gooszen (1991), "Population Trends 1795-1940", *Changing Economy in Indonesia*, Vol. 11, Royal Tropical Institute, Amsterdam.

--- and J.L. van Zanden (1990), "Food Crops and Arable Lands, Java 1815-1940", *Changing Economy in Indonesia*, Vol. 10, Royal Tropical Institute, Amsterdam.

Booth, A. (1988), *Agricultural Development in Indonesia*, Asian Studies Association of Australia; Southeast Asia Publication Series, No. 16, Allen & Unwin, Sydney (etc.).

Bouchon, G. and D. Lombard (1987), "The Indian Ocean in the Fifteenth Century", in: A. Das Gupta and M.N. Pearson (eds.), *India and the Indian Ocean 1500-1800*, Oxford University Press, Calcutta (etc.), pp. 46-70.

Brandes, J.L.A. and N.J. Krom (eds.) (1920), *Pararaton (Ken Arok) of het boek der koningen van Tumapel en van Majapahit*, Verhandelingen Bataviaasch Genootschap, No. 62, Nijhoff/Albrecht, 's-Gravenhage/Batavia.

Bray, F. (1986), *The Rice Economies; Technology and Development in Asian Societies*, Oxford.

Casparis, J.G. de (1986), "The Evolution of the Socio-Economic Status of the East-Javanese Village and its Inhabitants", in: Sartono Kartodirdjo (ed.), *Papers of the Fourth Indonesian-Dutch History Conference, Yogyakarta 24-29 July 1983*, Vol. I: Agrarian History, Gadjah Mada University Press, Yogyakarta, pp. 3-24.

Chaudhuri, K.N. (1985), *Trade and Civilisation in the Indian Ocean. An Economic History from the Rise of Islam to 1750*, Cambridge University Press, Cambridge (etc.).

Cheetham, R.J. and R.K. Peters (1991), "Poverty Reduction during the New Order Government", paper presented at the Colloquium on "Poverty and Development in Indonesia", The Hague, April 9-10.

Christie, J. Wisseman (1982), *Patterns of Trade in Western Indonesia: Ninth through Thirteenth Century A.D*, PhD dissertation, University of London, SOAS.

--- (1985), "Theatre States and Oriental Despotism: Early Southeast Asia in the Eyes of the West", The University of Hull, Centre for South-East Asian Studies", *Occasional Papers*, No. 10.

--- (1986), "Negara, Mandala, and Despotic State: Images of Early Java", in: D.G. Marr and A.C. Milner (eds.), *Southeast Asia in the 9th to 14th Centuries*, ANU & ISEAS, Singapore, pp. 65-93.

--- (1991a), "States without Cities: Demographic Trends in Early Java", *Indonesia*, Vol. 52, pp. 23-40.

--- (1991b), "Ikat to batik?: Epigraphic Data on Textiles in Early Java between the Ninth and the Fifteenth Centuries A.D.", draft paper.

Christie, J. Wisseman, in press (a), "Water from the Ancestors: Irrigation in early Java and Bali", in: J. Rigg (ed.), *Gift of Water*, SOAS, London.

--- in press (b), "Trade and Settlement in Early Java: Integrating the Epigraphic and Archeological Data", to appear in an Archeology Volume, edited by Ian Glover, White Lotus, Bangkok.

Clemens, A.H.P. and J.Th. Lindblad (1989), *Het belang van de Buitengewesten. Economische expansie en koloniale staatsvorming in de Buitengewesten van Nederlands-Indië 1870-1942*, NEHA, Amsterdam.

Cortesão, A. (ed.) (1967) [1944], *The Summa Oriental of Tomé Pires. An Account of the East, from the Red Sea to Japan, written in Malacca and India in 1512-1515*, Works Hakluyt Society, 2nd series (Reprint Nendeln/ Liechtenstein: Kraus).

Daghregister (1888/1931), *Daghregister gehouden int Casteel Batavia vant passerende daer ter plaetse als over geheel Nederlandts-India*, 30 volumes covering selected years between 1624 and 1682, Landsdrukkerij/Nijhoff, Batavia/'s-Gravenhage.

Gibb, H.A.R. (ed.) (1929), *Ibn Battuta: Travels in Asia and Africa 1325-1354*, London.

--- (ed.) (1971), *The Travels of Ibn Battuta AD 1325-1354*, Works Hakluyt Society, 2nd series, No. 141, Cambridge.

Hall, K.R. (1985), *Maritime Trade and State Development in Early Southeast Asia*, University of Hawaii Press, Honolulu.

Jones, A.M. Barrett (1984), "Early Tenth Century Java from the Inscriptions", *Verhandelingen KITLV*, No. 107, Foris, Dordrecht/ Cinnaminson.

Korthals Altes, W.L. (1991), "General Trade Statistics 1822-1940", *Changing Economy in Indonesia*, Vol. 12a, Royal Tropical Institute, Amsterdam.

Laanen, J.T.M. van (1989), "Per Capita Income Growth in Indonesia, 1850-1940", in: A. Maddison and G. Prince (eds.), *Economic Growth and Social Change in Indonesia, 1820-1940*, Verhandelingen KITLV, No. 137, Foris, Dordrecht/Providence, pp. 43-66.

Leur, J.C. van (1967) [1955], "Indonesian Trade and Society. Essays in Asian Social and Economic History", *Selected Studies on Indonesia*, No. 1, Van Hoeve (1st ed. 1955), The Hague.

Maddison, A. (1989), "Dutch Income in and from Indonesia 1700-1938", *Modern Asian Studies*, Vol. 23, No. 4, pp. 645-670.

McNeill, W.H. (1979), *Plagues and Peoples*, The Scientific Book Club, London.

Miller, J. Innes (1969), *The Spice Trade of the Roman Empire 29 B.C. to A.D. 641*, Clarendon Press, Oxford.

Naerssen, F.H. van and R.C de Iongh (1977), "The Economic and Administrative History of Early Indonesia" in: *Handbuch der Orientalistik*, Dritte Abteilung, Vol. 7, Brill, Leiden/Köln.

Nagtegaal, L. (1988), *Rijden op een Hollandse tijger. De noordkust van Java en de VOC 1680-1743*, PhD dissertation, University of Utrecht.

Pangestu, M. (1990), "Adjustment Problems of a Small Oil-Exporting Country: Did Indonesia Suffer from the Dutch Disease?", in: S. Naya and A. Takayama (eds.), *Economic Development in East and Southeast Asia; Essays in Honor of Professor Shinichi Ichimura*, Institute of Southeast Asian Studies/East-West Center, Singapore/Honolulu, pp. 121-137.

Pigeaud, T.G.T., (1960/1963), "Java in the 14th Century; a Study in Cultural History", *KITLV Translations Series*, No. 4, 5 Vols., Nijhoff, The Hague.

Reid, A. (ed.) (1983), *Slavery, Bondage and Dependency in Southeast Asia*, University of Queensland Press, St. Lucia (etc.).

--- (1988), *Southeast Asia in the Age of Commerce 1450-1680*, Vol. 1, The Lands below the Winds, Yale University Press, New Haven/London.

Ricklefs, M.C. (1981), *A History of Modern Indonesia; c. 1300 to the Present*, MacMillan, London, etc.

Setten van der Meer, N.C. van (1979), "Sawah Cultivation in Ancient Java; Aspects of Development during the Indo-Javanese Period, 5th to 15th Century", *Oriental Monograph Series*, No. 22, ANU Press, Canberra.

Warmington, E.H. (1974) [1928], *The Commerce between the Roman Empire and India*, Curzon/Octagon Books (1st ed. 1928), London/New York.

White, B. (1991), "Economic Diversification and Agrarian Change in Rural Java, 1900-1990", in: P. Alexander, P. Boomgaard and B. White (eds.), *In the Shadow of Agriculture; Non-Farm Activities in the Javanese Economy, Past and Present*, Royal Tropical Institute, Amsterdam, pp. 41-69.

Wicks, R.S. (1986), "Monetary Developments in Java between the Ninth and the Sixteenth Centuries: A Numismatic Perspective", *Indonesia*, Vol. 42, No. 1, pp. 42-77.

Wolters, O.W. (1967), *Early Indonesian Commerce; a Study of the Origins of Śrivijaya*, Cornell University Press, Ithaca, New York.

Explaining Economic Growth
A. Szirmai, B. van Ark and D. Pilat
© 1993 Elsevier Science Publishers B.V. All rights reserved.

Comparative Productivity in Manufacturing: A Case Study for Indonesia

*Adam Szirmai**
University of Groningen

1. Introduction and Summary of Main Results

1.1 Introduction

Starting from a very low level of industrialisation in 1966, Indonesia has experienced a very rapid and sustained process of industrialisation since then. The growth rates for manufacturing were among the highest in the East Asian region. Between 1965 and 1980 value added grew by 12.5 per cent per annum, between 1980 and 1990 by 12 per cent per annum (World Bank, 1992). In all but five years since 1970, Indonesia has had double digit manufacturing growth (Hill, 1992). Of the ASEAN countries Indonesia had the lowest industrial output in 1966. By 1984 it had the largest output, contributing 30 per cent of the region's manufacturing production. Nevertheless, in terms of manufacturing value added per capita and share of manufacturing in national income, Indonesia is still one of the least industrialised countries of South and East Asia (Poot, Kuyvenhoven and Jansen, 1990; Hill, 1987, 1992). In 1989, after more than two decades of rapid growth, the share of manufacturing (including the large petroleum refining and natural gas sector) was only 18.4 per cent of GDP at market prices (*National Income of Indonesia 1984-1989*).

The success story of Indonesian industrialisation has been analysed in several recent publications (Hill, 1988, 1990a, 1990b, 1992; McCawley 1981; Poot, Kuyvenhoven and Jansen, 1990; Roepstorff, 1985; Soehoed, 1988;

---

[*] I gratefully acknowledge extensive statistical assistance by Ineke van der Werf. I have benefited much from the advice and help of my colleagues Bart van Ark and Dirk Pilat. I thank Steven Keuning for useful comments. Preliminary results of this research project were presented at a staff seminar at the Department of Economics of the Universitas Indonesia and at a seminar of the Department of Economics of Universitas Sumatera Utara. In the process of data collection, I benefitted from discussions with Alec Hanson, Nurimansjah Hasibuan, Martani Huseini, Yahya Jammal, Alex Korns, Slamet Mukeno, Marcel Pommée, Gatot Pudjantojo, Kusmadi Saleh, Suwandhi Sastrotaruno, Pieter Snel and Paul Wymenga.

Thee, 1989, 1990, 1992). A number of the most important characteristics will be briefly recapitulated here.

Indonesian industrialisation started in the sixties with traditional light industries such as textiles and processing of agricultural products (food, beverages and tobacco products). The industrialisation strategy was heavily inward looking, relying on a plethora of tariff and non-tariff barriers. Under the post 1966 new order (*orde baru*), the economy was opened up to foreign investment, though investment, both foreign and domestic remained highly regulated. In addition to foreign investment there was a substantial inflow of foreign aid. The first phase of easy import substitution in consumer goods industries lasted till the mid seventies (Roepstorff, 1985).

In the seventies soaring oil revenues created an oil boom, which provided the government with ample funds for large scale industrial investment. The government, alone and in joint ventures with foreign firms, invested heavily in resource based capital intensive activities such as steel, aluminum, fertilisers, oil refining, LNG, petrochemicals and cement. The share of intermediate and capital goods industries in value added of intermediate and large scale manufacturing increased from 20 per cent in 1970 to 57 per cent at the end of the decade (Poot et. al, 1990; Hill, 1987, 1992). There was also rapid expansion of electronics (followed by stagnation in the eighties) and transport equipment, which benefitted from extreme protection. In spite of extensive government involvement in the economy, consumer goods industries were primarily left to private enterprise. Thee and Yoshihara (1987) speak of upstream socialism, down stream capitalism. Oil exports dominated exports, Dutch disease effects hampering non-oil exports.

The collapse of oil prices in 1982, however, gave rise to a policy switch. The government embarked on a policy of retrenchment, fiscal austerity, devaluation and gradual liberalisation. The approach became more outward looking. From May 1986 onwards there were a series of important reforms aimed at liberalising the economy, redressing the anti-export bias, reducing restrictions on imports, stimulating foreign investment and simplifying procedures for approvals of investment. The rupiah was devalued by 31 per cent in september 1986 and after that there was a managed gradual depreciation of the currency against the falling US dollar (Thee, 1992).

Before 1982 manufactured exports were almost non-existent. In 1982 manufactured exports accounted for 11 per cent of total exports. Since then, there has been very rapid growth in industrial exports, particularly in textiles, wood products and furniture. By 1989 manufactured exports accounted for 50 per cent of total exports (Thee, 1992). Nevertheless, the manufacturing sector is still highly protected and predominantly inward looking. In terms of exports per capita and shares of exports in manufactured output Indonesia was far behind Asian economies such as Korea, Thailand, Malaysia and the Philippines (Poot et. al, 1990). Liberalisation of the economy turns out to be a slow and painful process.

Most observers agree that Indonesia differs from resource poor Asian NICs, both old and new, in its resource richness. Besides having a comparative advantage in labour intensive industries due to very low wages, Indonesia has a comparative advantage in resource intensive production (Poot et. al., 1990). A final characteristic of Indonesian manufacturing is the existence of an enormous small scale and cottage industry, accounting for a modest part of output (14.9 per cent in 1986), but creating most of manufacturing employment (3.3 million workers or 56.8 per cent of the manufacturing employment in 1986, see table 2).

Summing up, Indonesia has a booming industrial sector, which has developed in a highly protective environment. At present the inefficiencies in this sector are becoming more manifest and Indonesia is struggling in the direction of a more outward looking pattern of industrialisation.

1.2 Comparisons of Levels of Economic Performance

Comparisons and references to other economies are continuously being made in the Indonesian industrialisation literature. In spite of the differences mentioned above, the models for Indonesia are Korea, Taiwan, Singapore and Hong Kong and the second generation of Asian industrialising countries, Thailand, Malaysia and to some extent the Philippines. It is difficult, however, to assess Indonesian economic performance in manufacturing, because so far few systematic comparisons of levels of economic performance are available. This article reports on the first results of a study of comparative labour productivity levels in medium and large scale Indonesian non-oil manufacturing. This study focuses on real output and labour productivity in Indonesia in comparison with the USA in the benchmark year 1987, in establishments employing more than 19 persons. Along with the costs of factors of production and other productivity indicators, labour productivity is one of the important determinants of comparative advantage. Also in the long run, there can be no increase in the standard of living without sustained increased in labour productivity.

I apply the standard ICOP[1] methodology for international comparisons, described in the contribution of van Ark to this volume, to Indonesian and US industrial census data for the benchmark year 1987. The characteristic of the ICOP approach is that it does not take exchange rates as the appropriate conversion factor for international comparisons, but derives specific purchasing power parities (PPPs) for different industries, branches and sectors

---

[1]   Acronym for International Comparisons of Output and Productivity.

of the economy. As in many other ICOP studies, the USA is taken as the reference country. Indirect comparisons with other countries can be made via the USA. At a later stage in this project, direct comparisons with other Asian countries will be made and multilateral techniques will be applied (see Pilat and Rao, 1991).

Though the methodology applied in this research is standard, there are specific problems involved in making comparisons between an advanced industrial economy and a developing economy. These difficulties involve among others: the quality of the statistical data, problems of coverage, the differences in economic structure and the problem of making adequate matches between products taking into account quality differences in products (see section 3).

The emphasis in this paper is on the presentation of new empirical results, rather than on their explanation. More work has to be done to check the plausibility and trustworthiness of the results, before engaging in a search for explanations in a next stage of this research project.

1.3 Main Results

The purchasing power parities (PPPs) derived in this study from the detailed comparisons of products and unit values from the industrial censuses, are generally quite a bit lower than the exchange rate. The PPP for manufacturing as a whole (geometric average) is 1059 rupiahs to the US dollar, compared to an exchange rate of 1644 rupiahs to the dollar in 1987. Thus, application of our PPPs as conversion factors will result in higher productivity ratios for Indonesia, than found in studies using the exchange rate as a conversion factor, such as e.g. Hill (1990a, table 8).

Gross value added per person employed in medium and large sized manufacturing in Indonesia as a whole is 9.7 per cent of that in the USA. Lowest relative labour productivity is found in branches such as food manufacturing (4.6 per cent of value added per person in the USA), beverages (4.9 per cent), tobacco products (3.9 per cent) and other manufacturing (4.9 per cent). Highest labour productivity vis à vis the USA is found in leather products and footwear (36.2 per cent), basic and fabricated metal products (25.2 per cent), electrical machinery and equipment (21.0 per cent), wood products, furniture and fixtures (20 per cent). Intermediate levels of relative productivity are found in branches such as textile mill products (12.7 per cent), machinery and transport equipment (14 per cent) and wearing apparel (17.1 per cent)

Relative labour productivity for non-oil manufacturing as a whole has remained about the same from 1978 to 1988. Comparisons between Indonesia and other Asian economies for which ICOP comparisons have been made, show that from 1978 to 1986 Indonesia has somewhat higher relative labour productivity in manufacturing than India, but substantially lower labour productivity than South Korea, a country which often stands as model for industrialisation processes in Asia.[2]

2. Methodology

The ICOP methodology has been described in detail in several publications (see van Ark's article in this book, see also Maddison and van Ark, 1988; Szirmai and Pilat, 1990). Here, I provide only a brief outline of the methods used.

The primary sources used in this study are the US *1987 Census of Manufactures* and the Indonesian *1987 Survey of Large and Medium Scale Manufacturing*. These sources provide information on product quantities and corresponding gross output values, making it possible to derive unit values for large numbers of products.

The basic approach is to match products in as many as possible sample industries. The sample industries consist of one or more four digit industries from the US census and one or more five digit industries from the Indonesian Survey. In this study matches have been made for 32 sample industries, representing fourteen branches of manufacturing.

The coverage ratios by branch of manufacturing are reproduced in table 1. In total 204 matches have been made, representing 54.1 per cent of gross value of output in Indonesia and 16.9 per cent of gross value of output in the USA. Lowest coverage was achieved in the USA in rubber and plastics, electrical machinery, non-metallic minerals and chemicals.

The unit value ratios of the matched products in a sample industry are used to derive purchasing power parities for each of the sample industries, by using quantities produced in either of the countries to weight the unit value ratios. In the binary comparison between Indonesia and the USA, we thus calculate two PPPs at every level of aggregation, one at Indonesian quantity weights, one at USA quantity weights. The Fisher average of the two PPPs is used as a summary measure.

The 32 sample industries represent 14 branches of manufacturing. For each branch of manufacturing branch PPPs are calculated as weighted averages of the sample industry PPPs in that branch (using value added as weights). The branch PPPs for the fifteenth branch of manufacturing, for which no sample industries are available, are the quantity weighted averages of all the unit

---

[2] These results are very preliminary. The data for India and Indonesia refer to medium, large scale manufacturing, while the data for the other countries are for total manufacturing. In the Indonesia/USA comparison, oil refining and liquid gas have been excluded. In the other comparisons, this sector is included.

values in the study.

Branch PPPs are used to convert branch value added data from the industrial censuses in order to make real output comparisons. Labour input data from the censuses are used to arrive at real labour productivity comparisons.

TABLE 1

Coverage Ratio: Gross Value of Matched Output as a % of Total Gross Value of Output in Branches of Manufacturing

Branch of Manufacturing	Indonesia 1987	USA 1987
Food manufacturing	51.9	28.9
Beverages	32.7	27.5
Tobacco and tobacco products	94.8	91.5
Textile mill products	60.3	49.2
Wearing apparel	85.9	36.1
Leather products and footwear	68.6	60.7
Wood products, furniture and fixtures	83.1	20.2
Paper products, printing & publishing	37.3	12.6
Chemicals, petroleum & coal products	35.7	8.4
Rubber and plastic products	10.3	2.6
Non-metallic mineral products	50.6	6.5
Basic and fabricated metal products	61.2	17.9
Machinery & transport equipment	29.8	16.0
Electrical machinery & equipment	25.2	4.6
Total manufacturing	54.1	16.9

3. Data Sources and Problems

3.1 Sources

The Indonesian Census of Manufacturing is part of the quinquennial *Economic Census*. The 1986 census for medium and large scale manufacturing actually refers to 1985, the census for small scale industry (establishments with 5 - 19 persons engaged) and for home industry (1 - 5 persons engaged) refers to 1986. The census for medium and large scale manufacturing contains a listing of quantities and output values of products. The census for small scale and home industries does not provide such information, so matches can only be made for medium and large scale manufacturing. Home industry statistics are only available by province and are not broken down by branch of manufacturing.

In intercensal years, there is an annual survey of medium and large scale manufacturing, aiming at complete coverage of all establishments. The primary source for this article was the *Statistik Industri, 1987* (Jakarta, 1989). This issue of the survey lists about 4200 products, with some double counting involved, as certain products are listed more than once and in more than one industry. For the USA, my source was the *1987 Census of Manufactures*, which lists approximately 11000 products.

For the comparison between the Indonesian survey and the US census the following points are of relevance:

1. The survey refers to establishments with 20 or more persons engaged. The US census provides information on value added, value of output and employment by size of employment, so that it is possible to make comparisons for establishments with 20 or more persons engaged.

2. The concept of value added in the US census is a rather gross concept of value added, including the cost of purchased services from outside the manufacturing sector. The concept of value added in the Indonesian survey is net of cost of purchased services. Fortunately, the survey provides separate information on input cost of 'non industrial services received', so one can readjust Indonesian census value added to the US census concept for purposes of comparison.

3. The gross value of output in the Indonesian product listing includes indirect taxes and subsidies, the gross value of output in the US census is at factor cost. At sample industry level, however, indirect taxes are given separately in the Indonesian survey. Using sample industry proportions, one can readjust sample industry PPPs, so as to exclude the effects of indirect taxes and subsidies.

4. The Indonesian survey provides no data on oil refining and liquid natural gas. Therefore, the US Indonesian comparison is made for manufacturing, excluding oil refining and natural gas. At a later stage, it may be possible to make matches on the basis of the *Petroleum Report 1990* of the US Embassy.

5. Employment figures per industry in the US census exclude head office and auxiliary employment. In the Indonesian survey, head offices and auxiliary establishments are explicitly included in the establishments covered by the census. Thus, I assume that head office and auxiliary employment are included in the Indonesian survey employment figures. At branch level, US employment figures can be readjusted to include head office and auxiliary employment, using figures from the General Summary. The assumption I make here is, that all head office and auxiliary employment can be imputed to establishments with 20 or more employees.

6. US census employment figures exclude unpaid family workers. This category is listed separately in the employment figures in the Indonesian survey, so they can be excluded for reasons of comparability.

3.2 Census and National Accounts.

For a discussion of the relationship of US census and US national accounts, the reader is referred to the ICOP publications quoted above. The following discussion focuses on Indonesian sources.

As in many developing countries, the census is the primary source for the national accounts. Nevertheless, there are several discrepancies between published census data and published national accounts for manufacturing. The relationships between census and national accounts are discussed in some detail in Hal Hill's extremely valuable 1990 article in the *Bulletin of Indonesian Economic Studies* (Hill, 1990a, 1990b).

Prior to the census of 1986, the manufacturing data were characterised by underenumeration of enterprises. Backcasting from the more complete coverage of establishments in the 1986 census resulted in an upward adjustment of previous survey data on value added in large and medium sized establishments by 22 per cent. Employment data have been adjusted upward by 9 per cent. Boldly assuming that the same underenumeration characterises the 1986 census data themselves, national accountants have applied the same ratios to make upward adjustments for 1986 (and subsequent years). They have also made the assumption that the same degree of underenumeration holds for statistics on small scale and cottage industry, as for large and medium sized industry. Hill concludes that after adjustment for underenumeration, census data and national accounts are broadly consistent. In 1986, value added in total manufacturing from the industrial census was 94.2 per cent of manufacturing value added in the national accounts. More serious problems arise with regard to the compatibility of census and national accounts employment figures, due to difficulties in estimating full time equivalent employment in cottage industries.

In table 2, I present a reconciliation for 1986 based on published figures, applying the adjustment techniques discussed in Hill's article. This table confirms Hill's conclusion that adjusted survey data are consistent with the national accounts. But here adjusted value added from the survey is 103.4 per cent of the national accounts figure, against 94.2 per cent in Hill's article. Hill's figure for value added in large and medium sized establishments in the survey is 10,197 billion rupiah, against 11,405 billion rupiahs in table 2. His figure for small scale industry is also somewhat lower, namely 899 billion rupiah against 946 billion rupiah in table 2. These discrepancies require further examination. Both Hill's article and table 2 bring out the crucial importance of the upward adjustment of value added by a factor of 1.22. Soon it will be possible to check the accuracy of this upward adjustment, when the results of new backcasting exercises based on later survey data become available.

TABLE 2
Reconciliation of Manufacturing Census and National Accounts, Indonesia, 1986

	Gross Value of Output at market prices (mill. Rps.)	Gross Value Added at market prices	Employment (persons)
	(1)	(2)	(3)
A. National Accounts			
Total national accounts incl. oil/gas	50,864,700	17,184,700	5,699,530
Medium and large scale industry,			
excl. oil/gas	32,081,212	10,747,049	2,439,575
Oil refineries	7,866,200	1,915,400	
Liquid natural gas	3,391,000	1,968,500	24,000
Small and cottage industry	7,526,288	2,553,751	3,235,955
Total national accounts, excl. oil/gas	39,607,500	13,300,800	5,675,530
B. Survey (market prices)			
Survey, large and medium, excl. oil/gas	25,877,340	9,348,483	1,691,435
Survey, Small Industry	2,182,821	775,304	770,144
Survey Cottage Industry	3,317,487	1,169,371	2,727,250
Survey, Total Manufacturing, excl. oil/gas	31,377,647	11,293,158	5,188,829
Survey Total as Percentage of National Accounts Total	79.22%	84.91%	91.42%
C. Adjusted Survey Data (market prices) (a)			
Survey, large and medium, excl. oil/gas		11,405,149	1,843,664
Survey, Small Industry		945,870	839,457
Survey, Cottage Industry		1,426,633	2,972,703
Survey, Total Manufacturing, excl. oil/gas		13,777,652	5,655,824
Survey Total as Percentage of of National Accounts Total		103.59%	99.65%

Note (a): value added multiplied by 1.22, employment by 1.09 (Hill, 1990a, table A1).
Sources: National accounts: from *National Income of Indonesia, 1984-1989*, Jakarta, 1990. Employment figures and data on small and cottage industry supplied by Mr. M. Asta of Biro Pusat Statistik. Survey: data for large and medium sized establishments from *Statistik Industri, 1986*, Vol I; small industry statistics from *Statistik Industri Kecil, 1986*; cottage industry figures from *Home Industry Statistics, 1986*, table 16b. Employment figures for oil refining and liquid gas estimated by Hill (1990a).

TABLE 3
Reconciliation Industrial Survey - National Accounts, 1987
(large and medium sized industries)

Branch	Gross Value Added at market prices (mill. Rps.)		Employment (persons)	
	Nat. Acc.	Survey	Nat. Ac.	Survey (a)
	(1)	(2)	(3)	(4)
Food Manufacturing	1,538,491	1,302,538	427,370	328,618
Beverages	218,462	162,657	14,586	11,766
Tobacco Products	2,236,437	1,927,380	261,371	202,745
Textile Mill Products	1,609,916	1,322,081	424,446	326,202
Wearing Apparel	272,557	203,424	98,762	79,677
Leather Products and Footwear	82,337	69,482	26,150	13,028
Wood Products, Furniture & Fixtures	1,579,998	1,524,726	299,440	210,858
Paper Products, Printing & Publishing	342,583	456,478	86,822	61,963
Chemical Products (b)	2,528,999	1,411,448	249,139	105,533
Rubber and Plastic Products	666,128	595,146	226,957	149,214
Non-metallic Mineral Products	777,870	581,623	132,268	82,492
Basic & Fabricated Metal Products (c)	1,322,182	1,735,525	126,846	88,415
Machinery & Transport Equipment	752,831	854,765	101,482	81,848
Electrical Machinery & Equipment (c)	357,169	262,489	79,464	29,599
Other Manufacturing Industries	52,102	58,831	32,289	16,367
Total, excl. oil/gas	14,338,062	12,468,592	2,587,392	1,788,325
Survey as percentage of national accounts		87.0%		69.1%
Adjusted survey data as percentage of national accounts (d)		106.1%		75.4%

Notes: (a) Employment including unpaid family workers.
   (b) Excl. oil refining and liquid gas.
   (c) Part of value added and employment in sample industry lamps and bulbs (electrical machinery) reallocated to metal products branch.
   (d) Value added adjusted upward by a factor of 1.22, employment by 1.09 (see Hill (1990a)).

Source: Breakdown of national accounts by branch for large and medium size manufacturing in 1983 rupiahs, supplied by Mr. Moh. Asta of BPS. Adjusted to current 1987 rupiahs using ratios of total 1987 value added in current rupiahs to value added in 1983 rupiahs from the published national accounts. Survey data from *Statistik Industri, 1987*, Vol. I, Jakarta, 1989.

Table 3 presents a reconciliation for 1987 between the national accounts and the 1987 Survey for Medium and Large Scale Industry. Census value added at market prices in non-oil manufacturing is 87 per cent of national accounts value added, employment is 69.1 per cent. If we adjust the survey data, using the adjustment factors suggested by Hill, the percentages become 106.1 per cent and 75.4 per cent respectively.

In principle, it would be preferable to make productivity comparisons within a national accounts framework. However, considering the discrepancies between national accounts and survey data, I have for the time being chosen to base our productivity comparisons on published survey data.

3.3 Specific Problems

Quality Problems

Hill (1990) concludes that "Indonesia's Industrial Statistics ... are now excellent". As regards the quality of the product listings (Volume II of the Survey), this conclusion is in need of some qualification. There is not yet a consistent product code for categorising products. Products have no identifying codes at all. They are listed per industry in order of gross value of output. The listings are not consistent from one year to another. One year products are lumped together. Another year they are not. The description of items in the survey is often vague and provides insufficient detail. The quantity information is often in terms of numbers of products, unspecified by size, weight or quality. Not infrequently, the largest product in a listing is a residual category. Translations of the same items differ from year to year.

This has consequences for the quality of matches with products from the US census. In the US census large numbers of precisely described products have to be lumped together to achieve matches with a few roughly described products in Indonesia. There may be a serious quality problem involved. The Indonesian survey provides insufficient detail to enable us to make quality adjustments, as were made in the case of the automobile industry in previous ICOP Studies (see Maddison and Van Ark, 1988; Szirmai and Pilat, 1990).

One would expect the average quality of manufacturing products produced in Indonesia to be lower than in the USA. If that is the case, our PPPs are too low and Indonesian productivity will be overestimated. However, one cannot be certain of this. In the wearing apparel branch, for instance, high quality products such as Arrow shirts, are produced for the export market, along with lower quality products for the domestic market. In a subsequent stage of this research project, it might therefore be necessary to go outside the framework of the industrial survey and to use industry specific information and studies to supplement the survey data on prices, quantities and qualities.

Primary and Secondary Products

In the US census, the product listing for an industry includes the products primary to an industry and products secondary to other industries. In the Indonesian product listings, the industry listing includes both the primary and secondary products of that industry. Sometimes, the primary products represent only a small percentage of gross value of output in an industry, leading to low matching percentages.

The listing of both primary and secondary products has as consequence that the same products are listed in different industries. In a few cases, I had to reallocate part of the output of an industry to another industry, to be able to make more matches and achieve adequate matching percentages. In order to do this, one has to make the not very realistic assumption that there are no differences in labour productivity within an industry.

Categorisation of Industrial Products

Not only are primary and secondary products listed together in the Indonesian survey. Also, some industry product listings consist of large amounts of products from widely disparate industries. For instance, 58 per cent of gross output of products in the lamps and bulbs industry consists of non-ferrous cables, wires and rods which are usually categorised as basic metal products. In another case all organic and inorganic chemical products were listed together. Unless one lumps together industries, such as organic and inorganic chemicals, or basic metals and fabricated metal products, one may get extremely low coverage ratios. As stated above, I have occasionally resorted to the expedient of reallocating part of an Indonesian industry, to achieve higher matching percentages.

Structural Differences

The more similar the economic structures of two economies, the less difference there is between PPPs at country weights of the one country or the other. When comparing a developing economy such as Indonesia with the United States, there will be important structural differences, both at branch level, within branches and within industries. The country weighted PPPs will tend to diverge substantially.

4. Results at Branch Level

Table 4 contains PPPs per branch of manufacturing. Branch PPPs are weighted averages of PPPs of the sample industries in a branch, using sample industry value added as weights. The PPPs for other manufacturing are quantity weighted price ratios of all the matches in the other branches. No matches were achieved in the residual category itself. The PPPs for total manufacturing are weighted averages of the branch PPPs, using branch value added as weights. For the sake of comparison, I have used both national accounts branch value added and census branch value added as weights. The differences between the PPPs based on census and national accounts weights are very small.

In most branches PPPs at US weights are much higher than those at Indonesian weights. This is only to be expected. Products which are cheap and common in the US, will tend to be expensive and rare in Indonesia. The greater the difference in industrial structure, the greater the divergence in PPPs. The geometric average of PPPs for manufacturing as a whole is 1059 rupiahs to the US dollar, compared to an exchange rate of 1644 rupiahs to the dollar in 1987. In the last column of table 4, the geometric average of the PPPs has been divided by the exchange rate to calculate relative price levels for each branch.

The basic data on value added and employment derived from the 1987 US census and the Indonesian survey of manufactures are summarised in table 5. Indonesian value added data have been adjusted to the US census concept of value added by adding the value of non-industrial services received. They have been adjusted to factor cost by deducting indirect taxes.

Unpaid family workers, who are excluded from the US employment figures, have been deducted on the Indonesian side. As the Indonesian survey also covers head office establishments (see *Statistik Industri, 1987*, Vol I, p. vi), I have assumed the employment data include head office employment. In the USA, the general summary provides information on head office and auxiliary employment at 2 digit division level. Using this information, I have adjusted our branch employment levels to include head office and auxiliary employment.

As the Indonesian survey data refer only to establishments with 20 or more persons engaged, the US data had to be readjusted to a similar basis. The data in the general summary of the US census are broken down by employment size, with the exception of data on head office employment. I have assumed that all head office and auxiliary employment is related to medium and large sized manufacturing. The exclusion of small scale industry from the productivity comparisons, will tend to bias Indonesian labour productivity performance in an upward direction. One would expect the large small scale industry sector to be characterised by lower labour productivity than medium and large sized manufacturing. This supposition needs to be examined further.

In Indonesia the large oil refining and liquid gas sector is not included in the Industrial Survey. On the US side I have therefore excluded petroleum and coal products from chemical products. In the Indonesian sample industry lamps and bulbs (38330), considerable part of the products listed (58 per cent)

230 *Adam Szirmai*

consisted of basic metal products. Therefore, I have reallocated 58 per cent of
the value added and employment in this industry to the metal products branch.

TABLE 4
Purchasing Power Parities and Price Levels by Major Manufacturing Branch
Indonesia/USA (Rp. to the US$)

	PPP (Rp./US$)			Relative Price Level Indonesia (USA = 100)
	at US Quantity Weights	at Indonesian Quantity Weights	Geometric Average	
Food Manufacturing	1,386.6	913.5	1,125.4	68.5
Beverages	1,735.3	1,734.5	1,734.9	105.5
Tobacco Products	807.2	827.3	817.2	49.7
Textile Mill Products	913.0	775.5	841.5	51.2
Wearing Apparel	510.4	508.5	509.4	31.0
Leather Products & Footwear	461.5	406.2	433.0	26.3
Wood Products, Furniture & Fixtures	1,238.0	621.7	877.3	53.4
Paper Products, Printing & Publishing	1,514.7	872.8	1,149.8	69.9
Chemical Products (excl. oil/gas)	1,529.6	1,122.9	1,310.6	79.7
Rubber & Plastic Products	1,086.6	606.4	811.7	49.4
Non-metallic Mineral Products	906.4	1,088.0	993.1	60.4
Basic & Fabricated Metal Products	1,511.0	1,175.3	1,332.6	81.1
Machinery & Transport Equipment	1,641.8	718.9	1,086.4	66.1
Electrical Machinery & Equipment	692.9	592.0	640.5	39.0
Other Manufacturing Industries	1,354.1	823.7	1,056.1	64.2
Total Manufacturing, Census Weights (a)	1,355.6	826.9	1,058.8	64.4
Total Manufacturing, National Accounts Weights (a)	1,335.4	834.9	1,055.9	64.2
Exchange Rate	1,644.0	1,644.0	1,644.0	

Note: (a) The PPP for total manufacturing is the weighted average of the PPPs of
all manufacturing branches, weighted with value added weights. It can
be based on census or national accounts weights, which give slightly
different results.

Source: The PPP for each branch is the weighted average of the PPPs of the
sample industries belonging to that branch. Sample industry PPPs are available on
request. The PPP for other manufacturing is the weighted average of all product
PPPs.

TABLE 5
Census Value Added and Employment, Indonesia and the USA, 1987
(large and medium sized manufacturing)

	Indonesia			USA		
	Gross Value Added at factor cost (a) (mill. Rps.) (1)	Gross Value Added in Branch as % of Total (2)	Employment (persons) (3)	Gross Value Added (mill. US$) (4)	Gross Value Added in Branch as % of Total (5)	Employment (persons) (6)
Food Manufacturing	1,224,845	10.72	325,684	95,349	8.8	1,319,572
Beverages	130,676	1.14	11,660	21,961	2.0	165,928
Tobacco Products	1,454,327	12.73	201,679	14,252	1.3	63,100
Textile Mill Products	1,261,881	11.04	323,930	24,808	2.3	680,717
Wearing Apparel	198,817	1.74	78,979	29,808	2.8	1,029,300
Leather Products and Footwear	65,355	0.57	12,842	4,155	0.4	128,000
Wood Products, Furniture & Fixtures	1,499,162	13.12	209,982	42,614	3.9	1,045,400
Paper Products, Printing & Publishing	423,704	3.71	61,667	129,488	12.0	1,952,600
Chemicals Products (excl. oil/gas)	1,346,838	11.79	105,294	115,717	10.7	979,041
Rubber and Plastic Products	536,935	4.70	148,696	42,080	3.9	811,200
Non-metallic Mineral Products	545,258	4.77	81,362	29,508	2.7	479,700
Basic & Fabricated Metal Products	1,641,071	14.36	88,078	113,481	10.5	2,048,600
Machinery & Transport Equipment	820,862	7.18	81,536	243,301	22.5	3,684,530
Electrical Machinery & Equipment	226,500	1.98	29,539	93,385	8.6	1,636,400
Other Manufacturing Industries	52,075	0.46	16,118	82,727	7.6	1,321,012
Total Manufacturing (excl. gas/oil)	11,428,304	100.00	1,777,046	1,082,632	100.0	17,345,100

Source: Col. 1 and 3 from *Statistik Industri 1987*, Vol. I, Biro Pusat Statistik, Jakarta, 1989, tables 9, 12 and 13. Col. 4 and 6 from US Dept. of Commerce, *US 1987 Census of Manufactures, General Summary*, Washington DC, 1990.
Notes: (a) adjusted to US census concept. Adjustment to factor cost by deducting indirect taxes and subsidies.

TABLE 6
Gross Value Added (Census Concept) per Person Employed
Indonesia and the USA, 1987

	at Indonesian Prices			at US Prices			Geometric Average
	Indo-nesia (mill. Rp.)	USA	Indo-nesia/ USA(%)	Indo-nesia (1000 US$)	USA	Indo-nesia/ USA(%)	Indo-nesia/ USA(%)
Food Manufacturing	3.8	100.2	3.8	4.1	72.3	5.7	4.6
Beverages	11.2	229.7	4.9	6.5	132.4	4.9	4.9
Tobacco Products	7.2	182.3	4.0	8.7	225.9	3.9	3.9
Textile Mill Products	3.9	33.3	11.7	5.0	36.4	13.8	12.7
Wearing Apparel	2.5	14.8	17.0	5.0	29.0	17.1	17.1
Leather Products & Footwear	5.1	15.0	34.0	12.5	32.5	38.6	36.2
Wood Products, Furniture & Fixtures	7.1	50.5	14.1	11.5	40.8	28.2	20.0
Paper Products, Printing & Publishing	6.9	100.5	6.8	7.9	66.3	11.9	9.0
Chemical Products	12.8	180.8	7.1	11.4	118.2	9.6	8.3
Rubber & Plastic Products	3.6	56.4	6.4	6.0	51.9	11.5	8.6
Non-metallic Mineral Products	6.7	55.8	12.0	6.2	61.5	10.0	11.0
Basic & Fabricated Metals	18.6	83.4	22.3	15.9	55.4	28.6	25.2
Machinery & Transport Equipment	10.1	108.4	9.3	14.0	66.0	21.2	14.0
Electrical Machinery & Equipment	7.7	39.5	19.4	13.0	57.1	22.7	21.0
Other Manufacturing Industries	3.2	84.8	3.8	3.9	62.6	6.3	4.9
Total Manufacturing	6.4	84.6	7.6	7.8	62.4	12.5	9.7

Source: Gross value added in national currencies and employment from table 5. Gross value added converted with PPPs from table 4.

The PPPs of table 4 have been used to convert the branch value added data in national currencies from table 5 into the currency of the other country.[3] Division by employment figures provides us with labour productivity comparisons in table 6. On average, Indonesian labour productivity in large and medium scale manufacturing is just under 10 per cent of the US level (geometric average). Low productivity is to be found in food manufacturing (4.6 per cent of the US level), beverages (4.9 per cent), tobacco products (3.9

---

[3] Both at sample industry level and at branch level output PPPs are used to convert gross value added. There are insufficient data to calculate separate PPPs for inputs.

per cent) and other manufacturing (4.9 per cent). High productivity is found in leather products and footwear (36.2 per cent), metal products (25.2 per cent), wood products (20.0 per cent) and electrical machinery and equipment (21 per cent). Two other branches with above average productivity are wearing apparel (17.1 per cent) and machinery and transport equipment (14 per cent).

Application of the PPP for manufacturing from table 4 to national accounts data results in somewhat higher relative labour productivity in Indonesia, than on a census basis. On a national accounts basis labour productivity in medium and large scale Indonesian manufacturing is 11.5 per cent of the US level, against 9.7 per cent on a census basis. This is due to the fact that the discrepancy between national accounts and the census is larger for value added than for employment.[4] For the time being, I prefer to stick with the census comparison as the Indonesian census provides so much more detailed information on concepts and subsectors than the published national accounts.

5. Trends in Relative Labour Productivity: Indonesia/USA 1978-88

Table 7 presents trends in relative labour productivity derived by applying index figures of growth of real value added and employment in the USA and Indonesia to the benchmark productivity comparisons of table 6.[5]. Table 8 shows index numbers of labour productivity for Indonesia and the USA separately, so one can relate changes in relative performance to trends in each of the countries.

Table 7 shows that relative labour productivity for Indonesian manufacturing as a whole remained at about the same level between 1978 and 1988. There was some increase in relative productivity till 1980, followed by a decline from 1980 to 1988. In 1988 labour productivity was 9.4 per cent of the US level, against 8.3 per cent in 1978. On the Indonesian side there was rapid productivity growth from 1978 to 1980, followed by stagnation in 1980-1983. This period of stagnation coincided with almost zero growth of production in 1982 and 1983 (Hill, 1992). After 1983 productivity growth in Indonesia resumed, with 1984 as positive outlier. Over the whole period

---

[4]   On a national accounts basis real value added at factor cost in medium and large scale manufacturing in Indonesia is 1.7% of the US level, against 1% on a census basis. On a national accounts basis employment in Indonesia is 14.5% of the US level, against 10.2% on a census basis.

[5]   Food manufacturing and beverages have been combined to form a single branch food and beverages. Labour productivity trends in the USA are for the whole of manufacturing, those for Indonesia for large and medium sized industry only. However, the share of small establishments in value added and employment in the USA is modest (5.5% of value added and 4.3% of employment in 1987).

1978-88 labour productivity increased by 59.2 per cent (table 8). In the USA labour productivity remained stagnant till 1982. Between 1982 and 1987 US labour productivity went up by 40 percentage points.

Table 7
Comparative Labour Productivity by Manufacturing Branch, 1978-1988
Indonesia/USA, 1978-1988, USA=100

	1978	1980	1982	1984	1986	1987	1988
Food & Beverages	4.8	4.4	4.4	4.2	3.5	4.3	4.8
Tobacco Products	1.5	1.6	2.0	2.3	2.7	3.9	5.6
Textile Mill Products	9.6	8.8	9.7	10.7	10.1	12.7	15.3
Wearing Apparel	10.9	9.4	13.4	13.6	13.1	17.1	17.4
Leather Products & Footwear	59.1	54.7	47.2	56.5	45.2	36.2	44.0
Wood Products, Furniture, Fixtures	13.2	12.4	16.4	14.3	15.3	20.0	20.9
Paper Products, Printing & Publishing	7.0	7.0	6.8	8.3	8.3	9.0	11.0
Chemicals, Petroleum & Coal Products	11.7	26.9	19.1	18.9	11.1	8.3	6.5
Rubber and Plastic Products	11.6	10.6	10.9	10.2	8.2	8.6	9.7
Non-Metallic Mineral Products	9.6	10.7	10.5	10.4	9.3	11.0	10.1
Basic & Fabricated Metal Products	13.2	15.5	20.0	26.8	24.9	25.2	26.5
Machinery and Transport Equipment	14.0	18.4	22.2	15.1	12.5	14.0	15.0
Electrical Machinery and Equipment	31.8	29.5	31.8	31.6	29.2	21.0	23.2
Other Manufacturing	8.9	8.5	7.7	6.8	4.8	4.9	4.1
Total Manufacturing	8.3	11.4	11.1	11.5	9.8	9.7	9.4

Sources: US GDP from *Survey of Current Business*, January 1991 and April 1991; employment from BEA, *National Income and Product Accounts, 1929-1982*, and *Survey of Current Business*; Indonesian GDP and employment from national accounts data for large and medium sized manufacturing in constant 1983 rupiahs provided by Mr. Moh. Asta of the Biro Pusat Statistik; benchmark productivity comparisons for 1987 from table 6.

Table 7 allows us to make a comparison at branch level for 1984 between the results of this study and exchange rate comparisons presented by Hill (1990). Hill's figures for Indonesian labour productivity relative to the USA are 4.0 per cent for food and beverages, 7.2 per cent for textile mill products, 7.2 per cent for wearing apparel, 4 per cent for paper products, 9.8 per cent for chemicals, 8.9 per cent for basic metals and 8.3 per cent for transport equipment. With the exception of food and beverages, his productivity comparisons place Indonesia one third to a half lower than comparisons based on ICOP PPPs.

Table 8
Index Numbers of Labour Productivity by Manufacturing Branch, 1978-1988
in Indonesia and the USA (1978=100)

	Indonesia	USA	Indonesia/ USA
Food & Beverages	125.7	126.7	99.2
Tobacco Products	178.0	46.9	379.7
Textile Mill Products	198.5	124.6	159.3
Wearing Apparel	203.9	127.5	159.9
Leather Products & Footwear	82.1	110.4	74.3
Wood Products, Furniture, Fixtures	195.7	124.0	157.9
Paper Products, Printing & Publishing	163.0	104.3	156.4
Chemicals, Petroleum & Coal Products	93.5	167.7	55.8
Rubber and Plastic Products	120.0	142.8	84.0
Non-Metallic Mineral Products	119.6	114.2	104.7
Basic & Fabricated Metal Products	257.5	128.4	200.6
Machinery and Transport Equipment	176.4	165.0	106.9
Electrical Machinery and Equipment	110.8	151.7	73.0
Other Manufacturing	60.6	130.8	46.3
Total Manufacturing	159.2	139.9	113.8

Sources: see source note for table 7.

There is considerable variation in productivity developments at branch level. Exceptionally rapid improvement in relative productivity took place in tobacco products and in basic and fabricated metal products. Productivity in basic and fabricated products rose from 13.2 per cent of the US level in 1978 to 26.5 per cent in 1988. Labour productivity in Indonesia improved by a factor of 2.6 in eleven years, undoubtedly due to large scale investment in capital intensive activities. In recent years Indonesia has even started exporting steel and aluminum products. In the USA productivity in metal products increased by only 28 per cent in the same period.

In tobacco products productivity rose from 1.5 per cent of the US level in 1978 to 5.6 per cent in 1988. In Indonesia productivity improved by 78 per cent. In the USA it declined by more than 50 per cent. The Indonesian tobacco sector is dominated by the very rapidly growing *kretek* cigarettes industry, where mechanisation is proceeding at a fast pace (Poot et. al., 1990; Hill, 1988). Nevertheless, relative labour productivity is still extremely low in this sector.

Four other sectors with a marked improvement in relative productivity performance were: a. textile mill products; b. wearing apparel; c. wood products, furniture and fixtures and d. paper products, printing and publishing. The gains in relative performance were due to large increases in labour productivity in Indonesia, accompanied by modest productivity increases in the USA. It is interesting to note that these four sectors were all involved in Indonesia's export drive since the mid 1980s, particularly textiles, wearing apparel and wood products (Thee, 1989, 1992; Hill, 1988).

Several authors have drawn attention to a technological revolution in textiles and garment production (McCawley, 1984; Hill, 1983; Poot et. al., 1990). The take-off in wood production dates from 1980 when the government introduced a ban on the export of primary wood products. Both production and exports of plywood have expanded rapidly since then. Since 1986 the exports of raw rattan have also been prohibited, with subsequent rapid growth of furniture production for export purposes (Thee, 1992). Paper products was another resource based industry which has grown rapidly in recent years.

On the other hand there were five branches, where relative productivity declined substantially between 1978 and 1988: a. leather products and footwear; b. electrical machinery and equipment; c. chemical products (including oil refining and natural gas); d. rubber and plastics and e. other manufacturing. The most intriguing pattern is to be seen in the branch with the highest relative productivity, leather products and footwear, where relative productivity declined from 59.1 per cent of the US level in 1978 to 44 per cent in 1988. Productivity declined not only in relative terms but also in absolute terms (by 18 per cent). Nevertheless, this sector still registered the highest labour productivity in Indonesian manufacturing in 1988. Until recently one very large foreign owned (Bata) plant produced two thirds of all Indonesian footwear (Hill, 1988), which provides a possible explanation of the exceptionally high productivity in this branch.

In chemical products relative labour productivity initially increased from 11.7 per cent of the US level in 1978 to 26.9 per cent in 1980, subsequently falling to 6.5 per cent by 1988.[6] In absolute terms labour productivity in Indonesian chemicals declined over the whole period. In this sector there has been considerable government investment among others in oil refining and fertilisers. These activities have frequently been criticised as inefficient and overprotected, in particular in the case of fertilisers. In electrical machinery and equipment relative productivity declined from 31.8 per cent of the US level in 1978 to 23.2 per cent in 1988.

6. Labour Productivity in Indonesian Manufacturing in Asian Perspective.

Though this study takes the USA, the leading country in world manufacturing,

---

[6]   The level comparison was made for chemical products only, excluding the large oil refining and liquid gas sector. In the time series oil and gas are included.

as the reference country, it is of particular interest to make comparisons between Indonesian productivity performance and that of other Asian economies.

Table 9 contains the results of binary comparisons of labour productivity per person engaged between four Asian economies so far included in ICOP and the USA. The comparisons are all made in the same fashion as in this paper, namely by taking the geometric average of the PPPs at country quantity weights as the conversion factor for value added. Table 9 shows that Indonesia is somewhat ahead of India in terms of labour productivity. However, it has not attained productivity levels comparable to those obtaining in South Korea in the early seventies. In spite of rapid industrial growth, Indonesia still has far to go, before it can embark on a path of industrialisation comparable to that of Korea.

TABLE 9
Real GDP per Person Engaged
in Manufacturing (USA=100)

	India (a)	Korea	Japan	Indonesia (a)	USA
1970	7.0	14.8	61.8		100
1971	6.3	15.8	60.7		100
1972	6.1	15.6	62.6		100
1973	6.0	15.6	65.1		100
1974	6.0	16.7	67.0		100
1975	5.8	16.9	69.2		100
1976	5.7	16.3	71.6		100
1977	5.8	17.3	72.2		100
1978	6.2	19.4	75.0	8.3	100
1979	5.7	20.7	81.5	9.3	100
1980	5.6	22.1	86.8	11.4	100
1981	6.1	24.9	88.5	11.2	100
1982	6.9	25.0	92.6	11.1	100
1983	7.1	24.7	87.5	10.4	100
1984	7.1	26.6	87.3	11.5	100
1985	7.7	26.1	88.8	10.1	100
1986	7.9	27.1	83.2	9.8	100
1987		26.3	85.4	9.7	100
1988		28.5	86.7	9.4	100
1989			90.3		100

Note: (a) The India/USA and Indonesia/USA are for large and medium sized industry (20 or more persons employed), the Korea/USA and the Japan/USA comparison are for total manufacturing.
Source: India/USA from van Ark (1991), Japan/USA from Pilat and van Ark (Nov. 1991), Korea/USA from Pilat (August, 1991). Revised US data, including latest revisions of US trends in value added from *Survey of Current Business*, Jan. and April, 1991

References

Ark, B. van (1991), *Manufacturing Productivity in India: A Level Comparison in an International Perspective*, IDPAD, Occasional Papers and Reprints, 1991-5, New Delhi, The Hague, September.
BPS (1989), *Sensus Ekonomi 1986, Statistik Industri Kecil 1986* (Small Scale Manufacturing Industry Statistics), Jakarta, January.
--- (1989), *Sensus Ekonomi 1987, Statistik Industri/Kerajinan Rumahtangga 1986* (Home Industry Statistics, 1986), Jakarta, January.
--- (1989), *Statistik Industri 1987. Survey of Manufacturing Industries Large and Medium*, Vol I, II and III, Jakarta, January.
BPS (1990), *Pendapatan Nasional Indonesia, Table-Table Pokok, 1984-1989* (National Income of Indonesia, Main Tables 1984-1989), Jakarta, September.
Hill, H. (1983), "Choice of Technique in the Indonesian Weaving Industry" *Economic Development and Cultural Change*, Vol. 31, No. 2, pp. 337-53.
--- (1987), "Survey of Recent Developments" *Bulletin of Indonesian Economic Studies*, Vol. 23, December, pp. 1-32.
--- (1988), *Foreign Investment and Industrialization in Indonesia*, Oxford University Press, Singapore.
--- (1990a), "Indonesia's Industrial Transformation, Part I", in: *Bulletin of Indonesian Economic Studies*, Vol. 26, No. 2, August, pp. 79-120.
--- (1990b), "Indonesia's Industrial Transformation, Part II", in: *Bulletin of Indonesian Economic Studies*, Vol. 26, No. 3, Dec., pp. 76-109.
--- (1992), "Manufacturing Industry", in: A. Booth (ed.), *The Oil Boom and After. Indonesian Economic Policy and Performance in the Soeharto Era*, Oxford University Press, Singapore.
Maddison, A. and B. van Ark (1988), *Comparisons of Real Output in Manufacturing*, World Bank, Working Papers, WPS 5.
McCawley, P. (1981), "The Growth of the Industrial Sector" in: A. Booth and P. McCawley (eds.), *The Indonesian Economy during the Soeharto Era*, Oxford University Press, Kuala Lumpur, pp. 62-101.
--- (1984), "A Slowdown in Industrial Growth", *Bulletin of Indonesian Economic Studies*, Vol., 20, No. 3, pp. 158-74. *Petroleum Report*, American Embassy, June, 1990.
Pilat, D. (1991), "Productivity Growth in South Korean Manufacturing. A Comparative Perspective, 1953-1988", *Research Memorandum No. 435*, Institute of Economic Research, Groningen, August.
--- and D.S. Prasada Rao (1991), "A Multilateral Approach to International Comparisons of Real Output, Productivity and Purchasing Power Parities in Manufacturing", *Research Memorandum, No. 440*, Institute of Economic Research, Groningen, September.
--- and B. van Ark (1991), "Productivity Leadership in Manufacturing,

Germany, Japan and the United States, 1973-1989", *Research Memorandum, No. 456*, Institute of Economic Research, Groningen, November.

Poot, H., A. Kuyvenhoven and J. Jansen (1990), *Industrialization and Trade in Indonesia*, Gadjah Mada University Press, Yogyakarta.

Roepstorff, T.M. (1985), "Industrial Development in Indonesia: Performance and Prospects", *Bulletin of Indonesian Economic Studies*, Vol. 21, No. 1, pp. 32-61.

Soehoed, A. R. (1978), "Reflections on Industrialization and Industrial Policy in Indonesia", *Bulletin of Indonesian Economic Studies*, Vol. 23, No. 2, August, pp. 43-57.

Szirmai, A. and D. Pilat (1990), "The International Comparison of Real Output and Labour Productivity in Manufacturing: A Study for Japan, South Korea and the USA for 1975", *Research Memorandum, No. 354*, Institute of Economic Research, Groningen, February.

Thee, K.W. (1989), "The Shift to Export-Oriented Industrialisation: Obstacles and Opportunities", *Prisma - The Indonesian Indicator*, No. 48, December, pp. 82-96.

--- (1990), "Indonesia: Technology Transfer in the Manufacturing Industry" in: H. Soesastro and M. Pangestu (eds.), *Technological Challenge in the Pacific*, Allen and Unwin, Sydney, pp. 200-232.

--- (1992), "Indonesia's Manufactured Exports: Performance and Prospects", in: N. Mihira (ed.), *Indonesia's Non-Oil Exports: Performance, Problems and Prospects*, IDE, Tokyo (Forthcoming).

--- and K. Yoshihara (1987), "Foreign and Domestic Capital in Indonesian Industrialization" *Southeast Asian Studies*, Vol. 24, No. 4, pp. 327-49.

US Dept. of Commerce (1990), *US 1987 Census of Manufactures*, General Summary and Industry Series, Washington DC.

--- (1986), Bureau of Economic Analysis, *National Income and Product Accounts, 1929-1982*, Statistical Tables, Washington DC., September.

---, Bureau of Economic Analysis, *Survey of Current Business*, various issues.

--- (1987), Bureau of Economic Analysis, "Gross National Product by Industry and Type of Income in Current Dollars and by Industry in Current Dollars and by Industry in Constant Dollars, 1947-1986", July.

World Bank (1992), *World Development Report 1992*, Oxford University Press, Oxford.

Explaining Economic Growth
A. Szirmai, B. van Ark and D. Pilat
© 1993 Elsevier Science Publishers B.V. All rights reserved.

Economic Development in Latin America in the 20th Century - A Comparative Perspective

*André Hofman**
Economic Development Division, ECLAC

1. Introduction

The objective of the present article is to make a comparative assessment of Latin American economic performance in the 20th century. Emphasis is given to quantitative supply-side analysis but the role of policy and institutions, both national and international, in economic performance will also be analysed.

The Latin American countries under consideration are: Argentina, Brazil, Chile, Colombia, Mexico and Venezuela. In 1989 they had a combined population of 331 million which is 75 per cent of the Latin American total (including the Caribbean). In terms of output the sample is even larger.

Latin American performance is compared with that of three other groups of countries: (a) three Asian countries - Korea, Taiwan and Thailand - whose economic growth in the past couple of decades has been remarkably fast; (b) Portugal and Spain, whose institutional heritage has a good deal in common with Latin America; and (c) six advanced countries (France, Germany, Japan, the Netherlands, UK and USA) whose level of income and productivity are amongst the highest in the world.

One can distinguish distinctive phases of economic development in the Twentieth century.[1] The first ended in 1913 when the world entered a period of

---

*   I would like to thank Angus Maddison who has been working with us at ECLAC in this project, helped to shape it, provided most of the data for the non-Latin American countries and whose encouragement and knowledge was a continuous source of inspiration. I am also grateful to Victor Urquidi and the participants of the Groningen conference "Explaining Economic Growth" in honour of Angus Maddison and to the participants of a seminar at ECLAC for their observations. The author is a staff member of the United Nations Economic Commission for Latin America and the Caribbean. The views expressed in this article are his responsibility and do not necessarily reflect those of the United Nations.

[1]   For this periodisation we used Maddison (1989) with some small adjustments especially for the interwar period, including for some exercises 1938. In the postwar period we included 1980, starting point of a severe economic crisis and therefore also a distinct marking point in the case of Latin America.

war and turmoil. This phase started around 1820 in the advanced countries when growth accelerated and around 1870 in developing countries under the influence of trade and capital flows. As the subject of this article is Latin American economic development in the 20th century, our starting point for the first phase is 1900. We next distinguish the 1913-50 period, subdivided into 1913-29, 1929-38 and 1938-50. During this period the world experienced two world wars and a great depression, causing huge losses in military and civilian casualties, a big fall in world aggregate output and "a collapse in world trade, capital markets and the international monetary system. It accentuated nationalism, autarky, and international conflict".[2] The pace of growth slowed down worldwide. However, although the whole world economy experienced these disasters, it was worse for Europe and Asia whilst Latin America was sheltered and remained relatively intact.

For the 1950-89 period, subdivided into 1950-73, 1973-80 and 1980-89, a growth accounting framework is presented using total factor productivity analysis. The years 1950 to 1973 were a golden age.[3] There are several interrelated factors which can explain this performance. The new world order which was created, had many more elements of stability than the one created after the first world war with its built-in elements of instability. This new order affected the options of most countries in a positive way, offering greatly enlarged opportunities for trade and specialisation, better access to foreign capital and technology. Domestic policies were directed to promoting high levels of demand and employment in the advanced countries and oriented to development objectives elsewhere. Finally there was a large increase in investment ratios and capital stocks, an accelerated educational effort and improvements in international trade and specialisation. In Latin America the change in policy attitudes and instruments was smaller, because it had fared relatively well in the previous period and there was therefore a tendency to follow more inward looking policies.

The last period (1973-89) cannot be characterised as clearly as the previous ones. OECD countries experienced a slowdown since 1973 but for the other countries of our sample this slowdown is not as straightforward. Latin America continued to grow until the beginning of the 80s with substantial help from increased capital inflows at low interest rates. However inflation increased and our results show clearly that productivity measures in most Latin American countries started to fall already as early as 1973. And since the beginning of the 1980s Latin America is experiencing a crisis only to be compared with the Great Depression.

---

[2] See Maddison (1989), p. 51.

[3] See Maddison (1989), p. 65.

The Asian countries also experienced some problems in the last period. Japan's growth rate fell dramatically, but the developing Asian countries have been able to continue to grow at a fast rate, in some cases even faster then during the golden age.

This study is built up as follows. The next section (2) gives a brief historical overview of the 1900-50 period. In section 3 we analyse labour productivity and the acceleration and slowdown of growth in the 20th century. Section 4 treats the postwar period from two angles: the first part (4.1) treats policy and performance in the postwar period; and the second part (4.2) presents the results of a growth accounting analysis for the 1950-89 period. In the final section some conclusions are drawn.

2. Historical Retrospect 1900-1950

The Liberal World Order

The period before the first world war, starting around 1870 (for some authors even earlier, around 1800) has been denominated the liberal world order with its characteristics of growth acceleration, through trade and capital flows. The period 1900-1913 in table 1 represents only the final years (1900-13) of a much longer phase.

Latin America experienced fast growth during the first years (until 1913) of the 20th century. This was a period of great prosperity for almost all countries of our sample (only the Asian developing countries grew rather slowly). On a comparative basis it was the best period in the 20th century for Latin America.

World Wars and Interbellum (1913-50)

The period 1913 to 1950 contained three major disasters on the world scale: the World Wars I and II and the "Great Depression". This period from 1913-1950 has been divided into three different subperiods with 1929 heralding the start of the "Great Depression", and 1938 forming the dividing point between the depression and the second world war. Below, we only enter into a detailed analysis of the subperiods when the data show marked differences between the periods, as is the case especially with the data on labour productivity.

For the period to 1929 when the liberal world trading order broke down, the expansion of per capita real income in different regions was not too different, with Asia as the laggard region. In 1929-50 when growth was interrupted by the collapse of international trade and the second world war, most areas of the world suffered major setbacks to growth, and their performance was generally very poor or, for our Asian countries[4], even negative.

TABLE 1
GDP per Capita 1900-1989
(average annual compound growth rates)

	1900-1913	1913-1929	1929-1950	1950-1973	1973-1980	1980-1989	1900-1989
Argentina	2.5	0.9	0.6	1.9	0.6	-2.5	0.9
Brazil	2.3	2.5	2.6	3.9	4.6	0.0	2.8
Chile	2.4	1.6	0.6	1.2	1.8	1.2	1.3
Colombia	2.1	2.1	1.6	2.2	2.6	1.2	1.9
Mexico	1.8	0.1	1.5	3.2	3.6	-1.0	1.6
Venezuela	0.4	2.3	3.2	2.6	0.6	-2.4	1.7
Average	1.9	1.6	1.7	2.5	2.3	-0.6	1.7
Korea	0.8	1.3	-1.4	5.2	5.4	7.2	2.5
Taiwan	0.3	2.1	-0.9	6.2	6.2	5.9	2.9
Thailand	0.3	-0.4	0.3	3.2	4.7	4.7	1.7
Average	0.5	1.0	-0.6	4.8	5.4	5.9	2.3
Portugal	0.8	-0.1	1.5	5.5	1.7	1.3	2.2
Spain	1.3	1.5	-0.8	5.1	1.0	2.4	2.0
Average	1.1	0.7	0.4	5.3	1.4	1.9	2.1
France	1.5	1.9	0.5	4.1	2.3	1.6	2.1
Germany	1.6	0.8	0.7	4.9	2.3	1.8	2.2
Japan	1.2	2.4	-0.2	8.3	1.8	3.5	3.2
Netherlands	0.9	2.1	0.2	3.5	1.7	1.2	1.7
UK	0.7	0.3	1.3	2.5	0.9	2.3	1.4
Average	1.2	1.5	0.5	4.7	1.8	2.1	2.1
USA	2.0	1.7	1.5	2.2	1.0	2.2	1.8

Source: Tables A1 and A2.

However, 1929-50 were good years for Latin America, considering the state of the world economy. From 1929-38 GDP per capita grew at around 1 per cent, the same growth rate as that of the developed countries (except the USA where per capita GDP fell), while our Asian countries grew rather rapidly. For the Iberian countries we only have data for Portugal, as Spain was merged in its Civil War. During the 1938-50 period Latin America did remarkably well, growing at average rates of 2.4 per cent per annum, while in other areas like

---

[4] The three countries selected in Asia are of course not at all representative for Asia and therefore summarising them as "the Asian case" is misleading. This is even more the case in the period before 1950 when Korea and Taiwan were colonies of Japan.

Asia, GDP per capita fell 2.7 per cent on average and was stationary in the developed countries except for the USA where growth accelerated.

From table 2, showing GDP per capita relative to the USA, it becomes clear that the whole period 1900-50 was, comparatively, a very prosperous period for Latin America. Its GDP per capita remained almost unchanged relative to the USA whilst the Asian group had fallen from an average of 18 per cent in 1900 to 9 per cent in 1950. The Iberian level which was 31 per cent in 1913, had fallen to 21 per cent by 1950. The advanced countries' level had also fallen drastically in this period.

TABLE 2
GDP Per Capita 1900-1989
(USA=100)

	1900	1913	1929	1950	1973	1980	1989
Argentina	44	47	41	35	32	31	21
Brazil	10	10	12	15	22	28	23
Chile	39	41	41	34	27	28	26
Colombia	18	18	19	19	19	22	20
Mexico	35	34	27	27	34	40	30
Venezuela	29	24	26	37	41	40	26
Average	29	29	28	28	29	32	24
Korea	19	16	15	8	16	22	29
Taiwan	15	12	13	8	19	27	32
Thailand	21	17	13	10	12	16	17
Average	18	15	14	9	16	22	26
Portugal	25	22	16	16	35	36	34
Spain	43	41	40	25	48	48	46
Average	34	31	28	21	41	42	40
France	55	51	54	44	68	74	71
Germany	54	51	44	37	69	75	74
Japan	23	21	24	17	64	67	71
Netherlands	74	64	69	53	71	74	68
UK	96	81	65	62	68	67	66
USA	100	100	100	100	100	100	100
Average	67	61	59	52	73	76	75

Source: Tables A1 and A2.

3. Labour Productivity, Growth Acceleration and Slowdown in the 20th Century

In table 3 we present labour productivity figures from 1913, the earliest year for which data were available, to 1989. One of the most important findings is that the process of acceleration of growth and labour productivity in Latin America already started around 1938, when GDP per capita and productivity growth accelerated at growth rates about four times as high as in the previous 1929-38 period. Especially in Argentina, Chile, Mexico and Venezuela growth accelerated from 1938 onwards. It was during this period that the combined effects of expansionary fiscal and monetary policy and import substitution, resulted in high growth of productivity per man hour and per capita GDP, some countries also benefiting from the positive effects of World War II.

As can be seen in table 1 in the developed countries and also in the developing Asian countries, this growth acceleration started only after the second world war, during the golden period of 1950-73. In the case of Korea growth accelerated in the late fifties. Another important finding is that the growth acceleration in this period was much stronger in the non-Latin American countries than in Latin America. The Asian developing countries had an average negative per capita growth in the 1929-50 period and grew at 4.8 per cent during the golden 1950-73 period. The Iberian countries had a comparable performance and the developed countries, excluding the USA, grew a mere 0.5 per cent during 1929-50 against 4.7 per cent in 1950-73.

Table 1 and tables A1 and A2 of Annex A show the long term growth record since 1900 for our sample of countries. In terms of total GDP growth for the 1900-89 period, the record was very respectable for Latin America. At 3.9 per cent per annum, it was a good deal faster than the 3.0 per cent recorded in the advanced OECD countries, and the 2.8 per cent in the two Iberian countries. It was, however, distinctly slower than the 4.5 per cent a year in the Asian group.

Since 1950, Latin American performance has been systematically much worse than in all the other areas with the exception of the 1973-80 period. The 1950-73 was a period of great expansion in Latin America, when growth per capita averaged 2.5 per cent a year (faster than the 1.7 average for 1929-50). However, other areas experienced a much greater acceleration of growth in the same period. In Asia growth averaged 4.8 per cent a year in 1950-73, in Iberia 5.3 per cent and in the advanced countries (excluding the USA), 4.7 per cent a year.

In 1973 the period of postwar expansion abruptly came to an end. The advanced and the Iberian counties settled on a much lower growth rate of 1.8 and 1.4 per cent respectively. The Asian countries continued to grow at extremely high average growth rates of above 5 per cent and Latin America slowed down its pace in 1973-80 to collapse completely in the 1980-89 period.

TABLE 3
Latin America: Growth and Productivity, 1900-1989
(annual average compound growth rates)

	1900-1913	1913-1929	1929-1938	1938-1950	1950-1973	1973-1980	1980-1989	1900-1989
GDP per Capita								
Argentina	2.5	0.9	-0.8	1.7	1.9	0.6	-2.5	0.9
Brazil	2.3	2.5	2.5	2.7	3.9	4.6	0.0	2.8
Chile	2.4	1.6	-0.9	1.7	1.2	1.8	1.2	1.3
Colombia	2.1	2.1	2.1	1.1	2.2	2.6	1.2	1.9
Mexico	1.8	0.1	0.1	2.5	3.2	3.6	-1.0	1.6
Venezuela	0.4	2.3	1.1	4.7	2.6	0.6	-2.4	1.7
Average	1.9	1.6	0.7	2.4	2.5	2.3	-0.6	1.7
Labour Productivity (GDP per Man Hour)								
Argentina		1.6	-0.2	2.7	2.2	1.5	-1.8	
Brazil		2.7	3.0	3.9	3.9	3.7	-1.6	
Chile		2.3	-0.7	2.0	2.9	1.5	0.0	
Colombia		4.2	0.6	2.3	3.2	2.8	0.7	
Mexico		1.5	0.9	3.3	4.2	2.3	-1.4	
Venezuela		0.8	1.0	4.5	3.6	-1.0	-2.4	
Average		2.2	0.8	3.1	3.3	1.8	-1.1	

Levels of Labour Productivity (USA=100)

	1913	1950	1973	1980	1989
Argentina	45	32	31	32	24
Brazil	13	17	24	29	22
Chile	44	31	34	36	31
Colombia	18	19	23	27	24
Mexico	41	30	45	51	38
Venezuela	47	41	53	47	33
USA	100	100	100	100	100
Average	35	28	35	37	29

Source: See Annex A.

Table 3 shows the development of labour productivity in our Latin-American countries in the 1913-89 period. The period 1913-50 has been analysed in a previous section. Remarkable is the growth performance during the 1973-80 period in Latin America. While GDP per capita continued to grow almost as rapidly as during the 1950-73 period, labour productivity growth declined markedly after 1973, heralding the crisis to come.

4. The Post-War Period

This section treats the postwar period from two angles. First we give a brief
impression of policy and performance during this period. Our most important
yardstick remains GDP per capita and we also give the most important
population developments. This period is subdivided into 1950-73, 1973-80 and
1980-89. In the second part of the section a growth accounting exercise for the
1950-89 period is presented.

4.1. Policy and Performance in the Post-War Period

The Postwar Golden Age (1950-73)

For the world economy 1950 to 1973 was a period of unparalleled prosperity
with GDP in the OECD countries of our sample (excluding the USA) growing
at 5.3 per cent on average, almost triple the rate of 1913-50. The Iberian
countries grew at 5.8 per cent compared with a mere 1.4 per cent for 1913-50
and the Asian countries grew at 7.7 per cent, 3.5 times as fast as in 1913-50.
The Latin American countries grew at 5.4 per cent compared to 3.8 per cent
during 1913-50.

In 1950 per capita real income in Latin America countries was three times
higher than that of developing Asia, somewhat higher than the Iberian countries
and about half that of the six advanced countries. Within Latin America real
income per capita ranged from around 35 per cent of the US level in Argentina,
Chile and Venezuela, 27 per cent in Mexico and 19 and 15 per cent respectively
in Colombia and Brazil.

In 1950 the international economy embarked on an expansion which was to
continue unabated until 1973, when the first petroleum price shock erupted.
Moreover the growth of world output was the highest ever recorded.

Latin America also achieved an expansion during this quarter century which
probably outstripped regional growth in any previous twenty-five year period.
Furthermore, the rate of growth of regional output between 1950 and 1973
exceeded both the rate of growth of world gross domestic product and the rate
of growth of output of the industrialised countries as a whole.

But there was a fundamental contrast between the growth performance of
Latin America and that of much of the rest of the world. In effect, while the
expansion of world commerce, and especially of industrial country trade, was
appreciably more intense than the growth of world output, the growth of Latin
America's exports was significantly less than the growth of its gross domestic
product and, during the final third of this period, considerably less than one-half
the rate of increase of its imports. And whereas the unprecedented expansion of
the industrialised countries was achieved together with an exceptional degree of
price stability, the acceleration of growth in Latin America was accompanied, in

a good number of countries, by sustained price instability.

While mildly expansionary monetary and fiscal policies, in combination with large devaluations, promoted the strong recuperation of Latin American economies from the Great Depression, expansionary monetary and fiscal policies continued to be pursued or even intensified in the 1950s and 1960s, i.e. long after output had returned to or approached its potential. Moreover, in a number of countries money supply growth far exceeded the potential rate of growth of output.

The evolution of the Latin American economies thus continued to diverge considerably from that of the Asian developing economies; but in this historical instance the departure entailed the progressive build-up of macroeconomic disequilibria (Bianchi and Nohara, 1988).

Income growth resulting from the expansion of primary exports led the rise of demand for manufactured consumer goods and their inputs in Latin America. This demand had become increasingly satisfied by domestic production that enjoyed the "natural protection" provided by transportation costs, complemented in some cases by tariff protection dating from before World War II. The foreign exchange scarcity created by the fall in primary exports during the Great Depression and limited access to foreign goods during World War II subsequently boosted import substitution. Only after the war, however, did import substitution become a doctrine, guiding policy making in much of Latin America.

TABLE 4
Latin America: Evolution of Nominal Tariffs, 1925-86, (percentages)

	1928	1938	1950	1965	1973	1980	1986
Argentina	26	24	12	148	94	34	38
Brazil		26	14	85	55	99	45
Chile	30	35		89	94	10	20
Colombia	23	25	17	48	36	28	
Mexico	28	17	11	20	28	12	27

Source: Bianchi and Nohara (1988), table 17.

Although average nominal protection gradually went up in the course of the 1950s, the average tariff in 1950 was still rather low in a number of Latin American countries.[5] However, between the mid-1950s and the mid 1960s tariff

---

[5] Table 4 should be interpreted cautiously as the figures for protection in the benchmark years included in the table normally represent an estimate of protection in a period immediately around the benchmark years. In some cases protection changes drastically from one year to another.

levels soared and reached extremely high protective levels (see table 4). The rates of effective protection come rather close to those of nominal protection, the former being lower in Argentina and Brazil, and much higher in Chile, Colombia and Mexico in the sixties.

Structural Problems Still Concealed (1973-80)

For the world economy 1973-80 meant the departure from the similarity of growth trends during the previous period of very high growth. The OECD countries as a whole experienced a sharp slowdown, GDP per capita growth rates being more than half as low as in the previous period. However, Latin America and Asian developing countries continued to grow.

During this period Latin America's GDP per capita continued to increase rather fast compared to the USA and its comparative level reached 32 per cent in 1980, the highest level of the entire 20th century. However if this performance is compared to that of other blocks, Latin America's performance is not as good as appears at first view. Asian developing countries more than doubled their level while the other OECD countries also markedly improved their relative stance vis à vis the USA. In Latin America the drastic changes which occurred in the world system at the beginning of the 1970s, such as the fall of the Bretton Woods fixed exchange mechanism (1971) and the action of the OPEC price cartel, did not have the same effect on policy-making as they had in the developed countries, where a sharp change in economic policy occurred. The new disturbance was simply a new variation on a familiar theme, and was not regarded as a razor's edge situation, calling for drastic policy changes (Maddison, 1989).

The combination of biased macroeconomic policies and compensatory sectoral subsidies with unlimited access to international capital markets, was accompanied by economic growth in the 1973-80 period. Eventually it created pervasive imbalances, including stagnation of exports and imports other than manufactured ones, overproduction of non-traded goods and services, uncommonly large resource gaps, unparalleled excess external debt and rampant domestic price instability, all of which contributed to the unusual severity of crisis of the 1980s (Bianchi and Nohara, 1988).

During this period several countries experimented with neoconservative economic policies i.e. the marriage of monetarist views concerning economic stabilisation with radical conservative approaches. Both ingredients have been present in varying degrees in the economic programs of Chile after 1973 and Argentina after 1976, both put into practice by strong military governments (Foxley, 1983).

The Lost Decade (1980-89)

During 1980-89 the world economy recuperated somewhat from the low growth of the previous period, with the exception of Latin America. Total GDP of the OECD countries grew on average 2.5 per cent a year compared to around 2 per cent in 1973-80. The Asian developing countries continued to grow at the same or somewhat higher growth rates. Latin American growth performance was abysmal.

In 1989 GDP per capita in Latin America had fallen, on average, to the lowest levels of the twentieth century. From a level of 32 per cent of the USA in 1980 it fell to 24 per cent in 1989. Argentina experienced the biggest decline from being a rather prosperous country in 1900 (ranking 6th among our 17 countries) to being one of the poorest in Latin America in 1989 (ranking 15th).

Between 1980 and 1989 Latin America experienced its deepest and longest economic crisis since the ill-fated years of the Great Depression. Indeed, so much ground has been lost that from the standpoint of economic welfare the 1980s turned out to be a "lost decade". On average GDP per capita fell from 3727 to 3492 constant 1980 international dollars with heavy per capita income losses in Argentina, Venezuela and to a lesser degree in Mexico, virtual stability in Brazil and (recently) some improvement in Chile and Colombia.

Another unique and disturbing characteristic of the crisis has been the generalised and simultaneous deterioration of virtually all main economic indicators. Many countries have not only experienced a decline in the level or in the rate of growth of total output but also a deterioration in the employment situation and decreases in real wages. Moreover inflationary processes intensified enormously and became more widespread.

4.2 The Growth Accounts

For the 1950-89 we present a growth accounting exercise using 1973 and 1980 as benchmarks. These kind of growth accounting exercises may serve different purposes such as explaining differences in growth rates between countries, illuminating processes of convergence and divergence, assessing the role of technical progress and calculating potential output losses.

The growth accounts go successively through the main features which could have significant explanatory value. For our sample of sixteen countries we will present the results with respect to the most traditional explanatory factors, i.e. changes in the quantity and quality of labour inputs and changes in the quantity and quality of capital inputs. We also include natural resources, although difficult to measure, as an explanatory factor because Latin America has abundant resources compared to other countries of our sample.

The decomposition of economic growth gives clues about the costs of increasing the growth rate. But growth accounting can only explain part of the process of economic growth. It does not deal with other factors such as economic policy, the national and international environment and non-economical factors such as natural disasters and war.

Labour

In this kind of international comparisons it is necessary to estimate labour input in hours worked and not only in employment due to the fact that the average annual hours worked per employee year varies enormously between the different countries. We have elaborated a consistent set of estimates with respect to annual hours worked per employee for Latin America (until now not available) and the other countries of our sample.

An important element with respect to labour is the adjustment for changes in the quality of labour input. In this study this change is represented by the increase in the level of education.

Table 5 summarises the main trends in labour quantity and quality. The first fact that jumps out immediately is the big difference in quantity growth between the developed and the developing countries, the Asian and Latin American countries growing at rates drastically higher than the developed countries. In the 1973-89 period labour quantity growth in the latter was negative on the average with Spain showing high negative growth (employment went down from 13.2 million persons in 1973 to 11.2 million in 1989) the USA growing rather rapidly during the whole period.

The real fast growers were the Asian countries where both elements that influence quantity growth, i.e. employment and hours worked, show very high growth rates. 1989 employment was two to three times as high as in 1950 and we estimated about a 10 per cent rise in hours worked during the 1950-89 period. Latin American employment also grew fast but annual hours worked declined steadily throughout the whole period.

Labour quality which is reflected by educational level shows a steady increase over the whole period for all countries, whereby the Asian countries again experienced by far the most rapid growth. Latin America and the Iberian countries also show rather high growth rates, whilst the developed countries which on the average already had rather high levels in 1950, grew at a much lower pace. We have used the average years of formal educational experience of the population as an indicator of labour quality. Due to the lack of data it was not possible to estimate the attained educational level of the labour force which, together with indicators of the efficiency of education, would probably give a less favourable picture of labour quality in Latin America compared to the Asian and developed countries.

The augmented labour input estimates in the last three columns of table 5 are the weighted sum (with an assumed factor share of 0.6) of the labour quantity and quality growth rates. Growth rates of augmented labour inputs are distinctly different between developed and developing countries and within our group of developing countries the Asian group show remarkably high growth rates.

TABLE 5
Labour Inputs 1950-1989
(average annual compound growth rates)

	Labour Quantity			Labour Quality			Augmented Labour Input		
	1950-1973	1973-1980	1980-1989	1950-1973	1973-1980	1980-1989	1950-1973	1973-1980	1980-1989
Argentina	1.35	0.77	0.63	0.84	1.25	1.28	1.31	1.21	1.15
Brazil	2.89	3.21	3.87	1.33	1.38	2.22	2.53	2.75	3.65
Chile	0.53	1.88	2.93	0.59	0.94	0.96	0.67	1.69	2.33
Colombia	1.90	2.13	2.56	0.65	0.79	0.83	1.53	1.75	2.03
Mexico	2.21	4.01	2.71	1.53	0.80	2.11	2.24	2.89	2.89
Venezuela	2.87	5.10	2.79	0.94	1.11	1.16	2.29	3.73	2.37
Average Latin America	1.96	2.85	2.58	0.98	1.05	1.43	1.76	2.34	2.41
Korea	3.11	3.74	1.54	1.55	1.94	2.85	2.80	3.41	2.63
Taiwan	4.25	3.31	1.58	1.55	2.05	3.00	3.48	3.22	2.75
Thailand	2.68	2.59	2.05	1.55	2.05	1.99	2.54	2.78	2.42
Average Asian countries	3.35	3.21	1.72	1.55	2.01	2.61	2.94	3.14	2.60
Portugal	-0.22	1.06	0.66	1.49	1.49	2.15	0.76	1.53	1.69
Spain	0.33	-2.36	0.12	0.79	0.79	1.72	0.67	-0.94	1.10
Average Iberian countries	0.06	-0.65	0.39	1.14	1.14	1.94	0.72	0.29	1.40
France	0.08	-0.40	-0.77	0.43	0.53	0.83	0.31	0.08	0.04
Germany	-0.05	-1.19	0.06	0.20	0.20	0.14	0.09	-0.59	0.12
Japan	1.55	0.30	0.95	0.62	0.51	0.54	1.30	0.49	0.89
Netherlands	0.37	-0.32	0.81	0.51	0.62	0.70	0.53	0.18	0.91
UK	-0.15	-1.11	0.54	0.24	0.37	0.39	0.05	-0.44	0.56
USA	1.22	1.41	1.43	0.48	0.18	1.19	1.02	0.95	1.57
Average Developed countries	0.50	-0.22	0.50	0.41	0.40	0.63	0.55	0.11	0.68

Source: See Annex A.

Capital

In order to make growth accounting possible, one needs capital stock estimates[6].

---

[6] These capital stock estimates have been generated in the context of the ECLAC project "Long Run Economic Growth in Latin America" and are published as a working paper of ECLAC, see Hofman (1991) and also Hofman (1992).

Capital stocks have been estimated according to the "Perpetual Inventory Method" developed by Raymond Goldsmith (see Goldsmith, 1951). The capital stock has been disaggregated into machinery and equipment, structures, and dwellings with respective service lives of 15, 40 and 50 years.

We have included technical progress in the form of quality improvement of the successive vintages of capital as was first suggested by Robert Solow. The basic argument is that physical investment is the prime vehicle by which technical progress is realised. This capital embodiment effect is not a "catch-all" effect of technical progress (as suggested initially by Solow) because part of technical progress is embodied in the labour force and organisational and other improvements.

Finally the factor share for capital was 0.30 for all countries. This may in fact be a rather crude assumption, as we know that in some cases the capital share has been higher especially in Latin American and probably also in some Asian countries.

Table 6 shows the rates of growth of the capital inputs (gross non-residential capital stock) in the 1950-89 period. The 1950-73 period shows a world of great homogeneity with annual average growth rates of capital stock around 6 per cent for our complete sample. The lowest growers were Chile and Colombia in Latin America and the USA. Fastest capital stock growth took place in Brazil, Mexico, Venezuela, Japan and Germany.

During the 1973-80 period capital stock growth showed two markedly different tendencies. In the developed countries capital stock growth decelerated markedly (except in France and the USA). In the developing and the Iberian countries growth increased, with exceptionally high rates in Korea and Taiwan.

In 1980-89 growth rates decelerated drastically in all countries with the exception of Colombia. Even with this exception the fall in Latin America's capital stock growth rate was the biggest of all regions. Asian capital quantity growth rates were double the Latin American ones in 1980-89.

The capital quality growth rates of table 6 show a uniform rate of about 1.6 per cent for all countries of our sample during 1950-73. From 1973-80 only the Asian countries had higher growth rates and during the 1980-89 period all countries except for Germany and Japan experienced a drastic fall in capital quality growth.

In the augmented capital input the quality and quantity effects are combined and weighted by 0.3, our assumed factor share of capital, and reflect the tendencies described above.

Land

Land has been included as an indicator of natural resources endowment for the different countries. Natural resources have been measured as the amount of land in use, with the following weights: arable and permaɹent crop land 0.7, permanent pasture 0.2 and forest land 0.1. At this stage it has not been possible to include more sophisticated measures of natural endowment which undoubtedly have had a great impact on economic growth especially in Latin America. The factor share for land was 0.1 for all countries.

TABLE 6
Capital Inputs 1950-1989
(average annual compound growth rates)

	Capital Quantity			Capital Quality			Augmented Capital Input		
	1950-1973	1973-1980	1980-1989	1950-1973	1973-1980	1980-1989	1950-1973	1973-1980	1980-1989
Argentina	4.53	4.50	1.08	1.35	1.39	0.85	1.76	1.77	0.58
Brazil	9.44	11.17	5.29	1.52	1.36	0.81	3.29	3.76	1.83
Chile	4.21	2.34	1.88	1.26	0.99	1.04	1.64	1.00	0.88
Colombia	3.79	5.14	4.80	1.19	1.32	1.26	1.49	1.94	1.82
Mexico	7.14	7.38	4.20	1.28	1.62	1.32	2.53	2.70	1.66
Venezuela	7.59	8.08	3.23	1.28	1.72	1.04	2.66	2.94	1.28
Average Latin America	6.12	6.44	3.41	1.31	1.40	1.05	2.23	2.35	1.34
Korea	6.04	15.50	11.83	1.52	1.88	1.37	2.27	5.21	3.96
Taiwan	5.91	12.42	7.58	1.67	1.83	1.31	2.27	4.28	2.67
Thailand	4.60	4.44	5.59	1.53	1.46	1.60	1.84	1.77	2.16
Average Asian countries	5.52	10.79	8.33	1.57	1.72	1.43	2.13	3.75	2.93
Portugal	5.52	5.44	4.48	1.64	1.43	1.36	2.15	2.06	1.75
Spain	6.30	6.74	3.91	1.61	1.72	1.17	2.37	2.54	1.52
Average Iberian countries	5.91	6.09	4.20	1.63	1.58	1.27	2.26	2.30	1.64
France	4.89	5.43	3.44	1.58	1.38	1.15	1.94	2.04	1.38
Germany	7.67	4.07	3.14	1.52	1.20	0.93	2.76	1.58	1.22
Japan	8.87	8.04	6.19	1.78	1.17	1.07	3.20	2.76	2.18
Netherlands	5.87	4.11	2.70	1.54	1.24	1.20	2.22	1.61	1.17
UK	5.05	3.38	2.69	1.61	1.78	1.35	2.00	1.55	1.21
USA	3.26	3.84	3.06	1.89	1.66	0.95	1.55	1.65	1.20
Average Developed countries	5.94	4.81	3.54	1.65	1.41	1.11	2.28	1.87	1.39

Source: See Annex A.

Levels of Explanation

Tables 7 and 8 summarise the results with respect to the growth accounting exercise. Table 7 presents the growth rates of joint factor productivity (JFP) which is the result of taking into account only the quantities of capital and labour

TABLE 7
GDP and Joint Factor Productivity 1950-89
(average annual compound growth rates)

	GDP			Joint Factor Productivity (JFP)			Doubly Augmented Joint Factor Productivity (DAJFP)		
	1950-1973	1973-1980	1980-1989	1950-1973	1973-1980	1980-1989	1950-1973	1973-1980	1980-1989
Argentina	3.59	2.29	-1.15	1.34	0.46	-1.86	0.43	-0.70	-2.88
Brazil	6.91	7.04	2.21	2.14	1.63	-1.74	0.89	0.39	-3.32
Chile	3.42	3.39	2.90	1.75	1.48	0.74	1.02	0.62	-0.15
Colombia	5.12	4.97	3.26	2.85	2.16	0.15	2.10	1.29	-0.73
Mexico	6.50	6.43	1.31	3.00	1.71	-1.47	1.70	0.74	-3.13
Venezuela	6.56	4.10	0.37	2.49	-1.38	-2.28	1.55	-2.56	-3.29
Average Latin America	5.35	4.70	1.48	2.26	1.01	-1.08	1.28	-0.04	-2.25
Korea	7.49	7.07	8.68	3.76	0.19	4.23	2.38	-1.53	2.11
Taiwan	9.32	8.28	7.41	4.99	2.63	4.22	3.55	0.85	2.02
Thailand	6.39	7.19	6.83	3.05	4.12	3.83	1.66	2.45	2.16
Average Asian countries	7.73	7.51	7.64	3.93	2.31	4.09	2.53	0.59	2.10
Portugal	5.50	3.22	2.55	4.00	1.00	0.82	2.62	-0.32	-0.87
Spain	6.12	2.08	2.85	4.05	1.51	1.62	3.10	0.51	0.24
Average Iberian countries	5.81	2.65	2.70	4.03	1.26	1.22	2.86	0.10	-0.32
France	5.13	2.83	2.03	3.65	1.45	1.43	2.91	0.72	0.58
Germany	5.92	2.18	1.92	3.62	1.67	0.98	3.05	1.19	0.62
Japan	9.55	2.90	4.06	5.93	0.36	1.64	5.03	-0.30	0.99
Netherlands	4.74	2.42	1.72	2.83	1.38	0.38	2.06	0.64	-0.40
UK	3.02	0.95	2.50	1.61	0.60	1.38	0.99	-0.15	0.74
USA	3.65	2.09	3.15	1.94	0.09	1.38	1.08	-0.52	0.39
Average Developed countries	5.34	2.23	2.56	3.26	0.93	1.20	2.52	0.26	0.49

Source: table A2, 4 and 5.
For the country blocks arithmetic averages were calculated.

and doubly augmented joint factor productivity (DAJFP) including capital and labour quality. In table 8 the residual (either as JFP or DAJFP) is given as a percentage of GDP. The remaining residual can be considered as an approximate measure of the effect of disembodied technical progress on long term growth, but in addition other unmeasured influences, statistical and other error are included in it. In comparing different kinds of growth accounting one must be aware that the residual may be quite different for different authors. Joint factor productivity (JFP) without quality augmentation is what is very often presented in these kind of studies. Table 8 shows that for the 1950-73 period an average of 43 per cent of GDP growth in Latin America cannot be explained by increases in factor inputs.

TABLE 8
Explaining Economic Growth 1950-89

	GDP (average annual compound growth rates)			Unexplained Residual (JFP as % of GDP)			Unexplained Residual (DAJFP as % of GDP)		
	1950-1973	1973-1980	1980-1989	1950-1973	1973-1980	1980-1989	1950-1973	1973-1980	1980-1989
Argentina	3.59	2.29	-1.15	37	20	162	12	-31	250
Brazil	6.91	7.04	2.21	31	23	-79	13	6	-150
Chile	3.42	3.39	2.90	51	44	26	30	18	-5
Colombia	5.12	4.97	3.26	56	43	5	41	26	-22
Mexico	6.50	6.43	1.31	46	27	-112	26	12	-239
Venezuela	6.56	4.10	0.37	38	-34	-616	24	-62	-889
Average Latin America	5.35	4.70	1.48	43	21	-103	24	-5	-176
Korea	7.49	7.07	8.68	50	3	49	32	-22	24
Taiwan	9.32	8.28	7.41	54	32	57	38	10	27
Thailand	6.39	7.19	6.83	48	57	56	26	34	32
Average Asian countries	7.73	7.51	7.64	50	31	54	32	8	28
Portugal	5.50	3.22	2.55	73	31	32	48	-10	-34
Spain	6.12	2.08	2.85	66	73	57	51	25	8
Average Iberian countries	5.81	2.65	2.70	69	52	44	49	7	-13
France	5.13	2.83	2.03	71	51	70	57	25	29
Germany	5.92	2.18	1.92	61	77	51	52	55	32
Japan	9.55	2.90	4.06	62	12	40	53	-10	24
Netherlands	4.74	2.42	1.72	60	57	22	43	26	-23
UK	3.02	0.95	2.50	53	63	55	33	-16	30
USA	3.65	2.09	3.15	53	4	44	30	-25	12
Average Developed countries	5.34	2.23	2.56	60	44	47	44	9	17

Source: table 7.
For the country blocks arithmetic averages were calculated.
Negative values indicate the existence of overexplanation.

Somewhat surprising is the fact that Brazil had the lowest unexplained residual in the 1950-73 period followed by Argentina, Venezuela and Mexico. Chile and Colombia were the countries with the highest unexplained residual. For 1973-80 Brazil, Argentina and Mexico remained in the group with low unexplained residuals. In this period Venezuela already had considerable levels of overexplanation, i.e. the growth of weighted factor inputs exceeded GDP growth, due to the recession of the late 1970s. With the exception of Chile and Colombia, the levels of overexplanation in Latin American countries became huge during the 1980-89 crisis. These negative residuals are an indication of the enormous economic loss of the "Lost Decade" for Latin America through a fall of capital and labour productivity.

When analysing the residual in a comparative perspective at least two striking results become clear. First the relatively small differences in the residual between Latin America and the Asian group for the 1950-80. In very general terms there are 10 percentage points difference between the Latin American and Asian group (the Asian countries using their inputs somewhat more efficiently) and an equal difference between Asia and the developed countries.

Secondly, during the 1980-89 periods the crisis in Latin America caused the residual to become highly negative indicating that total factor productivity growth was negative. The same thing however did not happen in either the Asian or the developed countries, where joint factor productivity remained positive although with declining growth rates. This supply analysis gives an indication of the huge losses in GDP growth experienced during the eighties in Latin America.

5. Conclusions

Latin America's relative position in GDP per capita compared to the USA remained practically unchanged during the first 80 years of the 20th century and fell sharply during the "Lost Decade" of the eighties. The relative position of the Asian countries in our sample worsened during the first half of the 20th century, to improve dramatically since 1950. The relative position of the Iberian and developed countries deteriorated during 1900-50, but improved gradually during the second half of the 20th century.

At the beginning of the 20th century Latin America was at the initial phase of the demographic transition with high death and fertility rates and actually the region is experiencing the effects of the third phase of the transition with the death rate down considerably and a fertility rate which is starting to fall (see Chackiel, 1991).

The results with respect to joint factor inputs and the resulting joint factor productivity are perhaps the most interesting and surprising results of this study. Joint factor productivity considered as an approximate measure of the effect of disembodied technical progress (together with other effects as mentioned above) shows a rather meagre role of technical progress in Latin American countries. Only in Colombia and Chile during the 1950-73 period did technical progress reach levels of 30 to 40 per cent of economic growth. During the same period, technical progress thus viewed, contributed 26 per cent to growth in Mexico and Venezuela, and just over 10 per cent in Argentina and Brazil. During the 1973-80 period, technical progress contributed almost 30 per cent to growth only in Colombia; it "explained" less than 20 per cent of growth in Chile, 12 per cent in Mexico and a mere 6 per cent in Brazil. In Argentina and Venezuela productive factors increased more than GDP during this period, somehow "erasing" previous technical progress.

In the Asian countries the role of technical progress has been somewhat more important than in Latin America. However, the contribution is only 10 per cent higher on average. Technical progress during the 1950-73 period contributed around 40 per cent to growth in Taiwan and about 30 per cent in Korea and Thailand. During the 1973-80 period these countries increased their joint factor input (especially capital) and the contribution of technical progress fell somewhat even causing overexplanation in Korea. During the 1980s the Asian countries continued to grow at a fast pace, with technical progress contributing around 30 per cent to growth.

Total factor productivity's role was more important in the developed countries than in the developing countries, due of course in great part to different factor inputs. In particular labour input growth was much smaller in developed countries than in developing ones. However, it also suggests that the strains of fast development and high resource mobilisation decreased the efficiency of allocation. Total factor productivity growth slowed down or even became dramatically negative in the 1980s in Latin America. Latin America's level of productivity is presently much lower than that of the developed countries. However, if Latin America is able to resolve its major macroeconomic problems and improve the unproductive allocation of resources, it still has the potential for a return to fast productivity growth on the basis of the incorporation and adaptation in the productive sector of the internationally available stock of technology.

Labour's participation in factor input was very different between regions during the 1950-89 period. Firstly there is a very clear distinction in the quantity of labour which was increasing rapidly (although in many cases not fast enough compared with demographic trends) in the developing countries while growth virtually came to a halt in the developed countries. Secondly within developing countries employment was growing rather fast over the whole range of countries but annual hours worked show markedly different trends for 1950-80, between Latin America with a clear downward trend, and the Asian group where annual hours worked per person increased substantially. Since around 1980 annual hours worked tend to fall, in the Asian countries as well.

With regard to the quality side of labour as represented by educational level, systematic improvements in most countries can be noted. Education grew by far the fastest in Asia, at about half the Asian rate in Latin America and the Iberian countries and at a much lower rate in the developed countries. One has to take into account that our measure of years of education of the population is rather crude due to lack of data. If a more refined measure such as attained educational level of the labour force were used in combination with indicators of the efficiency of education, than the results would probably change drastically especially in the Latin American case.

One of the major results within the present study is the fact that we have been able to generate capital stocks. Gross non-residential capital increased steadily at significant rates in most countries and the 1950-73 period shows great homogeneity with annual average growth rates of capital stock around 6 per cent for our complete sample. The lowest growers were Chile and Colombia in Latin America and the USA. Fastest capital stock growth took place in Brazil, Mexico, Venezuela, Japan and Germany.

During the 1973-80 period capital stock growth showed two markedly different tendencies. In the developed countries capital stock growth decelerated markedly (except in France and the USA), while in the developing and the Iberian countries growth increased, with exceptionally high rates in South Korea and Taiwan. In 1980-89 growth rates decelerated drastically in all Latin American countries with the exception of Colombia. Asian capital quantity growth rates were double the Latin American ones in 1980-89.

Capital quality grew at a uniform rate of about 1.6 per cent per year for all countries in our sample during 1950-73. From 1973 to 1980 only the Asian countries experienced higher growth rates than in the previous period. During the 1980-89 period all countries except Germany and Japan experienced a drastic fall in capital quality growth.

In our analysis we have included the effect of natural resources measured as the amount of land in use. Latin America increased cropped area (especially Brazil) while in the other regions land in use remained stable (the Asian countries) or declined as was the case in the developed countries. At this stage it has not been possible to include more sophisticated measures of natural endowments which undoubtedly have had a great impact on economic growth especially in Latin America.

ANNEX A

This annex presents tables A1 and A2 containing our estimates for population and total GDP and a description of the sources used to elaborate all the basic series used in the article. However a cautionary note with respect to the data is in order as the quality of the data is not the same for all countries. In general the data for the six most advanced countries are good. The data on the Iberian countries are probably the weakest (together with those on Thailand), as long run series have not yet been elaborated or are of poor quality. In these countries research by economic historians is advancing and new data will be incorporated as soon as they become available. Of our Asian group the data on Thailand are the weakest. For Latin America several new series (capital, hours worked and in some cases GDP) have been estimated. The historical data on Venezuela have to be used with caution and new data on that country, and also on the others, would be welcome.

TABLE A1
Population 1900-1989
(in thousands of midyear)

	1900	1913	1929	1950	1973	1980	1989
Argentina	4,693	7,653	11,592	17,150	25,216	28,237	31,929
Brazil	17,984	23,660	32,894	53,444	103,158	121,286	147,404
Chile	2,974	3,491	4,306	6,082	10,012	11,145	12,961
Colombia	3,998	5,195	7,821	11,946	22,939	26,906	32,317
Mexico	13,607	14,971	16,875	28,012	58,259	70,416	86,740
Venezuela	2,302	2,417	2,979	5,009	11,841	15,024	19,246
Total	45,558	57,387	76,467	121,643	231,424	273,014	330,597
Korea	8,772	10,277	13,397	20,557	34,103	38,124	43,100
Taiwan	2,858	3,469	4,493	7,882	15,427	17,642	20,107
Thailand	7,320	8,690	12,059	19,442	39,303	46,455	55,600
Total	18,950	22,436	29,949	47,881	88,833	102,221	118,807
Portugal	5,451	6,001	6,738	8,441	8,368	9,289	10,337
Spain	18,594	20,330	23,210	27,977	34,810	37,424	38,888
Total	24,045	26,331	29,948	36,418	43,178	46,713	49,225
France	40,731	41,690	41,230	41,836	52,118	53,880	56,160
Germany	34,162	40,825	43,793	49,938	61,976	61,566	61,990
Japan	44,103	51,672	63,244	83,662	108,660	116,800	123,116
Netherlands	5,142	6,164	7,782	10,114	13,439	14,150	14,849
UK	38,426	42,622	45,672	50,363	56,210	56,314	57,236
USA	76,391	97,606	122,245	152,271	211,909	227,757	248,777
Total	238,955	280,579	323,966	388,184	504,312	530,467	562,128

Sources: See Annex A.

TABLE A2
Total GDP 1900-1989
(million 1980 international dollars)

	1900	1913	1929	1950	1973	1980	1989
Argentina	6008	13491	23509	39705	89295	104603	94222
Brazil	5291	9371	19436	54068	251644	405222	493542
Chile	3398	5432	8577	13649	29560	37336	48307
Colombia	2037	3476	7273	15427	48680	68361	91207
Mexico	13955	19485	22287	50640	215684	333588	374942
Venezuela	2112	2323	4031	12329	53153	70416	72776
Average	5467	8930	14186	30970	114669	169921	195833
Korea	4817	6264	10035	11584	61058	98474	208340
Taiwan	1239	1571	2835	4145	32201	56190	106963
Thailand	4579	5666	7423	12705	52789	85802	155520
Average	3545	4500	6764	9478	48683	80155	156941
Portugal	3930	4894	5374	9251	31714	39599	49683
Spain	23302	31446	45817	47076	184589	213205	274592
Average	13616	18170	25596	28164	108152	126402	162138
France	65154	80636	108375	123052	388908	472689	566436
Germany	53259	77864	94293	125362	470687	547383	649361
Japan	29840	41102	73490	93343	760632	929027	1329735
Netherlands	11036	14794	26245	35951	104211	123162	143557
UK	107502	130623	146167	210042	416686	445162	556132
Average	53358	69004	89714	117550	428225	503485	649044
USA	222352	368132	600055	1019726	2326225	2688467	3554816

Source: See Annex A.

GDP and Capital

Our GDP and capital stock estimates for Latin America, Korea and Spain were
based upon the sources described in Hofman (1991) and (1992). The GDP
estimates for France, Germany, Japan, The Netherlands, Portugal, Taiwan,
Thailand, UK and the USA come from Maddison (1989) updated to 1989 for
OECD countries by OECD, *National Accounts*, various issues and up-dated to
1989 for Taiwan and Thailand using Council for Economic Planning and
Development (1990). The capital estimates for France, Germany, Japan, The
Netherlands, UK and the USA come from the worksheets of Maddison (1991)
slightly adjusted for changes in the benchmark year from 1985 to 1980 and for
the use of somewhat different asset service life assumptions. For Taiwan the
perpetual inventory methodology was used as described in Hofman (1991) and
(1992) using investment data for 1900-38 from Mizoguchi and Umemura (1988).
From 1939-51 total capital formation was estimated; 1939-42 15 per cent of

GDP, 1943 10 per cent, 1944-49 5 per cent and 1950-51 at 8.3 per cent. Total capital formation was disaggregated as follows: 30 per cent machinery and equipment, 60 per cent non-residential construction and 10 per cent residential construction. Total and disaggregated capital formation data for 1952-89 are from Council for Economic Planning and Development (1990). For Portugal no disaggregated data were available and we applied the short-cut method described in Hofman (1991) to estimate the capital stock using data from sources described in Maddison (1989).

Population

Latin America from 1900-49 from the sources mentioned in Maddison (1989). Venezuela from CICRED and 1950 onwards for all Latin American countries from CELADE (1990). Other countries for 1900-1987 from Maddison (1989) updated to 1989 with OECD (1991). Korea updated to 1989 with Council for Economic Planning and Development (1990). For 1900-49 the Maddison (1989) benchmarks; 1900, 1913, 1929, 1938 were used and the years in between directly interpolated, except in the case of Argentina where the yearly estimates for 1913-49 come from IEERAL (1986). In the case of Mexico I used INEGI (1985) for yearly estimates for 1900-10 and 1921 and interpolated these with the benchmarks of Maddison (1989). For 1950-85 CELADE gives 5-yearly estimates which were interpolated and 1986-89 come from yearly estimates of CELADE.

Employment

Employment figures for Latin America from ECLAC (1990). Estimates for the OECD countries from OECD, Labour Force Statistics, various issues. Other countries from Maddison (1989) updated to 1989 by using growth rate 1980-86. The estimates on hours worked for Latin America come from Hofman (1990). For the other countries Maddison (1989) updated to 1989 using growth rate 1980-86.

Land in use

The land in use data come from FAO, *Production Yearbook*, various issues, using a weighted average of arable land (weight 0.6), pasture land (weight 0.3) and forest (weight 0.1).

Education

Our data on average years of formal educational experience of population aged 15-64 come from Maddison (1989) and are equivalent years of education per person 15 years and over weighted primary education 1, secondary education 1.4

and higher education 2. Venezuela 1950 from Ministerio de Fomento, *Octavo Censo General de Población*, Caracas, 1957. Other years derived from OCEI, *Indicadores de la Fuerza de Trabajo, Total Nacional y por Regiones, Segundo Semestre 1987*, Caracas, 1988. Netherlands from Maddison (1987). Thailand estimated as arithmetic average of Korea and Taiwan. Portugal and Spain derived from OECD, *Educational Statistical Yearbook*, Vol.I, Paris, 1974. The estimates were extrapolated from 1986 to 1989 using the growth rates of 1980-86.

References

Altimir, O. and A. Hofman (1990), *Latin American Development Problems in Historical Perspective*, paper presented at the ECLAC/University of Lund symposium, Santiago.

Banco Central de Venezuela (1990), *La Economia Contemporánea de Venezuela: Ensayos Escogidos*, cuatro tomos, Compilación y Notas; T. Hector Vallecillos and Omar Bello Rodriquez, Caracas.

Balassa, B., G.M. Bueno, P.-P. Kuczynski and M.H. Simonsen (1986), *Towards Renewed Economic Growth in Latin America*, Washington, D.C.

Bianchi, A. and T. Nohara (1988), *A Comparative Study on Economic Development between Asia and Latin America*, JRP Series 67, Institute of Developing Economies, Tokyo.

Blades, D. (1989), *Capital Measurement in the OECD Countries: An Overview*, OECD, Paris.

Brazil, Fundacao IBGE (1970), *Contribuicoes Para o Estudo da Demografia do Brasil*, 2nd edition, Rio de Janeiro.

Bresser, P.L. (1984), *Development and Crisis in Brazil, 1930-1983*, Westview Press, Boulder and London.

Brito, F.F. (1966), *Historia Económica y Social de Venezuela: Una Estructura para su Estudio*, Universidad Central de Venezuela, Caracas.

Cardoso de Mello, J.M. and M. da Conceicao Tavares (1985), "The Capitalist Export Economy in Brazil, 1884-1930", in: R. Cortés Conde and S.J. Hunt (eds.), *The Latin American Economies*, Holmes and Meier, New York.

Cariola, C. and O. Sunkel (1985), "The Growth of the Nitrate Industry and Socioeconomic Change in Chile: 1880-1930", in: R. Cortés Conde and S.J. Hunt (eds.), *The Latin American Economies*, Holmes and Meier, New York.

CELADE (1990), *Boletín Demográfico*, Año XXIII, No. 45, Santiago.

CEPAL (1989), *Antecedentes sobre la Transformación Productiva y la Competitividad de la Economia Chilena en el Período 1939-1989*, Santiago de Chile.

--- (1990), *Transformación Productiva con Equidad*, Santiago de Chile.

Chackiel, J. (1991), *America Latina: Analisis de la Dinamica de la Población Orientado al Sector Salud. Periodo 1950-2000*, CELADE, Santiago, Chile.

CICRED, *La Población de Venezuela*, Caracas, Venezuela.

Collver, A.O. (1965), *Birth Rates in Latin America: New Estimates of Historical Trends and Fluctuations*, res. ser. no.7, Berkeley, Institute of International Studies, University of California.

Council for Economic Planning and Development (1990), *Taiwan Statistical Data Book 1990*, August.

Cortés Conde, R. and S.J. Hunt (eds.) (1985), *The Latin American Economies*, Holmes and Meier, New York.

Díaz Alejandro, C.F. (1975), *Ensayos sobre la Historia Económica Argentina*, Amorrortu editores, Buenos Aires.

Dornbusch, R. and S. Edwards (1990), " El Populismo Macroeconómico", in: E.L. Bacha and S. Edwards (eds.), "Sector Externo, Políticas Financieras y Proceso de Ajuste Macroeconómico" *El Trimestre Económico*, December.

Ferrer, A. (1977), *Crisis y Alternativas de la Política Económica Argentina*, Fondo de Cultura Económica, Mexico City.

Fishlow, A. (1972), "Origins and Consequences of Import Substitution in Brazil", in: L.E. Di Marco, *International Economics and Development: Essays in Honor of Raúl Prebisch*, New York, Academic Press.

Foxley, A. (1983), *Latin American Experiments in Neoconservative Economics*, University of California Press, Berkeley.

Furtado, C. (1963), *The Economic Growth of Brazil*, Berkeley.

Goldsmith, R.W. (1951), A Perpetual Inventory of National Wealth, *Studies in Income and Wealth*, Vol. 14, New York, National Bureau of Economic Research.

--- (1986), Brasil 1850-1984, *Desenvolvimento Financiero sob un Sécolo de Inflacao*, Harper and Row do Brasil, Sao Paulo.

Griffin, K. (1989), *Alternative Strategies for Economic Development*, OECD Development Centre, Macmillan Press.

Hofman, A.A. (1982), *Mexico's Current Economic Problems in Historical Perspective*, M.A. Thesis, mimeograph, Groningen, Netherlands.

--- (1990), *Note on Hours Worked*, ECLAC, Economic Development Division, mimeograph, Santiago.

--- (1991), *The Role of Capital in Latin America: A Comparative Perspective of Six Countries for 1950-89*, ECLAC Working Paper No.4, Santiago.

--- (1992), "Capital Accumulation in Latin America: A Six Country Comparison for 1950-89", *Review of Income and Wealth*, December, (forthcoming).

IEERAL (1986),"Estadísticas de la Evolución Económica de Argentina", *Estudios*, July/September.

INEGI (1985), *Estadísticas Historicas de México*, Tomo I, México, D.F.

Kuznets, S. (1974), *Population, Capital and Growth*, London.

Langoni, C.G. (1974), *As Causas do Crescimiento Economico do Brasil*, APEC.

Maddison, A. (1982), *Phases of Capitalist Development*, OUP, Oxford.

--- (1985), *Two Crises: Latin America and Asia 1929-38 and 1973-83*, OECD, Development Centre Studies, Paris.

Maddison, A. (1987), "Growth and Slowdown in Advanced Capitalist Economies", *Journal of Economic Literature*, June, pp. 649-698.

--- (1989), *The World Economy in the 20th Century*, OECD, Paris.

Mamalakis, M.J. (1976), *The Growth and the Structure of the Chilean Economy: From Independence to Allende*, Yale University Press, New Haven.

McGreevey, W.P. (1985), "The Transition to Economic Growth in Colombia", in: R. Cortés Conde and S.J. Hunt (eds.), *The Latin American Economies*, Holmes and Meier, New York.

Merrick, T.W. and D.H. Graham (1979), *Population and Economic Development in Brazil 1800 to the Present*, Johns Hopkins University Press, Baltimore.

Mizoguchi, T. and M. Umemura (1988), *Basic Economic Statistics of Former Japanese Colonies 1895-1938*, Toyo Keizai Shinposha, Tokyo.

OECD (1991), *Main Economic Indicators*, Paris.

Quero Morales, C. (1978), *Imagen-Objetivo de Venezuela: Reformas Fundamentales para su Desarrollo*, Banco Central de Venezuela, Caracas.

Ramos, J. (1986), *Neoconservative Economics in the Southern Cone of Latin America, 1973-83*, The Johns Hopkins University Press, Baltimore

Reynolds, L.G. (1983), "The Spread of Economic Growth to the Third World: 1850-1980", *Journal of Economic Literature*, September.

Solow, R.M. (1962), "Technical Progress, Capital Formation and Economic Growth", *American Economic Review*, Vol. 52, May.

Suzigan, W. (1976), "Industrialization and Economic Policy in Historical Perspective", in: IPEA/INPES, *Brazilian Economic Studies*, No. 2, Rio de Janeiro, Brazil.

Thomas, V. (1985), *Linking Macroeconomic and Agricultural Policies for Adjustment with Growth: The Colombian Experience*, World Bank, The Johns Hopkins University Press, Baltimore and London.

Urquidi, V. (1985), "The World Crisis and the Outlook for Latin America" in: Wionczek, M.S. (ed.), *Politics and Economics of External Debt Crisis, The Latin American Experience*, Westview Press, Boulder and London.

Villa, M. (1991), *Urbanización y Transición Demográfica en América Latina: Un Reseña del Período 1930-1990*, Celade, Santiago.

Villela, A.V. and W. Suzigan (1977), "Government Policy and the Economic Growth of Brazil, 1889-1945", *Brazilian Economic Studies*, No. 3, IPEA/INPES, Rio de Janeiro, Brazil.

World Bank (1991), *Proceedings of the World Bank Annual Conference on Development Economics 1990*, Washington, DC.

Explaining Economic Growth
A. Szirmai, B. van Ark and D. Pilat
© 1993 Elsevier Science Publishers B.V. All rights reserved.

The Dutch Economy in the Very Long Run - Growth in Production, Energy Consumption and Capital in Holland (1500-1805) and the Netherlands (1805-1910)

Jan Luiten van Zanden
Free University, Amsterdam

1. Introduction

The development of the Dutch economy between 1500 and 1914 has been the subject of much debate among economic historians. The most important of these debates focus on the periods of (relative) economic decline, particularly the period of stagnation between about 1670 and 1800, and the slow process of industrialisation during the nineteenth century (van Zanden, 1989). These debates are concerned with the question of how and why: uncertainty exists about the exact timing of economic development and about why growth ceased or failed to pick up again until the late nineteenth century. There is controversy, for example, concerning the question of when growth in the Dutch economy ceased after the period of rapid expansion that followed the revolt of 1572 and the fall of Antwerp (1585), and when economic stagnation set in, around 1620, 1650 or 1670. Or did per capita income grow continuously even after 1670, as Riley (1984) has argued? Those involved in the debate on industrialisation in the nineteenth century also fail to agree on when the process of modern economic growth began; Griffiths (1979) and de Meere (1982) suggest the 1820s, Brugmans (1961, pp. 201-214) argues for a later period (after 1850), while other scholars have claimed that the take-off of modern industry did not occur until after 1890 (de Jonge, 1968, pp. 339-360).

Until recently, most of the contributions to these debates were based on an evaluation of extremely partial - sometimes even mainly qualitative - sources relating to limited sectors of the economy. Jan de Vries, for example, based his estimates of the change in real income per capita in Holland between 1660 and 1800 on data on the number of passengers carried by Dutch barges in this period (de Vries, 1978, pp. 251-303; de Vries, 1984). For the years 1860-1910 Teijl estimated the level of national income from data on tax revenues, on the growth in energy use, and on the size of the labour force during this period (Teijl, 1971; see also Griffiths and de Meere, 1982). Brinkman, Drukker and Slot (1988) estimated growth in per capita income in the second half of the nineteenth century using data on the height of conscripts, which, for the period 1900-40 at least, appears to correlate with changes in the level of real income. Although these studies have increased our understanding of the long-term development of the Dutch economy, they have not provided us with a reliable picture of how the national economy developed, let alone an understanding of the determinants and the background to the process of economic growth. In order to identify and analyse these, the analysis has to be based as much as possible on the System of National Accounts. The great advantage of this system is, of course, that it forces the researcher to strive for **completeness** - to reconstruct the pattern of change in all sectors of the economy - and **consistency** - all the available data can be utilised and have to be reconciled. Moreover, it provides an understanding of the relationship between economic sectors and macroeconomic factors (investment, savings, government expenditure, etc.), which can serve as a starting point for an analysis of economic development.

In a number of earlier studies, I have tried to estimate growth in GDP in Holland (1500-1805) and the Netherlands (1805-1910), basing my approach as much as possible on the national accounting system and using a large number of quantitative sources (van Zanden, 1987a, 1987b, 1992). It was hoped thereby to provide an initial answer to the question of how the Dutch economy developed in the long run, and to illustrate the usefulness of the system of national accounting in analysing pre-industrial economic growth. The present paper aims to provide an outline of the long-term development of the Dutch economy based on this research. We shall not deal with the debate on the exact timing of economic growth, but instead concentrate on the characteristics of the process of economic growth before and after 1800. An attempt will be made to relate developments in two factors of production - energy and capital - to the process of economic growth in the pre-industrial and industrial periods. In this, we shall focus on the degree to which economic growth in the seventeenth and nineteenth centuries was a result of the availability of inexpensive (fossil) energy. In the literature, both the flourishing of the economy during the Golden Age and industrialisation during the nineteenth century are often associated with peat and coal respectively. Even more classic is the connection made in economic theory between capital accumulation and economic development. We shall consider whether this connection is equally unambiguous in the case of Holland. Our focus on energy and capital is not entirely an arbitrary choice. In the literature on the development of the Dutch economy it is often claimed that the relatively energy- and capital-intensive structure of the national economy is in a sense an inheritance of the Golden Age. Finally, the present study is intended to help encourage the systematic analysis of the long-term development of the Dutch economy, and to contribute to this analysis.

2. Growth of Production

The figures presented in this article are only rough estimates, and are based on a preliminary survey of the available sources. These estimates can certainly be improved upon. As far as the nineteenth century is concerned, attempts are already being made to calculate more detailed series of GDP. In 1991 a start was made on the "Reconstruction of the Dutch National Accounts, 1800-1940" project. This project aims to provide more reliable economic data for this period than those I published in 1987, and to replace these 1987 figures by annual estimates of national income. *Faute de mieux*, however, the present study draws on the 1987 data. Compared with my estimates for the period 1500 to 1805, though, these data are based on a relatively wide range of statistical sources.

A few qualifications to the data are necessary. Firstly, the figures for the sixteenth to the eighteenth centuries refer only to the region of Holland, where between 30 per cent (1500) and 40 per cent (1600-1800) of the population lived and where about 50 per cent of total income was generated in 1800 (Faber et al., 1965; van Zanden, 1987a, p. 55). For a number of reasons, Holland was not representative for the entire Republic, though it was typical in the sense that the economic development of the Republic was dominated by this region. Secondly, the estimates for the period 1500-1805 are narrowly based, particularly in the case of industry. Data on industrial output are available for only a few branches of industry, though, fortunately, these include the most important export industries. This problem was particularly evident for the period 1580-1650, a period of industrial diversification which saw the establishment of many new industries (sugar refineries, the silk and diamond industries, gin distilleries, etc.) as a result of the growth in international trade. In general, data on output are unavailable for these "new" types of industry, partly because they were not subject to the kind of duties levied on traditional export industries. As a result, industrial growth in the period 1580-1650 has tended to be underestimated. Finally, certain assumptions had to be made in the case of almost all sectors in order to translate the available quantitative data into estimates of GDP. These assumptions, discussed in detail in the articles referred to above, imply that the margin of error in calculating estimates of GDP is considerable. Nevertheless, the estimates of changes in the level of GDP calculated in this way do provide a reliable summary of the state of current research in this field. As far as we are aware, all the available data have been included in our calculations and provide more or less consistent estimates. Further, the results broadly correspond with what is already known about the long-term development of the Dutch economy in this period.

Tables 1 and 2 summarise the statistical findings of our earlier studies. In outline, they are as follows.

Jan Luiten van Zanden

TABLE 1

**Estimates of Growth in Output in the Most Important Sectors of the
Economy, Holland (1500-1805) and the Netherlands (1805-1910)
(average annual growth rates)**

	Holland				Netherlands	
	1500-1580	1580-1650	1650-1750	1750-1805	1805-1850	1850-1910
Agriculture	0.3	0.5	-0.3	0.5	0.7	1.3
Fisheries	1.0	0.4	0.3	-3.0	a	a
International Services	1.8	1.3	0.1	0.0	0.9^b	2.7^b
Industry	-0.3^c	1.7^d	-0.2	-0.4	1.2	2.7
Total Gross Output	0.5	1.2^d	-0.0	-0.1	0.9	2.3
Population	0.5	0.9	0.0	0.0	0.8	1.1
Output per Capita	0.0	0.3^d	-0.0	-0.1	0.1	1.2

[a] included in agriculture
[b] including domestic services
[c] export industries
[d] minimum estimate
Sources: Van Zanden (1987a, 1987b, 1992)

- The period 1500-80 was characterised by a rapid expansion in international
  services, particularly in the period 1540-65, when the size of the merchant
  navy increased fourfold. Agriculture, fishing and peat digging also grew
  throughout the period 1500-80. In contrast, urban export industries -
  predominantly breweries and the textile industry - faced a major crisis
  during these years. The decline in this sector almost offset the growth in
  the rest of the economy (see van Zanden, 1992, for more details).
- 1580-1650 was the classic period of growth and owed most to the rapid
  growth of industry (the exact extent of which is still underestimated), trade
  and shipping. Agriculture flourished too, partly because of huge land
  reclamation schemes, which increased the area of land available for
  agriculture (see, for instance, de Vries, 1974; Israel, 1989). The rapid
  growth of the economy was partly offset by an accelerated growth of
  population.
- The 150 years after about 1650 (or 1670) were years of stagnation:
  industry gradually declined after 1670, and agriculture suffered a severe

crisis (from which it did not recover until after 1750). Only growth in international services (together with an expansion in the whaling industry) prevented a sharp decrease in the level of GDP. In this period the Dutch economy showed all the features of the stationary state described by Adam Smith, in which economic growth has come to a standstill because of declining investment opportunities.[1]

- During the first quarter of the nineteenth century there was an economic crisis. It was severest during the years 1810-13 (Buyst and Mokyr, 1990, pp. 64-78). After 1820 the economy gradually recovered, in particular because of industrial growth and growth in the provision of international services. The growth in output in the period 1805-50 was hardly sufficient to match the growth of population, and per capita GDP increased only slightly.

- By international standards, the period after 1850 was characterised by "normal" economic growth, largely the result of the continuing expansion of industry and of international services. The level of GDP per capita doubled (van Zanden, 1987a, p. 68).

TABLE 2
Estimates of Per Capita GDP, Holland
(1500-1805) and the Netherlands (1805-1910),
(in 1985 US dollars)

	Netherlands	Holland
1500		1400-1730
1580		1400-1730
1650		2130
1750		2055
1805	1488	1935
1850	1551	
1880	2295	
1913	3178	

Sources: Maddison (1991) and table 1.

It is clear from this outline that economic growth - and certainly growth in per capita GDP - in Holland between 1500 and 1850 was not a "normal" phenomenon. During these 350 years there was only one period of substantial

---

[1]   The best survey is still that of de Vries (1968); Klein (1979) gives an excellent theoretical interpretation of the transition from growth to stagnation, inspired by the theory of the "stationary state". See also Wrigley (1987), pp. 21-45.

growth: between 1580 and 1650, when per capita GDP increased by at least 30 per cent, and possibly even by 60 per cent. When we extrapolate from Maddison's estimates of per capita GDP for 1913, then the conclusion must be that per capita GDP was already relatively high around 1500 (table 2) - higher than in many third world countries today. This might imply that economic growth between 1500 and 1805 has been systematically underestimated, but this is unlikely. It is more likely that the first major period of growth in the Dutch economy took place before 1500. The many relatively modern features of the Dutch economy around 1500 support such an interpretation (see below).

A second conclusion is that, in the centuries before 1850, economic growth occurred at the same time as demographic growth. The Dutch labour market was open and, particularly during the seventeenth century, large numbers of labourers migrated to Holland in search of work (Lucassen, 1991). In this respect, the development of Holland exhibited many of the features of Lewis' dual development model and was characterised by an unlimited supply of labour (Lewis, 1963). The growth in production led to a similar increase in employment levels, because labour demand could be met by almost inexhaustible reserves of labour in, for example, Germany, Scandinavia, and the east of the Netherlands. Consequently, as far as can be calculated, the growth in per capita output was modest. Another piece of evidence which supports our second conclusion is that even during the period of rapid growth between 1580 and 1650, real wages increased only modestly, and they did not show a clear long-term upward trend.

Economic growth was not only linked to demographic change, but also to the degree of urbanisation. Urbanisation stagnated between 1500 and 1580 as a result of the crisis in urban industries. Between 1580 and 1670, however, the proportion of the population living in cities increased from 45 to 59 per cent, stabilising between 1670 and 1800. Between 1800 and 1910 this pattern was repeated. At the beginning of the nineteenth century there may have been a slight fall in the extent of urbanisation, after which urbanisation stabilised between 1820 and 1850 and was succeeded by a period of urban expansion after about 1860 (van der Woude, 1980, pp. 135-8; Nusteling, 1989). Because of the close relationship between economic growth and urbanisation, one may conclude that the economy of Holland was already relatively modern by 1500: by then about 46 per cent of the population lived in cities and a considerable proportion of the rural population worked in industries other than agriculture (in the fishing industry, peat cutting, the merchant navy) (van Zanden, 1991, pp. 41-8). By 1500 the proportion of the total working population of Holland occupied in agriculture was probably not more than 30 to 40 per cent, an exceptionally low figure for a pre-industrial (late-medieval) society. This partly explains the relatively high level of per capita GDP. As research into the economic development of Holland during the early modern period progresses, it is increasingly apparent that Holland's advance probably has to be dated as far back as the period 1350-1400, much earlier than most historians have hitherto suggested (Jansen, 1978).

3. Economic Growth and the Supply of Energy

In an often-cited article, de Zeeuw (1978) maintained that the growth of Holland's economy during the Golden Age was to an important extent due to the availability of large quantities of cheap energy in the form of peat. He based his claim largely on estimates of peat production, which were in turn based on estimates of the area of land dug during the seventeenth century. De Zeeuw assumed that the energy equivalent of peat production per year was about 6×10^{16} kcal, considerably more than could be attributed to any other energy source, including wood and wind. Unger (1984) subsequently disputed de Zeeuw's estimates and demonstrated that, in general, they were too high. On the basis of more realistic assumptions, Unger concluded that the annual level of peat production was equivalent to 1.2×10^{16} kcal.

The thesis that the supply of energy was an important factor in economic growth has much currency in economic history. The industrial revolution in Great Britain is traditionally associated with the emergence of a new source of energy, coal, particularly on account of the development of the steam engine (von Tunzelmann, 1978, 1-14). The question of whether the availability of cheap energy provides an explanation for Dutch economic growth in the seventeenth and the nineteenth centuries will be approached in two ways. First, an attempt will be made to reconstruct levels of energy consumption in Holland (1600-1800) and the Netherlands (1807-1910) and to compare these figures with the growth in GDP. We then discuss changes in the relative price of energy sources and try to assess the validity of the energy thesis in the case of the Netherlands on the basis of the results of the two approaches.

It is remarkable that in their analyses de Zeeuw and Unger did not use data on actual levels of peat (and coal) consumption in Holland in the seventeenth and eighteenth centuries. These can be derived from the yield of duties (*imposten*) on peat, coal (often combined) and wood in 1608 and for the entire period 1650-1805, and they enable us to calculate rough estimates of the minimum level of energy consumption for these years. From 1807 onwards similar figures can be calculated from comparable data (and import and export statistics) for the Netherlands as a whole. The data for the period 1832-1913 are largely derived from Teijl's work.[2]

There are few problems associated with the figures for the nineteenth

---

[2] Teijl (1971) and (1973); use has been made of the data he collected, which are now in the NEHA archives in Amsterdam.

century. In general, however, the data for the period 1608-1805 probably underestimate real levels of energy consumption. The reasons for this are as follows.

- To a certain extent, the *imposten* were evaded like all taxes. We have no reliable data on the extent to which this occurred.
- Prior to 1750 the collection of these duties was contracted out and, therefore, only the net yield is known (thus excluding the costs of collection and the profits of those collecting these duties).
- A number of users were (partially) exempted from duties on peat; these included almshouses (in Amsterdam in 1752/3 the almshouses accounted for about 8 per cent of total peat use) and some energy-intensive industries (salt refining, stone and lime ovens, tile kilns), for which the duties on peat were 50 per cent lower.[3]
- For the years 1650-1805 we only have data on the total yield of duties on peat and coal. The overwhelming proportion was accounted for by peat consumption however (in 1608 the duty on coal raised only 0.9 per cent of that on peat).[4] For this reason, we based our calculations for 1650-1805 on the tariff per peat ton (and the number of kcal per peat ton). This leads to an underestimate of total energy consumption, however, because the duty per kcal of coal was lower.[5]
- The proportion of total energy supplies accounted for by wood has not been taken into account. In 1608 the estimated value of wood consumption - the *impost* was levied *ad valorem* - was about 6 per cent of the estimated value of peat consumption. In 1805-7 this figure was about 10 per cent for Holland. It seems that much earlier than in the case of its European competitors, wood was an almost negligible source of energy in Holland (Buis, 1985, p. 488).

Despite these problems, however, the broad pattern of energy consumption in Holland can be reconstructed. In 1608 the amount of peat consumed was at least 9.3 million peat tons. This probably rose to more than 10.5 million peat tons by 1651. From about 1670 peat consumption declined, and continued to do so until 1805, though there were considerable fluctuations from year to year. In the 1740s peat consumption reached more than 8 million tons, a level similar to that in 1805, more than half a century after the government had ceased (in 1750) to rely on the private sector to collect duties on peat.[6]

Peat consumption pretty much paralleled changes in GDP, which supports

---

[3]   Municipal Archives Amsterdam, *Archief Burgemeester*, No. 668.

[4]   The 1608 data are from A.R.A., Joh. van Oldenbarnevelt, No. 110.

[5]   Information on rates of *imposten* from Engels (1862), pp. 84-87.

[6]   A.R.A., *Financie van Holland*, No. 826-8.

the plausibility of the figures presented. Our estimates of total peat consumption are also similar to the revised estimates Unger published on the basis of his critical review of de Zeeuw's work. The data available on the yields of excise duties levied also suggest that the figures presented by de Zeeuw are overestimates.

The extent of the increase in coal use is less clear. In Holland in 1608 coal consumption amounted to about 3,600 tonnes. In the kingdom of Holland, an area more or less equivalent to the Netherlands today without the province of Limburg, an average of 110,000 tonnes of coal were consumed each year during the period 1803-7 (Horlings, unpublished). Much of this increase occurred after 1750, when peat prices rose sharply (see below).

TABLE 3
Estimates of Per Capita Energy Consumption and of the Energy-Intensity of Production, Holland and the Netherlands (1608-1910)

	GDP per Capita (1985 US $)	Energy Consumption per Capita Kcal. 10^9	Energy Intensity Kcal. 10^6/GDP
Holland			
1608	1500-2000	2.4	1.20-1.60
1650	2130	2.0	0.94
1750	2055	1.8	0.88
Netherlands			
1805	1488	1.25	0.84
1850	1551	2.41	1.55
1880	2295	6.52	2.84
1910	3178	10.24	3.22

Sources: GDP from table 2. Energy consumption for 19th century from Teijl (1973) and Teijl's data in NEHA archives in Amsterdam; for 17th and 18th century from A.R.A., *Financie van Holland*, No. 826-8, and Joh. van Oldenbarnevelt, No. 110 (The Hague). Information on rates of *imposten* from Engels (1862), pp. 84-87.

In table 3 these data have been converted to estimates of per capita energy consumption. In the seventeenth and eighteenth centuries per capita energy consumption in Holland was at best constant at around 2×10^6 kcal, taking into account the fact that the data on duties underestimate levels of use. There may have been a decline though between 1608 and 1650, when the rate of population growth exceeded the rate of increase in peat consumption. It was not until the nineteenth century that energy consumption increased markedly.

Per capita consumption increased eightfold, mainly because of the significant increase in coal use. In 1807 coal accounted for only 35 per cent of total energy consumption, and peat for 65 per cent. The corresponding figure for coal in 1840 was 41 per cent, and this rose to 58 per cent in 1860 and 92 per cent in 1910 (in that year oil accounted for 3 per cent and peat for the remaining 5 per cent).[7] The degree to which production was energy intensive had changed little in the seventeenth and eighteenth centuries, but it rose markedly in the course of the nineteenth century to a level in 1910 four times that of the corresponding figure for 1807 (table 3).

The relative price of energy sources can be considered a possible explanation for these changes. If the increase in the supply of peat had been an important factor in the economic prosperity of the Republic during the seventeenth century, then one may expect the price of peat to have declined in relation to general prices and wages. Entrepreneurs would then have been encouraged to increase the degree to which production was energy intensive and/or to replace labour by energy (setting aside the question of whether this was possible given the technology available in the seventeenth century). Drawing on the work of Posthumus, the relative price of peat in Utrecht can be calculated for the period 1500-80 (the data are drawn from the Kapittel Oudmunster and the Bartholomeï-Gasthuis) and in Leiden for the period of 1575-1800 (based on prices paid by two hospitals). Peat prices have been compared with an unweighted index of prices for a large number of (agricultural and non-agricultural) commodities, for Utrecht as well as for Leiden (figure 1). In Utrecht in the sixteenth century the relative price of peat rose quite markedly up to about 1565 and then declined, probably due to the fact that the large-scale export of peat from Holland and Utrecht to Antwerp ceased during the years following the *Beeldenstorm* (iconoclastic fury) of 1565-6 and the Revolt of 1572. It is worth noting that peat prices in Flanders during the same years reached record levels (VandenBroeke, 1988, pp. 109-10). Between 1580 and 1675 the relative price of peat rose almost continuously, falling, only briefly, around 1660. It seems to have declined again a little in the first half of the eighteenth century, but after 1750 it rose, and by the end of the eighteenth century the relative price of peat was almost double that around 1600. In short, relative peat prices rose throughout the entire period, except between 1565 and 1580, when prices fell considerably. This pattern of change suggests there was a growing shortage of peat (Buis, 1985, pp. 488-93). This may explain why the degree to which production was energy intensive seems to have decreased rather than increased in the course of the seventeenth and eighteenth centuries. It also implies that rapid growth

---

[7] See Teijl's data in the NEHA archives, Amsterdam.

in output during the Golden Age cannot easily be explained simply in terms of the availability of peat as a cheap source of energy.

FIGURE 1
Price of Peat Relative to Price Index of Agricultural
and Non-Agricultural Commodities, 1500/04-1795/99
(1503/04 = 100 and 1580/84 = 100)

Although comparable prices are lacking for the nineteenth century - remarkably, thanks to Posthumus we know more about prices during the seventeenth and eighteenth centuries than about prices in the nineteenth century - it is clear that the relative price of coal fell considerably during this century. The data we have on coal prices relate only to Amsterdam. They suggest, however, that coal prices fell by about 20 per cent between 1843/4 and 1910, while the cost of living increased by 30 per cent and nominal wages by almost 100 per cent in the same period (van Zanden, 1987c, pp. 86-91, pp. 134-41). So the real price of coal fell considerably. Furthermore, technical change led to an increase in the efficiency of steam engines, because of which the relative price of energy declined even more quickly than is suggested by the fall in the real price of coal. These developments led to an increase in the degree to which productivity was energy intensive, and in general they played a role as a factor in industrialisation during this period. In this respect, economic growth during the nineteenth century differed fundamentally from that during the seventeenth century.

4. Economic Growth and Capital Accumulation

The relationship between economic growth and capital accumulation is complex, and we must confine ourselves here to one aspect of that relationship, namely that between growth in output and changes in the capital wealth of individuals. It is possible to estimate the approximate value of capital holdings for a number of years (1500, 1650, 1790, and 1910) and to determine roughly the composition of private capital holdings - to what extent they consisted of "productive" capital (investment in agriculture, trade and industry), of capital invested in loans to the government, and of capital invested abroad. These estimates have been deflated to take into account changes in price levels. These data give an impression of long-term changes in personal wealth in Holland and the Netherlands in the period 1500-1910, rather than of changes in the stock of capital goods. In the period 1650-1790, for example, the real value of capital invested in agricultural land rose considerably because of the increase in the (relative) price of land - the number of hectares of farmland remained practically the same however. The rise in the relative price of farmland in turn partly resulted from the decline in interest rates. In table 4 estimates have also been included of the average rate of interest on government debt in the same years as those for which data on the value of capital holdings are known. These estimates suggest that there were three distinct periods.
- Between 1500 and 1650 - and probably especially after 1580 - economic growth and capital accumulation roughly paralleled one another. There was large-scale investment in the stock and quality of capital goods: the merchant navy grew tenfold, for example, and the amount of farmland increased significantly as a result of land reclamation, etc.. Per capita wealth tripled and the growing supply of capital led to a fall in interest rates.
- The period 1650 to 1790 was one of economic stagnation - per capita output declined slightly - while, on the other hand, capital accumulation continued. Savings were no longer used productively, but invested in government loans and abroad (mainly in loans to foreign governments). The demand for capital from the productive economy probably declined markedly because of the significant fall in net investment. This process of "accumulation without growth" explains why economic historians have come to such varying conclusions concerning this period. Most scholars argue that the period was one of stagnation. But Riley (1984), in particular, has argued, on the basis of the marked growth in the financial sector, for a more positive interpretation of the economic development of this period.
- Between 1790 and 1910, and especially after 1850, per capita wealth continued to grow. On average it probably doubled, and this was

accompanied by a strong rise in per capita output. In this period the rate of capital accumulation and economic growth more or less parallelled each other again. The amount of "productive" capital grew much more than the capital invested abroad and the capital invested in government loans. Because of the increasing demand for capital from the productive economy, interest rates no longer fell but stabilised at about 3 per cent (after 1900 they rose to about 3.5 per cent).

The most exceptional period was no doubt that between 1650 and 1790. During these years private sector savings continuously exceeded private investments, resulting in a significant decline in the rate of interest and in heavy lending abroad. The extent of the private sector savings surplus can be estimated from the increase in the size of the government debt and the level of investment abroad. On average this increase amounted to about 2.6 million guilders per year between 1650 and 1720, about 6 million per year between 1720 and 1770, and more than 21 million per year between 1770 and 1790, when capital investment abroad increased enormously (van Zanden, 1992). As a result, the eighteenth century saw the paradox of an increasingly (capital) rich society with an extremely fragile economic basis because of the decline in important sectors of the economy.

TABLE 4
Estimates of the Capital Holdings of Private Individuals and Interest Rates (1500-1910)

	Private Capital			Interest rate
	Total (million)	per Capita	in Prices of 1650	
1500	10-12	ca. 40	ca. 200	6.25
1650	450-500	ca. 600	ca. 600	5.00
1790	1600	ca. 2000	ca. 2000	3.00
1910	15000	ca. 2550	ca. 2550	3.50

Sources: 1500-1790: van Zanden (1992); 1910: Verrijn Stuart (1910-1917)

5. Conclusion: Comparing Pre-Industrial and Industrial Economic Growth

In the centuries between 1500 and 1914 the Dutch economy experienced two phases of rapid economic growth - between about 1580 to 1650, and after 1850. In this article we have compared a number of the features of pre-industrial and industrial growth (table 5). It is clear that during the period of pre-industrial growth, long-term real wages were at best more or less constant, interest rates were falling and land prices and energy prices increased markedly (van Zanden, 1992, for more details). If we ignore technical change during the period, then the growth in productivity can only be ascribed to the replacement of labour by capital, which occurred in Holland to a certain extent. Economic growth in the nineteenth century was of a radically different nature: after about 1850 labour costs increased more and more, while the cost of energy fell significantly partly because of the introduction of energy-saving techniques. As shown earlier, the change in relative prices was mirrored in the extent to which particular factors of production were used. The decline in the relative price of energy in the nineteenth century led to a marked rise in the degree to which production was energy intensive, and the increase in real wages in this period was linked to the growth in productivity. It would be wrong of course to argue that the process of economic growth was only determined by changes in the relative prices of the factors of production though. Other factors, such as technical change, specialisation, and economies of scale, were also important. It is not possible, however, to consider these in any detail within the scope of the present article.

TABLE 5

The Relative Prices of Labour, Capital, Energy and Farmland during the Pre-Industrial and Industrial Periods of Economic Growth

	Pre-industrial Growth (1500-1800)	Industrial Growth (1850-1910)
Labour	constant	rising
Capital	declining	constant?
Energy	rising	declining
Land	rising	rising

The comparison shows that somewhere in the 19th century - probably between 1800 and 1850 - the character of economic growth changed markedly. For instance, the "unlimited supplies of labour", characteristic of the pre-industrial period, disappeared. It is this transition from pre-industrial to industrial economic growth that will be the main focus of research in the ongoing project devoted to the "Reconstruction of Dutch National Accounts, 1800-1940".

(Translation from Dutch: C. Gordon, The English Word)

References

Brinkman, H.J., J.W. Drukker and B. Slot (1988), "Lichaamslengte en reëel inkomen: een nieuwe schattingsmethode voor historische inkomens-reeksen", *Economisch- en Sociaal-Historisch Jaarboek*, Vol. 51, pp. 35-79.

Brugmans, I.J. (1961), *Paardenkracht en mensenmacht*, Martinus Nijhoff, The Hague.

Buis, J. (1985), "Historia Forestis", *AAG Bijdragen*, Vol. 26.

Buyst, E. and J. Mokyr (1990), "Dutch Manufacturing and Trade during the French Period (1795-1814) in a Long Term Perspective", in: E. Aerts and F. Crouzet (eds.), *Economic Effects of the French Revolutionary and Napoleonic Wars*, Louvain, pp. 64-78.

Engels, P.H. (1862), *De belastingen en de geldmiddelen van den aanvang der Republiek tot heden*, Utrecht.

Faber, J.A., et al. (1965), "Population Changes and Economic Development in the Netherlands: An Historical Survey", *AAG Bijdragen*, Vol. 12, pp. 47-113.

Griffiths, R.T. (1979), *Industrial Retardation in the Netherlands 1830-1850*, Martinus Nijhoff, The Hague.

--- and J.M.M. de Meere (1983), "The Growth of the Dutch Economy in the Nineteenth Century: Back to Basics?", *Tijdschrift voor Geschiedenis*, Vol. 96, pp. 563-572.

Horlings (1991), De waarde van de Nederlandse koopvaardijvloot in 1850, unpublished, Free University, Amsterdam.

Israel, J.I. (1989), *Dutch Primacy in World Trade 1585-1740*, Clarendon Press, Oxford.

Jansen, H.P.H. (1978), "Holland's Advance", *Acta Historiae Neerlandicae*, Vol. 10, pp. 1-19.

Jonge, J.A. de (1968), *De industrialisatie in Nederland tussen 1850 en 1914*, Scheltema & Holkema, Amsterdam.

Klein, P.W. (1979), "De zeventiende eeuw", in: J.H. van Stuijvenberg (ed.), *De economische geschiedenis van Nederland*, Wolters Noordhoff, Groningen, pp. 79-118.

Lewis, W.A. (1963), "Economic Development and Unlimited Supplies of Labour", in: A.N. Agarwala and S.P. Singh (eds.), *The Economics of Underdevelopment*, Oxford University Press, New York, pp. 400-449.

Lucassen, J. (1991), *Dutch Long Distance Migration*, IISG, Amsterdam.

Maddison, A. (1991), *Dynamic Forces in Capitalist Development*, Oxford University Press, Oxford.

Meere, J.M.M. de (1982), *Economische ontwikkeling en levensstandaard in Nederland gedurende de eerste helft van de negentiende eeuw*, Martinus Nijhoff, The Hague.

Nusteling, H.P.H. (1985), *Welvaart en werkgelegenheid in Amsterdam 1540-1860*, De Bataafsche Leeuw, Amsterdam.

--- (1989), "Periods and Caesurae in the Demographic History of the Netherlands, 1600-1900", *Economic and Social History in the Netherlands*, Vol. 1, pp. 87-118.

Posthumus, N.W. (1936-1939), *De Geschiedenis van de Leidsche laken-industrie*, Vol. II and III, Martinus Nijhoff, The Hague.

--- (1964), *Nederlandsche prijsgeschiedenis*, Vol. II, Brill, Leiden.

Riley, J.C. (1984), "The Dutch Economy after 1650: Decline or Growth?", *The Journal of European Economic History*, Vol. 13, pp. 521-569.

Teijl, J. (1971), "Nationaal inkomen in Nederland in de periode 1850-1900", *Economisch- en Sociaal-Historisch Jaarboek*, Vol. 34, pp. 232-262.

--- (1973), "Brandstofaccijns en nijverheid in Nederland gedurende de periode 1834-1864", in: J. van Herwaarden (ed.), *Lof der historie*, Universitaire pers, Rotterdam.

Tunzelmann, G.N. von (1978), *Steam Power and British Industrialisation to 1860*, Oxford.

Unger, R.W. (1984), "Energy Sources for the Dutch Golden Age: Peat, Wind and Coal", *Research in Economic History*, Vol. 9, pp. 221-253.

VandenBroeke, C. (1988), "Zuinig stoken", *Economisch- en Sociaal-Historisch Jaarboek*, Vol. 51, pp. 93-125.

Verrijn Stuart, C.A. (1910-17), *Inleiding tot de beoefening der statistiek*, Haarlem.

Vries, Joh. de (1968), *De economische achteruitgang der Republiek in de achttiende eeuw*, Stenfert Kroese, Leiden.

Vries, J. de (1974), *The Dutch Rural Economy in the Golden Age, 1500-1700*, Yale University Press, New Haven.

--- (1978), "Barges and Capitalism", *AAG Bijdragen*, Vol. 21.

--- (1984), "The Decline and Rise of the Dutch Economy, 1675-1900", in: G. Saxonhouse and G. Wright (eds.), *Technique, Spirit and Form in the Making of the Modern Economies*, Greenwich, pp. 149-189.

Woude, A.M. van der (1980), "Demografische ontwikkeling van de noordelijke Nederlanden 1500-1800", *Algemene Geschiedenis der Nederlanden*, Vol. 5, Fibula-Van Dishoeck, Haarlem, pp. 102-168.

Wrigley, E.A. (1987), *People, Cities and Wealth*, Basil Blackwell, Oxford.

Zanden, J.L. van (1987a), "Economische groei in Nederland in de negentiende eeuw", *Economisch- en Sociaal-Historisch Jaarboek*, Vol. 50, pp. 51-77.

--- (1987b), "De economie van Holland in de periode 1650-1805: groei of achteruitgang?", *Bijdragen en Mededelingen Betreffende de Geschiedenis der Nederlanden*, Vol. 102, pp. 562-609.

--- (1987c), *De Industrialisatie in Amsterdam 1825-1914*, Octavo, Bergen.

Zanden, J.L. van (1989), "The Dutch Economic History of the Period 1500-1940: Review of the Present State of Affairs", *Economic and Social History in the Netherlands*, Vol. 1, pp. 9-31.

--- (1991), *Arbeid tijdens het handelskapitalisme*, Octavo, Bergen.

--- (1992), "Economic Growth in the Golden Age", *Economic and Social History in the Netherlands*, Vol. 4 (in press).

Zeeuw, J.W. de (1978), "Peat and the Dutch Golden Age", *AAG Bijdragen*, Vol. 21, pp. 3-32.

Explaining Economic Growth
A. Szirmai, B. van Ark and D. Pilat

Long-Run Economic Growth in Spain since 1800: An International Perspective

Leandro Prados de la Escosura
Universidad Carlos III, Madrid

1. Introduction.

Over the last two centuries Spain has evolved from a declining imperial power to an emerging, but still relatively backward nation in the Western European periphery. Despite being an interesting case of retarded or failed growth, Spain's economic performance has received only a tiny proportion of the attention paid to her political history during the interwar years and the Civil War (1936-1939).[1]

Spain's absence in historical debates on European industrialisation has been associated with the lack of quantitative research and economic analysis in Spanish economic history until recent times when progress along the lines drawn by quantitative and analytical economic historians has proceeded very rapidly.[2] Some shortcomings have still to be overcome. In the first place, there is no overall picture of economic performance in modern Spain.[3] Most historical research has dealt with the nineteenth century while post-World War I history has been abandoned to occasional explorations by economists.[4] As a consequence, perceptions of economic performance in modern Spain are derived from the nineteenth century experience despite the fact that growth and structural change are mostly twentieth century features.[5]

---

[1] Spain has been absent from major debates in modern European economic history. The impact of the Napoleonic Wars, the role of colonies in the metropolis' economic development, or late-comers' strategies of development, have all been analysed with no regard to the lessons that could be extracted from Spanish history.

[2] Modern economic history is a very young subject in Spain and most now classical works are less than a quarter of century old. Cf. Sánchez-Albornoz (1968); Tortella (1973); Nadal (1975); Donges (1976).

[3] Cf. recent attempts by Tortella (1992) and Prados (1992).

[4] Only in the last years has the interwar period captured some attention from economic historians. Cf. Martín Aceña (1984); Fraile (1991).

[5] Evidence to support such a statement can be derived from the lively debate on the causes of poor performance over the period 1815-1913 where endogenous and

A second feature of Spanish economic history is the lack of a consistent comparative approach despite occasional implicit comparison with an European pattern of development.[6] Explicit and systematic attempts to compare Spain's performance with other European experiences or models have hardly taken place.[7] In addition, most explanatory hypotheses have not been put to the test with the available quantitative evidence and the use of modern economics. A major obstacle to accomplish this has been the lack of consistent, reliable and homogeneous macroeconomic data, in particular, historical national accounts that prevented Spain's historians from making systematic comparisons with other European experiences. During the last decade quantitative evidence on major macroeconomic variables has been gathered and attempts to establish the pace of growth have taken place. Benchmarks and annual series are now available for GDP but strong discrepancies among alternative estimates suggest a still weak and incomplete quantitative basis.

It is the aim of this paper to provide a quantitative assessment of Spanish economic growth over the long run taking the Napoleonic Wars as a starting point, and to place her performance within the context of Western European industrialisation. Section two presents new evidence on trends in real gross domestic product per head. Section three compares economic performance between Spain and the leading European nations and provides evidence for an assessment of retardation and convergence. Historical explanations for Spanish relative backwardness are explored in section four. Finally, an agenda for further research is suggested.

2. New Evidence on Spain's Economic Growth.

Spanish national accounts started to be published in 1954 and more detailed accounts only appeared in 1964.[8] For earlier periods only index numbers of real output were built up by the official Consejo de Economía Nacional (CEN) estimates, that go back till 1906, and by Alcaide's revision of the CEN series

---

exogenous explanations for failure, retardation and underdevelopment are proposed in sharp contrast with the widely accepted consensus about twentieth century economic modernisation.

[6] When depicting pre-World War I Spain, historians emphasise the failure to replicate an industrial revolution along the British path, the retardation within the European setting or simply features of underdevelopment as shown in today's third world countries.

[7] Cf. as exceptions Tortella (1992); Molinas and Prados (1989); Fraile (1991).

[8] The best updated, homogeneous set of macroeconomic data is the 1980-based series by Corrales and Taguas (1989).

that start in 1901.[9] In the last decade an attempt to provide long-run GDP series from the expenditure side back to mid-nineteenth century was produced by Carreras.[10] A shortcoming of the three annual series for real product is the neglect of the service sector. In the CEN estimates physical output series for agriculture and manufacturing were weighted by 0.4 and 0.6 coefficients, and smoothed by a de-trended index of nuptiality to incorporate yearly fluctuations. Alcaide followed an analogous procedure for agriculture and industry and assumed that output in services moved with the labour force employed in this sector. The implication is that while CEN estimates implicitly assume that output per worker in services was a weighted average of agricultural and industrial labour productivity, Alcaide assumed no growth at all for services' labour productivity.[11] In the case of Carreras' estimates services are, in the best of the cases, clearly underrepresented. In addition to annual series, GDP estimates for seven benchmarks over the period 1800-1930 that included service output were built up by Prados de la Escosura.[12] A common feature of all available estimates is that they are real output indices and not direct calculations of gross domestic product. They all suffer from the index number problem and their economic significance declines as one moves away from the base year. Unfortunately, only contemporary observers have produced direct estimates of national income for the period prior to 1954.[13]

My purpose in providing a new yearly series of real output is to offer an alternative to existing series that incorporates some aspects previously neglected.[14] The new GDP index has been obtained from the output side and it starts from a desaggregated data base that incorporates the results of major independent research on agriculture, manufacturing and services over the last two decades. It has been built up from spliced homogeneous series for agriculture, manufacturing and services with 1913 and 1954 as base years in an attempt to include changes in the product mix and in the price structure.[15] Carreras' pathbreaking research on manufacturing provides the basis for an industrial

---

[9] CEN (1945, 1965); Alcaide (1976).

[10] Carreras (1985). In addition, annual estimates were derived for shorter periods by Schwartz (1977), for 1940-1960, and by Naredo (1991), for 1920-1954.

[11] Cf. Tortella (1987) for a critique of Alcaide's estimates.

[12] Prados de la Escosura (1988). Benchmark indices for real output for the 19th century were also obtained by indirect methods by Bairoch (1976) and Crafts (1984).

[13] Cf. Schwartz (1977).

[14] Prados de la Escosura, Dabán and Sanz (1992).

[15] In the case of industry three base years are used: 1913, 1929 and 1958.

output index updated and improved by recent work by Morellà.[16] Benchmark
estimates for agricultural final output built up by Simpson have been linked to
an annual series derived from a large sample of commodities in an attempt to
represent year-to-year fluctuations.[17] Service output has been derived from
independent physical indicators for a large sample of subsectors, including
transportation and communications, housing rents, public administration, banking, trade and liberal professions. Although only a step in the larger endeavour
of producing historical national accounts for Spain, the new index represents an
improvement in our perception of Spanish economic growth, reconciling scattered knowledge about performance at the sub-sectoral level with an aggregated
view of economic activity. In addition, the series has been constructed with a
method analogous to early nineteenth century benchmarks built up by Prados and
it allows us, therefore, to splice both sets of estimates in order to produce an
overall picture for one hundred and fifty years.[18] Finally, the series can be
linked to available national account series for the post-1954 period.[19]

Table 1 presents growth rates for the new series over significant periods in the
pre-national accounts era and compares the results to those derived from earlier
estimates.

The new series improves the picture of Spanish economic performance in the
century previous to 1950, in particular for the early twentieth century. After
negligible per capita growth over the early nineteenth century, in which increases
in output of goods and services were cancelled out by an acceleration in
population growth, a sustained gain in product per head took place up to World
War I.[20] There is a significant agreement between Carreras' estimates and my

---

[16] The sources for industrial output are Carreras (1984) and Morellà (1992).

[17] Simpson's benchmarks are averages for final output, that is, total production less seed
and animal feed, for the years 1891/95, 1897/1901, 1909/13 and 1929/33. The annual
series used to allow for short-term fluctuations, covers around 50 per cent of output
and includes cereals, pulses, olives and must and covers the period 1882-1935. A
physical output index is available for the 1940-1954 period. Lack of sources for the
years prior to the 1880's make highly conjectural any numbers for agricultural output.
Unsatisfactory fiscal data on crop taxes have been deflated by the price of wheat and
spliced with the post-1882 series. The results, however, are consistent with qualitative
and scattered quantitative evidence.

[18] Prados de la Escosura (1988), chapter 1.

[19] Corrales and Taguas (1989), revised and updated by the authors who kindly allow me
to use it.

[20] Population grew at 0.9 per cent between 1816 and 1857, according to Pérez Moreda
(1985), against 0.4 per cent over the 18th century. It appears that the main contribution
of growth in this period was escape from the Malthusian trap.

new ones on the late nineteenth century pace of growth despite discrepancies for shorter periods. The new series, by contrast with Carreras, emphasises the acceleration of growth in the free-trading years (1860-1890) and the decline that followed the closure of the economy brought by the return to high tariff barriers in 1891 and the delayed effects of giving up the peseta's gold convertibility.[21]

TABLE 1
Growth in real GDP per Head in Spain since 1800 (%)
(exponential fitting, annual growth rates)

	New	Carreras	CEN	Alcaide
1860-1890	1.5	1.0	-	-
1890-1913	0.8	1.0	-	-
1913-1929	1.4	0.8	1.1	1.2
1929-1935	-0.8	-1.4	-0.5	0.5
1935-1940	-2.5	-6.8	-7.6	-6.9
1940-1954	1.5	1.7	3.0	2.7
1929-1950	-0.7	-2.1	-2.1	-1.4
1800-1860	0.2[a]	-	-	-
1860-1913	0.9	0.9	-	-
1913-1950	0.1	-1.0	-0.8	-0.2
1800-1950	0.6[a]	-	-	-
1860-1950	0.8	0.3	-	-
1860-1990	1.4	1.0	-	-

[a] compound growth rate between centered three year averages.
Sources: Prados, Dabán and Sanz (1992a); Carreras (1985); CEN (1965); Alcaide (1976).

Much stronger discrepancies emerge over the poor early twentieth century performance. The new series suggests a slowing down in the rate of growth against the lack of growth or the absolute decline suggested by previous estimates. Substantial differences emerge compared to Carreras' series which represents the interwar years as a period of deceleration, while the new index suggests that a phase of remarkable acceleration in growth and structural change took place from 1913 till 1929. A milder intensity of the 1930s crisis, a less steep fall in the level of economic activity during the Civil War (1936-1939), and a slower growth in the autarkic post-war years, are responsible for the discrepancies between the new series and earlier estimates which showed a decline in output per head from 1929 to the early 1950s. To conclude: a more gradual, more optimistic picture emerges from the new estimates that depicts

---

[21] Cf. Tena (1992); Martín Aceña (1985).

early 20th century Spain as an accelerating economy up to the Great Depression, abruptly interrupted by the Civil War, from which it recovered only slowly under the Dictatorship's economic autarky that lasted until the late 1950s.

A last remark concerns regional dualism within Spain as suggested by strong deviation of regional output per head from the national average during the early twentieth century.[22] Such remarkable regional deviations from the national pattern suggests that the conclusions emerging from this section should be used with extreme caution when inferences at regional level are attempted.

3. Spanish Economic Growth: an International Perspective

Despite perceptions of retardation, backwardness or underdevelopment in Spanish history that implicitly suggest the existence of a European or international pattern, historical assessments of Spain's economic performance pay little regard to the international context. Evidence to support such a contention can be obtained from accounts of early industrialisation and progress in the 1830s and 1840s, of the Spanish "wirtschaftswunder" of the 1960s, or even of the expansion occurring since Spain's admission to the EEC in 1986. This section aims at providing the evidence to revise some of the "stylised facts" about long-run comparative growth of Spain.

The point of departure is Kuznets' definition of modern economic growth that emphasises sustained changes in real output per head and per worker accompanied by structural change, that allow us to define retardation as slower growth relative to neighbour countries together with deviations from patterns of structural change exhibited by leading industrialised countries.[23] Within this context Spain's levels and growth rates of real per capita income and labour productivity will be related to those of major Western European countries and the U.S.A. in order to establish her relative performance and to qualify previous historical assessments.

Figures 1, 2 and 3 and table 2 present evidence for Spain's comparative performance with real GDP per head expressed in 1990 "international" dollars and adjusted for the peseta's purchasing power parity.[24] Levels of real product

---

[22] Cf. Prados (1992), p. 34, the coefficient of variation remained over 35 per cent between 1900 and 1950.

[23] Kuznets (1966), p. 1.

[24] OECD's 1990 PPP "international" dollars were preferred to existing alternatives for 1985, where estimates by Summers and Heston (1991) show strong discrepancies with OECD's similar estimates or with Maddison's (1991) Paasche PPP estimates for Spain's real GDP per head (I am indebted to Angus Maddison for pointing out these discrepancies to me). Besides, the gap between the exchange rate and the PPP rate is narrower for 1990 than for 1985, making the resulting figures more easily

per person for 1990 as estimated by OECD were projected backwards with the new series for Spain's GDP per head and a similar procedure was used to derive annual series for other countries in 1990 "international" dollars.[25]

TABLE 2
Real GDP per Capita Growth in European Countries, 1860-1990
(annual rates. exponential fitting)

	Spain	Italy	France	Germany	U.K.
1860-1890	1.48	0.38	1.08	1.36	1.08
1890-1913	0.83	2.38	1.29	1.69	0.87
1919-1938	0.97[a]	1.01	1.66	2.71	1.34
1950-1960	4.09	5.13	3.59	6.51	2.39
1960-1973	5.73	4.08	4.57	3.48	2.42
1950-1973	5.11	4.79	4.23	4.52	2.38
1973-1990	0.99	2.76	1.53	1.98	2.02
1860-1913	0.91	0.90	1.09	1.55	1.03
1860-1938	0.93[b]	1.21	1.13	1.26	0.81
1950-1990	3.53	3.91	3.27	3.27	2.19
1860-1990	1.45	1.87	1.71	1.82	1.23

[a] For Spain, 1914-1935; [b] For Spain, 1860-1935;.
Notes: t coefficients are highly significant.
Sources: All countries, except Spain, Maddison (1991, 1992); Spain, Prados, Dabán and Sanz (1992b).

Unfortunately, index number problems arise as we move away from the present and are faced with the changes in relative prices and the composition of output that economies experience in the process of structural change.[26]

---

understandable.

[25] Together with OECD (1992) PPP levels of real product per head expressed in 1990 "international" dollars, annual indices of national real output derived from Maddison (1991, 1992), for all countries, and Prados de la Escosura, Dabán and Sanz (1992), for Spain.

[26] Cf. Eichengreen (1986) for a critique of the procedure followed.

Therefore, the evidence offered here only allows us to provide rough orders of
magnitude for Spanish economic performance within the international context.
    Several distinctive features of the Spanish economy emerge from placing it in
an international context. The remarkable tenfold increase in Spain's real per
capita income over one hundred and sixty years, only represents a moderate pace
of growth compared to industrial European nations if Britain is excluded. Spain
started from a lower point in terms of output per person since it practically
stagnated over the early decades of the nineteenth century while Western
European nations industrialised and, therefore, her international position
deteriorated. It appears, thus, that the catching-up hypothesis in which growth
rates correlate inversely to initial levels does not seem to apply to Spain's
historical experience. When evidence about the pace of growth is supplemented
by information on comparative levels of real output per head, the non-
convergence case is reinforced.

FIGURE 1
Real GDP per Head in Spain, 1860-1990

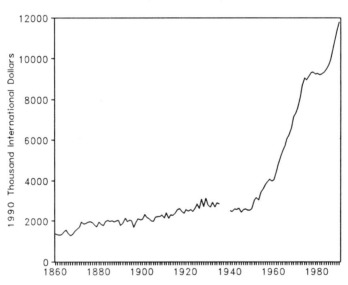

In the search for differentials in Spanish economic performance several
significant periods emerge. Within the period from the mid-nineteenth century
up to the Spanish Civil War (1936), only the moderately free-trading years
1860-1890 and to a lesser extent the late 1910s and the 1920s, represent a mild
attempt to catch up with Western European industrial nations. In the late
twentieth century the 1960-1975 period is another attempt at closing the gap.
Conversely, three periods appear to be responsible for the widening gap between

FIGURE 2
Real GDP per Head, USA=100

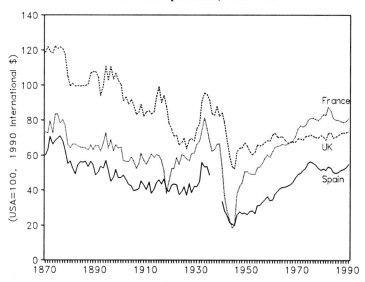

FIGURE 3
Real GDP per Head, USA=100

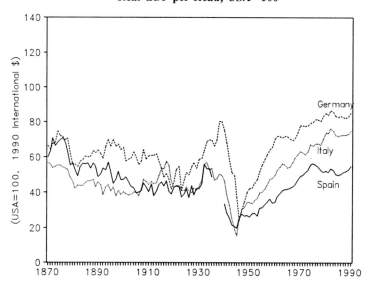

Spain and the advanced Western European nations: the turn of the century and the decade prior to World War I seems to be a lost opportunity for closing the gap as the comparison with Giolittian Italy suggests.[27] Despite traditional accounts stressing the poor economic performance under autarky in the 1940s, in comparative terms the 1950s emerge as a decade of failed catching-up, as the ups and downs in real output per head and the comparison with Italy's performance suggest. As forces making for growth and convergence were stronger in the 1950s, countries like Spain that failed to catch-up paid a heavier penalty than would have been the case in phases of slowing down.[28] Countries that remained closed and did not compete in international markets for similar goods did not share the productivity growth benefits deriving from the leading nations. However, the largest loss in relative levels of income per head during more than one and a half centuries appears to derive from the years between General Franco's death (1975) and the admission of Spain to the EEC (1986). Once again, the comparison with Italy seems to be particularly relevant. Research on the period is lacking and only superficial hypotheses relating poor performance to the difficult transition to a democratic regime are available as explanations. However, there seem to be deeper institutional reasons underlying poor economic performance, i.e. an over-regulated, heavily protected economy, cut-off from the international market. This explanatory hypothesis needs to be explored further.

When assessing differences in the level of efficiency across countries, partial or total factor productivity measures are used. Over the long run only reliable partial productivity estimates can be obtained for Spain. Labour productivity measurements provide a reasonable index for productive potential, influenced by both factor endowments, technology and organisation. Lower participation rates, largely unexplored, improve Spanish relative position but the picture of retardation drawn for real product per head remains basically unaltered.[29]

4. Retardation and Catching-Up in Spain: A Search for Determinants

Both Gerschenkronian explanations for backwardness and convergence and catching-up hypotheses are related to the search for the causes of growth.

---

[27] Not only Italy but Sweden, and Hungary and Russia, to a lesser extent, reduced distances with respect to Britain and France over the 1900-1913 period. Cf. Berend and Ranki (1982).

[28] Cf. Baumol (1986).

[29] Cf. Prados de la Escosura (1992) for a discussion and evidence. Gender and age structure of the labour force, urbanisation, educational patterns and levels of unemployment all influence participation rates and contribute to the explanation of differentials across countries.

Economists have emphasised the role of technological progress, partly embodied in new capital, and the social capability for innovative adoption of the leader's technology and organisation to the resource endowment and particular conditions of the follower, as crucial elements for reducing the productivity gap among countries.[30] The pace at which catching-up takes place depends on the diffusion of knowledge, the reduction of intersectoral disequilibria through structural change, physical and human capital accumulation, and the degree of openness, along with an institutional framework that favours economic progress through an adequate system of incentives.

Testing the plethora of explanatory hypothesis for growth and convergence in modern Europe is a challenge for economic historians that obviously goes beyond the scope of this paper. However, the definition of backwardness along Kuznetsian lines, allows us to identify the extent to which structural change in a peripheral country like Spain gave rise to a convergence process towards Europe's industrial nations.[31] Patterns of development for Spain within a European framework built up along the lines defined by Chenery and Syrquin and Crafts are offered in table 3.[32] Simulations allow us to compare structural change in Spain with structural change in an "ideal" European country with the same size and income per head as Spain. Convergence would take place if structural differences are reduced, as real income per head grows. Conversely, increasing structural differences would imply backwardness. In table 3 Spain's deviations from the European pattern are presented in percentage terms. The results seem to provide enough evidence to conclude that for most of the period under consideration human and physical capital accumulation in Spain remained below European standards and only converged towards them at high levels of per capita income not reached before the 1960s. A large agricultural sector in Spain, with relatively low productivity - up to 1913, and again in recent years -, together with a slower and delayed release of labour from the countryside, seem to be another explanatory element of retardation. Recent research on European agricultural productivity confirms our findings as it suggests that even in 1980 a large gap in value added per worker existed between Spain and Western European nations.[33]

---

[30] Cf. Baumol (1986); Abramovitz (1986); Dowrick and Gemmell (1991); Barro (1991).

[31] As defined above, it would imply a widening differential in per capita incomes with regard to advanced countries together with a structural divergence as real product per head grows.

[32] Chenery and Syrquin (1975); Crafts (1984). The underlying equations derive from a forthcoming paper by Prados, Dabán and Sanz (1992b).

[33] Cf. O'Brien and Prados de la Escosura (1992).

TABLE 3
Patterns of Development in Spain, 1860-1990
(centered five-year averages)

	1860	1890	1900	1913	1929	1950	1960	1975	1990
Y/pop	1359	1776	2079	2307	3133	2625	4022	8973	11791
Pop. (m)	15.6	17.8	18.6	20.3	23.2	27.9	30.3	35.5	39.2
%INVT/GDP	5.5	7.3	9.6	11.9	17.1	15.2	18.0	27.9	26.0
Dev.(%)	**-43**	**-35**	**-13**	**-1**	**13**	**-27**	**-13**	**24**	**4**
%CON/GDP	88.4	86.6	82.8	75.5	75.6	72.1	65.4	65.7	64.0
Dev.(%)	**2**	**11**	**9**	**2**	**-1**	**2**	**0.1**	**3**	**8**
%SCHOOL	39.0		36.0	30.6	26.0	30.1	49.0	76.0	86.0[a]
Dev.(%)	**26**		**-10**	**-41**	**-43**	**-33**	**-10**	**13**	**26**
%IND/GDP	14.9	20.0	21.2	21.6	21.9	25.8	35.2	41.9	39.1
Dev.(%)	**-56**	**-37**	**-34**	**-28**	**-35**	**-36**	**-7**	**10**	**1**
%AG/GDP	45.2	38.5	38.3	37.7	36.7	29.9	23.7	9.6	6.3[b]
Dev.(%)	**15**	**9**	**11**	**13**	**22**	**-2**	**-6**	**16**	**4**
%Lag/L	63.5	65.3	66.3	66.0	45.5	47.6	39.0	23.4	11.8
Dev.(%)	**17**	**25**	**27**	**25**	**10**	**4**	**4**	**29**	**-17**
Agriculture's relative productivity									
	0.71	0.59	0.58	0.57	0.81	0.63	0.56	0.41	0.34[b]
Dev.(%)	**-2**	**-16**	**-16**	**-15**	**12**	**-6**	**-10**	**-13**	**11**

[a] year 1980. [b] year 1985.
Notes: Dev.(%): deviation from the European norm (difference between the log of the actual value for Spain and the log of the European norm).
Y/Pop: real GDP per head in 1990 "international" dollars.
Pop. (m): million inhabitants.
%AG/GDP: agriculture's share in GDP.
%IND/GDP: industry's share in GDP.
%Lag/L: share of agriculture in total active population.
%INVT/GDP: share of domestic investment in GDP, expressed in real terms.
%CON/GDP: share of domestic consumption in GDP, expressed in real terms.
% SCHOOL: percentage of population aged 5 to 19 in school.
Sources: Prados, Dabán and Sanz (1992b).

A lower degree of openness up to the 1980s, divergent from the European pattern, completes a picture in which structural convergence is not clearly visible.[34]

---

[34] Cf. Tena (1992).

5. Conclusions

Moderate growth, retardation and incomplete attempts to catch up emerge from a brief quantitative assessment of Spain's economic performance over almost two centuries. No persuasive explanations have been provided but a long agenda for research emerges from the questions raised by the empirical evidence gathered. Why did the release of labour from the countryside take so long? Can this be explained by characteristics of the "urban" economy? Why did human and physical capital accumulation proceed at such a slow pace? What prevented Spanish industrialists from having access to international markets? Only a comparative, quantitative approach seems adequate to provide the answers.

References

Abramovitz, M. (1986), "Catching-Up, Forging Ahead, and Falling Behind", *Journal of Economic History*, Vol. XLVI, No. 2, pp. 385-406.

Alcaide, J. (1976), "Una revisión urgente de la serie de renta nacional en el siglo XX", in: *Datos básicos para la Historia financiera de España*, Instituto de Estudios Fiscales, Madrid, 2 Vols., pp. 1126-1150.

Barro, R. (1991), "Economic Growth in a Cross Section of Countries", *Quarterly Journal of Economics*, Vol. CVI, No. 2, pp. 407-447.

Baumol, W.J. (1986), "Productivity Growth, Convergence and Welfare: What the Long-Run Data Show", *American Economic Review*, Vol. LXXVI, No. 5, pp. 1072-1085.

Berend, I.T. and G. Ranki (1982), *The European Periphery and Industrialization, 1780-1914*, Cambridge University Press, Cambridge.

Carreras, A. (1984), "La producción industrial española, 1842-1981: construcción de un índice anual", *Revista de Historia Económica*, Vol. II, No. 1, pp. 127-157.

--- (1985), "Gasto Nacional Bruto y Formación de Capital en España, 1849-1958: primer ensayo de estimación", in: P. Martín Aceña and L. Prados de la Escosura (eds.), *La Nueva Historia Económica en España*, Tecnos, Madrid, pp. 17-51.

Chenery, H.B. and M. Syrquin (1975), *Patterns of Development 1950-1970*, Oxford University Press, Oxford.

Consejo de Economia Nacional (CEN) (1945), *La Renta Nacional de España*, 2 Vols., C.E.N., Madrid.

--- (CEN) (1965), *La Renta Nacional de España, 1906-1965*, C.E.N. Madrid.

Corrales, A. and D. Taguas (1989), *Series macroeconómicas para el período 1954-1988: un intento de homogeneización*, Instituto de Estudios Fiscales, Madrid.

Crafts, N.F.R. (1984), "Patterns of Development in Nineteenth Century Europe", *Oxford Economic Papers*, Vol. XXXVI, No. 4, pp. 438-458.

Donges, J.B. (1976), *La industrialización en España. políticas, logros, perspectivas*, Oikos Tau, Barcelona.

Dowrick, S. and N. Gemmell (1991), "Industrialization, Catching-Up and Economic Growth: A Comparative Study Across the World's Capitalist Economies", *Economic Journal*, Vol. CI, No. 1, pp. 263-275.

Eichengreen, B, (1986), "What Have We Learned from Historical Comparisons of Income and Productivity", in: P.K. O'Brien (ed.), *International Productivity Comparisons and Problems of Measurement*, Bern.

Fraile, P. (1991), *Industrialización y grupos de presión. La economía política de la protección en España*, 1900-1950, Alianza, Madrid.

Kuznets, S. (1966), *Modern Economic Growth: Rate, Structure, and Spread*, Yale University Press, Yale.

Maddison, A. (1991), *Dynamic Forces in Capitalist Development*, Oxford University Press, Oxford.

--- (1992), "El crecimiento económico italiano, 1861-1989: una revisión", in: L. Prados de la Escosura and V. Zamagni (eds.), *El desarrollo económico en la Europa del sur: España e Italia en perspectiva histórica*, Alianza, Madrid, pp. 81-100.

Martin Aceña, P. (1984), *La política monetaria en España, 1919-1935*, Instituto de Estudios Fiscales, Madrid.

--- (1985), "Déficit público y política monetaria en la Restauración 1874-1923", in: P. Martín Aceña and L. Prados de la Escosura (eds.), *La Nueva Historia Económica en España*, Tecnos, Madrid, pp. 262-284.

Molinas, C. and L. Prados de la Escosura (1989), "Was Spain Different? Spanish Historical Backwardness Revisited", *Explorations in Economic History*, Vol. XXVI, No. 4, pp. 385-402.

Morella, E. (1992), "Indices sectoriales de producción industrial de postguerra (1940-1958)", *Revista de Historia Económica*, Vol. X, No. 1.

Nadal, J. (1975), *El fracaso de la Revolución industrial en España, 1814-1913*, Ariel, Barcelona.

Naredo, J.M. (1991), "Crítica y revisión de las series históricas de renta nacional de la postguerra", *Información Comercial Española*, 698, pp. 133-152.

O'Brien P.K. and L. Prados de la Escosura, "Agricultural Productivity and European Industrialisation, 1890-1980", *Economic History Review*, Vol. XLV, No. 3, pp. 514-536.

Perez Moreda, V. (1985), "La evolución demográfica española en el siglo XIX (1797-1930): tendencias generales y contrastes regionales", in: *La popolazione italiana nell'Ottocento*, Bologna, pp. 45-113.

Prados de la Escosura, L. (1988), *De imperio a nación. Crecimiento y atraso económico en España (1780-1930)*, Alianza, Madrid.

Prados de la Escosura, L. (1992), "Crecimiento, atraso y convergencia en España e Italia: introducción", in: L. Prados de la Escosura and V. Zamagni (eds.): *El desarrollo económico en la Europa del sur: España e Italia en perspectiva histórica*, Alianza, Madrid, pp. 27-55.

---, T. Daban and J. Sanz (1992a), *An Index for Real GDP in Spain, 1860-1954*, Mº de Economía y Hacienda (mimeo).

---, L., T. Daban and J. Sanz (1992b), *Patterns of Development in Europe, 1820-1990*, Mº de Economía y Hacienda (mimeo).

Sanchez-Albornoz, N. (1968), *España hace un siglo: una economía dual*, Península, Barcelona.

Summers, R. and A. Heston (1991), "The Penn World Table (Mark 5): An Expanded Set of International Comparisons, 1950-1988", *Quarterly Journal of Economics*, Vol. CVI, No. 2, pp. 327-368.

Tena, A. (1992), "Protección y competitividad en España e Italia, 1890-1960", in: L. Prados de la Escosura and V. Zamagni (eds.), *El desarrollo económico en la Europa del sur: España e italia en perspectiva histórica*, Alianza, Madrid, pp. 321-355.

Tortella, G. (1973), *Los orígenes del capitalismo en España*, Tecnos, Madrid.

--- (1987), "El sector terciario en España antes de 1936: una nota de escepticismo sobre las estimaciones al uso", *Revista de Historia Económica*, Vol. V, No. 2, pp. 587-597.

--- (1992), "La Historia económica de España en el siglo XIX: un ensayo comparativo con los casos de Italia y Portugal", in: L. Prados de la Escosura and V. Zamagni (eds.), *El desarrollo económico en la Europa del sur: España e italia en perspectiva histórica*, Alianza, Madrid, pp. 56-80.

Explaining Economic Growth
A. Szirmai, B. van Ark and D. Pilat
© 1993 Elsevier Science Publishers B.V. All rights reserved.

Economic Growth in Eastern Central Europe after World War II

*Éva Ehrlich**
Institute for World Economics, Budapest

1. Introduction

The present study is only a rough outline of the problems of economic growth in Eastern and Central Europe. We still lack the necessary perspective required for a thorough scientific and historical evaluation, and reliable national statistics are only partly available.

In this article three questions are raised: first I sketch the Stalinist model's rise and fall (based on factual evidence whenever possible); secondly I briefly outline the nature of the Stalinist approach; and thirdly I offer a brief account of the present economic situation of the Eastern and Central European countries, the therapies proposed for the stabilisation of their economies, and the transition to a market economy.

The countries covered in this study are Czechoslovakia, Poland, Hungary and East Germany (up to 1990), in the north of the region, and Yugoslavia, Bulgaria and Romania in the south.

2. The More Distant Past

The countries of Eastern and Central Europe (hereafter Eastern Europe) do not constitute a homogenous region in terms of their geopolitical situation, history, or level of development. The present borders were mainly drawn up after the disintegration of the Austro-Hungarian Monarchy at the end of World War I, though there were important changes after World War II in Poland and minor ones in other countries. Czechoslovakia and Poland gained independence after World War I and Yugoslavia emerged then as a unified country. Transylvania, previously part of Hungary, was attached to Romania. Hungary, the former associate in the Austro-Hungarian Monarchy, lost two-thirds of its territory and half of its population. A large part of its old territory, inhabited partly by a purely Hungarian population and partly by a

---

* In writing this article, I borrowed material from a forthcoming volume *"Europe 1990"* (Eunaudi) coauthored with Révész (Ehrlich and Révész, 1992).

TABLE 1
Labour Force Structure between the Two World Wars
Total Active Population = 100%

Country	1920-1921			1930-1934		
	Agriculture	Industry[1]	Others	Agriculture	Industry[1]	Others
Czechoslovakia	40.3	36.8	22.9	37.0	37.1	25.9
Hungary	56.6	17.0	26.4	50.7	20.7	28.6
Poland	75.9	9.4	14.7	65.0	16.9	18.1
Romania	-	-	-	78.7	7.2	14.1
Yugoslavia	82.2	11.0[2]	6.8	78.7	11.1	10.2
Bulgaria	82.4	8.1	9.5	80.0	8.0	12.0

Notes: [1] Mining, manufacturing, construction, electricity, gas and water.
       [2] Transport and communications, including industry.
Source: Csernok, Ehrlich and Szilágyi (1975) pp. 351-355.

TABLE 2
Illiteracy between The Two World Wars
Percentage of Population (10 years and older)

Country group or country	1920	1929	1937
Western Europe	6.7	1.6	0.7
Southern Europe	47.4	38.4	36.0
Eastern Central Europe			
Czechoslovakia	5.5	4.1[1]	3.0
Hungary	13.0	9.3	7.0[2]
Poland	32.7[3]	23.1[8]	18.5[2]
Bulgaria	50.3	-	31.4[7]
Romania	58.0[4]	42.0[4]	-
Yugoslavia	62.0[5]	48.0[5]	39.0[5]
USSR			
European part	-	48.1[6]	-
Asian part	-	73.0[6]	-

Notes: [1] 1930; [2] Estimate; [3] 1921; [4] 7 years and older; [5] 11 years
         and older; [6] 1926. Census. 5 years and older; [7] 1934;
         [8] 1931
Source: Csernok, Ehrlich and Szilágyi (1975), pp. 330-334 and pp.
         305-318; Hauner (1985), p. 93; USSR: Uj idők Lexikona,
         Vol. II, p. 369.

mixed population, was granted to neighbouring countries (Czechoslovakia, Austria, Romania and Yugoslavia; some of the territory regained in World War II was ceded to the Soviet Union). Bulgaria and Romania had won territory from the Turkish Empire during the Balkan Wars right before World War I. All these changes later became the source of much national conflict.

In terms of economic development, only Czechoslovakia (primarily Bohemia) had a level approaching the Western European average. Hungary and Poland, on the periphery of Europe, had taken the road of industrialisation. The southern, Balkan countries - Yugoslavia (except Slovenia and Croatia), Bulgaria and Romania (principally the Eastern and Southern regions of the country) were just at the start of industrialisation. The economic and social heterogeneity of the region is well demonstrated by the tables showing the employment structure (table 1), the extent of illiteracy (table 2) and per capita national income (table 3).

Within the region, the inherited differences in the level of development remained after World War I. Czechoslovakia, (first of all the northern, Czech part of the country), the now smaller Hungary, and Poland, (a country formed just after World War I, primarily its Western regions, previously part of the Austro-Hungarian Monarchy), were relatively developed. The three Balkan countries, a large part of Yugoslavia, Romania and Bulgaria were relatively underdeveloped, and so they remained.

The area is therefore an entity only in that it became the sphere of interest of the Soviet Union after World War II. Countries were compelled to adopt the political and economic system and solutions developed in the Soviet Union during the Stalinist era. COMECOM an organ for "socialist integration" aimed at harmonisation of the central plans of member countries. Military integration was ensured by the power of the Warsaw Pact.

3. The Functioning and the Collapse of the Stalinist Model of Forced Economic Growth

The aim of the Stalinist model was to attain rapid economic growth. It was thought or at least proclaimed that the production level of the developed market economies would be attained within a few decades. The reality was different.

Before presenting some basic statistical data, attention must be drawn to the fact that macroeconomic indicators, such as national income or the rate of accumulation are not reliable in the majority of Eastern European countries (with the possible exception of Hungary and Yugoslavia). Where more reliable estimates are available, we present these alongside the official statistics in order to reveal at least the order of magnitude of the generally upward distortions. In many former socialist countries work on detecting

304   *Éva Ehrlich*

TABLE 3
Ranking of 33 Countries by Economic Development Level, 1937
(Calculated by PIM)

Country	National income (SNA) US$ per capita Expressed in current US$ measured at the exchange-rate scale, 1937		
	Rank	USA = 100	Czechoslo-vakia = 100
USA	1	100.0	335.0
United Kingdom	2	77.2	258.0
Australia	3	75.2	252.0
New Zealand	4	71.9	242.0
Sweden	5	70.2	235.0
Canada	6	62.5	210.0
Germany	7	59.6	200.0
Denmark	8	59.6	200.0
Belgium and Luxembourg	9	57.9	194.0
Switzerland	10	56.1	185.0
Netherlands	11	53.7	180.0
Norway	12	52.6	176.0
France	13	46.5	156.0
Argentina	14	38.6	130.0
Finland	15	37.5	126.0
Austria	16	33.3	112.0
Ireland	17	31.6	106.0
Czechoslovakia	18	29.8	100.0
South Africa	19	27.2	91.5
Chile	20	26.3	88.4
Italy	21	23.7	79.6
Japan	22	23.7	79.6
Hungary	23	21.1	70.8
USSR	24	18.4	61.7
Poland	25	17.5	58.7
Spain	26	16.7	56.0
Portugal	27	16.3	54.7
Greece	28	16.1	54.1
Mexico	29	15.3	51.4
Romania	30	14.2	47.7
Yugoslavia	31	14.0	47.0
Bulgaria	32	13.2	44.3
Turkey	33	10.5	35.2

Source: Ehrlich (1991)

distortions in the official statistics has not even begun.[1] But this work will have to be performed in every Eastern European country in the years to come.

The post - World War II economic development of the countries of the region can be roughly divided into three phases (if one disregards important but individual characteristics). The **first period** starts at the end of the 1940s and the beginning of the 1950s, and closes in the 1960s. Industrialisation advanced very rapidly in this period. The growth of the national economies was rapid even by international standards. In the period 1949-1953 the standard of living decreased, although the rate of accumulation was high. After that, the standard of living began to grow, although there were serious shortages in the consumer markets. An important role in the rise of living standards was played by budget-financed redistributory systems (free or highly subsidised day nurseries and kindergartens, free education, free or almost free health services, pensions for almost every citizen, state-subsidised housing) and full employment. According to both the official published figures and estimated data, the rate of growth was lower in the more developed (northern) countries than in less developed (southern) ones. Official growth rates for the period 1937-1960 are presented in table 4, and for the period 1951-1973 in table 5. Table 4 also presents the rates of growth calculated by Ehrlich by the Physical Indicators Method (PIM)[2] devised by the Economic Commission for Europe, which are lower but more reliable than the official rates.

---

[1]   According to my information, Hungary is the only country where the official rates of growth in the mid-1960s relative to pre- and post-World War II years have been reviewed. The revision considerably reduced the growth figures previously published.

[2]   PIM (Physical Indicators Method) is built on heuristic regressions between productive and personal consumption, stock-type physical indicators and per capita GDP in market economies. Regressions established for individual physical indicators then make it possible to estimate GDP for countries for which only physical indicators are known. If we rely on offical exchange rates when converting national GDPs into dollars for the establishment of the regression between market economies' physical indicators and per capita GDP we place development levels and ratios on the exchange rate scale. However, PIM can start from purchasing power parity GDPs too (e.g. those calculated by ICP using the repricing method). In this case, development levels and ratios are expressed on the purchasing power parity scale (as in Maddison's calculations). The exchange rate scale has a steeper slope than the purchasing power parity scale. If for some year we have GDP data on both scales, then values of the other can be converted (the same way as temperature in Fahrenheit is converted into temperature in Celsius). For more on the Physical Indicator Method (PIM), see Jánossy (1963), Ehrlich (1966, 1969, 1991 and 1991a), Comparative GDP levels (Economic Commission for Europe, 1980 and Marer, 1985).

TABLE 4

Per Capita National Income (SNA) and GDP Growth
Calculated and Official Rates, 1937-1960-1980
(Calculated by PIM, Annual % Growth Rates)

	Index per capita				Differences between official and calculated indices	
	Calculated		Official			
	National Income (SNA)	GDP	Produced National Income (MPS)		1960/1937	1980/1960
Countries	1937-60 (1)	1960-80 (2)	1937-60 (3)	1960-80 (4)	(3)/(1) (5)	(4)/(2) (6)
GDR	-	3.47	-	4.74	-	1.37
Czechoslovakia	1.94	3.11	2.57	3.92	1.33	1.26
Hungary	1.64	4.18	1.98[1]	4.78[3]	1.21	1.14[4]
Poland	1.81	3.52	3.20	4.85	1.77	1.38
Bulgaria	2.16	4.99	4.60[2]	6.73	2.13	1.35
Romania	1.52	4.25	2.26	7.78	1.48	1.83
Yugoslavia	1.60	4.55	1.90	4.99	1.19	1.10
USSR	2.10	4.38	4.47	4.92	2.13	1.12

Notes: [1] In 1968, four years after Ehrlich's calculation, the Central Statistical Office re-examined the official rates of growth of per capita national income (MPS) published earlier and reduced them. The recalculated index is used here.
[2] 1939-1960
[3] Per capita GDP growth: 4.5 percent
[4] Per capita GDP growth: 1.08 percent

Sources: 1960-1937: National Statistical Yearbooks; Ehrlich (1991)
1980-1990:
- OECD National Accounts 1960-1987
- CMEA Statistical Yearbooks
- Hungary per Capita GDP:
1960-1969: Népgazdasági méelegek 1960-1970, KSH
(Central Statistical Office) 1971
1969-1970: Népgazdasági mérleg 1970, KSH 1971
1970-1980: A népgazdaság fejlődésének fóbb mutatój 1985, KSH, 1987.

TABLE 5
Per capita GDP. Calculated and Official Rates, 1951-1973
(Calculated by PIM, Annual % Growth Rate)

Countries	1951-55		1956-60		1961-65		1966-70		1971-73		1951-73		
	1	2	1	2	1	2	1	2	1	2	1	2	3
GDR	5.2	13.7	4.7	8.0	3.5	3.7	3.2	5.1	3.4	5.4	4.0	7.2	1.80
Czecho-													
slovakia	3.7	6.9	4.5	6.2	4.0	1.1	3.7	6.5	3.5	4.5	3.9	5.0	1.28
Hungary	5.3	4.6	4.0	5.7	5.1	3.7	5.0	6.5	4.5	6.3	4.8	5.3	1.10
Poland	4.1	6.6	3.9	4.8	4.8	4.7	4.7	5.1	5.5	9.7	4.5	5.9	1.31
Bulgaria	7.2	8.1	7.9	8.7	7.4	5.9	6.1	8.0	3.4	7.2	6.6	7.6	1.15
Romania	5.7	12.6	4.9	5.6	7.5	8.3	5.8	6.5	5.8	10.2	5.9	8.5	1.44
Yugoslavia	4.2	4.2	6.0	7.5	6.2	5.8	5.0	5.4	5.1	5.1	5.3	5.6	1.06
USSR	5.1	9.1	5.2	7.7	5.4	5.1	4.4	6.5	3.9	5.1	4.8	6.7	1.40

Legend: 1 = Calculated growth rate
2 = Official growth rate
3 = Differences between official and calculated indices
Sources: Comparative GDP levels (1980); Economic Bulletin for Europe Vol. 31.,
No. 2., p. 26.

Adapting themselves to a model of extensive growth aimed at maximal utilisation of resources, and preparing themselves for a possible imminent war, the Eastern European countries in the early 1950s raised their net rate of accumulation (investment within national income) to 25-30 percent. This resulted in a sizeable decrease in real wages and personal consumption, despite increasing national income.

As a result of land reforms after World War II, small farms had become predominant, but they came under political and economic pressure by the beginning of the 1950s. The peasantry was harassed. Unlawful methods were employed against rich peasants and the upper stratum of middle-ranking peasants, aimed at bringing about their economic (and sometimes their physical) destruction. One of the important tools of economic pressure in the 1950s was compulsory delivery. Another was taxation. Taxes were determined not on the basis of the income but according to "productive capacity", which took into account the quantity and quality of land held. As a result, the peasantry lost its incentive to produce. From the early 1950s onwards, there were shortages of food and queues for food in all Eastern European Countries, something previously unheard of in the region in peacetime.

Following the Soviet example and Stalinist doctrine, necessity was turned into a principle. As the Soviet leadership had done in 1929-33, the leaders of state socialism in Eastern Europe tried to collectivise agriculture as fast as possible, in order to bring about a more productive, large-scale agriculture that would produce more national income and release workers for heavy industry and arms production. They hoped that economies of scale would allow agriculture to do better at supplying the rapidly increasing urban population with food. The ideology fabricated to justify this policy ran as follows: "Socialism cannot be built on two opposing principles: on state-owned industry and privately owned, small-scale agriculture, because the latter gives birth to day-to-day capitalism".

Collectivisation in Eastern Europe (Poland and Yugoslavia being exceptions) was completed by 1961. The predominant proportion of the area farmed came into the possession of large cooperative and state farms. The functioning of cooperatives and state monopolies in supplying and buying organisations, integrated agriculture into the unified system of the planned economy.

Constraints on rapid long-term growth manifested themselves in this initial period in ever more frequent underfulfilment of the quantitative targets of the central plans.[3] Quality and modernity of products were neglected. There were no quality goals in central plans. Deteriorating quality and a widening technological gap did not cause serious sales problems either at home or in CMEA exports; an environment of chronic shortage meant that sales problems were not a constraint on quantitative growth. Although the volume of unsold goods increased, this was attributed to poor planning or deviations from the plan. These and similar problems were considered by the leaders of the countries as infantile disorders of the new system, deriving from "bad execution of good decisions" and a series of subjective failures.

The **second period** covers the latter half of the 1960s and the first half or two-thirds of the 1970s. This period is marked by a gradual fall in the rate of economic growth from the previous period and an increase in hardship. By the early 1960s, the rulers of Eastern Europe made policy adjustments that had an important effect on conditions in agriculture and standards of living. Taxes became less onerous. Compulsory delivery was first eased and later abolished, but the state monopoly over procurement and buying organisations meant that the state still had the upper hand. The mechanisation of large-scale

---

[3] It is important to stress that our growth rates measure growth of individual countries not on a national but on a special international scale. This international scale evaluates changes in the development level of individual countries relying on physical indicators of several countries. In market economies the differences between my calculated growth rates and the official ones are not large but in the case of former socialist economies are relatively large, and in one direction only: my calculated rates of growth are always less than the official rates (See Table 4). For the methods used to calculate growth rates, see Economic Commission for Europe (1980) and Ehrlich (1991, 1991a).

agriculture continued. Restrictions on "household farms" (smallholdings granted to cooperative members and state-farm employees as a benefit in kind) were somewhat eased, and as a result the producers themselves appeared in town markets. Poverty in the countryside eased somewhat, but agriculture remained poor and deficient; the queues also remained.

The only true exception to this general picture was Hungary where cooperative and fairly unrestricted household agriculture had been integrated by the end of the 1960s. As a result, agricultural production began to increase in the mid-1960s in Hungary, the shortage of food ceased, and despite state-subsidised agricultural exports, the supply to the domestic market became plentiful (by East European standards). The standard of living of the peasantry and the whole population increased considerably, private housing construction, financed partly from credit, became widespread in villages, in small towns, and later also in larger cities.

National statistics suggest that the share of investment in national income decreased somewhat compared with the 1950s, and the share of personal and government consumption increased somewhat.

A characteristic of the second period is that the mode of functioning of the economy was changed in certain countries as a result of the decrease in the rate of growth. There were two types of change. In some countries the aim was to "perfect the existing system of the planned economy" which resulted in a reduction in the number of plan indicators, increased centralisation of corporate organisation, wider competence for firms, and greater importance for profit targets and financial incentives. Such changes were instituted in the second half of the 1960s in the Soviet Union, whose example was to a greater or lesser extent followed by the majority of countries in the region. The second type of change was aimed at an essential alteration in the way the economy functioned. Preserving the centralisation of strategic decision-making, the reformers tried to base day-to-day management of the economy on the market; that meant that bureaucratic coordination was replaced by market coordination. Such changes were undertaken in the second half of the 1960s by Yugoslavia, Hungary and Czechoslovakia. In Czechoslovakia, the process was tied up with demands for more democracy and an easing of contacts with the CMEA and the Warsaw Pact. As a result, the Soviet army (backed by some East German, Polish, Hungarian and Bulgarian troops) invaded Czechoslovakia in the summer of 1968 and stifled the reform process. With a Soviet-leaning, conservative elite in power in Czechoslovakia, the economic system of centralised distribution of resources and plan directives was restored.

All in all, the only Warsaw Pact country in which a market-oriented reform was realised was Hungary. Yugoslavia, the other reformer, had declared itself politically neutral and experimented with methods of self-management. No wonder Hungary's lone economic reform became bogged down in 1972. Nevertheless the appearance of market forces - the fact that managers had to take account of demand, supply and price effects and that recognition of market forces was incorporated into law - made it easier for Hungary and Yugoslavia, to adapt to the requirements for systemic change in 1989-1990. A retrograde effect was exercised in this period by the fact that the Soviet Union, precisely in order to neutralise endeavours to modify the management system, tried to reinforce the CMEA relations, and succeeded in raising their importance to the Eastern European economies.

By the end of the 1970s the rate of growth in the Eastern European region had slowed, but by comparison with the two decades that followed, it was still high. This is confirmed by our own calculations, which show lower rates of growth than the official ones (table 4).[4]

By the 1970s, the maintenance of growth, or more precisely the increase in domestic consumption that was a precondition for political stability, could be secured in the northern countries of the region only by reliance on outside resources. In the economically less developed southern region, however extensive type development still had some reserves to draw on, although the rate of growth diminished there also, and these countries were likewise compelled to rely on outside resources.

In the two decades following 1960, the countries in the region caught up somewhat with the more developed countries (table 6).

As is well known, new type economic processes started in the market economies after 1970-1973.[5] The leaders of the Eastern European countries, however, thought these epoch-making changes would be short-term, and so ignored them. They thought that socialist countries could continue to divorce themselves from world-market processes, and so the region tried even after 1973 to maintain its high rate of growth at all costs.

The halt in the rates of growth occurred in the 1975-78 period (table 7). These years may be considered as the starting point of the **third period**. This period stretches from the late 1970s to the late 1980s. It was a period of stagnation and recession, of the agony and final collapse of these economies. By the beginning of the period, huge debts had been amassed, particularly by Poland, Hungary and Yugoslavia (figures 1-3, pp. 316/7). As a result, the first priority in state economic policy became the maintenance of solvency. These efforts were successful only in Hungary. Yugoslavia, Poland and then Bulgaria

---

[4]   Our own calculations differ from the product volumes consumed in these countries, since the latter show growth even if higher utilisation is financed from foreign debt. It was characteristic for the 1970s, especially after 1975, for the maintenance of the growth of domestic consumption to be secured in the northern countries only by increased reliance on outside resources.

[5]   See Maddison (1989 and 1991).

TABLE 6
**Relative Changes in Selected Countries and Groups of Countries
Ranking by Economic Development Level, 1960, 1980, 1989
(Calculated by PIM, USA = 100)**

Country Groups[1]	Per capita GDP In current US$ in the corresponding years, measured on the exchange-rate scale		
	1960	1980	1989
I. Northern European developed market economies	54.7	74.7	75.7
II. The original Common Market (the Six)	39.7	60.2	58.2
III. The present Common Market (the Twelve)	39.1	54.3	53.4
IV. Southern European market economies (except Turkey)	15.6	31.3	31.4
V. Less developed European market economies	13.1	21.6	21.0
VI. European market economies	37.6	50.4	48.9
VI. Eastern and Central European countries[2]	19.8	27.7	-
(including the GDR)	22.1	30.0	25.6
Japan	24.8	56.8	64.0
Austria	38.0	60.4	58.8
FRG	50.0	71.2	69.0
GDR	35.1	45.9	48.4
Czechoslovakia	34.7	42.3	37.5
Hungary	21.1	31.7	29.5
Poland	20.7	27.3	19.9
Romania	14.0	21.3	16.0
Yugoslavia	13.6	21.9	17.0
Bulgaria	17.1	29.9	29.0
USSR	21.9	34.1	33.9

Notes: [1] The following countries belong to the individual groups:
I. Finland, Norway
II. Belgium, Luxembourg, France, FRG, Italy, the Netherlands
III. Belgium, Luxembourg, Denmark, France, FRG, Greece, Ireland, Italy, the Netherlands, Portugal, Spain and the UK.
IV. Greece, Portugal
V. Greece, Portugal, Spain
VI. Austria, Belgium, Luxembourg, Denmark, Finland, France, Greece, Ireland, FRG, Italy, the Netherlands, Norway, Portugal, Spain, Switzerland, Sweden, Turkey and the UK.
VII. Bulgaria, Czechoslovakia, GDR, Hungary, Poland, Romania, Yugoslavia
[2] Excluding GDR

In the case of market economies data for 1980 were extrapolated from official growth rates. In the case of Eastern and Central European economies official national income according to MPS was corrected. The correction was based on calculations for the period 1960-1980 (see Table 6); assuming that the calculated growth indices are closer to the real ones than the official indices for the 1980-1989 period, the official growth index for the 1980-1989 period is reduced by the difference.
Sources: 1960-1980: Ehrlich (1991); 1989: Ehrlich and Révész (1992)

became insolvent and were compelled to reschedule their debts. Inability to service debt had serious economic repercussions, and in the second part of the third period it was the cause of two and later three-digit inflation in Poland and Yugoslavia.

What Were the Outward Signs of Agony in the Eastern European Economic Model?

In the second half of the 1970s and particularly in the early 1980s, there was a drastic fall in the rate of growth (table 7). For first time since World War II several Eastern European countries registered absolute declines in their national incomes. After 1982, these countries were briefly able to liven up their economies, primarily by increasing exports to the West and restricting Western imports. After two or three years, however, declines set in and indebtedness worsened.

In the world economy there were epoch-making changes, with outside forces exacerbating the serious, decades-long economic problems of the Eastern European countries.

1. The **structural deformation** of the East European countries was intensified in the new situation. The prices of energy and raw materials multiplied in economies which were highly **energy and material-intensive**. The large share of heavy industry and arms production, and heavy, obsolete, energy-consuming machinery and equipment played their role. Since the Soviet Union could not even supply itself with energy and raw materials any more, its exports to Eastern Europe were reduced considerably. They were replaced by imports from the West, where prices were much higher. This contributed further to the problems of securing the investment goods necessary for modernisation and for renewal of the infrastructure from convertible currency areas .

The countries of the region reacted to the price shock not by abandoning energy and material-intensive production, or introducing efficient energy saving measures, but by increasing imports from other sources and by exploitation of their own resources, which required high investment.

2. By the 1980s 20-40 percent of national production (50 percent in Hungary) was being exchanged through foreign trade. The **terms of trade** deteriorated considerably in this period for every country in the region. The mass products they offered for export were not up to the requirements of the time and were unable to match the competition from South-East Asia and Latin America. A change in production structure and modernisation would have necessitated imports of Western capital goods, which could not be obtained because of their large foreign debts and the embargo on supplies of modern technology and equipment. It would also have required a switch from state ownership and administrative centralisation and obsolete technology in

TABLE 7
Net Material Product Used and Produced, 1970-1990
(1 = Used; 2 = Produced, Annual Percentage Change)

Year	GDR[1] 1	GDR[1] 2	Czecho-Slovakia 1	Czecho-Slovakia 2	Hungary 1	Hungary 2	Poland 1	Poland 2	Bulgaria[2] 1[2]	Bulgaria[2] 2	Romania 1	Romania 2	Eastern Europe[3] 1[3]	Eastern Europe[3] 2	Yugo-slavia 2	USSR[4] 1[4]	USSR[4] 2
1970	8.4	5.6	5.0	5.7	11.8	4.9	5.0	5.2	3.7	7.1	-	6.8	6.5	5.7	6.0	11.2	9.0
1971	3.4	4.4	4.9	5.5	11.3	5.9	9.8	8.1	1.6	6.9	-	13.5	6.7	7.3	9.0	5.1	5.6
1972	5.8	5.7	5.7	5.7	-3.7	6.2	12.5	10.6	9.8	7.7	-	9.8	7.3	8.0	5.0	3.5	3.9
1973	6.3	5.6	7.3	5.2	2.0	7.0	14.3	10.8	9.0	8.1	-	10.7	9.2	8.3	4.0	7.7	8.9
1974	6.5	6.5	8.1	5.9	12.7	5.9	12.0	10.5	11.8	7.6	-	12.3	10.0	8.6	9.0	4.1	5.5
1975	2.6	4.9	4.5	6.2	6.4	6.1	9.5	9.0	11.1	8.8	-	9.8	6.8	7.6	4.0	4.2	4.4
1976	6.3	3.5	3.1	4.1	1.2	3.0	6.5	6.8	0.3	6.5	12.3	11.3	6.0	6.1	4.0	5.0	5.9
1977	5.1	5.1	1.6	4.2	6.0	7.1	2.2	5.0	5.2	6.3	6.8	8.7	3.9	5.8	7.0	3.5	4.5
1978	0.8	3.7	2.7	4.1	9.2	4.0	0.5	3.0	0.2	5.6	9.6	7.2	3.2	4.2	6.0	4.5	5.1
1979	1.1	4.0	1.1	3.1	-5.8	1.2	-3.7	-2.3	3.5	6.6	5.5	6.5	-0.2	2.0	7.0	2.0	2.2
1980	5.1	4.8	2.7	2.9	-1.7	-0.9	-6.0	-6.0	5.1	5.7	0.8	4.2	-0.3	0.3	1.5	3.9	3.9
1981	1.1	4.8	-3.4	-0.1	0.7	2.5	-10.5	-12.0	7.7	5.0	-6.5	-0.4	-4.2	-2.3	0.8	3.2	3.3
1982	-3.4	2.6	-1.6	0.2	-1.1	2.6	-10.5	-5.5	1.9	4.2	-1.5	4.0	-4.2	0.3	-1.2	3.5	3.9
1983	-	4.6	0.6	2.3	-2.8	0.3	5.6	6.0	1.2	3.0	2.2	6.0	1.8	4.3	1.7	3.6	4.2
1984	3.4	5.5	1.2	3.5	-0.6	2.5	5.0	5.6	5.2	4.6	2.8	6.5	3.2	5.1	0.2	2.0	2.9
1985	4.8	5.2	3.2	3.0	-0.6	-1.4	3.8	3.4	2.3	1.8	4.8	-1.1	3.6	2.7	3.6	2.1	1.6
1986	4.2	4.3	4.9	2.6	3.9	0.9	5.0	4.9	8.4	5.3	-	3.0	5.0	3.7	-0.5	1.6	2.3
1987	4.5	3.3	2.8	2.1	3.0	4.1	1.8	1.9	0.4	5.0	-	0.7	2.6	3.2	-2.0	0.7	1.6
1988	5.1	2.8	2.0	2.4	-4.3	-0.5	4.7	4.9	3.7	2.4	-	-2.0	3.3	3.1	1.0	4.6	4.4
1989	1.6	2.1	3.4	1.3	-1.3	-1.1	0.1	-0.2	-5.5	-0.4	-	-7.9	0.4	0.5		3.2	2.4
1990	-	-19.5	1.4	-3.1	-7.5	-5.5[5]	-17.0	-13.0	-	-13.6	-	-10.5[5]	-	-12.0[5]	-	-	-4.0

Notes: [1] Calculated from rounded index numbers (1950 = 100); [2] Calculated from absolute volume figures at 1962 prices; [3] 1970-1975 and 1986-1988 excluding Romania; [4] 1970-1973 nominal; [5] Estimate

Sources: Economic Survey of Europe in 1990-1991. App. Table B.1., p. 221, and B.2., p. 222; Yugoslavia: National Yearbook, 1990.

the hands of large and very large firms producing mass products only, to more flexible small and medium-sized firms.[6]

3. Development of the **infrastructure and services** lagged behind the development of productive sectors of the economy, and behind the needs of the population. Repair and maintenance of the infrastructure (construction, railways, roads, telephones, sewage, water etc.) had been minimal. By the 1980s, areas of crisis had multiplied. Structures had decayed and there were frequent breaks in sewage and water pipes etc. Telephones and telecommunications were in a particularly bad shape. To obtain a telephone was and remains a privilege in these countries. Old technology, obsolete equipment and accompanying bad quality limited the utility of existing telephones as well. The latest developments in modern telecommunications (telefax etc.) were non-existent in the region at the end of the 1980s.

4. According to the official figures of the Eastern European countries, 98-100 percent of national income was produced by the socialist (state-owned and cooperative) sector. (The share was smaller - 83 and 84 percent respectively - in the case of Poland and Yugoslavia, where agriculture had not been collectivised.) One might conclude from these data that production and service activity outside the socialist sector was minimal. In the second half of the 1970s and in the 1980s, considerable changes came about. The economic structure ossified. There were visible signs of decay in the socialist sector and shortages opened up increasing opportunities for private activity, either registered (official), or more often unregistered.

The main causes of the development of the **unofficial economy** in the Eastern European countries were the unresponsiveness of the socialist economy to demand, the serious neglect of the need for services, the performance-restricting effects of wage regulation, the narrowing of wage differentials by state measures, and the general shortage of labour. The registered private sector which served to supply these needs, was held back by taxation and by frequent withdrawal of licences and tenancy rights to premises, thereby keeping it in constant uncertainty. At the same time, the rise of private housing construction and the spread of household durables, automobiles and tourism as a result of the gradual rise in the standard of living raised the demand for such services from the private sector. The increase in such activity was directed into quasi-legal (white), semilegal (grey) or totally illegal (black) channels. Towards the end of the 1980s, the liberalisation of tourism greatly expanded black-market trade and smuggling in every country in the region.

National economies were almost torn into two parts. In Hungary and

---

[6]   See Ehrlich (1985).

Yugoslavia this happened by the early 1980s, in the remaining countries (to differing degrees) by the second half of the 1980s. On one hand there was the first, official economy, in which the large state-owned firms and cooperatives of the socialist sector dominated. On the other hand there was the second (and third) economy which maintained itself at the expense of the first and was determined to a large extent by market relations. Unlike the official economy, this developed at spectacular speed. An intricate web of ventures, held back by strong constraints but evading them, only partly registered, pursued as a secondary job (alongside a main job in the socialist sector) produced sizeable incomes. The increasing dichotomy in the Eastern European economies could not be reversed, even though it was opposed by the authorities.

5. By the 1980s, one element of economic reality had become predominant: the frighteningly high level of **indebtedness and debt servicing**, principally in Poland, Yugoslavia and Hungary, but also in the East Germany and Romania (figures 1, 2 and 3). Great efforts were made to increase convertible-currency exports and hold back imports. As a result of this economic policy, the rate of growth of indebtedness had diminished by the second half of the 1980s, but it remained at a high level. By the end of the decade Romania had paid back almost all of its debt but the price had been high: the standard of living of the population was reduced to subsistence level.

6. By the second half of the 1980s, the rate of growth of production fell considerably. At the same time, the deteriorating terms of trade and burden of debt servicing caused considerable loss of income and a net outflow of capital. Domestic consumption diminished in every country. The answer by the economic policy-makers was a drastic alteration in the **shares of accumulation and consumption** (figure 4). Accumulation decreased abruptly from 1978 onwards. Then it stabilised at a low level, while consumption increased slowly throughout the period. Considering the whole of Eastern Europe except Yugoslavia, accumulation declined in 1979-82 to two-thirds of its 1978 level. Governments were unable to reduce consumption (due partly to the dichotomy in the economy) or did not dare to do so for fear of political turmoil. The process ended in the collapse of the Eastern European economies in 1989.

More than three decades of catching up had proved to be transitory for it was succeeded in the 1980s by a deterioration of relative position vis à vis the market economies (table 6). In 1980, the level of the development of the region was about 30 percent of the US. By 1989 it had fallen to a quarter. The distance to the twelve EC countries also increased. The gap with the three Southern EC members: Spain, Greece and Portugal increased even more from 4 percent in 1980 to 18 percent in 1989. Most important was the increasing lag relative to Japan. The ratio of per capita GDP increased from 1:1.9 in 1980 to 1:2.5 by 1989. Even the favourable official statistics show

FIGURE 1
Net Debt in Convertible Currencies in Eastern Central Europe,
1970-1990 (reflecting foreign currency reserves)

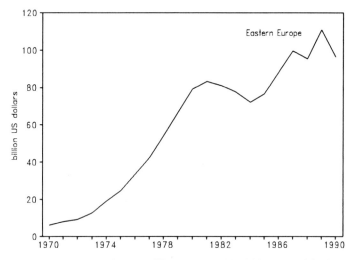

Source: *Economic Survey of Europe in 1990-1991.* App. table C11,
p. 250; Yugoslavia from Stiblar (1991), p. 4.

FIGURE 2
Net Debt in Convertible Currencies in the GDR, Czechoslovakia,
Hungary and Poland, 1970-1990 (reflecting foreign currency reserves)

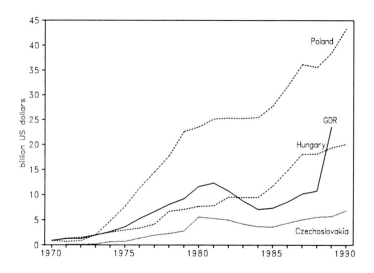

Source: same as figure 1.

FIGURE 3
Net Debt in Convertible Currencies in Bulgaria, Romania,
Yugoslavia and the Soviet Union, 1970-1990
(reflecting foreign currency reserves)

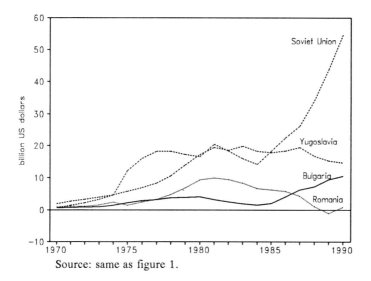

Source: same as figure 1.

FIGURE 4
Changes in Domestic Consumption and Accumulation
in Eastern Central Europe [a], 1970-1989 (1970 = 100)

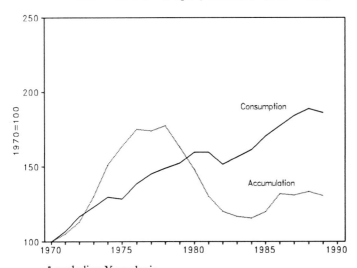

[a] excluding Yugoslavia.
Source: *Economic Survey of Europe in 1990-91*, App. table B2, p. 224

Éva Ehrlich

that the development strategy of the Eastern European countries, aiming at rapid growth and catching up with the developed countries, was not successful as the gaps increased rather than declined.[7]

The Soviet Union collapsed at the end of the 1980s. It neither could nor wanted to maintain the unity of the national economies and the authority of the communist parties. It had no political, ideological or economic weapons with which to defend the position of the power elites in Eastern Europe. So they ceased to exist. Gorbachev managed a self-instigated retreat by the Soviet empire and power system, opening up the possibility for the Eastern European countries to step out of their impossible situation and begin to make systemic changes.

4. The Nature of the Model

The flowering and decline of the system makes it clear that its collapse may be attributed to the characteristics of the Stalinist model. In this respect three interconnected problems have to be mentioned:

1. Under this model, economic growth **uses up all resources** at its disposal (raw materials, energy, capital and labour) and harnesses them to the quantitative growth of heavy industry and the arms industry (as part of the preparations for an imminent war). The areas of the economy where the quantity of output is less visible, however, get only minimal resources, scarcely enough to keep them functioning. The system destroys the infrastructure necessary for undisturbed production and normal life, depletes the services (transport, telecommunication, housing etc.) and ruins the environment.

2. Economies based on the model cannot utilise **technical development**, since they are isolated from the world economy (liquidation of market relations, autarky). The model is conservative not only in a technological sense, but in every other sense as well. Under bureaucratic coordination, already existing activities siphon resources from new activities, because resource allocation is determined basically by existing power positions. In allocation, economic selection is slow and cumbersome, since self-correcting economic (and political) mechanisms hardly exist.

3. The model reinforces **reactions** within social and human relations **opposed to dynamism**. Economic agents shun the risks indispensable to a rational economy. The model lacks internal and external competition and the

---

[7] Some countries (Romania, East Germany and Bulgaria) publish unrealistically high growth rates. I have corrected them by relying on my own calculations. This was still not enough, however, to cancel out the upward distortion of the official Eastern European figures.

spirit of enterprise. The actors in the economy are interested in acquiring the largest possible quantity of resources and obtaining the lowest possible plan targets. Capacity is concealed and resources hoarded, because this makes it possible to deploy extra capacity at the best possible moment. There is a vicious circle in the selection of managers. Managers have to perform under bureaucratic bargaining. So innovative personalities are relegated. People who can adapt flexibly to changing power relations, build up good relations with superiors, and shun risks are favoured.

The nature of the model sketched above demonstrates that it is able to mobilise resources in the short run, but that in the long run it is unsuited for modernisation and catching up. So inevitably, after a few decades of functioning it winds up its own growth potential without creating new sources of growth. The growth model exhausts itself after a shorter or longer period (depending on the conditions in the country concerned). That is why the model may be called the **growth-exhausting model**.

The question may arise whether the model was reformable or not, or to put it another way, whether the efforts made since the early 1960s to reform the model were based on an illusion.

I think that the model was reformable in principle. But in order to be successful, the initial reform measures should have generated further measures for which the historical situation was not yet ripe. It is a strange irony of history that in the northern countries of the region, the reform process stalled due to the opposition of the great power and its power elite whose long-term interest lay in the initiation of true reforms in the way the system functioned: the mobilisation of market forces in order to secure long-term economic growth. Looking back after 20-25 years, the reforms aimed at changing the mode of functioning of the economies seem to be of outstanding importance despite their failure. They initiated new types of management and attitudes that may ease and shorten the transition to the market economy now the political system has changed. (This is true above of all for Hungary.)

5. Changing the Political System. A Brief Look at the Present Situation: 1989-1991

At the end of the 1980s and the beginning of the 1990s, **the old power system** collapsed in one country after another. Changing the political system became the order of the day everywhere. In Hungary and Poland, the change of system was the result of negotiations between the old party-state (state socialism) and opposition forces. In Czechoslovakia and East Germany it took place as a result of peaceful demonstrations. In Romania and Bulgaria there was a coup by part of the old elite intent on saving itself. In Yugoslavia and the Soviet Union, the collapse involved the state organisation. In Yugoslavia, the autonomy endeavours of the member republics led to armed clashes and civil war. In the Soviet Union the drive for independence on the part of certain republics led to a clash of interests, tensions between nations. In certain areas armed struggle is still continuing. One can say that, the change of system is more or less over in the northern countries of the region, whereas it is still going on in the southern countries and the Soviet Union.

Macroeconomic indicators for the area signal an accelerated recession from 1989 onward, amounting to outright collapse in the southern countries. In 1989 the liquidity and ability to deliver of the Soviet Union, the largest commercial partner of the Eastern European countries, was shaken. This caused some Eastern European countries to amass sizeable, but unrealisable surpluses in their trade with the Soviet Union. From January 1, 1991. trade between the Soviet Union and the former CMEA countries switched to dollar settlements which further reduced the trade among them. The economic situation of countries in the region was further burdened by the disappearance of East Germany (in June 1990), destroying an old and settled pattern of economic cooperation from one day to the next.

The ending of export-import relations with sizeable partners is a hard blow even for healthy economies. The weak adaptability of Eastern European countries and their obsolete economic structures (adapted to the needs of the Soviet and the other CMEA markets) makes it difficult for them to replace lost markets with markets in the West or developing countries. An increase in their competitive exports to developed market economies is hindered on the one hand by the 1990-91 recession there and by protectionism of these countries (import quotas, tariffs etc.), on the other. In the second half of 1990, the Gulf-War reduced the Middle-East markets of these countries, and froze some of the debts due to them from this region. Indebtedness and the uncertain economic, social and power position of non-oil exporting developing countries makes it impossible to increase exports in that direction as a way of compensating for lost Soviet and CMEA exports. As a result, the macroeconomic figures for the region are unfavourable, showing an extremely rapid, accelerating relapse (table 8).

It may be seen from table 8 that national income and GDP is decreasing in every country, that gross industrial production is plummeting, and that the rate of inflation is high. Inflation is coming down perceptibly only in Hungary and to some extent in Czechoslovakia. In every country of the region there are levels of unemployment, unheard of since World War II, and unemployment is rising rapidly. By 1991 it was already higher than the OECD average. The rate of investment is decreasing further. Due to the sizeable foreign debt and debt servicing, a net outflow of capital is taking place in every country in the region except Romania. Real wages and incomes have fallen everywhere (in Poland, Czechoslovakia, Bulgaria and Romania considerably), and domestic demand is low and still decreasing. Large-scale bankruptcies and insolvencies of firms have considerably increased the internal

TABLE 8
Basic Economic Indicators, 1989-1991
(Percentage change over same period of preceding year)

	GDR	Czecho-slovakia	Hun-gary	Poland	Bul-garia	Romania	Yugo-slavia	Eastern[1] Europe	USSR
GDP									
1989	2.3	1.3	0.9	0.1[2]	-0.3	-5.8	-	-0.7	-2.4
1990	-19.5[2]	-2.0	-4.0	-11.6	-11.8	-7.3	-8.5	-8.4	-2.0
1991		-16.0	-7-8	-8-10	-20-25	-17.0	-25.0	-13-15	-13.0
Ind. Output									
1989	2.3	0.8	-2.5	-0.5	2.2	-2.1	0.9	0.2	1.7
1990		-3.7	-9.6	-25.0	-13.1	-19.8	-10.8	-16.5	-1.2
1991[3]		-18.8	-18.8	-12.0	-28.8	-17.7	-18.0	-18.0	
Agr. Output									
1989	1.6	-1.8	-1.3	1.5	0.4	-5.1	-		-0.8
1990		-3.7	-6.5	-1.4	-8.8	-3.0	-		-2.3
Gross Inv.									
1989	0.9	1.6	0.5	-2.4	-7.7	1.6		-1.5	-4.3
1990	-9.0	5.7[4]	-9.8	-6.7	-10.8[4]	-35.0[5]			-8.7
1991[3]		-29.4	-10-13	-11.0	-20.0	-24.0[5]			-4.0
Exports									
1989	0.5	-2.0	-	0.2	-3.4	-10.8	-	-2.1	-1.0
1990	-	-13.0	-4.3	14.9	-26.0	-46.0	-	-9.8	-12.1
1991[3]		-13.3[6]	-8.0	-5.6	-56.0[6]	-25.4	-8.0[6]		
Imports									
1989	2.4	2.7	1.0	1.5	-6.5	3.7	-	0.5	5.1
1990	15.0	-	-3.4	-15.6	-26.0	4.0	-		-3.1
1991[3]		-33.6[6]	1.0	41.3	-71.0[6]	-36.6	-12.2[6]		-45.2
Unempl. (%)									
Dec. 1990	7.3	1.0	1.7	6.1	1.6	1.3	13.6		1.4
Jan. 1991	8.6	1.5	2.1	6.6	1.8	-	13.9		
Mar. 1991	9.2	2.6	3.0	7.1	3.1	3.1	-		
June 1991		3.8	3.9	8.4	6.0	2.5	19.4		
Sep. 1991		5.6	6.1	10.4	9.0	3.3	20.1		
Consumer Price Increase									
1989	2.3	9.5	18.8	259.5	6.2	0.9	1252.0[11]		1.9
1990		10.0	28.9	584.7	50.6[8]	4.2	587.6		10.0
1991									
Jan-Jun[7]		61.5	35.7	77.1	317.0[9]	77.5[9]	69.0		55.8
Jan-Sep[7]		59.7	35.6	73.6	404.0[9]	219.0[10]	85.8		70.6

Note: [1] Including Czech-Slovakia, Hungary, Poland, Bulgaria and Romania; [2] Net material product; source ECE (1991), p. 221; [3] 1991 Jan.-Sept; [4] Current prices; [5] Investment from state funds; [6] In USD; [7] Previous period = 100; [8] Dec. against May; [9] June 1991 against Dec. 1990: Sept 1991 against Dec. 1990; [10] Sept. 1991 against Oct. 1990; [11] OECD Economic Surveys, Yugoslavia (1990), p. 15

Source: Gross national product: 1989 from national statistics; Industrial Output: 1989 from The ECE economics in mid-1991, p.4; Agricultural Output from ECE (1991a), p. 232; Gross Investment: 1989 from Economic Survey 1990-1991, p. 227; Exports and Imports: 1989 and 1990 from Economic Survey 1990-1991, p. 234; Unemployment: Dec. 1990 and Jan March 1991 from The ECE economics in mid-1991, p. 6; Rate of Consumer Prices: 1989 from Economic Survey 1990-1991, p. 226; Other entries from Garbisch, H. et al. (1992), p. 3-9.

debt expressed in national currencies. The phenomenon that "everybody is in debt to everybody" constitutes an objective obstacle to rational management and the prosperity of new ventures.

The export offensive to convertible-currency areas has been successful in Hungary, Czechoslovakia and Poland. Though their total exports decreased (because of the collapse of CMEA market), the direction of exports changed. The majority of their exports are already geared to developed and developing market economies, rather than to ex-CMEA countries.

There are signs that the abrupt recession in Soviet and other ex-CMEA trading partners, and the forced reduction in domestic demand, has resulted in a stronger economic recession than forecast.

6. Therapies for the Economic Ills

In this unprecedentedly grave situation, two characteristically different solutions to stabilising these economies and making the transition to a market economy have been put forward:

One solution is represented by Poland and Yugoslavia, and since January 1, 1991, by Czechoslovakia. In Poland and Yugoslavia a **shock therapy**[8] was applied to combat hyperinflation and the accelerating recession of the late 1980s, and to make the transition to a market economy. (The merger of the former GDR with West Germany also involved a severe shock therapy.) In Czechoslovakia, where inflation has been mild and the prior conditions were much more favourable than in the other two countries, the shock therapy was aimed at a rapid, abrupt transition.

After half a year of successful operation, shock therapy failed both in Poland and Yugoslavia. Although hyperinflation was checked in each country, the price was an abrupt across-the-table drop in production. Shortages were eased considerably and the general level of provision improved. However, the other side of the coin was a drastic reduction of demand and a 30-40 percent drop in real wages.

The dominant monopolistic state and other "socialist" large firms have not adapted as expected. The Polish and Yugoslav governments were not able - and this is an important aspect of the failure - to reduce radically the subsidies to loss-making state-owned firms. They were unable to withstand wage

---

[8] The essence of this method of stabilisation is to produce a forceful, instantaneous equilibrium between supply and demand by drastically reducing budget subsidies to loss-making state-owned firms, amassing convertible-currency reserves, strong devaluation of the domestic currency and hence internal convertibility, and restricting domestic demand through strict monetary and fiscal policies to break the high inflation or hyperinflation that disrupts the economic process.

claims, as they were frightened by the consequences of a rapid deterioration in the public's economic, social and political assessments. Although hyperinflation was ended, inflation rose again to double digits within six months after the beginning of the shock therapy. The public's faith in shock therapy was destroyed. As a result - although half the debt of Poland to Western governments was written off - the government fell. In Yugoslavia the social shock helped intensify the strife among republics and nationalities.

Shock therapy has been used in Czechoslovakia since early 1991. As already mentioned, the development level and the standard of living there were much higher than in the other two countries. There were no food shortages or hyperinflation even before the shock therapy began. The drastic, 20 percent reduction in domestic demand and the increase in unemployment did not do so much damage to public credibility as to jeopardise the shock therapy.

The other kind of stabilisation therapy is represented in Eastern Europe by Hungary, where stabilisation and transition to a market economy have been gradual, step by step. It is worth emphasising that Hungary's economy is in much better shape than those of Poland and Yugoslavia were after the shock therapy.

Although Hungary has a high foreign debt, it was able so far to service it by relying on the Western money market for rollover credits, but without rescheduling so far. It has also been able to contain inflation and proceed with the transition to a market economy. In this an important role has been played by Hungary's previous history of reforms, which for all their half-measures, compromises and foreign repressions, placed the actors of the economy under the control of market impulses and reduced shortages, abolishing food shortages altogether. The private sector had been allowed to function since the early 1980s, even though this permission was ambiguous and limited. By mid-1991, the black market exchange rate was very near the official exchange rate, without drastic measures being taken, and so internal convertibility could be achieved. All this has exacted a heavy price: real wages have decreased steadily over the past 10-13 years, and so has personal consumption since 1988.

It has to be stressed that slow and gradual advance is not without its disadvantages either. This road too is lined with unemployment, declines in real wages and consumption, increased inequalities in income and wealth, rising poverty and destitution, whereas the welfare net (state distributive systems: health, education, pension etc.) is loosening due to the great burden it places on public spending. Only history can tell whether shock therapy or a gradual approach causes more human suffering, and which will achieve durable success.

It is not clear yet which road to economic stabilisation and transition to a market economy will be taken by Bulgaria or Romania, where the change in political system is still not over.

Whatever therapy is chosen, one thing is certain: in the foreseeable future (5-10 years), only the northern countries of the region have a chance of completing the transition to a market economy. Due to their lower level of economic development and the weakness of the prior conditions, the southern countries of the region will need more time to make the transition. Practical experience with transition suggests that to differing degrees, political processes, political clashes of interests, and political in-fighting effectively hinder a rapid stabilisation of the economy and are sources of irrational economic behaviour in all countries in Eastern and Central Europe.

References

Csernok, A., É. Ehrlich and Gy. Szilágyi (1975), *Infrastruktura. Korok és országok*, Kossuth Könyvkiadó, Budapest.

Economic Commission for Europe (1980),"Comparative GDP levels", *Economic Bulletin for Europe*, Vol. 31., No. 2, Geneva/New York.

Economic Commission for Europe, U.N. (1991) *The ECE Economies in Mid-1991*, Geneva.

--- (1991) *Economic Survey of Europe in 1990-1991*, Geneva.

Ehrlich, É. (1966), "An Examination of the Inter-relation between Consumption Indicators Expressed in Physical Units and Per National Income", *Czechoslovak Economic Papers*, Academy Publishing House of the Czechoslovak Academy of Sciences, No. 7.

--- (1969), "Dynamic International Comparison of National Incomes Expressed in Terms of Physical Indicators", *Oesteurope Wirtschaft*, No. 1.

--- (1985), "The Size Structure of Manufacturing Establishments and Enterprises: An International Comparison", *Journal of Comparative Economics*, No. 9.

--- (1991), "Contest between Countries: 1937-1986", *Soviet studies*, Vol. 43.5., (In Hungarian as a closed study in 1985 and in 1987. Published first in Hungarian, "Országok versenye, 1937-1986", *Közgazdasági Szemle* (1990), No.1).

--- (1991a), *Országok versenye, 1937-1986*, Fejlettségi szintek strukturák, növekedési ütemek, iparosodási utak, (Contest between countries: 1937-1986. Economic Development Levels, Structure, Economic Growth and Paths of Industrialization), Közgazdasági és Jogi Könyvkiadó, Budapest.

--- and G. Révész (1992), "Collapse and Systemic Change in Eastern Central Europe", in: *Europe 1990*, Forthcoming, Eunaudi, Torino.

Gabrish, H. (et al.) (1992), *Depression and Inflation: Threats to Political and Social Stability. The Current Economic Situation of Former CMEA Countries and Yugoslavia*, Wiener Institut für Internationale Wirtschaftsvergleiche, No. 180, February.

Hauner, M. (1985), "Human resources", in: M.C. Kaser and E.A. Radice (eds.), *The Economic History of Eastern Europe 1919-1975*, Vol. I, Clarendon Press, Oxford.

Jánossy, F. (1963), *A gazdasági fejlettség mérhetősége és mérésének új módszere*, (The Measurability of the Economic Development Level and a New Method of Measurement), Közgazdasági és Jogi Könyvkiadó, Budapest.

Maddison, A. (1989), *The World Economy in the 20th Century*, OECD, Paris.

--- (1991), *Dynamic Forces in Capitalist Development. A Long-run Comparative View*, Oxford University Press, Oxford/New York.

Marer, P. (1985), *Dollar GNPs of the USSR and Eastern Europe*, The John Hopkins University Press, Baltimore/London.

Stiblar, F. (1991), *External Indebtedness of Yugoslavia and Its Federal Units*, Wiener Institut für Wirtschaftsvergleiche (WIIW), No. 175.

Explaining Economic Growth
A. Szirmai, B. van Ark and D. Pilat
© 1993 Elsevier Science Publishers B.V. All rights reserved.

Was the Thatcher Experiment Worth It?
British Economic Growth in a European Context

Nicholas F.R. Crafts*
University of Warwick

1. Introduction.

The British Conservative Government was elected in 1979 against the background of an economic performance in the 1970s widely perceived as deeply disappointing. The decade had seen a marked slowdown in economic growth, rising unemployment and record peacetime inflation; the overtaking of British income and productivity levels by other European countries had become apparent. The Conservatives under Mrs Thatcher promised institutional reform on the microeconomic front and for the macro-economy a disinflation through monetarist policies.

Among the key elements of this new policy stance were the following.
a) Supply-side policy moved towards increasing pressure for cost reductions and away from the pursuit of allocative efficiency. Government regulatory failures rather than market failures were targeted for policy action, subsidies were reduced, and eventually privatisation was given a high priority. This amounted to a rejection of the central thrust of postwar industrial policies.
b) The government finally abandoned counter-cyclical policy in the form of demand management as practised by the Keynesian policy-makers of the 1950s and 1960s. The Thatcherites, if not the Wets, accepted rapidly rising unemployment as the immediate consequence both of seeking to establish a credible anti-inflationary policy and of reducing the productivity gap between the UK and competitor countries.
c) There was a heightened emphasis on efficiency relative to equity in the resolution of policy conflicts. Thus, priority was given to cutting personal taxes rather than to expanding welfare spending and to faster growth and restructuring industry rather than income redistribution or support for lame

* I received excellent advice and comments from participants in the Explaining Economic Growth Conference, especially my discussant Rainer Fremdling, and from the Warwick Economic History Workshop. I am also grateful for helpful discussions with Steve Broadberry, Angus Maddison, Alan Manning, Robin Naylor and Mark Stewart. I am to blame for all errors and omissions.

ducks.

The government saw itself as escaping from the trade unions' veto on economic reform (Holmes, 1985), and many of the changes of the 1980s would have been regarded as inconceivable by informed opinion in the 1960s and 1970s - for example, the reduction of the top marginal income tax rate to 40 per cent, the privatisation of the major utilities, the decimation of the NUM and the indexing of benefits to prices rather than wages. Similarly, the government's re-election in 1983 and 1987 notwithstanding the very high levels of unemployment in those years flew in the face of the hitherto conventional wisdom.

The policy stance of the British Conservatives also contrasted sharply with the line taken by other major European governments. In France, the 1980s opened with the Mitterand government committed to Keynesian expansion and further nationalisation. In Germany, despite the initial rhetoric, structural and political constraints prevented Chancellor Kohl "from enacting more than a half-hearted imitation of the Thatcherite model" (Humphreys, 1989, p.128).

As table 1 shows, the 1980s were a period of relatively poor British performance in terms of inflation and unemployment. The Misery Index rose slightly compared with the 1970s on Layard et al.'s (1991) estimates and the UK remained in seventeenth position in the league table. There was virtually no improvement relative to Germany, although the UK avoided the spectacular deterioration in the Misery Index experienced by France. In fact, when the data are made comparable, the 1980s witnessed the worst British unemployment of any period on record, including the 1930s (Crafts, 1991). The 1970s stand out as a period of exceptionally high inflation but 1980s inflation was high by the standards of the early postwar period. The much used, though arbitrarily weighted, Misery Index shows only a marginal gain for the Conservatives in 1980-8 over the much derided Labour years of 1974-9.

If the Thatcher government is to be favourably regarded, it would seem that such an evaluation must be based on success in improving growth performance and, in particular, in raising productivity growth. Here, there is a *prima facie* case, as table 2 shows. Moreover, as section 4 suggests, the high Misery Index may in part be a corollary of policies which raised the growth rate.

Critics of the Thatcher government's achievements on growth and productivity point to a number of problems and weaknesses. These would include the failure to regain the productivity growth rate of the 1960s and the suggestion that, even though there was some improvement in productivity performance relative to sluggish European economies generally, the price paid for this growth revival was unacceptably high. In particular, it has been suggested that any improvement in growth was only temporary and involved large increases in inequality while failing to raise the quality of life for most people (Costello et al., 1989).

TABLE 1
Inflation and Unemployment Rates (per cent): A Comparative Picture

	Inflation Rate	Standardised Unemployment Rate (UR)	Equilibrium Unemployment Rate (UR*)	Misery Index
a) 1980-88				
Australia	8.42	7.67	6.10	16.09
Austria	4.17	3.14	2.95	7.31
Belgium	4.48	11.07	7.04	15.55
Canada	5.99	9.48	8.14	15.47
Denmark	6.92	8.56	6.30	15.48
Finland	7.57	5.01	4.65	12.58
France	7.82	8.98	7.81	16.80
Germany	2.99	6.07	4.04	9.06
Ireland	9.26	14.12	13.09	23.38
Italy	12.31	6.87	5.42	19.18
Japan	1.42	2.51	2.14	3.93
Netherlands	2.64	9.89	7.27	12.53
New Zealand	11.71	4.18	3.91	15.89
Norway	6.67	2.51	2.50	9.18
Spain	10.33	17.74	14.95	28.07
Sweden	8.12	2.21	2.36	10.33
Switzerland	3.89	1.87	1.44	5.76
UK	7.62	10.32	7.92	17.94
USA	5.00	7.38	6.36	12.38
b) 1969-79				
Australia	10.13	3.66	4.01	13.79
Austria	5.96	1.32	0.48	7.28
Belgium	7.21	4.53	4.82	11.74
Canada	7.85	6.44	7.01	14.29
Denmark	9.40	3.64	4.64	13.04
Finland	10.35	3.48	2.61	13.83
France	8.66	3.65	3.88	12.31
Germany	5.42	2.13	1.87	7.55
Ireland	12.22	6.72	9.13	18.94
Italy	11.73	4.37	4.94	16.10
Japan	7.46	1.61	1.82	9.07
Netherlands	7.58	3.67	4.28	11.25
New Zealand	11.88	0.58	1.96	12.46
Norway	7.91	1.75	2.22	9.66
Spain	13.58	4.12	9.73	17.70
Sweden	8.58	1.65	1.93	10.23
Switzerland	5.09	0.52	0.83	5.61
UK	12.18	4.30	5.15	16.48
USA	6.48	5.85	5.97	12.33

Sources: Based on Layard et al. (1991). Misery Index is the sum of the inflation rates and the standardised unemployment rates.

TABLE 2
Productivity Growth in the Business Sector of OECD Countries
(per cent per year)

	Labour Productivity			Total Factor Productivity		
	1960-73	1973-79	1979-88	1960-73	1973-79	1979-88
Australia	3.2	2.0	1.1	2.9	1.2	1.0
Austria	5.8	3.3	1.8	3.4	1.4	0.7
Belgium	5.0	2.8	2.1	3.7	1.5	1.1
Canada	2.8	1.5	1.5	2.0	0.7	0.3
Denmark	4.3	2.6	1.5	2.8	1.2	0.8
Finland	5.0	3.4	3.2	3.4	1.7	2.3
France	5.4	3.0	2.4	3.9	1.7	1.5
Germany	4.6	3.4	1.9	2.7	2.0	0.7
Greece	8.8	3.4	0.2	5.8	1.5	-0.7
Italy	6.3	3.0	1.6	4.6	2.2	1.0
Japan	9.4	3.2	3.1	6.4	1.8	1.8
Netherlands	4.9	3.3	1.5	3.1	2.0	0.6
New Zealand	1.8	-1.5	1.4	1.0	-2.2	0.6
Norway	4.1	0.1	2.0	3.6	-0.4	1.4
Spain	6.1	3.8	3.4	4.2	1.7	2.1
Sweden	3.9	1.4	1.6	2.5	0.3	0.9
Switzerland	3.2	0.7	0.9	1.6	-0.9	0.2
UK	3.5	1.5	2.6	2.2	0.5	1.9
USA	2.8	0.6	1.6	1.8	0.1	0.7

Source: Kendrick (1990).

This suggests four questions which the remainder of the paper will attempt to answer. i) What happened to the standard of living in the UK compared both with earlier periods and with Europe? ii) How good was British growth performance in the 1980s relatively speaking? iii) In so far as there was an improvement in relative growth performance, what were the reasons for this? iv) What was the overall effect of the Thatcher Experiment on economic welfare?

Four preliminary remarks are called for before proceeding to this agenda in order to avoid misunderstandings.

a) Evaluation of the Thatcher Experiment depends in a number of respects on the economic model which is thought applicable. Thus, the underlying growth model (Solow or Romer) matters as does the interpretation of unemployment (demand deficiency or higher natural rate) and the framework for explaining productivity change (bargaining model or growth accounting).

b) The outcome of the Thatcher Experiment was obviously not a Pareto Improvement. Attempts to measure the impact on economic welfare depend heavily on value judgments. Moreover, there is no consensus on how or whether the quality of life can be measured. Nevertheless, some quantification can be provided following well known procedures along the lines of Beckerman (1980) and Dasgupta and Weale (1992). It must be accepted, however, that there will always be scope for disagreement, as with the rather similar debate on the workers' standard of living during the British industrial revolution.

c) There is no way of specifying the counterfactual policy mix in ways which will satisfy everyone. For the purposes of this paper I have in mind a "mainstream European" model but the British Conservatives would no doubt prefer a Bennite model as their *anti-monde*.

d) Even if it is claimed that the Thatcher Experiment was worth it, it does not necessarily follow that other European countries should have done the same. Differing institutions and/or initial conditions at the start of the 1980s need to be taken into account.

2. Relative Economic Decline in Britain before 1979

From the 1870s to the 1970s the growth of output and productivity in the UK was slow by the standards of other advanced countries (Matthews et al., 1982, p. 31). The growth gap was particularly pronounced in the Golden Age from 1950-73 when the British growth rate was only about half the OECD average, although total factor productivity growth was higher than in any previous period of British economic history.

Moreover, in the post World War II period British manufacturing productivity levels were overtaken by France and Germany, as table 3 reports. Up to 1939 Britain's productivity lag was relative to the United States and, at least in terms of manufacturing, should be seen as a failure, in common with other leading European countries, to catch up with the leader of the second industrial revolution. In the 1950s through the 1970s there was a falling behind European rivals, particularly in manufacturing.

There are some persistent themes in the literature on relative economic decline in Britain which recur in all periods. These include low levels of investment, inadequate management, inappropriate education and training standards and industrial relations systems. In general, the problems can be regarded as coming from institutional arrangements which were not particularly conducive to longterm investments or effective in promoting good managerial performance and from bargaining equilibria between firms and their workers which led to poor productivity performance (Crafts, 1992b).

At the same time it would be a mistake to exaggerate the elements of continuity in the explanations for relatively slow growth over the century to the 1970s (Crafts, 1988). Thus natural resource endowments and market size probably played a much more important role in the Anglo-American productivity gap in the 1910s than in the 1970s (Nelson and Wright, 1992), while government interventions and distortions loomed large as a source of relatively poor performance only after World War II (Crafts, 1991).

The weaknesses listed above were well-known to policymakers by at least the 1950s. Their persistence over time reflected the inability of market forces and/or governments to eliminate them. At bottom then, there must have been market failures and/or political constraints inhibiting British growth performance. In the 1980s, however, there was a rapid narrowing of the manufacturing productivity gap between Britain and Europe, as table 3 shows. This is discussed in section 5 in the light of the historical background.

TABLE 3
Manufacturing Output per Person Employed
(UK = 100)

	France	Germany	USA
1913	79.3	119.0	212.9
1937	76.3	99.9	208.3
1950	83.9	96.0	262.6
1958	91.1	111.1	250.0
1975	124.0	132.9	207.5
1980	138.8	140.2	192.8
1989	112.2	105.1	177.0

Source: Broadberry (1992, table 1); comparisons are based on an industry of origin approach.

3. Recent Changes in Living Standards

In the 1970s it was a popular pastime to seek to modify estimates of the growth of real GDP to include other aspects of living standards in a broader measure of economic welfare. In this section I shall initially repeat an exercise of that kind for the more recent period before considering other aspects of the quality of life. I have adopted the approach of Beckerman (1980) for two reasons; his methodological position is as reasonable as that of anyone else in an area where there is no consensus and this will allow straightforward comparisons with the earlier postwar period using his results. The elements added to GNP for Beckerman's "measurable economic welfare" were allowances for changing income distributions and the growth of leisure time; in the end his overall conclusion was essentially that GNP is a fairly good indicator of relative growth rates of measurable economic welfare, i.e., when other quantifiable items are added relative performance is largely unchanged (Beckerman, 1980, p.59).

TABLE 4
Changes in Poverty and Inequality of Incomes

a) Poverty in the EC (per cent of total population)

	Mid 1970s	ca. 1980	1985
Belgium	7.9	7.6	7.2
Denmark	12.4	13.0	14.7
France	19.9	17.7	17.5
Germany	8.8	6.7	8.5
Greece	26.6	24.2	24.0
Ireland	16.4	16.9	22.0
Italy	10.6	9.4	11.7
Luxembourg	7.9	7.9	7.9
Netherlands	6.6	7.0	7.4
Portugal	23.4	27.8	28.0
Spain	20.0	20.5	20.0
UK	6.7	9.2	12.0
EUR12	12.8	12.6	13.9

b) Average Equivalent Weekly Gross Incomes of UK Households by Decile (1986 £) and Atkinson Indices

Decile	1971	1976	1981	1986
1	30.82	35.00	35.00	35.64
2	42.15	48.51	49.38	49.86
3	51.73	59.06	60.79	63.15
4	60.74	69.31	72.63	77.61
5	69.56	79.93	85.44	92.86
6	79.41	91.54	98.53	109.82
7	90.51	104.47	113.41	128.88
8	105.24	121.06	132.92	151.93
9	127.07	146.58	161.13	185.22
10	204.68	217.89	249.39	305.61
Atkinson index				
$\epsilon = 0.5$	0.073	0.067	0.078	0.094
$\epsilon = 1.0$	0.138	0.129	0.148	0.178

Sources:
Part a) taken from O'Higgins and Jenkins (1990); poverty is defined as less than 50% of average equivalent income. Part b) from Jenkins (1991, table 2). For the Atkinson index see footnote 1.

Table 4 reflects the sharp increase in inequality in the UK in the 1980s much stressed by critics of the government. Data on income distribution in OECD countries are not yet generally available for the 1980s but the estimates on poverty compiled by O'Higgins and Jenkins (1990) and also reported in table 4 suggest that the British experience was not repeated elsewhere in the EC. Depending how average income and an inequality measure are combined to form a social welfare index, it is quite possible toconclude that social welfare fell in the UK in the early 1980s. Most exercises of this kind have made use of the Atkinson index of inequality which allows the investigator an explicit redistribution preference.[1] Given the data of table 4b, Jenkins (1991) takes social welfare to be mean income multiplied by $(1 - \text{Atkinson}, \epsilon=1)^{\alpha}$ and considers $\alpha=0.25$ and $\alpha=4$. In the latter case where the greater weight goes to inequality reduction, the distributional trends between 1976 and 1986 imply a slight reduction in total welfare despite an increase of about a quarter in mean real income whereas with $\alpha = 0.25$, social welfare rises by about 20 per cent.

Beckerman (1980) also used the Atkinson index to adjust real GNP for changes in income distribution. He used the index directly to compute "equally distributed equivalent income" for several values of ϵ, the Atkinson inequality aversion parameter, including $\epsilon=0.5$ and $\epsilon=1.0$, which he regarded as about as far as people would accept in trading off equality against efficiency (1980, p.56). For the countries for which he could obtain data he found this generally made little difference in the 1950s and 1960s with the notable exception of France. Adopting Beckerman's procedure for the UK in the 1980s, taking the 1976 distribution of income as applicable to 1979 and the 1986 distribution for 1989, would significantly impact on measured growth. If $\epsilon=1.0$, a 2.1 per cent growth rate is reduced to 1.5 per cent or to

---

[1]   Atkinson's approach to the measurement of inequality is based on evaluating how much total income society is prepared to lose in order to carry out a given re-distribution of income; this depends on the marginal utility of income at different income levels. Atkinson assumes that marginal utility of income $= y^{-\epsilon}$. Then a transfer is acceptable if $dy_1/dy_2 = (y_1/y_2)^{\epsilon}$. Thus, if $y_1 = 2y_2$, if person 2 receives only half any income taken from person 1, i.e., $dy_1/dy_2 = 2$, this will be all right if $\epsilon=1$. Higher values of ϵ imply a greater degree of inequality aversion and thus a greater willingness to sacrifice total income for the sake of equality. This parameter is chosen by the investigator and can then be used with data on the whole income distribution to estimate the total income which if equally distributed would provide the same utility as the actual unequally distributed income. The **Atkinson index** is defined as the difference between total actual (unequally distributed) income and total redistributed income, expressed as a fraction of total actual income. Thus in Table 4b for $\epsilon=1.0$ the figure for the Atkinson index of 0.178 in 1986 means that, with this degree of inequality aversion and the Atkinson utility function, an equally distributed total income amounting to 82.2 per cent of actual total income would have yielded as much utility. Beckerman's adjustment to measured growth uses the Atkinson index in each year to calculate the growth of equally distributed income - a rise in the Atkinson index over time lowers this growth rate.

1.8 per cent if $\epsilon = 0.5$.

TABLE 5
Growth of Measurable Economic Welfare (MEW) per Head
(per cent per year)

	Real GDP per Head	Leisure Imputed	Inequality Adjustment	MEW per Head
a) 1950-73				
Belgium	3.6	-0.1	n.a.	3.5
Denmark	3.5	0.2	n.a.	3.7
France	4.3	-0.2	1.1	5.2
Germany	4.6	0.1	0.1	4.8
Italy	4.6	2.7	n.a.	7.3
Netherlands	n.a.	n.a.	n.a.	n.a.
UK	2.4	-0.6	-0.1	1.7
b) 1973-89				
Belgium	2.0	1.0	n.a.	3.0
Denmark	1.7	-0.4	n.a.	1.3
France	1.9	0.9	n.a.	2.8
Germany	2.0	0.7	n.a.	2.7
Italy	2.6	0.3	n.a.	2.9
Netherlands	1.3	1.1	n.a.	2.4
UK	1.9	0.5	-0.3	2.1
c) 1979-89				
Belgium	1.9	1.2	n.a.	3.1
Denmark	1.8	-0.2	n.a.	1.6
France	1.6	1.1	n.a.	2.7
Germany	1.7	0.3	n.a.	2.0
Italy	2.3	0.3	n.a.	2.6
Netherlands	1.0	0.9	n.a.	1.9
UK	2.1	0.5	-0.6	2.0

Sources:
1950-73 derived from Beckerman (1980). The leisure imputation excludes
pensioners' leisure, assumes no productivity increase in leisure time and allows
only for marginal increases in leisure. The inequality adjustment embodies an
Atkinson adjustment with $\epsilon = 1.0$.
1973-89 and 1979-89 are new calculations. The leisure imputation uses data on
hours and participation rates from Maddison (1982, 1991), excludes leisure of
pensioners and unemployed persons and assumes no productivity increase in
leisure. Changes in leisure are valued using wage data from Eurostat (1991).
The inequality adjustment for the UK uses data from Jenkins (1991) and
Beckerman's method with $\epsilon = 1.0$. Growth of real GDP per head is from
OECD (1991c).

This adjustment is entered in table 5 together with Beckerman's imputations where available for 1950-73. Until new data become available it is not possible to adjust other countries' growth for changing income distribution in the recent past but the evidence in table 4a suggests that any adjustments would either be much smaller than for the UK or even, as with France, would tend to **raise** the estimated growth rate.

Table 5 also includes imputations for changing leisure time. As is well-known the method used to deal with this aspect of economic growth has potentially very large effects on measured economic welfare and can seriously impinge on apparent relative performance. Key decisions required concern whether to value the whole of leisure or just the change between base and current years and what to assume about the productivity of leisure time. Since a substantial part of the changes in workyears per member of the labour force in the recent past has come from unemployment, a decision must also be made as to whether this time implies an increase in utility to be valued at the wage rate. My assumptions are listed in the notes to the table and follow in essence Beckerman's Method A (1980). Maddison (1991) reports large changes in working hours in the past 20 years and simply ignoring these does not seem good enough.

Several points come from table 5. First, in the recent period rankings of growth performance are much more sensitive to imputations than in the 1950s and 1960s. Second, although in general with these assumptions the estimated slowdown in growth since the 1960s is similar to that in GDP, the UK actually does better in 1973-89 than in 1950-73. Third, in the Thatcher period there are two generally offsetting and large imputations for the UK: the positive leisure component and the negative inequality one. With current assumptions they virtually cancel out but with different assumptions about leisure productivity or a different degree of inequality aversion this need not be the case. Fourth, it seems probable, however, that most economists compiling an index of measurable economic welfare would conclude that the UK's improvement relative to other European countries since the 1960s is appreciable.

Radical critics of the UK government stress that Conservative policy relied too much on markets and was driven too much by profits (Costello et al., 1989). Such suggestions would seem to imply that taking environmental damage/standards into account could also affect our perceptions of relative economic performance. GDP does not take account of the output of pollutants as a bad and in principle an adjustment would be required if welfare measures are desired, as has been recognised in the classic standard of living debate (Williamson, 1990) and by pioneers of adjusted national accounts (Nordhaus and Tobin, 1972). At present the data do not exist to perform this kind of calculation adequately. Table 6 suggests, however, that the outcome of the Thatcher Experiment left British citizens relatively satisfied with environ-

mental conditions and tends to question the desirability of making large
reductions in relative British growth performance due to environmental
problems.

TABLE 6
Survey Evidence on Dissatisfaction with the Environment
(Rank Order, 1 = least dissatisfied)

	Water Quality	Noise	Air Pollution	Waste Disposal
Belgium	6	7	6	3
Denmark	1	1	1=	1
France	7	5	5	2
Germany	9	11	11	6
Greece	10=	12	12	12
Ireland	5	2	3	9
Italy	12	8	10	10=
Luxembourg	4	6	9	4
Netherlands	2	4	4	7
Portugal	8	9	7	10=
Spain	10=	10	8	8
UK	3	3	1=	5

	Access to Open Space	Landscape Damage	Borda Ranking
Belgium	7	5	7
Denmark	1	1	1
France	6	4	4
Germany	8	7=	9
Greece	12	12	12
Ireland	3=	2	3
Italy	9	11	11
Luxembourg	2	7=	6
Netherlands	5	9	5
Portugal	10	6	8
Spain	11	10	10
UK	3=	3	2

Note: = indicates equal rank order.
Source: Based on Eurobarometer 1988 survey reported in Eurostat (1991, p.
106). The Borda Rule ranking is an ordinal aggregator and simply ranks on
the basis of the sum of the individual components' rankings.

Discussions of the quality of life generally consider mortality conditions to
be important and these are reflected in table 7. Table 7a suggests that taken as
a whole mortality experience by the mid 1980s was very similar in major
European countries.

TABLE 7
Some Aspects of Mortality

a) Life Expectancy at Birth

	1950	1970	1980	1986
Belgium	62.0	67.8	70.0	n.a.
Denmark	69.8	70.7	71.1	71.8
France	62.9	68.4	70.2	71.8
Germany	64.6	67.4	70.2	71.8
Greece	63.4	70.1	72.2	72.6 (1985)
Ireland	64.5	68.8	70.1	71.0
Italy	63.7	69.0	70.6	72.6
Luxembourg	63.4	67.1	69.1	70.6
Netherlands	70.6	70.7	72.7	72.2
Portugal	56.4	64.2	67.7	70.6 (1988)
Spain	59.8	69.2	72.5	73.1
UK	66.2	68.7	70.2	71.7 (1985)

b) Fatal Accidents at Work per 1000 Persons Employed

	Manufacturing			All Sectors
	1965-9	1975-9	1985-9	1985-9
Belgium	0.111	0.098	0.065	0.070
Denmark	n.a.	n.a.	0.035	0.030
France	0.117	0.088	0.059	0.079
Germany	0.152	0.117	0.075	0.090
Greece	0.115	n.a.	n.a.	0.058
Ireland	0.074	0.070	0.162	n.a.
Italy	0.093	0.080	0.033	0.084
Luxembourg	n.a.	n.a.	n.a.	n.a.
Netherlands	0.033	0.029	0.021	0.016
Portugal	n.a.	n.a.	n.a.	n.a.
Spain	0.063	0.112	0.131	0.138
UK	0.040	0.033	0.019	0.019

Sources: Part a) from Eurostat (1990); part b) from ILO (various years).

The first half of the 1980s shows virtually identical outcomes for France, Germany and the UK, for instance. Nevertheless, the Thatcher Experiment involved a weakening of trade unions and it has been convincingly argued that in manufacturing, given the ineffective policing of safety standards, such a change in bargaining power led to an increase inaccidents, including fatal accidents (Nichols, 1990). A precise evaluation of this argument is left to section 5; as far as levels of fatal accidents are concerned, table 7b compiles the available evidence.

TABLE 8
Rank Order of "Quality of Life" (1 = best)

	Poverty	Environ-ment	Misery Index	Produc-tivity	Mortality	Fatal Accidents
a) Rankings in the Late 1980s						
Belgium	1	5	4	3	6=	4
Denmark	6	1	3	8	4=	3
France	7	3	5	2	6=	5
Germany	3	6	1	4	6=	7
Italy	4	8	7	5	2=	6
Netherlands	2	4	2	1	2=	1
Spain	8	7	8	6	1	8
UK	5	2	6	7	4=	2
b) Rankings in the Late 1970s						
Belgium	4	[5]	3	2	7	6
Denmark	6	[1]	5	7	3	[3]
France	7	[3]	4	3	5=	5
Germany	2	[6]	1	4	8	8
Italy	5	[8]	6	5	4	4
Netherlands	1	[4]	2	1	1=	1
Spain	8	[7]	8	6	1=	7
UK	3	[2]	7	8	5=	2

c) Borda Index

	Late 1980s		Late 1970s	
	All	Without Col. 3 & 4	All	Without Col. 3 & 4
Belgium	2	4	3	5
Denmark	3	3	2	3
France	6	6	6	6
Germany	5	7	5	8
Italy	7	5	7	4
Netherlands	1	1	1	1
Spain	8	8	8	7
UK	4	2	4	2

Note: = indicates equal rank order. Sources: Basic procedure follows that of Dasgupta and Weale (1992). Data derived from tables 1, 3, 5, 6 and for output per person employed (col. 4) from Eurostat (1991). Environment is the Borda index of table 5 and has been assumed to be the same for the late 1970s in the absence of any specific information (see figures between brackets).

International comparisons of these statistics are surely not very reliable but, as far as these data show, reductions in fatal accident rates were achieved in the UK during the 1980s and both at the beginning and end of the period the UK compares favourably with most other European countries.

Dasgupta and Weale (1992) use the Borda rule to compute an overall ranking of the quality of life. Their concern is with developing countries and different categories are required to assess European countries effectively. Nevertheless, their method provides one way of comparing countries by aggregating ordinal rankings and I have used it in table 8 as a way of summarising and assessing the earlier tables in the paper. Table 8 suggests three observations. First, it would be wrong to be unduly pessimistic about the British quality of life compared with other countries either at the start or the end of the Thatcher period. Second, the UK tends to come out better in non-macroeconomic aspects of the quality of life. Third, for this group of advanced countries the rank order of relative productivity is not all that closely correlated with the rank order of the overall quality of life.It must be stressed that these are only preliminary findings. In particular, a research programme to widen the list of attributes in table 8 (to cover, for example, crime and health care) is highly desirable and might well change the results.

4. Recent Changes in Productivity Performance

This section turns to questions ii) and iii) posed in the introduction, namely how good was British growth performance in the 1980s relatively speaking and what were the reasons for any improvement. Both are essential ingredients in any attempt to evaluate the overall results of the Thatcher Experiment. I now return to considering the conventional estimates of real GDP growth rather than "measurable economic welfare". It will be recalled from table 2 that there is *prima facie* support for an improvement in British productivity growth from the Thatcher Experiment.

In order to assess this in its historical context, it is important to allow for differential scope for productivity growth between countries and also over time, as suggested by the influential literature on "catch-up" in OECD countries (Abramovitz, 1986; Dowrick and Nguyen, 1989). I experimented with a number of variants of Dowrick and Nguyen's econometric approach to obtain estimates of productivity performance normalised for "catch-up effects".[2] The results of a typical regression are shown in table 9 where

---

[2]   The inclusion of the Loglag variable allows this. The regression's prediction thus takes account of the effect of the initial productivity gap on growth performance. This can be thought of as normalising for "catch-up" potential - the negative coefficient on Loglag indicates that the bigger was the initial productivity gap, the higher was the growth rate *ceteris paribus*.

positive residuals indicate relatively good performance after allowing for the
included variables. The UK seems to have improved in the recent past, a
finding which is stronger if the equation's results are applied to sub-periods.
Thus, the UK residual is - 0.63 in 1960-73 but + 0.84 in 1979-88 whereas
Germany was 1.97 in 1950-60 but only 0.09 in 1979-88.[3]

TABLE 9
Regression Estimates of Catch-Up Effects and Residuals from the Equation

	1950-1973		1973-1987	
	Catch-Up	Residual	Catch-Up	Residual
France	1.5	0.4	0.5	0.5
Germany	1.8	0.7	0.6	0.4
Japan	3.0	1.4	1.1	-0.4
Netherlands	1.3	-0.3	0.3	0.5
UK	1.2	-0.7	0.5	0.4
USA	0.0	0.3	0.0	1.1

Sources: The equation estimated for a sample of 16 advanced countries for pooled data
on the periods 1900-13 (only 11 observations), 1923-38 (only 12 observations), 1950-
60, 1960-73 and 1973-87 is

$$\Delta Y/Y = 6.054 + 0.090\ I/Y + 0.861\ \text{Emptgr} - 1.350\ \text{Loglag}$$
$$(5.231)\quad (4.686)\qquad (7.751)\qquad\qquad (-4.941)$$

$$+ 1.281\ \text{RELYPW} - 1.282\ \text{RELYPWSQ}$$
$$(1.722)\qquad\qquad (-2.509)$$

$$+ 1.450\ \text{Dummy50s} + 2.280\ \text{Dummy60s}\qquad R^2 = 0.827$$
$$(5.267)\qquad\qquad (8.240)$$

where I/Y is the investment ratio, Emptgr is the growth rate of labour inputs measured
in hours, Loglag is the logarithm of the ratio of GDP per hour worked relative to that
in the USA in the initial year of each period measured at purchasing power parity,
RELYPW is income postwar relative to prewar multiplied by a dummy variable=1 for
1923-38 and 1950-60 to capture reconstruction effects and the dummy variables are
for 1950-60 and 1960-73. Data are taken from Maddison (1989), t-statistics in parentheses. Catch-up is estimated from the impact of loglag on the growth rate compared
to the United States. The justification for this basic approach can be found in Dowrick
and Nguyen (1989). Growth of human capital effects are not modelled explicitly.

---

[3] It should be noted that this better UK growth in the 1980s does not appear to be
the result of North Sea oil. North Sea oil output measured in 1985 prices was
about 4.5 per cent of GDP in both 1979 and 1988. The large arithmetic impact of
oil on measured growth was a phenomenon of the 1970s.

UK growth in the early postwar years nor the recovery of the Thatcher period is fully explained by the catch-up model in its "naive form". This should not be surprising because writers like Abramovitz have always stressed that catch-up is not an automatic process and that potential is sometimes not fully realised; thus Abramovitz argued that "(s)ocial capability [for catch-up] depends on more than the content of education and the organisation of firms ... it is a question of the obstacles to change raised by vested interests, established positions and customary relations among firms and between employers and employees" (Abramovitz, 1986, p.389).

Human capital and stock of knowledge variables are not included in the regression so it is appropriate to ask if these could be responsible for the relative improvement in British productivity growth. The literature is fairly unanimous in rejecting this possibility, although there would be a small effect of longer years of schooling in a conventional growth accounting framework such as Maddison (1991). Elsewhere in table 10 the evidence stubbornly fails to give any sign of relative British improvement. O'Mahony (1992) using a production function framework for manufacturing found that for 1987 human capital (approximated by measuring the skill structure of the labour force and weighting by relative wage levels) accounted for 12 percentage points of the gap between British and German labour productivity; in an attempt to replicate her estimate for 1979, I found it accounted for 14 percentage points whereas between the two dates the total decline in the productivity gap was 28 percentage points (O'Mahony, 1992, p. 55).

Similarly, it seems unlikely that growth discrepancies between Britain and Germany before 1979 are readily accounted for simply by the accumulation of factors of production emphasised by the new growth theory. Thus, Crafts (1992a) finds that an allowance for a Lucas-type human capital externality has no role at all in Anglo-German growth differences over 1950-73 while Crafts (1992b) looks at econometric estimates of the impact of R & D stock growth and equipment investment shares and concludes that they leave about half of the Anglo-German growth rate difference in 1960-73 unexplained.

At the same time there is evidence of a "behavioural" productivity gap between Britain and Germany resulting from the structure of industrial relations and from the political economy of the postwar period (Crafts, 1992b). This appears to have affected both levels (Pratten, 1976) and rates of growth of productivity (Prais, 1981). Indeed the consensus in the literature now appears to be that the British productivity surge of the 1980s - concentrated in manufacturing where output per worker rose by 50 per cent between 1979 and 1988 - owed little to greater investment in plant, people or research but came rather from more efficient use of existing factors of production and a shake-out of the inefficiencies which had accumulated in earlier decades.

TABLE 10
Comparisons Relating to Long Term Investments

a) R & D Expenditure as a Share of GDP (per cent)

	1970	1980	1989
France	1.91	1.84	2.32
Germany	2.06	2.41	2.88
Japan	1.85	2.18	3.04
UK	2.18	2.24	2.20
USA	2.65	2.39	2.82

b) Share of Patents Granted in the USA (per cent)

	1958	1973	1979	1988
France	10.4	9.4	7.9	6.8
Germany	25.6	24.2	22.7	17.4
Japan	1.9	22.1	27.8	41.3
UK	23.4	12.6	10.8	8.1

c) Labour Force with Intermediate Vocational Qualifications (%)

	1979	1988
France	32	40
Germany	61	64
UK	23	26

d) Years of Formal Schooling of Population, 15-64

	1950	1973	1989
France	8.2	9.6	11.6
Germany	8.5	9.3	9.6
Japan	8.1	10.2	11.7
UK	9.4	10.2	11.3
USA	9.5	11.3	13.4

Sources:
R & D data from Englander and Mittelstadt (1988, table 14) and
OECD (1991a, table 5). Patenting derived from Pavitt and Soete
(1982) and OECD (1991b, table 21). Vocational qualifications from
Steedman (1990). Schooling from Maddison (1987, table A12) and
Maddison (1991, table 3.8).

Econometric studies have suggested that this productivity advance in
manufacturing can be quite well explained along the lines of a model in which

adverse employment shocks and declining product market power of firms lead to new bargaining equilibria in which overmanning is reduced and/or work effort is increased (Bean and Symons, 1989; Machin and Wadhwani, 1989; Metcalf, 1989). It may well be that this stems from the idiosyncrasy of British industrial relations as both Crafts (1992c) and Weisskopf (1987) found that rises in unemployment have a strong pro-productivity effect in the UK but not in France or Germany. Thus a trade-off existed for the Conservatives under Mrs Thatcher between unemployment and productivity improvement which does not seem to have existed in the same way for the Christian Democrats under Herr Kohl.

Indeed, it might be more generally argued that the policy stance of the Conservatives on growth had some beneficial effects there while at the same time having an adverse impact on the Misery Index. By adopting the style of subjecting British industry to a "cold bath" both demand deficient and mismatch unemployment were raised (Layard et al., 1991) and de-regulating capital markets in pursuit of greater efficiency resulted in the excess demand and inflation of the late 1980s in the absence of other offsetting demand management strategies (Allsopp, Jenkinson and Morris, 1991).

The poor performance of the 1970s and fortuitous political circumstances gave a radical British government an extended "window of opportunity" to reform British productivity performance. The new policies led to changed bargaining equilibria with weaker trade unions and a major shakeout of inefficiencies. Other longstanding weaknesses and unfavourable institutions remained, notably in education and training and in short termism in investment decisions. The changes were, initially at least, more in conduct than in structure. Nevertheless, obstacles to "catch-up" in Britain were reduced and relative economic decline was ended for the time being. It is much harder to be confident that relative decline has permanently ended (Crafts, 1991).

5. Was the Thatcher Experiment Worth It?

In the light of the preceding sections, I shall interpret this question as follows. Were any gains in productivity attributable to the new policy stance post 1979 sufficient to outweigh the costs accruing through higher unemployment, reduced industrial safety and increased inequality of incomes? As noted in the introduction, the answer to this question depends on what social welfare function is adopted and assumptions about the counterfactual path of both the economy and economic policy.

Of the three negative effects identified, I shall argue that industrial safety can be regarded as unlikely to be a serious issue. Nichols (1990, p.328) gives regression evidence to suggest that declining bargaining power of workers raised industrial accidents in manufacturing by about 16 per cent per year in the first half of the 1980s, i.e. about an additional 32 deaths per year. His argument implies that non-fatal accidents in manufacturing would also have increased but data problems prevent effective measurement of this. Recent evidence on workers' valuations of safety (Marin and Psacharopoulos, 1982; Gegax et al., 1991) suggests that £100 mln. (0.02 per cent of 1989 GDP) might willingly be paid to avoid these increased safety risks. However, any such costs are surely more than offset for workers as a whole by the de-industrialisation of employment resulting from the Thatcher Experiment. Manufacturing employment fell by about a third while expansions of employment were in the much safer services sector.

The unemployment cost is potentially a serious one. I shall regard it as having two components and shall seek to establish an upper bound estimate. The Thatcher policy package can be thought of as producing more severe deflation and more structural change than that of the average European government. Consider the extra demand deficient component to be the value of UR - UR* for 1980-88 shown in table 1 compared with the average of other North European EC countries. Consider the extra structural unemployment element of UR* in the UK to be the 1.54 percentage point rise in mismatch estimated by Layard et al. (1991, p. 446). Together these would add up to an average Thatcher Experiment effect on unemployment of about an extra 2.5 per cent of the labour force relative to a "mainstream European" policy counterfactual. Evaluating the cost of this at average labour productivity implies an annual loss of the same fraction of GDP per person. This is likely to be an overestimate of the costs of unemployment because it values leisure of the unemployed at zero, because the unskilled disproportionately became unemployed, and because it assumes no rise in mismatch absent the Thatcher government.

Over the period 1980-88 even this upper-bound estimate of unemployment cost is, however, probably outweighed by the induced productivity gain in manufacturing from Thatcher Shock effects. The evidence for this includes improvements in "residual growth" shown by the cross-section regressions of table 9. Also, there are the positive effects of employment falls and competition increases generally noted in the literature (Crafts, 1991) and the regression results in Crafts (1992c) which indicate productivity gains induced by the new willingness to let unemployment rise. These all suggest a fairly substantial short-run impact on productivity. Other explanations for productivity increase are unpersuasive.

If the 15 per cent improvement in productivity in manufacturing relative to the average of France and Germany shown in Van Ark (1990) is regarded as a plausible lower bound guess, then the productivity gains from the Thatcher Experiment are worth at least 4.5 per cent of annual GDP by 1988 with more than half occurring by 1984. A more generous interpretation of changes in relative productivity growth, assuming a continuation of the 1960s negative residual in the table 9 regression - (i.e., below normal productivity growth after allowing for catch-up and factor accumulation) - as the counterfactual, could quite possibly triple this figure.

Whether such gains outweigh losses from a greater inequality of income depends, of course, on the investigator's degree of "inequality aversion" and the extent to which the greater inequality stemmed from the new policy stance. Table 4 suggests that welfare may have been reduced by about 5.6 per cent of GDP by rising inequality not experienced elsewhere in Europe if the Atkinson/Beckerman approach is adopted with $\epsilon = 1.0$ or about 2.9 per cent if $\epsilon = 0.5$.

It should be noted that there were big changes in inequality of original income and that the tax and transfer system operated somewhat to mitigate the impact on final income; the Gini coefficient for original income rose from 0.45 to 0.52 between 1979 and 1986 and for final income from 0.32 to 0.36 (Crafts, 1991, table 5). Moreover, it has been argued forcefully that the welfare state survived little changed through at least 1987, the main difference from earlier being that its increase relative to other areas of the economy stopped (Le Grand, 1990). There may, therefore, be some doubt as to the extent of the responsibility of the new policy stance for rising inequality of incomes.

Nevertheless, the Conservatives' willingness to promote reductions in personal income taxation, their tightening up of aspects of the benefit system, their acceptance of a return to a greater role for market forces in wage/salary determination and their tolerance of high unemployment make it likely that changes in economic policy relative to a "mainstream European" stance played a large role in the move to greater inequality of income in the 1980s. A provisional analysis by Johnson and Webb (1992) attributes about 80 per cent of the rise in inequality of incomes in 1980s Britain to these factors, with tax and benefit changes having by far the largest impact.

The implication of these various considerations is that evaluations of the Thatcher Experiment will differ; it would seem likely, however, that the majority of estimates based on these types of effect would fall in a range of plus 5 per cent to minus 3 per cent of GDP for the average annual effect in the mid 1980s. The pessimistic estimate would take a reduction of 5 per cent for greater inequality plus 2.5 per cent for greater unemployment offset by 4.5 per cent for productivity. The optimistic calculation would have the inequality loss equal to about 3 per cent of GDP, the unemployment loss at perhaps 2 per cent and the productivity gain at, say, 10 per cent of GDP.

Such calculations might need amendment, however, if a new growth theory view of these developments were taken rather than the implicitly Solow-type view which I have adopted thus far. If the changes of the early 1980s were to lead to permanently faster trend growth, then virtually everyone is likely to conclude that the present value of this welfare improvement would be worth the short run unemployment and inequality costs. It is exactly such possibilities that are contemplated by endogenous growth theory.

Two well-known variants of this approach are proposed in Lucas (1988) and Romer (1990). In these models a permanent re-allocation towards higher human capital formation and research and development respectively will permanently raise the growth rate. Neither of these eventualities appears to have been the result of adopting British rather than German style economic management during the 1980s and I am not optimistic that the Thatcher Experiment can be vindicated in this way. A third argument based on Romer (1986) would simply be that externalities to physical capital formation are large enough to obviate diminishing marginal productivity. If so, a positive productivity shock, which lowers the capital to output ratio and raises the growth rate of capital as a result, has a permanent growth rate effect. The available evidence seems, however, to refute this hypothesis (Crafts, 1992b). Overall then, it may be better at this point to accept the ambiguous result of the Thatcher Experiment on welfare implied by a Solow-type world.

6. Summary and Conclusions

In sum, the overriding impression is that both the claims of Thatcher enthusiasts like Matthews and Minford (1987) and critics like Costello et al. (1989) are greatly overstated.

More specifically, the findings of the paper are as follows.

i) UK productivity growth improved relative to comparator countries in the 1980s compared with the period of the long postwar boom. This improvement carries over into the growth of measurable economic welfare on a Beckerman-type approach.

ii) British economic performance in the 1980s included better growth but also higher unemployment and rising inequality of incomes. These latter may be regarded as costs of the Thatcher approach to faster growth. On the other hand, the "quality of life" in Britain still compared reasonably well with that elsewhere in the EC.

iii) There were positive impacts of the new policy stance on productivity performance in the UK which were largely unavailable for other European countries. It seems unlikely that these would have had a large permanent effect on the growth rate persisting into the 1990s and beyond.

iv) Assessment of the welfare effects of the Thatcher Experiment depends critically on the degree of "inequality aversion" of the investigator. Unless permanent growth rate effects can be established, most estimates are likely to be in an annual range of plus 5 per cent to minus 3 per cent of GDP.

References

Abramovitz, M. (1986), "Catching Up, Forging Ahead, and Falling Behind", *Journal of Economic History*, Vol. 46, No. 2, pp. 385-406.

Allsopp, C., T. Jenkinson and D. Morris (1991), "The Assessment: Macroeconomic Policy in the 1980s", *Oxford Review of Economic Policy*, Vol. 7, No. 3, pp. 68-80.

Bean, C. and J. Symons (1989), "Ten Years of Mrs. T.", *CEPR Discussion Paper*, No. 316.

Beckerman, W. (1980), "Comparative Growth Rates of 'Measurable Economic Welfare': Some Experimental Calculations", in: R.C.O. Matthews (ed.), *Economic Growth and Resources*, Vol. 2, Macmillan, London, pp. 36-59.

Broadberry, S.N. (1992), "Comparative Productivity Performance in Manufacturing since the Early Nineteenth Century: Europe and the United States", mimeo, University of Warwick.

Costello, N., J. Michie and S. Milne (1989), *Beyond the Casino Economy*, Verso, London.

Crafts, N.F.R. (1988), "The Assessment: British Economic Growth over the Long Run", *Oxford Review of Economic Policy*, Vol. 4, No. 1, pp. i-xxi.

--- (1991), "Reversing Relative Economic Decline? The 1980s in Historical Perspective", *Oxford Review of Economic Policy*, Vol. 7, No. 3, pp. 81-98.

--- (1992a), "Human Capital and Productivity in Advanced Economies", in: J. James and M. Thomas (eds.), *Capitalism in Context*, University of Chicago Press, Chicago, forthcoming.

--- (1992b), "Productivity Growth Reconsidered", *Economic Policy*, No. 15, forthcoming.

--- (1992c), "Productivity Growth in West Germany and the UK, 1950-1990: A British Perspective", in: K. Rohe, G. Schmidt and H. Pogge von Strandmann (eds.), *Deutschland-Grossbritannien-Europa*, Universitätsverlag Dr. N. Brockmeyer, Bochum, pp. 27-53.

Dasgupta, P. and M. Weale (1992), "On Measuring the Quality of Life", *World Development*, Vol. 20, No. 2, pp. 119-131.

Dowrick, S. and D.T. Nguyen (1989), "OECD Comparative Economic Growth 1950-85: Catch-Up and Convergence", *American Economic Review*, Vol. 79, No. 4, pp. 1010-1030.

Englander, A. and A. Mittelstadt (1988), "Total Factor Productivity: Macroeconomic and Structural Aspects of the Slowdown", *OECD Economic Studies*, Vol. 10, pp. 7-56.

Eurostat (1990), *Demographic Statistics*, Luxembourg.

--- (1991), *A Social Portrait of Europe*, Luxembourg.

Gegax, D., S. Gerking and W. Schulze (1991), "Perceived Risk and the Marginal Value of Safety", *Review of Economics and Statistics*, Vol. 73, No. 3, pp. 589-596.

Holmes, M. (1985), *The First Thatcher Government, 1979-1983*, Wheatsheaf, Brighton.

Humphreys, P. (1989), "Policies for Technological Innovation and Industrial Change", in: S. Bulmer (ed.), *The Changing Agenda of West German Public Policy*, Dartmouth Publishing, Aldershot, pp. 128-154.

ILO (various years), *Yearbook of Labour Statistics*.

Jenkins, S.P. (1991), "Income Inequality and Living Standards: Changes in the 1970s and 1980s", *Fiscal Studies*, Vol. 12, No. 1, pp. 1-28.

Johnson, P.S. and S. Webb (1992), "Recent Trends in UK Income Inequality: Causes and Policy Responses", mimeo, Institute for Fiscal Studies.

Kendrick, J.W. (1990), "International Comparisons of Productivity Trends and Levels", *Discussion Paper*, No. 90-02, George Washington University.

Layard, R., S. Nickell and R. Jackman (1991), *Unemployment*, Oxford University Press, Oxford.

Le Grand, J. (1990), "The State of Welfare", in: J. Hills (ed.), *The State of Welfare*, Clarendon Press, Oxford, pp. 338-362.

Lucas, R.E. (1988), "On the Mechanics of Economic Development", *Journal of Monetary Economics*, Vol. 22, No. 1, pp. 3-42.

Machin, S. and S. Wadhwani (1989), *The Effects of Unions on Organizational Change, Investment and Employment: Evidence from WIRS*, Centre for Labour Economics, London School of Economics, Discussion Paper, No. 355.

Maddison, A. (1982), *Phases of Capitalist Development*, Oxford University Press, Oxford.

--- (1987), "Growth and Slowdown in Advanced Capitalist Countries: Techniques of Quantitative Assessment", *Journal of Economic Literature*, Vol. 24, No. 3, pp. 649-698.

--- (1989), *The World Economy in the Twentieth Century*, OECD, Paris.

--- (1991), *Dynamic Forces in Capitalist Development*, Oxford University Press, Oxford.

Marin, A. and G. Psacharopoulos (1982), "The Reward for Risk in the Labour Market: Evidence from the UK and a Reconciliation with Other Studies", *Journal of Political Economy*, Vol. 90, No. 5, pp. 829-853.

Matthews, R.C.O., C.H. Feinstein and J.C. Odling-Smee, *British Economic Growth 1856-1973*, Stanford University Press, Stanford.

Matthews, K.G.P. and P. Minford (1987), "Mrs. Thatcher's Economic Policies 1979-1987", *Economic Policy*, Vol. 5, pp. 59-92.

Metcalf, D. (1989), "Water Notes Dry Up: The Impact of the Donovan Reform Proposals and Thatcherism at Work on Labour Productivity in

350 Nicholas F.R. Crafts

British Manufacturing Industry", *British Journal of Industrial Relations*, Vol. 27, No. 1, pp. 1-31.

Nelson, R.R. and G. Wright (1992), "The Rise and Fall of American Technological Leadership: The Postwar Era in Historical Perspective", *Journal of Economic Literature*, Vol. 29, forthcoming.

Nichols, T. (1990), "Industrial Safety in Britain and the 1974 Health and Safety at Work Act: the Case of Manufacturing", *International Journal of the Sociology of Law*, Vol. 18, No. 3, pp. 317-342.

Nordhaus, W. and J. Tobin (1972), *Is Economic Growth Obsolete?*, Columbia University Press, New York.

O'Higgins, M. and S.P. Jenkins (1990), "Poverty in the EC: 1975, 1980, 1985", in: Eurostat, *Analyzing Poverty in the EC*, Luxembourg, pp. 187-211.

O'Mahony, M. (1992), "Productivity Levels in British and German Manufacturing Industry", *National Institute Economic Review*, Vol. 139, pp. 46-63.

OECD (1991a), *Main Science and Technology Indicators*, Paris.

--- (1991b), *Basic Science and Technology Statistics*, Paris.

--- (1991c), *Historical Statistics, 1960-1989*, Paris.

Pavitt, K. and L. Soete (1982), "International Differences in Economic Growth and the International Location of Innovation", in: H. Giersch (ed.), *Emerging Technologies*, Mohr, Tubingen, pp. 105-133.

Prais, S.J. (1981), *Productivity and Industrial Structure*, Cambridge University Press, Cambridge.

Pratten, C.F. (1976), *Labour Productivity Differentials Within International Companies*, Cambridge University Press, Cambridge.

Romer, P.M. (1986), "Increasing Returns and Long-Run Growth", *Journal of Political Economy*, Vol. 94, No. 6, pp. 1002-1037.

--- (1990), "Human Capital and Growth: Theory and Evidence", *Carnegie-Rochester Conference Series on Public Policy*, Vol. 32, pp. 251-286.

Steedman, H. (1990), "Improvement in Workplace Qualifications: Britain and France, 1979-88", *National Institute Economic Review*, Vol. 133, pp. 50-61.

Van Ark, B. (1990), "Comparative levels of Manufacturing Productivity in Postwar Europe: Measurement and Comparisons", *Oxford Bulletin of Economics and Statistics*, Vol. 52, No. 4, pp. 343-374.

Weisskopf, T. (1987), "The Effect of Unemployment on Labour Productivity: An International Comparative Analysis", *International Review of Applied Economics*, Vol. 1, No. 1, pp. 127-151.

Williamson, J.G. (1990), *Coping with City Growth*, Cambridge University Press, Cambridge.

Part III

Measuring Levels of
Economic Performance

Explaining Economic Growth
A. Szirmai, B. van Ark and D. Pilat
© 1993 Elsevier Science Publishers B.V. All rights reserved.

What Can be Learned from Successive ICP Benchmark Estimates?

*Alan Heston and Robert Summers**
University of Pennsylvania

1. Introduction

The United Nations International Comparison Programme (ICP) is now 25 years old and has produced comparisons of currency purchasing power and real product for over 90 countries in seven different years during the period 1967-1990.[1] Each of the ICP's seven benchmark studies, one for each year, is a detailed analysis of the expenditure data of a group of countries for that year.[2] In this paper, we are concerned with what can be learned from the

---

* Support for this research by the National Science Foundation and the United States Agency for International Development is gratefully acknowledged, as is the computational assistance underlying the preparation of the tables by Bettina Aten and Joe Berger. We wish also to thank Robert Lipsey and Daniel Nuxoll for some very valuable discussions bearing on the main point of the paper.

[1] One part of the original mandate of the International Comparison Programme's when it was formed in 1968 was to prepare purchasing power comparisons from the production side as well as the final-product expenditure side. For many reasons, Irving Kravis and others formulating the early ICP agenda felt it would be too ambitious to begin with production side comparisons. In fact, to date the ICP's benchmark studies have dealt exclusively with final-product expenditure comparisons. The production-side work of Angus Maddison and his colleagues at Groningen has been a major contribution to world statistics. This paper ignores production-side work only because of the paucity of countries that have participated in multiple benchmark studies on the production side.

[2] The initial benchmark work, termed Phase I in the ICP, covered six countries for 1967 and those six plus four more for 1970. The Phase II study expanded the number of benchmark countries for 1970 to 16 and also updated them to 1973. Our work here will not use the 1967 or 1973 results because they are not altogether independent of those for 1970. Phase III covered 34 countries for 1975; Phase IV covered 60 countries for 1980; and Phase V covered 63 countries for 1985. Phase VI, still underway, covers 24 OECD countries for 1990,plus Czechoslovakia, Hungary, Poland and the USSR, and probably another 55 countries from Africa, Asia, and Latin America for 1993. At present the world comparisons have not been published for 1985, and only the OECD comparisons are available for 1990. For additional discussion of the countries and citations, see Summers and Heston (1991).

connections between the five major studies, those conducted in 1970, 1975, 1980, 1985, and 1990.

In the ICP's various benchmark studies, detailed price comparisons are made of final products (and in some important cases, input prices too) across countries for 150 to 200 detailed categories, or basic headings, of national output. These price comparisons are directed at producing for each country an overall purchasing power parity (PPP) covering aggregate gross domestic product (GDP), and price parities for the detailed basic headings and broader major components. The quantity counterpart of the price comparisons is a set of real product comparisons based on the PPPs which the ICP presents at both detailed and aggregate levels. Since a benchmark study deals with a single year's cross-section of price and final product expenditure data, it may be thought of as a point-in-time snapshot of how the collection of countries hang together in the benchmark year. (The price data come from price surveys conducted in each of the participating countries and the expenditure data are from the countries' national accounts; both the price and expenditure data relate to the benchmark year.) The premise of this paper is that it is instructive to investigate the country dynamics - that is, the motion pictures - that can be inferred from the successive benchmark studies.

We will be concerned here with the growth rate implications of multiple-benchmark results, and we will study further two propositions that emerged from our past examinations of cross-section relationships based on individual benchmark studies (see for example Kravis, Heston, and Summers, 1982). The first proposition is that the ratio of a country's PPP to its exchange rate, termed the comparative price level (CPL), is positively associated with the level of per capita income of the country; and the second is that the price similarity index for any pair of countries is inversely related to the difference in per capita income between them.

Three specific dynamic aspects will be examined:

1. The relative per capita GDP standings of pairs of countries in each of two benchmark studies imply the countries' relative growth rates between the years of the benchmark studies. In section 2, these growth rates will be compared with the almost independent relative growth rates embedded in the countries' national accounts.

2. The relationship between a country's exchange rate and its PPP has been a subject of great interest to international trade specialists dating back to the origins of the purchasing power parity doctrine. The multiple benchmark readings presented in section 3 on the departures of country PPPs from their exchange rates in a series of years help to clarify the underlying relationships.

3. Country's price structures change over time. Aspects of the character of that change over the period 1970-85 are explored in section 4.

The paper will conclude with a summary in section 5.

2. Growth Rates

We will deal empirically with the relative growth rates of eight OECD countries between 1970 and 1990. We will be concerned with how the relative growth rates implied by their standings in the 1970 and 1990 benchmark studies compare with the relative growth rates of the corresponding constant-price time series of the countries' own national accounts. To illustrate the question in a slightly different but perhaps more illuminating way, if the national accounts growth rates of GDP per capita in Japan and the United Kingdom between 1970 and 1990 are applied to their ICP benchmark standings in 1970, one would be led to expect that in 1990 Japan's GDP per capita would be 124 per cent of the United Kingdom's. However, in the 1990 benchmark study, Japan was found to be at 112 per cent of the United Kingdom. That is, the relative growth rate of the two countries in the national accounts was 1.1 per cent per year but the relative rate implied by the 1970 and 1990 benchmark studies was 0.6 per cent. Is this comparison in fact warranted? What should be made of the discrepancy? Some comment is called for before referring to table 1 which presents the details of the 1970-90 experience of all eight OECD countries participating in both benchmarks.

Background

We have discussed in detail elsewhere (Summers and Heston, 1991) possible explanations for differences between growth rates estimated from benchmark and national accounts data. Many reasons can partially explain such differences. For example, the weights and sample of items priced entering into country's intertemporal price indexes are by no means identical with the ICP's. However, it seems unlikely that such factors can explain the magnitudes of the discrepancies between ICP and national account growth rates as observed for both poor and rich countries and for market and planned economies.

We were originally led to consider questions of consistency of successive ICP benchmarks by an apparent pattern in the results for the participating East European countries, and later by what appeared to be a similar pattern (not observed in ICP benchmark studies, however) reported by the World Bank for China.[3] Since the character of the East European and Chinese experience and

---

[3] Perhaps the most striking illustration of a gross difference between   reported income levels and growth experience is for China. Most growth rates for China are inconsistent with place-to-place comparisons. The World Bank's *World Development Report* has since at least 1988 reported growth figures that are difficult to reconcile with level estimates at different points in time. For example,

Alan Heston and Robert Summers

the conclusions we have drawn from it are different from those for most ICP countries, their experience will not be explored further here.[4] Suffice to say, the national accounts growth rates - or really Western-source guesses about them - have been repudiated in varying degrees over the last few years for most of the East European countries.

The key question to be confronted is "How should one think about successive benchmark comparisons in dynamic terms?" Do they indeed reflect the relative movements of the income levels of countries over time, or do the secular and income-induced shifts in country price structures, and therefore the international price structure as well, make meaningful comparisons impossible? (Changes in price structures will be taken up below.) At least in gross terms, it is reassuring to find an additional fact in the Japan-UK illustration above: Japan's superiority was greater in 1990 than in 1970, since all evidence, including of course the national accounts, establishes Japan's faster growth over the intervening twenty years. However, does it follow from this that we would expect the 1985 and 1990 benchmark data to provide us with short-term information about the growth of Japan relative to other OECD countries that is not contained in national growth rates? In our previous work we have answered this question with "a little bit." Growth rates derived from constant-price output series based on **estimated** price indexes are hardly free of error. To put our view succinctly, if the Japanese-UK extrapolation from the 1970 benchmark study overshot the observed 1990 value, it should not be assumed automatically that either the 1970 benchmark comparison was too high or the 1990 benchmark comparison was too low. The estimated intertemporal price indexes might have been underestimated so the national accounts growth rates were overstated. We still hold this position but less strongly than in the past because the experience of successive benchmarks suggests that over short periods of five years, substantial variations may show up in the benchmarks that are not necessarily informative about growth in that five year period. These short-term variations are imperfectly understood. Our conjecture here is that they are probably related

---

the 1992 WDR (p. 218) puts the 1965-90 annual growth rate of per capita GNP of China at 5.8 per cent and at 1.9 per cent for India, along with estimates of 1990 GNP per capita at $370 and $350 respectively. These growth rates and income levels imply that their respective incomes in 1965 were $83 and $215, a relative standing generally regarded as highly implausible. The growth rates in China appear to pose problems like those that turn up in Hungary, Poland and Yugoslavia.

[4] We have argued that the macro explanation of why successive ICP benchmarks have produced lower and lower estimates for Hungary, Poland, and Yugoslavia is systemic, relating both to the nature of the prices used for the ICP and the nature of the growth rates in these economies (see Heston and Summers, 1991).

to exchange rate shocks that significantly affect relative prices.

Consider the effect of the appreciation of the dollar such as occurred between 1980 and 1985. The immediate effect is to lower the dollar price of imported tradables in the United States relative to non-tradables. If actual production is unchanged, real income rises because of the decline in the price of imports and a rise in the value of exports, a terms of trade effect. This is certainly the direction in which the comparisons move between 1980 and 1985 where the position of the United States improved relative to other OECD countries more than would be expected from just its constant-price growth rate. When the dollar declined between 1985 and 1990, we observed a reversal in the terms of trade effect. In this latter situation, for given production, real income would decline, and indeed the position of the United States did decline relatively. We will not elaborate further on the theoretical aspects of this topic here, but it is an important avenue of future research.

Growth Rates: A Comparison of Benchmark and National Accounts Estimates

Table 1 reviews the growth experience of the eight OECD countries that have participated in all five of the ICP benchmark studies.[5] Because these countries are fairly homogeneous with respect to economic structure and quality and type of price and output statistics, it is likely that observed differences are not simply a result of spurious errors in method or data.

The countries are arrayed in table 1 in order of their 1990 benchmark estimated per capita GDP.[6] These estimates in OECD prices appear in column (1)

---

[5] It must be mentioned that there is a significant methodological difference between the aggregation method used in calculating the 1990 benchmark OECD results reported here and the method used in the earlier benchmark studies, a difference that will be eliminated in later versions of the 1990 results. The so-called EKS method used in the 1990 study gives results very similar to those from the Geary-Khamis method used earlier, except that the EKS gives less weight to large countries. In the 1975 benchmark study, the consequences of using alternative aggregation methods were explored. It was found there that for the OECD countries the difference between EKS and Geary-Khamis was negligible. (For details, see Kravis, Heston, and Summers, 1982, chapter 3 and particularly table 3-6, pp. 96-7.) All in all, for the purposes served by table 1 here, the fact that the reported 1990 benchmark results were obtained by EKS rather than Geary-Khamis can be ignored.

[6] The numeraire country in ICP work has been the United States, and the currency in which all estimated magnitudes are denominated is termed the **international dollar**. The sense in which the United States is numeraire is that the value of the international dollar is defined to be such that the United States GDP measured in international dollars is equal to the United States GDP in American dollars. In this usage, the term **international**, modifying **dollar** means that the prices used to value each participating country's quantities are world average relative prices. That

358   Alan Heston and Robert Summers

TABLE 1
Long Term Comparisons of Benchmarks and National Growth Rates
Available OECD Countries, 1970 and 1990

Country	GDP per capita			Difference	
	In OECD Dollars 1990	Relative to OECD=100 ICP Benchmarks 1970	1990	Extrap. 1990	[(3)/(4)-1] Percent	Annual Rate Percent
	(1)	(2)	(3)	(4)	(5)	(6)
Belgium	16,405	92	97	109	-11	-0.52
Germany, F.R.	18,291	108	108	111	-3	-0.14
France	17,431	102	103	107	-4	-0.20
U.K.	15,720	94	92	90	2	0.10
Italy	16,021	87	94	89	6	0.29
Japan	17,634	81	104	112	-7	-0.34
Netherlands	15,766	103	93	94	1	0.05
U.S.	21,449	136	126	135	-7	-0.34

Columns (2) and (3) give their 1970 and 1990 GDP's per capita in percentage terms, relative to the average of all OECD countries. Column (4) provides an alternative estimate of each country's 1990 figure, obtained by extrapolating the 1970 figure of column (2) forward using the national growth rate of the country relative to the growth of the OECD countries at national prices. The difference between the two estimated relative per capita GDP's for 1990 appears in column (5). This difference is calculated as ([column (3)/column (4)] - 1.0). A negative difference means that the 1990 benchmark value is less than what would be expected from the 1970 reading, given the national growth rates between 1970 and 1990. Or equivalently, the growth rate implied by the 1970 and 1990 benchmarks is lower than the observed national growth rate. The implied difference in annual growth rates between benchmarks and national accounts is given in column (6). Those countries with negative

---

is, they are a weighted average of the relative prices of all countries of the world. The technical details of how this is done, using so-called **supercountry** weights is spelled out in Kravis, Heston and Summers (1982, pp. 79-82). It has been common for the OECD (and also for Africa and the Caribbean) to employ OECD (or African or Carribean), rather than international dollars as the currency unit. In OECD usage, the United States is still the numeraire country (the United States GDP in OECD prices is still the same as its GDP based on United States prices) but here all quantities are valued at the average relative prices of just the OECD countries. (The OECD prices are estimated using only information from the OECD countries, ignoring prices in the rest of the world.)

differences include slower growing countries like th U.S. as well as faster growing countries like Germany and Japan. A cursory examination of table 1 does not suggest any simple explanation of these differences.

For a comparison of the OECD countries over a twenty year period to be useful, the period should begin and end with normal years. It is reasonable to consider 1970 a normal year, with the system of fixed exchange rates still in place, but 1990 is less obviously a normal year. It is therefore fairly striking that by and large the differences are modest. The 7 per cent differences for the U.S. over twenty years means that the annual growth rate implied by the two benchmarks differs from the national growth rate by 0.34 per cent per annum. However, one overall pattern is that the column (3) benchmark estimates for 1990 display less dispersion of the countries from the OECD average than do the extrapolated estimates in column (4). Also, the two non-European countries, Japan and the United States retain their relative positions in columns (3) and (4) with each other, but not with various European countries.

Let us return to the question of whether successive benchmarks tell us anything about national growth rates. Probably, most observers would find column (3) a more plausible ranking of these countries than column (4) because in the former the relative position of Italy is higher and of Japan and the United States lower. If column (3) does seem more reasonable than column (4), it could be because the national growth rates are in error or that the 1970 benchmark is in error, or as we think, there are errors in both benchmarks and growth rates. In this paper we do not really deal with possible errors in national growth rates. Rather, what we wish to argue is that we should view the results of successive benchmark comparisons as informing us about the relative positions of countries throughout the period covered; or put another way, the latest benchmark may tell us less about that benchmark year than some mix of the information from that benchmark and previous benchmarks.

Up to now we have expressed the differences between national and ICP results in terms of growth rates. For the remainder of the paper we will discuss these differences in terms of comparative price levels. Using the Japan-U.K. 1970-1990 comparison again may be helpful in explaining our reason for changing the mode of exposition. According to constant price per capita national accounts series Japan grew 30 per cent more than the U.K. between 1970 and 1990. By contrast, between the 1970 and 1990 benchmarks Japan would appear to have gone from 95 per cent to 112 per cent of the U.K., the implicit growth rate of Japan exceeding that of the U.K. by only 18 per cent. The difference in the two growth estimates [1.0 - 1.18/1.30] is 9 per cent, namely the difference between the U.K. and Japan in column (5) of table 1.

Another way to look at this is to note that the yen/pound PPP was 322 in the 1990 benchmark and 801 in 1970. However, if the implicit deflators of GDP between 1970 and 1990 had been applied to the 1970 PPP, the implied PPP in 1990 would have been 293 yen/pound. The difference between the benchmark PPP of 322 and 293 yen/pound is of course 9 per cent, the mirror image of the difference in the implied and national accounts growth rates for Japan and the U.K. For most purposes the PPP of a country is less user friendly than a related concept, the comparative price level. The comparative price level (CPL) for a country is its purchasing power parity over GDP divided by the exchange rate.[7] Why CPLs instead of simply PPPs? After the freeing of exchange rates, it would be expected that exchange rates and PPPs would tend to move together for countries between benchmark years. If countries have very different inflation rates, then one would expect more temporal stability in CPLs than in PPPs so that over successive benchmarks their behavior would be easier to analyze.

In terms of the differences between benchmark and national statistics, it does not matter whether one works with growth rates and levels of output, or deflators and PPPs, or CPLs, deflators and exchange rates. For the purposes of this paper there is one advantage of working with the CPL, namely that we believe it is analytically more informative about what brings about differences between national statistics and successive benchmarks.

3. Comparative Price Levels of the OECD Countries

A. The 1990 Benchmark Results

Table 2 presents **comparative price levels** for OECD countries in the first 5 benchmark comparisons with the four largest EC countries, the **EC4** of France, Germany, Italy and the U.K. as numeraire. The countries in table 2 are ordered by increasing income with the figures in brackets giving the per capita GDP in the 1990 benchmark as a per cent with the U.S. = 100. The entry in each year is based upon the 1990 benchmark as published in volume I of the National Accounts (1992) of the OECD and their extrapolations to earlier benchmarks. Entries that are in italics indicate that the country did not participate in the ICP benchmark comparison for that year so that there is no independent check on the extrapolation. The U.S. row displays substantial

---

[7] In using **comparative price level** we are trying to conform to OECD usage and also disengaging ourselves from earlier nomenclature. In the first ICP volumes the reciprocal of the CPL (x 100) was termed the exchange rate deviation index, a usage that was certainly a red flag for many in the international trade and finance field. Use of the term price level of a country or national price level also was confusing to some who would associate these terms with temporal price indexes.

variation in the CPL over the benchmarks, with the 1970 and 1985 levels being over 55 per cent higher than the 1980 and 1990 levels. This is the reason that table 2 does not use the U.S. as the numeraire for the CPL, because this introduces variance in the CPLs of other countries, whereas the U.S. appears to be a main source of variation.[8]

Table 2 is based only upon the 1990 benchmark and does not illustrate differences between the various benchmarks and national data. Before returning to the consistency of benchmarks, there are several points to be made about the results in table 2. The first relates to the relationship between the CPL and the level of income of countries. As was mentioned earlier all benchmark comparisons for the world have exhibited a positive relationship between the CPL and the per capita income of a country. However, in table 2, this relationship is not at all strong, though the reader is again reminded that the entries in italics indicate that the country did not participate in the ICP in that year so the CPL is only observed with hindsight.

In the 1970 benchmark all countries including those in table 2, had CPLs below the U.S., and it was generally believed that as countries approached the level of income of the U.S. their CPL would approach that of the U.S. Had Canada, Norway and Sweden been in the 1970 benchmark, there might have been less attempt build upon this relationship. However, there is an intellectual tradition going back to Ricardo based on productivity differentials between non-tradables and tradables that suggested such a result.[9]

---

[8] The rows of table 2 indicated with an asterisk refer to EC4, France, Germany (as of 1990), Italy and the U.K. The main purpose of creating this entity is to provide an alternative numeraire to the United States, which is the numeraire for the ICP and the OECD. The reason we prefer the EC4 as numeraire is because it reduces the apparent variance in CPLs from benchmark to benchmark, and because these four countries were in all of the benchmarks. If the U.S. is numeraire, the coefficient of variation of the CPLs is usually over 20 per cent while with the EC4 as numeraire in table 2 it is more typically 5 per cent or 6 per cent. What this means is that the numeraire chosen greatly affects our perception of fluctuations in CPLs across benchmark years because the experience of the United States has been so variable. It should be mentioned that there are efforts to find an explanation for the U.S. fluctuations in terms of the data collection or other procedures in estimating the PPPs and CPLs between 1980 and 1990 for the United States. While such efforts to check on the basic data should be an essential part of the ICP, it is our guess that the variation displayed in table 2 for the United States is not fundamentally a data problem.

[9] For a discussion of the simple differential productivity model of Ricardo underlying this proposition, see Balassa (1964). Although benchmark countries are not ranked in table 2 by their 1970 income (which would put Italy and Japan near the UK) if one looks down the 1970 column for benchmark countries the general tendency for the CPL to rise with income can be observed. If low income countries like India were included the tendency would be even more pronounced.

TABLE 2
OECD Comparative Price Levels (EC4* = 100)

Benchmark year Country[a]	1970	1975	1980	1985	1990
Turkey (15.4)	*79.4*	*83.5*	*75.9*	62.9	47.4
Greece (34.3)	*105.7*	*92.0*	81.3	82.5	73.3
Portugal (39.1)	*67.2*	*68.5*	52.2	53.2	60.1
Ireland (49.7)	*99.8*	90.2	94.0	105.8	94.2
Spain (55.0)	*66.5*	76.2	80.9	72.2	88.6
N.Zealand (61.8)	*91.4*	*81.7*	*78.3*	87.2	78.9
U.K.* (73.3)	92.0	83.7	99.8	100.1	89.6
Netherlands (73.5)	97.6	114.5	111.9	103.5	98.1
Iceland (73.8)	*123.0*	*127.9*	*129.5*	*137.0*	119.6
Norway (74.2)	*144.1*	*154.7*	141.5	157.7	129.8
Australia (74.4)	*111.8*	*121.9*	*98.4*	117.0	90.0
Italy* (74.7)	89.9	82.2	79.3	90.3	104.0
Belgium (76.5)	112.0	121.3	114.2	96.8	97.5
Finland (76.7)	*110.5*	*124.8*	111.8	132.2	138.8
Austria (77.5)	*86.2*	98.0	97.1	100.3	101.7
Denmark (78.2)	*121.1*	138.4	123.0	122.2	125.9
Sweden (78.6)	*147.1*	*148.8*	*136.4*	130.9	130.8
Four EC* (78.6)	100.0	100.0	100.0	100.0	100.0
France* (81.3)	107.6	115.4	109.2	104.0	100.2
Japan (82.2)	94.7	98.6	95.1	131.0	112.2
Germany* (85.3)	110.7	118.6	111.5	105.5	106.3
Canada (89.1)	*148.9*	*121.3*	90.1	133.8	93.0
Luxembourg (90.2)	*116.1*	114.0	112.3	98.3	98.1
Switzerland (98.4)	*86.8*	*115.9*	*113.4*	*126.3*	130.7
U.S. (100.0)	140.6	104.6	86.4	144.3	82.9

[a] between brackets index numbers of 1990 GDP/capita (U.S. = 100)

When the results of the 1975 benchmark became available countries were adjusting to flexible exchange rates and we thought that when countries like France and Germany in table 2 had CPLs greater than the U.S., it was simply a temporary situation. However, in the 1980 benchmark countries like Argentina and Nigeria had CPLs greater than the U.S., and as can be seen in table 2, one of the poorest OECD countries, Ireland, also had a CPL above the U.S. in 1980. A glance at the 1990 column in table 2 suggests that the CPL is really quite variable with most countries having higher CPLs than the United States.

One variable clearly affecting the denominator of the CPL is the exchange rate and when it is driven by expectations and real interest rate differentials, it need not follow the PPP of a country. This is enough to produce substantial changes in the CPL of certain countries. Take for example, Switzerland, for which the initial benchmark estimate for 1990 and backward extrapolations are most interesting. Based on the 1990 benchmark Switzerland's per capita GDP would be 108 per cent of the U.S. in 1970, declining to 98 per cent in 1990, during which period the CPL of Switzerland was moving from 86.8 to 130.7 relative to the EC4, and from 61.7 to 157.7 relative to the U.S. From 1970 to 1990, Switzerland's economic level appears to be slightly declining compared to the U.S., while its price level is moving in the opposite direction, a result not consistent with the notion that CPLs should be inversely related to income. It is not hard to come up with reasons why Switzerland is special, e.g., expectation of low rates of inflation, and convenience of its financial environment for holding capital.

However, an examination of CPLs in 1990 does not suggest that those greater than the U.S. are necessarily found in countries with higher real interest rates.[10] Further many of these countries are not likely to have their

---

10   Real Interest Rates

Income Group		CPL > 110		110 > CPL > 90		90 > CPL > 75		75 > CPL	
Lower	1985			7.1	**(1)**	0.8	**(1)**	6.9	**(3)**
	1990			7.4	**(1)**	7.8	**(1)**	-3.0	**(3)**
Middle	1985	6.5	**(5)**	6.0	**(6)**				
	1990	6.2	**(4)**	7.2	**(5)**	4.8	**(1)**	6.0	**(1)**
Higher	1985	4.6	**(4)**	5.5	**(3)**				
	1990	2.2	**(2)**	5.8	**(4)**	2.6	**(1)**		

Our observations are based upon an examination of real interest rates computed as government borrowing rates less the consumer price increases in 1985 and 1990 of the countries in table 2 except Iceland. The countries were grouped into those less than 60 per cent of U.S. per capita GDP in 1990 (5 countries); those 60 to 80 per cent of the U.S. (11 countries); and the remaining 7 higher income countries.

exchange rates substantially affected by capital movements. How do we explain, for example, that countries with relatively similar per capita GDPs within Europe have CPLs 30 per cent or more higher than say Germany or France, e.g., Denmark, Finland and Sweden. In short, the notion implicit in one and two commodity convergence models that CPLs of countries approach the CPL of the country with the highest per capita income (accounting for real interest rates), seems quite at odds with OECD experience.

B. Comparisons of the Benchmarks

Let us now return to the consistency question on which more evidence is given in table 3. For each country a measure is provided of the ratio (times 100) of the benchmark CPL of a country for each benchmark year between 1970 and 1990 compared with the extrapolated CPL from 1990. An entry like 61 for Turkey in 1985 means that the benchmark PPP in 1985 was 61 per cent of the PPP extrapolated from 1990. Translated into economic level it means that the 1985 benchmark put Turkey over 60 per cent higher than was implied by the 1990 benchmark. (While a very large difference, 1985 was the first year that Turkey participated in the ICP, and typically there are larger errors in the first year of participation than subsequently). One other piece of information is provided in table 3 in brackets by each country; it is the ratio of the 1990 to 1970 per capita GDP of each country divided by the same factor for the United States. The entry of 1.21 for Turkey indicates that based on national statistics Turkey's per capita GDP grew 21 per cent more than that of the U.S. between 1970 and 1990. In interpreting table 3, how should one regard differences between two benchmark years other than 1990? If the entries are identical, it means that extrapolated results between the two benchmarks match the benchmark results. This is the case for Japan, for example, between 1970 and 1980, and between 1975 and 1985.

Four groupings were made by CPL, and the average real interest rate calculated for each group cell by income group and price level with the number of countries in each cell in brackets.The effect of high real interest rates would be to lower exchange rates and raise CPLs, other things equal. There is a weak positive association of higher real interest rates and CPLs for the lower income countries in both years, a still weaker association for the middle income countries, and no association for the higher income countries where the effect might be expected to be most pronounced. Middle income countries with CPLs above 90 do appear to have higher real interest rates than higher income countries with CPLs above 90, which is in support of attributing some explanation to real interest rates. Our conclusion is that real interest rates and real incomes help explain variations in CPL, but only partially.

TABLE 3
**Ratio of Benchmark Comparative Price Levels to those
extrapolated from 1990 (1990 = 100)**

Benchmark year Country[a]	1970	1975	1980	1985	1990
Turkey (1.21)				61	100
Greece (1.13)			90	89	100
Portugal (1.25)			106	95	100
Ireland (1.33)		95	88	94	100
Spain (1.15)		96	101	101	100
N.Zealand (0.88)				100	100
U.K.* (1.07)	102	107	100	95	100
Netherlands (0.98)	99	97	100	84	100
Norway (1.31)			79	83	100
Australia (1.01)				97	100
Italy* (1.18)	106	108	98	99	100
Belgium (1.14)	89	92	96	101	100
Finland (1.26)			99	95	100
Austria (1.21)		102	107	104	100
Denmark (1.04)		91	94	88	100
Sweden (0.98)				94	100
Four EC* (1.11)	100	100	100	100	100
France* (1.09)	96	94	100	101	100
Japan (1.39)	93	92	93	92	100
Germany* (1.09)	97	96	102	104	100
Canada (1.18)			85	87	100
Luxembourg (1.14)		95	92	97	100
U.S. (1.00)	93	95	94	90	100

[a] between brackets ratio of 1970 to 1990 GDP/capita (U.S. = 1.00)

Is there any simple pattern to these benchmark differences? Since the U.S. displays considerable variation between its last three benchmarks, we will take up this case first. In table 4 we try to bring out these relationships for the United States by reproducing the U.S. numbers from tables 2 and 3, and introducing information on U.S. exchange rates. In table 4, rows (1) and (2) correspond to the U.S. entries in tables 2 and 3, except that in table 4 row (2) has been normalized so that the average over the five benchmarks is 1.0. Three additional rows from IMF are also provided in table 4, the exchange rate to the SDR in row (3) and two measures of the effective exchange rate in rows (4) and (5).[11]

TABLE 4

Comparative Price Levels and Exchange Rates of the United States

Year Item	1970	1975	1980	1985	1990
(1) CPL(EC4 = 100)	140.6	104.6	86.4	144.3	82.9
(2) CPL Difference*	.98	1.01	1.00	.95	1.06
(3) US $/SDR	1.00	1.21	1.30	1.02	1.36
(4) Eff EXR-MERM	1.09	.91	.86	1.28	.85
(5) Eff EXR-REAL	n.a.	75.9	68.8	100	58.6

* Row (2) is the U.S. row of table 3 with the average value = 1.0; Row (4) has been expressed like row (2) so that the average of the 5 benchmarks is 1.0.

There are a number of relationships in table (4) that are suggestive. First, as would be expected, the exchange rate in row (3) and the CPL are inversely related and second, the CPL and the effective exchange rate in row (4) are positively related. Third, there is also an inverse relationship, that is particularly strong in the last three benchmarks between the benchmark and extrapolated CPL in row (2) and the effective exchange rate in row (4). The simple correlation coefficient, r, for the U.S. is 0.86 between row 2 and row 3, and -0.89 between row 2 and row 4. What this says is that when the dollar per SDR rate is falling significantly (and the effective exchange rafe is rising) the benchmark estimates produce a PPP that is low relative to that obtained from extrapolations.

Our present interpretation of this result is that when the dollar appreciates

---

[11] Row (3) is the annual average (geometric) exchange rate of the dollar to the SDR. Rows (4) and (5) are two measures of the effective exchange rate the first the IMF MERM rate and the second their real exchange rate series based upon movements of relative labor costs in manufacturing. The MERM rate is the only rate available back to 1970 and it is unfortunately some what less transparent than the other effective exchange rates of IMF as it is imbedded in a large econometric model.

relative to the SDR as in 1985, then the effective exchange rate declines because costs or prices in the U.S. have not changed relative to those in other countries by as much as have exchange rates. While this may represent a situation that is not viable in the long-run, in the short run of a benchmark comparison, it will make the U.S. look affluent relative to production. The more favorable dollar will allow a number of prices in the U.S. to decline relative to previous levels and permit an increase in income. We argue that this terms of trade effect is what is driving the relationships observed in table 4. The extrapolated value of the price level from 1990 to 1985 is 10 per cent higher than the 1985 benchmark because the latter incorporated a terms of trade effect and a lower set of prices.

Are the magnitudes of the terms of trade adjustment large enough to explain such difference? A conventional measure of the terms of trade adjustment as reported by the World Bank (World Tables, 1992) is to subtract from the capacity to import in a year (exports of goods and non-factor services deflated by the import price index) exports deflated by the export price index. With 1987 as the base, the adjustment as a per cent of GDP in the last three benchmarks is given below for the U.S. and several other countries. Between 1985 and 1990, the U.S. position went down relative to what was happening in the other countries above. For Germany, for example, the difference is fairly large, the U.S. losing 0.39 per cent of GDP and Germany increasing (reducing losses) by 3.87 per cent. For other countries, the gain, or reduced loss averaged about 1.25 per cent. The direction of the terms of trade adjustment is consistent with the benchmark results, though the magnitudes are not sufficient to explain all of the differences.

Country	1980	1985	1990
U.S.A.	-0.18	0.44	0.05
Japan	-2.10	-2.54	-1.22
Italy	-2.84	-2.22	-0.57
Germany, F.R.	-2.35	-4.10	-0.23
France	-1.66	-2.06	-0.34
U.K.	0.68	0.94	1.58

The pattern between 1980 and 1985 reveals a net improvement for the U.S. of 0.72 per cent and declines for all of the other countries except the U.K. (where North Sea oil presented a special situation). Again the magnitudes are not as large as the discrepancies between successive benchmarks given in table 3. The export and import price indexes that underlie estimates of the terms of trade adjustment are often not comparable across countries, are frequently based on unit values not on specification pricing, and are subject to major shifts in weights. However, we have no reason to believe the deficiencies of these indexes would systematically affect the terms of trade adjustments above. We are left with the conclusion that there is enough support for the proposition that differences between successive benchmark estimates and national growth rates are partially explained by terms of trade effects to justify future research in this direction.

4. Similarity in Price Structures

Earlier we mentioned the expectation that the CPLs of countries would tend towards 100 as their per capita income approached that of the higher income countries, an expectation that has certainly not been realized. Another proposition that appears to flow from the one and two commodity worlds of convergence models is that relative price structures of countries should tend to converge to those of the leader as countries approach the level of per capita GDP of the leading country. This is implicit in the **cost disease** approach of Baumol as more fully developed in Baumol, Blackman and Wolff (1989). This part of the paper, again using benchmark ICP data, looks directly at convergence of relative prices by asking whether similarity indexes of price structures have moved closer together over successive benchmarks.

What does it mean that countries have similar price structures. In our earlier work with Irving Kravis we looked at a way to measure similarity of price structures for the ICP benchmark countries (Kravis, Heston and Summers, 1982). Essentially for each country the basic heading parities were expressed relative to the PPP for GDP for each of the approximately 150 basic headings. Weighted raw correlation coefficients were computed as measure of similarity of prices between all possible pairs of countries, where the weights were the quantity structure at the basic heading level for all benchmark countries. Only one modification of our previous presentation of similarity indexes for a benchmark year has been made, namely to add a row (column) for the world, the average for all countries in the benchmark including their supercountry weight to approximate the distribution of expenditures of GDP of the world.[12]

The formula for the price similarity index is:

---

[12] In our previous work the similarity index was constructed to show only the relationship of price structures between each pair of countries. There is implicit in the aggregation method a structure of relative prices for all countries to which each country can be compared. The addition of an additional row to the similarity matrix allows this comparison.

$$S_{jk}^p = \frac{\sum\limits_i R_{ij} * R_{ik} * w_i}{[\sum\limits_i w_i * R_{ij}^2 * \sum\limits_i w_i * R_{ik}^2]^{1/2}}$$

where $R_{ij} = pp_{ij}/PPP_j$; pp_{ij} is the detailed heading parity for item i for country j, and PPP_j is the purchasing power parity over GDP of country j. The weights, w_i, are the share of world output of the heading out of world GDP.

Because the 1990 data at the basic heading level are not yet available, we have been unable to look at the most recent, and perhaps more normal terminal year for examining price similarity among major industrial countries. For weighting the relative prices at the level of basic heading we have used the quantity structure for all the countries for the benchmark year 1970 and for 1985. A case could be made for using the expenditure weights of the leader, the U.S., and perhaps for using the weights of the latest year. Our use of weights of each year should be viewed as a first approximation to further analysis that would involve all of the benchmark countries for 1985, not to mention 1990. While the half-life of our empirical findings may be short, we offer the following as suggestive of some of the complexities of the world.

The countries in table 5 include most benchmark countries in 1970 and 1985 for which we had available data at the basic heading level. The 12 countries in table 5 represent a broader range of per capita GDPs than in table 2; the countries are ordered by per capita GDP in 1985. The broad results of our earlier findings (Kravis, Heston and Summers, 1982) are evident in both years, namely that price similarity tends to increase the closer are two countries to the same level of income. In particular the results of regressing the similarity index in 1970 and 1985 on the difference in income (higher income minus lower income) between each pair of countries gives the following results:

$$S^{70} = 89.9 - .181 \text{ ydif} \qquad R^2 = .52$$
$$(.023) \qquad\qquad SEE = 5.50$$

$$S^{85} = 88.4 - .297 \text{ ydif} \qquad R^2 = .50$$
$$(.038) \qquad\qquad SEE = 8.62$$

In the equations **ydif** is the difference in income relative to the U.S. of the higher income country of the pair minus the lower income country. The coefficients in both years are negative and significant (standard errors in brackets) indicating that the closer are two countries in income the more similar will be their price structures.

TABLE 5
Price Similarity Indexes, 1970 and 1985

	IND	PHL	IRN	KOR	BEL	UK	ITL	JAP	NET	FRA	GER	USA	ALL
India													
1970	100	91	88	85	81	83	82	79	78	77	78	70	85
1985	100	80	82	70	69	72	71	72	67	69	64	60	79
Philippines													
1970		100	82	75	80	77	75	73	74	73	74	69	80
1985		100	80	76	68	72	70	72	69	68	66	66	80
Iran													
1970			100	81	83	82	82	79	81	80	81	82	87
1985			100	84	68	71	58	69	68	69	66	64	78
Korea													
1970				100	78	79	79	82	74	75	76	73	82
1985				100	72	71	71	87	68	73	67	64	76
Belgium													
1970					100	90	95	90	94	95	95	88	96
1985					100	97	95	93	98	98	97	92	95
U.K.													
1970						100	90	89	88	90	91	88	94
1985						100	95	86	96	97	96	91	95
Italy													
1970							100	90	95	97	98	88	96
1985							100	84	95	96	93	88	93
Japan													
1970								100	87	88	90	97	94
1985								100	84	89	82	77	86
Netherlands													
1970									100	96	96	87	94
1985									100	97	98	93	94
France													
1970										100	98	89	95
1985										100	97	92	94
Germany													
1970											100	90	96
1985											100	94	94
USA													
1970												100	93
1985												100	90
All													
1970													100
1985													100

Note to table: The indexes are based on the 16 benchmark countries of 1970 and on 30 of the 1985 benchmark countries. The indexes are calculated over from 140 to 148 basic headings; all categories with possible negative expenditures are excluded, and for each pair of countries only those headings for which both countries had parities were included. All refers to the average of **all** the countries in the 16 or 30 country aggregation. The aggregation affects the calculations only in providing the weights which is the distribution of the international dollar expenditure of 16 or 30 countries for each heading.

Does this relationship hold across benchmarks? Put another way does the similarity index between two countries decrease if their incomes get closer to each other over time? We examined these questions by regressing the change in the similarity index against the change in relative income between 1970 and 1985. There was no association between these variables over the successive benchmarks with R^2 being less than .001.

We conclude that a comparison of similarity indexes reveals a much more complicated world than one where followers were converging on the price structure of the leading country. Japan is a remarkable result, to say the least. The fact that Korea appears to be following Japan, suggests the role of geography and other homogenizing factors. However, there is only limited evidence that within the EC countries there is convergence on Germany. Belgium, the Netherlands and the U.K. (perhaps for other reasons) have price structures converging to Germany between 1970 and 1985, while France (trivially) and Italy diverge.

What can be made of the last column in table 5. First, we may note the plausible result that the countries closest to the world price structure are middle-high income countries, namely Belgium and Italy in 1970 and Belgium in 1985. A second result appears to be that the price structures of countries of the world are **not converging**, but diverging on average. The sum of the differences from 100 for 1970 for all of the countries is 108 and for the OECD countries 42; the corresponding sums in 1985 are larger, 146 and 59. The same result is evident in the somewhat less satisfactory fit for the regression equation above for 1985 than for 1970.

This evidence of diverging prices is supported by many studies of international trade which find countries buying and selling the same broad commodity groups to each other but where individual prices within the group are quite different. The point we wish to make is that most of our broad models of economic growth are for one, two or three sectors, and all point to convergence of price structures as per capita incomes come closer together. The real world does not seem that simple.

5. Conclusion

We have examined several facets of the benchmark ICP results in the context of the relative growth rates, comparative price levels, and relative prices of countries. Section 3 of the paper demonstrated that there has been no tendency between 1970 and 1990 for the comparative price levels (CPLs) of OECD countries to converge towards the CPL of the leading country. Countries with much lower incomes than the United States have higher CPLs over several benchmarks; further there is substantial variation in the CPLs within Europe not associated with income.

Finally in section 4 it was shown that between 1970 and 1985 there has been no tendency for the price structures of the 12 countries for which comparable benchmark data were available to converge. Rather measures of price similarity show greater variance in 1985 than in 1970, and countries that have grown more rapidly during this period do not have price structures closer to the leaders or the average in 1985.

All of this is not to say that per capita incomes have not come closer together for a large group of middle and high income countries in the past two decades. And we would agree that one can buy Big Macs in more countries in the 1990s than in the 1980s or 1970s. However, the Economist notwithstanding, the Big Mac is not a great measure of the purchasing power of currencies because it is bundled with an outlet and services that are not necessarily the same to consumers in different countries. What our results suggest is that the apparent homogenization of the world has not been accompanied by a convergence of price structures or overall price levels to those of the leader. To the extent that theories of convergence imply a coming together of price levels and relative price structures, they are in serious need of modification.

Finally, we have suggested that one might view successive ICP benchmarks as comparisons of incomes of countries at different points in time. National accounts data in constant prices are a comparison of real product at different points in time. Consequently, one might expect differences between growth rates in national accounts and those implied by successive benchmark comparisons if there have been forces leading to divergences between income and production over the period. We have suggested there is strong evidence of this occurring for the United States between the 1980, 1985 and 1990 benchmarks. Before such a conjecture can be accepted, however, it will be necessary to investigate the relationships for a larger number of benchmark countries.

References

Balassa, B. (1964), "The Purchasing Power Parity Doctrine: A Reappraisal", *Journal of Political Economy*, December.

Baumol, W., S.A.B. Blackman and E.N. Wolff (1989), *Productivity and American Leadership; The Long View*, MIT Press, Cambridge, Mass.

Heston, A. and R. Summers (1989), *An Evolving International and Inter-temporal Data System Covering Real Outputs and Prices*, NBER Growth Conference, Cambridge.

--- and --- (1991), "Some Issues in East-West Comparisons: Reform, Growth and Production versus Final Use", Paper presented to the Conference on "The Economic Contest Between Communism and Capitalism: What's Ahead", Institute for the Study of Free Enterprise, University of Buffalo, May 10-11, 1991.

Kravis, I.B., A. Heston and R. Summers (1982), *World Product and Income*, Johns Hopkins University Press, Baltimore.

--- and Robert Lipsey (1988), "National Price Levels and the Prices of Tradables and Nontradables", *NBER Working Paper No. 2536*.

Nuxoll, D. A. (1991), *Constant Returns to Scale Economies and Increasing Growth Rates*, Ph.D. Dissertation, Brown University, May.

OECD (1992), *National Accounts*, Vol. I, Paris.

Summers, R. and A. Heston (1991), "The Penn World Table (Mark 5): An Expanded Set of International Comparisons, 1950-88", *Quarterly Journal of Economics*, May.

World Bank (1992), *World Development Report 1992*, Oxford University Press, Oxford/New York.

World Bank (1992), *World Tables*, Johns Hopkins University Press, Baltimore/London.

Explaining Economic Growth
A. Szirmai, B. van Ark and D. Pilat
© 1993 Elsevier Science Publishers B.V. All rights reserved.

The ICOP Approach - Its Implications and Applicability

*Bart van Ark**
University of Groningen

1. Introduction

International comparisons of output per capita or per person employed have a history going back at least to the late seventeenth century. The first quantitative comparisons of per capita income are probably those by King (1696) and Davenant (1698) between England, France and Holland for 1688 and 1695. At the end of the nineteenth century Mulhall (1899) published estimates of per capita income including most West-European countries, North and South America and Oceania.[1]

Since the beginning of this century the quantitative approach to the study of economic growth and development received an important stimulus from the increased availability of official statistics on income, output and expenditure. It led to the creation of national accounts in most countries and to an upsurge in international comparisons of relative growth rates. However, so far only few studies have been concerned with cross-country comparisons of **levels** of per capita income and productivity. One main reason for this relative scarcity of level comparisons is the widely accepted notion that the use of currency exchange rates is not appropriate for such comparisons.

After the second world war some important studies appeared which compare levels of total GDP and per capita income on the basis of expenditure-based purchasing power parities (Gilbert and Kravis, 1954; Gilbert and Associates, 1958; Clark, 1957). Expenditure PPPs, including those from the International Comparisons Project (ICP) which have been compiled on a regular basis since 1967, also served in some studies as the basis for comparative productivity estimates.[2] However, expenditure PPPs

---

* Acknowledgements: I wish to underline here the cooperative nature of the ICOP research on which this article reports. I have benefited in particular from work done by Angus Maddison, Dirk Pilat and Eddy Szirmai. I am grateful to Dirk Pilat for his contribution to the statistical base of the present article.

[1] See Studenski (1958) for a historical review of national income and output estimates.

[2] See, for example, Maddison (1964, 1991).

cannot be applied directly to comparisons of real output and productivity by sector and industry. For that purpose detailed comparisons of physical output are required, or alternatively comparisons of output prices which can be used to convert value added by industry to a common currency.

Since 1983 a substantial research effort has been made at the University of Groningen towards the systematic development of this kind of industry-of-origin comparisons. The studies which have emerged so far have been brought under the heading of the International Comparisons of Output and Productivity (ICOP) project.

Industry-of-origin comparisons are particularly useful for the study of the reasons behind varying degrees of convergence of productivity levels among nation states, and for the analysis of the role of production factors and other variables in explaining productivity gaps. An alternative application is to study the relationships between productivity and the competitiveness of nation states on the world market. Finally, detailed productivity comparisons at industry level provide a link to more micro-oriented studies on the relative distance between average and best practice in productivity performance and on the process of technology diffusion among countries and industries.

The aim of the ICOP project has been threefold:
(1) to develop a systematic and transparent methodology for industry-of-origin comparisons of real output, productivity and purchasing power parities.
(2) to work towards a system of cross-country comparisons covering all sectors of the economy including services industries and the government sector.
(3) to make these comparisons for countries beyond the relatively small group of advanced countries.

Over the past years some 32 ICOP titles have appeared which represent the contribution of 10 past and present members of the research team.[3] The major aim of the present paper is to give an overview of the present "state of the art" of ICOP. Section 2 provides an account of the development of a methodology for industry-of-origin studies since the pioneering study by Rostas (1948). Sections 3 and 4 briefly outline the ICOP methodology. By way of illustration these sections present results for manufacturing comparisons of relative prices and productivity for seven countries in comparison with the United States. The seven countries are Brazil, Germany[4], India, Mexico, Japan, Korea and the United Kingdom. Most of the methodological points made in this section are also relevant for the ICOP

---

[3] For a complete bibliography see Angus Maddison and Bart van Ark, "The ICOP Project: A Progress Report", March 1992, Groningen. Available from the authors upon request. See also Maddison and Van Ark (1993).

[4] In this paper "Germany" refers only to the former Federal Republic of Germany.

studies covering other sectors of the economy, but for a detailed discussion of specific methodological aspects of ICOP studies of agriculture and services I refer to van Ooststroom and Maddison (1984) and Pilat (1991a) respectively. In section 5 one of the applications of ICOP, i.e. the explanation of productivity gaps, is elaborated in more detail for four of the advanced countries in the sample.

2. The Evolution of a Methodology for Cross-Country Productivity Comparisons

The first major study on comparisons of real output and productivity by industry of origin was by Laszlo Rostas (1948), comparing the United Kingdom and the United States. This study covered all sectors of the economy. But the most detailed comparison was for industry which included comparisons of physical output for 108 products in 31 industries, which were weighted by the number of employees in one of the two countries.[5]

Following the Rostas study a gradual shift in methodology has taken place. Nowadays production statistics report on so many product varieties of different qualities in each country that it has become impossible to cover all items by individual quantity comparisons. The alternative is to compare prices (or unit values) for a sample of products and to use the average price ratio to convert the total value of output to a common currency. A general consensus has emerged in the literature on national accounts and index numbers that the representativity of measured prices for unmeasured prices is better than that of measured quantities for unmeasured quantities.[6]

Nevertheless direct comparisons of physical output are still appropriate if a relatively small number of items of a fairly homogeneous nature are involved, such as for example in agriculture. In other cases the physical quantity method is still in use where price information is hard to come or very unreliable, for example for comparisons including developing countries or (former) socialist economies.

It would go beyond the scope of this article to provide a complete survey of studies on comparative productivity levels by sector which have used the industry-of-origin approach.[7] Below a brief overview will be given of the

---

[5] Rostas also included a comparison with Germany and (though based on much smaller samples) with some other countries including the Netherlands. For an "update" of the Germany/UK comparison of Rostas, see Broadberry and Fremdling (1990).

[6] For a more detailed treatment of this topic see Maddison and van Ark (1988).

[7] See for example the survey on international comparisons of productivity by Kravis (1976). See also my forthcoming book on cross-country productivity comparisons, van Ark (1993).

kind of studies which have emerged so far for agriculture, manufacturing and for all sectors of the economy.

Most cross-country comparisons of agricultural productivity have primarily used FAO or EC sources. The international statistics distinguish approximately 200 product items. Therefore physical quantity comparisons can be made more easily than for other sectors of the economy. Furthermore the agricultural comparisons mostly apply a double deflation procedure, which will be discussed in more detail for manufacturing in section three. Finally, comparisons on the basis of a multilateral weighting system have been applied mostly to agricultural comparisons.[8]

Studies on manufacturing productivity are now available for some 15 to 20 countries, including several developing countries (for example, India, Korea and Brazil) and (former) socialist countries.[9] These studies are mostly on a binary basis, usually with the United States as the "numéraire" country. The census of production is usually the basic source for such comparisons though in some cases use has been made of the national accounts. The use of national accounts has certain advantages, because in some countries (for example in the United States) the census only provides a somewhat anachronistic concept of "census value added", which includes non-industrial services inputs and is therefore "grosser" than national accounts GDP. However, the main advantage of census figures for productivity level comparisons is that output and input information is obtained from the same primary source.

Industry-of-origin studies covering all sectors of the economy are relatively scarce. The lack of quantity information on output in many services industries makes comparisons for this part of the economy very difficult. Rostas (1948) provided some comparative estimates for the UK and the USA for sectors other than industry. However, the pioneering study in this field is that of Paige and Bombach (1959). Their study involved meticulous comparisons of real output by sector, which has never been superceded in terms of coverage, transparency and clarity. For most sectors Paige and Bombach applied a mix of physical quantity indicators and real output measures obtained through price comparisons. Maddison (1970) provided industry of origin estimates for the total economy for 29 countries. His estimates included detailed comparisons of agriculture based on FAO sources. However, Maddison's comparisons for manufacturing and services were much cruder than the two-

---

[8] See section 3 for a more detailed discussion of the double deflation problem and the difference between bilateral and multilateral weighting systems.

[9] See also the contribution to this conference by Szirmai dealing with the specific problems of industry-of-origin comparisons for developing countries, describing the case of Indonesia compared to the United States. For a detailed overview of studies including the former USSR and Eastern European countries, see Laszlo Drechsler and Jaroslav Kux (1972).

country study of Paige and Bombach. Recently Pilat (1991a) has applied the industry-of-origin approach to a comparison of sectoral output and productivity for Japan and the United States. Clearly, this is an area in which more work is required, in particular, with regard to detailed studies for individual services industries.

During the past three decades a range of studies has emerged which provide short-cut methods or proxy measures. One short-cut method is to compare physical quantities for a limited number of commodities which are obtained from an international source such as UNIDO's *Statistical Yearbook*.[10] Unfortunately the information from these sources is incomplete and too aggregate for detailed comparisons.

A proxy approach to convert the sectoral output value to a common currency is to use expenditure PPPs.[11] There are at least four objections against the use of expenditure-based PPPs for output comparisons. Firstly expenditure by category adds up to national income and not to domestic output. Consequently prices include prices of imported products, which must be excluded for a comparison of domestic output. On the other hand, prices of exported products, which are part of domestic output, are excluded from the expenditure PPPs. Secondly PPPs refer to prices inclusive of transport and distribution margins. Third, expenditure PPPs are usually at market prices. For comparisons of the performance of production factors, value added should ideally be expressed at factor cost, and prices should therefore exclude indirect taxes and include subsidies. Finally, PPPs such as those from ICP relate to expenditure on final goods and not to intermediate products which make up an important part of domestic production.

3. International Price Comparisons for Manufacturing

Unit Value Ratios by Industry of Origin

In our ICOP studies, value added by manufacturing industry is converted to a common currency on the basis of average unit value ratios for product samples obtained from each country's census of production or industrial survey.

---

[10] See a study by Shinohara (1966) which compares output for 53 commodities in 89 countries weighted by census value added from Japan, the UK and the USA. Maddison (1970) uses a trade adjusted version of Shinohara's estimates at US prices for 29 countries in 1965.

[11] For the use of GDP PPPs for sectoral comparisons see for example Dollar and Wolff (1988). Proxy PPPs for specific expenditure categories are applied by Jones (1976), Roy (1982), Conrad and Jorgenson (1985), Roy (1987) and Hooper and Larin (1989).

In this article the basic comparisons are of a binary nature with the United States as the "numéraire" country. The benchmark years are either 1975 (for Brazil, India and Mexico) or 1987 (for Germany, Korea, Japan and the United Kingdom). The first step was to collect information on quantities and sales values for comparable product items. "Prices" were obtained by dividing the sales values by the corresponding quantities, so it is more accurate to call them "unit values". Unit values ratios (UVRs) for comparable products in two countries are obtained by weighting the unit values by the corresponding quantities of one of the two countries:[12]

$$UVR_j^{XU(X)} = \frac{\sum_{i=1}^{s} P_{ij}^X * Q_{ij}^X}{\sum_{i=1}^{s} P_{ij}^U * Q_{ij}^X} \tag{1}$$

at quantity weights of country X, and:

$$UVR_j^{XU(U)} = \frac{\sum_{i=1}^{s} P_{ij}^X * Q_{ij}^U}{\sum_{i=1}^{s} P_{ij}^U * Q_{ij}^U} \tag{2}$$

at quantity weights of country U (the United States).

$i=1...s$ is the sample of matched items in industry j.

The equations (1) and (2) are in fact traditional index numbers of the Paasche and Laspeyres type, depending on the weights chosen.

Apart from some quality adjustments discussed below, we made no attempt to collect specified prices from product catalogues, from the detail of official producer price indexes or directly from manufacturers. One major advantage of using unit values instead of specified prices is that the appropriate weights for the unit values are directly available in the form of the corresponding quantities of the same product.

The aggregation of the unit value ratios (UVRs) was carried out in a

---

[12] I have called the cross-country price ratios *unit value ratios* (UVRs) instead of the more familiar term "purchasing power parities" (PPPs) which we we used in other ICOP studies. The two terms are interchangeable, but for output comparisons my terminology seems preferable because it identifies more accurately the nature of the "prices" we use.

number of stages from industry level to the level of manufacturing as a whole by using value added as weights.[13] The advantage of stage-wise aggregation over single aggregation is that UVRs are more than once reweighted according to their relative importance in the aggregate. Table 1 shows the UVRs for total manufacturing for each binary comparison.

TABLE 1
Unit Value Ratios for Benchmark Years, Total Manufacturing,
national currency to US$ (1975 and 1987)

Binary Comparison with United States	US Quantity Weights (1)	Own Quantity Weights (2)	Geometric Average (3)	Exchange Rate (4)	Relative Price Level (US = 100) (3)/(4)
1975					
Brazil/USA[a] (Cr/US$)	8.77	6.91	7.79	8.13	95.8
India/USA[b] (Rs/US$)	12.77	6.70	9.25	8.65	106.9
Mexico/USA[a] (Ps/US$)	15.60	11.97	13.67	12.50	109.4
1987					
Korea/USA (Won/US$)	848.73	576.80	699.60	822.60	85.0
Germany/USA (DM/US$)	2.25	2.16	2.21	1.80	122.8
Japan/USA (Yen/US$)	218.80	150.59	181.52	144.64	125.5
UK/USA (£/US$)	0.748	0.670	0.708	0.612	115.7

[a] Original product data for the USA are for 1977, and were adjusted to 1975 at the industry level. See Maddison and van Ark (1988).
[b] Original product data for India are for 1973/74, and were adjusted to 1975 at the industry level. See van Ark (1991). For USA see footnote [a].
Sources: Brazil/USA and Mexico/USA from an expanded sample from Maddison and van Ark (1988); India/USA from van Ark (1991); Korea/USA from Pilat (1991b); Germany/USA and Japan/USA from Pilat and van Ark (1991); UK/USA from van Ark (1992); exchange rates from IMF, *International Financial Statistics*.

As might be expected, the two weighting systems represented by equations (1) and (2) do not lead to the same results, as can be seen from the first two columns in table 1. Unit value ratios for countries which are relatively close in terms of their level of industrial development are not very sensitive to the different weighting systems. However, for the developing countries, the UVRs at own quantity weights are substantially below those at weights of the USA. The use of the geometric average or Fisher index is a convenient way

---

[13] For details on the aggregation procedure see Maddison and van Ark (1988) and van Ark (1990a and b).

of showing a compromise indicator. Although the Fisher index has no theoretical meaning in analysing price structures, it has certain advantages over
Paasche and Laspeyres indexes. Firstly it compensates to some extent for the
"bias" created by single country weights. Secondly, an attractive property of
the Fisher index is that when used for extrapolation of price indexes to other
years it tends to show smaller margins of error than Paasche or Laspeyres
indexes (Krijnse Locker and Faerber, 1984).

The last column of table 1 shows the ratio of the UVR to the exchange rate
which provides an indication of the relative price levels in each country. For
the developing countries, relative price levels in 1975 are clearly above those
of the USA if the UVR is weighted by US weights, whereas it is close to or
below the US price level based on own country weights. Apart from Korea,
the 1987 relative price levels of the advanced countries are above those of the
USA irrespective of the weighting system. This reflects the relatively low
exchange value of the US dollar in 1987.

TABLE 2

**Unit Value Ratios, ICP Purchasing Power Parities and Proxy Purchasing Power
Parities for Manufacturing, national currency to US$ (1975 and 1987)**

Binary Comparison with United States	Unit Value Ratios for Manufacturing (1)	ICP PPPs for Total Economy (2)	Proxy PPPs for Manufacturing (3)	Exchange Rate (4)
1975				
Brazil/USA (Cr/US$)	7.79	5.40	7.77	8.13
India/USA (Rs/US$)	9.25	2.82	7.28	8.65
Mexico/USA (Ps/US$)	13.67	7.17	12.46	12.50
1987[a]				
Germany/USA (DM/US$)	2.21	2.57	2.64	1.80
Japan/USA (Yen/US$)	181.52	235.65	250.53	144.64
UK/USA (£/US$)	0.708	0.604	0.663	0.612

[a] ICP PPPs for Korea versus the USA are not yet published.
Note: Proxy PPPs for manufactured products were obtained from the Fisher or
multilateral average PPPs for the following categories: food, beverages and tobacco;
clothing and footwear; furniture; household textiles and appliances; personal transport
equipment and machinery and equipment. The PPPs were weighted at value added
weights derived from each country's production census.
Sources: UVRs are geometric averages taken from table 1. PPPs for 1975 are
"augmented" binary PPPs derived from Kravis, Heston and Summers (1982). PPPs for
1987 are Fisher binary PPPs for 1985 kindly provided by Eurostat, which are updated
to 1987 on the basis of national deflators.

Table 2 compares the unit value ratios for total manufacturing with PPPs for total expenditure derived from ICP, with "proxy PPPs" for manufacturing and with the exchange rate.

For the developing countries the expenditure PPPs are substantially below our manufacturing UVRs. This is not surprising because the former also measures the services prices of which are relatively low in developing countries. The proxy PPPs for these countries are much closer to the UVRs.

For the 1987 comparisons between Germany and Japan on the one hand and the USA on the other, the PPPs and proxy PPPs from table 2 are clearly above the UVRs, though the contrary is the case for the UK. This would imply that relative prices of manufactured goods in the USA were higher than for non-manufactured goods in comparison to Germany and Japan, but not in comparison to the UK.[14]

Binary versus Multilateral Weighting Systems

The comparisons presented in this paper are binary comparisons in a star pattern with the USA as the centre of the star. Comparisons between two or more countries which represent points of the star, are of course feasible when using identical weights, for example US weights. This would fullfill an important index requirement named **transitivity**, which in the present context means that the unit value ratio between two countries equals the ratio between the UVRs between each country and a third country. However, as discussed above, the use of single country weights creates biases in one or the other direction. In addition to transitivity, binary comparisons also create some other index-number problems such as **base country variance** and **matrix inconsistency**.[15]

Recently Pilat and Prasada Rao (1991) calculated multilateral indexes for a sample of countries covered by ICOP for the benchmark year 1975. Their study covers six originally binary comparisons with the United States, which include Brazil, India, Japan, Korea, Mexico, the United Kingdom and Japan. The multilateralisation was carried out at various levels of aggregation, i.e. at branch level, industry level and product level. The first index applied by the two authors is the Geary-Khamis index, which derives average international

---

[14] The relatively high price levels of manufactured goods in the United Kingdom are confirmed by intra-European comparisons of manufacturing productivity levels I presented for the Netherlands versus the UK and France versus the UK (van Ark, 1990a and b). See also the 1987 comparison for Germany versus the UK by O'Mahony (1992).

[15] For a discussion of index properties in international comparisons, see Kravis, Heston and Summers (1982) and Hill (1982). See also Pilat and Prasada Rao (1991).

prices at a disaggregated level simultaneously with a PPP for the aggregate on the basis of two interdependent equations. The Geary-Khamis procedure is mostly used for ICP comparisons. An alternative method is a multilateral version of the Theil-Tornqvist price index. The binary Theil-Tornqvist index is a weighted geometric average of detailed sectoral PPPs with average value shares of the two countries as weights. Transitivity is imposed on these binary indexes through a formula developed by Eltetö, Köves and Szulc (EKS) which creates a minimum distortion to the original binary indexes.

On the whole Pilat and Prasada Rao found that their multilateral results did not diverge strongly from the original Fisher indexes. However, the effect of multilateralisation depends on the countries included in the sample. For example, in the case of the Geary-Khamis method, the results were affected disproportionally by including India, which was characterised by a very different price structure from the other countries.

Despite the attractive properties of multilateral methods for comparisons between more than two countries and more than one industry, it should be emphasised that the major disadvantage of multilateralisation is the loss of a very important property of binary index numbers, i.e. **country characteristicity**.[16] For a comparison between any pair of countries, quantity weights of the two countries themselves most adequately reflect the relative price structures. This is the strongest argument in favour of binary comparisons. In particular if one is primarily interested in how each country compares to, and catches up with the leading country (which is the United States) in terms of manufacturing productivity performance, a comparison based on weights of the USA or the country itself is to be preferred.

The Quality Problem

In practice it is not possible to compare unit values for all products in manufacturing. Firstly, the specifications of the products in the censuses do not always match between two countries. Secondly, for some products no information on the sales values or quantities is reported in the census, generally because to do so would breach confidentiality. Finally, some products are too heterogeneous in terms of their defined characteristics. The unit values of products as specified in the census represent the average price for a mix of product qualities which might be present in different proportions in two countries.

On average the unit value ratios shown in this article are based on samples of between 130 and 200 product matches, apart from the India/USA comparison which is based on 108 matches and the Germany/USA

---

[16] The term was first coined by Laszlo Drechsler (1973).

comparison which consists of as many as 277 product matches. On average, coverage ratios are between 20 and 25 per cent of total sales, but quite some variation exists among branches. In some manufacturing branches, close to 50 per cent of sales or even more could be matched, but in some other branches, in particular in the engineering industries, coverage was much lower.

In the ICOP studies we have so far applied a conventional method to the quality problem by only comparing prices of "matcheable" products, i.e. products which are assumed to possess similar quality characteristics. In some cases industry and trade organisations were consulted to check the comparability of items between countries.

The quality problem is least present in manufacturing branches which produce relatively homogeneous goods such as paper, steel, cement, planed wood, etc. These goods largely represent intermediate stages of the production process. Beckerman (1966) considered the industry of origin comparisons to have an advantage over expenditure comparisons, because the latter exclude intermediate goods by definition. This also explains why in our UVR comparisons relatively high matching percentages are achieved in developing countries (e.g. Brazil, Mexico and Korea), where homogeneous items account for a larger share of output than in industrialised countries. On the other hand, broad descriptions of many product items in the censuses of developing countries and the lack of a product classification seriously hamper comparisons for some sectors, notably investment industries.

Detailed quality adjustments were made for our comparisons of passenger cars using information from secondary sources.[17] The production censuses of most countries only give the total sales quantity and value of passenger cars. Information from industry publications was therefore used to allocate passenger cars in each country to size classes on the basis of cylinder capacity. It was not possible to obtain ex-factory prices for different cylinder categories, but trade sources were consulted to obtain retail prices for domestically manufactured models, which were typical for each cylinder category in terms of certain quality characteristics. On average 3 to 4 specified prices were collected for each category. The average ex-factory unit value for each category was then inferred from the average retail prices in national currencies by class and the actual unit value for all passenger cars taken from the production census.

The Problem of Double Deflation

Industry of origin comparisons of real output and productivity face a major problem which is not encountered in comparisons from the expenditure side,

---

[17] For a detailed description of the methods, see Maddison and van Ark (1988) and van Ark (1990b).

namely that the former needs to distinguish between gross value of output and
value added. As value added is obtained by deducting the value of intermediate inputs from the gross value of output, one therefore ideally requires two
instead of one set of unit value ratios, i.e. one UVR to convert the gross
value of output (or sales) and the other UVR for deflating the value of the
inputs. Hence the term double deflation.

So far no cross-country comparison of manufacturing output has systematically applied the double deflation procedure because one faces serious data
limitations concerning separate UVRs for raw materials, fuels, electricity,
industrial and non-industrial inputs.[18] However, the production censuses are
not exhaustive. Input-output tables are of some help, but the level of
disaggregation is mostly insufficient to make adequate adjustments.

Apart from the practical reasons concerning the limitations of the data
base, there are at least two methodological objections against double deflation.
Firstly, the use of different weights for output-levels and input-levels lead to
"value added"-UVRs which at different country weights are far apart in
particular if the share of intermediate inputs in gross output is different
between countries. Secondly, relatively small measurement errors in the price
ratios of output or inputs tend to become magnified in the UVR for value
added, in particular when intermediate inputs make up a large part of gross
output.

Instead of applying an incomplete and unsatisfactory double deflation
procedure, we adopted the procedure proposed by Paige and Bombach (1959)
to weight the gross output UVRs for industry j by their corresponding gross
value added (VA), i.e.:

$$UVR_k^{XU(U)} = \frac{\sum_{j=1}^{r} [UVR_j^{XU(U)} * VA_j^{U}]}{VA_k^{U}} \qquad (3)$$

and:

$$UVR_k^{XU(X)} = \frac{VA_k^{X}}{\sum_{j=1}^{r} [UVR_j^{XU(X)} / VA_j^{X}]} \qquad (4)$$

j=1...r is the number of industries in manufacturing branch k

Although the industry UVRs refer to the gross output level, the aggregates for
branches and total manufacturing approximate the value added level using

---

[18] See Frank (1977) for a partial double deflation procedure including fuels, electricity
and raw materials. Paige and Bombach (1959) and Van Ark (1990a) adjusted their
productivity ratios for the use of fuels. Szirmai and Pilat (1990) experimented with
a full-scale double deflation procedure for their Japan/USA comparison for 1975,
which shows rather volatile results.

value added weights. This method, which is called the "adjusted single indicator" method, is based on the following assumptions:

1) for comparisons within an industry, i.e. at the product level, the value of intermediate inputs per unit of output compared to the output price of that unit is the same for all products within that industry and across countries.

2) the UVRs for inputs of industries and branches equal the corresponding UVRs for gross output or sales.

Paige and Bombach (1959) defended the superiority of the adjusted single indicator method which "although not so tidy and conceptually less satisfying" (p. 82) tends to provide more robust results than the double deflation method.

4. Comparative Levels of Labour Productivity

Manufacturing Productivity in the Postwar Period

Table 3 shows comparative levels of output per person-hour worked in manufacturing for seven countries relative to the United States from 1950 to 1989, ranked according to their relative productivity level to the USA in 1989. Briefly the procedure is as follows. Value added and labour input for benchmark years (1975 or 1987) are obtained from production censuses or surveys in each country. Value added is converted to US dollars on the basis of the unit value ratios presented in section 3. The relative productivity ratios for the benchmark years were then extrapolated forwards and backwards on the basis of time series of real value added and labour input for each country.[19]

The change in comparative labour productivity by country is also shown in figure 1. In interpreting the graph the reader should be aware that the relatively flat lines at the bottom of the productivity scale in some cases may still represent substantial productivity increases in absolute terms.

The United States has undoubtedly remained the productivity leader in manufacturing throughout the postwar period. Up to 1973 all advanced countries in the sample, and in particular Japan, caught up quickly with the US level of productivity. Growth slowed down in all countries during the 1970s, but the catch-up process continued in most cases. During the 1980s productivity growth in Japan, the UK and the USA clearly recovered compared to the 1970s. However, in Germany productivity growth stayed behind. By 1987 Japanese labour productivity in manufacturing was above that of Germany even after taking account of the fact that annual working

---

[19] For the extrapolation of the productivity levels to other years, I left out Mexico as there are problems in compiling a reliable long-run series on manufacturing value added and employment from the Mexican national accounts.

Bart van Ark

hours per person employed are 2,161 in Japan compared to 1,630 hours in Germany. Clearly the challenge to the overall US productivity leadership position in manufacturing comes primarily from Japan.

TABLE 3
Real Output per Person Hour Worked in Manufacturing,
1950-1989, USA = 100.0

	Census Value Added per Hour Worked				
	1950	1965	1973	1979	1989
India	4.2	4.9	4.9	5.0	5.7[c]
Korea	4.9[a]	6.8	11.2	14.6	19.8[d]
Brazil	20.0	31.8	39.7	36.0	28.6[c]
United Kingdom	40.0	44.4	52.4	53.7	60.5
Germany	39.3	60.5	75.5	91.3	79.4
Japan	18.4[b]	32.1	57.4	71.6	80.9
United States	100.0	100.0	100.0	100.0	100.0

[a] 1953; [b] 1955; [c] 1987; [d] 1988
Note: census value added is equivalent to gross value added plus non-industrial service inputs. Output is converted into US dollars on the basis of the geometric average of the unit value ratios for total manufacturing from table 1.
Source: Sources as for table 1; extrapolation of productivity in benchmark year is based on time series derived from national accounts and employment statistics (see van Ark, 1993 forthcoming).

In a recent study, Pilat and van Ark (1991) show that US leadership compared to Germany and Japan is still strong in light industries (food, beverages and tobacco, wearing apparel and wood products) but less so in investment industries, including engineering and transport equipment, where Japanese productivity levels are above those of the United States.

Compared to the advanced countries, present levels of comparative labour productivity for the developing countries in the sample (Brazil, Korea and India) are substantially lower. It appears that the absolute level of manufacturing productivity in Brazil is substantially above that of the two Asian developing countries. This striking difference between developing countries in Latin America and in Asia was also found in other ICOP comparisons. Census value added per hour in Mexico was estimated at 34.1 per cent of the United States for 1975. Pilat and Hofman (1990) arrived at an estimate of 22.3 per cent for Argentina compared to the United States. On the other hand, the article by Szirmai in this volume shows census value added per person employed in the manufacturing sector of Indonesia at 9.7 per cent of the United States.

For Brazil most of the catching-up on the US level of manufacturing productivity took place during the 1950s. Since the mid-1970s the relative productivity level in Brazilian manufacturing has strongly deteriorated in comparison to the USA and to the Asian countries. Comparative productivity in Korean manufacturing has steadily improved since 1968, and in India a significant improvement in productivity performance took place during the 1980s as well.

FIGURE 1

Census Value Added per Hour Worked in Manufacturing, 1950-1990, USA = 100

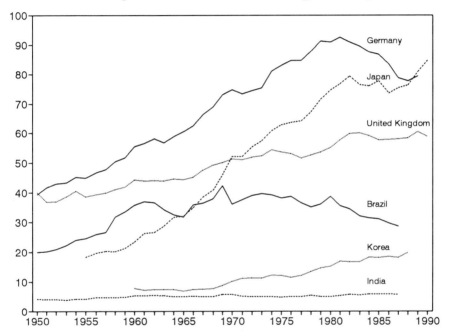

Source: see tables 1 and 3

Towards a Consistent System of Time Series and Benchmark Comparisons

In this section, time series of comparative productivity performance were obtained by linking the productivity ratios for the benchmark year, which was either 1975 or 1987, to series on real output and labour input for each country. These "extrapolation" results do not yield identical results compared to independent benchmark comparisons for different years. For example, by backcasting the 1987 benchmark result to 1975, I obtained a comparative productivity level for the United Kingdom of 53.6 per cent of the US level.

This implies a smaller gap than I obtained in a benchmark comparison for 1975, for which the UK/US productivity ratio was 46.0 per cent (see van Ark, 1990c).

There are at least three reasons why extrapolated figures cannot be expected to give identical results to a direct benchmark comparison:

(1) The inherent index number problems in time series and benchmark comparisons.

(2) Differences in methodology and basic data underlying the time series of real output and labour input betweem countries.

(3) Differences in methodology and basic data underlying the individual benchmark comparisons for different years.

The problems of inconsistency between time series and benchmark comparisons have also received attention in the ICP literature, as appears for example from the Heston and Summers-contribution to this volume.[20] Szilagyi (1984) argued that when using extrapolated series one should distinguish between two elements of the index number problem. The first element is that the prices of one base year are preserved as the weighting system for the complete time series. This element is called **price conservation**. The second element, which is called **weights inconsistency**, relates to the fact that the time series arc based on the national weights of each individual country whereas the benchmark estimate is based on a common weighting system for both countries. These elements of inconsistencies between benchmarks and extrapolated results, and which are referred to as the "tableau effect" by Summers and Heston (1991), need to be distinguished from the use of different sources and methods as described under (2) and (3).

Krijnse Locker and Faerber (1984) suggested various methods to smooth errors out between time series and benchmarks, by fixing one or more of the estimates and distributing the errors over the other variables. Summers and Heston (1988) have proposed to straighten out differences between bench-

---

[20] Blades and Roberts (1987) concluded that time series real income per capita show higher growth rates for the European countries compared to the USA than can be derived implicitly from a comparison of the 1980 and 1985 ICP benchmarks. They ascribed this difference primarily to an error in calculating the US purchasing power parity for 1980. However, Maddison (1991) found that by comparing the implicit growth rates between ICP II (for 1970) and ICP V (for 1985) with time series for the same period the relative productivity standing of European countries was also lower on basis of the former method. Furthermore a comparison of the most recent ICP benchmark result for 1990 with estimates updated from 1985 shows that the former overstates rather than understates 1985-90 growth rates for European countries relative to the USA (see OECD, *National Accounts, Main Aggregates, 1960-1990*, Paris, 1992). Interestingly, the extrapolated and benchmark results concerning the Japanese per capita growth rates relative to the United States do not show very different results.

marks and extrapolated time series by way of a statistical technique which distributes errors in measurement of the "true" values between the benchmarks and time series. These smoothing methods seem attractive, but they do not solve the problem, and tend to shift our attention away from the fundamental problem which is to establish the sources of differences between the various estimates.

The basic series which are used for extrapolation in the ICOP studies are real output series (usually GDP at constant prices) by industry from the national accounts which are combined with series on labour input, i.e. the number of employees or the total number of hours worked. The main reason to prefer national accounts over series which are directly derived from production censuses relates to the former's greater degree of consistency over time. For developing countries the national accounts are mostly not very different from census series, as the latter is often the only source on which the national accounts estimates by industry-of-origin can be based.[21] However, in advanced countries one can usually choose from a variety of sources to estimate output series for manufacturing. For example in the United States and the United Kingdom national accounts estimates of GDP are only very partially based on census information and to a larger extent on income and expenditure sources (see van Ark, 1993). It is therefore important that the sources of the differences between production censuses and national accounts are carefully analysed in order to reconcile "extrapolated" cross-country comparisons with independent benchmark estimates

It could be argued that the best approach to provide a dynamic perspective of cross-country comparisons is to make separate benchmark comparisons for each year. Apart from the practical problems of lack of resources to carry out time-consuming benchmark studies on an annual basis and the fact that production censuses are not always available annually, there are also methodological objections to such an approach. Annual cross-country comparisons affect the comparability of the comparative productivity ratios over time, because the weighting system changes each year.

It seems that a compromise needs to be sought between a regular updating of benchmark comparisons and the use of national time series for extrapolation. One cannot determine an unambiguous time pattern for updating these benchmarks. It partly depends on the relative change in growth rates between different countries. For example, if growth is much faster in one

---

[21] This point should not be confused with the fact that in absolute terms the national accounts in developing countries usually show substantially higher levels of output. This is primarily caused by the usual extension of the national accounts with "guesstimates" on small scale industries, which are not taken into account in the production censuses.

Bart van Ark

country than in another country there is more need to reconcile extrapolated
series with updated benchmarks, than if growth rates are fairly similar. In the
latter case the "bias" created by the time series can be expected to move in
the same direction for both countries.

5. Explaining Productivity Gaps

In the introductory section I mentioned various applications of ICOP measures
of comparative productivity. One of the most important of these is the search
for the explanatory causes behind productivity gaps. It is clear from
production and trade theory that only under very restrictive assumptions
productivity levels equalise among countries. In their quest to increase per
capita income, nation states look for clues to understand why their
productivity levels converge or diverge from that of the leading country. In
this section I will attempt to quantify the contribution of some factors for the
advanced countries in the sample, including the comparative level of capital
intensity and the composition and size effects to the productivity gaps.

TABLE 4
**Effects of Capital Intensity, Compositional Differences
and Establishment Size on Comparative Levels of Real Output per Person-Hour
in Manufacturing for 1987**

Binary Comparison with United States	Unadjusted Productivity Ratio (USA=100.0)	Percentage Explanation of Productivity Gap			
		Capital Intensity	Composition Effect	Size Effect	Unexplained
Germany/USA	78.7	1.4	-15.0	-25.4	-139.0
Japan/USA	75.5	19.6	13.5	52.3	14.6
UK/USA	58.0	11.7	0.2	-2.9	91.0

Note: Capital intensity equals the ratio of the capital stock to total labour input.
Capital stocks are obtained by a perpetual inventory method using official figures on
gross capital formation, and asset life assumptions of 45 years for buildings and 17
years for plant and vehicles. Assets were assumed to be retired uniformly between 20
per cent below and 20 per cent above the average service life.
Sources: Unadjusted productivity ratios same as for table 3. Gross capital formation
for Germany from Statistisches Bundesamt (1991), *Volkswirtschaftliche Gesamt-
rechnungen, Revidierte Ergebnisse 1950-1990*; for Japan (1965-1989) from EPA
(1991), *Gross Fixed Capital Stock of Private Enterprises*;, 1954-65 from MITI, *Census
of Manufactures*, various issues, with investment deflated at producer price index. for
UK from estimates provided by CSO; for USA from US Dept. of Commerce (1986),
Fixed Reproducible Tangible Wealth in the United States, 1929-1985, updated with
figures from *Survey of Current Business*.

Table 4 shows which part of the productivity gap is explained by these factors, which are discussed in more detail below. The effects for the three countries compared to the USA are surprisingly different. In the case of the Germany/USA comparison, differences in capital intensity play almost no role and an adjustment for the composition and size effect would in fact increase rather than reduce the productivity gap between Germany and the USA. It implies that 140 per cent of the productivity gap observed here is to be explained by other factors than those I measured here. The three effects have a limited influence on the UK/USA comparison, where 91 per cent of the productivity needs to be explained from other sources. Finally, in the case of the Japan/USA comparison the three factors, and in particular the size effect, play an important role and together "explain" 85 per cent of the productivity gap. A search for other explanatory causes, for example differences in skill intensity and institutional differences, has not been attempted in this article, but such factors clearly require further investigation.

The Role of Differences in Capital Intensity

It is often suggested that high labour productivity levels in the United States are primarily explained by the greater amount of capital per worker compared to other countries. As one can see from table 4 capital intensity accounted for one-third of the productivity gap between Japan and the USA, but for very little of the productivity between both European countries and the United States.

Capital has been calculated as the gross stock of buildings, machinery and vehicles in manufacturing in 1985 prices. For that year purchasing power parities on gross capital formation were available from ICP, and these were used to convert the capital stock to US dollars.[22]

In all four countries countries capital stock is compiled on the basis of the perpetual inventory method by which stock estimates are derived from cumulating investments over a long period. For my estimates I did not use the official capital stock estimates. Each country uses its own assumptions about asset lives and scrapping patterns which has a substantial impact on the level of the gross capital stock. In fact there is little hard evidence for very different asset lives between countries.[23] I therefore "standardised" the service lives of assets among countries on the basis of an average for 14

---

[22] For each binary comparison I used Fisher-weighted ICP PPPs for gross capital formation which were kindly provided by Eurostat.

[23] See for example Maddison (1991), Appendix D for reasons rejecting declining asset lives as assumed in the German and British estimates of the capital stock. See the contribution of Derek Blades to this volume for an alternative view (Blades, 1992).

OECD countries which was obtained from a detailed survey by Blades (1989, 1991). For asset lives I used 45 years for buildings and 17 years for machinery and vehicles. For scrapping I assume that the assets were retired uniformly between 20 per cent below and 20 per cent above the average service life. My "standardised" capital stock estimate for the USA is some 8 per cent above the official estimate for 1987. The estimates for Germany and Japan are 16 per cent and 22 per cent above the official figures respectively. Finally my UK estimate is more than 30 per cent below the official British estimate.[24]

I calculated the contribution of differences in capital intensity (K^X/L^X over K^U/L^U) to the labour productivity gap (Y^X/L^X over Y^U/L^U) by way of a simple Cobb-Douglas formula separating the effect of joint factor productivity (A^X/A^U) and capital intensity:

$$\ln\frac{Y^X/L^X}{Y^U/L^U} = \ln\frac{A^X}{A^U} + (1-a)\ln\frac{K^X/L^X}{K^U/L^U} \tag{5}$$

where "a" stands for the factor share of labour inputs in value added.

There are various ways to improve the estimates on the role of capital intensity. Firstly the capital stock estimate can be further refined, for example by applying the perpetual inventory method at a more detailed level of industries and assets to take account of different asset lives and compositional effects. This would also require more disaggregated PPPs to convert the gross capital stock value to a common currency. Secondly, alternative indexes to measure joint factor productivity could be tried, for example the transcendantal logarithmic index.

Compositional Effects

Differences in structure of the manufacturing sector between the countries is a second source which accounts for part of the overall productivity gap. Employment in country X can be more strongly concentrated in industries with relatively low absolute levels of labour productivity than employment in country U. To adjust for these compositional difference, output per person-hour in country X is weighted by the employment shares of either country X or country U before it is compared with output per person-hour in country U weighted by the same employment shares. This effect accounts for a modest

---

[24] In the official German estimate, asset lives are assumed to have declined over time. In the UK asset lives are approximately 60 instead of 40 years for buildings and 20 instead of 15 years for machinery and vehicles.

part of the productivity gap in Japan and the UK, whereas the structure of the German industry was in fact slightly favourable compared to the United States.

Size Effects

Employment in country X can also be more strongly concentrated in relatively small firms compared to country U. On average, output per person-hour is lower in small firms compared to large firms. An adjustment for the effect of size differences was made in a similar way as explained above for the compositional effect, using the employment shares by size category as weights for the productivity gap by size. In Japan employment has been concentrated relatively strongly in small firms. Size accounts for half of the productivity gap in Japanese manufacturing compared to the USA. However in Germany, a substantial part of manufacturing labour was concentrated in relatively large firms so that after the adjustment for size the productivity gap between this country and the USA increases compared to the unadjusted estimate.

6. Conclusion

The purpose of the present article was to describe the present "state of the art" of the International Comparisons of Output and Productivity (ICOP) project. The evolution of industry-of-origin comparisons was briefly presented in section 2. Sections 3 and 4 provided a birds-eye view on the ICOP methods and procedures as developed over the past decade. These methods and procedures, which are described in more detail in several ICOP studies underlying this article, comprise the first phase of the ICOP project. Further work is needed before this first phase can be finalised. For example, adjustments for quality differences will require more attention in the future. We aim also to expand our comparisons for services industries and to cover more countries. For example, ICOP studies are now being made for some former socialist countries in Eastern Europe for which the basic information on output and labour input requires more substantial adjustments before they can be used for our purpose.

In section 5 I presented some results of work which characterises the second phase of ICOP. Here the emphasis shifts towards applications of the ICOP results. Comparisons of relative joint factor productivity is only one such application. Alternatively one can use the productivity estimates in relation to the analysis of competitive advantage, which shifts the focus to relative cost levels in different countries. Finally, ICOP productivity estimates represent the "average" practice of one nation compared to another. To understand the process of technology diffusion between and within countries, one needs to measure the distance between average and best practice within industries. Such comparisons will require more micro-oriented studies of productivity performance at plant level.

The two phases of ICOP mentioned here are not chronological. A major aim of the research will remain to present methods and results in a transparent manner so that others can check them and are provided with the tools to replicate the method and apply it to other countries or industries.

References

Ark, B. van (1990a), "Comparative Levels of Labour Productivity in Dutch and British Manufacturing", *National Institute Economic Review*, No. 131, February, London.

--- (1990b), "Manufacturing Productivity Levels in France and the United o0 Kingdom", *National Institute Economic Review*, No. 133, August, London.

--- (1990c), "Comparative Levels of Manufacturing Productivity in Postwar Europe: Measurement and Comparisons', *Oxford Bulletin of Economics and Statistics*, November.

--- (1992), "Comparative Productivity in British and American Manufacturing", *National Institute Economic Review*, No. 141, November, London.

--- (1993), *The Economics of Convergence, A Comparative Analysis of Productivity Since 1950*, Edward Elgar, forthcoming.

Blades, D.W. (1989, 1991), "Capital Measurement in OECD Countries: An Overview", paper presented at International Seminar on Science, Technology and Economic Growth, June 1989. In revised form published in: *Technology and Productivity: The Challenge for Economic Policy*, OECD, Paris.

--- and D. Roberts (1987), "A Note on the New OECD Benchmark Purchasing Power Parities for 1987", *OECD Economic Studies*, No. 9, Autumn.

Broadberry, S.N. and R. Fremdling (1990), "Comparative Productivity in British and German Industry, 1907-37", *Oxford Bulletin of Economics and Statistics*, November.

Clark, C. (1957), *Conditions of Economic Progress*, 3rd edition, MacMillan.

Conrad K. and D.W. Jorgenson (1985), "Sectoral Productivity Gaps between the United States, Japan and Germany", in: H. Giersch (ed.), *Problemen und Perspektiven der Weltwirtschaftlichen Entwicklung*, Duncker and Humblot, Berlin.

Davenant, C. (1698), *Discourses on the Publick Revenues and on the Trade of England*, 2 Vols., London.

Dollar, D., and E.N. Wolff (1988), "Convergence of Industry Labor Productivity among Advanced Countries, 1963-1982", *The Review of Economics and Statistics*, Vol. LXX, No. 4, November.

Drechsler, L. (1973), "Weighting of Index Numbers in International Comparisons', *Review of Income and Wealth*, March.

--- and J. Kux (1972), *International Comparisons of Labour Productivity* (in Czech), SEVT, Prague.

Frank, J.G. (1977), *Assessing Trends in Canada's Competitive Position: The Case of Canada and the United States*, The Conference Board in Canada, Ontario.

Gilbert, M. and I.B. Kravis (1954), *An International Comparison of National Products and the Purchasing Power of Currencies*, OEEC, Paris.

--- and Associates (1958), *Comparative National Products and Price Levels*, OECD, Paris.

Hill, P.T. (1982), *Multilateral Comparisons of Purchasing Power and Real GDP*, Eurostat, Luxembourg.

Hooper, P. and K.A. Larin (1989), "International Comparisons of Labor Costs in Manufacturing", *The Review of Income and Wealth*, Series 35, No. 4, December.

Jones, D.T. (1976), "Output, Employment and Labour Productivity in Europe since 1955", *National Institute Economic Review*, London.

King, G. (1696), "Natural and Political Observations and Conclusions upon the State and Condition of England", in: G. Barnett (ed., 1936), *Two Tracts by Gregory King*, Johns Hopkins University Press.

Kravis, I.B., A. Heston and R. Summers (1982), *World Product and Income*, John Hopkins, Baltimore.

Krijnse Locker, H. and H.D. Faerber (1984), "On the Estimation of Purchasing Power Parities on the Basic Heading Level", *The Review of Income and Wealth*, Series 30, No. 2, June.

Maddison, A. (1964), *Economic Growth in the West*, Norton & Co., New York.

--- (1970), *Economic Progress and Policy in Developing Countries*, W.W. Norton & Co., New York.

--- (1991), *Dynamic Forces in Capitalist Development*, Oxford University Press.

--- and B. van Ark (1988), *Comparisons of Real Output in Manufacturing*, Policy, Planning and Research Working Papers, WPS5, World Bank, Washington D.C.

--- and --- (1993), "International Comparisons of Real Product and Productivity", paper presented at 105th Annual Meeting of the American Economic Association, 5-7 January, Los Angeles.

Mulhall, M.G. (1899), *Dictionary of Statistics*, 4th edition, London.

O'Mahony, M. (1992), "Productivity Levels in British and German Manufacturing Industry", *National Institute Economic Review*, February.

Ooststroom, H. van and A. Maddison (1984), "An International Comparison of PPPs, Real Output and Productivity in Agriculture in 1975', *Research*

Memorandum No. 162, Institute of Economic Research, Groningen.)

Paige, D. and G. Bombach (1959), *A Comparison of National Output and Productivity*, OEEC, Paris.

Pilat, D. (1991a), "Levels of Real Output and Labour Productivity by Industry of Origin, A Comparison of Japan and the United States, 1975 and 1970-1987", *Research Memorandum, No. 408*, Institute of Economic Research, Groningen.

--- (1991b), "Productivity Growth in South Korean Manufacturing, A Comparative Perspective, 1953-1988", *Research Memorandum, No. 435*, Institute of Economic Research, Groningen.

--- and A. Hofman (1990), "Argentina's Manufacturing Performance: A Comparative View', *Research Memorandum, No. 374*, Institute of Economic Research, Groningen.

--- and D.S. Prasada Rao (1991), "A Multilateral Approach to International Comparisons of Real Output, Productivity and Purchasing Power Parities in Manufacturing", *Research Memorandum, No. 440*, Institute of Economic Research, Groningen.

--- and B. van Ark (1991), "Productivity Leadership in Manufacturing, Germany, Japan and the United States, 1973-1989", *Research Memorandum, No. 456*, Institute of Economic Research, Groningen.

Rostas, L. (1948), *Comparative Productivity in British and American Industry*, National Institute of Economic and Social Research, Cambridge University Press, London.

Roy, A.D. (1982), "Labour Productivity in 1980: An International Comparison", *National Institute Economic Review*, London.

Roy, D.J. (1987), "International Comparisons of Real Value Added, Productivity and Energy Intensity in 1980", *Economic Trends*, June.

Shinohara, M. (1966), *Japan's Industrial Level in International Perspective*, Ministry of Foreign Affairs, Tokyo, March.

Studenski, P. (1958), *The Income of Nations, Theory, Measurement and Analysis: Past and Present*, New York University Press.

Summers, R. and A. Heston (1988), "A New Set of International Comparisons of Real Product and Price Levels, Estimates for 130 Countries, 1950-1985", *The Review of Income and Wealth*, Series 34, No. 1, March.

--- and --- (1991), "The Penn World Table (Mark 5): An Expanded Set of International Comparisons, 1950-1988", *Quarterly Journal of Economics*, Vol. CVI, No. 2, May.

Szilagyi, G. (1984), "Updating Procedures of International Comparison Results", *The Review of Income and Wealth*, Series 30, No. 2, June.

Szirmai, A. and D. Pilat (1990), "The International Comparison of Real Output and Labour Productivity in Manufacturing: A Study for Japan, South Korea and the USA for 1975", *Research Memorandum, No. 354*, Institute of Economic Research, Groningen.

Explaining Economic Growth
A. Szirmai, B. van Ark and D. Pilat
© 1993 Elsevier Science Publishers B.V. All rights reserved.

Comparing Capital Stocks

*Derek W. Blades**
OECD

1. What Makes Statistics Comparable?

Statistics for two or more countries, or for two or more time-periods, can be compared if they meet two basic conditions: i) they are based on the same definitions; ii) they are measured with similar degrees of accuracy.

For example, the Gross Domestic Products of two countries can legitimately be compared if they both use the same production boundary, and if they measure the activities occurring within that production boundary with similar levels of accuracy. Note that comparability does not depend on the methods used to estimate GDP. One country may rely entirely on data from administrative sources while another may use only statistical surveys and censuses; provided the statisticians produce estimates of similar accuracy from these quite different kinds of sources the two GDP figures will still be comparable. For most macro-economic measures, statisticians typically use a variety of sources and adjustment procedures. They assess the basic information available to them and then select those sources and methods which they judge will provide the most accurate estimate of the aggregates they are seeking to measure. Nothing would be gained in terms of comparability by insisting that both countries use the same sources and methods. On the contrary, by preventing a country from using the estimation procedure judged most accurate in that country, the comparability of the resulting figures would be reduced rather than enhanced. Statistical methodology is irrelevant to statistical comparability.

2. Comparing Capital Stocks

Turning to the topic at hand, the comparability of capital stock statistics can be assessed by examining how far they use common definitions and how accurately they are measured. To focus the discussion, this paper deals only

---

* The author is an administrator in the Statistics Directorate of the Organisation for Economic Cooperation and Development. The views expressed in this article are those of the author rather than those of the Organisation.

with statistics of gross capital stocks at replacement cost. The gross capital stock is the total value of assets at the prices at which they would be purchased if they were still new. Replacement costs can refer either to the current period or to a base year. The gross capital stock at constant replacement cost is the value of the stock of capital assets assuming that all assets were purchased new in the base year; the gross capital stock at current replacement cost shows the value of the capital stock if all assets were purchased new in the current year.

Coverage of Estimates

National estimates of capital stocks do not all cover the same basket of goods; in particular there are often differences with regard to non-reproducible assets such as land and subsoil assets and to assets owned by the public sector. For most countries, however, it is possible to obtain estimates of the capital stock covering most of the assets included in Gross Fixed Capital Formation (GFCF) broadly in line with the definitions of the UN-OECD System of National Accounts (SNA). In general, the SNA defines GFCF to include goods that are **durable** (lasting more than one year), **tangible** (intangible assets like patents and copyrights are excluded), **fixed** (inventories and work in progress are excluded, though mobile transport equipment is included) and **reproducible** (natural forests, land and mineral deposits are excluded). In addition to conventional assets such as plant, machinery, vehicles, buildings and construction, GFCF also includes livestock which are kept for breeding, for their milk or wool or for use as draught animals, as well as orchards, tree plantations and vineyards. GFCF should also include outlays on construction of defence assets if they have civilian as well as military applications; airfields and roads sometimes fall in this category, as do family housing for military personnel.

Several OECD countries do not follow the SNA rules strictly. Canada and Australia exclude livestock from GFCF; Sweden only treats goods that last three years or more as capital assets; and Australia classifies all defence expenditure as current. In addition, few countries strictly follow the SNA classification of capital formation so that, for example, non-residential buildings are often included in the "other construction" category (e.g. Netherlands) and livestock are sometimes included with machinery and equipment (e.g. Germany).

Quantitatively, all these are certainly minor departures from the SNA rules. Possibly more important is the treatment of "capital repairs". The SNA stipulates that repairs and extensions that either increase the service life of an asset beyond the lifetime expected for it at the time of purchase or that increase the productivity of assets are to be treated as capital repairs and included in GFCF. In most OECD countries, the tax authorities specify what kinds of repairs may count as investment for tax purposes and, in practice, national accountants are obliged to base their own definition of capital repairs on such legislation. It is possible that there are significant differences between countries in how capital repairs are defined.

Valuation at Replacement Cost

Valuation is another important aspect of the definition of the capital stock. For stock statistics to be comparable, assets must be valued at the prices at which they could be purchased (in their "as new" state) either in a base year or in the current year. In both cases, price indices are required to deflate assets from their years of purchase to the base-year (constant replacement cost) or to reflate them from the purchase year to the current year (current replacement cost). Price indices for GFCF are, therefore, indispensable for capital stock estimates. How reliable are they?

It is common ground among price statisticians that quality changes should be quantified. If this year's Ford has a higher price but has more comfortable seats, some part of the price increase should be discounted in calculating the (p_t/p_o) price relative used to calculate the price index for motorcars. How to quantify the improved seat-quality is very difficult and, because price indices have high political profiles, statisticians are generally conservative in quantifying quality changes. They tend to ignore minor quality changes and make lower-limit adjustments for those which they cannot ignore. Better to be criticised for sensible caution than for over-exuberance. Hedonic indices appear to be a practical method for quantifying quality changes, but the results are so sensitive to the choice of quality variables that only the United States has so far dared to use them in their official statistics. The indices obtained by hedonic regression confirm the suggestion above that indices based on traditional quality adjustment procedures tend to underestimate quality improvements and so overestimate price increases.

Overestimation of price inflation will always lead to underestimation of the capital stock at constant replacement cost; its measured value will be less than its actual value. At current replacement cost however, the problem may be less severe because the price index is applied twice in opposite directions - first to deflate to base year prices and then to reflate to the prices of the current year.

Note that if price indices are correctly measured, i.e. if all quality changes are quantified, the capital stock series will fully capture changes in the quality of assets. Analysts generally believe, probably correctly, that price indices are not fully adjusted for quality improvements. This must be why they sometimes introduce "vintage adjustments" into their calculations. These are supposed to capture improvements in the quality (i.e. productivity) of assets over time. Hofman (1991) uses a vintage adjustment for his estimates of

capital stocks in six Latin American countries. He assumes that the official
price indices used in his calculations overstate the true (quality adjusted) price
index by one percentage point each year over the period of estimation, so that
his vintage adjustment rises by 0.01 each year starting from 1.00 in 1910.
Two comments here. First his vintage adjustment implies steady deceleration
in quality improvements over the period; it is not clear why it should be
steady nor why it should decelerate. Second, if he believes that official price
indices overstate price inflation for capital goods, he may want to make the
same assumption for consumption goods and apply a "vintage adjustment"
(i.e. a price-index correction factor) to GDP as well. He seems not to have
done this. In general, it seems more sensible - and certainly more transparent
- to directly adjust the price indices[1].

3. Estimation procedures

In Central and Eastern Europe, capital stock estimates are based on
book-values of assets taken from enterprise accounts. Elsewhere, capital
stocks are estimated by the Perpetual Inventory Method (PIM) which involves
adding new investment to an initial stock estimate and subtracting assets when
they reach the end of their service lives. Application of the PIM involves
making a number of assumptions and these have been the object of close
scrutiny by analysts who have questioned the reliability (hence the
comparability), of capital stock statistics. In addition to concern with price
indices, attention has focused on average service lives, mortality functions
(which determine the dispersion of retirements around average service lives),
and on whether services lives should be kept constant over long periods.

Average Service Lives

In 1983, the OECD published a report on the service lives used in capital
stock estimates by Member countries (Blades, 1983). This showed that
countries were using very different service lives for what appeared to be very
similar kinds of assets. Table 1 is an updated version of a table from that
report. It shows the average service lives used by 9 countries for machinery
and equipment in certain manufacturing industries. Following publication of
this report some countries which had been using especially long service lives
brought them down closer to the OECD averages, but there was a clear
consensus among the national statisticians who have discussed the estimation

---

[1] In fairness to Hofman, it should be noted that his vintage adjustment is offered as
an optional extra. Hofman's very detailed tables also provide estimates for capital
stocks before adjusting or any "vintage effect".

TABLE 1
Average Service Lives of Machinery and Equipment in Selected Manufacturing Activities (years)

	Canada	United States	Japan	Australia	Finland	France	Norway	Sweden	United Kingdom
Food, beverages and tobacco									
Food and beverages	29	20	(11)	19	20	17	25	20	26
Tobacco	15	21	(11)	19	20	17	25	20	26
Textiles, clothing and leather									
Textiles	26	16	(10)	19	19	21	25	20	28
Clothing	21	15	(11)	19	19	21	25	20	24
Leather	15	15	(10)	19	19	21	25	20	24
Paper, paper products, printing, etc.									
paper and paper products	22	16	(12)	19	17	21	25	(30)	32
Printing and publishing	30	15	(12)	19	17	21	25	30	32
Chemicals, petroleum products, etc.									
Chemicals	22	16	(8)	19	18	17	25	15	29
Petroleum and coal products	26	22	(13)	19	18	17	25	30	23
Rubber	15	14	(9)	19	18	17	25	15	24
Plastic products	15	14	(9)	19	18	17	25	20	24
Basic metals	22	27	(13)	19	15	21	25	35	26
Fabricated metal products and machinery									
Metal products	21	24	(11)	19	15	17	25	25	26
Non-electrical machinery	21	25	(12)	19	15	17	25	25	25
Electrical machinery	22	14	(10)	19	15	17	25	25	25
Motor vehicles	30	14	(11)	19	15	17	25	15	27
Other transport equipment	30	17	(11)	19	15	17	25	15	27
Arithmetic Average	22	17	11	19	17	18	25	23	26

( ) average calculated by the author
Source: Blades (1991)

of service lives at OECD meetings that there really are differences between countries in average service lives. It was argued that these differences are partly due to a compositional effect. Service lives used for capital stock estimates are usually averages for groups of similar assets each of which may have lives longer or shorter than the average for the group as a whole. Within a given asset group the mix of short and long-life assets may be quite different between countries. But it was also noted that there can be differences between countries in service lives of identical assets. One of the main reasons for discarding an asset is the rising cost of maintenance as assets get older. If ratios of maintenance costs to new asset prices vary across countries, service lives will also vary. Tax legislation is often designed to encourage capital investment through authorising large amounts of depreciation to be charged against gross income in the years immediately after installation; as tax incentives for new capital investment vary between countries, so will incentives to discard existing assets.

Above all, however, capital stock estimators insisted on the fact that the service lives they use in the PIM models are empirically based. Admittedly, the evidence may be weak but their service life estimates are not guesses plucked out of thin air. Most countries consult engineers working in the industries that produce or purchase capital assets; several have carried out surveys to measure ages and life expectancies of assets in a small sample of companies; others have devised techniques for deducing asset lives from company accounts. None of this means that estimated service lives are precise, but it does suggest that they are reliable in a statistical sense - they are best estimates made from the limited information available and they are as likely to be too high as to be too low.

Before leaving this topic it is worth noting that too-long services lives will overstate the size of a capital stock and too-short service lives will understate it. However, for many analytic purposes, the growth rate rather then the size of the capital stock is the more important consideration. The service lives used in the PIM act like weights. A too-short service life for a fast growing (slow growing) asset will reduce (increase) the rate of growth of the capital stock as a whole, and vice-versa for a too-long service life. Changing from incorrect to correct service lives is as likely to increase as to decrease the growth rate of the capital stock and the use of erroneous service lives does not introduce any systematic bias into capital stock growth rates.

Mortality Functions

OECD Countries use a variety of mortality functions to describe how a group of similar assets installed in a given year are retired from the stock as they get older. Several studies have considered how the use of different mortality functions will affect estimates of the level and growth of the capital stock.

Figure 1 is taken from a Norwegian study and shows how the use of four different mortality functions affect estimates of the stock of machinery and equipment in metal manufacturing industries in Norway.

FIGURE 1
Gross Capital Stock Using Four Different Mortality Functions:
Machinery and Equipment in Metal Manufacturing Industries
(values in 100 million 1975 kroner)

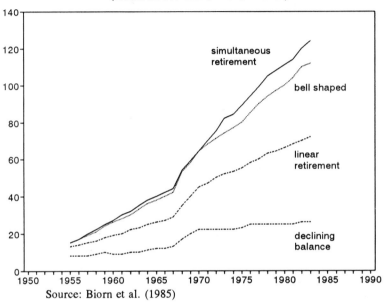

Source: Biorn et al. (1985)

At first sight it is rather disconcerting to see that these various mortality functions can produce such different results. The fact is, however, that the bell-shaped function is the only plausible candidate. Common sense, supported by a few empirical studies (notably Winfrey, 1935), suggest that retirements of assets will start gradually some years before their average service life, will rise to a maximum at, or near, the average and then gradually decline to zero. It is simply contrary common sense to assume that equal amounts of a given vintage are discarded each year starting immediately after installation (linear function) or, *a fortiori*, that the heaviest discards occur in the first years after installation (declining balance function).

In practice all OECD countries use either a bell-shaped function or one of two alternatives - simultaneous exit (e.g. Norway) and delayed linear (e.g. United Kingdom) - both of which can be regarded as approximations to a bell-shaped function. The conclusion is that OECD countries' capital stock estimates cannot be faulted for using inappropriate mortality functions.

Service Lives: Fixed or Variable?

Both the United Kingdom and Australia assume that service lives have been gradually declining since the 1950s. In the PIM estimates for Australia, service lives are assumed to be declining by about five per cent each decade, while in the United Kingdom's estimates, service lives of most types of long-life assets are reduced by just over one per cent each year. Lives of certain assets are also assumed to have fallen in Germany; declining service lives are assumed for housing, farm buildings, motor vehicles and certain types of industrial equipment. All other OECD countries assume that service lives have remained constant.

As regards specific types of assets, the evidence is mixed. A study by Hulten et al. (1988) of second hand prices for nine specific types of machine tools and construction equipment strongly suggests that, on average, these particular pieces of equipment continued to have the same service lives throughout the 15-year period of their study. Service lives of specific types of motor vehicles have been studied in Germany (Schmitz and Kramer, 1958; Schmitz, 1969 and Halstrick, 1986/87). Contrary to the results just cited, these studies suggest that service lives of passenger vehicles fell by just over 1 per cent per year from 1954 to the mid-1970s.

As noted earlier, however, the service lives used in PIM models refer to groups of assets, rather than to specific asset types. Service lives of groups of assets depend not only on the lives of the individual members of the group but also on the asset-mix within the group. Service lives of groups of assets have been studied in France and Italy by, respectively, Cette and Szpiro (1988) and Barca and Magnani (1989). For France, increases in service lives were found for capital assets in manufacturing and construction industries between 1972 and 1984, while for Italy declines were reported for lives of machinery and equipment in most manufacturing industries between 1969 and 1984.

When empirical evidence is as weak and contradictory as it is in this area, most capital stock estimators are showing sensible prudence in keeping service lives constant. It may be, of course, that service lives really are declining in Australia, Germany and the United Kingdom but are constant in other OECD countries. It seems more likely, though, that one or other group of countries is mistaken. This suggests some unreliability (hence non-comparability) in stock estimates, but it is hard to argue that this will be a major cause of non-comparability.

4. Capital Stock Estimates Based on Standard Methodologies

Because official statisticians use different variations of the Perpetual Inventory Method in estimating capital stocks, several economists have devised alternative estimates using standard versions of the PIM. The same service lives and the same mortality functions (usually simultaneous exit) are used for all countries in the study. Recent examples include studies by Paccoud (1983), Van Ark (1990), Maddison (1991), Hofman (1991) and Sentance and McKenzie (1992). The use of a standard mortality function does not seem a matter of great importance since all those currently in use give very similar results. But the use of the same service lives for similar assets in all countries is a very questionable procedure.

TABLE 2
Comparison of Capital-Output Ratios[a] Based on National and Standardised Capital Stock Estimates

	1970	1975	1980	1985	1986	1987	Annual growth rate[b]
United States							
National	3.94	4.19	4.16	4.11	4.10	4.07	0.2
Maddison	3.40	3.67	3.67	3.68	3.69	3.66	0.4
Japan							
National	1.92	2.60	2.85	3.07	3.16	3.20	3.1
Maddison	1.79	2.54	2.90	3.21	3.31	3.36	3.8
Germany							
National	4.08	4.52	4.45	4.68	4.66	4.69	0.8
Maddison	3.38	3.91	3.96	4.37	4.38	4.43	0.5
United Kingdom							
National	---	4.53	4.86	4.80	4.74	4.62	0.2
Maddison	2.42	2.61	2.76	2.84	2.83	2.78	0.6

Notes:
[a] Capital output ratios are gross capital stock at constant replacement cost divided by GDP at constant prices.
[b] Annual growth rates are for 1975 to 1987 for the United Kingdom, and for 1970 to 1987 for all other countries.
Sources: "National" estimates are taken from the OECD International Sectoral Data Base (see Meyer-zu-Schlochtern, 1988). "Maddison" estimates are taken from Maddison (1991).

In the case of the Hofman study, the author could justify the use of standard service lives by arguing that for his six Latin American countries there is no information from national sources on actual service lives and the same lives have had to be used *faute de mieux*. In the other studies cited above, however, standard service lives are used because the authors believe that this will actually improve the comparability of the estimates. It is argued above that comparability depends exclusively on definitions and reliability and that the estimation procedures are irrelevant. I would now go further and say that by ignoring the evidence that asset service lives really do differ between countries, and by imposing lives which have no empirical basis, the authors of these studies are deliberately introducing an element of unreliability and, by my definition, non-comparability into their capital stock estimates.

Table 2 compares ratios of gross capital stock to GDP from national sources with ratios based on Professor Maddison's standardised estimates of gross capital stocks. The differences are not trivial and analysts would draw quite different conclusions about the growth and size of capital-output ratios for these four countries depending on which series they chose to use. In what sense are "standardised" estimates more comparable than empirically-based national series?

References

Ark, B. van (1990), "Comparative Levels of Manufacturing Productivity in Postwar Europe: Measurement and Comparisons", *Oxford Bulletin of Economics and Statistics, Special issue: European Productivity in the 20th Century*, November.

Barca, F. and M. Magnani (1989), "L'industrie fra Capitale e Lavoro", *Il Mulino*, Bologna.

Biorn, E., H. Erling, H. and O. Oystein (1985), *Gross and Net Capital, Productivity, and the Form of the Survival Function - Some Norwegian Evidence*, Discussion Paper, No.11, Central Bureau of Statistics, Oslo.

Blades, D. (1983), *Service Lives of Fixed Assets*, ESD Working Paper No. 4, OECD, Paris.

--- (1991), "Capital Measurement in the OECD Countries: An Overview", *Technology and Productivity. The Challenge for Economic Policy*, OECD, Paris.

Cette, G. and D. Szpiro (1988), "La durée de vie des équipements industriels sur la période 1972-1984", *Cahiers Economiques et Monétaires*, No. 28, Paris.

Halstrick, M. (1986/87), "Zur Entwicklung der Neuzulassungen von Personenkraftwagen in der Bundesrepublik Deutschland bis zum Jahr 2000", *Mitteilungen des Rheinisch-Westfälischen Instituts für Wirtschaftsforschung*, Vol. 37/78.

Hofman, A.A. (1991), *The Role of Capital in Latin America: A Comparative Perspective of Six Countries for 1950-1989*, ECLAC, Santiago de Chile.

Hulten, C.R., J.W. Robertsons and F.C. Wykoff (1988), *Energy Obsolescence and the Productivity Slowdown*, Working Paper 176, United States Department of Labor, Bureau of Labor Statistics, Washington D.C..

Maddison, A. (1991), *Standardised Estimates of Fixed Investment and Capital Stock at Constant Prices: A Long Term Survey for 6 Countries*, University of Groningen, mimeographed.

Meyer-zu-Schlochtern, F.J.M. (1988), *An International Sectoral Data Base for Thirteen OECD Countries*, ESD Working Paper No. 57, OECD, Paris.

Paccoud, T. (1983), *Le Stock de Capital Fixe Industriel dans les Pays de la Communauté Européenne; vers une Comparabilité Accrue*, Eurostat, Etudes de comptabilité nationale, Luxembourg.

Sentance, A. and D. Mckenzie (1992), *Financial Times*, 27 January 1992.

Schmitz, E. and H. Kramer (1958), "Absterbeordnung für Kraftfahrzeuge", *Problematik, Berechnung und Anwendung*, Rheinisch-Westfalischen Instituts für Wirtschaftsforschung.

Schmitz, E. (1969), "Sterbetafeln für Lastkraftwagen und Kraftfahrzeuganhanger", *Mitteilungen des Rheinisch-Westfalischen Instituts für Wirtschaftsforschung*, No. 1.

Winfrey, R. (1935), *Statistical Analyses of Industrial Property Retirements*, Bulletin 125, Iowa Engineering Experiment Station, Iowa State College.

Part IV

Policy Perspectives

Explaining Economic Growth
A. Szirmai, B. van Ark and D. Pilat
© 1993 Elsevier Science Publishers B.V. All rights reserved.

Liberalism and Economic Growth

Alan Peacock
The David Hume Institute, Edinburgh

"Little else is required to carry a state to the highest degree of opulence from the lowest barbarism, but peace, easy taxes, and a tolerable administration of justice; all the rest being brought about by the natural course of things".

Adam Smith in 1755 as reported in Dugald Stewart, *Account of the Life and Writings of Adam Smith LL.D.* (1793), reprinted in Adam Smith, *Essays on Philosophical Subjects*, edited by W.P.D.J.C. Bryce and L.S. Ross, Oxford University Press, 1980, p. 322.

1. Introduction

Liberalism is a political creed which embraces a distinct economic philosophy or "political economy" using the term liberalism in the Anglo-Saxon sense. The political economy of liberalism therefore comprehends a particular stance towards society's objectives, a particular view about the way the economic system works and therefore a particular view of the role of government in relation to liberalist objectives.

My agenda is based on this three-fold division between objectives, economic constraints and policy instruments. So far as objectives are concerned, I must try to achieve the impossible and encapsulate liberal economic philosophy within a few sentences; for it does turn out to be necessary to recognise that the place of growth in the list of objectives and the "trade-off" between these objectives is quite distinct (see section 2 below). I then consider what will be more familiar to "growthmen", namely the particular emphasis placed by Adam Smith and his followers on economic freedom as a factor in promoting economic growth (see section 3 below). I can then consider how far liberals have been correct in their claim that the role of the state in promoting growth should be a much more restricted one than that promoted by growthmen in general (see section 4 below).

I must warn the reader that liberalism is a wide-ranging political philosophy and that disagreement between liberals about the precise content of economic policy towards growth is quite common. I have not explored these differences in detail but consider that a synthetic view of liberalism does not give an entirely misleading picture of the liberalist position and enables me to proceed directly towards issues more germane to the theme of this conference volume. What I can say is that, whatever one's political philosophy, the profession owes an immense debt to Angus Maddison for his long devotion to the study of comparative economic development which combines the talents of economist, statistician and historian to a unique degree. My own debt to him will soon become apparent.

2. The Growth Objective

Liberalism embodies an important initial proposition - the comprehension of how the economy behaves or ought to behave cannot be understood without reference to the actions of individuals. There is no society which is independent of the individuals who compose it. The basic model of the economy is derived from the study of individuals' tastes and preferences which lead them to try to "better their condition", as Adam Smith put it, within the limitations imposed by resource constraints, lack of knowledge and information and by the uncertainties surrounding the attempt to overcome these limitations. We shall examine later how this view influences liberalist growth models as a contribution to positive economics, but must first of all note that underlying the concept of the individual acting to further his own interests is an ethical principle - the individual is the best judge of his own welfare. Such a principle certainly does not rule out co-operation between individuals in order to resolve conflicts between them about the distribution of property rights and about how further matters of collective interest are to be decided. The "decision rules" to be applied in cases where voluntary transactions between individuals do not achieve individuals' aims are themselves subject to the liberal prescription that they must minimise the use of compulsion. Where state action is regarded as necessary, all must have an equal share in making the law and there must be equality before the law (for further discussion, see Barry, 1986).

Given this individualist philosophy, one cannot derive from it a commitment to economic growth as an objective which requires collective action. Growth is not an end in itself. It is simply the outcome of individual work and savings patterns. The idea of an optimal growth rate has no meaning. Moreover the individual is not accountable to "society" for his actions, once the rule of law is established. Consequently, it is illiberal to seek to impose some collective saving objective which would be necessary in order to pursue some target rate of growth set by government.

Of course, if one strand of liberal philosophy requires that there is an equal share in making the law, then it could be that one outcome of voting system which conformed with liberal principles could be strong support for a government that wished to encourage a "satisfactory" rate of growth. In short the economic policy paradigm need not be one in which the government simply dictates the policy agenda by identifying "desirable" movements in target economic variables such as the rate of growth, the unemployment rate and the rate of inflation and specific trade-offs between them, if appropriate. The policy paradigm becomes one in which a bargaining situation exists between those who supply policies, the politicians, and those who demand them, the voters. Is it contrary to liberal philosophy if voters demand that the government specifies for them a collective growth target which, when voted upon, has their full support?

There are two ways of answering this question. The first is to agree that liberal support for a political system which seeks to reflect individual preferences as near as is possible does not guarantee that illiberal policies will not be introduced. However, this does not mean that those who regard liberalism as identified with individual self-reliance would wish to "force men to be free". If the liberalist political process produces support for collectivist action, then the only course open to the liberal idealist is to try to persuade voters to change their minds (see Rowley and Peacock, 1975).

The second way of answering this question is to enquire further what forms of intervention are necessary in order to achieve a "satisfactory" rate of growth. Indeed, the liberal idealist placed in the position of persuader need not adopt a defensive stance. First of all, (s)he could emphasise that consumption and not growth (as measured by GDP per head) is the object of most interest to individuals; and their welfare functions can sensibly include concern for the consumption opportunities of the less fortunate and for the endowment of resources which protect the consumption standards of future generations. Second, (s)he could emphasise that the pattern of consumption at a point of time and through time is an important argument in individual welfare functions. Third, if the liberal perception of human action is correct then there is a strong presumption that market economies characterised by limited state intervention will be better able to achieve a satisfactory rate of growth and consumption per head than those which capture a large proportion of annual output for government use. This last proposition leads naturally to an analysis of a liberal perception of the growth process.

3. Liberalism and Growth Models

The "liberal slant" on the comparative growth performance of countries is evident at the very beginning of the professional discussion of long-term economic growth. Indeed it could be argued that the father of economic liberalism, Adam Smith, first put forward a coherent growth model of a kind which is readily translatable into the aggregate production function form commonly found in modern growth theory.[1] I use a stylised version of

---

[1] See, for example, Adelman (1961), Simpson (1983), Reid (1989), Stern (1991) and, of course, Maddison (1991).

Smith's model in order to bring out the points where this distinct liberal slant may be detected. Of course, Smith did not adopt a mathematical formulation even of the simple kind presented below; the input of scholarship which would justify this formulation has been prodigious and may be found in the references cited in footnote 1.

The Smithian aggregate production function can be specified as follows:

$$Y = f(L, K, N, T), \ where \ f_l, \ f_k, \ f_n, \ f_t > 0 \qquad (1)$$

Y = output, K = capital stock, L = labour force, N = "natural resources", T = level of technique

Y is an increasing function of capital and labour input and natural resources and the state of technology with partial second derivatives of each factor negative. I shall follow other writers and regard N as a "bit of a nuisance" (Higgins) and treat it as part of the capital stock. This makes no difference to the general argument though it would be important to consider N separately if one were closely concerned, as I am not, with highlighting all the main characteristics of Smith approach (for critical discussion, see Reid, *op. cit.*).

The particular contribution of Smith in the specification of the aggregate production function which attracts attention is his treatment of T. Smith rather dismisses philosophy and speculation as an important influence on T and concentrates on endogenous influences. Imagine that, for reasons to be gone into later, K increases relative to L, Y/L may increase initially but, *cet.par.* , diminishing returns to capital must eventually set in, the capital/output ratio rises, and the process of growth is halted. However, T is itself a function of the extent of the market (Y/L) and the capital labour ratio (K/L). The growth in the extent of the market facilitates specialisation, offering greater opportunities for learning by doing which pays off in greater efficiency. The increase in capital per head is associated with an increase in the number of production processes and therefore with an extension of experience of specialisation. It follows that:

$$T = T(Y/L, K/L), \ where \ t'(Y/K), \ t'(K/L) > 0 \qquad (2)$$

We can represent the Smithian process of growth which is **technologically possible** as being self-sustaining over some range of output (see figure 1). Curve A1, represents the relationship between an increase in capital per worker and output per worker for a given state of technology. For given L, Y/K increases but at a decreasing rate, i.e. the capital/output ratio rises, Curve A2 and A3 are similarly drawn for successively higher levels of T. Given equation (2), the potential growth path can be represented by a locus of points on successive A curves, as T increases in response to market expansion

(Y/L) and the increase in capital per worker (K/L). Expressed in this way Smithian analysis recognises the distinction between a growth effect produced by some permanent increase in K/L and a level effect produced by endogenous technical change (cf. Lucas, 1988).

FIGURE 1
Technological Change According to Adam Smith

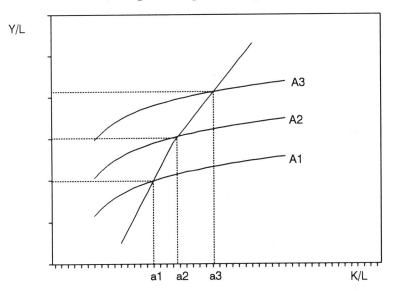

It is hardly necessary for our argument to go into detail on the length and timing of the process of growth. Sufficient to say that Smith places primary emphasis on capital accumulation. The reaching of a maximum Y/L with a subsequent stationary state or even a decline in Y/L is closely related to the motives for capital accumulation. This is not to neglect the limitations that might be placed on the growth process from growing scarcity of that "bit of a nuisance", land, or what was to become famous as the Malthusian effect, namely that population growth could be a function of growth in income per head.

The liberal slant in growth modelling first becomes evident in the insistence on understanding the micro-foundations of the growth process. What makes a society start moving along a growth path? The answer cannot be provided by specifying a technological relationship but depends on individual motivations. As we have already observed, Adam Smith put great emphasis on men's desire to "better their condition". Human action is both purposive and rational, a theme which is endlessly repeated in liberal political economy. With capital accumulation playing such a major part in Smith's model, how do we translate individual motivations into an increase in K/L? By an increase in resources set aside from personal consumption, in short by frugality. Indeed, Smith's prime example of bettering one's condition is that of saving, "a desire which, though generally calm and dispassionate, comes with us from the womb, and never leaves us till we go into the grave". The intended result is an increase in wealth and "an augmentation of fortune is the means by which the greater part of men propose and wish to better their condition" (Smith, 1776/1976, p. 341).

In short:

$$S = s(Y), \; s'(Y) > 0 \qquad (3)$$

$$S = \delta K$$

Where S = Saving and δK = the increase in capital stock. It follows that if saving increases with income, so will investment, so does the capital stock and with it T increases, as previously explained.

The next element in the liberal slant is to define the conditions which will favour an increase in K without an offsetting rise in K/Y, the capital/output ratio. It is important that entrepreneurs envisage investment opportunities which offer profits over and above compensation for risk.[2] Smith is the first of many liberal writers to emphasise the importance of good government and particularly institutional arrangements which favour security of property and the legal enforcement of contracts. Stable and wise government would be a necessary but not a sufficient condition for growth. A further condition would have to be some incentive to use capital efficiently so as to maximise profits. Competition which would allow freedom of entry into new markets at home and abroad and which would encourage process innovation would be an important supplement. Stern (1991, p. 128) actually observes that it goes "beyond the standard theory" to add management and organisation as an argument in the aggregate production function. May be; but this is an important theme in Smith who observes that "monopoly (...) is a great enemy of good management, which can never be universally established but in consequence of that free and universal competition which forces everybody to have recourse to it for the sake of self-defence" (Smith, 1776/1976, pp. 163-164).

The liberal slant is carried over into the Smithian recommendations regarding the role of the state in promoting growth. His is not an extreme laissez-faire position, as the following list clearly indicates:
i) Remove barriers to competition, such as granting of monopoly privileges and - constantly emphasised - barriers to communication. Good roads, canals and navigable rivers are means for breaking down local monopolies. These require state action to remove barriers to private provision and even financial

---

[2] On this point, see the excellent discussion by Adelman (1961).

support by government - but not a state-run communications system.[3]
ii) Keep the growth of the public sector in check to prevent reduction in
saving through increasing tax burdens;
iii) Insofar as the state has to provide services which promote good
government, try to relate effort to reward in public as well as in the private
sector.

Again it should be noted, that Stern states that it goes beyond the standard
theory to pay attention to infrastructure, in the widest sense, highlighting such
impediments to growth as slow, costly and hazardous transport and corrupt
and inefficient bureaucracy as impediments to growth, but credit for
emphasising such matters, which appear frequently in Smith, is only attributed
to writings first published in the 1980s!

Smith's emphasis on good government as a pre-condition for growth and
limited government as a cardinal element in maintaining it ran into trouble
long before more sophisticated models appeared as rival products in the
intellectual market-place. The doubts and reservations are well known and I
only briefly mention those that emanated form liberal writers.

The first set of criticisms is associated with the Classical debate about
whether or not economies would reach a stationary state. In this respect, the
most that Smithian limited measures of intervention would achieve would be
to postpone the day when the standard of living would gravitate to the
subsistence minimum, even taking account of the benefits which could accrue
from extending the market through encouragement of free trade. Smith's
critics did not, however, envisage any solution which rested on further state
intervention, and had different views about when the exact moment would
come when, in Mill's words, "the condition of the poorest class sinks, even in
a progressive state, to the lowest point which they will consent to endure"
(Mill, Toronto Edition, 1965, p. 753). It is worth parenthetic mention that
Mill broke ranks amongst those who had an "unaffected aversion" for the
stationary state: "I confess that I am not charmed with the idea of life held out
by those who think that the normal state of human beings is that of struggling
to get on; that the trampling, crushing, elbowing, and treading on each other's
heels... are the most desirable lot of human kind, or anything but the most
disagreeable symptoms of the phases of industrial progress" (Mill, *loc. cit.*),
adding later: "...the best state for human nature is that in which, while no one
is poor, no one desires to be richer, nor has any reason to fear being thrust
back by the efforts of others to push themselves forward". Many liberals
would say "Amen".

The second set of criticisms offers different reasons for the inadequacy of

---

[3] For further discussion, see Peacock (1979).

Smith's views on "natural liberty" as the mainspring of economic growth. I
need hardly dwell on Marx's attempt to use the stationary state of argument to
demonstrate that the inevitable emergence of intolerable inequalities of income
and employment opportunities would bring about the demise of capitalism.
The influence of Marx on Schumpeter, a liberal convert, is manifest.
Schumpeter accepted Marx's view that "internal forces" would bring about a
transformation of capitalism, though not as Marx predicted. The transformation to socialism would be gradual rather than violent. Increasing
industrial concentration would separate ownership from control and remove
the mainspring of capitalism - the proprietary interest in the use of capital. In
its place would emerge state socialism fostered by the bureaucratic attitudes
resulting from the organisational changes in large business enterprises.
Schumpeter, unlike Marx, did not relish what he believed would come to
pass.[4]

Nevertheless, what is striking about Smith's approach is that important
vestiges of it still remain in the modern growth literature, though this is not
the result of the passing down of a Smithian torch from one generation of
liberals to another.[5] The intellectual battle between liberalist and socialist
economists changed its form in the later 19th century and concerned such
questions as the determination of factor shares according to the principle of
marginal productivity and whether market socialism could be made to
conform with principles of allocation based on consumer sovereignty. Indeed,
I know of no specifically liberal model of economic growth to lay alongside
the many variants of aggregate production models of the post-World War II
era. That is not to say, as we shall soon observe, that there is not a liberal
disposition towards such models, and particularly towards some of the policy
conclusions that have been drawn from them. Thus, the Solow-type growth
models adapted to include endogenous technological change have a clear
affinity to the Smithian model, although the role of the entrepreneur is often
not spelt out in the detail which Smith and later Schumpeter considered
necessary.

The crucial question is whether the growth theories of today require
liberals to modify their view about the Smithian conception of the role of the
state in promoting economic progress. In the case of the Solow-type models
with variable capital/output ratios and flexible factor and product prices,
clearly the Smithian "canons" are pre-conditions for the growth process to
take place, but, in the primary version of the model, with no "built-in"
technological progress, no fiscal or monetary measures can influence the

---

[4]   For further elaboration, see Schumpeter (1950).

[5]   For detailed discussion, see Reid (1988), Chapter 9.

growth rate, in the long run anyway. Keith Shaw and I (1976) have shown that if consumption rather than income per head is taken as the target variable, the fiscal policy could influence its growth rate; and it is well known that fiscal policy models have been produced to show how the natural rate of growth can be reached more swiftly by compensatory finance. But these are not much more than theoretical curiosities.

Once the model is developed along Smithian lines with technological improvements made a function of the growth in capital stock, then fiscal stimuli, so it is claimed, could both raise the natural rate of growth and also within the time horizon which would make such a policy of interest to vote-maximising governments (see Streissler, 1979; Peacock and Shaw, 1976). I suspect that liberals, assuming that they accepted that evidence supported this position, would be divided on the desirability of buttressing the Smithian "canons" with fiscal stimulation. Those who considered growth as the most important argument in some widely agreed welfare function might consider that liberal principles would not be violated. Others would argue that the fiscal policy was in effect promoting the collectivisation of saving for raising the rate of capital formation would imply a rise in the rate of saving above that sanctioned by a freely working capital market. The additional argument might be used that stimulation of investment by tax reliefs and grants would take the pressure off entrepreneurs to be efficient and innovative.

However, the recent emphasis on knowledge and therefore on research and education and training as a cardinal factor in growth (cf. Romer, 1986; Solow, 1991) presents a more interesting challenge to liberal thinking. Entrepreneurs may only have a limited interest in investment in knowledge and education because of the claimed difficulties of capturing the benefits. Thus the familiar argument that the externalities created by research and knowledge require public support if not public production. The additional twist provided by Romer is that, even if externalities can be internalised, the introduction of increasing returns to scale throws doubts on the encouragement of competition, notably through trade liberalisation, as a measure which would promote economic growth. It is beyond my competence to pass any judgment on the strength of this line of argument. What can be said is that a liberal who was convinced by the argument and accompanying evidence would wish to look very closely at how far the externalities created by knowledge required public support, and the efficiency of the delivery systems for education, training and research relying on such support; unless, of course, (s)he judged that such collective action would be contrary to liberal principles in the first place, whatever growth benefits might follow from it.

I have probably given the impression that the liberal position vis-a-vis growth economics is that of the critical bystander; and to some extent I believe that to be the right description. There is one area, however, in which liberal economists have been very much on the attack, namely with regard to

growth models which assign a large role to collective action in raising growth
rates in "developing" countries. This attack is of more than passing interest
because liberal thinkers, notably Bauer (1969) and Lachmann (1973), have
questioned the very existence of a phenomenon labelled "growth" and
"historicist prophecies" (Bauer) which claim to be able to map its progress
and identify the forces which promote it. For example, Bauer argues: "(m)any
of the concepts used..., notably capital output ratios, are exceedingly vague.
But even if they were more precisely defined they could not serve as the basis
for scientific prediction as they are only simple descriptions of past
occurrences and not variables between which functional and causal
relationships have been established. And casual collection of a few statistics is
not serious historical study, nor does simple extrapolation of arbitrarily
chosen trends reflect scientific activity" (Bauer, *ibid.*). Latterly, liberal
economists have been less "Austrian" and more "Smithian" in their attitude to
macro-economic modelling. It has become accepted that national income
accounting and input-output analysis have considerably improved our
knowledge of the workings of developing countries, though themselves
originating in the need for development plans which have been, so it is
claimed, conspicuously unsuccessful. Indeed, it is maintained by Deepak Lal,
in a phrase which encapsulates the growing acceptance of the importance of
efficient markets in development countries, that "efficient growth which raises
the demand for unskilled labour by 'getting the prices right' is probably the
most important means of alleviating poverty" (Lal, 1983, p. 102). Space
prevents me adumbrating further the precise policy measures implicit in Lal's
prescription of "getting the prices right"; sufficient to note that his conclusion
is that administrators in developing countries have much to learn still from
"that oft-neglected work, *The Wealth of Nations*, both so relevant and so
modern" (Lal, 1983, p. 108). Adam Smith still lives and not only in Chicago!

4. The Size of the State and Economic Growth

The corollary of the Smithian prescriptions must be that, whereas it will be
generally accepted that some state intervention is a necessary condition for
long-term growth, an increase in the proportion of resources absorbed by
government will exercise both a negative effect on the rate of economic
growth and growing misallocation of resources. The latter proposition has
been extensively investigated by public choice liberals employing the theory of
rent-seeking. The former has received less attention though it has received
more prominence with the marriage of hypotheses with empirical testing.

That well known proposition known as Baumol's Law postulates that the
opportunities for employing new technologies in service sectors (notably in
government) are limited whereas wage rates in these sectors are not likely to
fall out of line with those in manufacturing sectors, if the normal forces of

competition operate in the labour market. It follows that, even if the proportion of real resources absorbed by government is constant, government expenditure will rise as proportion of GNE. It follows further that if the proportion of real resources rises, a progressive rise in the proportion of G to GNE will be associated with a lower rate of economic growth than would otherwise be the case.[6]

The proposition that purely technological factors account for the differences in economic performance of the public and private sector seems suspect. I would not deny that welfare and environmental services, commonly produced within the public sector, contain a large element of personal service so that the physical presence of labour input is a necessary constituent of output. However, I refuse to believe that in the age of "info-tech" and computers that the technical limitations on factor substitution are of paramount importance in the public sector. A more plausible argument for the existence of labour intensive public services lies in the barriers that can be erected to prevent or to control the speed of introduction of new technologies. In the private sector, given competition, product and process innovation are necessary for firms to survive. The pressures to introduce new technologies are much less in circumstances where, as with government undertakings, there is a monopoly or near-monopoly of the output of a particular service and the product is not sold on the market. The barriers to improving productivity in the public sector therefore reflect the behaviour of rent-seekers, particularly bureaucrats, and do not have their origin in technological constraints.

My criticism of Baumol's thesis has been elevated into a more general hypothesis that echoes Adam Smith's complaint of "want of parsimony" in public spending. Buchanan (1980) argues that the incidence of rent-seeking and the associated diversion of resources is a function of the increased size of government resulting in a decline in economic growth. The effect is cumulative for the growth in the relative size of the public sector itself reduces incentives in the private sector through higher and higher taxes. In other words, the more an economy moves away from the Smithian ideal of limited government input to promote free trade, the lower its rate of growth; if this were true, then the economic prescriptions of Classical liberalism should command wide appeal.

This hypothesis should be testable and, indeed, there is an attempt by Scully (1989) to do so. Here I only report his results in summary form in table 1. He uses World Bank data for 115 market economy countries which record economic growth, as measured by the growth rate of real GDP over the period of 1960-1980, alongside the growth in the share of government in

---

[6] For a simple proof, see Peacock (1979).

GDP. The relation between government share and economic growth was estimated using linear OLS and the error term is assumed to be normally distributed, it being claimed that tests for heteroscedasticity validate this assumption. In equation (1), the "simpliste" version of the hypothesis is presented, in which only the government share variables appear as regressors. Both the size of government share (GOVT 60) and the change in that share (CHGGOVT) are of the right sign, which accords with earlier studies. However, as Scully points out, account has to be taken of the change in the capital/labour ratio over the relevant period. Public investment has a positive effect on the growth rate, though less productive than private investment. To neglect this factor may be to overstate the negative effect of the government share on growth. In equation (2) the compound rate of growth in the capital/labour ratio (KLGWTH) is introduced as a regressor but GOVT60 and CHGGOVT still have the correct sign and are statistically significant in a one-tail test at better than the 1 per cent level.

TABLE 1
**Growth Rates of Real GDP per Capita in Relation to
the Share of Government Expenditures in GDP, 1960-1980.**

	Compound Growth Rate of Real GDP per Capita (CAPGWTH)	
	Equation 1	Equation 2
Constant	.0467	.0372
	(7.04)	(6.70)
Change in capital/labour ratio 1960-1980 (KLGWTH)		.4752
		(7.61)
% Share government expenditures in GDP 1960 (GOVT60)	-.1123	-.0889
	(3.15)	(3.05)
Change in government expenditure share 1960-1980 (CHGGOVT)	-.1140	-.0871
	(3.66)	(3.41)
R^2	.1007	.4039
(N)	(115)	(115)

Notes:
CAPGWTH = Compound Growth Rate of Real Per Capita GDP from 1960-1980.
KLGWTH = Compound Growth Rate in the Capital/Labour Ratio from 1960-1980.
GOVT60 = Government Expenditures as a % of GDP, 1960.
CHGGOVT = Government Expenditures as a % of GDP, 1980 - GOVT60.
Student t values are in parenthesis below the coefficients.
Source: G.W. Scully, 1989, p. 156.

I have only reproduced the results which are sufficient to further discussion of the economics, and certainly not the econometrics, of such an approach. Here are the points for discussion that occur to me:

i) As Scully recognises, his approach really requires that the economy-wide growth rate should be a weighted average of the growth rates of each sector, with separate production functions estimated for both private sectors and the public sector. The increased size of the government sector and its effect on the growth rate could then be directly measured. Scully rejects this approach, simply because data are not available. There is a much more important problem than this. Ignoring any attribution of the relation between growth in public investment and output in the private sector, how is one to measure the real output of public sector services which are not priced? Conventional measures based on input changes "adjusted" to take account of productivity changes are notoriously arbitrary.

ii) Government expenditure as a percentage of GDP cannot embrace all the influences of government actions on the private economy. As is often argued, government by statute and regulation can exercise a major effect on private incentives and the allocation of resources. At the very least, any complete empirical study should take account of non-budgetary forms of government intervention. It cannot be assumed that growth in regulation is complementary to the growth in overall government expenditure. It could be; but account would then have to be taken of the influence of the composition as well as the amount of government expenditure on the complexity of the regulatory system. Matters are further complicated by the propensity of western governments embarking on privatisation programmes to subject privatised concerns which were previously public monopolies to strict regulatory control. The size of the public sector relative to the rest of the economy will decline, *cet. par.*, but will its influence be diminished?

iii) One should be careful not to conclude that a western-type economy which embarked on a vigorous programme of cutting government services in order to improve growth prospects would necessarily achieve its aim. As Maddison (1991, pp. 79-80) has emphasised, extensive state action to equalise the primary distribution of income has been a pre-requisite for widespread acceptance of capitalist property relations and the operation of market forces, making them more legitimate by removing most of the grievances which motivate proponents of a socialist alternative. This is not to deny that potential efficiency gains would not accrue from reductions in social transfers and subsidies with disincentive effects on individuals and firms respectively, but the perceived distribution effect could engender strong opposition to major cutbacks. While it is arguable whether Maddison is right in claiming that the efficiency losses from the growth in public spending are likely to be insignificant, one can certainly agree with him that they are modest in comparison with those experienced in command economies where the level of state intervention has been very much higher.

5. Concluding Observation

The thing that strikes me most about conducting this review of the liberal stance towards economic growth both as an objective and as a variable which may be influenced by policy is the change in the intellectual climate. When growth economics became a fashionable subject in economic theory in the 1950s, anti-Keynesianism was so strong amongst Continental and some, but by no means all, Anglo-Saxon liberals that friendly discourse was almost impossible. I can even recall being accused by Ludwig von Mises at a liberal meeting in 1958 of being tainted with "national socialism" because I used the term national product! An appeal to the "Introduction and Plan" of, *The Wealth of Nations* which starts with a definition of a nation's annual produce fell on deaf ears. That has all changed, I am glad to say, and it may be worth saying a word or two as to how this has come about.

Firstly, whatever one's views on policy, any fair-minded economist could not fail to be impressed by the careful empirical work which has vastly improved our knowledge of the process of growth and thrown light on its determinants. This work has been influenced by and has influenced growth modelling. Angus Maddison has played a major part in this comparatively recent development. Liberal speculation on the effects of public sector growth on economic development has been given a much better focus by growth accounting.

Secondly, it has become accepted that any macroeconomic theory that deserves the name has to have firm micro-economic foundations; and this applies to growth models as well as to short-term forecasting models. As I have argued, the methodological bias in liberal economics towards the importance of individual motivation has made us all more wary of models which treat economic actors as automatons.

Lastly, economists of very different persuasions with experience of advice giving have been brought face to face with the harsh realities of political action. Growth policy cannot be based on the presupposition that correction of market failure is imply a matter of choosing the right policy instruments. Whatever the value judgments underpinning the approach of public choice theorists, the move towards an economic analysis of government which studies the motivation of politicians and bureaucrats and their relations with firms and individuals must influence our attitude to the feasibility of growth policies that rely on large-scale government intervention. Government failure is a reality to be faced and not an uncomfortable fact to be ignored. But then that is one of the most important messages to be found in *The Wealth of Nations* which we are in the process of re-learning.

References

Adelman, I. (1962), *Theories of Economic Growth and Development*, Stanford University Press, Stanford, Chapter 3.

Barry, N. (1986), *On Classical Liberalism and Libertarianism*, Macmillan, London, Chapter 5.

Bauer, P. (1969), "Development Economics: The Spurious Consensus and its Background", in: Erich Streissler (ed.) *Roads to Freedom: Essays in Honours of Friedrich A. von Hayek*, Routledge and Kegan Paul, London, pp. 5-46.

Buchanan, J. (1980), "Rent Seeking and Profit Seeking", in: J. Buchanan, G. Tullock and R. Tollison (eds.), *Toward a Theory of a Rent Seeking Society*, Texas A. and M. University Press.

Lachmann, L. (1973), *Macro-Economic Thinking and the Market Economy*, Hobart Paper, No. 56, Institute of Economic Affairs, London.

Lal, D. (1983), *The Poverty of "Development Economics"*, Hobart Paperback, No. 16, Institute of Economic Affairs, London.

Lucas, R.E. (1988), "On the Mechanics of Economic Development", *Journal of Monetary Economics*, Vol. 22, pp. 3-22.

Maddison, A. (1991), *Dynamic Forces in Capitalist Development*, Oxford University Press.

Mill, J.S. (1848/1965), *Principles of Political Economy*, Toronto Edition, V. Bladen and J. Robson (eds.) (1965), University of Toronto Press Book IV, Chapter VI.

Peacock, A. (1979), *The Economic Analysis of Government*, Martin Robertson, Oxford, Chapter 3.

--- and G.K. Shaw (1976), *The Economic Theory of Fiscal Policy*, R e v i s e d Edition, Allen and Unwin, London, Chapter V.

Reid, G. (1989), *Classical Economic Growth: An Analysis in the Tradition of Adam Smith*, Basil Blackwell, Oxford.

Romer, P. (1986), "Increasing Returns and Long-Run Growth", *Journal of Political Economy*, No. 94, pp. 1002-1037.

Rowley, C. and A. Peacock (1975), *Welfare Economics: A Liberal Re-Statement*, Martin Robertson, London/Oxford.

Schumpeter, J. (1950), *Capitalism, Socialism and Democracy*, 3rd Edition, Harper, New York, preface.

Scully, G. (1989), "The Size of the State, Economic Growth and the Efficient Utilization of National Resources", *Public Choice*, Vol. 63, No. 2, November, pp. 149-164.

Simpson, D. (1983), *The Political Economy of Growth*, Basil Blackwell, Oxford, Chapter 4.

Smith, A. (1776/1976), *An Inquiry into the Nature and Causes of the Wealth of Nations, 1776*, R.H. Campbell and A.S. Skinner (general eds.) (1976), Clarendon Press, Book II, Chapter 3.

Solow, R. (1991), "Growth Theory", in: *Companion to Contemporary Economic Thought*, D. Greenaway, M. Bleaney and I. Stewart (eds.), Routledge, London, Chapter 19.

Stern, N. (1991), "The Determinants of Growth", *Economic Journal*, Vol. 101, No. 404, January, pp. 122-133.

Streissler, E. (1979), "Growth Models as Diffusion Processes", *Kyklos*, Vol. 32, pp. 251-269 and pp. 571-586.

Explaining Economic Growth
A. Szirmai, B. van Ark and D. Pilat
© 1993 Elsevier Science Publishers B.V. All rights reserved.

429

Keynesian Stabilisation Policy and Post War Economic Performance

*Jan A. Kregel**
University of Bologna

1. Keynesian Stabilisation Policy and Deficit Spending

In conditions in which economic debate is dominated by the "New Keynesian" Economics and New Macroeconomics and governments claim that they can do nothing to remedy the enduring conditions of recession in the industrialised countries because of the excessive size of their budget deficits it seems pure folly to discuss the role of "Keynesian" policy to further economic growth. But, as the current recession persists, pressures build for something to be done, and as Dennis Robertson noted of highbrow opinion, if you stand in one place long enough it comes back round to you. It thus seems appropriate to recall a number of generally overlooked aspects of Keynes' approach to economic policy so that if like the hunted hare, opinion does come this way again, it might be diverted from past errors.

The first problem is to define Keynes' economic policy views. Even before Keynes published the *General Theory* proposals for public works financed by public debt to combat the depression were promoted by a wide range of economists of various political persuasion. Public spending as an anti-cyclical policy tool was part of the economic legacy of the Hoover administration, and Franklin Roosevelt's first presidential campaign was based on balancing the budget (providing Ronald Reagan with cutting quotations for the same purpose). Something more precise than deficit spending is required.

2. Offensive Policy to Cure an Existing Depression

Keynes supported those who proposed deficit spending, but made a sharp distinction between what I will call "defensive" and "offensive" economic policy. The latter relates to the policy to apply in depressed conditions, while the former is to be ever-present in order to provide a defence against depressions.

---

* The research underlying this paper has been supported by a MURST-University of Bologna (60%) grant.

On the offence Keynes tried to shock received views by suggesting such schemes as burying jars filled with banknotes in order to dig them up again. Many critics did not notice that although this was "make-work", at least it was "work" and not an entitlement or a handout. They also failed to notice that Keynes quickly added that such schemes were rather foolish, and that the "make-work" should better be "real" work on things that might actually serve some useful purpose such as schools, hospitals and the like. Keynes' humorous sarcasm was not meant to be taken seriously. The holes in the ground were to make the point that productive labour power was being lost; it was not a practical proposal. Keynes also recommended that deficit spending policies supporting investment should be preferred to increasing consumption.

"Offensive" policies were considered temporary; they would eventually restore "normality" and could then be replaced by "defensive" policies. It was not blind faith in deficit spending that brought Keynes to this conclusion, but rather his theoretical[1] analysis of the disequilibrium operation of price adjustment in durables markets. It is often repeated (unfortunately by some of his closest collaborators) that he knew nothing about price theory. Yet, the theoretical foundation for the success of offensive policy is based on his analysis of price determination in the *Treatise on Money*. The conditions of "normality" in price relations is what that book defines as "Normal Backwardation".

3. The Outline of Offensive Policy and the Short Period Price Equation

The buyer of a futures contract profits (loses) if the price of the commodity rises (falls) over the life of the contract. Since a futures contract represents the equivalent of spot delivery of the commodity at maturity, its price should not differ from the spot price when it reaches maturity. Thus, over its life, the price of a futures contract "converges" to the spot price. This means that in conditions of expectations of stable spot prices holders of long futures contracts will profit only if they buy futures when their prices are at a discount on spot prices.

If supply and demand of a durable commodity are currently in balance and expected to remain constant individuals should not pay a price for future delivery which is different from the current spot price. However, the seller of a futures contract who hedges his position will have to buy the commodity spot and hold it until delivery, incurring carrying costs composed of storage, insurance and wastage. Sellers will thus only be willing to enter a contract if the futures contract price is sufficiently above the current spot to provide a

---

[1] As well as practical - recall that during the 1914-18 war Keynes virtually controlled the international commodity markets.

fall in price as the contract approaches maturity which yields a profit sufficient to offset the carrying costs. Buyers of futures contracts would then be paying a price above the current spot price and suffer a loss equal to the fall in the price as the future converges to the spot price. They would only be willing to buy contracts if the loss on the contract is just equal to the carrying costs that they would have had to pay had they held the physical commodity.

But commodity markets are in general one-sided. Producers of commodities have a natural long position in commodities and will normally incur both carrying costs and the risk of changes in spot prices. If they want to hedge this risk by selling futures contracts they will have to offer speculators, who do not have an inherent demand for the commodity, a return equal to the risk-free rate plus a premium for the risk of a change in spot prices. Since the buyer of a contract can only profit if prices rise this means that long hedgers will have to offer to sell futures contracts to speculators at prices which are below the current spot price, guaranteeing speculators a profit as the futures price rises to converge to spot. Keynes argued that "backwardation"[2], future prices below spot prices, was the "normal" state of affairs in balanced market conditions dominated by long hedgers.[3]

On the other hand, if there is a shortage of existing output, the spot price may be driven above the futures price and produce backwardation[4]. But, as long as current costs of production are below the futures price, producers can

---

[2] The source of these terms is the settlement procedure in the London Stock Exchange: backwardation representing the payment that a seller of a stock speculating on a fall in price which has not yet materialised has to pay the buyer for the right not to deliver (or to pay an owner of the stock to borrow it in order to make delivery) in order to wait for the expected fall, while contango is the payment the buyer expecting a rise in price which has not yet materialised makes to the seller to postpone receipt (or to someone short the stock to receive it in his place). If on balance speculators expecting a fall dominate those expecting a rise, the latter will pay the former to "carry over" settlement into the next account and vice versa. Thus the seller's effective price is lower than the actual price or spot price by the amount of the backwardation payment. If this were greater than his expectation of the fall in price he would not be willing to carry over the bargain. Backwardation thus represents a shortage in the spot market.

[3] Keynes believed that producers would have less flexibility in changing production plans than consumers will have in changing their consumption plans; therefore the former will be more risk averse and dominate in seeking to hedge their positions - since producers are long and consumers are short of output, the sales of futures contracts will dominate the purchase, causing excess supply and pressure on future prices relative to spot.

[4] These same relations are spelled out in Chapter 17 of the *General Theory*; I have argued in a number of articles (e.g., Kregel, 1982) that they may be considered as a general theory of pricing for Keynes's system.

sell their output forward and still make a profit equal to the futures discount. But, if there is an excess supply of commodities the spot price will be driven down and eventually create a position of "contango" in which it becomes profitable to buy commodities at the spot price and hold them for sale at the higher expected future spot price. When "speculation" on the expected return of holding existing output exceeds the return on producing new output, current production is halted and employment falls. How long will such conditions last?

Instead of asking what contango premium of future over spot prices will be necessary to produce equilibrium, Keynes instead starts his analysis from a given expected future equilibrium price and asks what fall in price relative to expected normal prices would be required to convince speculators to buy the redundant output and hold it until normal conditions are restored. From the above analysis, it is clear that it must cover carrying costs, which will depend on interest rates, storage and insurance, plus the length of time that the position has to be held until it can be unwound at a profit.

Let X represent the annual per unit interest, storage and insurance costs for holding an excess supply of commodity stocks given by S. Let A represent the expected number of years until the position can be unwound. Then the required decline in the current price, P_1, relative to the normal price P_2 must be such that $(P_1-P_2)S = AXS$ or, the expected gain from the rise in price is equal to the total costs of the position. The per cent decline relative to the expected normal price, p, is then $(P_1-P_2)/P_2$ and will be equal to AX/P_2.

It remains to determine the value of A. If Q is normal annual output, and normal annual consumption is C, then if output falls to zero and consumption remains unchanged, the excess supply would be worked off in $y = S/C$ years. However, if current output remains positive then $A > y$ because the surplus will be reduced by only $C-(1-q)Q$ in each period, where q is the proportionate reduction in normal output actually being produced due to the fall in price below normal. This effect will be offset if at the same time annual consumption increases because of the fall in prices for then the surplus would be reduced by $(1+c)C - (1-q)Q$, where c is the proportionate increase in consumption due to the fall in prices. For y to be finite $(1+c)C > (1-q)Q$.

Assuming[5] that $Q = C$ and $q = c$ and substituting accordingly, $y = S/[(1+q)Q-(1-q)Q] = S/Q(1+q-1+q) = S/Q(2q)$. If P_1 rises smoothly to P_2 over time, then both q and c will be declining towards zero. At the beginning of the adjustment period the rate of reduction of stocks will be 2q and at the end zero; on average over the period it will be 2q/2, so that A can be defined

---

[5] Keynes, in a 1923 article in the Manchester Guardian Supplement (XII) suggests that production will fall off more quickly than consumption rises (or may even fall, although at a lower rate than production).

in terms of y and q as $A = y/(2q/2) = y/q$. The answer that Keynes gives is then found by rewriting $p = AX/P_2$ as $[(y/q)X]/P_2$ or $pq = xy$ where x is the cost of carry as a proportion of the expected normal price. This equation is what Keynes calls the overlooked theory of "short-period prices".[6]

From this relation it is clear that the required fall in price s will be higher the higher is x, determined by the rate of interest, insurance and storage costs; the higher is y, determined by the size of excess stocks relative to normal consumption and the lower is C, annual consumption, and the lower is q, the reduction in annual production relative to normal. The crisis will then be shorter the lower the costs of carry, the higher current consumption, and the lower current output[7].

Keynes' price equation thus provides an indication of the action to be undertaken in an offensive strategy against the slump. It is clear that there is a trade off between the fall in production q, and the fall in prices, p. If prices are sticky, then the fall in production will have to be larger, and given multiplier considerations will have an impact on excess of supplies of other goods as well. Recalling that $A = y/q$ there is also a trade off between the length, y, and the severity, q, of the slump. Finally, the higher are interest rates and the other factors entering into carrying costs, the larger the required decline in prices or the greater the reduction in output or the longer the slump. Thus, restrictive monetary and fiscal policies, which increase interest rates and reduce the normal levels of consumption will cause spot prices to be driven down lower relative to expected future prices and increase the cost of

---

[6] Had Keynes used the more normal notation of the futures market this would have required asking what rate of return could be expected from buying spot at P_1 and selling the future at P_2 for a return of $(P_2-P_1)P_1$ which would be established by borrowing P_1S for a cost of $i(T/360)P_1S$ and earning $-c(T/360)P_1S$ over the holding period, T, and i is the borrowing rate on money and c the rate of carrying costs per unit. Thus $(P_2-P_1)S = P_1S [(1+i(T/360)) -(1-c(T/360))] = P_1S ((i+c)T/360)$ and $(P_2-P_1)/P_1 = (i+c)T/360$. In Keynes' terms: $x = i+c$ and $T = y/q$ and his equation could be written as $f = (i+c)T/360$ and P_2 is the expected future spot price which should be equal to the price paid for a future contract. Since $x > 0$, $P_2 = P_1(1 + x)$, $P_2 > P_1$ which is a contango.

[7] The formula can also be applied to the production of investment goods and thus to investment expenditures by considering current costs of production relative to the discounted present value of the expected earnings of existing capital goods. Investment will be positive when it is profitable to hedge futures contracts for future delivery of capital goods by producing them, rather than buying existing goods and holding them for delivery. Thus, in a slump, the same argument made about excess stocks of commodities may be made about investment goods, with their spot prices falling below expected future prices by an amount determined by the cost of carry and investment coming to a halt when the return on holding existing investment goods exceeds the return to producing new goods.

carry, both of which will delay the return to "normal" conditions of back-wardation.

There is no immediate way out of such a situation. But, there are ways to influence the variables in the equation in order to influence the way in which equilibrium is re-established. The value of x can be lowered by lowering interest rates, storage and insurance costs, thus decreasing the required p. Even y and q can be lowered by reducing the outstanding stocks - giving them away (burying them in the ground?) or better, by creating purchasing power which increases the rate of normal sales. Another alternative, which Keynes was to return to in the post second World War period was creation of an agency to "invest" in excess stocks and hold them until recovery; for commodities this means buffer stocks.

This is difficult when it comes to productive capacity: better to use it than to hold it idle (user costs come into the calculation of the cost of carry here). The only way to use it is to insure demand for its output, which requires increasing current expenditures, either on consumption or capital goods. Thus, government policy to expand demand for the output of productive capacity, or by directly increasing government demand for investment. Thus, either increasing consumption expenditures via policies to increase household incomes (burying banknotes) or by direct government investment projects. Keynes clearly preferred the latter.

It is thus possible to trace most of the "offensive" strategy to an attempt to influence short-period inter-temporal prices, not by direct intervention on prices, as with tariffs and subsidies, but indirectly by operating on the rate of run off of existing stocks and on the costs of carry. The main concern was to get the system back to conditions of normal backwardation. Permanent intervention was not envisaged, for once normal conditions were restored, it was presumed that private investment would again become profitable and be resumed. Then the only question became the problem of liquidity preference, setting the rate of interest on alternative employments of capital at a rate which was higher than that on productive investment.

Since the alternative to holding positions in commodities or productive capacity was to hold money, a forward discount on commodities was a forward premium on money. This is precisely how Keynes was to define the rate of interest in the *General Theory*, the difference between the spot and forward price of money. If the forward premium on money was too high, investors would choose to hold positions in money, rather than in productive assets, leading to an insufficient level of investment. The defensive strategy against the slump was thus to make sure that liquidity preference was kept sufficiently low to ensure the full employment level of investment. This was not a question of deficit spending, but of keeping a high and stable level of income so as to make consumers and investors confident in their predictions of future conditions regarding their incomes and rates of return on investment respectively.

There were thus two points: one concerned the stability of prices, or better the stability of normal backwardation representing profitable conditions for new investment expenditures, the other concerned the relation between the discount of future prices of investment goods and the premium on the future price of money. The latter is now better known as the relation between the rate of interest and the marginal efficiency of capital or between the demand price and supply price of capital. It involved the supply of money and expectations. The former was subject to policy control, the latter could only be influenced indirectly by influencing general economic conditions.

4. From Offence to Defence

It was to be the role of "defensive" policy to insure that general economic conditions do not get out of control. In this respect Keynes proposed that the government budget be divided, as any business budget, into a capital and current expenditure budget. Keynes envisaged that the current expenditure budget would be kept broadly in balance. He argued that this was necessary "to preserve sound accounting, to measure efficiency, to maintain economy and to keep the public properly aware of what things cost" (Keynes, 1980, pp. 224-5).

It will certainly come as a surprise to the denigrators of Keynes, but his "defensive" policy was to "aim at having a surplus on the ordinary Budget, which would be transferred to the capital Budget, thus gradually replacing dead-weight debt by productive or semi-productive debt .... I should not aim at attempting to compensate cyclical fluctuations by means of the ordinary Budget, I should leave this to the capital Budget" (pp. 277-8). It was thus capital expenditures, which should be largely self-financing, which should deal with the problem of offensive policy. Over the long run, the government budget on both ordinary and capital account should be roughly in balance, although when demand fell off, the capital expenditures would increase, creating a temporary deficit which would be eliminated as the capital projects paid off in terms of higher tax receipts and surpluses on the ordinary budget.

I have tried to give a summary (Kregel, 1985) of Keynes' various pronouncements on "defensive" budgetary policy:

1. Long-term full employment in conditions of laissez-faire will require substantial government control of investment in order to make investment a more stable proportion of national output.

2. This process of government control should be undertaken through "semi-autonomous" public corporations and publicly owned joint stock corporations which are independent from direct government intervention.

3. In order to facilitate policy the government budget should be divided into a current and capital account budget. The current account budget should be

in balance or run a surplus which is transferred to the capital budget which is to be used to offset exogenous cyclical changes in investment spending. The capital budget may exhibit deficits, but should be balanced over the long run.

4. The proportion of total investment which is subject to government control through the capital budget should be in the range of 7.5 per cent to 20 per cent of national income.

5. Investment spending on government capital budget account should be counter cyclical relative to national income and vary inversely with cycles in private spending on plant and equipment.

6. The capital and current account budgets should both be balanced at the long-run target unemployment rate of between 3-5 per cent. If this is achieved, both outstanding debt and the deficit should become a declining proportion of national income.

7. Those services and transfers which are provided by the state should be "technically social", i.e. those which the private sector is unwilling and/or unable to provide in amounts and prices considered socially acceptable.

8. All state services should be furnished efficiently, which means that they should cover all costs, capital charges and should not include on or off-budget subsidies.

Most economists, as well as laymen, are so convinced that Keynes was a wild-eyed deficit spender bent on planning the minute details of the economy that this presentation will seem strange. It certainly falls awkwardly in the current professional debate between those who argue that no policy can improve the performance of the economic system and the New Keynesians who argue in terms of direct government intervention by means of tariffs, subsidies and all sorts of fine-tuning devices. There may be good reasons for such direct intervention in the economy, but they are not founded in Keynes' policy pronouncements. Since they usually deal with some sort of externality, they are perhaps closer to the views of Abba Lerner's "Functional Finance" approach. It is clear that Keynes was never a "fine-tuner", and it is somewhat paradoxical that current attempts to give modern justification to government intervention should resurrect this particularly inappropriate version of his views on government policy.

In addition to budget policy, Keynes had a long-standing position in favour of low interest rates, this predates both the *Treatise* and the *General Theory*. This is a position which he never relinquished and which was also developed on the basis of the short-period pricing equation given above. What did change was his early belief that money policy alone would be sufficient to offset recession and excessive liquidity preference. "It is not quite correct that I attach primary importance to the rate of interest ... I should regard state intervention to encourage investment as probably a more important factor than low rates of interest taken in isolation" (Keynes, 1980,

p. 350). Keynes thus eventually concluded that operating on x might not be sufficient to offset changes in expectations concerning future normal prices so that direct intervention capable of influencing expectations would be necessary. But, this intervention is not of the kind that adjusts real relative prices by means of taxes, tariffs or price subsidies, but the kind which changes the overall level of investment through government spending, thus acting directly on the values of both y and q in hopes of limiting the decline in p or the fall in q, and thus placing a floor on expectations of future profits.

It is for this reason that Keynes stressed point 4 in the list given above: in order to place a floor under price and profit expectations. On the other hand, there was no question that these government agencies should operate on a profitable basis. Public investments provide public services which are operated through the ordinary budget, and this budget is presumed to charge economic prices for these services. Thus, much as a firm will have a rising proportion of debt when it engages in an active investment programme, which, if successful will generate profits which will repay interest and principal, government agencies were presumed to operate in the same way. The only difference was that they should increase their indebtedness in periods when private firms' investments were low and when the general economy appeared to be falling away from the desired levels of employment because of structural, demographic or external reasons.

As already mentioned, Keynes' views on the use of the government budget for stabilisation policy were formulated with the post-war reconstruction in view. It is also interesting to note that Keynes envisaged three phases in this process of reconstruction (cf. Guger and Walterskirchen, 1988):

1) A five-year transition period in which formal constraints would have to be placed on both consumption and investment spending;
2) A twenty-year phase in which government would be active in ensuring full employment - this is the period to which the proposals outlined above referred;
3) A third phase in which, after twenty years of investment at more than 20 per cent of GNP, there was the possibility of saturation of investment and stagnation was a risk. Here offensive policies to discourage savings and increase consumption might become necessary, and Keynes accepted the possibility of permanent deficits: "I should expect for a long time to come that the government debt or government-guaranteed debt would be continually increasing in grand total" (1980, p. 278).

5. Has the Post War Period Been Offensive or Defensive?

All this is far from the simple idea of "deficit spending". If we ask the question, has any economy applied Keynes' policy in the post-war period, the answer must be no. No country has ever tried to separate its current and

capital account budgets, although this has been suggested a number of times
in the past[8] and is currently gaining a following as a way of surmounting the
impasse created by the large deficits of the 1980's. Indeed, most governments
have acted in precisely the opposite fashion, allowing their budget balances to
develop more or less independently of underlying economic conditions. When
growth in the government deficit appeared too large to be sustainable, the
response was to cut capital expenditures to create more room for deficits
caused by overspending for transfers on the ordinary budget. Table 1 shows
the decline in overall government influenced spending on gross fixed capital
formation, i.e. by all levels of government and by public-owned enterprises.
The reversal in policy in the UK is clearly influenced by the privatisation of
state enterprise; the reversal in Japanese policy is even more striking, but
given the behaviour of the economy, explicable as a counter-cyclical activity.

TABLE 1
**General Government and Public Enterprises Gross
Fixed Capital Formation as a percent of GDP**

	1962-72	1973-9	1977-9	1980-9
USA	3.50	2.81	2.83	2.48
Japan	8.78	9.46	9.85	7.69
UK	7.94	7.46	6.08	3.62

Source: OECD National Accounts, Detailed Tables,
Vol. II, 1981, 1991.

However, the importance of government investment policies in the post-war
period may be seen in tables 2 and 3(a) and 3(b), which deals with a wider
sample of countries.

---

[8] Sidney Weintraub (1981) proposed this in the early 1980's in response to the
rhetoric of the new Reagan administration, but as far as I know it was without any
knowledge of Keynes' post-war policy proposals.

TABLE 2
Ratio of General Government Gross Fixed Capital
Formation to GDP (averages)

	1955-64	1962-72	1973-9
USA	3.25	2.75	2.83
Japan	9.78	4.62	5.63
Austria	5.45	4.84	5.11
France	2.75	3.91	3.28
Germany	3.80	4.07	3.50
Italy	2.53	2.88	3.14
Netherlands	4.63	4.76	3.65
UK	2.07	4.47	4.08

Source: OECD National Accounts, Detailed Tables,Vol. II,
1981, 1991.

In general, high and stable ratios of government investment to output produced a more stable growth performance as measured by employment performance and growth variability.

TABLE 3(a)
Ratio of Unemployment to Total Labour Force
(averages)

	1962-72	1973-79	1977-79
USA	4.65	5.66	6.30
Japan	1.22	1.45	2.00
Austria	1.67	1.50	1.66
France	1.86	4.24	5.26
Germany	0.80	3.21	3.70
Italy	4.62	6.00	6.70
Netherlands	1.82	5.61	6.30
UK	3.08	4.61	5.60

Source: adapted from Maddison (1982), pp. 207-8.

TABLE 3(b)
Variability of GNP and Unemployment: USA

	Standard deviation of GNP Gap*	Unemployment rate: mean	standard deviation
Period			
1920-41	12.99	11.52	7.59
1900-45	13.58	7.77	6.51
1946-76	3.56	4.95	1.34
1962-73	2.46	4.74	0.88
1966-76	2.26	5.25	1.66

* GNP Gap = (GNP/trend GNP)-1
Source: Baily (1978).

Table 4 shows the extent to which social security transfer expenditures by government rose as a proportion of GDP as investment expenditures dropped. Only in Germany does the upward trend seem to be stopped, although not reversed. The increases in transfers are generally larger then the reductions in investment.

TABLE 4
Social Security Transfers as a Proportion of GDP

	60-7	68-73	74-9	80-9	60-89
USA	5.4	7.7	10.3	11.1	8.7
Japan	4.2	4.8	8.4	7.3	
Austria	14.3	15.6	17.8	20.1	17.2
France	15.5	15.6	17.5	21.3	17.8
Germany	12.4	13.2	16.7	16.5	14.8
Italy	11.1	13	15.4	16.7	14.2
Netherlands	17.7	23.5	26.7	23.4	
UK	7.3	8.8	10.7	13.2	10.3

Source: OECD 1991 Table 6.4, p. 67.

This has brought the increase in total government outlays noted in table 5. Even in the US, where the official policy was to decrease the role of government in the economy, the ratio rose in the 1980's. In the UK, similar policies have, however, stabilised the figure. It is still the US and Japan, however, which show similar, and substantially lower, proportions than those for the major European countries.

TABLE 5
Ratio of Total Government Outlays to GDP

	60-7	68-73	74-9	80-9	60-89
USA	28.3	31.1	32.6	36	32.3
Japan	18.7	20.5	28.4		25.6
Austria	37.6	40.2	46.7	51	44.4
France	37.4	38.9	43.3	50.3	43.2
Germany	35.7	39.8	47.5	47.6	42.8
Italy	29.3	34.7	39.2	45	37.6
Netherlands	37.8	44.8	52.8	59.6	49.5
UK	34.7	39.5	44.4	44.9	41

Source: OECD, 1991 Table 6.5, p. 68.

This rise in expenditures has not been matched either by cuts in spending or increases in taxation, leading to ever increasing borrowing by general government given in table 6. The UK is the sole exception, and much of this is explained by the policy of financing expenditure by the sale of public assets.

TABLE 6
Government Borrowing Requirements as a Proportion of GDP

	60-7	68-73	74-9	80-9	60-89
USA	-0.6	-0.6	-1.4	-3.4	-1.7
Japan	1.0	0.9	-3.4	NA	-0.8
Austria	0.6	0.8	-2.1	-3	-1.1
France	0.5	0.5	-1.1	-2.1	-0.7
Germany	0.8	0.2	-3	-2.1	-1
Italy	-1.8	-4.8	-9.2	-11	-6.9
Netherlands	-0.7	-0.5	-2.3	-5.7	-2.7
UK	-1.1	-0.4	-4.1	-2.4	-2

Source: OECD, 1991 Table 6.7, p. 69.

Looking at the employment experience, and recalling Keynes' projections of 3-5 per cent as the standard for full employment in the UK, there are a number of countries that have done substantially better than this. The UK clearly has paid for its budget reductions through rising unemployment, while the rising budget deficit does not seem to have had any positive impact on the US level of unemployment.

TABLE 7
Standardised Unemployment Rates

	64-67	68-73	74-9	80-9	60-89
USA	4.2	4.6	6.7	7.2	6.0
Japan	1.2	1.2	1.9	2.5	1.9
Austria	2.0	2.5	6.3	10.8	6.5
France	1.7	2.6	4.5	9.0	5.4
Germany	0.6	1	3.2	5.9	3.3
Italy	5.1	5.7	6.6	9.5	7.3
Netherlands	0.8	1.5	4.9	9.7	5.3
UK	2.5	3.3	5	10	6.1

Source: OECD: 1991 Table 2.20, p. 45.

The other side of Keynes's argument concerns the control of liquidity preference and the impact of interest rates on carrying costs. Tables 8 and 9 give figures for the inflation corrected growth in M1 + quasi money. It is interesting that in all countries except the US the rate of increase has fallen throughout the period.

TABLE 8
Real Money Supply: M1 and Quasi Money
(annual rate of growth)

	60-8	68-73	73-9	80-9	60-89
USA	5.8	4.5	2.5	3.6	4.1
Japan	11.9	12.4	3.6	7.4	8.7
Austria	9.5	8.4	9.3	4.1	7.4
France				2.4	
Germany	5.4	6.6	2.4	3.6	4.4
Italy	8.1	9.3	3	-0.1	4.4
Netherlands	3.5	4.6	2.7	5.5	4.2
UK			-2.3	8.2	

Source: OECD, 1991 Table 10.4 p. 103: M1+ Quasi money/ GDP Implicit Price Index.

Accompanying the fall in the rate of growth of real money was a rise in real long term interest rates, which in some countries was substantial.

TABLE 9
Real Long-Term Interest Rates

	68-73	74-9	80-9
USA	0.6	-0.6	5.5
Japan	0.5	0.1	4.8
Austria	2.3	2.6	4
France	1.6	-0.4	4.7
Germany		3	4.5
Italy	0.2	-4.2	2.7
UK	2	-2	3.4

Source: OECD, 1991. Table 10.10, p. 106.

The combination of high interest rates and rising budget deficits has, however, brought another change, the sharp increase in interest payments in government transfers. Table 10 shows the proportion of gross interest paid by general governments to GDP and to general government expenditures. The first two columns should be read in comparison to the figures given in table 6 showing government borrowing requirements as a proportion of GDP. Most governments are now in classic conditions of what Minsky has called "Ponzi finance", i.e. they have to borrow in order to be able to pay interest on their outstanding debt. This is the major problem facing most governments, and which is the obstacle to the use of expenditure policy, not the absolute value of the outstanding debt.

TABLE 10
Gross Interest Payments of General Government
in Proportion to GDP

	77-9	80-9	77-9	80-9
USA	2.63	4.51	8.17	12.4
Japan	2.23	4.01	7.19	12.12
Austria	2.13	3.38	4.39	6.61
France	1.30	3.50	-	-
Germany	1.61	2.66	3.35	5.56
Italy		7.57		15.31
Netherlands	4.02	6.70	7.46	11.36
UK	4.30	4.54	10.08	10.16

Source: OECD, 1991 Vol II (Germany to 1988).

The difficulty can be remedied only by means of lower outstanding indebtedness or lower interest rates. The former requires net government surpluses which can be achieved by cutting net expenditures, which in current conditions means a high probability of simply increasing deficits. The latter course is the only possibility.

6. Keynes and Stabilisation Policy for the Current Recession

Might we apply Keynes' policy as a means of current policy? A positive impact could be achieved by reversing the trend towards increasing transfer payments and offsetting this with increased capital expenditures. The possible decline in defence expenditure should make this easier. This shift in the composition of expenditure would require the introduction of separate ordinary and capital budgeting. It is interesting to see that this idea is starting to be discussed in the United States (cf. Levy and Levy, 1992).

The current recession in the US may be explained by means of Keynes' short-period pricing equation presented above. During the 1980's peculiar legislation effectively reduced the financing costs of investment in commercial real estate and speculative purchase of publicly quoted companies to zero, or negative, despite high real rates of interest so that the US is experiencing conditions of excess supply of certain types of capital goods. The p in the equation given above has been driven down by the high values of x and y despite the fact that q has been reduced to near zero. The only way that y can be reduced is by increasing government capital expenditures. This seems paradoxical in the presence of excess capacity, but might be achieved by increasing expenditures on social overhead capital which does not create additional capacity in the areas of excess, but only increased incomes. The other factor is the reduction in interest rates, which continue to remain high despite the recent reductions and should be reduced further. With inflation now expected to settle around 3 per cent, long term real rates are currently (June, 1992) above 5 per cent. Table 10 above shows that there is still a possibility of a 300 basis point (3 percentage points) fall in long rates. The current opinion is that long rates are being held up by the size of the rise in the expected borrowing requirement due to the continued recession and the level of long-term interest rates abroad, in particular in Germany. The increase in capital spending, by reducing the value of y/q brings recovery nearer and thus reduces the expected borrowing requirement. At the same time, the announcement that the government was proposing to split the ordinary budget from the capital budget and balance the former should have a positive impact on market expectations. A similar move in Germany, to cut transfer expenditures associated with unification, and to increase public investment expenditures in the former East German Länder, should have similar effect (it is interesting that the German government did not have a ready plan of public investment in the East at the moment of unification).

Thus the first priority is government expenditure switching, and the second the further decline in interest rates. Keynes's approach suggests that this can be achieved without a sustained depression, which is the only other alternative that has worked in the past, aside from massive destruction of human and fixed capital.

References:

Baily, M.N. (1978), "Stabilization Policy and Private Economic Behavior", *Brookings Papers on Economic Activity*, No. 1.

Guger, A. and E. Walterskirchen (1988), *Fiscal and Monetary Policy in the Keynes-Kalecki Tradition*, in: J.A. Kregel, E. Matzner and A. Roncaglia (eds.), Macmillan, London.

Keynes, J.M. (1923), "Some Aspects of Commodity Markets", reprinted in: *Economic Articles and Correspondence: Investment and Editorial*, Collected Writings of J.M. Keynes, Vol. XII, Macmillan, London, for the Royal Economic Society, 1983.

--- (1930), *A Treatise on Money*, Macmillan, London.

--- (1980), *Activities 1940-46 shaping the Post-War World: Employment and Commodities*, Collected Writings of J.M. Keynes, Vol. XXVII, Macmillan, London, for the Royal Economic Society.

Kregel, J.A. (1982), "Money, Expectations and Relative Prices in Keynes' Monetary Equilibrium", *Economie Appliquée*, Vol. 36, No. 3.

--- (1985), "Budget Deficits, Stabilisation Policy and Liquidity Preference: Keynes's Post-War Policy Proposals", in: F. Vicarelli (ed.), *Keynes's Relevance Today*, Macmillan, London.

Lerner, A. (1943), "Functional Finance and the Federal Debt", *Social Research*, Vol. 10, February.

Levy, S. Jay and D. Levy (1992), *How to Restore Long-Term Prosperity in the United States and Overcome the Contained Depression of the 1990s?*, The Jerome Levy Economics Institute, Annandale-on-Hudson, New York.

Maddison, A. (1982), *Phases of Capitalist Development*, Oxford University Press, Oxford.

Minsky, H.P. (1986), *Stabilising an Unstable Economy*, Yale University Press, New Haven.

OECD (1981), *OECD National Accounts: Detailed Tables Volume II 1962-1979*, Paris.

--- (1991), *OECD National Accounts: Detailed Tables Volume II 1977-1989*, Paris.

--- (1991), *OECD Historical Statistics 1960-1989*, Paris.

Weintraub, S. (1981), "Where Red Ink Is a False Alarm", *The New York Times*, December.

The Developmentalist View

Victor L. Urquidi
El Colegio de Mexico

1. Is Developmentalism an Issue?

This is an occasion to review ideas - and policies deriving from them - , that emerged some 45 years ago but have fallen into desuetude, even into disrepute, particularly since the 1980s. Market forces, private enterprise, less intervention by government, even mild taxation, have replaced planning, public enterprise and initiatives, government regulation of economic affairs and attempts at direct taxation as mainstays of development policy. On the basis of new theorising, developmentalist approaches have been abandoned as a prescription for rapid growth and development. The concept of "Development" itself has changed in nature, when it has not been simply left by the wayside. "Growth" under market forces and allocations seems to reign supreme; "development" has almost become a dirty word.

Yet it can be argued that the demise of a theory of development should not be exaggerated. The question is: what is left of it? Is there some life in the notion? Or, as Professor Sen exclaimed some years ago: Which way now? (Sen, 1984, Chapter 19, pp. 485-508) In briefly going over some of the literature that many of us had taken for granted as a thesis to explain and justify development policies, particularly the so-called structuralist approach, one is struck by the relative simplicity of "developmentalism". This view, this approach, appears to have been held mainly in the Latin American region (Little, 1982, p. 19; Seers, 1981, pp. 13-14), but not exclusively, for who can deny the antecedents in India or the obvious background originating in the Soviet Union (Little, 1982, pp.47-53)?

I am more familiar with the Latin American developmentalist view, on which there is much literature, and shall have it chiefly in mind in what follows, with occasional references to other developmentalist views. Two questions will be considered: (i) how valid an approach was developmentalism to achieve a process of development? (ii) is there anything left in it that could offset the negative social consequences of the present prescriptions to achieve "growth" through market forces alone? I shall deal with these two questions throughout, intermingling them rather than treating them consecutively.

2. Some background

For present purposes, I shall define **developmentalism** as a political-economy concept which epitomises a will, under an authoritarian system, to expand and indeed push public sector expenditure for development purposes, outside the confines of the market system, in the expectation that both economic and social benefits will result for society as a whole, and in particular for the lower income and disadvantaged strata. In an effort to dissolve structural constraints, developmentalism normally has little regard for conventional budget planning, relies on debt creation more than on efforts to raise taxation, is less than rigorous about a non-inflationary monetary policy, expects some external financing, and postpones correction of inflationary consequences until such time as the full result of the investment period matures. It does not exclude a role for private enterprise and even establishes considerable incentives for domestic investment, but does not rely on the private sector as a prime mover of growth.

As to the origin of developmentalism, I find it puzzling that, for instance, this approach - under a less specific definition than the one I have advanced in the previous paragraph - appears to be attributed almost wholly to the Secretariat of the UN Economic Commission for Latin America and, in particular, to the writings of Raúl Prebisch and his associates in Santiago de Chile (Little, 1982, p. 19; Seers, 1981, pp. 13-14). Apart from earlier formulations of the economic planning approach - which Professor Little, for instance, attributes to Feldmann in the Soviet Union and to Mahalanobis and others in India - , it can be argued that, if not in refined formal terms, the developmentalist view of growth arose out of necessity in the minds of political leaders in the Latin American region in the second and third decades of this century, and even earlier in some instances, as was expressed in certain policies during the late 19th century.

The history of Mexico is illustrative. Liberal political régimes prevailed - with the exception of the Emperor Maximilian interlude - for almost two decades under the Constitution of 1857. The long-lasting strong administrations and, finally, the dictatorship of General Porfirio Díaz embraced the trappings of a developmentalist policy, especially from the 1880s onward. It was the Mexican régime's way at the time to "insert the national economy into the expanding world economy" - to use the phrase now current. Public works, subsidies for transportation and other infrastructure, concessions to develop resources such as minerals and oil, and measures favoring industrialisation - **fomento**[1] was the term then, now replaced by "development" - were the essence of economic policy. Very little reliance was

---

[1] It is interesting that as late as 1944, the World Bank was born with the following legal name in Spanish: Banco Internacional de Reconstrucción y **Fomento**. In the 19th century and deep into the 20th, development ministries in Latin America were called **Ministerios de Fomento**.

placed on the "market". In fact, there was no integrated national market, nor was there much financial development. Such policies were, in any event, moderate, and they relied on a net inflow of external capital, through borrowing and by attracting foreign investment. One could argue that, in the context of those notions as a whole, those policies did not go far enough, for hardly anything was done to organise modern agriculture and nothing at all to reform the land tenure system based on very high concentrations of private ownership - the famous **latifundia**. For what it was worth, however, the developmentalist approach of the Díaz régime was fairly successful in raising national product and particularly in augmenting exports at a high rate... until the Mexican Revolution broke out in 1910, on both political and economic grounds.[2]

A review of the economic history of, say Argentina (Díaz-Alejandro, 1988), or Brazil, will no doubt reveal similar experiences and ideas. All this was not the "full" developmentalism of later years, but it had an underpinning. Perhaps one of the guiding forces was the realisation that these economies, as they progressed in the late 19th century, were what Prebisch was later to call extremely "vulnerable" to external economic and financial fluctuations - the old "trade cycle" that has been written so much about. In times of world trade expansion, fired from the "center" (mainly the United Kingdom), booms arose in the "dependent" countries - the "periphery" of Prebisch - based on exports of two or three commodities; and when the reverse occurred, these economies were left high and dry, with over-expansion of credit, a decline in tax revenues and a stubborn demand for imports, which led to devaluations (off gold) and recessions, until the cycle picked up again (Prebisch, 1944).

These ups and downs culminated in the Great Depression of the 1930s, when politicians and a few economists in some of the major Latin American countries began to formulate nationalistic economic policies designed to protect the local economies from the ravages caused by the decline in world demand. Meanwhile, population had grown, and social demands had become more vocal and had, in many countries, found expression in new political movements and parties. In Mexico, as early as the 1920s, the reconstruction period of the Revolution had been characterised by partial developmentalist endeavors, partly out of necessity - there was little private enterprise willing

---

[2] The standard reference for this expansionary period of Mexico's history is Cosío Villegas and associates (1965). There are many accounts in English, including Maddison (1992), who estimated that in the period 1870-1910 Mexican GDP per capita increased at an average 0.9 per cent annually, while the volume of exports rose at an astounding rate of 6.1 per cent per year. Cf. also Coatsworth (1978, 1981), and for the 20th century, Reynolds (1970). Maddison's work is an important contribution to measuring growth and analysing development in Mexico since 1929.

to go into larger-scale risk ventures - and in any event as a means of implementation of the new 1917 Constitution which established the responsibility of the state to undertake development policies. The economic objectives were coupled with radically new social policies in the spheres of land tenure, education and the rights of labor. In addition, the influence of external events in the 1930s, and structural shifts such as the decline of the foreign-owned oil industry, pushed the government in the direction of "planning", state enterprise, regulation and, generally, intervention in the market.

World War II, for Latin America, added to these trends. Not only were the wartime economies of both camps highly regulated ones, but scarcities of imports, export surpluses, sizeable increases in currency reserves and inflation, gave new impetus to developmentalism. It translated into strong support for rapid industrialisation, expansion of infrastructure, various policies to guard against a resumption of the old trade patterns, and, again, the need for the state to meet social demands. Some plans for the postwar period were formulated before ECLA even existed. Many writers in the US and elsewhere foresaw a "new world development", and Latin Americans were not indifferent to the role their region might play in this new world. Their hopes were soon dashed, however, by the US position, first expressed in 1945 at the so-called Chapultepec Conference and later, by General Marshall himself, in early 1948 at the Conference of Bogotá which gave birth to the Organisation of American States (successor to the Pan-American Union). At these meetings, Latin America was advised to return to the "free" market for its exports of basic commodities, to invite foreign direct investment rather than demand a "Marshall Plan for Latin America", and to lower its tariffs and espouse free multilateral trade. The Havana Conference on Trade and Employment in 1948 resulted only in the adoption of GATT, to which few Latin American, and indeed few developing nations, subscribed (Urquidi, 1964, Chapter 11).

In this connection, it should not be missed that developmentalism in Latin America has always been associated with the lack of sufficient external resources, be they obtained through trade or from outside financial centers, and later, from bilateral official sources and multilateral agencies. And at every international conference, the Latin American countries have consistently pressed for international financial cooperation. In the postwar years, this was not forthcoming from the only source that had the power to provide it, the United States; the Bretton Woods institutions having barely begun their operations in the Latin American region. In the absence of sufficient external resources, many countries went ahead with budget deficits, inflation and devaluations.

3. Some Theoretical Underpinnings and Some Ramblings

No wonder then that developmentalism did not abate, but began to take on a new drive. It lacked, however, a consistent theoretical underpinning, and this is where Prebisch and the ECLA secretariat provided some basic ideas. The so-called ECLA doctrine has been considered widely as giving a "rationale" to later development policies in Latin America - at least until some ten years ago. Recent writings tend to give less credit to Prebisch himself than was the fashion some years ago (Hodara, 1987). At least some connections can be traced between Prebisch and the writings and policy proposals of Central European authors. Certainly at the UN, and even before, Professor Hans Singer had formulated similar ideas on trade and on the terms of trade. Put simply, Prebisch held, in a UN-ECLA document specifically attributed to him (Prebisch, 1949) that the Latin American economies faced an adverse trend in the terms of trade (as Singer also argued generally), that therefore the outlook for exports of basic commodities was unfavourable as a source of foreign exchange to finance growing needs of imported capital and other goods, and that an expanding labor force and new urban demands required a higher rate of industrialisation. Moreover, in many countries the expansion of a modern industrial base became a matter of national prestige. Export pessimism combined with high import-elasticity to a growing GDP to make for an unstable balance of payments prospect. Import substitution was thus necessary both for balance of payments and for employment reasons. Import substitution was to be understood as a fall in the share of imports relative to aggregate domestic demand for a product or a group of products, not merely a shutting out of specific imports because domestic production existed or could be developed. Reasonable tariff and other forms of protection and stimulus to industrial expansion were therefore justified, as they had been in the historical experience of all industrialising countries. There was a need to render these policies consistent and to coordinate them. The "market" could not be relied upon to perform this function, and consequently it became the responsibility of the state to promote or plan development along these lines.

Much has been written going far beyond the Prebisch formulation and also to denigrate it. I shall not go into that here. Prebisch himself never espoused the ultraprotectionism of the 1950s and 1960s that brought upon him the scorn of Professor Viner or, later, the voluminous critique of Béla Balassa and others. At an early stage he recognised the need for export promotion and not only import substitution, and warned against excessive and mindless protectionism, as Hirschman pointed out in a well-known essay (Hirschman, 1968). Prebisch cannot be held responsible for what others wrote independently nor for what governments actually did.

In the early 1950s ECLA put out a so-called "programming technique", to which economists such as Jorge Ahumada, Celso Furtado, Julio Melnick and others contributed, as a methodology for governments to formulate coherent development policies. Studies were carried out on a number of Latin American countries to diagnose the national situation and suggest the policies needed to achieve rapid industrialisation. A UN regional institute was set up in Santiago in the mid-1950s to train "planners" in the Latin American region and to carry out research on social and economic planning. Sometimes it was called "programming", to deflect immediate reactions from certain quarters. But it was not predicated on state ownership of all enterprise, nor on farm collectivisation, nor on absolute controls over foreign trade and foreign exchange. It was largely an elaboration of the Harrod-Domar formulation, and was intended to give guidance on trade and industrialisation policies, on public and private investment requirements, savings requirements, and, naturally, the "savings gap", as well as the "external gap" to be filled by an inflow of, preferably, multilateral capital.

No special emphasis was given to foreign direct investment, mainly because its history in Latin America was one of concentration in the area of natural resources, with all its political and social implications, and for which in any event the export outlook was bleak. At the 1953 and 1954 conferences at Quitandinha and Rio de Janeiro, both of which were based on documents prepared by the ECLA secretariat, the final governmental recommendations went in the direction of urging the creation of the Inter-American Bank. This was the only concrete result of these meetings, with a dissenting vote of the United States and Peru, and it took a good six more years to achieve the establishment of the IDB.

As it turned out, the export pessimism of the late 1940s was not realised. The Marshall Plan and Europe's recovery bolstered the demand for Latin American commodity exports. Growth and industrialisation got under way fairly successfully in most Latin American countries. Nevertheless, industrialisation soon got out of hand, especially as recurring foreign exchange crises reinforced ultra-protectionism and exchange controls. Deficit spending and inflation did not help, and fed back into excessive protectionism. Currency overvaluation became the norm, and the IMF could only offer modest support in the hope that devaluations might be accepted and the disequilibria might be reversed. Floating or "real" exchange rates were unheard of. A complex network of over-protected industries arose. Many of the strategic industries were state-owned, and eventually became uncompetitive and inefficient. Also the major privately owned manufacturing industries followed the same path and were to a large extent socially inefficient. Vested interests and quick profitability prevailed over long-term social benefit. In any event, there was no consistent industrialisation plan anywhere and the export markets, and the consequent need for competitiveness, were sorely neglected. Foreign exchange policies, with a penchant for overvaluation, did not encourage manufactured exports.

The flow of foreign loans and other forms of external capital was quite modest. In 1958 an Operation Pan-America was urged on the US by President Kubitschek of Brazil - a developmentalist if there ever was one -, which resulted only in a small Inter-American Fund for Social Progress set up two years later. Finally, the arrival of the Castro régime in Cuba and John F. Kennedy's election in 1960 created the atmosphere for bringing into being the Alliance for Progress, a scheme in the formulation of which members of the ECLA secretariat and US and Latin American economists participated. The Alliance comprised more or less agreed external financial support for economic and social development in exchange for commitments on land reform, tax reform, urban and rural improvement and... planning! The plans were to be evaluated by an independent Committee of Nine, operating from the Organisation of American States. Despite its many faults, the Alliance met some of its goals - an average of about US$ 2 billion in external financial cooperation was actually achieved in the decade (Scheman, 1988) - , but the programme soon petered out; it never enjoyed sufficient commitment on the part either of the US or of many Latin American governments (Urquidi, 1964). It barely survived the death of President Kennedy.

In the end, today, developmentalism has been blamed for all Latin America's ills. But meanwhile another actor appeared on the scene: dependency or **dependencia**. According to Dudley Seers, dependency theory

"is very much a product of a particular place and particular historical period. Since the war, Latin Americans have come to see themselves as 'underdeveloped', which naturally carries implications for economic ideology. These were worked out during the 1950s in the Economic Commission for Latin America (ECLA), led by Raúl Prebisch: the central theme there, at that time, was a forerunner of 'dependency' theory, 'structuralism'. This was a response to the 'monetarism' of neo-classical economists which had become manifest in policies the International Monetary Fund was requiring of many Latin American governments to follow." (Seers, 1981, pp. 13-14).

Thus Seers finds a significantly close connection between developmentalism/structuralism à la ECLA and dependency theory. But, as he himself and others avow, **dependencia** went in other directions, on a highly politicised level, and largely led nowhere. He deals extensively with the problems of policy and its results, and the role of dependency "theory" (Seers, 1981, pp. 135-149).[3] It was not actually applied to policy in Latin

---

[3]   The literature on dependency is vast. I only mention the classical study by Cardoso and Faletto (1979), and essays by Palma and others in Seers (1981).

454   *Victor L. Urquidi*

America. To some extent, developmentalism can stand on its own.

4. Some Basics on Development; Different and Converging Views

What then, leaving aside the excesses in the policies of many governments, can be rescued?

It is useful to review what various authors meant by development. For Professor Gunnar Myrdal, for example - and I quote him at some length because I fear his writings are being forgotten - "development"

> "means a process of moving away from 'underdevelopment', of rising out of poverty; it is sought and perhaps actually attained by means of 'planning of development'. ... in (an underdeveloped country) there is ... a constellation of numerous undesirable conditions for work and life; outputs, incomes, and levels of living are low; many modes of production, as well as attitudes and behavioral patterns, are disadvantageous; and there are unfavorable institutions ranging from those at the state level to those governing social and economic relations in the family and the neighborhood;... There is a general causal relationship among all these conditions, so that they form a social system. 'Development' means the movement upward of that whole system." (Myrdal, 1971, pp. 427-8).

Myrdal, having India in mind, goes on to spell out some of the characteristics of underdevelopment: low productivity, low capital intensity and low savings and low living conditions, including much deprivation. He argues for an "institutional approach" in moving from underdevelopment to development "through planning for development". Planning is seen as a "coordination of policies". It is also a "political program", subject to many counteracting factors. However, "development from a traditional to a modern economy is largely the creation and expansion of a sphere of instrumental valuations where previously only independent valuations reigned. Development thus leads to a widening of choice... which stems from an increasing understanding of circular causation and greater readiness to regard change as a means to further ends." And he argues: "Planning, in the final instance, can never be a substitute for policy-making... (it) involves political choices". A plan requires "a big push"[4] applied to "all parts of the social

---

[4]   The "big push" idea, usually attributed to Professor Paul Rosenstein-Rodan in connection with South-Eastern Europe, gained ground in the developmentalist approaches of the 1960s and 1970s in Latin America. On the "big push", cf. Little (1982, pp. 38-9).

system". "Unless conditions are changed by specific, powerful, and coordinated efforts, they will not change at all or perhaps change in the wrong direction". There must be "a positive feedback of effects". Underdeveloped countries cannot rely on a "gradualist approach" (Myrdal, 1971, pp. 427-440, *passim*). In passing, Latin American countries by that time had already become developmentalist, rather than gradualist.

And - Myrdal concludes - economic policies "are undoubtedly easier to carry out than are social policies that challenge vested interests, violate deep-seated inhibitions, offend cherished traditions and beliefs, and work against the heavy weight of social inertia. Yet if development policies are mainly directed at economic development in the narrow sense, they will prove less than effective" (Myrdal, 1971, pp. 442-3). These ideas were already prevalent in many Latin American countries and were in fact included in the Alliance for Progress formulation referred to above.

Professor Little's approach is more cautious and indeed somewhat skeptical. If value judgments are taken into account - he argues - "there can be no objective definition of development and therefore no universally acceptable indicator. The best one might hope for would be to get some rough consensus on objectives and hence on how progress towards those objectives can be measured..." (Little, 1982, p. 6). For him, a liberal economic definition of development would be: "Economic development (or economic progress or real economic growth) occurs if there is a rise in the present value of average (weighted) consumption per head." Different weights can be attached, or social weights. He recognised the complications arising with the introduction of welfare aspects, political freedom, political values ('economic values are not separate from political values') (Little, 1982, p. 6). He seems to identify economic development with economic growth as such, but he recognises nevertheless that most LDC policymakers "were not simply aiming at growth of output per head. ...They were trying to satisfy many other objectives, of both a national and a sectional character". He also emphasises the role of nationalistic objectives and nation-building (Little, 1982, pp. 13, 17).

Developmentalism, as Little sees it, has its roots in structuralism, which "first came into use in the 1950s with reference to structuralist explanations of inflation in Latin America, as opposed to the monetary explanations and policies largely identified with the IMF" (Little, 1982, pp. 19ff.; also Seers, 1981). He quotes Chenery with reference to Rosenstein-Rodan, Nurkse, Lewis, Prebisch, Singer and Myrdal. "The structuralist sees the world as inflexible. Change is inhibited by obstacles, bottlenecks and constraints. In economic terms, the supply of most things is inelastic." The view of the structuralists was that "to achieve development, (the) structure had to be changed, and to achieve rapid development (the) structure had to be changed rapidly."

Again, for Professor Little: '(t)he structuralists' view of the world provides a reason for distrusting the price mechanism and for trying to bring about change in other ways... (However), if short run reaction can negate the required price change, the long run never arrives. It follows ... that there is no such thing as a structuralist theory of growth" (Little, 1982, p. 21).

This is a strong statement, and seems to fly in the face of reality, for over the long run events have shown that structural problems prevail. If they were not solved, that is another matter. It does not invalidate the theory.

Dudley Seers was apparently a convert to structuralism. "The basic argument of the structuralists" - he wrote - "... (was that) inflation (and) related foreign exchange shortages... were attributable basically to supply inelasticities, in the face of widespread **political** (sic, my emphasis) pressures for development... (The) ability of those with strong bargaining power (especially monopolistic manufacturers and trade unions) to protect their real incomes propagated the primary inflation". (Seers, 1981, p. 14). He laid special emphasis on the external factors as contributing to structural rigidity and as preventing precisely the solution of structural development problems. He regarded them as largely uncontrollable, that is, a developing country rarely has the capacity to influence the policy of an industrialised country or of the so-called First World. According to Seers and others, fluctuations and other events - external economic constraints - have always derailed development plans; worse still, there have often been no contingency plans even in times of strong booms such as the oil boom of the 1970s, or - in more recent times for instance - the 1985-86 sharp decline in petroleum prices.[5]

Seers' views are in many respects similar to the ECLA view in the approach to development, and to the instinctive views of politicians. It does not mean that external aid (and trade) should solve any or all domestic structural problems, nor that the latter can be solved in isolation, without external aid and trade. It is part of the reality, and has to be weaved into the development policy considerations. Seers also dwells on the importance of population policy and the negative impact of military expenditures, which (in my opinion also) have never been taken seriously by the ECLA secretariat.

However, Seers ends, as does Little, on a note of caution and skepticism:

---

[5] A few countries in Latin America have at different times tried to establish "counter-cyclical" funds (Argentina, with some success in the 1930s; Venezuela, in the late 1940s, on paper only), or emergency or contingency funds (Mexico in the late 1970s). The Gulf War of 1991 spurred Mexico to put the higher proceeds of oil into a contingency budget fund.

"...we may have to face the very real possibility that human reality is so constructed that no model can be devised for its analysis (especially a dynamic one) which is both realistic and simple enough to provide a universal development ideology that could be applied with safety in any nation at all, especially if we allow, as we surely must, for demographic and geographical factors, as well as a range of economic and cultural (factors)." (Seers, 1981, p. 146).

Celso Furtado sees development as a transformation process that encompasses the whole of society. It relates to the creation of wealth and to efficiency, so that a fuller satisfaction of human needs may be possible. But the starting point is a certain structure, subject to a process of change. He ascribes a heavy weight to innovation, to values, and to the "social surplus" that makes further development possible but which is open to different allocations according to political and other pressures from the different social strata. The state plays a role in helping to create basic industries - with the help of moderate protectionism - as well as specialised financial institutions which otherwise would not come into existence. However, in practice transnational enterprises, owners and managers of know-how and R and D capability, which are also shrewdly able to use available domestic savings, end up by taking over the sectors with dynamic demand for their products. Nevertheless, state enterprises play the role of "socialising part of the costs of production", which helps modernisation in all sectors; they also assume responsibility where capital turnover is slower and economies of scale more important. Hopefully, they contribute to the process of capital accumulation (Furtado, 1983, *passim*).

For Furtado, "the industrial economies arising in the periphery within the import substitution framework are the result of an effort to pursue modernisation in the face of unfavourable external conditions" (Furtado, 1983, p. 161). Eventually, transnational enterprises, oriented to meeting final demand that is related closely to a new "style of development" predicated on high income concentration and low wages, take charge within the domestic market and may even engage in exports of manufactures. The manufacturing transnationals benefit from low wages in order to carry out a part of their production in the periphery. This is characteristic of the new international division of labor and of the modernisation process in a semi-industrialised developing economy. And herein lies the new role of the State in aiding this process but also in shaping a new social structure (Furtado, 1983, pp. 163-5).

Thus, an ambiguous role emerges for the state and, in fact, for developmentalism. For, to say the least, in so far as an industrialising economy begins to rely increasingly on exports of manufactures by transnationals - due to the narrowness of the domestic market - it follows that industrial operations must be internationally competitive and that macroeconomic policies, including the exchange rate policy, must be consistent with this purpose. In recent terminology, "real" rates of exchange must prevail. Here, in my view, we see the seeds of a transition to a market-oriented industrial development as it now appears to be shaping up in the major Latin American countries (and which has already taken place in Southeast Asia and the Pacific Rim countries).

Finally, Raúl Prebisch's thinking evolved from his early formulations. It is not possible here to make a full presentation of his critique of neo-classical economics as applied to the developing economies of the "periphery", and of his advocacy of a transformation which should fully take into account market forces but which should emphasise increasingly a new role for the state in influencing the use of the "social surplus" to deal with the structural problems of development, including the social ones (Prebisch, 1981).[6] Suffice it to say that he recognises the extreme complexity and distortions that arose (in Latin America) under the previous developmentalist approaches, with an abusive role played by the state and sore neglect of inequality, but also with increasing conflict among business (transnational and local) and labor interests, and the public sector, in their struggle to appropriate a lion's share of what the economies could be capable of generating as a social surplus for the benefit of wage-earners, peasants and others in the lower strata of society. The answer can only be found - Prebisch argued - in a (democratic) transformation of society involving new forms of enterprise based on incentives and on market signals, and on taxes and other disincentives to conspicuous consumption. The change must come from the bottom up but also from the top down. The state has to engage in "collective rationality" to assist this process, even through "the planning of the surplus", but the role of the state must be cut down to size. All this seems rather Utopian, but that is Prebisch's final prescription and legacy.[7]

According to this new gospel of Prebisch, there seems to be no way out for developmentalism, except the reduced role of the state in promoting growth and development in a context in which market incentives are used to redress the inequities of previous development experience, as exemplified in Latin America. His ideas were largely developed and expressed, incidentally, before the external debt crisis of the 1980s and the severe adjustment processes that followed.

The ECLA Secretariat, in a report published in 1990, has apparently taken inspiration from Prebisch and in other analysts concerned with development,

---

[6] Much of his later writings dealt also with these issues; texts in English can be found in UN-ECLA publications, particularly in the *CEPAL Review* published in Santiago de Chile. Cf. also Hodara (1987).

[7] For a critical comment on the new Prebisch "thesis", cf. Hodara (1987, 1988).

and has also responded to the wave of neo-liberal approaches to development (UN-ECLAC, 1990). It purports to show the way to "(transforming) productive structures in the region in a framework of increasing social equity". ECLA interprets "productive transformation" as embracing actually several processes of change.[8] Through more open trade policies, short-term adjustments to lower the rate of inflation, reallocation of public sector resources, and rapid incorporation of technological innovations - under less government intervention and accepting stringent limitations on the scope of the public sector - the result is expected to be enhanced competitiveness of industry: international, regional and domestic. But "transformation" also appears to mean the **deliberate** expansion of manufacturing and other industries for the supply of international markets, with the aid of foreign direct investment and a redirection of domestic and international financial resources. Competitiveness is assumed to automatically enlarge the share of Latin American manufactured exports in world markets. In fact not much is said about the domestic market or about the intra-sector or inter-sector adjustment problems.

Moreover, "transformation with equity" seems to imply that the difficult process of turning around from inward-looking ultra-protectionism to outward, export-led industrial expansion, must take place at the same time that serious attention is given to programs to redress the long-standing inequality and poverty, and the ten-year backlog in the meeting of basic needs. Perhaps this is somewhat optimistic in present circumstances, for the indiscriminate opening to imports has hardly abated inflation but rather has contributed to a higher rate of open unemployment, adding to the problems of absorbing a high rate of increase in the labor force. Increased exports of manufactures and other "non-traditional" exports may or may not offset the expanded volume of imports. The Latin American economies are "late late exporters", to paraphrase Albert Hirschman. In any event, export-promotion certainly requires a concerted effort on the part of the state and private business and labour in breaking away from past patterns and engaging in new programs to induce the desired increase in exports. This will involve a change in the "management culture" of local private enterprise, especially-oriented technological research, and a policy towards the transnationals to induce joint ventures and technology sharing. So far it is the transnationals that are participating with a large share of the additional exports of manufactures. A ten-year lag in educational, health, housing, urban infrastructure, science and

---

[8] It is regrettable, by the way, that the expression **transformación productiva** in the title of the ECLA report has been rendered into English by the official translators as **changing production patterns**, which hardly does justice to the original concept or conveys the dynamic content.

technology and other basic aspects of development, will take some time to recoup under circumstances of financial stringency or austerity.

5. Is the Developmentalist Approach Merely in a State of Hibernation, or is it Moribund or Actually Already Dead?

A recent reformulation in terms of "neo-structuralism" has been made by Osvaldo Sunkel and Joseph Ramos (Ramos and Sunkel, 1991, pp. 15-32, 35-80). Is there an alternative to neo-liberalism and to the prescriptions emanating from the IMF and the World Bank (and others)? In their view, there is. A basic premise is to start from an assessment of a country's own potential and its ability to find new ways of insertion into a difficult but not impenetrable international context. The role of the state must be carefully evaluated in terms of its present crisis and of the need for deep restructuring. Social policies and their efficiency must be re-examined. Financial and tax policies must be reformed. And so on.

Neo-structuralism is seen by these authors not as an answer to the shortterm neo-liberal "solutions", but as a return to the notion that the central problems of underdeveloped are not due to economic policies but are endogenous or structural. There is need to move outward to a new transformation curve. The market thus needs to be supplemented by an active and dynamic action by the state that should promote markets that are lacking (e.g., long-term capital markets), strengthen incomplete markets (e.g., the "market" for technology), offset structural distortions (e.g. productive heterogeneity, high concentration of real assets), and compensate for market failures (e.g., economies of scale, externalities). Caution demands, also, that the new theory should not assume too much benefit from **dirigisme** nor should it disregard short-term policy requirements.

The new approach concurs with the renewed ECLA position on transformation with equity and tries to build on a renewed development strategy **"from within"**. To be guided simply by import substitution in the old sense would lead to a *cul-de-sac*. Options should be open to orient industrial development towards selected domestic and external markets in which the Latin American countries may have a special advantage. Such a strategy requires adequate financial support, which on the external side might come from reducing part of the debt service and channelling such savings into a reconstruction fund for economic and social development. Basic macroeconomic equilibria should accompany the whole process, which clearly implies adjustment programs. However, programs to alleviate extreme poverty should in any event have priority, as should also programs to create employment and to deal with the informal sector.[9] The mere functioning of the market is not expected to solve these issues. Exports of manufactures should be subsidised where necessary, and transnationals should be encouraged to export their manufactures. Neither agriculture nor environmental concerns should be left out of the strategy.

In my view, this brand of neo-structuralism does not yet seem quite convincing. It absorbs some of Prebisch's latter-day ideas, and goes a little further than the ECLA 1990 position, but it is not clear whether it is more than a sort of pragmatic adaptation of the old structuralism to certain realities of the new situation arising in the 1980s in the Latin American region, with much wishful thinking. If understood as a framework for a higher and qualitatively better rate of private and public investment, then perhaps it is helpful. It is a break, in any case, from the crude structuralism, based on the omnipresent and allpowerful state, that was supposed, some years ago, to generate a steady development process.

On the other hand, neo-structuralism contrasts with the gross advocacy of the free market and the private sector that comes from certain international agencies and other quarters. One particularly unfortunate assessment and recommendation for Latin America came from what I call, for short, the "Babukusi" Report (Balassa et al., 1986). Apart from insisting on an almost idealised version of the Pacific Rim paradigm, especially Korea, and from its indulgence in obvious exaggerations, overstating the case for export promotion strategies, this report fails to deal with the concept of development as such and even with the external debt problem. It seems to have had little influence.

But since this was merely a speculation by certain economists, let me refer to a recent article published by a World Bank Vice-president, Dr. Lawrence Summers (Summers, 1992, pp. 6-9). Although having in mind mainly Sub-Saharan Africa, he makes some bold generalisations, namely: in the developing world as a whole, 36 countries with a combined population of over half a billion people have actually regressed, because first, "national development failures are the fault of national policies - they cannot be blamed on a hostile international environment, or physical limits to growth", and second, "national policies have failed when governments thwarted progress, supplanting markets rather than supporting them". As simple as that!

---

[9] I have difficulty with poverty programs which are essentially designed to alleviate extreme poverty. From a humane point of view they are of course necessary and should be supported. The long-term question, however, is how to set in motion a development process that will permanently raise the income levels of the lower income strata and provide opportunities for individual initiative, thus preventing poverty from spreading and helping to eliminate it.

The author goes on to minimise the lack of foreign aid, the decline in the terms of trade, the lack of resources and the external debt burden - the latter being "a consequence, not a cause, of the miserable return (sic) that has been earned on the investments that debt financed". He blames war and the threat of war (in regions such as Africa), large budget deficits and overvalued currencies, government monopolies, punitive regulations, price controls on basic products, high tariffs and quotas, disastrous public management of enterprise due to intrusion of politics (Nigeria being a textbook example), overinvestment in new physical facilities, underinvestment in maintenance, neglect of human investment, heavy-handed government policies, subsidies and exchange controls.

His conclusion and recommendations: "Nations control their own economic destiny... At a minimum it is high time that as African governments act to provide a sensible framework for private production and cut wasteful spending, major creditors respond by negotiating substantial reductions in debt". It is essential that a large reduction in private (sic) and official debt be achieved for Africa, and that aid flows should increase, on condition that "resources are likely to be used wisely, not squandered on inappropriate industries, unnecessary public spending, or in support of overvalued exchange rates". The fear that attention is being turned to the former Soviet bloc is "overdone", and it is compounded by "the perception that too many African governments are 'kleptocracies' (sic)". Well, it may not be fair to compare these statements with some of the academic material I have quoted earlier, since they were not developed for academic consumption, but they clearly call into question their wisdom. I shall refrain from any other comment except to say that these are hardly the elements of a theory worthy of battle with developmentalism or neo-structuralism.

6. Conclusions ... of a Sort

I realise that I have probably omitted important statements in explanation of developmentalist views or directed at demolishing or modifying them. I have in mind mainly a general debt to the writings of Albert O. Hirschman, which range fairly widely into the non-economic aspects of development, that I unfortunately cannot go into here. I should like, however, before putting together a few concluding remarks, to recall a few basics insisted upon by one of the authors quoted earlier in this paper, Amartya Sen:

"...(The) following have been among the major strategic themes pursued (under development economics): (1) industrialisation, (2) rapid capital accumulation, (3) mobilisation of under-employed manpower, and (4) planning and an economically active state" (Sen, 1984, pp. 486-7). "Trying to interpret the South Korean economic experiment as a triumph of unguided market mechanisms, as is sometimes done, is not easy to sustain... aside from having a powerful influence over the direction of investment through control of financial institutions (including nationalised banks), the government of Korea fostered an export-oriented growth on the secure foundations of more than a decade of intensive import substitution, based on trade restrictions, to build up an industrial base... The pattern of South Korean economic expansion has been carefully planned by a powerful government." (Sen, 1984, pp. 493-4).

"(Despite) **average** achievements, the performances of different countries are highly divergent. There is still much relevance in the broad policy themes which traditional development economics has emphasised. The strategies have to be adapted to the particular conditions and to national and international circumstances, but the time to bury traditional development economics has not yet arrived." (Sen, 1984, p.495).

Sen goes on from there to discuss the need for social indicators, programmes, policies, entitlements and capabilities. "Ultimately, the process of economic development has to do with what people can or cannot do" (Sen, 1984, pp. 497-500).

From all the above I infer that development is a still a meaningful concept, not only in terms of economic improvement but in the social dimension which is both cause and effect. But developmentalism in practice was something different, which in some countries, especially in the Latin American region - and not only in the tradition of Ibero-American culture, witness Jamaica and Haiti - , involved irrational and inconsistent macroeconomic policies, including oversized and inefficient public sectors and overprotection for badly planned import substitution.

In my view, the worst features of developmentalism can and should be corrected. Such corrections, many of them painful socially and politically, do not invalidate a policy of development which includes government responsibility and overall coordination (planning) and takes into account the structural rigidities that cannot be resolved merely through the efficient functioning of the market. I believe a useful start has been made by the ECLA Secretariat's propositions of 1990 already referred to.

I cannot conceive of growth without structural transformation. This was long ago aptly described by Professor Colin Clark (Clark, 1940) and it appears in all works analysing modern development, in comparative census statistics and in comparative country studies. It means, briefly put, that a relative shift of output and the labor force from the primary to the secondary, tertiary and quaternary sectors takes place, while output and productivity rises in all sectors. Social change is largely meant to be the relative redistribution of income and property in favor of wage-earners or other groups earning low or subsistence incomes - the newly designated "poor" and "extreme poor" - , the strengthening of the weaker sectors of society through improvement of their material wellbeing and through education, health, housing and social protection programmes for their benefit and to raise their capability, and the enhancement of the share of these groups in the overall economic and social functioning of society. It is also essential that productive capacity - total factor productivity - should rise as a consequence of real capital investment and the incorporation of autonomous and imported technology, the evolution of financial and fiscal institutions to channel more real domestic savings and external savings into productive investment, and the creation of higher capacity to export goods and services in order to pay for imports of goods and services, especially of capital goods. To the above processes, there is great need to integrate value and ethical considerations regarding the role of individuals and of societal groups.

References

Balassa, B., G.M. Bueno, P.P. Kuczynski and M.H. Simonsen (1986), *Toward Renewed Economic Growth in Latin America*, Institute of International Economics, Washington, also available in Spanish.

Cardoso, F.H. and E. Faletto (1979), *Dependency and Development in Latin America*, University of California Press, Berkeley/Los Angeles, translated from Spanish.

Clark, C. (1940), *The Conditions of Economic Progress*, Macmillan, London.

Coatsworth, J. (1978), "Obstacles to Economic Growth in Nineteenth Century Mexico", *American Historical Review*, Vol. 83.

--- (1981), *Growth Against Development: The Economic Impact of Railroads in Porfirian Mexico*, University of Chicago Press, Chicago.

Cosío Villegas, D. and associates (1965-1980), *Historia Moderna de México* (A Modern History of Mexico), 10 Vols., Editorial Hermes, Mexico.

Díaz-Alejandro, C. (1988), "No Less Than One Hundred Years of Argentina Economic History plus Some Comparisons", Chapter 12 in: A. Velasco (ed.), *Trade, Development and the World Economy: Selected Essays of Carlos Díaz-Alejandro*, Basil Blackwell, New York.

Furtado, C. (1983), *Breve Introducción al Desarrollo: Un Enfoque Interdisciplinario* (Brief Introduction to Development: An Inter-disciplinary Approach), translated from the Brazilian edition, Fondo de Cultura Económica, Mexico.

Hirschman, A.O. (1968), "The Political Economy of Industrialization through Import Substitution in Latin America", *Quarterly Journal of Economics*, Vol. LXXXII, February, reprinted in: *A Bias for Hope*, Yale University Press, New Haven/London, 1971.

Hodara, J. (1987), *Prebisch y la CEPAL: Sustancia, Trayectoria y Contexto Institucional* (Prebisch and ECLA: Substance, Evolution and Institutional Context), El Colegio de México, Mexico.

--- (1988), "El capitalismo periférico tardío según Prebisch: reflexiones" (Late Capitalism in the Periphery, According to Prebisch: Some Thoughts", *El Trimestre Económico*, Vol. LV, No. 219, July-September, Mexico.

Little, I.M.D. (1982), *Economic Development: Theory, Policy and International Relations*, Basic Books, New York.

Maddison, A., and Associates (1992), *The Political Economy of Poverty, Equity and Growth, Brazil and Mexico*, Oxford University Press.

Myrdal, G. (1971), *Asian Drama: An Inquiry Into the Poverty of Nations*, abridgment by Seth S. King, Vintage Books, New York.

Palma, G. (1981), "Dependency and Development: A Critical Overview", in: D. Seers (ed.), *Dependency Theory: A Critical Reassessment*, Frances Pinter, London.

Prebisch, R. (1944), *El patrón oro y la vulnerabilidad económica de nuestros países* (The Gold Standard and the Economic Vulnerability of Our Countries), Jornadas, No. 11, El Colegio de México, Mexico.

Prebisch R. (1949), *El Desarrollo de la América Latina y Algunos de sus Principales Problemas* (The Development of Latin America and some of its Principal Problems), United Nations/Economic Commission for Latin America, Doc. E/CN.12/89, May 14, 1949; later reprinted in English and in Spanish in ECLA publications.

--- (1981), *Capitalismo Periférico: Crisis y Transformación* (Capitalism in the Periphery: Crisis and Transformation), Fondo de Cultura Económica, Mexico.

Ramos, J. and O. Sunkel (1991), "Introducción: Hacia una Síntesis Neo-estructuralista" (Introduction: Towards a Neo-structuralist Synthesis), in: O. Sunkel (ed.), *El Desarrollo Desde Dentro: Un Enfoque Neo-estructuralista para la América Latina* (Development From Within: A Neo-structuralist Approach for Latin America), Serie Lecturas, No. 71, Fondo de Cultura Económica, Mexico.

Reynolds, C.W. (1970), *The Mexican Economy: Twentieth Century Structure and Growth*, Yale University Press, New Haven, Conn.

Scheman, R. (1988), *The Alliance for Progress: A Retrospective*, Frederick A. Praeger, New York.

Seers, D. (1981), "Introduction" and "Development Options: The Strengths and Weaknesses of Dependency Theories in Explaining Government's Room to Manoeuvre", in: D. Seers (ed.), *Dependency Theory: A Critical Reassessment*, Frances Pinter, London.

Sen, A. (1984), "Development: Which Way Now?", Chapter 19 in: *Resources, Values and Development*, Harvard University Press, Cambridge, Mass.

Summers, L.H. (1992), "The Challenges of Development: Some Lessons of History for Sub-Saharan Africa", *Finance and Development*, Vol. 20, No. 1, March.

Sunkel, O. (1991), "Del Desarrollo hacia Adentro al Desarrollo Desde Dentro" (From Inward-looking Development to Development from Within), in: O. Sunkel (ed.), *El Desarrollo Desde Dentro: Un Enfoque Neoestructuralista para la América Latina*, Fondo de Cultura Económica, Mexico.

United Nations, Economic Commission for Latin America and the Caribbean (1990), *Changing Production Patterns and Social Equity* (in Spanish: Transformación Productiva con Equidad: La Tarea Prioritaria del Desarrollo de América Latina y el Caribe en los Años Noventa), Santiago de Chile.

Urquidi, V.L. (1964), *The Challenge of Development in Latin America*, Frederick A. Praeger, New York.

Explaining Economic Growth
A. Szirmai, B. van Ark and D. Pilat
© 1993 Elsevier Science Publishers B.V. All rights reserved.

The "Socialist Experiment" and Transformation Towards the Market

*Stanislav Menshikov**

Introduction

The economies of the former Soviet Union and Eastern Europe are in a deep crisis and some of them are on the verge of collapse. Falling real incomes and mass impoverishment are creating acute social tensions. Economic dislocations and controversies are helping aggravate ethnic conflicts, breed rising separatism, promote the disintegration of multinational states. The old socio-economic and political system, that was based on central planning, communist political monopoly and totalitarianism is undergoing a complete breakdown. A totally new internal situation is created and substantial changes are emerging in the global geopolitical picture.

A number of important issues are worth considering in this respect. Is the socialism-communism dead, as claimed by many authors? Was socialism a historical anomaly, a social order that was not viable from its very birth? If the transformation to a market economy is inevitable, can socialism adapt to the market, can they co-exist peacefully, or would "market socialism" be just another "cripple", a "half-pregnant lady", as some authors put it? Is transformation to a market-oriented system possible without experiencing economic recessions, crises, shocks? Whether crises can be avoided or not, what kind of economy and society is actually emerging as a result of the transformation?

The paper contains five sections. Section 1 compares the formal model of socialism followed by Soviet communists and later on in other socialist countries with the theoretical model described by Marx and Engels. The purpose is to show that it was an experiment with only one of the possible socialist models and that its demise cannot be construed as the final judgement of history on the fate of socialism in general. A full-fledged model of market socialism, for instance, was never implemented and tested.

Section 2 compares the formal, largely Stalinist, structure of "real socialism" with the informal, or real structure, that included both the bureaucratic managerial bargaining power lobbies and the shadow economy. The resulting structure of the economy and society was in many ways

---

* Currently Visiting Professor at Erasmus University Rotterdam.

completely different from what the Marxist theoretical model wanted it to be. This, then, rather than the formal socialist system, was the actual starting point for reforms aimed at its transformation.

Section 3 traces the steps made under Gorbachov and shows some of the reasons why both his economic policies and attempts at reform were largely destructive due to the fact that they were not only piecemeal and controversial, but also based on largely ignoring the major significance of the informal structure of "real socialism".

Section 4 continues the analysis of Section 3 into the Yeltsin period showing that the very sequence of reforms undertaken by his government, though different in direction and content from the Gorbachov reforms, makes the same error of ignoring the informal structure and the peculiar character of its transformation.

Section 5 explores the inertia of the socialist structure, formal and informal, and the effects it is having on the emerging new types of economy and society. As a result of unrealistic and ill-devised policies a perverse capitalism is developing which is too far from a free market, let alone a system that combines efficiency with social justice. A more realistic course to take in economic policies is suggested.

1. An Experiment in Non-Market Socialism

The type of centrally-planned economy that is now disintegrating was first set up in 30s in the former Soviet Union. In the 50s it was adopted, with modifications, in Eastern Europe and, with larger changes, in China, North Korea and later in Cuba. We shall confine ourselves largely to the Soviet model with the understanding that certain corrections and reservations should be made with respect to the other socialist countries.

It was always claimed by the Russian communists that they were following, with some adjustments, the theoretical model that Marx and Engels had suggested for a socialist society. There is some truth to this assertion. Both Lenin and most of his followers believed in nationalising most of the industry, all banks and land as necessary conditions for creating socialism. They were not so sure about farms. It was only later that Lenin suggested his plan for transforming private farms into co-operatives (Lenin, 1922). In any case, he and his followers were pretty certain that private property of means of production was inconsistent with socialism and should be largely eliminated. It could be tolerated for a certain time, as a *force majeur*, for economic and political reasons. This would be called the **New Economic Policy** (NEP) by Lenin.

The Stalinist model which was maintained from the 30s until the late 80s was thus a "two form" model that recognised state and co-operative (*kolkhoz*) property, as the only two legitimate forms of property consistent with "pure socialism". The establishment of this model and the elimination of private property were among the gravest errors and disservices to socialism that the Soviet communists ever committed.

They were also true to the Marxist faith when they tried to eliminate the market and the law of value from the new society they were building. This was, of course, in contradiction with reality. Even after the private sector was eliminated, employees of state-owned factories and organisations continued to receive compensation in cash money, not coupons or any other instruments of direct distribution. In fact, as the government quickly discovered, it was more practical to pay money wages than provide consumer goods in kind, since the latter tended to be in short supply. But, more importantly, due to money labour incomes a consumer's market was created with government retail trade units acting as sellers and state-sector employees as buyers.

Throughout the 30s Soviet economists failed to recognise this reality as a theoretical category. In 1940 Stalin startled the learned community by flatly stating that the law of value, and thus the market and commodity production remained under socialism and were consistent with it. In 1952, shortly before he died, Stalin reiterated this assertion (Stalin, 1952), thus completely negating Friedrich Engels, who claimed that there was no place for either commodity relations or money or the law of value, once socialist planning became the law of the land (Engels, 1878). But the market and its instruments were to remain subordinate to the plan.

Limiting the extent to which market relations and institutions were permitted to develop was a necessary condition to restrict consumption in favour of investment, defense and heavy industry. The non-market approach was instrumental in helping make "real socialism" chronically deficient in food and most consumer goods though, at least before the advent of Gorbachov, relative shortages tended to fluctuate rather than increase exponentially.

Thus, in eliminating private property and strangling the market, the Soviet communists were indeed following, with some deviations, the basic Marxist prescriptions. But not so when they built up the many-storied Babylonic Tower of government institutions vested with the task of managing a centrally-planned economy. Marx and Lenin never dreamed that the socialist state would become a Leviathan giving birth to a new ruling class of bureaucratic managers. In fact, they wrote enough to make one sure they wanted to avoid this outcome. But they did not foresee that once the non-private, non-market model became dominant, it would inevitably create the all-powerful bureaucracy they feared and detested.

The experiment that was pursued in the USSR and later in Eastern Europe was socialist only in a limited and formal sense. It was an experiment with a certain socialist model. The defeat of this particular model does not mean the defeat of all and any other socialist variants. It may be difficult politically and psychologically to return to a different socialist model very soon. But from the vantage point of a scholarly approach it should be clear that socialism *per se* is neither dead, nor doomed. No untried model can be considered impractical unless put into practice and tested. Whether a fresh approach to creating socialism is feasible and when, is a separate issue which is not our immediate concern in this paper.

One further point needs to be mentioned. In the recent past experiments with different variants of the socialist model also took place, particularly with those called "market socialism". In practice, this meant a limited introduction of the private sector in small-scale industry and retail trade and granting state enterprises more freedom in making their own business decisions. Hungary can be credited with the longest experience in "market socialism" dating as far back as 1968. A different variant was followed in China and Yugoslavia, and some elements of it have been tried in Poland and the Soviet Union. Janos Kornai (Kornai, 1990) claims that these experiments have been unsuccessful in all cases and that, therefore, no further attempts in this direction should be made anywhere. There is no real choice, he claims, between market socialism and capitalism. The only alternative left is to move away from socialism.

This, however, is an ideological position rather than a scientifically proven fact. The Hungarian experience, as Kornai shows in a number of his previous works (Kornai, 1986), is not so much that of market socialism in any true sense, but rather a variant of "liberal Stalinism" in which the state controlled most of its enterprises by indirect and invisible means rather than by direct intervention and directives.

As to China, it is doubtful or, at least, premature to conclude, that its experience is "unsuccessful". Its economy continues to grow rapidly, living standards are improving, the environment for foreign private investment is mostly favourable. In Poland only a limited version of market socialism was used in the 70s and 80s under the Communists and no true market was set up. In the USSR under Gorbachov there was more talk about the market than actual deeds, so that this example proves nothing.

2. The Starting Point: Whatever Became of "Real Socialism"?

From our short discussion of the Soviet model it is already clear that the society built on that basis was not strictly the model that Marx or Engels had in mind when they conceived "scientific socialism". The real structure was closer to a hierarchical and monopolistic managerial bureaucracy than to a society where workers were the ruling class. It retained the formal features of socialism: property was collective (owned by the public at large or by separate collectives) and the economy was run by central planning. For a while, at least until the early 60s, this was also largely true in a substantative way. But later on both collective property and central planning became somewhat fictitious. The non-private non-market system deteriorated into a semi-private non-planned system well before Gorbachov appeared with plans for its "perestroika". This point is crucial in understanding what kind of economy and society really failed in the former Soviet Union and Eastern Europe and what was the starting point of their transformation to the market economy.

The Soviet model had a formal structure which we have largely described above. But there was also an informal structure that became more important than the formal one though the latter was retained. Two elements of the informal structure are particularly important: bureaucratic bargaining power lobbies and the shadow economy.

Central planning was meant to keep the economy in balance without having to go through the vagaries of market competition to achieve equilibrium. The theoretical issue of whether this is at all possible in the absence of free pricing dates back to the early 20s and is still largely unresolved (Mises, 1920; Hayek, 1940; Lange, 1938; Friedman, 1984; Nove, 1983). The bureaucratic "solution" was to order the ministries and the plants within their domains to produce more than they were able to and to provide them with fewer material supplies and capital resources than were necessary to meet the planned quotas. Therefore, to bring their performance as close to the plan as possible, the ministries and plants had to either correct their official plans downward by influencing the right people at the appropriate level, or falsify their accounts by making phantom "additions" (the notorious *pripisky*), or over-exploit the clearly inadequate resources available and thus destroy them in the long run, or obtain more resources by every means, which necessarily involved peddling interests and working to acquire more power. Ministries became power lobbies fighting each other for more resources and more power.

The result was that the central plan that was initially meant to keep the economy in balance deteriorated into a register of the relative power of competing lobbies. Planned anarchy took over from planned equilibrium. A system that strove for more power to create even more power also lacked a built-in mechanism of self-correction and was inherently unstable. It became highly susceptible to crises caused by internal and external shocks and to catastrophes of various kinds. Given time, central planning deteriorated into a self-serving and highly inefficient bureaucratic system with a very weak potential for economic growth, technical progress and for provision of the well-being of the population. This transformation would have doomed the system even if it were not further corrupted by the shadow economy.

As a rule, the latter is treated in literature either as mafia groupings originating in economic cultures and traditions foreign to socialism (e.g. oriental societal values prevailing in Soviet Georgia or Uzbekistan), or as supressed private enterpreneurship fighting to survive inside the "two-form" system and even tending to correct some of its deficiences. Both approaches have a ring of truth in them. But I would go further and claim that the Stalinist model itself tends to create and re-produce the shadow economy and, in time, leads to the degeneration of the non-market socialist model.

The formal structure of "pure socialism" suggests that all ownership of the means of production is collective, or common. But this can be true only in the formal and very abstract legal sense. Actually, when everybody co-owns property, without definite provision for everybody to gain directly from this co-ownership and control it, the collective property becomes in effect owned by nobody. In the former Soviet Union and socialist Eastern Europe this was certainly the case. In such a property-less society assets that formally belonged to the state were *de facto* appropriated by persons or groups of persons who were in the position of actual control and management of these assets and who could use them, in part, for their own personal pecuniary benefit.

Under the "two-form" socialist model private appropriation of public property was completely illegal but practiced by the absolute majority of the managerial class. The typical manager of a plant would have part of his product officially unaccounted for and sold to customers with no revenues whatsoever accruing to the state. He would save part of his material supplies and then either sell them directly or produce even more unaccounted product. He accepted bribes and kick-backs for supplying clients with goods they were entitled to by the plan and even more bribes for doing so quickly and above the official allocation. He would also be able to sell some non-produced, or "phantom" goods to clients and account for them as real products and would share with the clients in the final proceeds from such sales.

As a result of these activities a growing part of factories formally belonging to the state became *de facto* private enterprises. This became the rule in most industries, whether they were consumer-oriented or not. Retail trade was a particularly susceptible area since it was selling for cash-money, unlike most other state enterprises. By the mid-Gorbachov period the shadow economy, according to my estimates, accounted for 15-20 per cent of Soviet GDP (Menshikov, 1990). Other private Soviet estimates are in line with this figure. Later on, when the formal system started breaking-up, the share increased to perhaps 25 per cent or more.

While the shadow economy corrupted the formal system, it did not improve its operation, as some authors claim. It added very little or close to nothing to the supply of goods and services produced and made available to the consumer. Far outweighing the positive contribution of the shadow economy, was its very definite negative contribution to the tendency to create more shortages. By using the resources that were intended for the formal economy it tended to make them less available for regular and legal production. By creating illegal incentives for managers it helped ruin their legal incentives to work better. The shadow economy was speculative, rather than creative. It aimed mainly for short-term financial gains. I do not know of a single instance where the shadow economy *per se* created a newer and better product than the official economy. To maximise profits, the shadow economy was interested in maintaining shortages and creating new ones. It was not simply appropriating the difference between the low government fixed price and the market clearing price. It was intentionally destroying free competition, dividing markets and creating monopolistic situations which produced a maximum return.

With the growth of the shadow economy under Brezhnev and particularly under Gorbachov the shortages of everything became much worse driving the economy to the brink of collapse. And it also resulted in the merger of the shadow economy operators with the managerial class, including the official authorities. A new ruling elite was born which became crucial in shaping the impending transition to a market economy.

In Eastern Europe, with the probable exception of Poland, the extent of corruption was much smaller than in the former Soviet Union. Living in Czechoslovakia and observing the adequate supply of meat in the shops I always wondered why? Then I understood the phenomenon that I called The Law of the Butcher: shortages tend to increase with the rise in the number of non-productive officials who have to be bribed. The non-private butcher in the socialist system starts with naive forms of private profiteering, i.e. he underweighs. If he does not exceed the marginal norm of the consumer's vigilance which is estimated at 5 to 7 per cent, he probably needs protection only from the local policeman for rare cases of excessive vigilance. But if more and more officials insist on "protecting" him, he will certainly reach a point when he will have to hide meat under the counter to be able to maintain his minimum level of profitability after paying-off the bunch of parasites. The Law of the Butcher applies, of course, to all goods, not just meat. In Czechoslovakia, a small country, the corrupted bureaucracy was smaller per capita and "per-butcher" so that the shadow economy in many areas tended to stay within the bounds of "naivité". Not so in the USSR or Poland.

This real structure, rather than the formal model of socialism was the starting point for reforms oriented towards a market economy.

3. Transformation: Plans and Reality

In most countries of Eastern Europe the Communists, while in power, were reluctant to change the formal structure too much unless they were forced to do so by political events, like those in Hungary (1956), and Poland (1956, 1970 and 1980). When they were thus forced to introduce "market socialism", they did so only within certain limits, taking care not to loose their political power. But in East Germany, Czechoslovakia, Romania, Bulgaria no drastic

changes occurred until the former communist regimes were overthrown. The
new governments that came in in 1989-1990, were mostly anti-communist and
did not wish to reform socialism at all for political and ideological reasons.
Their chosen course and stated goal was to move away from socialism and
effect a transformation to capitalism. The only issue was how to do it: in what
sequence, with what speed and intensity?

In the former Soviet Union where the communist regime largely survived
until late 1991 and where "perestroika" started much earlier (in 1987) the
dominant issue was how to reform socialism? Most economists and
politicians, at least until 1990, were thinking along these lines. All the
programmes that were put forward and publicly discussed were those of
transformation to the market, not necessarily to capitalism. They were
programmes for the creation of a new kind of socialism in which the private
sector would co-exist and compete with the public sector. The new model
would be that of a mixed economy but with prevailing socialist ownership and
liberalised central planning (Galbraith and Menshikov, 1988; Menshikov,
1990). None of these plans worked. Why?

First and foremost, because they were never fully put into practice. Many
changes occurred from 1987 to 1990 but of a less general magnitude. State
enterprises were given more freedom to plan their own production, but not to
set prices. Control by the ministries over factories was somewhat liberalised
but the production units still had to deliver most of their output to the
government in accordance with obligatory "state contracts". The controversial
nature of these measures led to open warfare between the plants and the
ministries and to the initial serious breakdown of clear lines of authority
within the formal structure. Later on, the ministries in charge of industries
were partly eliminated or reorganised into state "concerns". The private sector
was permitted, initially under the guise of co-operatives, but with a lot of
legal and other limitations. It was a movement towards the market but
piecemeal and in a very cautious and inconsistent way.

Not belonging to the adventurist creed, I can personally only applaud the
cautious approach if it is realistic and consistent. The trouble with the
Gorbachov reforms was not so much that they were cautious and piecemeal,
but that they were in many ways unrealistic and destructive. The most
destructive element was the absence of any serious effort to consciously create
a market infrastructure by which I mean, first and foremost, freely competing
commercial wholesale trade companies in all sectors of the economy and
territorial units. It is clear that there can be no normal circulation of goods in
a market economy without wholesale trade. Once centralised distribution is
eliminated (and it was eliminated step by step), the circulation of goods is
bound to be largely disorganised due to the absence of trade intermediaries.
And this is exactly what happened even before the country, as a federation,
started to fall apart into separate states. Barter between factories became a

rule. Many saw the principal reason in "bad money". The real reason was the absence of a market infrastructure.

Even before trying to reform socialism, Gorbachov, on the advice of Abel Aganbegian and others (Aganbegian, 1988) attempted to accelerate economic growth by making investment in machine-building and heavy industry a top priority at the expense of the consumer sector. An attempt was made by re-allocating capital investment from the production of consumer goods to the heavy industry and machine-building sector to accelerate overall economic growth. This initial Gorbachov policy did not succeed in ending stagnation, but helped reduce consumer supplies, both domestic and imported, overstrained the government budget and started off a series of unprecedentedly large budget deficits that eventually ruined government finance and money circulation.

According to official data, average annual GDP growth in 1986-1990 was down to 2.3 per cent as compared to 3.6 per cent in 1981-1985. More realistic private estimates showed zero growth continuing and then turning into negative growth in 1989-1990 (Narkhoz, 1989). Average annual government budget deficits were only 7.6 billion roubles in 1981-1985, but 80.8 billion roubles in 1986-1990, an increase of more than ten times (Izvestia, 1992). By 1989 the deficit exceeded 12 per cent of the GDP, a catastrophically high level (Menshikov, 1990). Gorbachov's greatest error in pursuing this policy was, perhaps, his misunderstanding of the informal system of bureaucratic power bargaining. Acceleration, as a grand strategic planning operation, could not work because there was, in fact, no real central planning left.

The other major mistake was Gorbachov's misunderstanding of the increased importance of the shadow economy. When he initiated the anti-alcohol campaign in 1986, little did he realise the destructive consequences. The state budget lost a significant part of its revenues (close to 10 per cent) derived from the turnover tax on vodka; the formal economy was not able to provide other consumer goods to fill the fiscal vacuum created; but, most importantly, the shadow economy grabbed the opportunity to make large profits for itself by expanding the production of illegal alcohol and by buying up and reselling whatever remained of government alcohol, now in great shortage, at very high black market prices. A further consequence was that sugar, never in short supply before "perestroika", suddenly became scarce because of its additional use for producing illegal alcohol and as an additional object of shadow market operations. The vodka and sugar bonanzas started off a series of other artificially created and never fully explained shortages unheard-of under Gorbachov's predecessors. The government's experiments created an extremely profitable environment for the illegal private sector. Estimated gross revenues of the shadow economy grew from 52.5 billion roubles in 1980 to 74.3 roubles in 1985 and 120 billion roubles in 1989, a sharp escalation in the Gorbachov years (Menshikov, 1990).

Something similar happened with the appearance of the co-operatives. Gorbachov's idea was to open-up personal initiative and introduce enterpreneurship under a collective, presumably socialist, flag. He was, alas, still thinking in Stalinist categories of permitting only two forms of socialist property, state and collective. But the co-operatives that appeared in 1987-1988 were mostly private partnerships or family firms. For some shadow economy operations this was a good opportunity to legalise, a new channel for speculative rather than productive activity.

Most co-operatives centered their activities not so much on producing new goods and services but rather on extracting profits out of shortages and good connections. Since co-operatives could legally sell their products at market prices, they also started repeating the old trick of buying up government-produced or imported goods at official prices plus a kickback to the producer or distributor and reselling them through co-operative outlets at monopolistic prices. This practice led to the sharp deterioration of the regular supply of consumer goods sold through state-owned retail outlets, created additional shortages and started off a new wave of inflation. This activity would very soon completely disorganise and cripple the consumer market.

To make a long story short, Gorbachov's reforms were clearly unrealistic and based on a gross misunderstanding of the nature of the "illness" that these policies were supposed to cure. It was as if laxatives were prescribed to a patient who suffered from insomnia and needed sleeping pills instead. With the wrong diagnosis it was no wonder that the sick man was very quickly approaching a condition when only intensive therapy could help him survive.

Does this prove that reformist policies were impractical and out of order, at all? There is no hard evidence to support this claim. Other leaders with better professional advice could have had done a better job. Gorbachov could have started with reforms in agriculture and with policies to promote consumer goods supply rather than with "acceleration" and the accent on heavy industry. His reform to give more freedom to state enterprises could have been more consistent and less contradictory. He could have sought to eliminate the bureaucratic ministries earlier than he did and make special efforts to create a market infrastructure, including wholesale trade. He could have made a special effort to de-monopolise rather than permit the reorganisation of the ministries into new monopolies. He could have permitted private enterprise at an earlier stage and created a favorable policy environment for the operation of those co-operatives that were willing to produce more rather than to speculate on price differentials and artificially created surpluses.

4. Transformation: The Yeltsin Approach

When Gorbachov's reforms proved to be unsuccessful, his days were doomed and it was only a matter of time before he would be deposed. But the Gorbachov-Yeltsin struggle for power throughout 1991 had the additional effect of totally disorganising the economy. Not only was the Union falling apart politically, but the governments of the republics, while still formally within the Union, and particularly the Russian government, went on a spending spree while failing to provide for the necessary tax revenues. Together with high federal spending this raised the total budget deficit to 394 billion roubles, a three-fold increase in one year. Money in circulation rose from 139.4 billion roubles at the end of 1990 to 263 billion roubles at the close of 1991, a 89 per cent increase (Izvestia, 1992). Inflation leaped to 300 per cent from an annual rate of 15-20 per cent even before prices were liberalised by Yeltsin. Inflationary expectations brought about even greater shortages. Output was collapsing. The economy got out of hand.

The advent of Yeltsin to power in late 1991, signalled something totally new in the country: the refusal to follow socialist reforms and a decision to move away from socialism at any cost. Not surprisingly, Yeltsin embraced "shock therapy" as suggested by Jeffrey Sachs. Whether or not he himself realised the full implications of his decision, is a different matter. Those who formulated the policy took the conscious decision to start with "liberalising prices" not because this would lead to economic stabilisation soon, but because they thought it would help create the economic foundations for a capitalistic society on a crash basis.

In fact, no stabilisation came about. In early 1992 prices rose by another 7-10 times, leaving wages far behind. Up to 80 per cent of the population found their incomes falling below poverty levels. Personal consumption decreased by 40 per cent Shortages persisted in spite of drastically lower demand. Producers and traders preferred to reduce output and supply rather than lower prices. It was difficult to believe that the government was really expecting to stabilise the economy this way.

In simple terms, the Yeltsin reforms, seen from a longer-term perspective, are meant to redistribute income and wealth in such a way as to promote a new enterpreneural class and to eliminate the general feeling of job and income security enjoyed by the working population in a society with practically full employment and a developed welfare state. Whether this rough experiment in "capitalism-creation" and "primitive accumulation" was actually needed is highly doubtful. The shadow economy, as it grew under Brezhnev and particularly under Gorbachov, was already rich enough to take care of itself.

In technical terms, there was also the difficult issue of the sequence of measures to be implemented on the way to the market. The two basic measures are, of course, economic stabilisation, where necessary, and creating the private sector. It is fairly obvious from East European experience that privatising is a difficult matter that can only proceed slowly. Kornai believes it will take at least twenty years to reach the point at which the private sector is dominant in the economy (Kornai, 1990). Perhaps, the Czechoslovakian "coupon privatisation", which aspires to make every citizen a small-scale shareholder fast, may introduce some corrections. But unless the economy is sufficiently privatised and de-monopolised it is hard to see how a free competitive market can really work.

Stabilisation in this context means gaining short- and medium-term equilibrium by means of fiscal, monetary and price policy. It cannot wait for privatisation to be completed. On the other hand, to be truly successful, price liberalisation, for instance, needs a substantial private sector to be in place and the government sector thoroughly de-monopolised. Otherwise it leads to abnormally high initial price leaps which tend to impoverish the majority of the population and create unaffordable social tension. That is why, I believe, attempting price liberalisation in Russia before privatisation took place was a gross misjudgement on the part of the Yeltsin government. In Poland the outcome was better due to the ability of the private sector to quickly increase the supply of consumer goods. No such possibility was available in Russia and other parts of the former Soviet Union.

However, stabilisation by fiscal and monetary policies could proceed from the very beginning without having to wait for anything else. In fact, in the Soviet Union it should have been started as soon as the first "socialist-reformist" measures were taken. These policies are very much the same in market and non-market economies: cutting military expenditure, improving the tax system, separating commercial banking from central bank money management, pursuing restrictive credit policies, introducing a free foreign exchange market. The fact that the communist authorities and their economic experts did not follow this course is explained partly by the failure to understand the proper means of macroeconomic management and also by their fear of "rocking the socialist boat" too much. Military expenditure was cut too late, capital investment financed from the central budget was reduced only marginally, the new tax laws were inadequate, interest rates were raised reluctantly and too late again, and the currency exchange system was kept intact for no reason at all. And so, instead of getting closer to the equilibrium, the system was floating further and further away from it.

The greatest difficulty in stabilising the Soviet economy was and still is striking a balance between supply and demand of consumer goods. Apart from attempting to import more consumer goods by earning more hard currency there are a few different ways of approaching this issue. One, and probably the easiest, is to reduce consumer demand. This can be done by by inducing the public to buy state-owned assets or gold or invest in government securities, or, in its more radical versions, by a monetary reform which would destroy the "money overhang", or by sharply raising prices through administrative measures or through price liberalisation. The latter road is the most brutal because it destroys current real incomes along with accumulated past savings and serves as a continuous, rather than a one-time rip-off.

The more difficult way is to try to increase supply of consumer goods. In principle, raising prices or having them liberalised should stimulate additional supply. But this is true only in a freely competitive market, not in one dominated by government or private monopolies. In the former Soviet Union state-owned firms are unable to follow the price signals for various reasons: they are restricted in their capacity to expand quickly; they are not sure their additional income will not be taxed away by the government; they are uncertain about prices of the materials they need to buy to produce more. The private sector is reluctant to invest in production because it is less risky and more profitable to operate quick commodity or financial deals in the politically and economically unstable situation of "transition". For these reasons higher prices do not lead to higher supply. And, when and if incomes catch up with price increases, the shortages, which are temporarily reduced by higher prices, tend to reappear and make new price rises inevitable.

Unless supply is increased, there is no way the stabilisation package will work. The greatest task of any government that attempts transition to the market is to find ways of promoting production of consumer goods. The Gorbachov government (under Prime-Minister Ryzhkov) tried to do it by decree. It did not work. It tried to do it by raising prices (under Pavlov). No reaction. It offered paying hard currency to the farmers for extra deliveries. Still little, if any response. Yeltsin liberalised prices. Supply fell instead of rising. Why?

Apart from other reasons, the answer is that Russia is in transition to a system that is not free market capitalism, but a continuation of the preceding structure that dominated the economy. Pro-market reforms have destroyed many remnants of the old formal structure of central planning and distribution. But they are far less effective in destroying the informal structure. The bureaucratic power lobbies and the shadow economy operators are still there. Moreover, their economic power and ability to exploit shortages has increased. It will take much more effort than the current reforms envisage to have their practices destroyed and induce them to convert to more civilised forms of economic behaviour.

5. Where Are We Transitting to?

Any economic structure has great inertia. It will not change on a leader's whim. Years and even decades will be needed to change it by well prepared reforms. These reforms have to take into account the inertia of both the formal and informal business structures left over from the centrally-planned economy. Reforms cannot be based simply on a primitive desire to destroy the previous structures. But some reformers in the former Soviet Union and in Eastern Europe are thinking exactly in this simplistic way. "Shock therapy" is claimed to be the "easiest" way of destroying the old and bringing about a new system. But is it not some kind of reverse "neo-bolshevism"? The communist anthem ran as follows: "We will destroy the old world to its foundation, and then we will build a new world". Very soon, though, they discovered from sad experience that the dead system was holding on to the new one and not letting it go. They had to re-introduce private property and the market, if only for a while. Something similar is happening with the current reverse transition. Both the formal and informal structures of the "two form" model are imposing themselves on the market and will continue to do so for quite a while.

As shown above, the pro-market reforms largely destroyed the centralised planning and distribution system. But the state monopolies remained largely untouched. Ministries and their sub-divisions were largely reorganised into monopolistic "concerns" that were even less controlled from above than the former ministries had been. The concerns did not have to ask for money from the central government budget and they had no parliament to account to. They became, for all practical purposes, self-controlled monopolistic managerial structures. The demise of the Communist Party changed nothing in this respect, except that it destroyed yet another controlling and profit-sharing nuisance.

Any policy of transformation, if it is to be realistic and effective, has to know how to deal effectively with this reality. Price liberalisation will not work if monopolistic managerial structures are still in control of the economy. The monopolies will not be bound by any obligation to act as freely competing units. They will continue to exploit shortages, charge monopolistic prices, remain largely price-inelastic as far as supply is concerned and will readily pass on to the consumers any upward price shock originating in the economy whether it comes from the government, the volatile currency exchange market or from anywhere else. They will continue to act as a powerful inflation-prone economic engine.

Privatisation, to be effective, should take special pains to first separate monopolies into competing but technically viable units. Then it has to be seen that the principal stockholders of the competing units are different from one another. Former monopolies (and the new private commercial structures) tend to buy large chunks of each others' shares and thus become interlocked financial-industrial groupings which are even more powerful than production monopolies. Policies will have to be devised limiting the powers of these groupings and their ability to dominate markets.

The other process to have in mind is the transformation of the former shadow economy into a legalised private sector. The Russian private enterpreneur of today is largely yesterday's shadow operator. Those who formerly reaped their benefits working from within the former state-owned sector have now either stayed in their old positions and transformed their former illegal methods of profiteering into legal ones inside the new monopolies, or chose to create their own new businesses ("commercial structures") outside of managerial monopolies. The best known cases of building up large fortunes have occurred exactly in this area. As to shadow operators whose main business was outside the formal structures, they largely formed the ranks of new entrepreneurs in their old spheres of interest: retail trade and consumer services. Finally, a large number of people, mostly but not necessarily young, who had no part in the former shadow economy, eagerly joined the ranks of the new entrepreneurs by becoming commercial bank managers, commodity brokers, etc., and quickly learned to make significantly more money than they ever could have in their former occupations. Many people fled into private business from the academia, universities and other respectable institutions. Rapidly rising prices and meager salaries in their old occupations led them to change their professions and way of life in a dramatic way.

While many of the newcomers are largely unspoiled by previous experience, a much larger part of the new private sector is formed by the former shadow economy. It is very difficult for them to shed their old ways. They were always profiting from shortages and monopolistic pricing, not from producing or selling in large quantities. The idea of selling bigger quantities at relatively low profit margins is foreign to their particular culture. Bribing and kickbacks are their natural way of doing business. They are quickly corrupting the new "democratic" and "anti-communist" authorities because in the current difficult economic environment and absence of a developed market infrastructure they see it as the only way of getting things done. One knowledgeable observer recently estimated that 85 per cent of the new officials he has to deal with are bribe-takers, while the remaining 15 per cent are "bribe-demanders". Many new commercial structures are thriving only due to good connections with the new authorities. It is a peculiar new form of state-capitalism, not too different from the former pseudo-socialist system of corruption.

It is a very unattractive, corrupted and in many ways perverse capitalism that is emerging instead of the old "two-form" model. It is perverse because it lacks the civilised features of the largely capitalistic mixed economy that is prevalent in the West. It is in many ways the same informal Stalinist model, but devoid of its communist-Marxist ideology and therefore quite cynical, shamelessly greedy and not constrained even by modern capitalistic ethics.

Can this be changed? Yes, but not quickly. One way has already been mentioned: breaking up the monopolies in the course of privatisation and seeing to it that new ones do not emerge. A second group of measures is to consciously create and promote wholesale trade companies which would be competitive with one another from the start.

I disagree with Kornai who claims that state-owned companies in a predominantly state-owned economy will never be bound by the hard-budget constraint and that the formerly centrally-planned countries will have to re-live through the painful experience of developing capitalism from the predominantly individual private proprietor all the way upwards to the modern big and impersonal, but private corporation (Kornai, 1990). Formally independent government companies may happen to be big spenders under a sympathetic government largely controlled by the same managerial bureaucracy. Under former Communist governments this may have been the rule. Under the non-Communist governments it need not be so.

A third group of measures should be specifically aimed at restoring price elasticity of supply. In a recent publication (Menshikov, 1990) I suggested that the producing and trading units would have to be induced to increase their profits by raising output and sales volumes rather than raising prices. This does not mean that prices should remain what they were in the past, i.e. largely unflexible. A price reform that would change relative prices is necessary to bring them in line with costs and international price structures. But after this has been achieved there should be a lengthy controlled price learning period in which the production and trading units will learn to work with greater volumes and slimmer profit margins. It is crucial that these units fully benefit from such activities and are certain that their profits are not taxed away.

Is it not too late in the day to pursue such corrective measures? I do not think so. It is much better to assist government and private firms in determining what their proper prices should be than hope for the perverted market to teach them this lesson. It is not the private enterpreneur, though, who suffers most from "perverted capitalism". It is the population at large. It is unnecessary and socially dangerous to drive it into mass impoverishment for the sake of some "pure market" utopia.

Conclusions

1. It is far too early to consider socialism to be dead. The "demise of communism" is the result of the disintegration of a particular case, the "bi-form" Stalinist non-market model of socialism. Other forms, particularly the different possible forms of "market socialism" have not, as yet, been adequately tested. They may turn out to be viable and may have a better role to play in the future.

2. When considering economic policies meant to transform socialism due account has to be taken not only of its formal structure, but also of the

informal structure. Policies and reforms that ignore this reality have helped de-stabilise the former centrally-planned economies and made it impossible to effect a relatively smooth transformation, rather than a "crash landing" which is erroneously believed to be the "price" of socialistic experiments.

3. Due to the strong inertia of economic systems, transformation has to be looked upon as a relatively slow process in the course of which the existing structures can only gradually adjust to new conditions created by government policies and reforms. Ignoring this inertia leads to unforeseen and undesirable effects, including the emergence of perverse structures, increase of economic and social insecurity and political instability. A closer look is necessary into the nature of future economic structures and societies, their mutual interaction and integration.

References

Aganbegian, A. (1988), "Soviet Economy: A Glance into the Future", *Ekonomika*, Moscow.

Bukharin, N. (1928), *The Politics and Economics of the Transition Period*, (English edition: Routledge & Kegan Paul, (1979), London.

Engels, F. (1878), *Anti-Duhring*, English edition: London (1934), latest German edition (1971), Frankfurt.

Friedman, M. (1984), *Market or Plan?*, Centre for Research into Communist Economics, London.

Galbraith, J.K. and S. Menshikov (1988), *Capitalism, Communism, Co-Existence*, Houghton Mifflin, Boston.

Hayek, F. (1940), "Socialist Calculation: The Competitive 'Solution'", *Economica*, New Series, Vol. VIII, No. 26, pp. 125-149.

Ivestia, (1992), March 5, p. 2.

Kornai, J. (1986), "The Hungarian Reform Process", initially published in 1986, reproduced in: J. Kornai (1990), *Vision and Reality, Market and State*, Routledge.

Kornai, J. (1990), *The Road to a Free Economy*, W.W. Norton, New York and London.

Lange, O. (1938), "On the Economic Theory of Socialism", in: O. Lange and F. Taylor, *On the Economic Theory of Socialism*, University of Minnesota Press, Minneapolis.

Lenin, V. (1922), "On Co-operatives", reproduced in: V.I. Lenin (1960), *Collected Works*, Politizdat, Moscow.

Mises, L. (1920), "Economic Calculation in the Socialist Commonwealth", in: F.A. von Hayek, (ed.) (1935), *Collectivist Economic Planning*, Routledge & Kegan Paul, London, originally published in German in the *Archiv für Sozialwissenschaften* (1920).

Menshikov, S. (1991), *Catastrophe or Catharsis, The Soviet Economy Today*, Inter-Verso, Moscow.

Narkhoz, (1989, 1990), *Narodnoie Khoziaistvo* (USSR Statistical Yearbook), Statizdat, Moscow; *Annual Reports* of Goskomstat (USSR Government Office of Statistics).

Nove, A. (1983), *The Economics of Feasible Socialism*, Allen & Unwin, London and Boston.

Stalin, J. (1952), *Economic Problems of Socialism in the USSR*, Gospolitizdat, Moscow.

Author Index

Abramovitz, M. 2, 6, 10, 41, 43, 56, 104, 105, 186, 295, 340, 342
Abu-Lughod, J.L. 201
Adelman, I. 415, 418
Aganbegian, A. 475
Aghion, P. 107, 108
Alcaide, J. 286, 287, 289
Ames, E. 105
Anderson, D. 84
Ark, B. van 4, 18, 24, 25, 171, 173, 219, 221, 227, 237, 345, 407
Arrow, K. 107

Baily, M.N. 51, 440
Bairoch, P. 287
Balassa, B. 361, 451, 461
Barro, R. 8, 148, 295, 406
Barry, N. 414
Bauer, P. 422
Baumol, W.J. 186, 294, 295, 368, 422, 423
Becker, G.S. 9, 45, 58
Beckerman, W. 5, 23, 41, 42, 53, 331, 332, 334-336, 346, 347, 385
Bellwood, P. 196, 197
Benhabib, J. 149
Blackman, S.A.B. 186, 368
Blades, D. 4, 24, 25, 390, 393, 394
Bliss, C.J. 131
Bombach, G. 378, 379, 386, 387
Boomgaard, P. 1, 3, 14-17
Booth, A. 195, 210-212
Brinkman, H.J. 267
Briscoe, J. 86
Broadberry, S.N. 327, 332, 377
Brugmans, I.J. 267
Buchanan, J. 423

Buyst, E. 271

Cairncross, A. 47, 58
Cardoso, F.H. 19, 453
Carreras, A. 287-289
Cas, A. 52
Cette, G. 406
Chaudhuri, K.N. 199
Chenery, H.B. 295, 455
Christensen, L.R. 7, 51, 55, 178, 185, 186
Christie, J.W. 196-199, 201, 202, 204
Chung, W.K. 53, 54, 138, 171, 173-175, 177-180, 185
Chung, A. 148
Clark, C. 375, 463
Clark, J. 103, 108
Clemens, A.H.P. 210
Conrad, K. 379
Cornwall, J. 104
Corrales, A. 286, 288
Costello, A. 328, 336, 347
Crafts, N.F.R. 3, 5, 13, 15, 18, 21, 22, 287, 295
Csernok, A. 302
Cummings, D. 7, 178

Dabán, T. 287, 289, 291, 295, 296
Daly, D. 43, 53
Dasgupta, P. 93, 96, 331, 339, 340
David, P.A. 74, 158
Denison, E.F. 2, 6-10, 14, 18, 132-135, 137, 138, 142, 171, 173-175, 177-180, 185
Dholakia, B.H. 54, 55
Dollar, D. 379

Donges, J.B. 285
Dore, R. 190
Dowrick, S. 13, 104, 295, 340, 341
Drechsler, L. 378, 384
Drukker, J.W. 267
Dubois, P. 44

Ehrlich, I. 8
Ehrlich, E. 3, 20, 21, 29
Eisner, R. 131
Engels, F. 467-470
Englander, A.S. 171, 343

Fabricant, S. 41
Faerber, H.D. 382, 390
Faletto, E. 19, 453
Feinstein, C.H. 44
Ferranti, D. de 86
Foss, M. 50, 142
Foxley, A. 250
Fraile, P. 285, 286
Fraumeni, B. 51
Freeman, C. 103, 104, 108
Fremdling, R. 377
Furtado, C. 451, 457

Gemmell, N. 295
Gerschenkron, A. 102, 147, 186
Gilbert, M. 38, 42, 375
Gittleman, M. 114
Goldsmith, R.W. 134, 254
Gollop, F. 51
Gomulka, S. 104, 109
Gorbachov, M. 468-477, 479
Griffin, J. 94
Griffiths, R.T. 267
Griliches, Z. 50-52
Grossman, G. 107
Guger, A. 437

Habakkuk, H. 105
Hall, K.R. 197-199, 201
Halstrick, M. 406
Helliwell, J.F. 148
Helpman, E. 107
Heston, A. 4, 12, 18, 22, 23, 25, 42, 111, 115, 153, 156, 157, 290, 382,

383, 390
Hill, H. 217, 218, 220, 224-227, 233-236,
Hill, P. 383
Hirschman, A.O. 451, 459, 462
Hobsbawn, E.J. 105
Hodara, J. 451, 458
Hofman, A. 3, 6, 14, 18-22, 26, 28, 388, 401, 402, 407
Hofstede, G. 14
Holmes, M. 328
Hooper, P. 379
Howitt, P. 107, 108
Hulten, C.R. 49, 171, 173, 185, 406

Ishikawa, T. 189

Jánossy, F. 305
Jansen, H.P.H. 273
Jansen, J. 217
Jenkins, S.P. 333-335
Johnson, H.G. 141
Jones, A.M.B. 196-199
Jones, D.T. 379
Jonge, J.A. de 267
Jorgenson, D.W. 7, 37, 50, 51, 55, 57, 134, 135, 178, 185, 186, 379

Kamien, M. 107
Kanamori, H. 53, 56, 172
Kendrick, J.W. 2, 6-9, 37, 53, 56, 57, 174, 330
Kenessey, Z. 42
Keynes, J.M. 27, 429-438, 441, 442, 444, 445
Kim, K.S. 55
King, G. 375
Klein, P.W. 271
Kornai, J. 470, 478, 482
Korthals Altes, W.L. 210
Kramer, H. 406
Kravis, I.B. 22, 23, 42, 353, 354, 357, 358, 368, 369, 375, 377, 382, 383
Kregel, J. 4, 26-29
Krijnse Locker, H. 382, 390
Kux, J. 378

Kuyvenhoven, A. 217
Kuznets, S. 2, 9, 37, 41, 43, 102, 103, 147, 290

Laanen, J.T.M. van 195
Lal, D. 27, 422
Landes, D. 105
Larin, K.A. 379
Layard, R. 328, 329, 344, 345
Lenin, V.I. 468, 469
Leur, J.C. van 201
Levy, S. and D. 444
Lewis, M. 42
Lewis, W.A. 272, 455
Lichtenberg, F. 148
Lincoln, E.J. 189, 190
Lindblad, J.T. 210
Little, I.M.D. 447, 448, 454-456
Lucas, R. 8, 52, 58, 107, 342, 347, 417

Maddison, A. 1-4, 6, 10, 13, 15-17, 19-21, 23-25, 30, 37, 39, 41, 48, 57, 65, 77, 101, 102, 105, 106, 108, 115-117, 124, 138, 148, 153, 171-173, 175, 178, 179, 185-187, 195, 227, 241, 242, 250, 262-264, 271, 272, 290, 291, 305, 310, 335, 336, 341-343, 353, 375-379, 381, 385, 390, 393, 407, 408, 414, 415, 425, 426, 439, 449
Magnani, M. 406
Mahalanobis, P.C. 448
Malinvaud, E. 44-46
Mankiw, F. 11, 147, 148
Marer, P. 305
Martín Aceña, P. 285, 289
Marx, K. 69, 420, 467-470
Matthews, R.C.O. 44, 331, 347
McCawley, P. 217, 236
McGillivray, M. 93
McNeill, W.H. 199
Meadows, D.H. 79, 80
Meer, C.L.J. van der 19
Meere, J.M.M. de 267
Menshikov, S. 4, 26, 29, 30
Metcalf, D. 344

Meyer-zu-Schlochtern, F.J.M. 407
Mill, J.S. 419
Miller, J.I. 196
Minford, P. 347
Mises, L. von 426, 471
Mishan, E.J. 78
Mittelstadt, A. 171, 343
Mokyr, J. 271
Morellà, E. 288
Myrdal, G. 9, 454, 455

Nadal, J. 285
Naerssen, F.H. van 197, 201
Nagtegaal, L. 208
Nelson, R.R. 33
Nguyen, D.T. 13, 104, 340, 341
Nichols, T. 338, 344
Nishimizu, M. 171, 173, 185
Nohara, T. 249, 250
Nordhaus, W. 84, 95, 131, 336
North, D. 2, 9, 13, 14, 41, 45
Nurkse, R. 9, 455

O'Mahony, M. 8, 9, 25, 343, 383
Odling-Smee, J.C. 44
Ohkawa, K. 44, 53, 171, 172, 174, 175
Olson, M. 45
Ooststroom, H. van 377

Paige, D. 378, 379, 386, 387
Palma, G. 453
Park, J.K. 55
Pasek, J. 81, 95
Patrick, H. 53
Pavitt, K. 343
Peacock, A. 4, 26, 27
Pearce, D. 96
Pigou, A.C. 132
Pilat, D. 3, 6, 18, 19, 24, 220, 221, 227, 237, 377, 379, 381, 383, 384, 386, 388
Poot, H. 217-219, 235, 236
Posthumus, N.W. 276, 277
Prados de la Escosura, L. 3, 17, 18, 22
Prais, S.J. 342

Prasada Rao, D.S. 24, 383, 384
Pratten, C.F. 342
Prebisch, R. 28, 448, 449, 451, 453, 455, 458, 461
Prince, G. 3

Ramos, J. 460
Reid, G. 415, 416, 420
Reid, A. 199, 203, 204, 209
Révész, G. 301, 311
Ricardo, D. 361
Ricklefs, M.C. 203, 209
Riley, J.C. 267, 278
Robinson, E. 46
Robinson, J. 133
Roepstorff, T.M. 217, 218
Roman, Z. 37, 53, 55
Romer, D. 11, 147, 148, 421
Romer, P.M, 8, 13, 52, 107-109, 330, 347
Rosenberg, N. 104, 105
Rosenstein-Rodan, P. 454, 455
Rosovsky, H. 44, 53, 171, 172, 174, 175
Ross, D. 107, 413
Rostas, L. 24, 376-378
Roy, D.J. 379
Roy, A.D. 379
Rymes, T.K. 52, 53, 59

Sala-y-Martin, X. 148
Sánchez-Albornoz, N. 285
Sanz, J. 287, 289, 291, 295, 296
Scherer, F. 107
Schmitz, E. 406
Schultz, T.W. 9, 141
Schultze, C.L. 41, 51, 56
Schumpeter, J. 102, 103, 420
Schwartz, C.F. 107, 287
Scott, M.F. 37, 52
Scully, G. 27, 423-425
Seers, D. 28, 447, 448, 453, 455-457
Sen, A. 29, 447, 462, 463
Shinohara, M. 188, 379
Simon, H. 14, 73
Simpson, D. 288, 415
Singer, H. 29, 451, 455

Slot, B. 267
Smith, A. 26, 27, 58, 271, 413-420, 422, 423
Soete, L. 2, 4, 9, 11, 12, 22, 343
Solow, R 8, 9, 33, 42, 48, 50, 52, 106-108, 254, 330, 346, 347, 420, 421
Spengler, J.D. 87
Spiegel, M. 149
Stalin, J. 469
Steedman, H. 343
Stein, H. 37, 41
Stern, N. 415, 418, 419
Stewart, I. 413
Stone, R. 38, 58
Streissler, E. 421
Studenski, P. 375
Summers, L. 461
Summers, R. 4, 12, 18, 22, 23, 25, 42, 111, 115, 153, 156, 157, 290, '353-358, 368, 369, 382, 383, 390
Sunkel, O. 460
Syrquin, M. 295
Szilágyi, G. 390
Szirmai, A. 3, 16, 171, 221, 227, 378, 386, 388
Szpiro, D. 406

Taguas, D. 286, 288
Taylor, C. 94, 99
Teijl, J. 267, 273, 275, 276
Thatcher, M. 13, 15, 21, 22, 327, 328, 330, 331, 336, 338, 340, 342, 344-347
Thee, K.W. 218
Thomas, R.P. 67
Tobin, J. 95, 131, 336
Tortella, G. 285-287
Tunzelmann, G.N. von 105, 273

Unger, R.W. 273, 275
Uno, K. 7, 10, 171, 173, 188
Urquidi, V. 4, 20, 26, 28, 29, 241
Usher, D. 134

Vaizey, J.E. 45, 46
Verspagen, B. 2, 4, 9, 11, 12, 22

Viner, J. 451
Vries, J. de 267, 270

Wallerstein, I. 15
Walters, D. 43, 55
Warmington, E.H. 196
Weale, M. 93, 331, 339, 340
Weil, D. 11, 147, 148
Weisskopf, T. 344
White, B. 211
Wolff, E.N. 2, 4, 11, 12, 22, 114, 165, 186, 368, 379

Wolters, O.W. 196-198
Wright, G. 331

Yakushiji, T. 105
Yeltsin, B. 29, 468, 477-479
Yoshihara, K. 218
Young, A.H. 133

Zanden, J.L. 1, 3, 16, 17, 195, 210
Zeeuw, J.W. de 273, 275

Subject Index

Age-sex 175-177, 180, 182-184, 189
    age-sex composition 54, 177,
    182-184
    age-sex distribution 175
    age-sex effects 180, 184
Agriculture 15, 18, 21, 25, 83, 134,
172, 173, 175, 177, 179, 184, 188,
197, 204, 208, 211, 212, 270, 272,
278, 287, 296, 302, 307-309, 314,
377, 378, 449, 461, 476
    collectivisation 21, 308, 452
    irrigation 202, 206, 210, 211
    kolkhoz 468
    rice cultivation 15, 197, 198,
    202, 203, 206
Atkinson index 333-335, 346
Autarky 242, 290, 294, 318

Backwardation 430, 431, 434, 435
Backwardness 12, 18, 147, 186, 187,
286, 290, 294, 295
    backward countries 9, 104, 147,
    285, 363
    underdevelopment 28, 213, 286,
    290, 454
Balance of payments 451
Bargaining model 330
Borda rule 337, 340
Bretton Woods 250, 450
Bureaucracy 29, 69, 201, 419, 469,
470, 473, 482
    Bureaucratic bargaining 29, 319,
    471

Capacity 129, 132-134, 141, 307,
319, 434, 444, 464
    productive capacity 174, 187,

307, 434
    utilisation 6, 7, 50, 51, 134, 138,
    141, 142, 144, 179, 307, 310
Capital
    capital accumulation 19, 22, 138,
    204, 268, 278, 279, 295, 297,
    417, 438, 439, 457, 462
    capital compensation 129, 130,
    137, 138, 143
    capital consumption 38, 51, 129,
    138, 143, 177
    capital expenditures 435, 438,
    444
    capital flows 242, 243
    capital formation 13, 60, 173,
    187, 189, 190, 212, 262, 263,
    347, 347, 392, 393, 400, 421
    capital income 51, 177, 178
    capital intensity 25, 392-394, 454
    capital market 421
    capital share 129, 130, 137, 178,
    186, 254
    depreciation 23, 25, 26, 39, 51,
    52, 95, 131, 133, 134, 137, 138,
    218, 404
Capital stock 6-8, 10, 18, 20, 21, 25,
26, 38, 48, 49, 52, 95, 130, 131,
133, 134, 138, 141, 172-178, 184,
187, 242, 253, 254, 260, 262, 263,
392-394, 399-402, 404-408, 416, 418,
421
    asset lives 392-394, 404
    capital goods 131-133, 135, 138,
    142, 218, 278, 312, 392, 402,
    433, 434, 444, 464
    equipment 50, 131, 132, 254,
    263, 312, 314, 354, 400, 402,

403, 405, 406, 436
intangible capital 7, 53, 142, 143
inventories 48, 50, 133, 175-177,
182-184, 400
mortality function 407
non-residential capital 18, 172,
177, 182-184, 254, 260
obsolescence 49
perpetual inventory 25, 132, 133,
175, 254, 262, 392-394, 402, 406
rectangular retirement 175
replacement cost 400, 401, 407
residential capital 18, 48, 50,
172, 174, 175, 177, 178,
182-184, 254, 260
service lives 25, 26, 50, 254,
262, 392-394, 400, 402-408
standardisation 26
structures 50, 131, 133, 137,
254, 314
tangible capital 7, 8, 14, 77, 78,
130, 132, 135, 142, 392, 400
vintages 48, 49, 254, 401, 402
Capitalism 69, 218, 308, 420, 468,
470, 474, 477, 479, 481, 482
Catch-up 4, 6, 10-13, 18, 23, 101,
104-106, 109-116, 118-120, 122, 124,
141, 147-149, 154, 159, 179, 292,
294, 295, 315, 318, 319, 340-342,
344, 346, 387, 389
Census of production 204, 219, 221,
223, 224, 231, 377-379, 392
Cluster analysis 11, 111-115
Colonialism 14, 16, 19, 203
colonies 17, 206, 211, 244, 285
Competitiveness 376, 452, 459
Convergence 2, 4, 8, 10-13, 15, 17,
23, 24, 105, 110, 115-124, 147-149,
153, 154, 156, 158, 159, 164, 251,
286, 292, 294-296, 364, 368, 371,
372, 376
coefficient of variation 149, 150,
152, 290, 361
conditional convergence 11-13,
148
convergence coefficient 115, 116
entropy coefficient 116

unconditional convergence 11, 12,
148, 154
Convertibility 289, 322, 323
convertible currency 312
Co-operatives 468, 474, 476
Cost disease approach 368

Debt 77, 250, 278, 279, 310, 312,
315-317, 320, 322, 323, 429,
435-437, 443, 448, 458, 460-462
debt crisis 458
foreign debt 310, 320, 323
indebtedness 312, 315, 320, 437
Dependency theory 453
Developmentalism 26-29, 447-464
Divergence 1, 2, 4, 8-13, 15, 19, 24,
155-122, 125, 229, 251, 295
Diversification 200, 205, 269
Division of labour 37, 38, 69
Dualism 290
dual development 272
Dutch disease 212, 218

Economic growth
constraints on growth 79
extensification 210
extensive growth 195, 307
growth-exhausting model 21, 319
growth model 109, 319, 330, 415
growth theory 8, 9, 11, 13, 26,
52, 101, 103, 106, 108, 109, 342,
346, 347, 415
intensification 205, 208, 210
stationary state 271, 417, 419,
420
sustainable growth 81, 95, 96
Economic reform
liberalisation 29, 30, 218, 314,
421, 478-480
perestroika 471, 474, 475
privatisation 29, 30, 327, 328,
425, 438, 478, 480, 481
reforms 307, 319, 323, 468, 473,
474, 476, 477, 479, 480, 483
shock therapy 29, 322, 323, 477,
480
stabilisation 29, 118, 250, 301,

322-324, 477-479
 transition 26, 29, 258, 294, 301,
 319, 322-324, 458, 473, 479, 480
Economic structure 24, 25
 compositional effect 395, 404
 structural change 18, 101, 102,
 179, 186, 187, 285, 289-291,
 295, 345, 463
 structural differences 228, 295
 structural divergence 295
Economies of scale 6, 9, 10, 13, 40,
47, 48, 54, 68, 142, 179, 182, 183,
185, 186, 205, 280, 308, 457, 460
 (increasing) returns to scale 8-10,
 40, 106, 107, 421
 scale economies 69
Education
 educational attainment 12, 148,
 151-154, 156, 158, 159, 164-166,
 175
 educational levels 5, 12, 135,
 148-150, 152-154, 158, 159, 162,
 163, 252, 259
 educational requirements 46, 187
 enrolment 12, 148-166
Efficiency 13, 14, 20, 40, 46, 47,
69-71, 103, 142, 252, 259, 277, 294,
327, 334, 344, 416, 421, 425, 435,
457, 460, 468
 adaptive efficiency 14, 69, 70
 allocative efficiency 14, 70, 327
 efficiency offset 40
Energy 10, 17, 21, 44, 57, 82-85,
92, 97, 179, 190, 267, 268, 273-277,
280, 312, 318
 energy consumption 17, 83, 97,
 267, 273-276
Environment 5, 22, 56, 69, 70, 77-
97, 318, 336, 337, 339, 423, 461
Exchange rate
 appreciation 23, 357
 devaluation 218, 322
 effective exchange rate 366, 367
 real exchange rate 366
External effects 8, 13, 26, 69, 70,
74, 75, 78, 97, 107, 342, 347, 421,
436, 460

Factor endowments 294
Firm size 25

Global warming 5, 77, 82-84, 92, 97
 global climate 81, 82
 global environment 89
 greenhouse effect 77, 82
Government budget 27, 435, 437
 budget deficit 441, 477
Government expenditure 27, 268,
423-425, 444
 deficit spending 27, 429, 430,
 434, 437, 452, 475, 480
Government policy 14, 15, 19, 28,
187, 189, 434, 436
 budget policy 436
 development policy 447, 456
 economic policy 3, 4, 26-28, 30
 fiscal policy 421
 government control 211, 435, 436
 monetary policy 63, 242, 246,
 249, 322, 420, 433, 436, 448,
 453, 455, 478, 479
Great Depression 28, 117, 137, 242,
243, 249, 251, 290, 449
Growth accounting 2, 3, 5, 6, 9, 10,
13, 18, 26, 37-59, 138, 141, 171,
173, 186, 190, 242, 243, 248, 251,
253, 255, 256, 330, 342, 426
 residual 6-8, 10, 18, 39, 45-47,
 51, 54, 56-58, 101, 133, 135-137,
 140-143, 256-258, 341, 345

Human capital 8, 9, 12, 13, 85, 95,
104, 134, 138, 142, 143, 148, 149,
156, 295, 341, 342, 347
 labor quality 135, 251, 252
 skills 13, 70, 74, 75, 149, 158,
 165, 208
 skill intensity 393
 training 7, 134, 142, 165, 189,
 331, 344, 421

ICOP 24, 25, 219-221, 224, 227,
234, 237, 375-377, 379, 380, 383,
385, 388, 391, 392, 395, 396
ICP 22-24, 305, 353-361, 364, 368,

371, 372, 375, 379, 382-384,
390, 393
Income distribution 103, 333, 334,
336
    Gini coefficient 346
Index numbers 233, 235 286, 287,
291, 362, 377, 380, 384
    characteristicity 384
    double deflation 24, 25, 378,
    385-387
    EKS 357, 384
    Fisher index 381, 382
    Geary-Khamis 357, 383, 384
    hedonic price indices 132, 401
    index number problem 287, 390
    multilateralisation 383, 384
    tableau effects 390
    Theil-Tornqvist 384
    transitivity 383, 384
Industrial relations 331, 342, 344
    trade unions 79, 328, 338, 344,
    456
Industrial revolution 158, 273, 286,
331
Industrialisation 16, 17, 21, 28, 86,
104, 106, 114, 212, 213, 217-219,
221, 237, 267, 268, 277, 285, 286,
290, 303, 305, 345, 448, 450-452,
462
    heavy industry 189, 308, 312,
    318, 469, 475, 476
Inequality 5, 22, 104, 328, 333-336,
344, 346, 347, 458, 459
Inflation 59, 189, 190, 242, 312,
320, 322, 323, 327-329, 344, 360,
363, 401, 402, 415, 442, 444, 450,
452, 455, 456, 459, 476, 477, 480
    hyperinflation 322, 323
Infrastructure 21, 27, 29, 30, 85,
312, 314, 318, 448, 450, 459
Input
    capital input 6, 39, 53, 134, 177,
    179, 182, 183, 185
    intermediate inputs 185
    labour input 5, 9, 13, 18, 172,
    174-180, 182-186, 189, 222, 252,
    253, 259, 387, 389-392, 395,

416, 423
    total factor input 7, 9, 20, 50, 53,
    54, 134, 135, 137, 156, 175, 176,
    182-186, 254, 255
Institutions 2, 7, 9, 14, 21, 26, 41,
43, 51, 65-75, 130, 132, 178, 186,
187, 201, 241, 331, 344, 450, 454,
457, 463, 464, 469, 481
    financial institutions 187, 457,
    463
    institutional change 45, 65, 75,
    132
    institutional framework/structure
    11, 20, 70, 71, 72, 74, 75, 105,
    295
    market institutions 26
    non-profit institutions 178
    political institutions 41, 67
International comparisons 3, 4,
22-25, 219, 252, 339, 375-377, 383,
395
    benchmark comparisons 356,
    359-361, 372, 389-392
    benchmarks 251, 263, 286-288,
    355, 356, 358-361, 364, 366-368,
    371, 372
    bilateral comparisons 42
    cross-country comparisons 375,
    376, 378, 391
    expenditure comparisons 353, 385
    industry of origin 4, 16, 24, 37,
    52, 53, 57, 332, 376-381,
    383-387, 391, 395
    level comparisons 23, 22-25, 375,
    378
    productivity comparisons 24, 222,
    227, 229, 232-234 376, 377
International monetary system 242
Investment
    foreign investment 147, 218, 449
    gross investment 39, 49, 321
    investment rate 148, 156, 157,
    160-164
    net investment 39, 278

Keynesianism 9, 26-29, 327, 328,
426, 429

Keynesian economic policy 28
Keynesian stabilisation 429, 437,
444
Knowledge 8, 9, 11, 13, 14, 43-50,
70, 73-75, 95, 104, 107, 158, 295,
342, 414, 421
advances in knowledge 18, 19,
39, 48, 52, 54, 56, 58, 102, 107,
181-184, 187
learning by doing 66, 67, 142,
190, 416, 426
scientific knowledge 67
state of knowledge 44
technical knowledge 7, 95, 141,
147
transfer of knowledge 50, 51,
147

Labour
hours worked 130, 135, 172,
174, 175, 177, 180, 182-185,
252, 259, 261, 263, 287, 294,
391
labour force 5, 46, 67, 105, 148,
164, 165, 172, 174, 175, 184,
188, 252, 254, 259, 263, 267,
287, 294, 302, 336, 342, 343,
345, 416, 439, 451, 459, 463
labour hoarding 179
labour income 178, 180
labour share 177, 180
participation 103, 189, 211, 259,
294, 335, 364
unemployment 22, 294, 320,
321, 323, 327-330, 336, 344-347,
414, 436, 439-442, 459
Liberalism 413-415, 423, 460
liberal world order 243

Malthusian 4, 67, 288, 417
Management 14, 20, 46, 57, 105,
187. 207, 208, 210, 310, 319, 322,
331, 418, 459
managers 68, 310, 319, 457,
469, 472, 481
Manufacturing 16, 18, 21, 50, 107,
173, 217-237, 287, 302, 331, 332,

338, 342-345, 366, 376-395, 402,
403, 405, 406, 422, 452, 457, 459
Market economies 12, 26, 29, 57,
70, 71, 109, 113, 149-151, 159-162,
164, 301, 303, 305, 308, 310, 311,
315, 319, 320, 322-324, 415, 423,
467, 471, 473, 474, 478
Misery index 328, 329, 344
Monetarism 453
Monopolies 30, 199, 200, 202, 209,
308, 418, 423, 425, 462, 467, 476,
479-481
Multinational/transnational
corporations 57, 147, 457, 459, 461

National accounts 50, 131, 217,
224-227, 229, 230, 232-234, 262,
267-269, 280, 286, 288, 336,
353-361, 364, 368, 372, 375, 377,
378, 387, 388, 390, 391
System of National Accounts 39,
131, 268, 304, 306, 400
Material Product System 306, 311
Natural resources 4, 28, 105, 132,
251, 254, 260, 452
non-renewable resources 79
resource endowment 295, 331
Neo-classical 65, 71-73, 102, 106,
453, 458
neo-classical economics 71, 73,
458
neo-classical model 8, 102, 106
neo-classical theory/framework 6,
8, 9, 11, 13

Organisations 14, 22, 44, 67, 69-71,
74, 75, 185, 308, 469

Periphery 15, 17, 285, 303, 449,
457, 458
Phases of growth/development 20,
195, 241
Physical Indicator Method 21, 305,
307, 308
Planning 21, 26-29, 308, 447, 448,
450, 452-454, 458, 462, 463, 467,
469-471, 474, 475, 479, 480

centrally planned economies 67,
113, 355, 468, 469, 480, 483
centralisation 309, 312
Pollution 5, 77, 78, 82, 85-87, 91,
92, 337
   acid rain 5, 77
   air pollution 86, 87, 91
   air quality 86, 89-92, 97
Population
   demographic transition 258
   immigration 14, 19, 105, 272
   migration 212, 213
   population density 197
   population growth 111, 113, 115,
   116, 147, 188, 204, 205, 208,
   210, 275, 288, 417
Potential output 19, 38, 55, 58, 187,
251
Poverty 1, 22, 78, 212, 309, 323,
333, 339, 422, 454, 459-461, 477
Pre-industrial 268, 272, 279, 280
Price level 23, 229, 230, 278, 354-
372, 381-383
   comparative price level 354, 360,
   361, 363, 364, 366, 371
   price levels
   relative price level 229, 354-359,
   363, 366-369, 371, 372, 382
Price structure 23, 287, 356, 371,
382, 384
   similarity index 354, 368, 369,
   371
Probit model 11, 103, 104
Production function 8, 10, 14, 342,
415, 416, 418
   Cobb Douglas 10, 394
Productivity
   capital productivity 134
   labour productivity 131, 137,
   140, 141, 172, 219-222, 228,
   229, 232, 233-237, 243, 246,
   247, 258, 287, 290, 294, 342,
   345, 387, 388, 393, 394
   marginal productivity 39, 46, 48,
   49, 134, 347, 420
   productivity gap 25, 147, 295,
   327, 331, 332, 340, 342, 392-395

productivity growth 20, 21, 50,
   103, 131, 136, 140, 141, 233,
   294, 147, 148, 165, 246, 247,
   258, 259, 328, 330, 331, 340,
   342, 345, 347, 387
   productivity leader 17, 18, 21,
   190, 387
   productivity level 147, 179, 378,
   387, 389
   productivity performance 147,
   229, 235, 237, 328, 331, 340,
   344, 347, 376, 384, 389, 396
   total factor productivity 6, 7, 18,
   20, 21, 134, 135, 136, 137, 140-
   142, 173, 179, 181-183, 185, 186,
   242, 255, 256, 258, 259, 294,
   331, 394, 395, 464
Purchasing power parities 22, 23,
153, 219-221, 230, 233, 290, 291,
305, 341, 354, 359, 360, 363, 364,
366, 368,369, 375, 376, 380, 382,
384, 390, 393
   basic headings 354, 368, 370
   international prices 156, 383
   unit value ratio 382, 383, 385,
   386

Quality 380, 384, 385, 395, 401, 402
   quality adjustment 401
   quality change 6, 49, 132
   quality problem 24, 25, 227, 384,
   385

Rationality 14, 73-75, 458
   instrumental rationality 14, 73, 74
   procedural rationality 14, 73, 74
Resource allocation 13, 18, 20, 21,
26, 142, 259
   misallocation 44, 46, 47, 422
Returns
   diminishing returns 4, 8-10, 21,
   52, 67, 416
   increasing returns 67, 74

Sanitation 85-89, 96, 97
   safe water 86, 100
   sewerage 88

water supply 86, 87, 96
Savings 9, 19, 27, 188, 268, 278,
  279, 414, 437, 452, 454, 457,
  460, 464, 479
  household savings 188
  savings rate 188
Shadow economy 29, 30, 467,
471-473, 475-477, 479, 481
Social capability 186, 295
Social indicators 5, 22, 463
  composite index 93-95
  Human Development Index 93
  quality of life 77, 93, 94, 98,
  103, 328, 330, 332, 337, 338,
  340, 347
Socialism 29, 30, 218, 307, 308,
319, 420, 426, 467-475, 477, 482
  communism 467, 482
  market socialism 29, 420, 467,
  468, 470, 473, 482
  Stalinist model 20, 21, 29, 30,
  301, 303, 318, 468, 472, 481
  socialist countries 377, 378, 395,
  467, 468
  socialist economies 303, 308,
  310, 314
Sources of growth
  (proximate) sources of growth 2,
  5, 9, 10, 13-15, 18, 37-43, 45,
  46, 53-56, 58, 138, 171, 173,
  179, 182, 183, 186-190
  ultimate sources/causes 2, 13,
  14, 18, 21, 30, 44, 45, 65, 70,
  71, 171, 186, 190
Standard of living 88, 102-104, 108,
219, 305, 309, 314, 315, 323, 330,
331, 336, 419
Structuralist approach 28, 447, 453,
455, 456, 460-462
  neo-structuralism 460-462

Taxation 27, 208, 307, 314, 346,
441, 447, 448
Technology
  diffusion 2, 9, 11, 14, 102-106,
  108, 109, 115, 120, 147, 154,
  190, 295, 376, 395
  embodied/disembodied 6, 7, 9,
  20, 67, 68, 48, 49, 132, 133, 254,
  256, 258, 295
  imitation 102, 103, 105, 118,
  120, 122, 124, 328
  innovation 9, 55, 101-103, 107,
  108, 118, 120-122, 124, 418, 423,
  457
  patents 11, 115, 116, 120-123,
  343, 400
  research and development/R&D
  intensity 7, 8, 10, 13, 37, 42, 43,
  45, 47, 52, 53, 57, 104, 105,
  107-109, 111, 115, 116, 118,
  120-124, 147, 190, 347
  technical change 9, 20, 21, 84,
  92, 102, 103, 106, 108, 124, 133,
  186, 187, 212, 251, 254, 256,
  258, 259, 277, 278, 295, 417,
  420, 471
  technological distance 11, 105
  technological frontier 104, 110,
  124
  technological leader 123
Trade
  export promotion 451, 461
  foreign trade 179, 213, 312, 452
  import substitution 19, 28, 218,
  246, 249, 451, 457, 460, 463
  maritime trade 196, 200, 201,
  207-209
  protection 218, 249, 250, 451,
  464, 473
  protectionism 320, 452, 457, 459
  tariffs 107, 218, 249, 274, 289,
  320, 450-452, 462
  terms of trade 28, 312, 315, 357,
  367, 368, 451, 463

Urbanisation 14-17, 86, 88, 202-204,
206, 208, 213, 272, 294
  cities 77, 79, 85, 86, 89-92, 199,
  201-204, 206, 213, 272, 309
  urban degradation 5